SEVENTH EDITION

CASES TO ACCOMPANY CONTEMPORARY STRATEGY ANALYSIS

ROBERT M. GRANT

WILEY

A John Wiley & Sons, Ltd, Publication

First published by Blackwell Publishing Ltd 1996, 1999, 2003, 2005, 2008
Copyright © Robert M. Grant

This edition Copyright © 2010 by Robert M. Grant
Published by John Wiley & Sons, Ltd

Registered office
John Wiley & Sons, Ltd, The Atrium, Southern Gate, Chichester, West Sussex, PO19 8SQ, United Kingdom

For details of our global editorial offices, for customer services, and for information about how to apply for permission to reuse the copyright material in this book please see our web site at www.wiley.com.

Library of Congress Cataloging-in-Publication Data

Grant, Robert M., 1948-
    Cases to accompany Contemporary strategy analysis, seventh edition / Robert M. Grant.
        p. cm.
    Rev. ed. of: Cases to accompany Contemporary strategy analysis. 2008.
    Written to accompany the 7th ed. of Contemporary strategy analysis, published in 2009.
    Includes bibliographical references.
    ISBN 978-0-470-68633-1 (pbk.)
    1. Strategic planning—Case studies. 2. Decision making—Case studies. I. Grant, Robert M., 1948- Contemporary strategy analysis.   II. Title.
    HD30.28.G716 2010
    658.4'012—dc22

                                                                                    2009052135

A catalogue record for this book is available from the British Library.

Set in 10/12pt Classical Garamond by Thomson Digital, India
Printed in Spain by Grafos Sa, Barcelona

bankruptcy. Ford's ability to survive the next five years depends critically on the state of the world automobile industry. The case asks you to advise Ford's head of strategic planning on the direction of profitability in the industry based on an analysis of the evolving structure of the global automobile industry and its implications for competition. It shows how internationalization and maturity in an industry can combine to create intense competition and weak margins. It also calls for an examination of why some companies are consistently more profitable than others and for the identification of key success factors in the industry.

From its humble origins in Bentonville, Arkansas, Wal-Mart has grown to be the world's largest retailer and the world's biggest corporation (in revenue). In the intensely competitive world of discount retailing, what is the basis of Wal-Mart's competitive advantage? Understanding the basis of Wal-Mart's success requires careful analysis of the resources and capabilities that Wal-Mart has built over time. What does the future hold for Wal-Mart? Will growing size and success blunt Wal-Mart's drive for cost efficiency? Will Wal-Mart's competitive advantage be undermined either by imitation by competitors or by changing market circumstances?

For nearly two decades, Manchester United has been the most successful English soccer club. The club faces the prospect of the retirement of the primary architect of that success: veteran team manager, Sir Alex Ferguson. What should be the approach of the Manchester United board and CEO in planning the continued development of the club? The case probes the interaction between financial and team performance in professional sport and explores the determinants of team-based capabilities in the intensely competitive world of European professional soccer. A critical issue for Manchester United—and for any professional sports team—is whether exceptional team-based capabilities are the result of superior resources (players in particular) or of superior coordination of the resources.

Eastman Kodak faces the challenge of adjusting to the transformation of technology in the photographic imaging industry. Kodak has staked its future on being a leader in digital imaging. Despite massive investment, a string of acquisitions and strategic alliances, Kodak's ability to establish competitive advantage within the digital imaging sector and to generate satisfactory returns from its investments remains in doubt. The case describes Kodak's digital imaging strategy and explores the challenges faced by CEO Antonio Perez in developing the organizational capabilities required to succeed in the fast-moving digital imaging sector.

requires an analysis of key success factors in this winner-take-all industry. The success of Nintendo's Wii points to a significant change in the dynamics of competition in the industry. The balance of power between hardware and software suppliers has shifted; online game playing has grown and the industry has lost several of its winner-take-all attributes. The three leading players—Nintendo, Microsoft, and Sony—are gearing up for the next generation of video-game consoles. To recommend strategies for each of the participants, the case requires an analysis of the potential for network externalities, the implications of changing technology and demographics, and the resource and capability strengths of each firm.

Toshiba's February 19, 2008 announcement that it was stopping production of its HD-DVD marked the end of the standards war between Sony and Toshiba for leadership in the next generation of high-capacity DVDs. This account of the two-year struggle between Toshiba and Sony offers insight into the dynamics of standards war, and allows us to consider what Toshiba might have done differently in order to succeed against Sony's Blu-ray.

During 2009, the New York Times Company is struggling against declining revenues, large losses and difficulties in refinancing its borrowings. These problems reflect both the current recession and the long-term decline in newspaper readership. The group addresses its financial problems through cost reduction while also seeking a new business model that addresses the shift of news readership and advertising from print media to the internet.

Eni's metamorphosis from a widely diversified, inefficient, state-owned corporation to a highly profitable, shareholder-owned, international energy major is a tale of corporate transformation over a 15-year period. In 2009, CEO Paolo Scaroni is considering Eni's strategy for the next four years and beyond. Despite Eni's outstanding operational and financial performance, Eni faces important questions of corporate strategy. Which businesses should it include within its corporate portfolio? How should it allocate its investment budget between them? What geographical scope is appropriate for the company? What is the scope for managing linkages between Eni's different businesses? Answering these questions requires analysis of the determinants of profitability in the oil and gas sector, and an assessment of Eni's resources and capabilities relative to other integrated energy majors.

American Apparel is an unusual company. While most U.S. fashion clothing is produced offshore in low-wage countries, American Apparel's tee-shirts are designed and manufactured in downtown Los Angeles then sold in company-owned retail stores. The case outlines the logic of American Apparel's strategy of vertical integration and considers the challenges facing

the company as it grows in size and international scope, and as the diversity
of its product range increases.

During the early 1990s, Outback Steakhouse became one of America's most
successful restaurant chains as a result of a strategy that was unusual but fitted
well with Outback's targeted niche, and its resources and capabilities. In 1994,
the prospect of market saturation in the U.S. and awareness of opportunities
overseas, encouraged Outback to explore international expansion. To what
extent is the Outback restaurant concept, strategy, and business system suited
to overseas markets? To what extent can Outback recreate its U.S.-based
resource and capability strengths overseas, and—given the answers to these
questions—what sort of international strategy makes sense for Outback? The
case offers an overview of the fundamental considerations relevant to the
decisions of whether, and how, to expand internationally.

Euro Disneyland was Disney's biggest and riskiest project since the EPCOT
Center a decade earlier. What considerations explained the complex mode of
entry that Disney adopted for Euro Disney? Unlike Tokyo Disneyland, in
which Disney held no equity stake, and the U.S. parks that were wholly
owned, Disney held minority ownership in Euro Disney as well as licensing
and management contracts. Diagnosing the reasons for Euro Disney's dismal
performance has important implications both for the future management of
the park and for Disney's plans to build another theme park in Asia. The case
requires analysis of two complex sets of questions: first, the choice of foreign
market entry mode; second, adaptation to a different national culture.

In early summer 2009, CEO Vittorio Colao addressed Vodafone's dismal
profitability record. Despite Vodafone's leading position in the world's
market for mobile communications, Vodafone was struggling against
increasing competition, maturing markets, and asset write downs. A critical
issue for Colao is the extent to which Vodafone can benefit from its
extensive international scope. Vodafone offers service in 25 countries and
has partner agreements in a further 39 countries, yet the potential for
reducing costs or providing superior service through cross-border
integration appear limited in wireless telecommunication. The case requires
an analysis of the potential benefits from international scope in wireless
telecommunications and the development of strategy recommendations for
Vodafone—especially in relation to its presence in the U.S. and France.

Richard Branson's Virgin Group of companies has continued to diversify into
an ever-widening set of industries—wireless telephony, a U.S. domestic airline,
health clubs, bio fuels, even space travel. Despite the success of the airlines and
mobile phone businesses, several businesses were making losses. As the Virgin

empire grows larger and more complex, and Branson himself grows older and becomes less directly involved, he needs to consider the corporate strategy of his loose-knit corporate empire. What is the logic, if any, that links together this motley collection of business ventures? Should any of the businesses be divested? What criteria should be used to guide future diversification? Are changes needed in the financial and management structure of the group?

Cases to Accompany Contemporary Strategy Analysis, Seventh Edition represents an ongoing commitment to the examination of the concepts and techniques of business strategy analysis in the context of real business situations. The cases have been written to accompany the seventh edition of my *Contemporary Strategy Analysis* textbook. Each case illuminates the ideas, concepts, and analytical techniques contained in one or more chapters of the textbook. Most important, the cases promote deep learning by students of strategic management by requiring these ideas, concepts, and techniques to be applied to the situations described in the cases. To achieve this, the cases are closely linked to the textbook chapters. For example:

- Case 1 (*Madonna*) offers an opportunity to explore some of the key themes of Chapter 1 of the textbook—namely, the nature of strategy as a dynamic, emergent phenomenon—and considers the factors that make such a strategy successful (in terms of delivering outstanding performance).
- Case 2 (*Starbucks*) is a vehicle for deploying the tools of performance diagnosis outlined in Chapter 2 of the textbook, and illustrates the potential for integrating financial and strategic analysis.
- Cases 3 and 4 (*The U.S. Airline Industry in 2009*, and *Ford and the World Automobile Industry in 2009*) give students the opportunity to apply the tools of industry and competitive analysis outlined in Chapters 3 and 4 of the textbook (notably Porter's "five forces of competition" framework).
- Cases 5, 6, and 7 (which relate to *Wal-Mart*, *Manchester United*, and *Eastman Kodak*) require the analysis of resources and capabilities outlined in Chapters 5 and 6 of *Contemporary Strategy Analysis*.

Similarly, each of the other cases has been designed to illustrate and apply the tools in one or more of the chapters of *Contemporary Strategy Analysis*—right through to the last case (*W. L. Gore & Associates*), which explores the novel approaches to strategic management discussed in the final chapter of the textbook.

The cases include a number that appeared in the earlier edition of the casebook—all of these have been revised and most of them updated to 2009. There are also a number of entirely new cases. These include the cases on Starbucks, the DVD war, *New York Times*, American Apparel, Vodafone, Google, Bank of America's acquisition of Merrill Lynch, and W. L. Gore & Associates. Cases that have been displaced from earlier editions can be found on the web site: **http://www.contemporarystrategyanalysis.com.**

Most of these cases refer to recent situations. Nevertheless, no matter how up to date they are at the time of writing, by the time the book reaches the reader they will be history. Teaching cases from the recent past rather than the present inevitably involves loss of both immediacy and uncertainty. The challenge for students and their instructors is to address the business situation as it existed at the time of the case without letting hindsight cloud assessment of the situation that prevailed at the time. However, I do recognize that teachers and students will want to know "what happened next". For this reason, the teaching notes and Web support offer guidance on current sources of information.

Most of the cases are focused around a strategic decision. How can Wal-Mart sustain its competitive advantage in discount retailing? What can Sony do to regain its leadership in video-game consoles? Should Bank of America's board pull the plug on the Merrill Lynch takeover? However, the key learning is not about what is the right decision; it is about gaining deep insight into the business situation that underlies the strategic decision. None of the cases have a single right answer. The performance of individual students and the class as a whole is not to be judged on the basis of reaching the best recommendation but upon the analysis and judgment that underlies the recommendation.

I have tried to make these cases as concise as possible by being more focused than is typical for strategy cases. Brevity limits the amount of information that is supplied to students. Does this mean that students should seek out additional information? Preferably not—the cases provide all the data needed to identify and analyze the key issues. More data permit more detailed analysis but at the cost of slowing and overloading the decision process. For most companies, strategic decisions must be taken with only a fraction of the relevant information available—events are moving too quickly to allow the luxury of extensive, in-depth research.

We hope that you will find the cases instructive and enjoyable. The process of case development is continuous, so please check the web site for new and updated cases. The web site also offers teaching notes for instructors and contains relevant video clip questions.

I appreciate any comments and suggestions—including proposals for new cases.

Robert Grant
Email: grant@unibocconi.it; grantr@georgetown.edu

The author and publisher gratefully acknowledge the permission granted to reproduce the copyright material in this book:

Tables 5.1, 5.5, and the Appendix in Chapter 5. Extracts taken from walmartstores.com. Used with permission of Wal-Mart Corporate Communications.

Tables 9.4 and 9.5. Taken from S. Buchholz, N. Fabio, A. Ileyassoff, L. Mang, and D. Visentin, "AirAsia – Tales from a Long-haul Low Cost Carrier," coursework submitted as part of the MSc international management degree, Bocconi University, May 31, 2009. Used with permission of the authors.

Case 17 draws extensively on M. L. Taylor, G. M. Puia, K. Ramaya, and M. Gengelback, "Outback Steakhouse Goes International," in A. A. Thompson and A. J. Strickland, *Strategic Management: Concepts and Cases*, 11th edn, McGraw-Hill, New York, 1999. Copyright © 1997 by case authors and North American Case Research Association. Used with permission of Marilyn L. Taylor.

Exhibit 19.1. Extract taken from "When Global Strategies Go Wrong," *Wall Street Journal Asia*, April 4, 2002. Used with permission.

Exhibit 22.2. Extract taken from Jordi Canals, "Universal Banks Need Careful Monitoring," *Financial Times*, October 19, 2008. Used with permission of Jordi Canals.

Appendix 22.3. Taken from Shawn Tully, "The Golden Age for Financial Services is Over," *Fortune*, September 29, 2008. Used with permission.

Exhibits 24.1 and 24.2. Extracts taken from www.gore.com. Used with permission of W. L. Gore & Associates.

Every effort has been made to trace copyright holders and to obtain their permission for the use of copyright material. The publisher apologizes for any errors or omissions in the above list and would be grateful if notified of any corrections that should be incorporated in future reprints or editions of this book.

Case 1 Madonna*

Desperately Seeking a Start

In July 1977, shortly before her nineteenth birthday, Madonna Louise Ciccone arrived in New York City with $35 in her pocket. She had left Ann Arbor where she was majoring in dance at the University of Michigan. The third of eight children, she was raised in the suburbs of Detroit; her mother had died when she was six years old. Her prospects in the world of show business looked poor. Apart from her training in dance, she had little musical background and no contacts.

Life in New York was a struggle. "I worked at Dunkin' Donuts, I worked at Burger King, I worked at Amy's. I had a lot of jobs that lasted one day. I always talked back to people and they'd fire me. I was a coat-check girl at the Russian Tea Room. I worked at a health club once a week."[1] She spent a few months training with the Alvin Ailey Dance Theater and had a succession of modeling engagements for photographers and artists. During 1979, Madonna began to explore New York's music and acting scenes. With boyfriend Dan Gilroy, his brother Ed and bassist Angie Smit, "Breakfast Club" was formed—Madonna sharing vocals and drums with Dan. For six months she was dancer and backup singer to French singing star Patrick Hernandez, accompanying him in Europe and North Africa. In August 1979, Madonna was offered the lead role in underground movie director Stephen Lewicki's low-budget film A *Certain Sacrifice*. She was paid $100.

After breaking up with Dan Gilroy, Madonna invited her former Michigan boyfriend, Steve Bray, to New York. They moved into the Music Building—a converted 12-storey building crammed with studios, rehearsal rooms and striving, impoverished young bands. Together they worked on writing songs and developing their sound while Madonna maintained a continuous stream of calls to managers, agents, record companies and club owners. Camille Barbone offered a management contract—but only for Madonna. However, Barbone was unable to deliver success fast enough for Madonna and after 18 months Madonna fired her.

Finding a Sound, Finding a Style

During 1981, Madonna's music and image moved in a new direction. Influenced by the emerging dance scene in New York, Madonna moved increasingly from Pretenders/Pat Benatar rock to the dance music that was sweeping New York clubs. In addition to working with Steve Bray to develop songs and mix demo tapes, she worked on her image—a form of glam-grunge that featured multilayered, multicolored combinations of thrift-store clothing together with scarves and junk jewelry. She adopted "Boy Toy" as her "tag name" and prominently displayed it on her belt buckle. It was a look that she would continue to develop with the help of jewelry designer Maripole. Her trademark look of messy, badly dyed hair, neon rubber bracelets, black lace bras, white lace gloves, and chunky belt buckles would soon be seen on teenage girls throughout the world.

Madonna was quick to recognize the commercial implications of the new musical wave. The dance clubs were crucial and the DJs were the gatekeepers. Armed with her demo tapes, Madonna and her friends frequented the hottest dance clubs where they would make a splash with their flamboyant clothing and provocative dancing. At Danceteria, one of the staff referred to her as a "heat-seeking missile targeting the hottest DJs." DJ Mark Kamins introduced her to Mike Rosenblatt and Seymour Stein of Sire Records, a division of Warner Records. A recording contract and $5000 were soon hers. The first release was a 12-inch single with different versions of *Everybody* on each side. The record was played extensively in dance clubs.

Madonna began working on her first album. Although she had allegedly promised longtime friend and music collaborator Steve Bray and DJ Mark Kamins the job of producer, she dumped both in favor of Warner Records' house producer, Reggie Lucas. Together with Warner Records' national dance promoter, Bobby Shaw, Madonna began a relentless round of courting DJs and pushing her record for play time. Central to the promotion plan was New York's number one DJ, John "Jellybean" Benitez, who Madonna began dating in November 1982.

Her second single, *Burning Up,* released in March 1983 was a dance-club hit, reaching number three in the dance charts. With the attention and resources of Warner Brothers, and a network of DJs, Madonna had most of the pieces she needed in place— but not quite. Early in 1983 she flew to Los Angeles to visit Freddie DeMann, then manager of megastar Michael Jackson. DeMann remembers the meeting vividly: "I was knocked off my feet. I've never met a more physical human being in my life." In a short time DeMann dropped Michael Jackson in favor of managing Madonna.

Breakthrough

The album *Madonna* was released in July 1983. By the end of 1983, the record was climbing the U.S. album charts supported by the success of single release *Holiday.* In April 1984, another single from the album, *Borderline,* reached the top ten. At Madonna's national TV debut on *American Bandstand,* presenter Dick Clark asked her, "What do you really want to do when you grow up?" "Rule the world," she replied.

Within little more than a year Madonna was part way there. The fall of 1984 saw Madonna filming in *Desperately Seeking Susan.* Although initially hired as support for the movie's star, Rosanna Arquette, Madonna progressively hijacked the movie. By the time the shooting was complete, it was essentially a movie about Madonna playing herself, wearing her own style of clothes, and featuring her own music. Its release coincided with a surge of Madonna-mania. Her second album, *Like a Virgin,* had gone triple platinum (over 3 million copies sold) in February 1985, while the singles charts featured a succession of individual tracks from the album. Madonna's first concert tour was a sell out. Her marriage to bad-boy actor Sean Penn on August 16, 1985 further reinforced her celebrity status. When Madonna took up residence in Los Angeles during 1985 she was already a star and seldom far from the popular press headlines.

Fame, Fortune, Notoriety

In the next two decades, little came between Madonna and her quest for fame. She released six albums between 1986 and 1990. The 16 single releases from these albums gave her a near-continuous presence in the charts, including a remarkable seven number-one hits. In the process, Madonna rejected the industry's conventional wisdom of "Find a winning formula and stick to it." Madonna's career was a continuous experimentation with new musical ideas and new images, and a constant quest for new heights of fame and acclaim. Having established herself as the queen of popular music, Madonna did not stop there. By the end of the 1980s she was destined to be "the most famous woman on the planet."

Madonna in Charge

Madonna's struggle for fame revealed a drive, determination and appetite for hard work that would characterize her whole career. "I'm tough, I'm ambitious, and I know exactly what I want—and if that makes me a bitch, that's okay," she told the

London *News of the World* newspaper in 1985. On the set of *Desperately Seeking Susan* she maintained a blistering pace. "During the shoot we'd often get home at 11:00 or 12:00 at night and have to be back at 6:00 or 7:00 the next morning. Half the time the driver would pick up Madonna at her health club. She'd get up at 4:30 in the morning to work out first."[2]

There was never any doubt as to who was in charge of managing and developing Madonna's career. While Madonna relied on some of the best minds and strongest companies in the entertainment business, there was little doubt as to who was calling the shots. Her swift exit from her marriage with Sean Penn further emphasized her unwillingness to allow messy personal relationships to compromise her career goals. For her third album—*True Blue*, released in June 1986—Madonna insisted on being co-producer.

The documentary of her 1990 "Blonde Ambition" tour, *Truth or Dare*,[3] clearly reveals her hands-on management style. The tour itself was a masterpiece of the pop concert as multimedia show embracing music, dance and theater. The tour's planning began in September 1989. Madonna was involved in every aspect of the show's design and planning, including auditioning dancers and musicians, planning, costume design, and choice of themes. For example, Madonna worked closely with Jean-Paul Gaultier on the metallic, cone-breasted costumes that became one of the tour's most vivid images. On the tour itself, the *Truth or Dare* movie revealed Madonna as both creative director and operations supremo. In addition to her obsessive attention to every detail of the show's production, she was the undisputed organizational leader responsible for building team spirit among the diverse group of dancers, musicians, choreographers and technicians; motivating the troupe when times were tough; resolving disputes between her fractious and highly strung male dancers and establishing the highest standards of commitment and effort.

The "Blonde Ambition" tour in the summer of 1990 marked new heights of international obsession with Madonna. The tour coincided with the release of *Dick Tracy*, the Disney movie that was a vehicle for the high-profile lovers, Madonna and Warren Beatty. The film did much to rectify a string of Hollywood flops and scathing reviews of Madonna's own acting capabilities. Madonna's portrayal of Breathless Mahoney exuded her natural talents for style and seductiveness.

Fame and Controversy

As a superstar, Madonna began increasingly to court notoriety, and push up against the boundaries of acceptability. Her overt sexuality together with audacious, expletive-laced talk, and use of crucifixes as items of jewelry raised disquiet within conservative and religious circles. Madonna's explanation only added fuel to the fire: "Crucifixes are sexy because there's a naked man on them." Among her efforts to enthrall and shock the American public, her *Like a Prayer* album, released in March 1989, proved to be a landmark.

Piggy-backing on Madonna-mania, Pepsi-Cola paid Madonna $5 million for a commercial based on the album's title track *Like a Prayer*. What Pepsi had not taken into account was that Madonna was making her own music video of *Like a Prayer* to accompany the launch of the record. The day after the first broadcast of the Pepsi commercial, Madonna's own *Like a Prayer* video appeared on MTV. The video was a stunning mixture of sex and religion that featured Madonna dancing in front of burning crosses, making love on an altar, and revealing stigmata on her hands.

Threatened by boycotts from Christian groups and the American Family Association, Pepsi pulled its Madonna commercial.

The explicit sexuality of the "Blonde Ambition" tour and its mixing of sexual and religious imagery resulted in Madonna achieving new heights of controversy—and public awareness. In Toronto, city authorities threatened to cancel the show. The Vatican condemned the show as "blasphemous." The *Justify My Love* video released in November 1990 set a new record for Madonna—it was banned by MTV for its portrayal of homosexuality, voyeurism, nudity, sado-masochism, and oral sex. Again, Madonna was quick to turn controversy into profit: the *Justify My Love* video was rush-released for retail sale, and the single soon topped the charts.

Sex also provided the basis for Madonna's entry into book publishing. Her photographic "art" book, *Sex,* featured Madonna in an array of sexual poses. Despite its high price ($49.95 for 120 pages) the book sold half a million copies in its first week.

Evita

Madonna has been compared to previous superstars and goddesses of sex and glamour—Greta Garbo, Marilyn Monroe, Mae West, Brigitte Bardot—but she has gone further in creating a persona that transcends her work as an entertainer. Those female superstars were defined by their movie roles. The big names in popular music, from Lena Horne to Janet Jackson, have been famous primarily for their music. Madonna achieved a status that was no longer defined by her work. By the 1990s, Madonna was no longer famous as a rock singer or an actress—she was famous for being Madonna. For the next decade she worked to reinforce this status. Strategically, superstar status has much to commend it. Joining the pantheon of superstars acts as insulation from comparison with lesser mortals. As her web site proclaims, she is "icon, artist, provocateur, diva, and mogul."

In her acting roles the key was to take roles that were primarily vehicles for Madonna to be Madonna. Her successes in *Desperately Seeking Susan* and *Dick Tracy* were the result of roles where Madonna could be herself. However, both these roles were to be eclipsed by Madonna's portrayal of Eva Peron in the movie version of the Andrew Lloyd Webber musical *Evita*. Madonna had coveted the role for years and mounted a vigorous campaign to gain the support of director Alan Parker and Argentine President Carlos Menem. While in previous roles Madonna had been able to use her talents as a singer, a poser, a sharp talker and a seductress; in *Evita* Madonna could present her own life. Like Madonna, Evita had working-class origins, a burning ambition, and had used sex and shrewd judgment to become a legend in her time. The film, released in December 1996, was a huge commercial and critical success. As *Q* magazine's Paul Du Noyer remarked, "If ever there was an ideal vehicle for Madonna's dream of transcendent stardom, this must be it."[4]

Motherhood and More

During most of the filming of *Evita*, Madonna was coping with her pregnancy. On October 14, 1996, she gave birth to Lourdes Maria Ciccone Leon at the Good Samaritan Hospital in Los Angeles. The baby's father was Carlos Leon, Madonna's personal trainer.

In terms of her life, image, and career, motherhood was a major discontinuity for Madonna. The press began reporting a host of lifestyle changes. Madonna abandoned pumping iron in favor of yoga. She began to study Kabbalah (a " mystical interpretation of the Old Testament," she explained). She developed a closer circle of women friends. She spent increasing amounts of time writing music. She became less available to the media. Her interviews were amazingly devoid of sex, expletives and shock value. "I think [motherhood] made me face up to my more feminine side. I had a much more masculine view of the world. What I missed and longed for was that unconditional love that a mother gives you. And so, having my daughter is the same kind of thing. It's like that first, true, pure, unconditional love."[5]

The clearest revelation of these changes was in Madonna's new album, *Ray of Light*, which was unlike any previous Madonna album. Working with William Orbit, the album incorporated a host of new influences: electronic music; traditional Indian music; Madonna's musings on the troubles of the world and the hollowness of fame; reflections on her own emotional development and her unhappy childhood. In performing tracks from the album both on TV and on video, Madonna revealed a series of entirely new looks including Madonna as Goth-girl (black hair, black clothes, black nail polish), Madonna as Shiva (multi-armed with henna tattoos on her hands), Madonna as geisha (straight black hair, kimono and white makeup).

The new persona was the most ambitious and risky reinvention of Madonna's career, insofar as it was the first that was not founded on sexuality and sexual aggression. Yet this transformation was met with no loss of popularity or worldwide acclaim. *Ray of Light* hit number two on the album charts and went triple platinum on the basis of U.S. sales alone. At the MTV Video Music Awards Madonna walked away with a total of six awards followed by three Grammy Awards.

Madonna as Mogul

Madonna's preoccupation with her "art" and her "freedom of artistic expression," has extended to an acute interest in her intellectual property rights. London's *Sunday Times* noted:

> Her early hits, "Holiday," "Like a Virgin" and "Papa Don't Preach," had been written by professional songwriters, who pocketed a quarter of the monies earned. Since 1986, and despite her limited musical ability, Madonna's has always been the first name to appear on her song credits. Her co-writers, meanwhile, have often been talented unknowns, like Pat Leonard, with whom she composed and performed her most successful album, the 24m-seller from 1986, True Blue. As soon as their names have benefited from the connection with her hits—and their asking price has consequently risen—she drops them and hires somebody new, and usually cheaper. [6]

Not only did Madonna maintain control over her own content—she increasingly wanted a cut in distribution. In April 1992 she signed a $60 million deal with Time Warner, Inc. The joint venture, Maverick Records, was a music production company (together with TV, video, and music publishing wings) that was to provide a vehicle for Madonna's creative and promotional talent. Warner Records provided distribution.

Although Madonna remained contracted to Warner Records for her own recordings, Maverick offered an avenue for her to develop and promote other singers and musicians. Among Maverick's early signings included Alanis Morissette, whose *Jagged Little Pill* album sold over 30 million copies, William Orbit, Prodigy, the Deftones, and Michelle Branch. Madonna also assisted in the U.S. launch of British comedian Sacha Baron Cohen (of Ali G and *Borat* fame).

Madonna's interest in new musicians and producing their music was linked to her own widening musical interests. Following *Ray of Light* Madonna became increasingly involved in both in electronic and world music, including collaboration with the French electro-boffin, Mirwais.

The Reinvention Goes On

During the first decade of the twenty-first century, neither Madonna's career nor her command over media attention showed much sign of flagging.

Madonna's family life continued to be a major focus of media interest. The birth of her second child, Rocco, was followed by marriage to Rocco's father, British actor and director Guy Ritchie. As a British resident, "Madge" became a staple feature for the British tabloid press.

Madonna also showed her ability to extend her media appeal beyond the celebrity-obsessed tabloids. Her adoption of a 13-month-old Malawian, David Banda, in October 2006, created a furor that engaged Third World politicians, anti-globalization activists, religious leaders and assorted intellectuals. Madonna became immersed in a global debate over "cash for babies" and "one law for the rich; another for the poor." A second adoption attempt, two years later, was blocked by the courts in Malawi.

On the career front, Madonna was quick to recognize the emerging business model in popular music. In the pre-digital world, live performances were primarily vehicles to publicize new album releases. Seeing the emergence of concert tours as dominant revenue stream, Madonna returned to concert touring in 2001. The "Drowned World" tour was followed by the "Re-invention" tour of 2004 and the "Confessions" tour of 2006.

When music revenues shifted from recordings to concerts, Madonna reorganized her own commercial arrangements. When Maverick began losing money (along with most other record companies), Madonna's exit was credited by industry observers as strategic brilliance. Maverick sued Warner Music for "improper accounting." Afraid of bad publicity and long-running litigation, Warner resolved the matter by buying out Madonna's share of Maverick for $10 million in 2004.

Free of Maverick, Madonna was able to court a new business partner. In 2007, she signed a $120 million, 10-year contract with Live Nation, the world's largest concert promotion company. "The business paradigm has shifted," she said upon signing. "As a creative artist and a businesswoman I have to acknowledge that." There seemed little doubt as who had gained the better part of the deal. Dismayed at the near-impossibility of making a profit from the deal, Live Nation was reported to be considering licensing Madonna's next album back to her old record company, Warner.

Madonna's "Sticky and Sweet" tour, which began in August 2008, set new standards in global scope, longevity, and revenue generation. With 85 concerts spanning every continent of the world except Australia over 14 months, the tour was forecast to gross over $400 million. Madonna's sell-out performances confirmed her ability to recruit a whole new generation of fans, many of whom had not been born when she recorded her debut album.

Outside of music, Madonna's artistic efforts met less success. A London stage performance in the comedy *Up for Grabs* and a movie co-starring with Guy Ritchie, *Swept Away*, were disasters. *The English Roses*, the first in series of children's books achieved modest commercial success.

Following the final concert of her "Sticky and Sweet" tour in September 2009, it seemed likely that Madonna would begin her next metamorphosis. With her divorce from Guy Ritchie finalized early in 2009, her "English gentlewoman" period was over. Part of the divorce settlement included the transfer of her 120-acre Wiltshire country mansion to Ritchie. What her next reincarnation would be was anyone's guess, however, as the London *Telegraph* noted: "What doesn't change, and hopefully never will, is Ms. Ciccone's hypercaffeineated zeal to make the world pay attention."[7]

Notes

1 M. Bego, *Madonna: Blonde Ambition,* Cooper Square, New York, 2000, p. 46.
2 C. Arrington, "Madonna," *People,* March 11, 1985.
3 Released as *In Bed With Madonna* outside North America.
4 "Commanding" (Review of Evita), *Q,* December, 1996, see www.pauldunoyer.com/pages/journalism/journalism_item.asp?journalismID=250, accessed October 29, 2009.
5 M. Murphy, "Madonna Confidential," *TV Guide,* April 11–17, 1998.
6 "Why Madonna's Still a Material Girl," *Sunday Times,* April 5, 2009, http://entertainment.timesonline.co.uk/-tol/arts_and_entertainment/music/article6015124.ece, accessed October 5, 2009.
7 "Madonna, Mistress of Metamorphosis," *Daily Telegraph,* August 10, 2008.

Case 2   Starbucks in 2009: The Coffee Goes Cold

After 20 years of continuous expansion accompanied by rising profits and a soaring stock price, Starbucks' downturn was unexpected and rapid. Starbucks' stock-market valuation was the leading indicator of the problems to come. After reaching a peak of $40 in October 2006, the share price declined by more than 75% over the next two years (see Figure 2.1). During 2007 growth of same-store sales and operating profits slowed. Amidst increasing concern over Starbucks' current strategy and future prospects, chairman and founder, Howard Schultz, returned as CEO at the beginning of 2008. His turnaround strategy comprised a sharp cutback in planned U.S. new store openings, revised operational and human resources practices aimed at improving customer service, "reigniting the connection with customers," and reallocating resources from the U.S. to overseas. In the summer of 2008, Schultz announced the closure of 600 U.S. stores and withdrawal from Australia.

FIGURE 2.1 Starbucks' share price and trading volume, 2000 to February 2009

Source: www.bigcharts.com

Starbucks' financial results for the year ending September 2008 revealed the damage being done by the economic downturn to same-store sales and margins. However, it was the results for the final quarter of 2008 that showed just how badly Starbucks was being hurt: net income was down by almost 70% and the company had experienced its first ever decline in quarterly revenues. Tables 2.1 and 2.2 show annual and quarterly results. The announcement prompted a 33c decline in Starbucks' share price to $9.33. Chairman and CEO Howard Schultz commented:

> In the midst of the weakening global consumer environment, Starbucks is following a well-developed plan to strengthen our business through more efficient operations and by preserving the fundamental strengths and values of our brand. We remain focused on driving the discipline and rigor necessary to create long-term shareholder value, and we are taking aggressive steps to excite customers by providing relevant value and innovation, even during this challenging time.[1]

CFO Troy Alstead, added:

> With a solid balance sheet, strong cash flow and healthy liquidity, Starbucks is well-positioned to weather the challenging global economy. We will continue to take the actions necessary to scale our cost structure to meet current business trends while positioning the company to drive margin expansion when the environment improves.[2]

Further retrenchment measures included: 300 store closures, 6700 job losses (including 700 in corporate and support positions), $500 million in operating cost savings for 2009 and a reduction in new openings of company-owned stores from 270 to 170. Schultz cut his own salary from $1.2 million to $10 000 and put two of Starbucks' three corporate jets up for sale.[3]

While deteriorating sales and profit performance could be blamed primarily on the global economic recession, Starbucks' languishing share price reflected broader concerns about the company's future. Had Starbucks' U.S. expansion resulted in excessive store density in some metropolitan areas? Had the growth of competition—not just from other specialist coffee chains but also from major fast-food chains such as McDonald's

TABLE 2.1 Starbucks Corporation: financial and operating performance 2004–8

Year ended September 30 (in $, millions)	2008 (52 weeks)	2007 (52 weeks)	2006 (52 weeks)	2005 (52 weeks)	2004 (53 weeks)
RESULTS OF OPERATIONS					
Net revenues:					
Company-operated retail	8771.9	7998.3	6583.1	5391.9	4457.4
Specialty:					
Licensing	1171.6	1026.3	860.6	673.0	565.8
Foodservice and other	439.5	386.9	343.2	304.4	271.0
Total specialty	1611.1	1413.2	1203.8	977.4	836.8
Total net revenues	10383.0	9411.5	7786.9	6369.3	5294.2
Cost of sales	4645.3	3999.1	3178.8	n.a.	n.a.
Store operating expenses	3745.1	3215.9	2687.8	n.a.	n.a.
Other operating expenses	330.1	294.2	253.7	n.a.	n.a.
Depreciation and amortization expenses	549.3	467.2	387.2	n.a.	n.a.
General and administrative expenses	456.0	489.2	479.4	n.a.	n.a.
Restructuring charges	266.9	—	—	n.a.	n.a.
Total operating expenses	9992.7	8465.6	6986.9	n.a.	n.a.
Operating income	503.9	1053.9	894.0	780.5	606.5
Net earnings	315.5	672.6	564.3	494.4	388.9
Net cash provided by operations activities	1258.7	1331.2	1131.6	922.9	862.9
Capital expenditures (net)	984.5	1080.3	771.2	643.3	416.9
BALANCE SHEET					
Working capital (deficit)	(441.7)	(459.1)	(405.8)	(17.7)	604.6
Total assets	5672.6	5343.9	4428.9	3513.7	3386.3
Short-term borrowings	713.0	710.3	700.0	277.0	—
Long-term debt	550.3	550.9	2.7	3.6	4.4
Shareholders' equity	2490.9	2284.1	2228.5	2090.3	2469.9
STORE INFORMATION					
Percentage change in same store sales:					
United States (%)	(5)	4	7	9	11
International (%)	2	7	8	6	6
Consolidated (%)	(3)	5	7	8	10
Stores opened during the year (net) of closures):					
United States					
Company-operated stores	445	1065	810	580	521
Licensed stores	438	723	733	596	417
International					
Company-operated stores	236	286	240	177	160
Licensed stores	550	497	416	319	246
Total	1669	2571	2199	1672	1344

TABLE 2.2 Starbucks Corporation: consolidated statement of earnings, final quarter 2008

($ millions)	13 weeks to: Dec 28, 2008	Dec 30, 2007
Net revenues:		
Company-operated retail	2176.2	2351.5
Specialty:		
Licensing	334.3	304.8
Food service and other	104.7	111.3
Total specialty	439.0	416.1
Total net revenues	2615.2	2767.6
Cost of sales (including occupancy costs)	1196.8	1186.0
Store operating expenses	936.6	927.3
Other operating expenses	72.6	85.7
Depreciation and amortization expenses	134.3	133.2
General and administrative expenses	105.2	125.9
Restructuring charges	75.5	—
Total operating expenses	2521.0	2458.1
Operating income	117.7	333.1
Interest expense	(13.0)	(17.1)
Earnings before income taxes	98.3	326.7
Income taxes	34.0	118.6
Net earnings	64.3	208.1

and Dunkin' Donuts, which had added gourmet coffee to their menus—fundamentally changed the attractiveness of the retail market for brewed coffee? Had Starbucks failed to maintain the uniqueness of the "Starbucks Experience," which had differentiated the company from its competitors? And was this "Starbucks Experience" something that was really recognized and valued by consumers?

The Starbucks Story[4]

The rise of Starbucks from a single coffee store in Seattle's Pike Place market to a Fortune 500 company (number 261 on Fortune's 2009 listing) is now an American business legend.

Howard Schultz lived in New York where he managed the U.S. operations of a Swedish kitchenware company. Intrigued as to why a small Seattle company, Starbucks Coffee, Tea and Spice, was ordering large quantities of an unusual kind of coffee filter—a plastic cone on top of a thermos—he visited the store in 1981. The cup of coffee he was given there, made with freshly ground Sumatra beans, was a revelation. "I realized the coffee I had been drinking was swill." The owner-managers of Starbucks were Gerald Baldwin and Gordon Bowker, former University of San Francisco students who had been running the company for 10 years. Schultz was captivated by the vision of a national chain of coffee stores. Despite their reservations about the threat of Schultz's energy and ambition to the mellow ambiance of their business, Baldwin and Bowker eventually hired Schultz as their head of marketing.

Within a year of joining Starbucks, Schultz's vision of the company shifted radically. On a business trip to Milan he discovered "the romance of the Italian coffee bar" and recognized the opportunity for Starbucks to be a place where people would come to share the experience of drinking great coffee rather than to simply buy coffee beans. "It crystallized in my mind that coffee brought people together . . . and that as far as I could envision, at the time there did not exist in the U.S. a place that brought people together with coffee as the conduit."

Unable to convince his Starbucks bosses of his vision, Schultz left to open his own Italian coffee bar, Il Giornale, in 1986. A year later he bought the Starbucks company and its six stores, merged it with his three Il Giornale bars and adopted the Starbucks name for the enlarged company. By the time Starbucks went public in 1992 it had grown to 165 outlets. With the $27 million raised from the stock offering, Starbucks accelerated its expansion. From its west-coast bases in Seattle and Vancouver, Starbucks expanded nationally in both the U.S. and Canada. Expansion followed a cluster pattern—opening multiple stores in a single metro area. The idea was to increase Starbucks' local brand awareness and facilitate customers' ability to find a Starbucks anywhere within their home town. International expansion included entry into Japan in 1996 and the U.K. in 1998.

Starbucks' organic growth was augmented by selected acquisitions: the U.K.-based Seattle Coffee Company in 1998, Seattle's Best Coffee and Torrefazione Italia in 2003, and Diedrich Coffee in 2006.

Starbucks' Strategy

The Appendix describes Starbucks' business and provides data on its performance.

The Starbucks Experience

Central to Starbucks' strategy is Schultz's concept of the "Starbucks Experience." Starbucks stores—like the original Il Giornata coffee bars—were founded on Schultz's idea of creating a "third place": somewhere other than home and work where people could engage socially amidst the shared experience of drinking good coffee. Despite his original idea of replicating Italian coffee bars where customers mostly stand to drink coffee, Schultz adapted his vision to "the American equivalent of the English pub, the German beer garden and the French café."[5] With the addition of wi-fi, Starbucks stores become a place to work as well as to socialize. The Starbucks Experience combined a number of elements:

- The coffee beans of high, consistent quality. As explained in the Appendix under "Product Supply," Starbucks forms long-term arrangements with coffee growers in order to ensure that Starbucks' requirements are met while ensuring the economic viability of the growers.
- Employee involvement. The counter staff at Starbucks stores—the baristas— played a central role in creating and sustaining the Starbucks Experience. Their role was not only to brew and serve excellent coffee but to engage customers in the unique ambiance of the Starbucks coffee shop. Starbucks' human-resource practices with regard to firing, training and remunerations

were very different from those of other U.S. restaurant chains. "Schultz felt he had to make employees partners in his vision. He had to infuse them with the Starbucks culture, provide them with personal security, and give them a reason to be involved in the success of the business."[6] Starbucks' employee selection was careful and rigorous—placing a heavy emphasis on adaptability, dependability, capacity for teamwork and willingness to further Starbucks' principles and mission. Its training program extended beyond basic operating and customer-service skills to educating employees abut coffee. Unique among catering chains, Starbucks provided health insurance for almost all regular employees.

- Community relations and social purpose. Schultz's approach to human resource management was not simply about the role of Starbucks' employees as key agents in transmitting the Starbucks' Experience, but also part of a broader vision of a common humanity: "I wanted to build the kind of company my father never had the chance to work for, where you would be valued and respected wherever you came from, whatever the color of your skin, whatever your level of education. Offering heathcare was a transforming event in the equity of the Starbucks brand that created unbelievable trust among our people. We wanted to build a company that linked shareholder value to the cultural values that we want to create with our people."[7] Schulz's vision was of a company that would earn good profits but would also do good in the world: "Perhaps we have the opportunity to be a different type of global company. One that makes a profit but at the same time demonstrates a social conscience."

- The layout and design of Starbucks stores were seen as critical elements of the experience. Starbucks has a store design group that is responsible for the design of the furniture, fittings and layout of Starbucks' retail outlets. Like everything else at Starbucks, store design is subject to meticulous analysis and planning—following Schultz's dictum that "retail is detail." While every Starbucks store is adapted to reflect its unique neighborhood, "there is a subliminal unifying theme to all the stores that ties into the company's history and mission—"back to nature" without the laid-back attitude; community-minded without stapled manifestos on the walls. The design of a Starbucks store is intended to provide both unhurried sociability and efficiency on-the-run, an appreciation for the natural goodness of coffee and the artistry that grabs you even before the aroma. This approach is reflected in the designers' generous employment of natural woods and richly layered, earthy colors along with judicious high-tech accessorizing . . . No matter how individual the store, overall store design seems to correspond closely to the company's first and evolving influences: the clean, unadulterated crispness of the Pacific Northwest combined with the urban suavity of an espresso bar in Milan."[8]

- Starbucks' location strategy—its clustering of 20 or more stores in each urban hub—was viewed as enhancing the experience both in creating a local "Starbucks buzz" and in facilitating loyalty by Starbucks' customers. Starbucks' analysis of sales by individual store found little evidence that closely located Starbucks stores cannibalized one another's sales. Recognizing that convenience of location was critical to driving sales, Starbucks began adding drive-though windows to some of its stores and locating stores specifically to capitalize on drive-through customers.

Diversification

Broadening Starbucks' product range was partly about responding to customer demand (for example, requests for iced coffee eventually led to Frappuccino) and partly about building the Starbucks Experience. "The overall strategy is to build Starbucks into a destination," explained Kenneth Lombard, then head of Starbucks Entertainment. This involved adding food, music, books and videos. As a music publisher and retailer of CDs, Starbucks was hugely successful—particularly its "Artists Choice" series where well-known musicians chose their favorite tracks. "I had to get talked into this one," says Schultz. "But then I began to understand that our customers looked to Starbucks as a kind of editor. It was like, 'We trust you. Help us choose.'"

However, Starbucks was also expanding beyond its company-owned stores. As the Appendix illustrates, Starbucks expansion has included:

- Licensed stores. The desire to reach customers in a variety of locations eventually caused Starbucks to abandon its policy of only selling through company-owned outlets. Its first licensing deal was with Host Marriot, which owned a number of food and beverage concessions in U.S. airports. This was followed by licensing arrangements with Safeway and Barnes & Noble for opening Starbucks coffee shops in their stores. Overseas, Starbucks increasingly relied upon licensing arrangements with local companies.
- Distribution of Starbucks retail packs of Starbucks coffee through supermarkets and other retail food stores.
- Licensing of Starbucks brands to PepsiCo and Unilever for the supply of Starbucks bottled drinks (such as Frappuccino and Tazo teas).
- Financial services, notably the Starbucks/Bank One Duetto Visa card, which combined a store card with a Visa credit card.
- *Via* instant coffee. On February 12, 2009, news broke of Starbucks' plan to introduce an innovative instant coffee. The product was the result of long-term R&D project that had been revived by Schultz as part of his drive to reinvigorate innovation at Starbucks. *Via* was based upon a proprietary patented process which allowed the company to "absolutely replicate the taste of Starbucks coffee." It would sell through Starbucks stores at $2.95 for a pack of three. Other commentators were less sanguine. Andrew Hetzel of coffee consultancy Cafemakers, stated: "I have an expectation of what it will be like, and I think it will be harmful for the brand."[9]

Managing Turnaround

Since his return as CEO in January 2008, Schultz's redirection of Starbucks' strategy has involved more than retrenchment. Central to his hyperactive leadership was his belief that the company needed to rediscover and revitalize the "Starbucks Experience" and reestablish its connection with its customers.

During 2008, Starbucks employees from all parts and all levels of the company met to reconsider the company's purpose and principles. The result was a revised mission statement (see the Appendix). Also important to the reaffirmation of Starbucks' core identity was a renewed emphasis on corporate social responsibility.

In October 2008, Starbucks held its annual leadership meeting in New Orleans—the first time the meeting had been held outside Seattle. Starbucks used the convention as an opportunity to field 10 000 volunteers on a variety of community projects ranging from repainting damaged houses to cleaning up neighborhoods. Other initiatives included:

- *Starbucks Shared Planet*— a set of environmental sustainability, community service and ethical targets to be achieved by 2011.
- Increased commitment to small-scale coffee farmers by doubling Starbucks purchases of Fair Trade Certified Coffee in 2009.
- Partnership with Bono and the Global Fund to donate 5 cents from the sale of each serving of certain Starbucks' beverages to support AIDS programs in Africa.

Schultz also reviewed operating practices to examine their consistency with the Starbucks Experience and Starbucks image. One key change was a return to "hand-made" coffee. To speed coffee making Starbucks had replaced its La Marzocco espresso machines, which required baristas to grind coffee for each cup, with automatic Verismo machines, which merely required baristas to press a button. During 2008, Starbucks spent millions installing new coffee machines where cups of coffee were made individually from freshly ground beans. Schultz also insisted on revising Starbucks' food menu—notably withdrawing toasted breakfast sandwiches whose aromas masked those of the coffee: "The breakfast sandwiches drive revenue and profit but they are in conflict with everything we stand for in terms of the coffee and the romance of the coffee."

Most of all, Schultz traveled Starbuck's far-flung empire meeting with employees ("partners") with a view to reinforcing Starbucks' values and reigniting their drive and enthusiasm. Jenny Wiggins of the *Financial Times* describes an October 2008 meeting at London's Barbican Center for 1000 Starbucks store managers from Britain and Ireland. In addition to inspiring tales that exemplified the "humanity of Starbucks" and the role that managers played in creating an experience that "values and respects" customers, Schultz challenged his store managers with the severity of the current situation and the need to return to the values and practices that had made Starbucks a special place.[10]

By re-emphasizing Starbucks' core values, reversing store expansion, eliminating non-core products and returning to the quality of the coffee and customer service, Schultz was doing much to correct the errors of the past. The question is whether the Starbucks concept has the same distinctiveness and appeal in the second decade of the twenty-first century as in the last decade of the twentieth century. According to Don Williams, CEO of brand consultants Pi Global: "Starbucks must seriously and rapidly re-evaluate what the brand stands for, what it sells, and what the consumer experience should be. Far from exuding an air of everyday indulgence, the often slightly dog-eared assembly line that is your average Starbucks store is suffering the double whammy of being both too familiar and overpriced."

Even if Schultz succeeds in reinvigorating Starbucks, it is clear that the market for gourmet coffee, especially in North America, has changed greatly over the past two decades. Despite a widely held view that Starbucks has saturated its market, it is clear that competition is strong, with Starbucks being attacked from below (McDonald's, Dunkin' Donuts) and above (Illy, Lavazza) (see Exhibit 2.1).

EXHIBIT 2.1
Competition in the U.S. Coffee Shop Market

Sales of premium, brewed coffee were estimated to have grown by 157% between 2000 ($3 258 million) and 2005 to reach some $8 372 million. The total number of coffee shops in the U.S. increased by 70% between 2000 and 2005, bringing the total to a staggering 21 400 or one coffee house for every 14 000 Americans.

Although Starbucks was the primary driver of this growth and far-and-away the market leader, it was also subject to competition from numerous directions.

- Starbucks' traditional competitors were independent coffee shops and cafes, some of which had grown into local chains.
- Starbucks had also spawned a number of imitators who aspired to grow into national chains. Of these Caribou Coffee, with 495 coffee shops in 15 states, was its nearest competitor.
- Starbucks competed with a range of catering establishments that supplied coffee as part of a broader menu of food and beverages. Increasingly these outlets were seeking to compete more directly with Starbucks by adding premium coffee drinks to their menus. McDonald's had introduced a premium coffee (which *Consumer Reports* rated more highly than Starbucks' coffee) and was adding *McCafes* to many of its burger restaurants. Burger King and Dunkin' Donuts had also moved upmarket in their coffee offerings. McDonald's and Dunkin' Donuts both targeted Starbucks in their advertising.

The McDonald's web site, Unsnobbycoffee.com implicitly identified Starbucks as overpriced and "snobbish." Dunkin' Donuts' web site, DunkinbeatStarbucks.com, encourages emailed messages such as: "Friends don't let friends drink at Starbucks."

Outside of the U.S., Starbucks faced different competitive situations country-by-country. In most of them competition was even more intense than in the U.S. Starbucks' withdrawal from Australia was a consequence of a highly sophisticated coffee market developed and educated by immigrants from southern Europe (Italy in particular) and the Middle East.

High standards of coffee preparation and strong local preferences were also a feature of most European markets. Moreover, Starbucks also had to contend with international expansion by the Italian coffee roasters—most notably Illy, which had successfully established itself at the pinnacle of quality. A key challenge that Starbucks faced is that, once it had educated North Americans about the joy of good coffee, these new coffee connoisseurs would go on to seek superior alternatives to Starbucks.

Competition was not only in the form of other coffee-shop chains. Increasingly coffee drinkers were being introduced to the secrets of good coffee at home. A widening range of home espresso makers included sophisticated, easy-to-use coffee systems introduced by Nescafé (Nespresso) and Lavazza (A Modo Mio).

TABLE 2.3 Starbucks, Caribou Coffee and McDonald's: Financial Comparisons, 2005–8

	Starbucks, year ended				Caribou Coffee, year ended				McDonald's, year ended			
	August 2008	August 2007	August 2006	August 2005	December 2008	December 2007	December 2006	December 2005	December 2008	December 2007	December 2006	December 2005
Sales ($m)	10383	9411	7787	6369	253.9	256.8	236.2	198.0	23522	22787	20895	19117
Depreciation and amortization ($m)	549	467	389	n.a.	24.9	32.2	21.5	16.4	1208	1193	1191	1172
General and admin. expense ($m)	456	489	479	n.a.	29.1	32.3	25.9	22.7	2355	2367	2296	2118
Operating income ($m)	504	1,054	894	781	(15.5)	(30.4)	(9.5)	(4.1)	6443	3879	4433	3984
Net income ($m)	316	673	564	494	(16.3)	(30.7)	(9.1)	(4.9)	4313	2395	3544	2602
Company operated outlets	9217	8536	7185	6135	414	432	440	386	6502	6906	8166	8173
Total outlets	16680	15011	12440	10241	511	484	464	395	31967	31377	31046	30766
Sales per co. outlet	0.988	1.018	0.988	0.953	0.553	0.551	0.546	0.554	2.547	2.204	1.885	1.715
Total assets ($m)	5673	5344	4429	3514	89.6	111.8	136.3	148.0	28462	29392	28974	29989
Shareholders' equity ($m)	2491	2284	2229	2090	43.9	59.3	88.4	96.9	13382	15280	15458	15146

Appendix: Extracts from Starbucks Corporation 10-K report for Fiscal Year 2008

Part I

Item 1: Business

General   Starbucks Corporation was formed in 1985 and today is the world's leading roaster and retailer of specialty coffee. Starbucks (together with its subsidiaries, "Starbucks" or the "Company") purchases and roasts high-quality whole bean coffees and sells them, along with fresh, rich-brewed coffees, Italian-style espresso beverages, cold blended beverages, a variety of complementary food items, a selection of premium teas, and coffee-related accessories and equipment, primarily through Company-operated retail stores. Starbucks also sells coffee and tea products and licenses its trademark through other channels such as licensed retail stores and, through certain of its equity investees and licensees, Starbucks produces and sells a variety of ready-to-drink beverages. All channels outside the Company-operated retail stores are collectively known as specialty operations.

The Company's objective is to establish Starbucks as one of the most recognized and respected brands in the world. To achieve this goal, the Company plans to continue disciplined expansion of its retail operations, to grow its specialty operations and to selectively pursue other opportunities by introducing new products and developing new channels of distribution.

Revenue Components   The following table shows the Company's revenue components as a percentage of total net revenues and related specialty revenues for the fiscal year ended September 28, 2008:

Revenues	Percentage of total net revenues	Percentage of specialty revenues	
Company-operated retail	84		
Specialty:			
Licensing:			
Retail stores	8	48	%
Packaged coffee and tea	3	21	%
Branded products	1	4	%
Total licensing	12	73	%
Foodservice and other:			
Foodservice	4	25	%
Other initiatives	<1	2	%
Total foodservice and other	4	27	%
Total specialty	16	100	%
Total net revenues	100		

Company-operated Retail Stores   The Company's retail goal is to become the leading retailer and brand of coffee in each of its target markets by selling the finest quality coffee and related products and by providing each customer a unique

Starbucks Experience. The *Starbucks Experience*, or third place beyond home and work, is built upon superior customer service as well as clean and well maintained Company-operated retail stores that reflect the personalities of the communities in which they operate, thereby building a high degree of customer loyalty.

Starbucks' strategy for expanding its retail business is to increase its market share by selectively opening additional stores in existing markets and opening stores in new markets to support its long-term strategic objectives. As described in more detail in Management's Discussion and Analysis in this 10-K, the Company committed in June 2008 to close approximately 600 underperforming Company-operated stores in the U.S. The decision was an integral part of its transformation strategy, first announced in January 2008, and was a result of a rigorous evaluation of the U.S. Company-operated store portfolio. The store closures were initiated in the fourth quarter of fiscal 2008 and are expected to be completed by the end of fiscal 2009.

Starbucks Company-operated retail stores accounted for 84% of total net revenues during fiscal 2008. The following table summarizes total Company-operated retail store data for the periods indicated:

	Net stores opened year ended		Stores open as of	
	Sept. 28, 2008	Sept. 30, 2007	Sept. 28, 2008	Sept. 30, 2007
United States	445	1065	7238	6793
Canada	104	97	731	627
United Kingdom	84	66	664	580
China	37	42	178	141
Germany	27	36	131	104
Thailand	24	18	127	103
Singapore	12	8	57	45
Australia	(64)	4	23	87
Other	12	15	68	56
Total international	236	286	1979	1743
Total Company-operated	681	1351	9217	8536

At the end of fiscal 2008, the Company operated approximately 2800 drive-through locations, compared to approximately 2300 at the end of fiscal 2007, representing approximately 35% and 31%, respectively, of Company-operated stores in the U.S. and Canada combined.

All Starbucks stores offer a choice of regular and decaffeinated coffee beverages, a broad selection of Italian-style espresso beverages, cold blended beverages, iced shaken refreshment beverages, a selection of premium teas and distinctively packaged roasted whole bean coffees. Starbucks stores also offer a variety of fresh food items, including several healthy choice selections. Food items include pastries, prepared breakfast and lunch sandwiches, and salads as well as sodas, juices, and bottled water. Starbucks continues to expand its food warming program in the United States and Canada, with approximately half of these stores as of September 28, 2008 providing warm food items, primarily breakfast sandwiches. A range of coffee-making equipment and accessories are also sold in the stores. Each Starbucks store varies its product mix depending upon the size of the store and its location. Larger stores carry a broad selection of the Company's whole-bean coffees in various sizes and types of packaging, as well as coffee and espresso-making equipment and accessories. Smaller Starbucks stores and kiosks typically sell a full line of coffee beverages, a limited selection of whole-bean coffees and a few accessories such as travel tumblers and logo mugs.

Retail sales mix by product type for Company-operated stores was as follows:

Fiscal year ended	Sept. 28, 2008	Sept. 30, 2007	Oct. 1, 2006
Beverages (%)	76	75	77
Food (%)	17	17	15
Coffee-making equipment and other merchandise (%)	4	5	5
Whole bean coffees (%)	3	3	3
Total (%)	100	100	100

Specialty Operations Specialty operations strive to develop the Company's brands outside the Company-operated retail store environment through a number of channels. Starbucks strategy is to reach customers where they work, travel, shop and dine by establishing relationships with prominent third parties that share the Company's values and commitment to quality. These relationships take various forms, including licensing arrangements, foodservice accounts and other initiatives related to the Company's core businesses. In certain situations, Starbucks has an equity ownership interest in licensee operations. During fiscal 2008, specialty revenues (which include royalties and fees from licensees, as well as product sales derived from specialty operations) accounted for 16% of total net revenues.

Licensing—Retail Stores In its licensed retail store operations, the Company leverages the expertise of its local partners and shares Starbucks operating and store development experience. Licensee partners provide improved and, at times, the only access to desirable retail space. Most licensees are prominent retailers with in-depth market knowledge and access. As part of these arrangements, Starbucks receives license fees and royalties and sells coffee, tea and related products for resale in licensed locations. Employees working in licensed retail locations are required to follow Starbucks detailed store operating procedures and attend training classes similar to those given to employees in Company-operated stores.

During fiscal 2008, 438 Starbucks licensed retail stores were opened in the U.S. and, as of September 28, 2008, the Company's U.S. licensees operated 4329 stores. During fiscal 2008, 550 International licensed stores were opened. At September 28, 2008, the Company's international operating segment had a total of 3134 licensed retail stores. Product sales to and royalty and license fee revenues from U.S. and international licensed retail stores accounted for 48% of specialty revenues in fiscal 2008.

At fiscal year end 2008, Starbucks total licensed retail stores by region and specific location were as follows:

Asia Pacific		Europe/Middle East/Africa		Americas	
Japan	814	Turkey	107	United States	4329
China	269	Spain	76	Mexico	241
South Korea	254	Greece	76	Canada	231
Taiwan	221	United Arab Emirates	69	Other	44
Philippines	150	Saudi Arabia	65		
Malaysia	113	Kuwait	57		
Indonesia	69	France	46		
New Zealand	43	Switzerland	42		
		Other	147		
Total	1933	Total	685	Total	4845

Licensing—Packaged Coffee and Tea   Through a licensing relationship with Kraft Foods, Inc. ("Kraft"), the Company sells a selection of Starbucks and Seattle's Best Coffee branded packaged coffees and Tazo® teas in grocery and warehouse club stores throughout the United States. Kraft manages all distribution, marketing, advertising and promotion of these products.

The Company sells packaged coffee and tea internationally both directly to warehouse club customers, such as Costco, and through a licensing relationship with Kraft in Canada and the U.K.

By the end of fiscal 2008, the Company's coffees and teas were available in approximately 37 000 grocery and warehouse club stores, with 33 000 in the U.S. and 4000 in international markets. Revenues from this category comprised 21% of specialty revenues in fiscal 2008.

Licensing—Branded Products   The Company licenses the rights to produce and market Starbucks branded products through several partnerships both domestically and internationally. Significant licensing agreements include:

- the North American Coffee Partnership, a joint venture with the Pepsi-Cola Company in which Starbucks is a 50% equity investor, manufactures and markets ready-to-drink beverages, including bottled Frappuccino® beverages and Starbucks DoubleShot® espresso drinks;

- licensing agreements for the manufacturing, marketing and distribution of Starbucks Discoveries®, a ready-to-drink chilled cup coffee beverage, in Japan and South Korea;

- a licensing agreement established in August 2008 with Unilever and Pepsi-Cola Company for the manufacturing, marketing and distribution of Starbucks super-premium Tazo® Tea ready-to-drink beverages in the U.S. and Canada;

- the International Coffee Partnership, another joint venture with the Pepsi-Cola Company, to manufacture, market and distribute ready-to-drink beverages internationally, which currently includes bottled Frappuccino® beverages in China and Mexico.

Collectively, the revenues from these branded products accounted for 4% of specialty revenues in fiscal 2008.

Foodservice The Company sells whole bean and ground coffees, including the Starbucks and Seattle's Best Coffee brands, as well as a selection of premium Tazo® teas and other related products, to institutional foodservice companies that service business and industry, education, healthcare, office coffee distributors, hotels, restaurants, airlines and other retailers. The majority of the Company's direct accounts are through national broadline distribution networks with SYSCO Corporation and U.S. Foodservice. Starbucks foodservice sales, customer service and support resources are aligned with those of SYSCO Corporation and U.S. Foodservice.

The Company's total foodservice operations had over 19 000 accounts, primarily in the U.S., at fiscal year end 2008. Revenues from foodservice accounts comprised 25% of total specialty revenues in fiscal 2008.

Product Supply Starbucks is committed to selling only the finest whole-bean coffees and coffee beverages. To ensure compliance with its rigorous coffee standards, Starbucks controls its coffee purchasing, roasting and packaging, and the distribution of coffee used in its operations. The Company purchases green coffee beans from coffee-producing regions around the world and custom roasts them to its exacting standards for its many blends and single origin coffees.

The supply and price of coffee are subject to significant volatility. Although most coffee trades in the commodity market, high-altitude *arabica* coffee of the quality sought by the Company tends to trade on a negotiated basis at a substantial premium above commodity coffee prices, depending upon the supply and demand at the time of purchase. Supply and price can be affected by multiple factors in the producing countries, including weather, political and economic conditions. In addition, green coffee prices have been affected in the past and may be affected in the future, by the actions of certain organizations and associations that have historically attempted to influence prices of green coffee through agreements establishing export quotas or by restricting coffee supplies.

To help ensure sustainability and future supply of high-quality green coffees in Central America and to reinforce the Company's leadership role in the coffee industry, Starbucks operates the Starbucks Coffee Agronomy Company.

SRL is a wholly owned subsidiary located in Costa Rica. Staffed with agronomists and sustainability experts, this first-of-its-kind Farmer Support Center is designed to respond proactively to changes in coffee-producing countries that impact farmers and the supply of green coffee. During fiscal 2008, the Company expanded this sustainability program to Africa by establishing a Farmer Support Center in Rwanda.

The Company buys coffee using fixed-price and price-to-be-fixed purchase commitments, depending on market conditions, to secure an adequate supply of quality green coffee. Due to volatility in green coffee commodity prices, the Company has historically used fixed-price purchase contracts in order to bring greater certainty to its cost of sales in future periods and promote sustainability by paying an equitable price to coffee producers. When green coffee commodity prices are high for sustained periods of time, the Company is less likely to enter into fixed-price contracts on favorable terms and more likely to increase the use of price-to-be-fixed contracts to meet its demand for coffee. These types of contracts state the quality, quantity and delivery periods and fix the price relative to a green coffee commodity benchmark, but allow the benchmark price to be established after contract signing. An increased use of price-to-be-fixed contracts instead of fixed-price contracts decreases the predictability of coffee costs in future periods until the price of green coffee becomes "fixed" by either Starbucks or the seller.

The Company depends upon its relationships with coffee producers, outside trading companies and exporters for its supply of green coffee. The Company believes, based on relationships established with its suppliers, the risk of non-delivery on such purchase commitments is remote.

Operating Segments   Segment information is prepared on the same basis that the Company's management reviews financial information for operational decision-making purposes. Starbucks has three reportable operating segments: U.S., international and CPG . . .

United States   The U.S. operating segment sells coffee and other beverages, complementary food, whole bean coffees, and coffee-brewing equipment and merchandise primarily through Company-operated retail stores. Specialty operations within the U.S include licensed retail stores, foodservice accounts and other initiatives related to the Company's core business.

Fiscal year ended	Sept. 2008 ($ millions)	Sept. 2007 ($ millions)	Change (%)	Sept. 2008	Sept. 2007
				(As percentage of U.S. total net revenues)	
Net revenues:					
Company-operated retail	6997.7	6560.9	6.7	88.7	89.3
Specialty:					
Licensing	504.2	439.1	14.8	6.4	6.0
Foodservice and other	385.1	349.0	10.3	4.9	4.7
Total specialty	889.3	788.1	12.8	11.3	10.7
Total net revenues	7887.0	7349.0	7.3	100.0	100.0

Company-operated retail revenues increased primarily due to the opening of 445 new Company-operated retail stores in the last 12 months, partially offset by a 5% decrease in comparable store sales for fiscal 2008. The U.S. Company-operated retail business continued to experience deteriorating trends in transactions during the year, driven by the U.S. economic slowdown.

Licensing revenues increased primarily due to higher product sales and royalty revenues as a result of opening 438 new licensed retail stores in the last 12 months. Foodservice and other revenues increased primarily due to growth in new and existing foodservice accounts.

Fiscal year ended	Sept. 2008 ($ millions)	Sept. 2007 ($ millions)	Change (%)	Sept. 2008	Sept. 2007
				(As percentage of U.S. total net revenues)	
Cost of sales including occupancy costs	3371.7	2956.2	14.1	42.8	40.2
Store operating expenses[a]	3081.0	2684.2	14.8	39.1	36.5
Other operating expenses[b]	219.6	204.8	7.2	2.8	2.8
Depreciation and amortization expenses	401.7	348.2	15.4	5.1	4.7
General and administrative expenses	72.7	85.9	(15.4)	0.9	1.2
Restructuring charges	210.9	—	nm	2.7	—
Total operating expenses	7357.6	6279.3	17.2	93.3	85.4
Income from equity investees	(1.3)	0.8	nm	—	
Operating income	528.1	1070.5	(50.7)%	6.7%	14.6%

[a] As a percentage of related Company-operated retail revenues, store operating expenses were 44.0% and 40.9% for the fiscal years ended September 28, 2008 and September 30, 2007, respectively.

[b] As a percentage of related total specialty revenues, other operating expenses were 24.7% and 26.0% for the fiscal years ended September 28, 2008 and September 30, 2007, respectively.

Operating margin contracted significantly primarily due to restructuring charges incurred and to softer revenues due to weak traffic, as well as higher cost of sales including occupancy costs and higher store-operating expenses as a percentage of revenues. Restructuring charges of $210.9 million had a 270 basis point impact on the operating margin. The increase in cost of sales including occupancy costs was primarily due to higher distribution costs and higher rent expenses as a percentage of revenues. Higher store operating expenses was due to the softer sales, higher payroll-related expenditures and charges from canceling future store sites and asset impairments.

International   The international operating segment sells coffee and other beverages, complementary food, whole-bean coffees, and coffee brewing equipment and merchandise through Company-operated retail stores in Canada, the U.K. and nine other markets. Specialty operations primarily include retail store licensing operations in nearly 40 other countries and foodservice accounts, primarily in Canada and Japan. The Company's international store base continues to increase and Starbucks expects to achieve a growing contribution from established areas of the business while investing in emerging markets and channels. Many of the Company's international operations are in early stages of development that require a more extensive support organization, relative to the current levels of revenue and operating income, than in the U.S. This continuing investment is part of the Company's long-term, balanced plan for profitable growth.

Fiscal year ended	Sept. 2008 ($ millions)	Sept. 2007 ($ millions)	Change (%)	Sept. 2008	Sept. 2007
				(As a percentage of international total net revenues)	
Net revenues:					
Company-operated retail	1774.2	1437.4	23.4	84.3	84.7
Specialty:					
Licensing	274.8	220.9	24.4	13.1	13.0
Foodservice and other	54.4	37.9	43.5	2.6	2.2
Total specialty	329.2	258.8	27.2	15.7	15.3
Total net revenues	2103.4	1696.2	24.0	100.0	100.0

Company-operated retail revenues increased due to the opening of 236 new Company-operated retail stores in the last 12 months, favorable foreign currency exchange rates, primarily on the Canadian dollar, and comparable store sales growth of 2% for fiscal 2008. In the fourth quarter of fiscal 2008, Company-operated retail revenues grew at a slower rate year-over-year of 12% and comparable store sales were flat compared to the same quarter in fiscal 2007, both driven by slowdowns in the U.K. and Canada, due to the weakening global economy.

Specialty revenues increased primarily due to higher product sales and royalty revenues from opening 550 new licensed retail stores in the last 12 months.

Fiscal year ended	Sept. 2008 ($ millions)	Sept. 2007 ($ millions)	Change (%)	Sept. 2008	Sept. 2007
				(As a percentage of international total net revenues)	
Cost of sales including occupancy costs	1054.0	824.6	27.8	50.1	48.6
Store operating expenses[a]	664.1	531.7	24.9	31.6	31.3
Other operating expenses[b]	88.5	69.9	26.6	4.2	4.1
Depreciation and amortization expenses	108.8	84.2	29.2	5.2	5.0
General and administrative expenses	113.0	93.8	20.5	5.4	5.5
Restructuring charges	19.2	—	nm	0.9	—
Total operating expenses	2047.6	1604.2	27.6	97.3	94.6
Income from equity investees	54.2	45.7	18.6	2.6	2.7
Operating income	110.0	137.7	(20.1)	5.2	8.1

[a] As a percentage of related Company-operated retail revenues, store operating expenses were 37.4% and 37.0% for the fiscal years ended September 28, 2008 and September 30, 2007, respectively.

[b] As a percentage of related total specialty revenues, other operating expenses were 26.9% and 27.0% for the fiscal years ended September 28, 2008 and September 30, 2007, respectively.

Operating margin decreased primarily due to higher cost of sales including occupancy costs driven by continued expansion of lunch and warming programs in Canada, higher distribution costs and higher building maintenance expense due to store renovation activities. In addition, restructuring charges of $19.2 million recognized in fiscal 2008 had a 90 basis point impact on the operating margin, nearly all due to the closure of 61 Company-operated stores in Australia.

Global Consumer Products Group   The Global Consumer Products Group (CPG) operating segment sells a selection of whole bean and ground coffees and premium Tazo® teas through licensing arrangements in the U.S. and international markets. The CPG also produces and sells a variety of ready-to-drink beverages through its joint ventures and marketing and distribution agreements.

Fiscal year ended	Sept. 28, 2008	Sept. 30, 2007	Change (%)	Sept. 28, 2008	Sept. 30, 2007
				As percentage of CPG total net revenues	
Net revenues:					
Licensing	392.6	366.3	7.2	100.0	100.0
Total specialty	**392.6**	**366.3**	**7.2**	**100.0**	**100.0**

Total net revenues increased primarily due to higher royalties and product sales in the international ready-to-drink business and increased sales of U.S. packaged tea and international club packaged coffee.

Fiscal year ended	Sept. 28, 2008 ($ million)	Sept. 30, 2007 ($ million)	Change (%)	Sept. 28, 2008	Sept. 30, 2007
				As a % of CPG total net revenues	
Cost of sales	219.6	218.3	0.6	55.9	59.6
Other operating expenses	22.0	19.5	12.8	5.6	5.3
Depreciation and amortization expenses	—	0.1	—	—	—
General and administrative expenses	6.4	6.3	1.6	1.6	1.7
Total operating expenses	248.0	244.2	1.6	63.2	66.7
Income from equity investees	60.7	61.5	(1.3)	15.5	16.8
Operating income	205.3	183.6	11.8	52.3	50.1

Growth of operating margin was primarily due to lower cost of sales as a percentage of related revenues, partially offset by lower income from equity investees. Lower cost of sales was primarily due to a sales mix shift to more profitable products.

Notes

1 Starbucks Corporation, press release, Starbucks Reports First Quarter Fiscal 2009 Results, January 28, 2009.

2 Starbucks Corporation, press release, Starbucks Reports First Quarter Fiscal 2009 Results, January 28, 2009.

3 Starbucks Corporation, press release, Starbucks Reports First Quarter Fiscal 2009 Results, January 28, 2009.

4 This draws upon information from "Starbuck's Timeline and History," www.starbucks.com/aboutus/timeline.asp, accessed October 6, 2009 and J. Wiggins "When the Coffee Goes Cold," *Financial Times*, December 13, 2008.

5 J. Wiggins "When the Coffee goes Cold," *Financial Times*, December 13, 2008.

6 *Trouble Brews at Starbucks* (Ivey School of Management, University of Western Ontario, Case No. 9B09A, 2009).

7 Quoted in: *Howard Schultz: Building the Starbucks Community* (Harvard Business School Case No. 9-406-127, 2006).

8 "Starbucks: A Visual Cup o' Joe," Contemporary Design Foundation, www.cdf.org/issue_journal/starbucks_a_visual_cup_o_joe.html, accessed May 15, 2009.

9 "Starbucks Instant: Will It Pass The Taste Test?" Fortune, February 13, 2007, http://money.cnn.com/2009/02/13/news/companies/starbucks_instant.fortune/, accessed May 19, 2009.

10 J. Wiggins "When the Coffee goes Cold," *Financial Times*, December 13, 2008.

Case 3 The U.S. Airline Industry in 2009

Here's a list of 129 airlines that in the past 20 years filed for bankruptcy. Continental was smart enough to make that list twice. As of 1992, in fact—though the picture would have improved since then—the money that had been made since the dawn of aviation by all of this country's airline companies was zero. Absolutely zero.

Sizing all this up, I like to think that if I'd been at Kitty Hawk in 1903 when Orville Wright took off, I would have been farsighted enough, and public-spirited enough—I owed this to future capitalists—to shoot him down. I mean, Karl Marx couldn't have done as much damage to capitalists as Orville did.

WARREN BUFFETT, CHAIRMAN, BERKSHIRE HATHAWAY

The year 2009 marked a century of passenger air travel. On November 19, 1909, Deutsche Luftschiffahrt AG had been formed to fly passengers by Zeppelin airships between Berlin, Potsdam and Dusseldorf.[1] The centenary passed without commemoration or celebration in the U.S. airline industry. Most airline executives were too busy struggling to remain solvent in the face of the worst economic downturn since the 1930s.

The financial crash of 2008 was a disaster for the airline industry: passenger traffic declined sharply and profit margins evaporated. All the leading airlines with the exception of Southwest reported large losses for 2008 (see Table 3.1). It was a dramatic end to the mood of optimism that had prevailed during 2006–7 when the industry had experienced a sharp upturn in profitability and was anticipating a rare period of financial stability. But dashed hopes were business-as-usual for the airlines. The previous period during which the industry had experienced a resurgence in profitability was 1999 to mid-2001. September 11, 2001 had brought a decisive end to that interlude of prosperity.

The short-term prospects for the industry looked grim. In March 2009, the International Air Transport Association (IATA) raised its estimate of total 2008 losses for the global industry from $5 billion to $8.5 billion. For 2009, revenues were expected to decline by 12%— steeper than in 2002 following September 11, 2001; net losses were forecast to be $4.7 billion. "The state of the airline industry today is grim. Demand has deteriorated much more rapidly with the economic slowdown than could have been anticipated even a few months ago . . . The industry is in intensive care."[2] The only comparative bright spot was the U.S., where airlines had shrunk capacity in line with demand. As a result IATA was forecasting a small profit for 2009.

First quarter results for U.S. airlines for 2009 confirmed IATA forecasts. While most leading U.S. airlines reported revenue reduction of between 10% and 20% on the year-ago period, all reported smaller losses.

The results of these capacity cuts were visible from satellite pictures of the deserts of California and Arizona where the majority of the world's 2300 surplus airliners were parked. The secondhand market for commercial jet planes also reflected this excess capacity: in March 2009, Air New Zealand was trying to sell one of its Boeing 747-400 jumbos for $5 million—compared to a new price of about $240 million.[3]

Despite fragments of evidence that the U.S. economy might be bottoming out by late 2009, the immediate prospects for any sustained revival in demand looked bleak. The efforts by the Treasury Department and the Federal Reserve Board to support

TABLE 3.1 Revenues, profits, and employment of the seven largest U.S. airlines

	Revenue		Net margin		Return on assets[a]		Employees	
	2007 $ billion	2008 $ billion	2007 (%)	2008 (%)	2007 (%)	2008 (%)	2002	2008
AMR	22.9	23.8	2.3	(9.3)	2.5	(7.9)	109 500	84 100
UAL	19.1	19.3	2.0	(27.1)	2.6	(24.2)	72 000	53 000
Delta	19.2	22.7	8.4	(12.2)	0.3	(10.0)	76 100	83 822
Northwest	12.6	13.8	16.7	(45.6)	9.1	(29.6)	44 300	38 000
Continental	13.1	14.6	5.1	(4.4)	5.8	(5.1)	43 900	40 120
U.S. Airways Group	11.7	12.1	3.6	(17.7)	6.1	(26.4)	46 600	32 671
Southwest	9.9	11.0	6.5	1.6	7.0	3.8	33 700	35 512

[a] Return on assets = net income/total assets.

Source: 10-K Reports of companies.

the financial system and unfreeze credit markets appeared to be successful but the aftermath would be strained balance sheets for government, business and households. It looked as though air travel would be a major casualty of budget cuts by both firms and individuals. In addition, the relief provided by lower fuel prices was drawing to a close: during the first five months of 2009, the price of crude had almost doubled from its December 2008 low.

The primary focus for most CEOs in the industry was short-term survival. Not only were most airlines losing money but these losses were being borne by weak balance sheets. Years of operating losses, restructuring costs and support for underfunded retiree benefits had resulted in an erosion of equity and build-up of debt. However, as prospects for reaching breakeven improved, so the attention of senior executives turned to the longer term prospects for the industry. Was the U.S. airline industry doomed to endure the fierce price competition, low margins and frequent encounters with bankruptcy that had been the norm for most of its history, or was there a prospect that airlines might become a "normal" industry where firms were able to cover their cost of capital most of the time?

Among industry executives and investment analysts, opinions on the prospects for the U.S. airline industry were mixed. Some pointed to a new climate of realism and financial prudence in the industry. As a result of losses and competition from low-cost carriers (LCCs) such as Southwest and Jet Blue, the "legacy carriers" had made major progress in getting cost under control. In particular, they had confronted the labor unions and gained substantial concessions on pay, benefits and working practices. They had gained efficiency benefits from outsourcing, made better use of information technology and retired many of their fuel-inefficient older planes. The speed with which the airlines reduced capacity and the way in which they avoided costly fare wars as demand plummeted in 2008–9 showed that they had learned from harsh experience. Consolidation in the industry was also conducive to profitability, both through exploiting scale economies and reducing the pressure of competition. Following America West's merger with U.S. Airways in 2005 and Delta's merger with Northwest in 2008, many airline executives believed further consolidation was both desirable and inevitable: "We think consolidation is good for the industry, and if it makes sense for us to participate, we will. Consolidation is a natural phase for the evolution of an industry as mature as ours," observed Jack Brace, UAL's CFO, predicting that the domestic airline industry would consolidate around two to four legacy network carriers, with three being the most likely number.

Others were less sanguine. The problems of the airline industry could not be attributed to the specific circumstances of the time: international terrorism, high fuel prices and the credit crunch of 2007–9. For decades the industry had generated poor returns on capital invested in it—not just in the U.S. but in other countries too. Nor could poor industry performance be attributed to inept management. It was notable that, while the legacy carriers (such as AMR, UAL, Delta, U.S. Airlines, and Continental) struggled to remain solvent, few of the LCCs were successful and the low-cost carriers were beginning to struggle. Jet Blue and Air Tran both lost money during 2008 and Southwest only just broke even. The pessimists pointed to two unfortunate features of the industry. First, when times were bad, airlines entered Chapter 11 bankruptcy but seldom liquidated. Second, whenever demand began to revive, airlines would add capacity and new airlines would enter the business, setting up the conditions for the next profit slump. "We've been here before, many times," observed one industry veteran. "Just when the industry seems to be climbing out of the mire, the industry's dire economics reassert themselves."

From Regulation to Competition

The history of the U.S. airline industry falls into two main phases: the period of regulation up until 1978, and the period of deregulation since then.

The Airlines Under Regulation (Pre-1978)

The first scheduled airline services began in the 1920s—primarily for carrying mail rather than passengers. By the early 1930s, transcontinental routes were controlled by three airlines: United Airlines in the north, American Airlines in the south, and TWA through the middle. New entry and growing competition (notably from Delta and Continental) led to the threat of instability in the industry, and in 1938 Congress established the Civil Aeronautics Board (CAB) with authority to administer the structure of the industry and competition within it. The CAB awarded interstate routes to the existing 23 airlines, established safety guidelines and priorities, and strict rules for fares, airmail rates, route entry and exit, mergers and acquisitions and interfirm agreements. Fares were set by CAB on the basis of cost plus a reasonable rate of return. The outcome was an ossification of industry structure—despite more than 80 applications, not a single new carrier was approved between 1938 and 1978.

During the 1970s, a major shift occurred in political opinion as increasing support for economic liberalism resulted in demands for less government regulation and greater reliance on market forces. Political arguments for deregulation were supported by new developments in economics. The case for regulation had been based traditionally on arguments about "natural monopoly"—competitive markets were impossible in industries where scale economies and network effects were important. During the early 1970s, the *theory of contestable markets* was developed. The main argument was that industries did not need to be competitively structured in order to result in competitive outcomes. So long as barriers to entry and exit were low then the potential for "hit-and-run" entry would cause established firms to charge competitive prices and earn competitive rates of return. The outcome was the Airline Deregulation Act, which, in October 1978, abolished the CAB and inaugurated a new era of competition in the airline industry.[4]

The Impact of Deregulation

The abolition of controls over entry, route allocations and fares resulted in a wave of new entrants and an upsurge in price competition. By 1980, 20 new carriers—including People Express, Air Florida, and Midway—had set up.

Deregulation was also accompanied by increased turbulence in the industry: the oil shock of 1979, recession and the air traffic controllers' strike of 1981. During 1979–83, the industry incurred widespread losses that triggered bankruptcies (between 1978 and 1984 over 100 carriers went bust) and a wave of mergers and acquisitions. Despite strong expansion from 1982 onwards, the industry experienced a profit slump in 1990–4. Figure 3.1 shows industry profitability since deregulation. Profitability is acutely sensitive to the balance between demand and capacity—losses result from industry load factors falling below the breakeven level (see Figure 3.2). The role of competition in driving efficiency is evident from the near-continuous decline in real prices over the period (see Table 3.2).

FIGURE 3.1 Profitability of the U.S. airline industry, 1978–2008

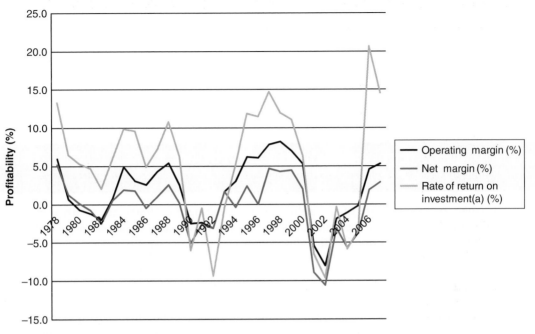

Source: Bureau of Transportation Statistics.

FIGURE 3.2 Load factors in the U.S. airline industry, 1978–2007

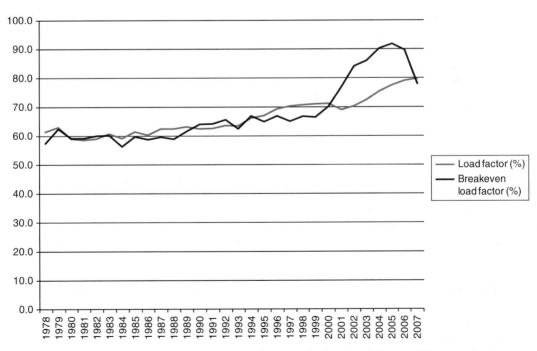

Source: Air Transport Association, Annual Economic Reports (Various Years); Bureau of Transportation Statistics.

TABLE 3.2 The falling price of air travel: revenue per passenger seat mile (cents)

	1960	1965	1970	1975	1980	1985	1990	1995	2000	2008
At nominal prices	6.1	6.1	6.0	7.7	11.5	12.2	13.4	13.5	14.6	12.7
At constant 1984 prices	20.3	19.4	15.4	14.3	14.0	11.3	10.2	8.9	8.5	6.1

Source: Bureau of Transportation Statistics.

Firm Strategy and Industry Evolution after Deregulation

Changes in the structure of the airline industry during the 1980s and 1990s were primarily a result of the strategies of the airlines as they sought to adjust to the new conditions of competition in the industry and gain competitive advantage.

Route Strategies: The Hub-and-Spoke System

During the 1980s the major airlines reorganized their route maps. A system of predominantly point-to-point routes was replaced by one where each airline concentrated its routes on a few major airports linked by frequent services using large aircraft, with smaller, nearby airports connected to these hubs by shorter routes using smaller aircraft. This "hub-and-spoke" system offered two major benefits:

- It allowed greater efficiency through reducing the total number of routes needed to link a finite number of cities within a network and concentrating traveler and maintenance facilities in fewer locations. It permitted the use of larger, more cost-efficient aircraft for interhub travel. The efficiency benefits of the hub-and-spoke system were reinforced by scheduling flights so that incoming short-haul arrivals were concentrated at particular times to allow passengers to be pooled for the longer haul flights on large aircraft.
- It allowed major carriers to establish dominance in major regional markets and on particular routes. In effect, the major airlines became more geographically differentiated in their route offerings. Table 3.3 shows cities where a single airline held a dominant local market share. The hub-and-spoke system also created a barrier to the entry of new carriers who often found it difficult to obtain gates and landing slots at the major hubs.

The hub-and-spoke networks of the major airlines were extended by establishing alliances with local ("commuter") airlines. Thus American Eagle, United Express and Delta Shuttle were franchise systems established by AMR, UAL and Delta, respectively, whereby commuter airlines used the reservation and ticketing systems of the major airlines and coordinated their operations and marketing policies with those of their bigger partners.

TABLE 3.3 Local market share of largest airline for selected U.S. cities (by number of passengers), 2009

City	Airline	Share of passengers (%)
Dallas-Forth Worth	American	73
Miami	American	71
Minneapolis-St. Paul	Northwestern	59
Detroit	Northwestern	54
Houston	Continental	62
Atlanta	Delta	53
Charlotte	U.S. Airways	55
Baltimore	Southwest	53
Newark	Continental	52
San Francisco	United	37
Denver	United	37
Cincinnati	Delta	33

Source: Bureau of Transportation Statistics.

Mergers

New entry during the period of deregulation had reduced seller concentration in the industry (see Table 3.4). However, the desire of the leading companies to build national (and international) route networks encouraged a wave of mergers and acquisitions in the industry—some triggered by the financial troubles that beset several leading airlines. Consolidation would have gone further without government intervention on antitrust grounds; however, Department of Justice approval of the Delta-Northwest merger pointed to a more lenient approach to airline mergers. Figure 3.3 shows some of the main mergers and acquisitions. During 2002–5, concentration declined as a result of capacity reduction by the major bankrupt

TABLE 3.4 Concentration in the U.S. airline industry

Year	CR4 (%)	Year	CR4 (%)
1935	88	1987	64.8
1939	82	1990	61.5
1949	70	1999	66.4
1954	71	2002	71.0
1977	56.2	2005	55.4
1982	54.2	2008	49.1

Note: The four-firm concentration ratio measures the share of the industry's passenger-miles accounted for by the four largest companies. During 1935–54, the four biggest companies were United, American, TWA, and Eastern. During 1982–2005, the four biggest companies were American, United, Delta, and Northwest. The 2008 data relate to American, United, Delta and Southwest.
Source: U.S. Department of Transportation.

FIGURE 3.3 Mergers and acquisitions among major U.S. passenger airlines, 1981–2009

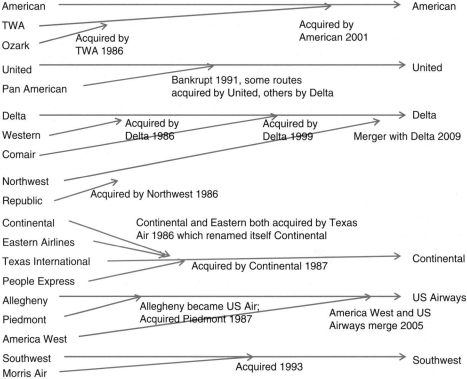

Source: Updated from S. Borenstein, "The Evolution of U.S. Airline Competition," *Journal of Economic Perspectives*, 6(2), 1992, p. 48.

airlines (United, Delta and Northwest) and market share gains by low-cost carriers.

Prices and Costs

Intensification of competition following deregulation was most apparent in the pricing of air tickets. Price cutting was typically led either by established airlines suffering from weak revenues and excess capacity, or by low-cost carriers. The new, low-cost entrants played a critical role in stimulating the price wars that came to characterize competition after deregulation. People Express, Braniff, New York Air and Southwest all sought aggressive expansion through rock-bottom fares made possible by highly efficient cost structures and a bare-bones service (the low-cost carriers economized on in-flight meals, entertainment and baggage handling). Although most of the low-cost newcomers failed during the early years of airline deregulation, they were soon replaced by new entrepreneurs eager to start up their own airlines.

In response to the price initiatives of the low-cost airlines, the major carriers sought to cut prices selectively. Fare structures became increasingly complex as airlines sought to separate price-sensitive leisure customers from price-inelastic business travelers. As a result, fare bands widened: advanced-purchased economy fares with Saturday night stays were as little as one-tenth of the first-class fare for the same journey.

Price cuts were also selective by route. Typically the major airlines offered low prices on those routes where they faced competition from low-cost rivals. Southwest, the biggest and most successful of the economy carriers, complained continually of predatory price cuts by its larger rivals. However, the ability of the major airlines to compete against the budget airlines was limited by the majors' cost structures—in particular, restrictive labor agreements, infrastructure and commitment to extensive route networks. To meet the competition of low-cost newcomers, several of the majors set up new subsidiaries to imitate the strategies and cost structures of the budget airlines. These included: Continental's Continental Lite (1994), UAL's Shuttle by United (1995), Delta's Song (1993) and United's Ted (1994). The closure of United's Ted airline in 2008 marked the end of attempts by the legacy carriers to create their own budget airlines.

During the crisis years of 2001–9, the major airlines made strenuous efforts to cut costs. Union contracts were renegotiated, inefficient working practices terminated, unprofitable routes abandoned and employment numbers reduced. Nevertheless, the budget airlines still maintained a substantial cost advantage over the majors. Higher fuel prices hit the major airlines more heavily than the low-cost carriers. Not only did the low-cost carriers have newer, more fuel-efficient planes but their stronger financial positions allowed them to make forward purchases to protect against escalating fuel prices.

The Quest for Differentiation

Under regulation, the inability to compete on price resulted in airline competition shifting to nonprice dimensions—customer service and in-flight food and entertainment. Deregulation brutally exposed the myth of customer loyalty: most travelers found little discernible difference among the offerings of different major airlines and were becoming more indifferent as to which airline they used on a particular route. As airlines increasingly cut back on customer amenities, efforts at differentiation became primarily focused upon business and first-class travelers. The high margins on first- and business-class tickets provided a strong incentive to attract these customers by means of spacious seats and intensive in-flight pampering. For leisure travelers it was unclear whether their choice of carrier was responsive to anything other than price and the low margins on these tickets limited the willingness of the airlines to increase costs by providing additional services.

The most widespread and successful initiative to build customer loyalty was the introduction of frequent flyer schemes. American's frequent-flyer program was launched in 1981 and was soon followed by all the other major airlines. By offering free tickets and upgrades on the basis of miles flown, and setting threshold levels for rewards, the airlines encouraged customers to concentrate their air travel on a single airline. By the end of 2006, airlines' unredeemed frequent-flyer distance had surged to over 10 trillion miles. By involving other companies as partners—car rental companies, hotel chains, credit card issuers—frequent-flyer programs became an important source of additional revenue for the airlines, being worth over $10 billion annually.

The Industry in 2009

The Airlines

At the beginning of 2009, the U.S. airline industry (including air cargo firms) comprised 151 companies, many of them local operators. Table 3.5 lists those with annual revenue exceeding $100 million. The industry was dominated by seven major passenger airlines—United, American, Delta, Northwestern, Continental, U.S. Airways, and Southwest (see Table 3.6). The importance of the leading group was enhanced by its networks of alliances with smaller airlines. Given the perilous financial state of so many of the leading airlines, most observers expected that the trend towards consolidation in the industry would continue.

Market for Air Travel

At the beginning of the twenty-first century, airlines provided the dominant mode of long-distance travel in the U.S. For shorter journeys, cars provided the major alternative. Alternative forms of public transportation—bus and rail—accounted for a small proportion of journeys in excess of a hundred miles. Only on a few routes (for example, between Washington, New York and Boston) did trains provide a viable alternative to air.

Most forecasts pointed to continued growth in the demand for air travel—but at a much slower rate than in earlier decades. During the 1980s and 1990s, passenger miles flown grew at a rate of 5% per annum, then slowed during the next decade. In March 2009, the FAA predicted a fall in passenger miles flown of 7.8% for 2009, with a long-term trend rate of growth of 2% to 3% through 2025.[5] Several observers thought this overoptimistic: economizing by both firms and consumers would depress demand. Moreover, an upsurge in video conferencing suggested that the long-anticipated shift from face-to-face business meetings to virtual business meetings had finally arrived.

Important changes were occurring within the structure of demand. Of particular concern to the airlines was evidence that the segmentation between business and leisure customers was breaking down. Conventional wisdom dictated that the demand for air tickets among leisure travelers was fairly price elastic; that of business travelers was highly inelastic. Hence, the primary source of airline profit was high-margin business fares. During 2008–9, increasing numbers of companies changed their travel policies to limit or eliminate employee access to premium-class air travel.[6]

Some of the increased pressure on prices could be attributed to changes in the distribution of airline tickets. The advent of the internet had decimated traditional travel agencies—retailers that specialized in the sale of travel tickets, hotel reservations and vacation packages. Meanwhile the companies were developing their direct sales organizations using both telephone and Web-based reservations systems. However, the airlines were slower than e-commerce startups in exploiting the opportunities of the internet. Despite the launch of Orbitz (the airlines' own online reservations service) in June 2001, Expedia and Travelocity lead online air ticket sales. As well as wielding greater bargaining power than traditional travel agencies, they also provided consumers with unparalleled price transparency, permitting the lowest price deals to be quickly spotted.

TABLE 3.5 The U.S. airline companies in 2008

	Employees		Employees
Major carriers			
ABX/Airborne Express	4983	Federal Express	144 237
Airtran	7825	Frontier	4850
Alaska Airlines	10 195	Jet Blue	11 852
American	75 074	Mesa	2940
American Eagle	9976	Northwest	29 137
Atlantic Southeast	4454	Skywest	9889
Comair	5720	Southwest	35 852
Continental	37 720	United	48 571
Delta	48 248	United Parcel	6115
Express Jet	5403	US Airways	33 809
National carriers			
Air Transport Int'l	409	Mesaba	4374
Air Wisconsin	2930	Miami Air	418
Allegiant	1560	Midwest Express	1183
Amerijet	559	North American	840
Arrow	514	Omni Air	1074
Astar	895	Pinnacle	4204
Astar Air Cargo	895	Polar Air Cargo	366
Atlas Air	1249	PSA Airlines	990
Continental Micronesia	1250	Ryan Int'l	576
Evergreen	484	Spirit	2410
Executive	1891	Sun Country	766
Florida West	61	USA 3000	556
Hawaiian	3707	USA Jet	191
Horizon	3751	World	1494
Kalitta Air	962		
Large regional carriers			
Aerodynamics	244	Lynx	375
Aloha Air Cargo	393	Northern Air Cargo	235
Capital Cargo	217	Pace	482
Casino Express	123	Republic Airlines	1432
Centurion Air Cargo	625	Shuttle America	1255
Colgan	1324	Southern Air	544
Compass	761	Tatonduk	291
GoJet	445	Tradewinds	69
Gulf & Caribbean	63	Virgin America	1305
Lynden Air Cargo	160		

Source: Bureau of Transportation Statistics.

TABLE 3.6 The cost structure of the U.S. airline industry by activity, 2002, 2005, and 2007

	Percentage of total operating costs		
Cost item	2002	2005	2007
Flying operations	30.1	36.5	37.9
Aircraft and traffic servicing	15.9	14.1	13.6
Maintenance	12.2	10.3	10.2
Promotion and sales	9.3	5.7	5.2
Transport related	10.0	16.7	16.9
Passenger services	8.3	6.2	5.4
Administrative	7.5	6.0	6.5
Depreciation and amortization	6.7	4.5	4.3
TOTAL	100.0	100.0	100.0

Source: Air Transport Association.

The decline of the traditional travel-agent sector was hastened by the reduction or elimination of commissions paid to travel agents. By 2008, commissions paid by airline companies to resellers fell to less than 1% of operating expenses (see Table 3.6), down from 6.2% in 1991. By 2008, the traditional travel agency industry was dominated by a few global leaders such as American Express and Thomas Cook.

Airline Cost Conditions

A little more than one-third of airline operating costs are accounted for by flying operations whereas servicing and maintenance account for another one-quarter (see Table 3.6). Labor and fuel costs are by far the biggest individual cost items

TABLE 3.7 Operating costs in the U.S. airline industry, 2006 and 2008

	Increase in cost (%)	Percentage of total operating expenses	
Cost item	2002–8	2006	2008
Labor	−6.0	23.8	24.36
Fuel	327.9	25.5	35.94
Professional services	49.9	7.8	8.07
Food and beverage	−11.4	1.5	1,25
Landing fees	31.4	2	1.93
Maintenance material	34.6	1.4	2.29
Aircraft insurance	−52.0	0.1	0.48
Passenger commissions	−27.0	1.3	0.97
Communication	4.3	0.9	1.01
Advertising and promotion	2.2	0.8	0.60
Transport-related expenses	167.4	14.7	19.23
Other operating expenses	93.6	7.6	3.86

Source: Bureau of Transport Statistics.

(see Table 3.7). A key feature of the industry's cost structure is the very high proportion of costs that are fixed. For example, because of union contracts, it was difficult to reduce employment and hours worked during downturns. The majors' need to maintain their route networks added to the inflexibility of costs—the desire to retain the integrity of the entire network made the airlines reluctant to shed unprofitable routes during downturns. An important implication of the industry's cost structure is that, at times of excess capacity, the marginal costs of filling empty seats on scheduled flights are extremely low.

Labor The industry's labor costs are boosted by the high level of employee remuneration—average pay in airlines was $55 950 in 2007; almost 40% higher than the average for all private industries.[7] Labor costs were also boosted by low labor productivity that resulted from rigid working practices agreed with unions. Most airline workers belong to one of a dozen major unions, the Association of Flight Attendants, the Air Line Pilots Association, and the International Association of Machinists and Aerospace Workers being the most important. These unions have a tradition of militancy and have been highly successful in negotiating pay increases far above the rate of inflation.

Between 2002 and 2009, the airlines forced major concessions from their employees. As a result, average compensation (including benefits) declined from $79 356 in 2003 to $74 786 in 2007. Industry employment fell from a peak of 680 000 in 2000 to 532 000 in 2008.[8]

Fuel How much a carrier spends on fuel depends on the age of its aircraft and its average flight length. Newer planes and longer flights lead to higher fuel efficiency. The fuel efficiency of different aircraft varies widely, primarily dependent on the number of engines. Fuel prices represent the most volatile and unpredictable cost item for the airlines due to fluctuations in the price of crude oil. Between January 2002 and June 2008, New York spot crude prices rose from $19 to $140 a barrel before falling to $40 in December 2008. By April 2009, crude prices were back above $50 a barrel.

Equipment Aircraft were the biggest capital expenditure item for the airlines. At prices of up to $250 million each (the A380 sells at around $350 million), the purchase of new planes represented a major source of financial strain for the airlines. While Boeing and Airbus competed fiercely for new business (especially when their order book was low, as in 2002–4), aggressive discounts and generous financing terms for the purchase of new planes disguised the fact that a major source of profits for the aircraft manufacturers was aftermarket sales. Over the past 20 years the number of manufacturers of large jets declined from four to two. Lockheed ceased civilian jet manufacture in 1984; McDonnell Douglas was acquired by Boeing in 1997. The leading suppliers of regional jets were Bombardier of Canada and Embraer of Brazil. During 2005–8, Boeing's return on equity averaged 21.3%.

Airport Facilities Airports play a critical role in the U.S. aviation industry. They are hugely complex, expensive facilities and few in number. Only the largest cities are served by more than one airport. Despite the rapid, sustained growth in air transport since deregulation, Denver is the only major new airport to have been built. Most airports are owned by municipalities; they typically generate substantial revenue flows for the cities. Landing fees are set by contracts between the airport and the airlines and are typically based on aircraft weight. New York's La Guardia airport has the highest landing fees in the U.S., charging over $6000 for a Boeing 747 to land. In 2007, the airlines paid over $2 billion to U.S. airports in landing fees and a further $3.0 billion in passenger facility charges.

Four U.S. airports—JFK and La Guardia in New York, Chicago's O'Hare, and Washington's Reagan National—are officially "congested" and takeoff and landing slots are allocated to individual airlines where the airlines assume *de facto* ownership. The cutback in airline capacity during 2008 and 2009 has temporarily relieved problems of congestion and reversed the escalation in the value of takeoff and landing slots.

Cost Differences between Airlines One of the arguments for deregulation had been that there were few major economies of scale in air transport; hence large and small airlines could coexist. Subsequently, little evidence has emerged of large airlines gaining systematic cost advantages over their smaller rivals. However, there are economies associated with network density—the greater the number of routes within a region, the easier it is for an airline to gain economies of utilization of aircraft, crews, and passenger and maintenance facilities. In practice, cost differences between airlines are due more to managerial, institutional and historical factors rather than the influence of economies of scale, scope, or density. The industry's cost leader, Southwest, built its strategy and management systems around the goal of low costs. By offering services from minor airports, with limited customer service, a single type of airplane, job-sharing among employees and salary levels substantially less than those paid by other major carriers, Southwest together with Jet Blue has one of the industry's lowest operating costs per available seat mile (CASM) despite flying relatively short routes. Conversely, U.S. Airways has the highest operating costs among major airlines—partly because of route concentration in the north-east (short routes, adverse winter weather) but also as a result of low productivity arising from restrictive union agreements. Table 3.8 shows differences in unit costs, unit revenues and capacity utilization among the airlines.

A critical factor determining average costs is capacity utilization. Because most costs, at least in the short run, are fixed, profitable operation depends on achieving breakeven levels of capacity operation. When airlines are operating below breakeven capacity there are big incentives to cut prices in order to attract additional business. The industry's periodic price wars tended to occur during periods of slack demand and on routes where there were several competitors and considerable excess capacity. The industry's ability to reduce losses during the first quarter of 2009 was a result of the airlines reducing capacity in line with falling demand.

Achieving high load factors while avoiding ruinously low prices is a major preoccupation for the airlines. All the major airlines have adopted yield-management systems—highly sophisticated computer models that combine capacity and purchasing data and rigorous financial analysis to provide flexible price determination. The goal is to earn as much revenue on each flight as possible. Achieving this goal has meant a proliferation of pricing categories.

Entry and Exit

Hopes by the deregulators that the U.S. airline business would be a case study of competition in a "contestable market" were thwarted by two factors: significant barriers to both entry and exit and evidence that potential competition was no substitute for actual competition in lowering fares on individual routes.[9] The capital requirements of setting up an airline can be low (a single leased plane will suffice)

TABLE 3.8 Operating data for the larger airlines, 2006 and 2008

	Available seat miles (billions)		Load factor (%)		Operating revenue per available seat mile (cents)		Operating expense per available seat mile (cents)	
	2006	2008	2006	2008	2006	2008	2006	2008
American	175.9	150.4	82.0	82.2	12.48	14.50	12.47	15.73
United	139.8	123.2	82.1	81.3	13.13	14.88	13.08	16.18
Delta	133.5	117.3	77.8	82.3	12.98	16.25	13.57	16.25
Northwest	91.8	72.0	82.7	85.0	14.33	16.63	14.47	17.35
Continental	85.5	91.4	83.1	81.4	13.51	15.15	13.26	15.53
Southwest	85.2	94.9	73.0	71.2	9.52	10.65	8.46	10.25
U.S. Airways	83.9	68.3	77.6	81.8	15.68	16.80	15.20	19.18
Air Tran	15.4	21.9	74.4	78.9	10.10	10.70	9.79	10.98
Jet Blue	23.8	29.7	82.5	80.5	7.55	10.48	7.48	10.18
Alaska	23.2	22.3	76.4	77.3	11.32	13.30	11.52	13.40

Source: Bureau of Transportation Statistics; 10-K reports of companies.

but offering an airline service requires setting up a whole system comprising gates, airline and aircraft certification, takeoff and landing slots, baggage handling services and the marketing and distribution of tickets. At several airports, the dominance of gates and landing slots by a few major carriers made entry into particular routes difficult and forced start-up airlines to use secondary airports. Despite the challenges of entry barriers and the dismal financial performance of the industry there seemed to be no shortage of willing entrepreneurs attracted to the apparent glamour of owning an airline. International airlines were also potential entrants into the U.S. domestic market. However, the depressed state of the industry has prevented a comprehensive E.U.–U.S. open skies agreement that would allow access by European airlines to intra-U.S. routes.

A key factor intensifying competition in the industry has been the barriers to exit that prevent the orderly exit of companies and capacity from the industry. The tendency for loss-making airlines to continue in the industry for long periods of time can be attributed to two key exit barriers: first, contracts (especially with employees) give rise to large closure costs; second, Chapter 11 of the bankruptcy code allows insolvent companies to seek protection from their creditors (and from their existing contracts) and continue operation under supervision of the courts. A critical problem for otherwise financially healthy airlines was meeting competition from bankrupt airlines, which had the benefit of artificially lowered costs.

Looking to the Future

At the end of May 2009, most industry observers were pessimistic about the outlook for the industry. While it looked as though the U.S. economy would avoid an outright depression, the first fruit of the "green shoots" of economic recovery was a rebound in the price of oil.

The mood of pessimism was reflected in stock-market valuation of airline companies and in their credit ratings. The total market capitalization of all quoted U.S. passenger airline companies at the end of May 2009 was $17.4 billion—less than half the value of its largest supplier, Boeing, and a mere 4% of the market value of Exxon Mobil. The market's view of the airlines' debt was similarly bleak. Only Southwest had an investment grade credit rating; all other airline debt was rated "junk" (below BBB−) by S&P. In the second quarter of 2009, Fitch downgraded the debt ratings of both AMR and UAL to CCC.

On the positive side, the legacy airlines had been successful in reducing their cost base through productivity improvements and reductions in compensation and benefits. As a result the cost gap between the LCCs and the legacy airlines had narrowed. However, although this had improved the competitive situation of the legacy airlines relative to the LCCs, it appeared that industry-wide cost reductions—whether from lower fuel prices or greater efficiency—did little to improve the profitability of the airline industry as a whole. The intensity of price competition meant that industry-wide cost reductions tended to be passed on to customers in lower fares.

The key issue was whether industry consolidation and a greater willingness to reduce capacity might lead to firmer pricing on the industry. The speed of capacity adjustment during 2008 and 2009 suggested that the airlines were more willing to adjust capacity to demand—and also more able to do so as a result of more flexible union agreements. The key issue was whether the new discipline would survive the next upturn in the industry. It was possible that the tightening of credit markets might help maintain a more cautious approach to capacity expansion. The long-term failure of the industry to earn a rate of return that came close to covering its cost of capital was likely to imply continuing difficulties for the airlines in financing new planes and other capital equipment. Doug Parker, U.S. Airways CEO, observed: "We have in this business been able to fund long-term losses with outside capital . . . and that is going to be harder to do in the future," citing "fundamental" changes for airlines' financial partners such as banks, aircraft makers, lessors and other suppliers.[10]

The evidence of past revivals in the industry suggested that they came to an end either as a result of external events or by the industry's own propensity to overinvest. In the case of the two previous upturns—1996-99 and 2006-08—external events were the critical factors (the September 11 terrorist attacks and the financial crisis of 2008). But even without adverse external events, the industry had shown a tendency towards over-optimism and lack of financial discipline that has fuelled investment in new capacity both by established airlines and new start-ups. With forecasts that demand for air travel would pick up gradually during the latter part of 2009 and into 2010, the key question was whether the airlines would be able to maintain the disciplined approach to cost control, capacity, and pricing that they had shown since the onset of the financial crisis.

Most encouraging was the success of the airlines in cost cutting. Yet, the efforts of the major airlines in improving operational efficiency also raised some perplexing questions. The widespread assumption had been that, if the major airlines could reduce their costs to the level of Southwest and the other low-cost carriers, they could enjoy profit levels similar to those experienced by Southwest. Despite the efforts of the majors, Southwest, Jet Blue and the other budget airlines still retained a substantial cost advantage over the legacy carriers. Even if the major airlines could continue to reduce costs, who would the beneficiaries be—the long-suffering shareholders of the companies, or travelers as competition to fill seats encouraged the airlines to pass on cost reductions to customers in the form of lower prices?

Notes

1 U.S. Centennial of Flight Commission, "The Early Years of German Commercial Aviation," www.centennialofflight. gov/essay/Commercial_Aviation/germany/Tran19.htm, accessed October 7, 2009.

2 "Airline Industry in Intensive Care," *Financial Times,* March 25, 2009.

3 "Deserts Littered by State of Airline Industry," *Financial Times,* March 5, 2009.

4 Abolition of the CAB meant that the primary responsibility for airline regulation was with the Federal Aviation Administration, which was responsible for airline safety.

5 "FAA: Air Travel will Fall 7.8% in '09," CNN, March 31, 2009, http://money.cnn.com/2009/03/31/news/companies/ Airlines/index.htm, accessed October 29, 2009.

6 "Business Travel Blues," *Washington Post,* March 17, 2009, http://www.washingtonpost.com/wp-dyn/content/ article/2009/03/17/AR2009031701280.html, accessed October 209, 2009.

7 Air Transport Association, *2008 Economic Report,* ATA, Washington DC.

8 Air Transport Association, *2008 Economic Report,* ATA, Washington DC.

9 On the principles of contestability and its application to the U.S. airline industry see: S. Martin, "The Theory of Contestable Markets," discussion paper, Department of Economics, Purdue University, July 2000.

10 "Airlines: Where Capital Goes to Die," *Business Week,* May 5, 2009.

Case 4 Ford and the World Automobile Industry in 2009

Ford in Crisis

By June 2009, Ford Motor Company was the only remaining member of Detroit's "Big Three" to have escaped bankruptcy. Chrysler had filed for Chapter 11 protection on April 30; General Motors had followed on June 1. For Chief Financial Officer, Lewis Booth, the eight months since his appointment in November 2008 had involved unremitting pressure. The financial crisis that followed the collapse of Lehman Brothers in September 2008 had engulfed the entire U.S. automobile sector. By the time President Obama took office in January 2009, U.S. auto sales were half of those a year previously. This fall in demand was unprecedented in the industry's history. Ford reported a $14.7 billion loss for 2008; a result of which was the elimination of stockholders' equity.[1]

TABLE 4.1 Ford estimates of U.S. sales and its own financial needs

	Forecast U.S. auto sales (million units)			Ford's estimated additional financing requirement ($ billion)
	2009	2010	2011	
GDP decline of 3%; recession persists throughout 2009	11.0	12.5	14.0	9
More severe slump persisting into 2010	10.5	11.0	12.0	13

Source: Ford Motor Company, Business Plan Submitted to the Senate Banking Committee, December 2, 2008.

Booth's attention had, by June 2009, shifted from short-term survival to the longer term financial outlook for Ford. The evidence that Ford had submitted to the Senate Banking Committee in December 2008 had estimated the company's financing needs on the basis of "current-rates" and "worst-rates" growth scenarios (See Table 4.1). Since then the world economy had stabilized and some forecasters were predicting that the U.S. economy would begin growing again in 2010. For the world auto industry, government incentives for scrapping old cars and purchasing new, fuel-efficient models had done much to stabilize demand—especially in Europe. Ford's results for the first quarter of 2009 showed signs of improvement: despite a continuing fall in sales, its $1.4 billion loss for the quarter was much smaller than the loss in each of the previous two quarters.

As the short-term threat of insolvency receded, Booth turned increasingly to Ford's longer term financial outlook. In December 2008, Booth had forecast that Ford would break even in 2011. Ford's cost-reduction measures had already begun to bear fruit— it had started its restructuring long before GM and Chrysler. During 2009 it would see the benefits of its plant closures, its early switch to smaller, more fuel-efficient cars and the sale of its loss-making Jaguar, Land Rover and Aston Martin subsidiaries.

However, Booth recognized that Ford's return to profitability would depend not only on its own efforts, but also upon the state of the automobile industry in a post-recessionary world. While the short-term outlook of the industry improved over the later part of 2009, the long-term outlook became more alarming.

Booth had taken comfort in the fact that Ford's stronger operational and financial performance would allow it to emerge as one of the survivors of the crisis while weaker competitors failed. A similar view was taken by Daimler Benz's CEO who predicted that 2009 would be a "Darwinian year" for the auto industry. Yet, by June 2009, there was little evidence of competitive selection:

> [I]nstead of natural selection, something else happened: governments around the world, from Canada and Brazil to Russia and South Korea, stepped in with prodigious amounts of cash to keep car plants open and assembly lines running.
>
> All told, automakers have benefited from well in excess of $100 billion of direct bail-out funds or indirect state aid, such as scrappage schemes, since global sales collapsed last October—in nominal terms, the biggest ever short-term intervention in manufacturing.
>
> All this money has preserved jobs in car making, still the linchpin of many industrial economies. But the money has also prevented a necessary shake-out in an industry that has long had too many producers. Consultants at PwC

estimate the industry has the capacity to build 86 million units this year, almost a record—and 31 million more than the 55 million vehicles that it will sell. "What appeared to be a unique opportunity to address the industry's biggest issue—excess capacity—has been missed," says Michael Tyndall, an analyst with Nomura. In Europe not a single plant has closed permanently, thanks to bail-outs.

"The shape of the industry looks all but the same, except that governments have tipped lots of money in and prevented Darwinian selection," says Max Warburton, analyst at Sanford Bernstein. "It has been a good reminder of what this industry is: a government-supported job creation scheme."

Long-term observers of the industry point out that it has never operated on the pure free-market principles. Governments have always intervened in hard times. The status of many carmakers as national champions is bolstered by dynastic family owners at about half the big producers, who often rank continuity and control above shareholder value. Both they and governments form a big obstacle to consolidation.[2]

The thought of an industry structure that was barely changed from that of the past decade was profoundly depressing to Booth: between 1990 and 2008 the world's five biggest auto makers (GM, Toyota, Ford, Daimler-Chrysler and Volkswagen) had earned on average net margin of 1.1%; their return on invested capital had been far below their cost of capital and together they had destroyed billions in shareholder value. However, even in the absence of consolidation among existing auto makers, it was clear that the structure of the industry was far from remaining static. The shifting of demand from the mature industrial nations to the growing markets of Asia, Eastern Europe and Latin America was accompanied by the emergence of new competitors from these same regions. At a more fundamental level, the combined forces of technology and environmental concerns were redirecting the industry's evolutionary path. Ford planned to introduce all-electric commercial vans in 2010 and all-electric automobiles in 2011.[3]

Development of the World Automobile Market[4]

The Evolution of Market Demand

During the 1880s, the first internal-combustion powered vehicles were produced in Europe—notably by Gottlieb Daimler and Karl Benz in Germany. By the turn of the century hundreds of small companies were producing automobiles both in Europe and in America. The subsequent 120 years saw the industry developing at different rates in different parts of the world. The U.S. market saw its fastest rates of growth during 1910–28 and then after the Second World War. Since the mid-1960s, the combined output of autos and trucks was broadly stable—despite cyclical fluctuations (see Figure 4.1). Western Europe and Japan also experienced maturing of their markets with production peaking in 1989–90. In all the advanced industrial countries, the tendency for cars to last longer created a downward trend in the demand for motor vehicles well before the 2008 recession (see Figure 4.2).

As a result, the automobile producers looked increasingly to the newly industrializing countries for market opportunities. During the 1980s and 1990s,

FIGURE 4.1 U.S. motor vehicle production, 1900–2008

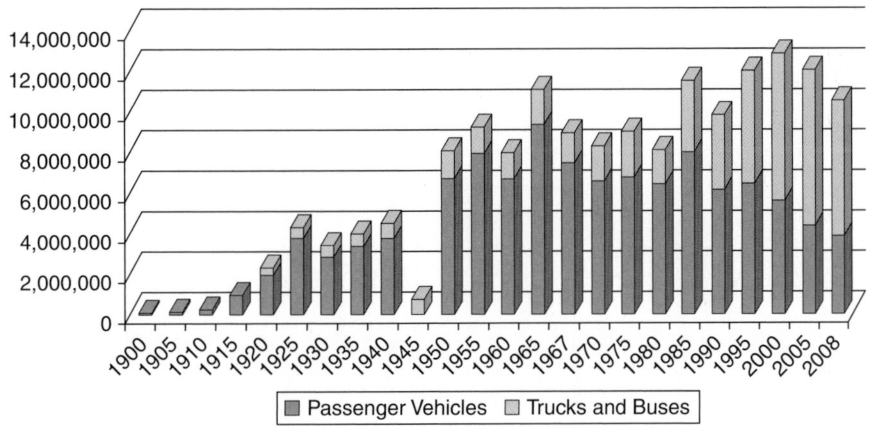

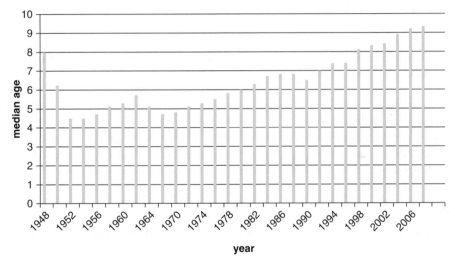

FIGURE 4.2 Median age of passenger cars in the U.S.

Source: R. L. Polk & Co.

newly industrializing countries such as Korea, Malaysia, Thailand, Turkey, and Argentina offered the best growth prospects. During 2000 to 2009, the BRIC countries (Brazil, Russia, India, and China) were the world's primary growth markets. As a result, the world production of cars and trucks continued to grow (see Figure 4.3).

The Evolution of the Automobile

The early years of the industry were characterized by considerable uncertainty over the design and technology of the motorcar. Early "horseless carriages" were precisely that—they followed design features of existing horse-drawn carriages and buggies.

FIGURE 4.3 World motor vehicle production, 1950–2008

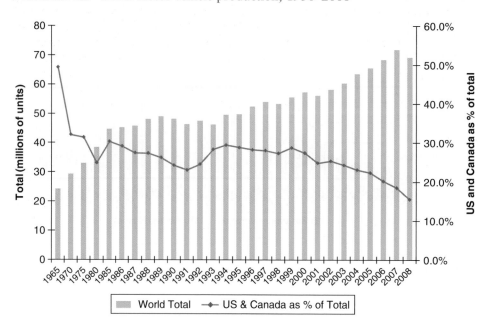

Early motorcars demonstrated a bewildering variety of technologies. During the early years, the internal-combustion engine vied with the steam engine and eclectic motors. Internal combustion engines featured a wide variety of cylinder configurations. Transmission systems, steering systems and brakes all displayed a remarkable variety of technologies and designs.

Over the years, technologies and designs tended to converge as competition relegated many once-promising designs to the scrapheap of history. The Ford Model T represented the first "dominant design" in automobiles—the technology and design features of the Model T set a standard for other manufacturers to imitate. Convergence of technologies and designs continued throughout the twentieth century. During the 1920s, all manufacturers adopted enclosed, all-steel bodies. The final decades of the twentieth century saw the elimination of most distinctively different designs: the VW Beetle with its rear, air-cooled engine, the Citroën 2-CV and its idiosyncratic braking and suspension system, Daf with its "Variomatic" transmission, and the two-stroke engines favored by some Soviet-bloc manufacturers. Engines became more similar: typically four cylinders arranged in line, with V-6 and V-8 configurations for larger cars. Front-wheel drive became standard on smaller cars; suspension, steering, braking systems and body shapes became more similar. Technological progress was incremental: innovations primarily involved new applications of electronics, new materials and new safety features. The main advances were multi-valve cylinders, traction control systems, all-wheel drive, electronic fuel injection, variable suspensions, intercooled turbos, satellite navigation systems, collision-avoidance radar and intelligent monitoring systems.

Despite less differentiation between manufacturers, new product segments have continued to appear. New vehicle types include a number of "crossovers" such as luxury SUVs and "mini-SUVs."

Convergence also occurred across countries. The same market segments tended to emerge in different countries. The major differences between countries were in the *sizes* of the various segments. Thus, in the U.S., the "mid-size" family sedan was the largest segment, with the Honda Accord and Toyota Camry the leading models. In Europe and Asia, small family cars ("subcompacts") formed the largest market segment. Yet for all the emphasis by manufacturers on global models, distinctive national differences persist. For example, during 2000–8 light trucks (pickups and SUVs) outsold passenger cars in the U.S. In Japan, microcars, such as the Suzuki Cervo, have grabbed 35% of the total car market.

This trend toward design convergence and slowing of technological change was interrupted by one major technological development. In 1997 both Toyota and Audi introduced mass-production hybrid cars—almost 100 years after Ferdinand Porsche had developed the first hybrid car in which an internal combustion engine powered an electric motor. By 2009, hybrids accounted for 12% of the Japanese market and 3% of the U.S. market. Several major automobile manufacturers, including GM, Daimler, Mitsubishi, and Subaru, planned to launch all-electric cars in the latter part of 2009 through to 2010, once more revisiting the early years of the auto industry—in 1900, 28% of all automobiles produced in the U.S. were all electric.

The Evolution of Manufacturing Technology

At the beginning of the twentieth century, car manufacture, like carriage-making, was a craft industry. Cars were built to order according to individual customers' preferences and specifications. In Europe and North America there were hundreds of companies producing cars, few with annual production exceeding 1000 vehicles. When Henry Ford began production in 1903, he used a similar approach—even for early versions of his Model T. His vision of an affordable, mass-produced automobile depended on the development of more precise machine tools that would permit interchangeable parts. By 1913, he had overcome the technical challenges of his new system of production. Components were produced either in batches or continuously and were then assembled on moving assembly lines by semi-skilled workers. The productivity gains were enormous. In 1912 it took 23 man-hours to assemble a Model T; just 14 months later it took only four. The resulting fall in the price of cars opened up a new era of popular motoring.

"Fordism" was the first major revolution in process technology; Toyota's "lean production" was the second. The system was developed by Toyota in postwar Japan at a time when shortages of key materials encouraged extreme parsimony and avoidance of inventories and waste. Key elements of the system were statistical process control, just-in-time scheduling, quality circles, teamwork and flexible production (more than one model manufactured on a single production line). Central to the new manufacturing was the transition from static concepts of efficiency optimization towards continuous improvement to which every employee contributed. During the 1980s and 1990s all the world's car manufacturers redesigned their manufacturing processes to incorporate aspects of Toyota's lean production.

New process technologies reduced the extent of scale economies in assembly. Optimal manufacturing efficiency once required giant assembly plants with outputs of at least 400 000 units a year. After 1990, most new assembly plants had capacities of between 150 000 and 300 000 units per annum. Scale economies in components and subassemblies were much more important. The minimum efficient scale for an engine plant was around 1 million units annually.

New Product Development

Scale economies were far more important in new product development: huge development costs needed to be amortized over large numbers of vehicles.

Increasing design complexity, the application of electronics, and new safety and environmental standards caused the cost of developing new models to rise steeply. By the 1990s the cost of creating an entirely new, mass-production passenger car from drawing board to production line was in excess of $1.5 billion. Ford's Mondeo/Contour—its first entirely global model—launched in 1994 cost a total of $6 billion (including tooling costs).

Smaller manufacturers could survive only by avoiding these massive product development costs. One way was to avoid new model changes. Prior to its acquisition by Ford, Jaguar's two models, the XJ6 and XJS, were almost two decades old. The tiny Morgan car company has made the same model since the late 1930s. The alternative was to license designs from larger manufacturers. Thus, Tofas of Turkey built Fiat-designed cars. Proton of Malaysia built Mitsubishi-designed cars. Maruti of India produced Suzuki-designed cars.

The cost of new product development has been the major driver of mergers and acquisitions in the industry. Economies from sharing development costs also encouraged increased collaboration and joint ventures. In 2009, the automobile industry was a global network of collaborative arrangements. These included joint-venture plants, technology alliances, component supply agreements and joint marketing agreements. In emerging market countries, most new auto plants were joint ventures between local and overseas companies. Figure 4.4 shows Ford's alliances with other automobile producers.

During the 1990s, new product development emerged as the critical organizational capability differentiating car manufacturers. Designing, developing and putting into production a completely new automobile was a hugely complex process involving every function of the firm, up to 3000 engineers, collaboration with several hundred suppliers and up to five years from drawing board to market launch. The team-based approach to new product development put in place by Toyota and Honda became models for all the major manufacturers. The result was a significant reduction in product development time.

Attempts to lower product development costs focused around three concepts. First, modular designs: the disaggregation of the vehicle into a number of separate subassemblies. Second, "virtual prototyping": the use of 3D computer graphics to design and test prototypes. Third, the development of shared platforms for multiple models. A "platform" comprised a vehicle's architecture including its floorpan, suspension system and layout of powertrain and major components. From 2000 to 2009 there was an important trend towards building multiple models on a single platform in order to exploit scale economies and to facilitate new product development. For example, Ford's C1 platform is used for the Ford Focus, the Mazda 3, the Ford C-max, and the Volvo S40 and G50. In engines, Ford moved to three engine families: V-8/V-10, V-6 and I-4 (four in-line cylinders). The I-4 engine has over 100 variations; it has an annual volume of 1.5 million and is built at three

FIGURE 4.4 Ford's alliances with other automakers

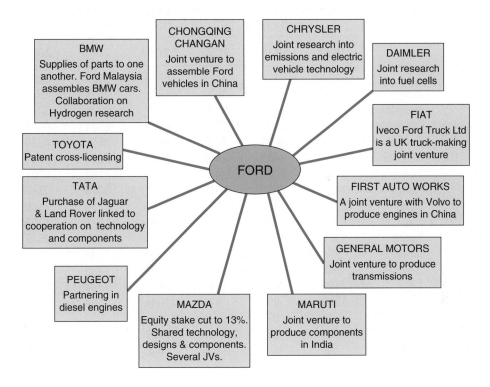

different plants—one in North America, one in Europe and one in Japan. *Automotive News* explained: "The idea is to share systems in areas that customers can't see and feel, and differentiate the brands in areas they can."

The Industry

The Manufacturers

The major automobile manufacturers are shown in Table 4.2. The ranks of the leading producers were dominated by U.S., Japanese, and European companies; outside of these countries only Hyundai of Korea was among the leading manufacturers. All the major manufacturers are multinational: both GM and Ford produce more cars outside the U.S. than within it; Honda produces more Accords in the U.S. than in Japan. As a result some countries—notably Canada, Spain, and the UK—are significant auto-producing countries without having any significant domestic auto companies. Over the past two decades the industry has consolidated through mergers and acquisitions (see Table 4.3). The financial problems of Japanese and Korean auto companies during the late 1990s accelerated this process. As a result, U.S. and European carmakers acquired significant proportions of the Japanese and Korean auto industries. The financial crisis of 2008–9 resulted in little consolidation: Fiat's acquisition of Chrysler was the only major merger. In fact, the

TABLE 4.2 The world's leading auto manufacturers

		Production ('000s of autos and commercial vehicles)						
		1992	1996	2000	2002	2004	2005	2007
GM	U.S.	6764	8176	8114	8326	9221	9200*	9350
Toyota	Japan	4249	4794	5897	6626	7674	7974*	8534
Volkswagen	Germany	3286	3977	5106	5017	4785	5243*	6268
Ford	U.S.	5742	6611	7206	6729	6721	6818*	6248
DaimlerChrysler	Germany	2782	4082	4666	4456	4551	4829*	4635
Hyundai[a]	S. Korea	874	1402	2488	2642	2283	2534*	3987
Honda	Japan	1762	2021	2469	2988	3141	3391*	3912
Peugeot	France	2437	1975	2879	3262	3078	3375	3457
Nissan	Japan	2963	2712	2698	2719	3226	3569*	3431
Fiat	Italy	1800	2545	2639	2191	1776	1708*	2679
Renault[b]	France	1929	1755	2515	2329	2490	2533*	2669
Suzuki	Japan	888	1387	1434	1704	2392	2630	2596
BMW	Germany	598	641	835	1091	1255	1328*	1542
Mitsubishi	Japan	1599	1452	1613	1821	1334	1381	1412
Mazda	Japan	1248	984	972	1044	1104	1149*	1287
Daihatsu	Japan	610	691	n.a.	n.a.	870	909	856
AvtoVAZ	Russia	674	562	756	703	727	732	736
FAW	China	n.a.	n.a.	n.a.	n.a.	n.a.	n.a.	691
Tata	India	n.a.	n.a.	n.a.	n.a.	n.a.	n.a.	588
Fuji (Subaru)	Japan	648	525	581	542	555	571	585
Isuzu	Japan	473	462	572	437	578	642	532

n.a. = not available.

* Sales data.

[a] Including Kia.

[b] Including Dacia and Samsung.

Source: Ward's Automotive Yearbook

main outcome was further fragmentation (e.g. GM's attempts to sell its Saab and Opel subsidiaries). In the meantime, a number of domestically focused manufacturers—especially from China and India—were building a global presence.

Outsourcing and the Role of Suppliers

Henry Ford's system of mass production was supported by heavy backward integration. At Ford's giant River Rouge plant, iron ore entered at one end, Model Ts emerged at the other. Ford even owned rubber plantations in the Amazon basin. The trend of the past 30 years has been towards increasing outsourcing of materials, components, and services in order to achieve lower costs and increased flexibility. At the end of the 1990s GM and Ford both spun off their component manufacturing businesses as separate companies: Delphi and Visteon, respectively. Relationships with suppliers also changed. The Japanese model of close,

TABLE 4.3 Mergers and acquisitions among automobile manufacturers, 1986–2009

Year	Acquirer	Target	Notes
2009	Volkswagen	Suzuki	Acquires 20% stake
2009	Fiat (Italy)	Chrysler	
2009	Volkswagen	Porsche	Merger agreed
2009	Beijing Automotive Industry Corp.	Fujian Motor; Changfeng Motor	
2008	Tata (India)	Jaguar Cars, Land Rover (U.K.)	Acquired from Ford
2008	SAIC Motor Group (China)	Nanjing Automobile	SAIC now owns both MG and Rover brands
2005	Nanjing Automobile (China)	Rover (U.K.)	
2005	Toyota	Fuji Heavy Industries	Acquired 8.7% stake from GM
2002	GM (U.S.)	Daewoo (South Korea)	42% of equity acquired
2000	Renault (France)	Samsung Motors (South Korea)	70% of equity acquired
2000	GM (U.S.)	Fiat (Italy)	20% of equity acquired
2000	DaimlerChrysler (Germany)	Hyundai (South Korea)	10% of equity acquired
2000	DaimlerChrysler (Germany)	Mitsubishi Motors (Japan)	34% of equity acquired
1999	Renault (France)	Nissan (Japan)	38.6% of equity acquired
1999	Ford (U.S.)	Volvo (Sweden)	Acquires car business only
1999	Ford (U.S.)	Land Rover (U.K.)	Acquired from BMW
1998	Daimler Benz (Germany)	Chrysler (U.S.)	Biggest auto merger ever
1998	VW (Germany)	Rolls Royce Motors (U.K.)	Acquired from Vickers plc
1998	Hyundai (South Korea)	Kia (S. Korea)	
1998	Daewoo (South Korea)	Ssangyong Motor (South Korea)	
1998	Daewoo (South Korea)	Samsung Motor (South Korea)	
1997	Proton (Malaysia)	Lotus (U.K.)	
1997	BMW (Germany)	Rover (U.K.)	
1996	Daewoo (South Korea)	FSO (Poland)	
1996	Daewoo (South Korea)	FS Lublin (Poland)	
1995	Fiat (Italy)	FSM (Poland)	
1995	Ford (U.S.)	Mazda (Japan)	
1994	Daewoo (S. Korea)	Oltcit/Rodae (Romania)	
1991	VW (Germany)	Skoda (Czech Republic)	
1990	GM (U.S.)	Saab-Scandia (Sweden)	50% of equity acquired
1990	Ford (U.S.)	Jaguar (U.K.)	
1987	Ford (U.S.)	Aston Martin (U.K.)	
1987	Chrysler (U.S.)	Lamborghini (Italy)	
1986	VW (Germany)	Seat (Spain)	

Source: newspaper reports.

collaborative long-run relationships with their "first-tier" suppliers has displaced the U.S. model of contract-based, arm's-length relationships. United States' and European automakers now have long-term relationships with a far smaller number of suppliers. As the leading component suppliers have gained increasing responsibility for technological development—especially in sophisticated subassemblies such as transmissions, braking systems, and electrical and electronic

TABLE 4.4 Revenues and profitability of the biggest automotive component suppliers

	Revenues ($ billion)			ROA (%)
	1994	2000	2008	2008
Robert Bosch (Germany)	19.6	29.1	58.5	1.7
Denso Corp. (Japan)	11	18.2	40.3	6.7
Johnson Controls (U.S.)	7.1	17.2	35.9	0.6
Aisin Seiki (Japan)	7.3	8.9	27.1	4.4
Magna International (Canada)	–	10.5	23.7	0.1
Delphi Automotive (U.S.)	–	29.1	18.1	n.a.
Eaton (U.S.)	4.4	8.3	15.4	6.6
Lear Corp (U.S.)	3.1	14.1	13.6	(1.0)
Valeo SA (France)	3.8	8.9	11.4	(3.2)
Visteon (U.S.)	–	19.5	9.5	1.2
Dana (U.S.)	5.5	12.7	8.7	n.a.

n.a. = not available.

Source: Company financial statements, Forbes.

equipment—they have also grown in size and global reach. Bosch, Denso, Johnson Controls and Delphi are almost as big as some of the larger automobile companies (see Table 4.4).

The Quest for Cost Reduction

Increasing competition in the industry has intensified the quest for cost reduction among automobile manufacturers. Cost-reduction measures have included:

- *Worldwide outsourcing*. Outsourcing has grown from individual components to major subassemblies (such as engines and steering systems) to complete cars as has been noted above. In addition, auto firms have developed original equipment manufacturer supply arrangements amongst themselves: Chery of China and Hyundai each produce cars for Chrysler, which are sold under the Dodge badge in North America.
- *Just-in-time scheduling*, which has radically reduced levels of inventory and work-in-progress.
- *Shifting manufacturing to lower-cost locations*. VW's North American production is based in Mexico and it moved production from Germany to the Czech Republic, Spain, and Hungary; Japanese companies have moved more and more production to lower cost locations in Southeast Asia; Mercedes and BMW developed greenfield plants in the deep south of the U.S.
- *Collaboration*. Ford's alliances (see Figure 4.4) are typical of the joint technology and product development among automobile companies intended to share costs.

Despite constant efforts at lowering costs, the major automakers were unable to achieve the unit costs of upstart producers in China, India, and other low labor cost countries. Tata Motors' launch of its Nano model in 2009 underlined the challenges faced by the global majors. The Nano was a four-seater, 623cc city car, which achieves almost 70 miles per gallon of gasoline. However, what gained the attention of all the world's automakers was its price: at 115 000 rupees ($2420) it was the world's cheapest new car.

Excess Capacity

The greatest structural problem of the industry was excess capacity. Ever since the early 1980s, the growth of production capacity had outstripped the growth in the demand for cars. Import restrictions had exacerbated the problem. During the 1980s and early 1990s, North American production capacity grew substantially as a result of Japanese companies building greenfield "transplants." The opportunities presented by the growth of private motoring in Eastern Europe, Asia and Latin America during the 1990s resulted in a rush by all the world's leading automakers to build new plants in these countries. Further big additions to world production capacity resulted from the expansion of the Korean car industry during 1992–7. Even where demand was growing fastest—such as China, where sales grew annually by almost 50% between 2002 and 2008—growth of capacity outstripped growth in demand. At the beginning of 2009, CSM Worldwide estimated global excess capacity at 34 million units (see Table 4.5).

Looking ahead, it appeared as though capacity reductions by Ford, GM and a few other companies would be more than offset by the new plants that would begin production during 2007–9. These included three new Toyota plants (one in India, two in China), two new Honda plants in North America, Hyundai plants in the Czech Republic and U.S., PSA in Slovakia, and at least a dozen other new plants in China and India.

Internationalization

Accessing growing markets, exploiting scale economies in purchasing, technology, and new product development were the main drivers of international

TABLE 4.5 Automobile production capacity, January 2009

	Production capacity (millions of units per year)	Production (millions of units per year)	Excess capacity (millions of units per year)
North America	17.3	10.1	7.2
South America	5.5	3.7	1.8
Europe	27.3	17.8	9.5
Middle East and Africa	2.5	1.7	0.8
Japan and Korea	17.3	13.9	3.4
South Asia	8.3	4.7	3.6

Source: CSM Worldwide.

expansion. Although Ford and General Motors began international expansion back in the 1920s, until the 1970s the world auto industry was made up of fairly separate national markets where each national market was dominated by indigenous producers. Each of the larger national markets was supplied primarily by domestic production and manufacturers tended to be market leaders. Internationalization has meant that, while there are now far fewer automakers in the world as a whole, concentration has declined in most national markets. For example, in 1970 the "Big Three" (GM, Ford, and Chrysler) held close to 85% of the U.S. market, VW and Daimler Benz dominated the market in Germany, as did Fiat in Italy, British Leyland (later Rover) in the U.K., Seat in Spain, and Renault, Peugeot, and Citroën in France. Internationalization meant that all the world's leading manufacturers were competing in most of the countries of the world. As a result, the market dominance of local firms was undermined (see Table 4.6).

The rise of new markets and the quest for low production costs has resulted in major shifts in global distribution of production (see Tables 4.7 and 4.8). Between

TABLE 4.6 Automobile market shares in individual countries (%)

	1988	2006		1988	2006
U.S.			**U.K.**		
GM	36.3	23.5	Ford	26.3	18.5
Ford	21.7	16.7	GM (Vauxhall)	13.7	12.7
DaimlerChrysler	11.3	10.8	Peugeot	8.7	10.0
Toyota	6.9	13.9	VW	n.a.	12.9
Honda	6.2	8.8	BMW/Rover	15.0	4.6
France			**Japan**		
Renault	29.1	24.8	Toyota	43.9	40.4
Peugeot	34.2	28.2	Nissan	23.2	14.0
VW	9.2	11.6	Honda	10.8	12.2
Ford	7.1	6.0	Suzuki	n.a.	12.1
Italy			**Korea**		
Fiat	59.9	28.5	Hyundai	55.9	50.0
VW	11.7	10.8	Kia	25.0	23.3
Ford	3.7	7.8	Daewoo	19.1	10.0
Peugeot	n.a.	9.6			
Renault	7.1	6.4			
Germany					
VW/Audi	28.3	27.8			
GM (Opel)	16.1	9.7			
Ford	10.1	8.0			
Mercedes	9.2	11.3			

n.a. = not available.

Sources: Japan Automobile Manufacturers Association; Korean Automobile Manufacturers Association; A. K. Binder (ed.), Ward's Automotive Yearbook, 2009, Wards Communications, Southfield MI, 2009.

TABLE 4.7 World motor vehicle production by countries and regions (percentage of world total)

	1960	1989	1994	2000	2005	2008
U.S.	52.0	23.8	24.5	22.2	20.0	18.6
Western Europe	38.0	31.7	31.2	29.9	28.4	20.7
Central and E. Europe	2.0	4.8	4.3	4.6	5.4	9.5
Japan	1.0	18.2	21.2	17.7	17.0	16.7
Korea	–	1.8	4.6	5.0	5.3	5.5
Other	7.0	19.7	14.4	20.6	24.0	29.0
Total units (millions)	12.8	49.5	50.0	57.4	66.8	69.4

Source: A. K. Binder (ed.), Ward's Automotive Yearbook, 2009, Wards Communications, Southfield MI, 2009.

1990 and 2008, China, Korea, Brazil and India established themselves among the world's leading motor-vehicle producers as a result of rapidly growing domestic markets and low production costs. Nevertheless, the continued leadership of Germany, Japan and the U.S., despite their high costs, pointed to the power of agglomeration effects in maintaining the competitiveness of long-established production centers.

TABLE 4.8 Top-15 automobile-producing countries, 2008 (thousands of cars; excludes trucks)

	1987	1990	1995	2000	2005	2008
Japan	7891	9948	7664	8363	9017	9916
China	n.a.	n.a.	356	620	3118	6341
Germany	4604	4805	4360	5132	5350	5532
U.S.	7099	6077	6338	5542	4321	3777
Brazil	789	663	1312	1348	2009	2561
Korea	793	987	1893	1881	2195	2436
France	3052	3295	3051	2883	3113	2144
Spain	1403	1679	1959	2445	2098	2014
India	n.a.	n.a.	n.a.	541	999	1507
Russia*	1329	1260	834	967	1288	1469
U.K.	1143	1296	1532	1641	1596	1448
Mexico	266	346	710	1130	846	1217
Canada	810	1072	1339	1551	1356	1195
Poland	301	256	260	533	527	840
Italy	1701	1874	1422	1442	726	659

*U.S.S.R. in 1987 and 1990.

Sources: Japan Automobile Manufacturers Association; Korean Automobile Manufacturers Association; A. K. Binder (ed.), Ward's Automotive Yearbook, 2009, Wards Communications, Southfield MI, 2009.

TABLE 4.9 Hourly compensation for motor vehicle workers (U.S.$ per hour, including benefits)

	1975	1984	1994	1998	2002	2004	2006
Germany	7.89	11.92	34.74	34.65	32.20	44.05	45.93
U.S.	9.55	19.02	27.00	27.21	32.35	33.95	35.12
U.K.	4.12	7.44	15.99	20.07	21.11	29.40	29.95
France	5.10	8.20	18.81	18.50	18.73	26.34	29.41
Japan	3.56	7.90	25.91	22.55	24.22	27.38	27.84
Spain	–	5.35	15.37	15.34	15.11	21.55	24.18
Korea	0.45	1.74	7.81	7.31	12.22	15.82	19.04
Italy	5.16	8.00	16.29	16.44	15.67	21.74	18.62
Mexico	2.94	2.55	2.99	2.21	3.68	3.50	3.73

Source: U.S. Department of Labor, Bureau of Labor Statistics.

The Outlook

As he revisited his financial forecasts for the next planning period, Booth realized that Ford's ability to generate profit would depend not just upon the recovery of demand in the world automobile market but also upon how competition would affect the kinds of profit margin that the industry would be earning over the next four years. What would happen in terms of mergers, capacity rationalization, and entry by emerging market manufacturers into world markets would clearly have a major impact on the overall margins that the industry would earn. As of June 2009, there was little evidence that the structural changes anticipated by many industry insiders were materializing. In particular, there was no evidence that recession and scale economies were pushing the industry towards radical consolidation. Despite the widely held belief that the minimum efficient scale for a full-line automobile producer was five million units annually, some of the industry's most successful companies— such as BMW, Suzuki, SAIC, and Tata Motor—had output far below this threshold. Meanwhile, General Motors and Ford with output well in excess of five million units annually were struggling for survival.

Booth also recognized that, despite the appearance of the industry becoming ossified by government support for existing carmakers, there was also the potential for radical change. The combination of environmental concerns and technological change might lead to a number of different scenarios. With global warming accelerating, government regulation and consumer preferences seemed likely to accelerate the shift from large to small cars and hasten the obsolescence of the internal combustion engine. The transition to electric vehicles would offer opportunities for a range of new entrants into the industry—particularly those companies with well-developed capabilities in electrical engineering. Environmental concerns—particularly rising urban congestion—might also result in a dramatic decline in private transportation in favor of public transportation, or possibly private motoring based upon short-term rental rather than car ownership.

Booth was particularly cognizant of the industry's propensity to retain outmoded assumptions concerning the automobile market and its economic drivers—indeed, this was a primary reason why the Detroit "Big Three" were in such a dire predicament. These deeply entrenched assumptions included: the belief that scale economies were the primary drivers of competitiveness, that there was no viable alternative to the internal combustion engine, that efficiency required offering a full range of models, that big cars were more profitable than small cars, and that consumers always preferred more—in terms of size and accessories—to less. Recent events had confounded many of these assumptions. Conventional notions about the attractiveness of different product segments appeared to be breaking down: some of the most popular—and profitable—new product launches had been small cars: the BMW Mini and Fiat Cinquecento in particular. The global success of the Toyota Prius and Honda Insight pointed to environmental awareness among consumers even in the absence of government inducements. New approaches to product development—including virtual prototyping, modular design and collaborative design and development—have the potential to overturn conventional relationships between scale and competitiveness. The efficiency-based logic of mass production is also being challenged by new developments in flexible manufacturing and increased opportunities for customization. Part of the appeal of the BMW Mini and Fiat Cinquecento has been their vast potential for customization.

Appendix

TABLE 4.10 Company sales ($ billion)

	1980–4[a]	1985–9[a]	1990–4[a]	1995–9[a]	2000-4[a]	2005	2006	2007	2008
GM	68	110	128	169	186	193	207	181	149
Ford	42	77	96	149	166	177	160	172	146
Chrysler	13	28	39	58	–	–	n.a.	60	n.a.
Daimler[b]	12	34	59	71	166	177	200	146	135
Toyota	18	42	82	107	125	173	179	203	265
VW	16	28	48	64	96	113	138	160	160
Honda	8	18	35	50	62	80	84	94	121
Fiat	18	27	42	50	59	55	68.4	86.1	83.7
Nissan	16	26	51	57	58	81	89	109	91
Peugeot	13	19	28	35	58	67		89	77
Renault	15	31	31	37	44	47	55	60	53
BMW	5	10	21	34	45	55	65	82	
Mitsubishi	12	14	25	32	27	20	41	43	61
Hyundai Motor	n.a.	n.a.	n.a.	18	38	58	68	74	
Mazda	n.a.	12	21	18	19	25	25	28	35

[a] Annual average.

[b] Daimler Chrysler 2000–6.

n.a. = not available.

Source: Company financial statements; Hoovers.

TABLE 4.11 Company profitability (return on equity, %)

	1980–4[a]	1985–9[a]	1990–4[a]	1995–9[a]	2000–4	2005	2006	2007	2008
GM[b]	11.4	11.8	3.2	27.5	11.7	n.c.	n.c.	n.c.	n.c.
Ford	0.4	21.8	5.9	35.4	(7.7)	18.8	n.c.	(48.2)	n.c.
Chrysler	66.5	20.8	2.0	24.5	–	–	n.a.	n.a.	n.a.
Daimler	24.3	18.3	6.9	22.1	7.7	8.0	9.5	13.1	5.5
Toyota	12.6	10.6	6.1	6.8	10.1	13.6	12.6	12.9	(5.0)
VW	1.6	6.3	(0.4)	11.1	6.8	4.7	7.3	13.0	13.4
Honda	18.1	11.8	5.3	15.1	13.2	11.9	11.3	11.1	1.3
Fiat	10.9	18.7	6.8	7.6	(24.2)	3.5	16.0	28.3	23.3
Nissan	10.3	4.7	3.6	(0.1)	29.3	17.2	13.0	13.7	(8.9)
Peugeot	(15.2)	36.7	12.5	3.0	13.4	n.a.	n.a.	5.8	(3.8)
Renault	(152.4)	51.1	9.1	11.0	14.7	17.6	14.2	12.7	3.2
BMW	14.8	10.4	9.7	(4.0)	15.4	13.2	14.5	11.8	12.7
Mitsubishi	10.0	7.9	4.8	(5.3)	(113.3)	(131.7)	3.7	11.2	(25.7)
Hyundai Motor	n.a.	n.a.	n.a.	4.4	10.6	n.a.	10.7	12.5	11.0
Mazda	n.a.	4.8	5.0	6.3	(34.2)	17.1	4.9	12.0	15.8

[a] Annual average.

[b] GM made a net loss of $2billion in 2006, $39 billion in 2007 and $31 bn. in 2008.

n.a. = not available.

n.c. = not calculable (shareholders' equity negative).

Source: Company financial statements; Hoovers.

Notes

1 Ford's stockholders' equity was negative $17.3 billion at the end of 2008.
2 "U.S. Car Industry: Back on the Road," *Financial Times*, June 17, 2009.
3 Ford Motor Company, Business Plan Submitted to the Senate Banking Committee, December 2, 2008, p. 16.
4 Note that different statistical authorities apply different definitions of "automobile." The basic distinction is between automobiles (or "passenger cars") used to transport people and commercial vehicles ("trucks") used to transport goods. The problem is that, in the U.S., sport-utility vehicles and pick-up trucks used primarily for personal transportation are classed as light trucks. Ideally we would like to define the automobile industry as comprising automobiles and light trucks (vans, pick-up trucks, SUVs, passenger vans), i.e. excluding heavy trucks and large buses. However, most of the statistics we use aggregate automobiles and all commercial vehicles.

Case 5   Wal-Mart Stores Inc., 2009

If you don't want to work weekends, you shouldn't be in retail.

—SAM WALTON (EXPLAINING THE SATURDAY CORPORATE MEETING)

On February 1, 2009, Mike Duke took over from Lee Scott as CEO of Wal-Mart Stores, Inc., the world's biggest retailer. His new office—the same CEO office that had been occupied by founder, Sam Walton—typified the contrast between Wal-Mart's vast size, $401 billion in sales and over two million employees, and its values of parsimony and simplicity. *Fortune* described the office as "no bigger than a child's bedroom."[1]

Wal-Mart's transformation from a small chain of discount stores in Arkansas, Missouri and Oklahoma in 1970 to the world's second largest company (in terms of revenue) was one of the most remarkable corporate success stories of the twentieth century. Its founder, Sam Walton, had combined folksy charm and homespun business wisdom with cutting-edge information technology and supply-chain management to create the world's most efficient retail organization. Under Lee Scott's leadership, Wal-Mart had embarked on its next stage of development. During his nine years as CEO, Scott had hugely expanded Wal-Mart's operations outside the U.S. and had engineered a transformation in Wal-Mart's external image through embracing social and environmental responsibility and a less aggressively anti-labor union stance. The success of Scott's leadership was apparent in the financial results for the financial year that closed on January 31, 2009: in the face of America's worst economic downturn in 60 years, Wal-Mart reported revenue growth of 7.2% and net income growth of 5.3%.

Despite this transformation, Duke's first report to Wal-Mart's shareholders placed primary emphasis on continuity in the company's leadership:

> My first day in the new job fell on the first Sunday in February. So my wife Susan and I took a few hours to move some boxes and belongings into my new office. But we didn't replace the carpet, furniture, or even Sam Walton's old wood paneling. With the exception of a couple of pictures on the wall, we kept it as the same office in which Sam Walton, David Glass and Lee Scott made the decisions that built our great Company. I could not be more honored or more humbled to sit at their desk now.[2]

The strategy he outlined suggested little deviation from that of his predecessor:

> Our Company is well positioned for today's difficult economy and tomorrow's changing world. We have an exceptionally strong management team, able to execute our strategy, perform every single day, and deliver results . . .
>
> Our team is very focused on working to improve return on investment (ROI). Our capital efficiency process drives expansion decisions. The Company has stepped up investments in technology to maintain leadership in an area that always has been a driver of our success. These efforts will contribute to Wal-Mart's increased efficiency through our use of capital, technology and logistics . . .
>
> Our strategy is working, and we're building more and more momentum. We will maintain our focus on price leadership in every market, whether we're talking to the working mom in São Paulo or the businessman in Tokyo. . .
>
> I'm certain of our strategy, our opportunity and our ability to perform as individuals and as a Company. By executing well and adhering to our values, we plan to distance ourselves even further from the competition and do even more to "save people money so they can live better."[3]

At the same time, Duke wondered whether a "more-of-the-same" strategy would be sufficient to maintain Wal-Mart's remarkable performance record during the new decade. During the decade 2000–9, Wal-Mart had grown sales at an average annual rate of 10% and earned an average return on equity of 21%—remarkable in the mature, intensely competitive business of discount retailing. Yet, maintaining that performance would become increasingly difficult.

As Wal-Mart continually expanded its range of goods and services—into groceries, fashion clothing, music downloads, online prescription drugs, financial services and health clinics—so it was forced to compete on a broader front. While Wal-Mart could seldom be beaten on cost, it faced competitors that were more stylish (T. J. Maxx), more quality-focused (Wholefoods), more service oriented

(Lowe's, Best Buy), and more focused in terms of product range. In its traditional area of discount retailing, Target was proving an increasingly formidable competitor. In March 2009, Target signaled its competitive intent by opening a store in Rogers, Arkansas—the site of the first ever Wal-Mart discount store.[4] Wal-Mart was also facing a "return of the zombies": several retailers that it had crushed earlier—Kmart, Sears and J. C. Penney—had been revitalized by new management. In warehouse clubs, its Sam's Clubs ran a poor second to Costco.

Increasing size boosted Wal-Mart's buying power but it also brought problems. Wal-Mart's success had rested heavily upon its ability to combine huge size with remarkable speed and responsiveness. Critical to this was its short chain of command and close relationship between the top management team and individual store managers. A key component in this linkage had been Wal-Mart's Saturday-morning meeting at its Bentonville HQ. In January 2008, the growing size of the meeting and increasing difficulty of getting all Wal-Mart executives back to Bentonville resulted in the company changing these meetings—which the company had described as "the pulse of our culture"—from weekly to monthly.[5]

Increased size also made Wal-Mart a bigger target for opponents. For years Wal-Mart had been under attack by organized labor seeking to unionize Wal-Mart's two million employees. More recently, "The Beast of Bentonville" has attracted the ire of environmentalists, antiglobalization activists, women's and children's rights advocates, small-business representatives and a growing number of legislators of varying political hues. Under Duke's predecessor, Wal-Mart had become increasingly image conscious and was a late but enthusiastic convert to social and environmental responsibility. The result was a series of senior appointments to new executive positions—a head of global ethics and a new executive vice president of government relations—plus more top management time spent in Washington and with the media.

Wal-Mart's growing geographical scope also raised complex strategic and organizational issues. Unlike other successful global retailers (such as IKEA), Wal-Mart did not have a consistent approach to different national markets. Moreover, its success varied greatly from country to country. Overall, its profitability was significantly lower internationally than in the U.S. What were the implications of the growing importance of its overseas operations for Wal-Mart's identity and culture, both of which were firmly rooted in Wal-Mart's Southern U.S., small-town heartland?

Looking ahead, Mike Duke realized that his first challenge would be to maintain and strengthen the principles and capabilities that had driven Wal-Mart's success for four decades: its unremitting quest for cost efficiency, its leading-edge logistics, its commitment to customers and ability to instill loyalty and commitment within its employees. His second challenge was to prepare Wal-Mart for a future that would inevitably be different from the past, would require meeting new customer requirements and new competitive challenges, and would inevitably require developing new capabilities.

History of Wal-Mart

Between 1945 and 1961, Sam Walton and his brother, Bud, developed a chain of 15 Ben Franklin franchised variety stores across rural Arkansas. Experiencing increasing price competition from newly established discount retailers with large format stores offering a broad range of products, Sam and Bud began developing their own discount store concept. At the time discount stores were located within large towns—it was believed that a minimum population of 100 000 was necessary to support a discount store. Sam Walton believed that, if the prices were right, discount stores could be viable in smaller communities: "Our strategy was to put good-sized stores into little one-horse towns that everyone else was ignoring."[6] The first Wal-Mart opened in 1962; by 1970 there were 30 Wal-Mart stores in small and medium-sized towns in Arkansas, Oklahoma, and Missouri.

Distribution was a problem for Wal-Mart:

> Here we were in the boondocks, so we didn't have distributors falling over themselves to serve us like our competitors in larger towns. Our only alternative was to build our own distribution centers so that we could buy in volume at attractive prices and store the merchandise.[7]

In 1970, Walton built his first distribution center, and in the same year took the company public in order to finance the heavy investment involved. Replicating this structure of large distribution hubs serving up to 100 discount stores formed the basis for Wal-Mart's expansion strategy. By 1980, Wal-Mart had 330 stores across the South and into the Midwest. By 1995, Wal-Mart was in all 50 states. Geographical expansion was incremental. In developing a new area, Wal-Mart built a few stores that were served initially by extending distribution from a nearby cluster. When a critical mass of stores had been established, Wal-Mart would build a new distribution center. As Wal-Mart became a national retail chain, so it entered more developed retailing areas, including larger cities, where it met stronger competition from other discount chains. In its early days, the local Wal-Mart was the only discount store in town—by 1993, 55% of Wal-Mart stores faced direct competition from Kmart and 23% from Target.[8]

Diversification

Wal-Mart experimented continuously with alternative retail formats. Some, like Helen's Arts and Crafts and Dot Deep Discount Drugstores, were unsuccessful. Others—Sam's warehouse clubs and the Supercenters—grew rapidly to become important components of Wal-Mart's business.

Sam's Clubs imitated a distribution concept established by Price Club. The warehouse clubs were not retailers as they were not open to the public. They were clubs where access was through membership. They carried a small number of lines and most items were available in multipacks and catering-size packs. The clubs were literally warehouses with products available on pallets and minimal customer service. The rationale was to maximize economies in purchasing, minimize operating costs and pass the savings on to members through very low prices. Competition among warehouse clubs was ferocious, resulting in rapid consolidation of the sector. Wal-Mart acquired The Wholesale Company in 1991 and Kmart's PACE clubs in 1993, while Costco Wholesale and PriceCo merged in 1993.

Supercenters were Wal-Mart's large-format stores (averaging 187 000 square feet, compared with 102 000 square feet for a Wal-Mart discount store and 129 000 square feet for a Sam's Club). Supercenters were modeled on the European concept of the "hypermarket" that had been pioneered by the French retailer Carrefour.

A Supercenter combined a discount store with a grocery supermarket: in addition, a Supercenter incorporated a number of specialty units such as an eyeglass store, hair salon, dry cleaners, and photo lab. The Supercenters were open for 24 hours a day, seven days a week. The Supercenter stores and Sam's Clubs were supplied through a separate distribution network from the Wal-Mart discount stores. In 1998, Wal-Mart opened the first of its Neighborhood Markets—supermarkets with an average floorspace of 42 000 square feet.

Wal-Mart also built a substantial online business through its web sites walmart.com and samsclub.com. Its online presence was extended through its online pharmacy and music download service.

International Expansion

Fear of saturation at home encouraged expansion abroad. In 1992, Wal-Mart established a joint venture with Mexico's largest retailer, Cifra S.A., and began opening Wal-Mart discount stores and Sam's Clubs in several Mexican cities. In 2000, Wal-Mart acquired 51% of Cifra and took control of the joint venture. By 2003, Wal-Mart Mexico was the country's biggest retailer.

In 1994, Wal-Mart entered the Canadian market by acquiring 120 Woolco stores from Woolworth and converting them to its own discount stores format. Again, Wal-Mart established itself as the country's largest retailer.

In Europe, Wal-Mart has struggled. In the U.K. its Asda subsidiary failed to take sales from market leader Tesco. In Germany, Wal-Mart sold its 85 stores to Metro after eight years of losses.

During the past decade, its international expansion has concentrated upon Latin America and Asia. Asia has been a mixed experience. Wal-Mart withdrew from South Korea in 2006 and at its Seiyu chain in Japan (51% Wal-Mart owned) its low-price strategy met a poor response from Japan's quality-obsessed shoppers.[9] In China, greenfield entry consisted of 138 Wal-Mart Supercenters and three Sam's Clubs. Moreover, through its 30% stake in the Chinese supermarket chain Trust-Mart, Wal-Mart owned 102 Trust Mart stores. Table 5.1 shows Wal-Mart's international development.

Overall, Wal-Mart's performance in overseas markets has been inconsistent. Its strongest performance was in adjacent countries—Mexico and Canada.

Sam Walton

Wal-Mart's strategy and management style was inseparable from the philosophy and values of its founder. Until his death in 1992, Sam Walton was the embodiment of Wal-Mart's unique approach to retailing. After his death, Sam Walton's beliefs and business principles continued to be the beacon that guided Wal-Mart's development. As Harry Cunningham, founder of Kmart Stores, observed: "Sam's establishment of the Walton culture throughout the company was the key to the whole thing."[10]

For Sam Walton, thrift and value for money were a religion. Undercutting competitors' prices was an obsession that drove his unending quest for cost economies. Walton established a culture in which every item of expenditure was questioned. Was it necessary? Could it be done cheaper? He set an example that few of his senior colleagues could match: he walked rather than took taxis, shared

TABLE 5.1 Wal-Mart stores by country, January 2009

Country	Stores	Notes
U.S.	3960	Included 2176 Supercenters, 1100 discount stores, 574 Sam's Clubs, and 110 Neighborhood Markets
Mexico	1197	Entered 1991: JV with Cifra. Chains include Wal-Mart, Bodegas, Suburbia, Vips and Mercamas
Puerto Rico	56	Entered 1992
Canada	318	Entered 1994: acquired Woolco
Argentina	28	Entered 1995: greenfield venture
Brazil	345	Entered 1995: JV with Lojas Americana. Includes Todo Dias, Bompreço, and Sonae stores
China	243	Greenfield entry in 1996; acquired 35% of Trust-Mart and 102 stores in 2006
U.K.	358	Entered 1999 by acquiring Asda. Operates Wal-Mart superstores and Asda supermarkets/discount stores
Japan	386	Entered 2002: acquired 38% of Seiyu. Mainly small stores but some superstores
Costa Rica	164	Acquired 30% of
El Salvador	77	CARHCO, a subsidiary
Guatemala	160	of Royal Ahold in 2005
Honduras	50	Shareholding later
Nicaragua	51	increased to 51%.
Chile	197	Entered January 2009 by acquiring Distribución y Servicio SA
Total	**7590**	

Source: www.walmartstores.com.

rooms at budget motels while on business trips and avoided any corporate trappings or manifestations of opulence or success. For Walton, wealth was a threat and an embarrassment rather than a reward and a privilege. His own lifestyle gave little indication that he was America's richest person (before being eclipsed by Bill Gates). He was equally disdainful of the display of wealth by colleagues: "We've had lots of millionaires in our ranks. And it drives me crazy when they flaunt it. Every now and then somebody will do something especially showy, and I don't hesitate to rant and rave about it at the Saturday morning meeting. I don't think that big mansions and flashy cars is what the Wal-Mart culture is supposed to be about."[11]

His attention to detail was legendary. As chairman and chief executive, he was quite clear that his priorities lay with his employees ("associates"), customers and the operational details through which the former created value for the latter. He shunned offices in favor of spending time in his stores. Most of his life was spent on the road (or in the air piloting his own plane), making impromptu visits to stores and distribution centers. He collected information on which products were selling well in Tuscaloosa; why margins were down in Santa Maria; how a new display system for children's clothing in Carbondale had boosted sales by 15%. His passion for detail extended to competitors' stores as well as his own: as well as visiting their stores, he was known to count cars in their parking lots.

Central to his leadership role at Wal-Mart was his relationship with his employees—the Wal-Mart associates. In an industry known for low pay and hard working conditions, Walton created a unique spirit of motivation and involvement. He believed fervently in giving people responsibility, trusting them, but also continually monitoring their performance.

After his death in 1992, Sam Walton's habits and utterances became hallowed principles guiding the company and its employees. For example, Wal-Mart's "10-foot attitude" pledge is based on Sam Walton's request to a store employee that: "I want you to promise that whenever you come within 10 feet of a customer, you will look him in the eye, greet him and ask if you can help him."[12] The "Sundown Rule"—that every request, no matter how big or small, gets same-day service—has become the basis for Wal-Mart's fast-response management system. Sam Walton's contribution to the management systems and management style of Wal-Mart is reflected in Wal-Mart's web site's description of "The Wal-Mart Culture" (see the Appendix).

Sam Walton's ability to attract the affection and loyalty of both employees and customers owed much to his ability to generate excitement within the otherwise sterile world of discount retailing. He engendered a positive attitude among Wal-Mart employees and he reveled in his role as company cheerleader. Wal-Mart's replacement of its mission slogan, "Everyday Low Prices" by "Save Money, Live Better" was intended to reflect Walton's insistence that Wal-Mart played a vital role in the happiness and well-being of ordinary people.

Wal-Mart in 2009

The Business

Wal-Mart described its business as follows:

> Wal-Mart Stores, Inc. operates retail stores in various formats around the world and is committed to saving people money so they can live better. We earn the trust of our customers every day by providing a broad assortment of quality merchandise and services at everyday low prices ("EDLP") while fostering a culture that rewards and embraces mutual respect, integrity and diversity. EDLP is our pricing philosophy under which we price items at a low price every day so that our customers trust that our prices will not change under frequent promotional activity.
>
> Our operations comprise three business segments: Walmart U.S., International and Sam's Club.
>
> - Our Walmart U.S. segment is the largest segment of our business, accounting for 63.7% of our fiscal 2009 net sales and operates stores in three different formats in the United States, as well as Wal-Mart's online retail operations, walmart.com. Our Walmart U.S. retail formats include:
>   - Discount stores, which average approximately 108 000 square feet in size and offer a wide assortment of general merchandise and a limited variety of food products;

- Supercenters, which average approximately 186 000 square feet in size and offer a wide assortment of general merchandise and a full-line supermarket; and

- Neighborhood Markets, which average approximately 42 000 square feet in size and offer a full-line supermarket and a limited assortment of general merchandise.

- At January 31, 2009, our International segment consisted of retail operations in 14 countries and Puerto Rico. This segment generated 24.6% of our fiscal 2009 net sales. The International segment includes numerous different formats of retail stores and restaurants, including discount stores, supercenters and Sam's Clubs that operate outside the United States.

- Our Sam's Club segment consists of membership warehouse clubs in the United States and the segment's online retail operations, samsclub.com. Sam's Club accounted for 11.7% of our fiscal 2009 net sales. Our Sam's Clubs average approximately 133 000 square feet in size.[13]

Table 5.2 shows sales and profits for these three business segments.

Performance

Table 5.3 summarizes some key financial data for Wal-Mart during the period 1994 to 2006. Table 5.4 shows Wal-Mart's recent performance compared with other discount retailers.

TABLE 5.2 Wal-Mart: performance by segment (year ending January 31)

	2000	2001	2002	2003	2004	2005	2006	2007	2008	2009
Sales ($ billion)										
Wal-Mart Stores	108.7	121.9	139.1	157.1	174.2	191.8	209.9	226.3	239.5	255.7
Sam's Clubs	24.8	26.8	29.4	31.7	34.5	37.1	39.8	41.6	44.4	46.9
International	22.7	32.1	35.5	40.8	47.6	56.3	62.7	77.1	90.6	98.6
Sales increase										
Wal-Mart Stores (%)	14.0	12.1	14.1	12.9	10.9	10.1	9.4	7.8	5.8	6.8
Sam's Clubs (%)	8.4	8.1	9.7	7.8	8.8	7.5	7.3	4.5	6.7	5.6
International (%)	85.6	41.4	10.6	14.9	16.7	18.3	11.4	30.2	17.5	9.1
Operating income ($ billion)										
Wal-Mart Stores	8.70	9.70	10.30	11.80	12.90	14.20	15.30	16.62	17.52	18.76
Sam's Clubs	0.85	0.94	1.03	1.02	1.13	1.30	1.40	1.48	1.62	1.61
International	0.82	1.11	1.46	2.00	2.40	3.00	3.30	4.26	4.77	4.94
Operating income/sales										
Wal-Mart Stores (%)	8.0	8.0	7.4	7.5	7.4	7.4	7.3	7.3	7.3	7.3
Sam's Clubs (%)	3.4	3.5	3.5	3.2	3.3	3.5	3.5	3.6	3.6	3.4
International (%)	3.6	3.5	4.1	4.9	5.0	5.3	5.3	5.5	5.2	5.0

Source: Wal-Mart Stores Inc., 10-K Reports.

TABLE 5.3 Wal-Mart Stores Inc.: financial summary 1998–2009 (year ended January 31)

	1998	1999	2000	2001	2002	2003	2004	2005	2006	2007	2008	2009
Net sales	118.0	137.6	165.0	191.3	217.8	229.6	256.3	285.2	312.4	345.4	374.5	401.2
Net sales increase (%)	12.0	17.0	20.0	16.0	4.0	5.0	12.0	11.3	9.5	11.7	8.6	7.2
U.S. same-store sales increase (%)	6.0	9.0	8.0	5.0	6.0	6.0	4.0	3.3	3.4	2.0	1.6	3.5
Cost of sales	93.4	108.7	129.7	150.3	171.6	178.3	198.7	219.8	240.4	264.2	286.5	306.2
SG&A expenses	19.4	22.4	27.0	31.6	36.2	40.0	44.9	51.2	56.7	64.0	70.3	76.7
Interest expense	0.6	0.5	0.8	1.1	1.1	0.8	0.7	0.9	1.2	1.6	1.8	1.9
Income taxes	2.1	2.7	3.3	3.7	3.9	4.4	5.1	5.6	5.8	6.2	6.9	7.1
Operating income	3.4	4.2	5.4	6.1	6.4	7.8	8.9	10.5	11.4	12.2	12.9	13.3
Net income	3.5	4.4	5.4	6.3	6.7	8.0	9.1	10.3	11.2	11.3	12.7	13.4
Current assets	19.4	21.1	24.4	26.6	28.2	30.7	34.5	38.9	43.8	47.0	47.6	48.8
Inventories	16.8	17.5	20.2	21.6	22.7	24.4	26.6	29.8	32.2	33.7	35.2	34.5
Fixed assets	23.6	26.0	36.0	40.9	45.8	51.4	58.5	68.1	79.3	88.4	97.0	95.7
Total assets	45.4	50.0	70.3	78.1	83.5	94.8	104.9	120.2	138.2	151.6	163.5	163.2
Current liabilities	14.5	16.8	25.8	28.9	27.3	32.5	37.4	43.2	48.8	52.2	58.5	55.3
Long-term debt	7.2	6.9	13.7	12.5	15.7	16.6	17.1	20.1	26.4	27.2	29.8	31.3
Long-term lease obligations	2.5	2.7	3.0	3.2	3.0	3.0	3.0	3.2	3.7	3.5	3.6	3.2
Shareholders' equity	18.5	21.1	25.8	31.3	35.1	39.5	43.6	49.4	53.2	61.6	64.6	65.3
Current ratio	1.3	1.3	0.9	0.9	1	0.9	0.9	0.9	0.9	0.9	0.8	0.9
Return on assets[a] (%)	8.5	9.6	9.5	8.7	8.5	9.0	9.0	9.3	8.9	8.8	8.5	8.4
Return on equity[b] (%)	19.8	22.4	22.9	22.0	20.1	21.0	21.0	22.6	22.5	22.0	21.0	21.2
Other year-end data (number of units)												
U.S. discount stores	1921	1869	1801	1736	1647	1568	1478	1353	1209	1075	971	891
U.S. Supercenters	441	564	721	888	1066	1258	1471	1713	1980	2256	2447	2612
U.S. Sam's Clubs	443	451	463	475	500	525	538	551	567	579	591	602
U.S. Neighborhood Markets	–	4	7	19	31	49	64	85	100	112	132	153
International units	601	715	1004	1071	1170	1272	1355	1587	2285	2757	3121	3615
Employees (000s)	825	910	1140	1244	1383	1400	1400	1600	1800	2100	1900	2100

[a] (Net income before minority interest, equity in unconsolidated subsidiaries and cumulative effect of accounting change)/Average assets.

[b] Net income/Average shareholders' equity.

Source: Wal-Mart Stores Inc., 10-K Reports.

TABLE 5.4 Wal-Mart and its competitors: performance comparisons ($ billions except where noted)

	Wal-Mart		Target		Dollar General		Costco	
	2007	2008	2007	2008	2007	2008[a]	2007	2008
Income								
Sales revenue	348.7	378.8	59.5	63.4	9.2	5.6	56. 5	63.5
Gross profit	84.5	92.3	20.1	21.5	2.4	1.6	8.0	9.0
Gross profit margin (%)	24.2	24.4	33.8	33.9	26.1	28.6	12.3	12.4
Sales, general &	58.5	64.0	13.5	14.5	2.1	1.0	5.8	6.4
administrative expense	5.5	6.3	1.5	1.8	0.28	0.15	0.57	0.66
Depreciation and amortization								
Operating margin (%)	5.9	5.8	8.5	8.3	2.7	6.6	2.5	2.7
Total net income	11.3	12.7	2.8	2.8	−0.008	−0.005	1.08	1.28
Net profit margin (%)	3.2	3.4	4.7	4.5	−0.3	−0.1	1.7	1.8
Financial position								
Cash	7.37	5.57	0.81	2.45	0.12	0.22	3.36	3.28
Inventories	33.69	35.18	6.25	6.78	1.43	1.29	4.88	5.04
Total current assets	46.59	47.59	14.71	18.91	1.74	1.52	9.32	9.46
Total assets	151.19	163.51	37.35	44.56	3.04	8.66	19.61	20.68
Short-term debt	8.28	11.27	1.36	1.96	0.008	0.003	0.11	0.14
Total current liabilities	51.75	58.45	11.12	11.78	0.83	0.86	8.58	8.87
Long-term debt	30.74	33.40	8.68	15.13	0.26	4.28	2.11	2.21
Total liabilities	89.62	98.91	21.72	29.25	1.29	5.95	10.98	11.49
Shareholder's equity	61.57	64.61	15.63	15.31	1.75	2.70	8.62	9.19
Financial ratios								
Total asset turnover	2.31	2.32	1.59	1.42	21.18	8.37	2.88	3.07
Inventory turnover	8.51	7.51	6.70	5.81	6.43	4.34	13.01	11.20
Debt/equity	1.46	1.53	1.39	1.91	0.74	2.20	1.27	1.25
Return on assets (%)	7.46	7.79	7.46	6.39	4.54	−0.15	5.52	6.20
Return on equity (%)	18.33	19.70	17.83	18.61	7.90	−0.47	12.56	13.95

[a] 47 weeks only.

Wal-Mart Stores' Operations and Activities[14]

Purchasing and Vendor Relationships

The size of Wal-Mart's purchases and its negotiating ability means that Wal-Mart is both desired and feared by manufacturers. Being accepted as a Wal-Mart vendor offers access to a huge share of the U.S. retail market. At the same time, Wal-Mart buyers are well aware of their ability to take full advantage of economies of scale available to their suppliers and to squeeze their margins to razor-thin level. Purchasing is centralized. All dealing with U.S. suppliers takes place at Wal-Mart's Bentonville headquarters. Would-be suppliers are escorted to one of 50 cubicles on "Vendor Row." Furnishings comprise just a table and folding chairs—sometimes no chairs. Suppliers regarded the experience of selling to Wal-Mart as intimidating and grueling: "Once you are ushered into one of the spartan little buyers' rooms, expect a steely eye across the table and be prepared to cut your price."[15] Another vendor commented: "All normal mating rituals are verboten. Their highest priority is making sure everybody at all times in all cases knows who's in charge . . . They talk softly, but they have piranha hearts, and if you aren't totally prepared when you go in there, you're in deep trouble."[16] The requirements that Wal-Mart imposes on its suppliers extend well beyond low prices. Increasingly Wal-Mart involves itself in its suppliers' employment policies, including workplace safety, working hours and absence of child labor.

All negotiations are directly between manufacturers and Wal-Mart: Wal-Mart refuses to do business with manufacturers' representatives and agents. To avoid dependence on any one supplier, Wal-Mart limits the total purchases it obtains from any one supplier. The result is an asymmetry of bargaining power. Thus, Wal-Mart's biggest supplier, Procter & Gamble, accounts for about 3% of Wal-Mart's sales—but this represents 18% of P&G's sales.

International expansion has allowed Wal-Mart to increase its purchasing muscle through global procurement. By 2003, Asda was sourcing over 2000 products from Wal-Mart's global network. This network included 23 procurement offices in 23 countries.[17]

Wal-Mart combines ruthless bargaining with close collaboration with its bigger suppliers. Wal-Mart's cooperation with Procter & Gamble provided a model for these relationships. The companies began electronic data interchange (EDI) at the beginning of the 1990s, and by 1993 there were 70 P&G employees working at Bentonville to manage sales and deliveries to Wal-Mart.[18]

By the mid-1990s, Wal-Mart had extended EDI to cover about 70% of its vendors. Through Wal-Mart's "Retail Link" system of supply-chain management, data interchange included point-of-sale data, levels of inventory, Wal-Mart's sales forecasts, vendors' production and delivery schedules, and electronic funds transfer.

Collaboration with Cisco Systems enabled Retail Link to move to the internet during the mid-1990s, allowing suppliers to log on to the Wal-Mart database for real-time store-by-store information on sales and inventory for their products. Suppliers could then collaborate with Wal-Mart buyers forecasting, inventory management, and shipping. The result was faster replenishment, lower inventory, and a product mix tuned to local customer needs. A key benefit to suppliers is in matching production schedules to Wal-Mart's sales.

Warehousing and Distribution

Wal-Mart is regarded as one of the world's leaders in logistics. It distributed a higher proportion of goods to its own stores than any other discount retailer. While most discount retailers relied heavily upon their suppliers to undertake distribution to individual stores, 82% of Wal-Mart's purchases were shipped to Wal-Mart's own distribution centers from where they were distributed in Wal-Mart trucks. The efficiency of the system rested on Wal-Mart's "hub-and-spoke" configuration. Distribution centers ("hubs") spanned over a million square feet, operated 24 hours, and served between 75 and 110 stores within a 200 mile radius. Deliveries into distribution centers were either in suppliers' trucks or Wal-Mart trucks, then deliveries were made to Wal-Mart stores. Grouping of Wal-Mart stores allowed trucks to deliver partial loads to several Wal-Mart stores on a single trip. On backhauls, Wal-Mart trucks would bring returned merchandise from stores and also pick up from local vendors. As a result, trucks were more than 60% full on backhauls. Unlike other retailers (and many manufacturers), which outsourced trucking, Wal-Mart owned over 4000 trucks and some 15 000 trailers.

Wal-Mart was continually seeking ways to make its logistics system cheaper, faster and more reliable. It was an early adopter of "cross-docking"—a system where goods arriving on inbound trucks were unloaded and reloaded on outbound trucks without entering warehouse inventory. In 2005, Wal-Mart introduced its "Remix" system designed to reduce inventories, speed deliveries to stores, and eliminate stock-outs. The new system created a new tier to Wal-Mart's distribution system. Third-party logistic companies were made responsible for making smaller, more frequent pickups from suppliers, establishing "consolidation centers" throughout the U.S., then making frequent deliveries to Wal-Mart's distribution centers. The new system would allow Wal-Mart to order from suppliers on a five-day rather than four-week basis and would lead to lower inventories in both distribution centers and retail stores.

In 2005, Wal-Mart extended its supply chain internationally. Its "direct import" initiative involved, first, purchasing directly from overseas suppliers rather than through importers and, second, taking control of import logistics. Covering 4 million square feet, its import distribution center in Baytown, Texas was America's largest distribution facility devoted to a single company's products. Not only did the new distribution center give Wal-Mart the opportunity to exert greater control over its supplies of imports—it allowed it to avoid the delays and congestion of west-coast ports such as Long Beach.[19]

In 2003 Wal-Mart announced the adoption of radio frequency identification (RDFI) and became the leading pioneer of this technology. However, slow adoption of RDFI by its suppliers has meant that, by 2009, Wal-Mart has been unable to eliminate manual bar code scanning for inventory control purposes.

Wal-Mart continuously seeks incremental improvements to its logistics systems. In the year ended January 2009 it reported higher inventory turnover and lower distribution costs as a result of packing its trucks more tightly.

In-Store Operations

Wal-Mart's management of its retail stores was based upon its objective of creating customer satisfaction by combining low prices, a wide range of quality products carefully tailored to customer needs and a pleasing shopping experience. Wal-Mart's management of its retail stores was distinguished by the following characteristics:

- *Merchandising.* Wal-Mart stores offered a wide range of nationally branded products. Between 2006 and 2009 it had expanded its range of brands—with a quest for more upscale brands in particular. Wal-Mart has become an important distribution partner for Apple, Dell, Sony, Dyson, and Kitchen Aid. Traditionally Wal-Mart placed less emphasis on own-brand products than other mass retailers; however, during 2008–9, Wal-Mart made major investments in its range of *Great Value* private-label products. Under its "Store of the Community" philosophy, Wal-Mart has long sought to tailor its range of merchandise to local market needs on a store-by-store basis. Over time, greater sophistication in analyzing point-of-sale data for individual stores has greatly increased Wal-Mart's responsiveness to local needs (see below).

- *Decentralization of store management.* Individual store managers were given considerable decision-making authority in relation to product range, product positioning within stores, and pricing. This differed from most other discount chains where decisions over pricing and merchandising were made either at head office or at regional offices. Decentralized decision-making power was also apparent within stores, where the managers of individual departments (for example, toys, health and beauty, consumer electronics) were expected to develop and implement their own ideas for increasing sales and reducing costs.

- *Customer service.* Discount stores were open 9 a.m. to 9 p.m. weekdays, with shorter hours on weekends. Supercenters were open continuously. Despite the fanatical emphasis on cost efficiency, Wal-Mart went to great lengths to engage with its customers at a personal level. Stores employed "greeters"—often retired individuals—who would welcome customers and hand out shopping baskets. Within the store, all employees were expected to look customers in the eye, smile at them and offer a verbal greeting. To encourage customer loyalty, Wal-Mart maintained a "Satisfaction Guaranteed" program. This program assured customers that Wal-Mart would accept returned merchandise on a no-questions-asked basis.

Marketing

Wal-Mart had been founded on Sam Walton's belief that: "There is only one boss: the customer." For Wal-Mart, the essence of customer service was low prices. Hence, Wal-Mart's marketing strategy was built upon its slogan "Everyday Low Prices": Wal-Mart's customer appeal was as a price leader across its entire product range, all the time—it did not engage in promotional price cutting.

The centrality of "Everyday Low Prices" to Wal-Mart's relationship with its customers had important implications for its marketing activities. Wal-Mart was able to rely on word-of-mouth communication of its merits and was able to spend comparatively little on advertising and other forms of promotion. Advertising typically involved one home-delivered advertisement circular per month by each store and some television advertising. As a result, Wal-Mart's advertising/sales ratio during the past three financial years was 0.55%—most of its rivals had advertising/sales ratios of between 1.5% and 3.0%. Nevertheless, with an advertising budget of over $2 billion, Wal-Mart was among the world's biggest advertisers.

Beyond its emphasis on serving customers by providing unbeatable value-for-money, the values that Wal-Mart projected were traditional American virtues of hard work, thrift, individualism, opportunity, and community. This identification with core American values was buttressed by a strong emphasis on patriotism and national causes.

However, as Wal-Mart increasingly became a target for politicians and pressure groups, former CEO Lee Scott initiated a major shift in the image that Wal-Mart projected to the world. In 2004, Wal-Mart issued its first annual report on ethical sourcing where it published results of its audit of suppliers' adherence to its code of conduct. In November 2005, Scott committed Wal-Mart to a program of environmental sustainability and set ambitious targets for renewable energy, the elimination of waste and a shift in product mix towards environmentally friendly products.[20] Two years later, Wal-Mart published the first of its annual sustainability reports.

Commitment to social and environmental responsibility can be seen as part of a wider effort by Wal-Mart to broaden its consumer appeal and counter the attempts by activist groups to characterize Wal-Mart as a heartless corporate giant whose success was built upon exploitation and oppression. Wal-Mart broadened its customer base to include more upper income consumers and expanded its geographical base into the more politically liberal parts of the U.S. (for example, the west coast and New England) and beyond U.S. borders, so building an appeal that extended beyond "everyday low prices."

In 2008, Wal-Mart launched a company-wide image makeover that involved a new corporate logo and a redesign of its stores. The new logo replaced upper-case characters by lower-case, eliminated the star-hyphen ("Wal*Mart"), and added a "sunburst" design. According to branding consultant, Marty Neumeier: "The new "sunburst" looks organic. My sense is they are trying to say, 'we're an eco-aware company,'" Tobias Frere-Jones, a professor of typography, observed that lower case letters tend to be interpreted as more casual and approachable.[21] The new logo coincided with a program of store redesign that included wider aisles, improved lighting, and lower shelves.[22]

Information Technology

Wal-Mart was a pioneer in applying information and communications technology to support decision making and promote efficiency and customer responsiveness. During the 1970s, Wal-Mart was among the first retailers to use computers for inventory control, to initiate EDI with its vendors, and to introduce bar code scanning for point-of-sale and inventory control. To link stores and cash register sales with supply chain management and inventory control, Wal-Mart invested $24 million in its own satellite in 1984. By 1990, Wal-Mart's satellite system was the largest two-way, fully integrated private satellite network in the world, providing two-way interactive voice and video capability, data transmission for inventory control, credit card authorization, and enhanced EDI.

During the 1990s Wal-Mart was pioneering the use of data-mining for retail merchandising:

> At Wal-Mart, information technology gives us that knowledge in the most direct way: by collecting and analyzing our own internal information on exactly what any given shopping cart contains. The popular term is "data-mining," and Wal-Mart has been doing it since about 1990. The result, by now, is an enormous database of purchasing information that enables us to place the right item in the right store at the right price. Our computer system receives 8.4 million updates every minute on the items that customers take home—and the relationship between the items in each basket.
>
> Data analysis allows Wal-Mart to forecast, replenish, and merchandise on a product-by-product, store-by-store level. For example, with years of sales data and information on weather, school schedules and other pertinent variables, Wal-Mart can predict daily sales of Gatorade at a specific store and automatically adjust store deliveries accordingly.[23]

Point-of-sale data analysis also assisted in planning store layout:

There are some obvious purchasing patterns among the register receipts of families with infants and small children. Well-thought-out product placement not only simplifies the shopping trip for these customers—with baby aisles that include infant clothes and children's medicine alongside diapers, baby food and formula—but at the same time places higher-margin products among the staples . . . Customers who buy suitcases are likely to be looking for other items they might need for traveling too—such as travel alarms and irons, which now, logically enough, can be found displayed alongside luggage at many Wal-Mart stores.

The common thread is simple: We are here to serve the customer; and customers tend to buy from us when we make it easy for them. That sounds like a simple idea. But first you must understand the customer's needs. And that's where information comes in.[24]

The role of IT was most important in linking and integrating the whole of Wal-Mart's value chain:

Wal-Mart's web of information systems extends far beyond the walls of any one store. Starting from the basic information compiled at the checkout stand, at the shelves, and gathered by associates equipped with hand-held computer monitors, Wal-Mart works to manage its supplies and inventories not only in the stores, but all the way back to the original source. Wal-Mart has given suppliers access to some of our systems, which enables them to know exactly what is selling, and to plan their production accordingly. This not only helps us keep inventories under control, but also helps the supplier deliver the lowest-cost product to the customer. With sales and in-stock information transmitted between Wal-Mart and our supplier-partners in seconds over the internet, buyers and suppliers are privy to the same facts and negotiate based on a shared understanding—saving a significant amount of time and energy over more traditional, low-tech systems.

Our buyer benefits from the supplier's product knowledge, while the supplier benefits from Wal-Mart's experience in the market. Combine these information systems with our logistics—our hub-and-spoke system in which distribution centers are placed within a day's truck run of the stores—and all the pieces fall into place for the ability to respond to the needs of our customers, before they are even in the store. In today's retailing world, speed is a crucial competitive advantage. And when it comes to turning information into improved merchandising and service to the customer, Wal-Mart is out in front and gaining speed. In the words of Randy Mott, Senior Vice President and Chief Information Officer, "The surest way to predict the future is to invent it."[25]

Human Resource Management

Wal-Mart's human-resource practices in 2009 were based upon Sam Walton's beliefs about relations between the company and its employees and between employees and customers. All employees—from executive-level personnel to checkout clerks—were known as "associates." Wal-Mart's relations with its associates were to be founded on respect, high expectations, close communication and clear incentives.

Wal-Mart's employees received relatively low pay—the median rates for hourly paid retail workers in 2009 was between $8.46 and $12 an hour. However, these rates were, on average, slightly above those paid in the retail trade generally. Employee benefits included a company health plan that covered 94% of Wal-Mart employees and a retirement scheme, which covered all employees with a year or more of service.

A key feature of Wal-Mart's compensation system was its profit incentives, which extended to hourly employees. A stock purchase plan was also available to employees. Wal-Mart retirees included a large number of millionaires—not all of whom were managers: in 1989, the first millionaire hourly associate retired from the company.

Wal-Mart resisted the unionization of its employees in the belief that union membership created a barrier between the management and the employees in furthering the success of the company and its members. Despite strenuous efforts by unions to recruit Wal-Mart employees, union penetration remained low. Between 2000 and 2008, the United Food and Commercial Workers union together with AFL-CIO fought a concerted campaign to recruit Wal-Mart workers, but to little effect.[26]

Associates enjoyed a high degree of autonomy and received continuous communication about their company's performance and about store operations. Every aspect of company operations and strategy was seen as depending on the close collaboration of managers and shop-floor employees. To control "shrinkage" (theft), the company instituted a system whereby a store's cost savings from reduced shrinkage were shared between the company and the store's employees. Wal-Mart's shrinkage was estimated to be just above 1%, versus an industry average of 2%.

Wal-Mart's approach to employee involvement made heavy use of orchestrated demonstration of enthusiasm and commitment. The central feature of Wal-Mart meetings from corporate to store level was the "Wal-Mart Cheer"—devised by Sam Walton after a visit to Korea. The call and response ritual ("Give me a W!" "Give me an A!" . . .) included the "Wal-Mart squiggly," which involved employees shaking their backsides in unison.

Fortune suggested that the Wal-Mart Cheer's mixture of homespun and corporate themes provided an apt metaphor for what it called "the Wal-Mart paradox":

> The paradox is that Wal-Mart stands for both Main Street values and the efficiencies of the huge corporation, aw-shucks hokeyness and terabytes of minute-by-minute sales data, fried-chicken luncheons at the Waltons' Arkansas home and the demands of Wall Street.
>
> Critics of Wal-Mart call the homespun stuff a fraud, a calculated strategy to put a human face on a relentlessly profit-minded corporation. What is paradoxical and suspect to people outside Wal-Mart, however, is perfectly normal to the people who work there. It reflects a deal that Sam Walton, Wal-Mart's founder, made with the people who worked for him.
>
> The deal was a lot more than just a matter of the occasional visit from Mr. Sam. Wal-Mart demonstrated its concern for workers in many ways that were

small but specific: time-and-a-half for work on Sundays, an "open-door" policy that let workers bring concerns to managers at any level, the real chance of promotion (about 70% of store managers started as hourly associates).[27]

The paradox of Wal-Mart's human resource practices continues. The enthusiasm it generates among employees supports a level of involvement and empowerment that is unique among large retail organizations. At the same time, the intense pressure for cost reduction and sales growth frequently results in cases of employee abuse. Wal-Mart suffered reversals in class action lawsuits by current and former employees. In a series of adverse court decisions, Wal-Mart was forced to compensate current and former employees for unpaid overtime work, for failure to ensure that workers received legally mandated rest breaks, and for systematically discriminating against women in pay and promotion.

Organization and Management Style

Wal-Mart's management structure and management style had been molded by Sam Walton's principles and values. As Wal-Mart grew in size and geographical scope, Walton was determined that corporate executives should keep closely in touch with customers and store operations. The result was a structure in which communication between individual stores and the Bentonville headquarters was both close and personal. Wal-Mart's regional vice presidents were each responsible for supervising between 10 and 15 district managers (who, in turn, were in charge of eight to 12 stores). The key to Wal-Mart's fast-response management system was linkage between the stores and headquarters. Former CEO, David Glass explained the system:

> The idea is very simple. Nothing very constructive happens in the office. Everybody else had gone to regional offices—Sears, Kmart, everybody—but we decided to send everybody from Bentonville out to the stores Monday though Thursday. And bring them back Thursday night. On Friday morning we'd have our merchandising meetings. But on Saturday morning we'd have our sales for the week. And we'd have the other information from people who'd been out in the field. They're telling us what our competitors are doing, and we get reports from people in the regions who had been traveling though the week. So we decide then what corrective action we want to take. And before noon on Saturday the regional manager was required to be hooked up by phone to all his district managers, giving them direction as to what we were going to do or change. By noon on Saturday we had all our corrections in place. Our competitors, for the most part, got their sales results on Monday for the week prior. Now, they're already ten days behind, and we've already made the corrections.[28]

The Saturday morning meeting was preceded by three other key corporate meetings. The operations meeting was on Thursday afternoon. This was attended by 70 senior executives and logistics, planning, and information managers. The meetings reviewed non-merchandising matters—including inventory management, supply chain efficiencies, and new store development. The meetings were held standing to encourage brevity.

Fridays began with the 7 a.m. management meeting, which involved Wal-Mart's 200 most senior managers. To attend these meetings Wal-Mart's 39 regional vice presidents needed to return on Thursday evening from their territories to the Bentonville "home office." The meetings dealt with strategic and critical operational matters. At lunchtime, in the same auditorium, the merchandising meeting took place. Here, buyers and corporate executives meet. The purpose of the meeting was, first, to give buyers direct insights into what was selling and what was not; second, to give the regional VPs a means to get instant action to solve merchandising problems in their stores; third, to report on what the competition was doing. The meeting dealt with stockouts, excess inventory, new product ideas, and a variety of merchandising errors. By the early afternoon, the regional VPs and merchandisers were emailed a "priority note" of specific actions that they should take action on by the end of the day.

It was the two-and-a-half-hour Saturday morning meetings, however, that were the week's high point and the clearest representation of Wal-Mart's unique management style:

> The meeting is the soul of this behemoth . . . It is the template for other vital gatherings that have evolved throughout the company, ranging from the daily shift-change meetings at the stores to the weekly management, merchandising, and operations meetings at the home office to the five company-wide mega-meetings each year that draw more than 10 000 participants apiece. Not only do these assemblies reinforce and personalize Wal-Mart's almost evangelical culture among its 1.5 million "associates" worldwide, but they are also largely responsible for the retailing giant's amazing agility in the aisles. The meetings enable the company to continue to operate its entire business on a weekly and sometimes a daily basis, just as the founder managed his first five-and-dime, moving quickly to outflank competition and growing almost as a matter of routine.[29]

The Saturday meetings were a mixture of information sharing, educational inputs and motivation recharging. They began with a review of the week's performance data, then involved question-and-answer sessions targeting examples of good and bad performance. They also included presentations that focused on merchandising best practices or new product lines and guest appearances that might include CEOs such as Carlos Ghosn, Steve Jobs, or Jack Welch, or celebrity entertainers or sports stars. The meetings closed with a talk from the CEO. By 2008, it became apparent that Wal-Mart's increasing size was making these meetings increasingly cumbersome—not to mention the fact that Wal-Mart's largest auditorium could no longer accommodate the participants. In January 2008, Wal-Mart announced that its legendary Saturday meeting would occur monthly and would be held at nearby Bentonville High School.

Some managers saw the downgrading of the Saturday morning meeting as a long-overdue recognition that one of the world's biggest corporations could no longer be run with the same personalized, Arkansas-focused management style put in place by Sam Walton. Others interpreted it differently: Wal-Mart was losing the unique spirit and driving force that had been the basis of its success for four decades.

Appendix: The Wal-Mart Culture[30]

As Wal-Mart continues to grow into new areas and new mediums, our success will always be attributed to our culture. Whether you walk into a Wal-Mart store in your home town or one across the country while you're on vacation, you can always be assured you're getting low prices and that genuine customer service you've come to expect from us. You'll feel at home in any department of any store . . . that's our culture.

Sam Walton's Three Basic Beliefs

Sam Walton built Wal-Mart on the revolutionary philosophies of excellence in the workplace, customer service and always having the lowest prices. We have always stayed true to the Three Basic Beliefs Mr. Sam established in 1962:

Respect the Individual

"Our people make the difference" is not a meaningless slogan—it's a reality at Wal-Mart. We are a group of dedicated, hardworking, ordinary people who have teamed together to accomplish extraordinary things. We have very different backgrounds, different colors and different beliefs, but we do believe that every individual deserves to be treated with respect and dignity. (Don Soderquist, Senior Vice Chairman, Wal-Mart Stores, Inc.)

Service to Our Customers We want our customers to trust in our pricing philosophy and to always be able to find the lowest prices with the best possible service. We're nothing without our customers.

Wal-Mart's culture has always stressed the importance of Customer Service. Our Associate base across the country is as diverse as the communities in which we have Wal-Mart stores. This allows us to provide the Customer Service expected from each individual customer that walks into our stores. (Tom Coughlin, President and Chief Executive Officer, Wal-Mart Stores division.)

Strive for Excellence New ideas and goals make us reach further than ever before. We try to find new and innovative ways to push our boundaries and constantly improve. "Sam was never satisfied that prices were as low as they needed to be or that our product's quality was as high as they deserved—he believed in the concept of striving for excellence before it became a fashionable concept." (Lee Scott, President and CEO.)

Sam's Rules for Building a Business People often ask, "What is Wal-Mart's secret to success?" In response to this ever-present question, in his 1992 book *Made in America*, Sam Walton compiled a list of ten key factors that unlock the mystery. These factors are known as "Sam's Rules for Building a Business."

Rule 1. Commit to your business. Believe in it more than anybody else. I think I overcame every single one of my personal shortcomings by the sheer passion I brought to my work. I don't know if you're born with this kind of passion, or if you can learn it. But I do know you need it. If you love your work, you'll be out there every day trying to do it the best you possibly can, and pretty soon everybody around will catch the passion from you—like a fever.

Rule 2. Share your profits with all your Associates, and treat them as partners. In turn, they will treat you as a partner, and together you will all perform beyond your wildest expectations. Remain a corporation and retain control if you like, but behave as a servant leader in a partnership. Encourage your Associates to hold a stake in the company. Offer discounted stock, and grant them stock for their retirement. It's the single best thing we ever did.

Rule 3. Motivate your partners. Money and ownership alone aren't enough. Constantly, day-by-day, think of new and more interesting ways to motivate and challenge your partners. Set high goals, encourage competition, and then keep score. Make bets with outrageous payoffs. If things get stale, cross-pollinate; have managers switch jobs with one another to stay challenged. Keep everybody guessing as to what your next trick is going to be. Don't become too predictable.

Rule 4. Communicate everything you possibly can to your partners. The more they know, the more they'll understand. The more they understand, the more they'll care. Once they care, there's no stopping them. If you don't trust your Associates to know what's going on, they'll know you don't really consider them partners. Information is power, and the gain you get from empowering your Associates more than offsets the risk of informing your competitors.

Rule 5. Appreciate everything your Associates do for the business. A paycheck and a stock option will buy one kind of loyalty. But all of us like to be told how much somebody appreciates what we do for them. We like to hear it often and especially when we have done something we're really proud of. Nothing else can quite substitute for a few well-chosen, well-timed, sincere words of praise. They're absolutely free—and worth a fortune.

Rule 6. Celebrate your successes. Find some humor in your failures. Don't take yourself so seriously. Loosen up, and everybody around you will loosen up. Have fun. Show enthusiasm—always. When all else fails, put on a costume and sing a silly song. Then make everybody else sing with you. Don't do a hula on Wall Street. It's been done. Think up your own stunt. All of this is more important, and more fun, than you think, and it really fools the competition. "Why should we take those cornballs at Wal-Mart seriously?"

Rule 7. Listen to everyone in your company. And figure out ways to get them talking. The folks on the front lines—the ones who actually talk to the customer— are the only ones who really know what's going on out there. You'd better find out what they know. This really is what total quality is all about. To push responsibility down in your organization, and to force good ideas to bubble up within it, you must listen to what your Associates are trying to tell you.

Rule 8. Exceed your customers' expectations. If you do, they'll come back over and over. Give them what they want—and a little more. Let them know you appreciate them. Make good on all your mistakes, and don't make excuses—apologize. Stand behind everything you do. The two most important words I ever wrote were on that first Wal-Mart sign, "Satisfaction Guaranteed." They're still up there, and they have made all the difference.

Rule 9. Control your expenses better than your competition. This is where you can always find the competitive advantage. For 25 years running—long before Wal-Mart was known as the nation's largest retailer—we ranked No. 1 in our industry for the lowest ratio of expenses to sales. You can make a lot of different mistakes and still recover if you run an efficient operation. Or you can be brilliant and still go out of business if you're too inefficient.

Rule 10. Swim upstream. Go the other way. Ignore the conventional wisdom. If everybody else is doing it one way, there's a good chance you can find your niche by going in exactly the opposite direction. But be prepared for a lot of folks to wave you down and tell you you're headed the wrong way. I guess in all my years, what I heard more often than anything was: a town of less than 50 000 population cannot support a discount store for very long.

Notes

1 "Changing of the Guard at Wal-Mart," *Fortune,* February 18, 2009.
2 Wal-Mart, Annual Report, 2009, p. 3.
3 Wal-Mart, Annual Report, 2009, pp. 2–3.
4 "Target Thrives in Wal-Mart Country," *Fortune,* June 10, 2009.
5 "Wal-Mart Alters Regular Saturday Meeting," *Morning News,* January 14, 2008, www.nwaonline.net/articles/ 2008/01/14/business/011508bizsatmeetings.txt, accessed October 16, 2009.
6 S. Walton, *Sam Walton: Made in America,* Bantam Books, New York, 1992.
7 *Forbes,* August 16, 1982, p. 43.
8 *Wal-Mart Stores, Inc.* (Harvard Business School Case No. 9–974–024, 1994).
9 "Why Wal-Mart Can't Find Happiness in Japan," *Fortune,* July 27, 2007.
10 From the Wal-Mart web site: www.walmart.com.
11. S. Walton, *Sam Walton: Made in America,* Bantam Books, New York, 1992.
12 See www.walmart.com/cservice/aw_samsway.gsp, accessed October 16, 2009.
13 Wal-Mart Inc., 2009 10-K Report.
14 This description of Wal-Mart's retailing operations refers primarily to its U.S. discount stores.
15 Bill Saporito, "A Week Aboard the Wal-Mart Express," *Fortune,* August 24, 1992, p. 79.
16 Bill Saporito, "A Week Aboard the Wal-Mart Express," *Fortune,* August 24, 1992, p. 79.
17 "At Wal-Mart, Less is More," *Journal of Commerce,* November 2005. Reprinted in *DSC Logistics and Supply Chain Management,* http://www.dsclogistics.com/

newsrelease_05NovJournalofCommerce.php, accessed 29 October 2009.
18 For an insightful account of the development of Wal-Mart's relationship with P&G see: "Lou Pritchett: Negotiating the P&G Relationship with Wal-Mart" (Harvard Business School Case No. 9-907-011, 2007.)
19 "Inside the World's Biggest Store," *Time Europe,* January 20, 2003.
20 "The Green Machine," *Fortune,* July 31, 2006.
21 "Wal-Mart Gets a Facelift," *Business Week,* July 2, 2008, http://www.businessweek.com/innovate/content/jul2008/i d2008072_324653.htm, accessed October 29, 2009.
22 "Wal-Mart Moves Upmarket," *Business Week,* June 3, 2009, http://www.businessweek.com/innovate/content/ jul2008/id2008072_324653.htm?campaign_id=rss_daily, accessed October 29, 2009.
23 Wal-Mart Stores, Annual Report, 1999, p. 9.
24 Wal-Mart Stores, Annual Report, 1999, p. 9.
25 Wal-Mart Stores, Annual Report, 1999, p. 11.
26 "Unions vs. Wal-Mart: Up against the Wal-Mart," *Fortune,* May 17, 2004.
27 "Sam Walton Made us a Promise," *Fortune,* March 18, 2002.
28 "The Most Underrated CEO ever," *Fortune,* April 5, 2004, pp. 242–8.
29 "Wal-Mart's $288 Billion Meeting," *Fortune,* April 18, 2005.
30 "The Wal-Mart Culture" from www.walmartstores.com; "Sam's Rules for Building a Business," from Sam Walton and John Huey, *Made in America.* (New York: Doubleday, 1992).

Case 6   Manchester United: Preparing for Life without Ferguson*

In July 2009, David Gill, the Chief Executive of Manchester United Football Club Limited (MUFC), was accompanying the Manchester United team on its Asia Tour. The series of matches against local teams in Malaysia, Indonesia, Korea, and China was ostensibly part of the team's pre-season training—in reality its goals were almost wholly commercial.

The tour's itinerary was determined primarily by existing deals: the game in Kuala Lumpur was a reward for Telekom Malaysia's £2 million sponsorship of the tour; the games in South Korea, China and Indonesia reflected deals with Kumho Tyres and Hi Seoul (Korea), Aigo (China) and 3 Indonesia. It was most important to maintain the

---

* This case was written by Robert M. Grant with assistance from Simon I. Peck, Christopher Carr and Timothy Smith. Copyright © 2010 Robert M. Grant.

enthusiasm and commitment of Manchester United's vast army of fans in these countries. In Asia as a whole, Manchester United estimated that it had 80 million supporters. "Our fans in Asia generate money for the club, and the reception United get in Asia is unlike anywhere else on earth," observed David Gill.[1] In South Korea there were 1.2 million Manchester United credit-card holders.

When the Manchester United plane touched down at Kuala Lumpur on July 16, the 73 people on board included a number of Manchester United employees who had no direct involvement in the next day's game against the Malaysia national team. They included a group from Manchester United's commercial office in London led by commercial director Richard Arnold. Their role was to finalize a series of lucrative sponsorship deals, partnerships and territory-specific agreements.

Manchester United's Asian fan base was a key factor for their £80 million four-year sponsorship deal with AON—whose corporate logo would replace that of AIG on Manchester United shirts. According to David Prosperi, AON's VP of Global Public Relations:

> The first year after AIG's sponsorship agreement began, they came from nowhere on the list of the world's top 100 brands to 47th. Manchester United has no equal in sports when it comes to global brand awareness, particularly in Asia. We believe that Asia, particularly India and China, are prime targets for revenue growth and being associated with the Manchester United brand will, we believe, help us to greatly build our brand and grow our business in this region.[2]

For David Gill, the number one issue on his mind was not Manchester United's commercial deals. So long as the team kept winning games and playing exciting football the commercial revenues—from shirt sales, broadcasting and sponsorship—would continue to flow. The biggest cloud on Manchester United's horizon was the imminent retirement of its veteran team manager, Sir Alex Ferguson—the prime architect of the team's success over the past 23 years and winner of more honors for Manchester United than in their entire history prior to his appointment. Although Ferguson had given no indication of his intention to retire, Gill thought it likely that Ferguson would choose to go at the end of the 2009-10 season. Even if Ferguson did decide to stay on beyond the end of next season, Gill could not imagine that it would be for long—at the end of 2009 Ferguson would be 68 years old.

The implications of Ferguson's departure for Manchester United were far reaching. In his 23 years at the club, Ferguson had built an entire infrastructure of scouting, training, team discipline, and team tactics and strategy. In seeking a successor to Ferguson, Gill was forced to look beyond the desirable characteristics for a new team manager and to ponder the fundamental issues of what determined success in English and European soccer.

The Competitive Environment

The English League

The top league in English professional football is the Premier League, comprising the 20 best English teams. Each team plays every other team twice, once at home and once away, with teams receiving three points for a win, one for a tie, and zero for a loss. At the end of every season, the three teams at the bottom of the Premier

TABLE 6.1 The top performing clubs in English football, 1980–2005

	League champion	Second place	Third place	FA Cup winner
2009	Manchester United	Liverpool	Chelsea	Chelsea
2008	Manchester United	Chelsea	Arsenal	Portsmouth
2007	Manchester United	Chelsea	Liverpool	Chelsea
2006	Chelsea	Manchester United	Liverpool	Liverpool
2005	Chelsea	Arsenal	Manchester United	Arsenal
2004	Arsenal	Chelsea	Manchester United	Manchester United
2003	Manchester United	Arsenal	Newcastle United	Arsenal
2002	Arsenal	Liverpool	Manchester United	Arsenal
2001	Manchester United	Arsenal	Liverpool	Liverpool
2000	Manchester United	Arsenal	Leeds United	Chelsea
1999	Manchester United	Arsenal	Chelsea	Manchester United
1998	Arsenal	Manchester United	Liverpool	Arsenal
1997	Manchester United	Newcastle United	Arsenal	Chelsea
1996	Manchester United	Newcastle United	Liverpool	Manchester United
1995	Blackburn Rovers	Manchester United	Nottingham Forest	Everton
1994	Manchester United	Blackburn Rovers	Newcastle United	Manchester United
1993	Manchester United	Aston Villa	Norwich City	Arsenal
1992	Leeds United	Manchester United	Sheffield Wednesday	Liverpool
1991	Arsenal	Liverpool	Crystal Palace	Tottenham Hotspur
1990	Liverpool	Aston Villa	Tottenham Hotspur	Manchester United
1989	Arsenal	Liverpool	Nottingham Forest	Liverpool
1988	Liverpool	Manchester United	Nottingham Forest	Milton Keynes Dons
1987	Everton	Liverpool	Tottenham Hotspur	Coventry City
1986	Liverpool	Everton	West Ham United	Liverpool
1985	Everton	Liverpool	Tottenham Hotspur	Manchester United
1984	Liverpool	Southampton	Nottingham Forest	Everton
1983	Liverpool	Watford	Manchester United	Manchester United
1982	Liverpool	Ipswich Town	Manchester United	Tottenham Hotspur
1981	Aston Villa	Ipswich Town	Arsenal	Tottenham Hotspur
1980	Liverpool	Manchester United	Ipswich Town	West Ham United

Source: www.european-football-statistics.co.uk.

League are replaced by the top three in the league below. The Premier League team that accumulates the most points throughout the season wins the English League Championship.

The governing body for English football is the Football Association (FA). The FA Cup pits teams from all the English leagues in a single elimination tournament—allowing little-known teams from the lower divisions to compete (and sometimes win) against the top clubs. Table 6.1 shows the top performing teams in the English league between 1980 and 2009.

The European League

The Champions League is composed of the 32 top teams in European football. Teams qualify by finishing at or near the top of their respective national leagues.

TABLE 6.2 The top 25 European football clubs 2000–2009

Club	Total points 2000–9	Club	Total points 2000–9
Manchester United (England)	1460	Olympique Lyonnais (France)	1076
Barcelona (Spain)	1411	Olympiakos SF Pireas (Greece)	1001
Real Madrid (Spain)	1314	FK Dynamo Kyiv (Ukraine)	948
Bayern München (Germany)	1314	SV Werder Bremen (Germany)	923
Arsenal (England)	1310	Glasgow Celtic (Scotland)	921
Chelsea (England)	1276	Deportivo de La Coruña (Spain)	919
Liverpool (England)	1199	Juventus (Italy)	917
AC Milan (Italy)	1178	Ajax Amsterdam (Netherlands)	914
Internazionale FC (Italy)	1177	Panathinaikos AO Athina (Greece)	910
FC do Porto (Portugal)	1170	FK Shakhtar Donets'k (Ukraine)	903
Valencia (Spain)	1105	Sporting CP (Portugal)	881
PSV (Netherlands)	1088	Glasgow Rangers (Scotland)	872
AS Roma (Italy)	1083		

Note: Points are based upon club performance in national leagues, national cup competitions and European Champions League and Intertoto cup. National performance is adjusted according to the standard of competition in the national leagues.

Source: www.european-fooball-statistics.co.uk.

In England the top four teams qualify for the Champions League; in Scotland, the top two teams qualify. Qualifying for the Champions League is a critical objective for the aspiring clubs in each of the major national leagues because of the substantial TV and gate revenues that it offers. The latter phase of the Champions League season is a knockout competition that results in one team winning the European Cup. Winning this championship represents the highest accomplishment in European club football, both competitively and financially.

Table 6.2 shows the top teams in Europe based on performance in both national and European competitions.

The inauguration of the European Champions League in 1992 and the revenues and prestige that it conferred had a major impact on English league football. A widening financial gap appeared between the top performing teams—Manchester United, Chelsea, Liverpool, and Arsenal—and the rest as revenues from the European competition fueled the purchases of top-class players, reinforcing the tendency for the leading group of clubs to break away from the pack.

The Players

The critical determinant of team performance in professional soccer is the quality of the players that make up the team. The world's leading players in 2008–9 are shown in Table 6.3.

Competition for superstar players has intensified in recent years as a result of two factors. First, the growing global market for football and football merchandise has greatly increased the value of top-class players in terms of their contribution to team performance and their individual market pull. Second, there has been an influx of new finance into football—especially into the acquisition of English Premier League clubs

TABLE 6.3 FIFA world player rankings, 2008–9

Rank	Player	Nationality	Team
1	Cristiano Ronaldo	Portugal	Manchester United
2	Lionel Messi	Argentina	Barcelona
3	Fernando Torres	Spain	Liverpool
4	Kaká	Brazil	Milan
5	Xavi	Spain	Barcelona
6	Steven Gerrard	England	Liverpool
7	Samuel Eto'o	Cameroon	Barcelona
8	Iker Casillas	Spain	Real Madrid
9	Andrés Iniesta	Spain	Barcelona
9	David Villa	Spain	Valencia
11	Andrei Arshavin	Russia	Zenit St. Petersburg
12	Frank Lampard	England	Chelsea
13	Didier Drogba	Cote d'Ivoire	Chelsea
14	Michael Ballack	Germany	Chelsea
14	Cesc Fàbregas	Spain	Arsenal
16	Zlatan Ibrahimović	Sweden	Internazionale
17	Emmanuel Adebayor	Togo	Arsenal
18	Franck Ribéry	France	Bayern Munich
19	Ruud van Nistelrooy	Netherlands	Real Madrid
20	Sergio Agüero	Argentina	Atlético Madrid
21	John Terry	England	Chelsea
22	Gianluigi Buffon	Italy	Juventus
23	Deco	Portugal	Barcelona and Chelsea

Note: Based on assessment by 157 managers and 145 captains of national teams.

Source: www.fifa.com.

from U.S., Middle East and Russian investors. As a result, despite the global recession, transfer fees hit new highs during the summer of 2009. Table 6.4 shows some of the biggest transfer deals.

Football Finances

If the critical resource determining a team's performance is the quality of its players, then the ability to acquire quality players depends on a club's financial resources. There are two major sources of a club's financial resources: its cash flows from its commercial activities and its financing by investors and lenders.

Revenues

The principal revenue sources for a club are:

- *Matchday revenues*. Revenues from the sale of tickets are determined by the number of home games played, the average attendance and average seat

TABLE 6.4 Biggest player transfers in European football (prior to the end of June 2009)

Rank	Player	From	To	Transfer fee ($ millions)	Year
1	Cristiano Ronaldo	Manchester United	Real Madrid	93.1	2009
2	Zinédine Zidane	Juventus	Real Madrid	76.0	2001
3	Zlatan Ibrahimović	Internazionale	Barcelona	66.0	2009
4	Kaká	Milan	Real Madrid	65.1	2009
5	Luís Figo	Barcelona	Real Madrid	58.5	2000
6	Hernán Crespo	Parma	Lazio	53.6	2000
7	Gianluigi Buffon	Parma	Juventus	49.2	2001
8	Robinho	Real Madrid	Manchester City	49.0	2008
9	Christian Vieri	Lazio	Internazionale	48.3	1999
10	Andriy Shevchenko	Milan	Chelsea	46.5	2006
11	Dimitar Berbatov	Tottenham	Manchester United	46.4	2008
12	Pavel Nedvěd	Lazio	Juventus	46.2	2001
13	Rio Ferdinand	Leeds United	Manchester United	43.9	2002
14	Gaizka Mendieta	Valencia	Lazio	43.8	2001
15	Ronaldo	Internazionale	Real Madrid	43.0	2002
16	Juan Sebastián Verón	Lazio	Manchester United	42.4	2001
17	Karim Benzema	Lyon	Real Madrid	34.9	2009

Source: www.wikipedia.org

price. Among the leading teams in Europe, attendance depends upon stadium capacity. In recent years most of the leading teams have redeveloped their stadiums—others (e.g. Arsenal) built entirely new ones. The great majority of income from tickets was from season tickets. A major source of revenue growth was the sale of corporate boxes and VIP hospitality packages.

- *Broadcasting revenues.* Outside of North America and Japan, football is the world's most popular televised sport. The world's most popular sporting event is the Football World Cup. The 2006 World Cup was televised in 213 countries to a cumulative audience of 26 billion viewers; the final was watched by an audience of 715.1 million. Club-level games are broadcast on national TV and increasingly on overseas TV networks. In England, broadcasting rights are negotiated between the Premier League and the TV networks. In 2006, TV rights to Premier League games were sold to Sky TV, Sentana, the BBC, and overseas TV networks for a total of £2.7 billion—each Premier League club receiving an average of £45 million annually between 2007 and 2010. TV rights for the Champions League are managed by the European governing body for football, UEFA. The international TV audience for Champions League games resulted in a massive revenue boost for those teams that qualified for the league. During 2008/9, Manchester United, Barcelona, Chelsea and Bayern Munich each received more than €30 million from UEFA.

- *Sponsorship and commercial revenues* comprise payments from companies for advertising rights at stadiums and on club web sites, sponsorship agreements and licensing arrangements—payments to license a club's trademarks for the manufacture of official club merchandise (replica shirts, scarves, games, drinking mugs, toys, and various other products). Most clubs had two leading sponsors: the supplier of team apparel (Nike, Addidas or Puma) and the company whose corporate logo appeared on the team's shirts. Major sponsorship deals included Juventus and Tamoil (€110 million over 5 years), Arsenal and Emirates (£100 million over 15 years), Manchester United and Aon (£80 million over 4 years), and Chelsea and Samsung (£50 million over 5 years). Sponsorship revenues are concentrated on a few leading clubs. In Spain Real Madrid and Barcelona accounted for over 60% of the Primera Liga's sponsorship revenue, while AC Milan, Inter, and Juventus accounted for over 50% of the Serie A's total. The leading European clubs have become increasingly sophisticated in marketing, merchandising and brand management with Real Madrid and Manchester United the leaders in promoting and exploiting their brands globally.

A club's potential sponsorship and commercial revenues depends on both the brand equity of the club and that of its leading players. Real Madrid's signing of superstar players Zidane, Beckham and Cristiano Ronaldo gave massive boosts to the club's licensing and merchandising revenues. Foreign players are especially important in building support in those players' home countries. Manchester United's commercial revenues from South Korea grew substantially after Ji-Sung Park joined the team.

Of the European leagues, England's Premier League is the biggest earner with revenues of €2.4 billion in 2007/08 (up 26% in Sterling terms). Italy's Serie A, Spain's La Liga, and Germany's Bundesliga each had revenues of about €1.4 billion. For the English Premier League during 2007-8, broadcasting contributed £931 million (an increase of 43% on the previous year), commercial revenues £447 million (up 12%), and matchday revenue £554 million (up 3%).[3]

Table 6.5 shows financial data for Europe's leading clubs.

Costs

Wages and salaries—most of which are accounted for by players' salaries—are the biggest cost item for European clubs. During 2007-8, wages as a percentage of revenues were 62% for the Premier League as compared with 68% for Serie A and 63% for La Liga. Among the English clubs Chelsea had the highest wage bill, accounting for 81% of total revenue. Manchester United and Arsenal each paid out about half of their revenues in wages. In 2008/9, the world's highest paid footballers were: David Beckham (Los Angeles Galaxy/AC Milan—$42.7 million), Lionel Messi (FC Barcelona—$37.7 million), Ronaldinho (AC Milan—$25.8 million), and Cristiano Ronaldo (Manchester United—$24.1 million).[4]

Other major cost items for the leading soccer clubs are:

- *Player transfer fees*. Players are transferred between clubs both on terms agreed between the two clubs and with the player concerned. Players are signed to clubs on contracts of up to five years. At the end of their contracts they become free agents. Transfer fees are determined primarily by the acquisitions of a few big-spending clubs. During 2000-2, Real Madrid was the key driver; during 2004-6, Chelsea was main inflationary force; during

TABLE 6.5 Financial data from the leading European football clubs

	Country	Revenue €m.	EBITDA[1] €m.	Club Value £m.	Debt £m.
Real Madrid	Spain	365.8	51.6	850	196
Manchester Utd	England	324.8	101.9	1.140	616
Barcelona	Spain	308.8	68.8	960	41
Bayern Munich	Germany	295.3	37.6	774	0
Chelsea	England	268.9	(8.3)	486	447
Arsenal	England	264.4	51.0	690	896
Liverpool	England	210.9	33.3	704	415
AC Milan	Italy	209.5	36.9	691	0
Roma	Italy	175.4	43.9	266	24
Internazionale	Italy	172.9	17.2	258	199
Juventius	Italy	167.5	29.3	419	21
Lyon	France	155.7	59.9	295	53
Schalke 04	Germany	148.4	26.1	356	135
Tottenham	England	145.0	44.6	310	90
Hamburg	Germany	127.9	28.0	n.a	n.a

[1] Earnings before interest, taxes, depreciation and amortization.

[2] Value of team based on fixed assets and player contracts.

Source: www.forbes.com/lists/2009/34/soccer-values-09_soccer-team-valuations_value.html

2008–9, Manchester City's lavishing of £185 million on new players had taken player valuations to yet new heights.

- *Stadiums*. Leading clubs have invested substantially in upgrading and expanding their facilities. In some cases this has involved building completely new stadiums. Arsenal's new stadium opened in 2006, cost a total of £430 million.

Sources of Finance

Only a small minority of European football clubs are publicly listed companies (these include Ajax, AS Roma, Celtic, and Lazio), most are privately owned. Traditionally, football club owners have been rich local businessmen. For example, Juventus is owned by the Agnelli family (Fiat), AC Milan by Silvio Berlusconi, Inter Milan by Massimo Moratti, Olympique Marseille by Robert Louis-Dreyfus. In recent years European football has attracted international sources of equity. Among British clubs owned by foreign-born billionaires include Chelsea (Roman Abramovitch), Manchester City (Sheikh Mansour bin Zayed Al Nahyan), Queen's Park Rangers (Lakshmi Mittal of Alcelor Mittal Steel) and Fulham (Mohammed Al Fayed of Harrods). Manchester United and Liverpool were both owned by U.S. investors (the Glaser family and Tom Hicks, respectively), however, because these investors had financed their purchases primarily through debt, neither club had received the influx of cash that permitted the massive investments in new players that had been made by Chelsea or Manchester City.

TABLE 6.6 Profitability of European football clubs 2000–2006

Club	Return on sales (%)[a]
Arsenal	5.6
Chelsea	(60.4)
Liverpool	(1.2)
Man. United	12.6
Celtic	(4.0)
Rangers	(20.9)
Bayern Munich	4.7
Inter-Milan	(78.4)
Juventus	(17.0)
Real Madrid	0.4

[a] Pre-tax profit over sales revenue.

Profitability

Despite its rapid growth in popularity and revenues, European professional football remains a highly unprofitable business. Deloitte's estimates of operating profitability show that the English and German leagues have earned significant levels of operating profit, but the French and Italian leagues earned substantial (and growing) operating losses. Moreover, these measures of profit are before taking account of interest, tax and depreciation (depreciation of players is a particularly important cost). In terms of net profit, Manchester United, Arsenal, and Bayern Munich were the only leading clubs earning significant profits (see Table 6.6).

Teams and Team Building

Measured by the number and ranking of leading players in Table 6.3, Europe's most star-studded teams were Barcelona and Chelsea. There were two routes to acquiring world-class players: to buy them or to develop them. The extent to which a club is reliant upon buying players is indicated by its expenditure on player transfer fees. Table 6.7 shows that Real Madrid and Chelsea were distinguished by their massive expenditures on star players. Other top-performing teams—notably Bayern Munich, Barcelona, Arsenal, and Valencia had placed the emphasis on developing their own players. A few leading clubs were able to generate revenues from developing and selling players—for Porto, AC Milan, and PSV, revenues from selling players exceeded expenditure on players by a sizable margin.

Coaching, Management and Organization

Running a professional football club involves two distinct areas of management: managing the team for on-the-pitch performance and managing commercial activities to generate revenue and profit. Most English and Scottish clubs are organized to achieve a clear separation between these two. Governance is the responsibility of the board of

TABLE 6.7 Expenditures on player transfers

Club	Performance points 2000-9	Gross transfer fees, 2003-9 (£m)[a]	Net transfer fees, 2003-9 (£m)[a]	Size of squad, July 2009	Average age of squad, July 2009 (years)
Barcelona	200.0	362	249	24	26.8
Manchester United	192.5	322	100	34	25.6
Real Madrid	183.0	626	438	29	26.2
Bayern München	179.5	197	122	25	26.5
AC Milan	169.0	164	(66)	30	28.6
Liverpool	162.5	303	157	33	24.5
Arsenal	162.0	173	22	31	23.3
Valencia	155.5	163	98	30	26.5
Chelsea	144.5	589	430	29	27.4
Internazionale	142.0	294	140	31	27.4
Porto	140.0	132	(173)	31'	25.4
Olympique Lyonnais	139.0	127	18	34	24.4
PSV	124.5	75	(17)	25	26.5
Roma	123.0	140	75	46	25.0
Juventus	115.5	233	68	29	28.1

[a] Covers transfers from the beginning of the 2003–4 season to the end of June 2009.

Source: www.transfermarkt.co.uk.

directors, which would appoint a chief executive officer to take charge of administrative and commercial matters and a team manager who would be responsible for coaching, team selection, and recommending the purchase and sale of players (subject to budgets determined by the board).

For some English clubs this separation of management between the team and commercial matters is less clear. The usual cause of a blurring of boundaries is the owners' desire to involve themselves in managing the team. At Chelsea, for example, the departure of team manager Jose Mourihno was the result of friction with owner Roman Abramovitch over matters of player acquisition, team selection and playing style.

In continental Europe, clubs have different organizational structures. Barcelona and Real Madrid are both owned by their local supporters who elected the club president. These presidents oversee both commercial and team management. Real Madrid's recent presidents, Jose Calderon and Florentino Pérez, have been heavily involved in team selection and player acquisition. As a consequence, the tenure of coaches has been short—Real Madrid hired and fired 10 head coaches between 2003 and July 2009.

A second organizational feature of many Continental European clubs is the division of team management between the coach and a "director of football" (or "sporting director"). The rationale is to enable the coach to focus his efforts on the first team, while the director of football handles the management of reserve and youth teams, scouting for new players, and acts as an interface between the coach and the board. The introduction of directors of football at some English clubs has often resulted in conflict with the coach/manager (for example, at Chelsea and Newcastle).

A critical constituency for every club is its fans. Not only are the fans the primary source of club revenues—they are the custodians of a club's culture and heritage, and their support can play a key role in team performance. The commitment and fanaticism of fans can be a two-edged sword—the fans can lift team performance at critical junctures; it can also be disruptive when they turn against the club's coach or owner. At Barcelona, the fans' adulation for coach Josep "Pep" Guardiola has fueled their support for the team as well as bolstering his authority over his team of superstars.

Despite the different roles of coaches (managers) at different clubs, it is apparent that their role in team success is critical. As the primary architect of the team, the principal motivator and disciplinary force, and the source of team strategy and tactics, the coach is the single person most responsible for its success. Sustained success by a team over a series of seasons is almost always associated with a single coach (see Table 6.8).[5] Yet, what determines a great coach is hard to judge. Coaches succeed with very different leadership styles. Ferguson's tough, aggressive style contrasted sharply with Sven Eriksson's (Lazio, England) calm, controlled demeanor, with Arsene Wenger's (Monaco and Arsenal) intellectual approach, or with Jose Mourinho's (Porto, Chelsea, Inter) obsessive, idiosyncratic style. Certain coaching styles are appropriate to different teams and to different circumstances; coaches that achieve outstanding success with one team are often dismal failures with another.[6]

TABLE 6.8 The world's most highly regarded coaches, 1990–2007

Alex Ferguson	St. Mirren 1974–8; Aberdeen 1978–86; Manchester United 1986–
Arsene Wenger	Nancy 1984–7; Monaco 1987–94; Arsenal 1994–
Arrigo Sacchi	Parma 1985–7; AC Milan 1987–91, 1996–7; Italy 1991–6; Athletico Madrid 1998–9; Real Madrid 2004.
Johan Cruyff	Ajax 1986–8; Barcelona 1988–94
Jose Mourinho	Leiria 2001–2; Porto 2002–4; Chelsea 2004–7; Inter 2008–
Marcello Lippi	Cesena 1989–91; Lucchese 1991–2; Atalanta 1992 –3; Napoli 1993–4; Juventus 1994–9, 2001–4, Inter 1999–2000; Italy 2004–6, 2008–
Luiz Felipe Scolari	Juventude 1986–7; Al Quadisiya 1988–90, 1992; Gremio 1993–6; Palmeiras 1997–2000; Cruzeiro 2000–1; Brazil 2001–2, Portugal 2003–8, Chelsea 2008–9
Vicente Del Bosque	Real Madrid 1999–2003; Besiktas 2004–5.
Fabio Capello	AC Milan 1991–6, 1997–8; Real Madrid 1996–7, 2006–7; Roma 1999–2004; Juventus 2004–6; England 2008–
Franz Beckenbauer	West Germany 1984–90; Olympique Marseille 1990–1; Bayern Munich 1994, 1996
Aime Jacquet	O. Lyonnais 1976–80; Bordeaux 1980–9; Montpellier 1989–90; Nancy 1990–1; France 1993–8
Guus Hiddink	PSV Eindhoven 1987–90, 2002–6; Valencia 1991–4; Netherlands 1995–8; Real Madrid 1998–9; Real Betis 1999–2000; S. Korea 2000–2; Australia 2005–6; Chelsea 2008–9; Russia 2006–
Giovanni Trapattoni	Milan 1974–6; Juventus 1976–88, 1991–4; Inter 1986–91; Bayern Munich 1994–5, 1996–8; Fiorentina 1998–2000; Italy 2000–4; Benfica 2004–5; Salzburg 2006–8; Ireland 2008–
Bobby Robson	Ipswich 1969–82; England 1982–90; PSV Eindhoven 1990–2, 1998–9; Sporting Lisbon 1992–4, Porto 1994–6; Barcelona 1996–7; Newcastle 1999–2004
Carlo Ancelotti	Parma 1996–9; Juventus 1999–2001; AC Milan 2001–9; Chelsea 2009–

Source: "Top 50 Managers of All Time," *Times on Line*, September 12, 2007.

However, some common factors are apparent. An eye for talent appears to be critical. The ability to recognize outstanding football potential before it is fully developed is essential to nurturing that talent within a team context. Second, the ability to mix and balance individual players into effective team combinations is critical to team design and development. Finally, all great coaches are able to motivate their players and inspire respect and loyalty from them.

Among Europe's top teams in 2005, it was possible to observe a variety of strategies at work. Real Madrid's approach was simply to buy the world's best players. Real's president Florentino Perez explained: "It's the only possible economic and sporting model for this club . . . We have the best players and we have an important image in the world. Our strategy is for the best players to come and everyone knows who the best players are." AC Milan relied on mature talent: their team included several players in their 30s. Arsenal's Arsene Wenger ("The Professor") focused on molding a group of talented young players into a flexible, interactive team that played fast-moving, attacking football. Manchester United has emphasized the development of outstanding young talent and blending it with mature, highly experienced players.

Despite over a hundred years of football experience by thousands of professional clubs throughout the world, the determinants of team performance remained a mystery. Why one team outplayed another and why the same team could play brilliantly in one game and abysmally in the next depends on a complex mix of factors that defies analysis. Certainly team performance is not simply a product of the quality of the players in the team. Probably the greatest achievement for any coach is to build a great team out of unknown players with meager financial resources. Thus, Alex Ferguson's achievement at Aberdeen, Jose Mourinho's at Porto, Alf Ramsey's at Ipswich, and Jock Stein's at Glasgow Celtic were triumphs of team building from humble resources. Conversely, Real Madrid and Chelsea's lavishing of vast sums of money to build star-studded teams has yielded teams that have failed to achieve greatness.

Manchester United's History

Manchester United was founded in 1878 and became a professional club in 1885. Old Trafford, Manchester United's stadium, saw its first game in 1910. During the 1950s and 1960s, Manchester United rose to prominence under the leadership of its legendary team manager, Matt Busby. However, in 1958, on a return flight from a European game, a plane crash killed eight of the "Busby Babes." Busby's rebuilding of the team was rewarded in 1968 when Manchester United became the first English team to win the European Cup. After Busby's retirement in 1969, Manchester United went into decline and Liverpool became England's pre-eminent club. During the 18 years before the arrival of Alex Ferguson, Manchester United did not win a single league championship and was runner up just once.

The Ferguson Era

Alex Ferguson was recruited by Manchester United in 1986 as a result of his remarkable success at Aberdeen where he had broken the historical dominance by Rangers and Celtic of Scottish football and had taken Aberdeen all the way to the European Cup.

Ferguson was born into a working-class family in Govan, a tough, shipbuilding community close to Glasgow—a city famous for the passion and loyalty of its football fans. Ferguson's life was built around soccer. After a playing career that included the Scottish clubs St. Johnston, Glasgow Rangers and Aidrie, Ferguson took to coaching. He began with bottom-of-the-league East Stirlingshire, moved to St. Mirren, then to Aberdeen.

During his first six years at Manchester United, Ferguson systematically rebuilt the team. Ferguson culled the existing squad, keeping outstanding talent such as Bryan Robson and jettisoning those whom he judged as lacking the necessary talent or commitment, or who simply didn't fit. Despite a new era of team discipline and the acquisition of several talented new players (including Mark Hughes, Paul Ince, Eric Cantona and Roy Keane), success came slowly. In 1990, Manchester United achieved his first major success: the FA Cup, and next year the European Cup Winners' Cup but it was not until 1993 that Ferguson achieved his primary objective: the English Premier League Championship.

While reconfiguring and augmenting Man United's first team, Ferguson was also developing a stable of talented youth players. In 1990, Manchester United won the English League youth team championship with a team that included Ryan Giggs, David Beckham, Nicky Butt, Gary and Phil Neville, and Paul Scholes. Between 1994 and 2003, these homegrown young players formed the nucleus of a Manchester United team that dominated English football. This golden era culminated in 1999 when Manchester United achieved a triumph unprecedented in English football history: the team won the English league championship, the FA Cup, European Cup, and the Intercontinental Cup when they defeated the South American champions, Palmeiras.

Between 2003 and 2008, Ferguson rebuilt the Manchester United team. Key members of the trophy-winning team of 1999 season were sold, including David Beckham, Roy Keane, Peter Schmeichel, Andy Cole, Teddy Sheringham, and Jaap Stam. Their replacements included a number of highly talented young players: Rio Ferdinand, Cristiano Ronaldo, Wayne Rooney, Louis Saha, Edwin van der Sar, Patrice Evra, Nemanja Vidic, Owen Hargreaves, and Michael Carrick, who would play key roles in Manchester United's winning the European Cup in 2008.

Ownership

Between 1991 and 2003, Manchester United FC was a public company, listed on the London Stock Exchange. In 2005, Manchester United was acquired by the American businessman, Malcolm Glazer, owner of the Tampa Bay Buccaneers—a National Football League franchise. The deal created outrage among Manchester United fans; not only was Glazer "a yank who knows nothing about football" but his purchase was financed mainly by debt. Under Glazer's ownership, the board of Manchester United Ltd comprised Glazer's six children with Joel Glazer as chairman.

Despite transitional difficulties, the new ownership created less friction than expected—and much less than at other foreigner-owned clubs, such as Chelsea and Liverpool. The key was the willingness of the Glazer family to play a back seat role in managing the club. Team manager Alex Ferguson and CEO David Gill were given considerable decision making freedom. Moreover, the primary fear—that Manchester United's heavy indebtedness would limit Ferguson's ability to acquire new players—proved groundless.

Ferguson's Management Style

In a business where the performance expectations of owners and fans were focused on the short term, Ferguson's emphasis was on success over the long term:

> My aim in management has always been to lay foundations that will make a club successful for years, or even decades . . . When I joined United on 6 November 1986, they had gone 19 years without a title. No-one had to tell me that if I did not end that drought I would be a failure. Putting them in a position to challenge consistently would, I knew, be a long haul. I would have to build from the bottom up, rectifying the flaws I had recognized and spreading my influence and self-belief through every layer of the organization. I wanted to form a personal link with everyone around the place—not just the players, the coaches and the backroom staff but the office workers, the cooks and servers in the canteen and the laundry ladies. All had to believe that they were part of the club and that a resurgence was coming.[7]

The starting point was training and team discipline. Ferguson declared war on alcohol—a problem endemic to British professional soccer and an indulgence that Ferguson viewed as incompatible with professional sport. The new, more rigorous training regime included meticulous attention to attendance, punctuality and effort. His training sessions built individual and team skills through continuous repetition: "refining technique to the point where difficult skills become a matter of habit."

In terms of long-term team building, Ferguson focused heavily on identifying and developing new talent: "From the moment I became manager of United, I was committed to the creation of a youth policy that would be the envy of every other club in Britain. The first imperative was to find the raw talent."[8]

One of Ferguson first initiatives at Manchester United was to expand the scouting staff from five to over 20 and instructed them to seek only the most outstanding talent. Manchester United's Youth Academy was built into what Ferguson declared was the finest youth coaching program in the country. Increasingly, Manchester United's scouts would scour the world for new players. In 2008, the club appointed two full-time scouts to seek out new players in Brazil.[9]

To Ferguson, team building was much more than acquiring and developing talented players, developing their skills and building coordination between them:

> The best teams stand out because they are teams, because the individual members have been so truly integrated that the team functions with a single spirit. There is a constant flow of mutual support among the players, enabling them to feed off strengths and compensate for weaknesses. They depend on one another, trust in one another. A manager should engender that sense of unity. He should create a bond among his players and between him and them that raises performance to heights that were unimaginable when they started out as disparate individuals.[10]

Ferguson's approach to motivating his players involved a combination of loyal support and, where he identified unnecessary mistakes or lack of effort, withering criticism. His ability to induce exquisite performances from the brilliant but volatile

Frenchman, Eric Cantona, owed much to Ferguson's unflinching support during Cantona's conflicts with authority. At the same time, Ferguson was renowned for his temper and the ferociousness of his verbal tirades. These were delivered to players at such close range that they became known as "Ferguson's hairdryer." One confrontation resulted in David Beckham requiring stitches above his eye—the result of Ferguson kicking a football boot at him. Ferguson's half-time talks to his team could have a powerful effect in re-energizing their second-half efforts. At the European Cup Final in 1999, Man United was losing 1–0 at the end of the first half. He told his team: "At the end of this game, the European Cup will be only six feet away from you and you'll not even be able to touch it if we lose. And for many of you that will be the closest you will ever get. Don't you dare come back in here without giving your all."

Central to Ferguson's approach to managing players has been his insistence that no player is bigger than the club. The result has been well publicized clashes with some of his leading players—typically resulting in them being dropped from the first team for several games or being sold to other clubs.

In terms of team strategy and match tactics, Ferguson was committed to control over the midfield. This required "controlled, sustained possession that calls for players adept at holding the ball and spreading calculated and accurate passes . . . A high standard of passing in central midfield was the core of United's football."[11] Ferguson had long admired the ability of the top Italian teams to vary the pace of their game—to slow the game with a period of low-energy, possession football, followed by a sudden, lightning attack. Ferguson's team design was characterized as a closely coordinated midfield group built around players such as Keane, Scholes, Beckham, Giggs and Ronaldo supporting creative strikers such as Cantona, van Nistelrooy, Cole and Rooney.

Ferguson has been a pioneering exponent of "squad rotation"—reconfiguring a team to rest players and to adapt tactics in order to exploit opponents' vulnerabilities. During consecutive games, Manchester United's starting team can vary substantially and, in the course of a game, Ferguson made extensive use of substitutes. This team flexibility calls for players to develop broad repertoires of coordination—they must get used to playing in different combinations and adapting their style of play according to the different talents of different team mates.[12]

Although Manchester United was one of Europe's top spending teams on new players, Ferguson's purchases were matched by a willingness to sell players that were valued more by other teams. Major sales have included: David Beckham, Juan Veron, van Nistelrooy and Ronaldo (for a world record transfer fee of £80 million). As a result, Manchester United's net expenditure on player transfers has been relatively modest compared to other leading European clubs.

Manchester United's Commercial and Financial Performance

Manchester United and Real Madrid are regarded as the most commercially focused clubs in European football. In building a global fan base then converting that support into revenues, Manchester United was a model for other European clubs.

"We're not just a sports club, we are an international brand . . . and building that brand is very important," former commercial director Andy Anson observed. In addition to the overall Manchester United brand, the club developed several sub-brands: "Fred the Red" was designed to appeal to children; the "MUFC" brand is targeted at teenagers, while "Red Devil" products are directed mainly towards adults. Other brands are associated with specific licensing deals – notably "Red Cafes" and "Theatre of Dreams" restaurants. A subsidiary, Manchester United International, was created in 1998 for the purpose of developing Man United's business opportunities outside the U.K.—in North America and Asia especially.

In addition to primary sponsors Nike and AIG (to be replaced by Aon in 2010) Manchester United's sponsors have included:

- Budweiser, "the official beer of Manchester United."
- Audi, "the official car supplier to Manchester United."
- Betfred, "the official betting partner of Manchester United."
- Hublot Watches, "official timekeeper of Manchester United."
- Tri Indonesia, "official telecommunications partner of Manchester United for Indonesia."
- Bharti Airtel, "official telecommunications partner of Manchester United in India."
- There were seven other sponsors.

Commercial initiatives have included:

- MU Finance, which offered credit cards, mortgages, and retirement planning products.
- MU Mobile, which offered SMS and video streaming services to Manchester United fans.
- MUTV, which showed Manchester United games on webTV.
- Manchester United Soccer Schools, offered in Manchester and other locations within the U.K. and in the U.S., Canada, Switzerland, Singapore, Malaysia and other countries. There are also Manchester United soccer schools at Disneyland in Paris and Hong Kong.
- The Manchester United Superstore offers a wide range of Manchester United licensed products both through the Old Trafford retail store and online through http://store.manutd.com.
- Manchester United's Old Trafford stadium hosts a wide variety of events. Regular attractions include the Manchester United museum and stadium tour. In addition, suites, bars and a ballroom can be rented for conferences, receptions, parties, weddings and dinners. Expansion of the stadium in 2006 gave a substantial boost to Manchester United's revenues—primarily from the 7500 additional seats.

It was one of the first of the English clubs to go public and the most successful in establishing effective corporate governance. The Glazer acquisition changed the club's financial structure but otherwise had limited impact on Manchester United's financial performance. The club continued to grow its commercial revenues—especially from overseas—however, it was not evident that Manchester United derived any significant benefit from Malcolm Glazer's much lauded promotional expertise.

The Appendix shows financial information for Manchester United plc.

July 2009

As the "Reds" returned from their Asia tour on July 28, 2009, media interest focused upon whether the club would spend the cash from the sale of Cristiano Ronaldo on a bid for Bayern Munich's Franck Ribery. Meanwhile, Sir Alex was setting out his expectations for the forthcoming season: at least 100 goals to be scored of which Rooney was expected to score at least 18 and new signing, Michael Owen 15.

At the same time, anticipation that Sir Alex would retire in the summer of 2010 was attracting a number would-be candidates for his job. Ferguson's former assistant and coach to the Portuguese national team, Carlos Queiroz, had made no secret of his desire to lead Manchester United. Ferguson's former adversary and current coach of Inter Milan, Jose Mourinho, also announced his interest in the post.[13] Another favored candidate was Gordon Strachan, one of Ferguson's former players who had been a highly successful manager of Celtic.

As Manchester United's CEO, David Gill, evaluated the possible successors to Sir Alex, he realized that the club faced a difficult dilemma. After 24 years of Ferguson's leadership, it was important to maintain as much as possible of the system of training, scouting, and team development that Sir Alex had put in place. This would favor appointing Ferguson's former assistants, Queiroz, or one of his current ones, Mike Phelan, Ole Gunnar Solskjær, or Brian McClair. The problem was whether anyone who had been successful as an assistant to Ferguson could have the presence and strength of personality needed to exert leadership and authority over Manchester United's high profile soccer stars. Conversely, if Manchester United was to appoint a manager with proven leadership skills—Jose Mourinho, for example—it was likely that this would involve a revolutionary change in coaching strategy in which much of Ferguson's infrastructure would be taken down and rebuilt.

Appendix: Manchester United: Selected Financial Data, 2000–2008 (£, thousands)

	2008[a]	2007[a]	2006[a]	2005[a]	2004[b]	2003[b]	2002[b]	2001[b]	2000[b]
Turnover	257 118	212 189	167 751	157 171	169 080	173 001	146 062	129 569	116 005
Group operating profit before depreciation and amortization	86 005	79 786	46 254	46 131	58 340	57 269	41 402	38 194	35 125
Depreciation	(7271)	(7630)	(5147)	(6054)	(6591)	(7283)	(6923)	(6514)	(5052)
Amortization of players	(35 481)	(24 252)	(23 427)	(24 159)	(21 839)	(21 018)	(17 647)	(10 173)	(13 092)
Exceptional costs				(7286)	—	(2197)	(1414)	(2073)	(1300)
Group operating profit	42 821	47 797	17 680	8632	29 910	26 771	15 418	19 434	15 681
(Loss)/profit on disposal of players	21 831	11 760	12 462	(556)	(3084)	12 935	17 406	2219	1633
Net interest receivable/ (payable)	462	343	722	2477	1066	(316)	27	727	456
Profit on ordinary activities before taxation	66 416	59 627		10 764	27 907	39 345	32 347	21 778	16 788
Taxation	(19 916)	(17 338)	(9222)	(4224)	(8486)	(9564)	(7308)	(7399)	(4838)
Profit for the period	46 754	42 289	21 603	6540	19 421	29 781	25 039	14 379	11 950
Fixed assets	267 452	283 020	228 989	202 823	204 504	n.a.	n.a.	n.a.	n.a.
Current assets	179 236	115 310	71 765	83 465	24 258	n.a.	n.a.	n.a.	n.a.
Creditors	(81 421)	(82 494)	(31 356)	50 304	53 430	n.a.	n.a.	n.a.	n.a.
Equity Shareholders' funds	294 018	245 304	202 666	180 846	173 354	156 418	137 443	120 457	114 950

Note: The data relate to Manchester United plc for 2000 to 2005 and Manchester United Limited for 2006–2008. Due to accounting changes, the data for 2000–4 are not comparable to those for 2005–8.

[a] 11 months to June 30.

[b] 12 months to July 31.

Source: Annual reports.

Notes

1 "Manchester United's global appeal goes from strength to strength," *Daily Telegraph* (July 16, 2009), www.telegraph.co.uk/sport/football/leagues/premierleague/manutd/, accessed July 25, 2009.

2 "Manchester United's global appeal goes from strength to strength," *Daily Telegraph* (July 16, 2009), www.telegraph.co.uk/sport/football/leagues/premierleague/manutd/, accessed July 25, 2009.

3 Deloitte, *Annual Review of Football Finance, 2009,* highlights, see www.deloitte.com/dtt/cda/doc/content/UK_SBG_ARFF2009_Highlights.pdf, accessed July 29, 2009.

4 "Beckham Again World's Best-paid," *Sports Illustrated,* March 30, 2009.

5 In British football, these included Manchester United under Matt Busby, Liverpool under Bill Shankly and Bob Paisley, Celtic under Jock Stein, Leeds under Don Revie and Nottingham Forest under Brian Clough.

6 Claudio Ranieri was less successful at Chelsea, Athletico Madrid and in his second stint at Valencia than he had been at Fiorentina and his initial term at Valencia; Brian Clough was unable to replicate his remarkable performance at Derby and then Nottingham Forest at either Brighton or Leeds; Bobby Robson's 37-year coaching career included outstanding success at Ipswich, Porto, and Barcelona and poorer team performance at PSV, Sporting Lisbon and Newcastle. "Big Phil" Scolari survived less than one season at Chelsea.

7 Alex Ferguson, *Managing My Life,* Hodder & Stoughton, London, 1999, p. 242.

8 Alex Ferguson, *Managing My Life,* Hodder & Stoughton, London, 1999, p. 274.

9 "Manchester United Invest in Brazilian Talent," *Independent,* October 17, 2008.

10 Alex Ferguson, *Managing My Life,* Hodder & Stoughton, London, 1999, p. 274.

11 Alex Ferguson, *Managing My Life,* Hodder & Stoughton, London, 1999), p. 437.

12 "Sir Alex Ferguson Proves Mastery at Manchester United with Rotation System," *The Times,* May 11, 2009.

13 "Jose Mourinho Wants to Succeed Sir Alex Ferguson at Manchester United," *DailyTelegraph,* July 28, 2009.

Case 7 Eastman Kodak: Meeting the Digital Challenge

On June 1, 2005, Antonio Perez, Eastman Kodak's chief operating officer, took over as CEO from Dan Carp. It was quite clear to him why he had been appointed and what the Kodak board expected from him. He had been recruited from Hewlett-Packard (HP) two years earlier because of his successful leadership of HP's digital imaging initiatives. There he had run HP's inkjet printing business and, subsequently, as CEO of consumer business, he had led HP's efforts to build its business in digital imaging and electronic publishing. As CEO of Eastman Kodak (Kodak) his task was to continue the journey begun by his predecessors, George Fisher and Dan Carp, in transforming Kodak from a photographic company into a world leader in digital imaging.

His first eight months in the job showed progress towards this goal. In 2005, Kodak was U.S. market leader in digital still cameras and ranked third worldwide (see Table 7.1). With its 75 000 retail photo kiosks and the leading online digital

TABLE 7.1 Brand shares of the world market for digital still cameras (by units)

Brand	2005	2004	2003	2002	2001	2000
Sony (%)	15.2	16.7	18	20	25	26
Canon (%)	17.4	17.1	16	14	10	9
Olympus (%)	9.8	7.7	13	16	11	18
Kodak (%)	14.2	11.8	12	10	14	11
Hewlett-Packard (%)	4.4	n.a.	n.a.	3	8	7
Fuji Film (%)	7.8	8.5	10	15	14	12
Total units sold (million)	78	64	48	28	17	n.a.

Source: IDC, The NPD Group/NPD Techworld.

photography service (EasyShare Gallery), Kodak led the retail market for printing digital photographs. In commercial printing, Kodak consolidated its global leadership in high-resolution, color printing systems. In healthcare, Kodak was a leader in digital dental imaging and was expanding its market share in digital X-rays.

However, the financial results told a very different story. Kodak posted an operating loss of $600 million and a net loss of $1362 million for 2005. While Kodak's cash flows from its traditional film business shrank much more quickly than Kodak had anticipated, its digital business—with its intense competition, compressed product cycles and declining product prices—failed to fill the gap. Since hitting a high of $99 in July 1998, Kodak's shares had continued their downward track, closing at $24 at the end of January 2006.

Perez's response was to accelerate Kodak's reallocation of resources from conventional business into digital imaging. In July 2005 he had called for 10 000 job cuts in addition to 15 000 previously announced in order to staunch Kodak's "bleeding year after year." Kodak's manufacturing capacity would be cut by two-thirds. He also called for the phasing out of film: "We need to establish an end point for this transformation and we need to get there soon."[1]

At the Consumer Electronics Show in Las Vegas in January 2006, Perez went further in reorienting perceptions of Kodak: "Soon, I'm not going to be answering questions about film because I won't know. It will be too small for me to get involved." He also played down Kodak's future as a digital imaging hardware company. He described digital cameras as "dinosaurs that cannot evolve as fast as the environment around them." He went on to argue that the future of digital imaging would not be based upon stand-alone cameras but on "technology that allows consumers to search, share and display images on different media such as mobile phones and the internet."[2] Software would play a central role in the industry; it was needed for storing, organizing and sharing digital images:

> Soon you're going to have 10 000 pictures on your computer. It's a complete nightmare . . . If you look at the people we're hiring, you'll be surprised by the number of software people we have. We have human interface experts and people who understand sentiment produced by different colors and shapes. We're becoming a very modern company.[3]

Perez's ambition and optimistic outlook did little to impress the stock market. Chris Whitmore of Deutsche Bank pointed to the difficulty of making money in digital imaging: "They're entering markets that are highly competitive and have low margins and levels of profitability." Commercial printing and medical imaging offered better potential for profitability but it was not clear that Kodak could build a strong competitive advantage in these markets. In commercial printing, Citigroup's Matthew Troy doubted Kodak's ability to integrate its various acquisitions. In medical imaging, he saw Kodak as lacking the critical mass to compete with GE and Siemens: "They're trying to upsell into the field with larger players with much broader expertise . . . They lack the comprehensive scale to compete."[4]

Kodak's History, 1880–1993

George Eastman transformed photography from an activity undertaken by professional photographers working in studios into an everyday consumer hobby. His key innovations were silver halide roll film and the first fully portable camera. In 1901 he established the Eastman Kodak Company in Rochester, New York, to provide the full range of products and services needed to support the amateur photographer. The emphasis was ease of use: "You push the button, we do the rest" was its first advertising slogan. By the time George Eastman died in 1932, Eastman Kodak was one of the world's leading multinational corporations with production, distribution and processing facilities throughout the world with one of the world's most recognizable brand names.

After the Second World War, Kodak entered a new growth period fueled by growing affluence and increased leisure time. Exploiting its polymer technology, its subsidiary, Eastman Chemical, became a major plastics producer. However, by the end of the 1970s, Kodak was facing its first competitive challenges. In cameras, Kodak's leadership was undermined by the rise of the Japanese camera industry, with its sophisticated yet easy-to-use 35 mm cameras. In film, Fuji Photo Film Company embarked on a strategy of aggressive international expansion. Most striking were the new imaging technologies that were emerging. Polaroid pioneered instant photography, Xerox led the new field of electrostatic plain-paper copying, and the personal computer was ushering in an array of new printing technologies.

Early Moves in Electronics, 1980–93

Under Colby Chandler and Kay Whitmore, Kodak launched a series of diversification moves including expansion into healthcare (Eastman Pharmaceutical was established in 1986) and a slew of new imaginative initiatives. These included:

- Eikonix Corp., acquired in 1985, which gave Kodak a leading position in commercial imaging systems that scanned, edited and prepared images for printing.
- Kodak developed the world's first megapixel electronic image sensor with 1.4 million pixels (1986). This was followed by a number of new products for scanning and electronic image capture, including Imagelink for document imaging and Optistar for micrographic digital image capture (1989).
- Kodak became a leader in image storage and retrieval systems. Its KAR4000 Information System provided computer-assisted storage and retrieval of

microfilm images (1983). The Ektaprint Electronic Publishing System and Kodak Image Management System offered integrated systems to edit, store, retrieve, and print text and graphics (1985).

- Kodak became involved in a range of data storage products including floppy disks (Verbatim was acquired in 1985), a 14-inch optical disk capable of storing 6.8 billion bytes of information (1986), and magnetic recording heads for disk drives (through the 1985 acquisition of Garlic Corp.).

- Kodak acquired IBM's copier services business.

- As a result of its collaboration with Philips, Kodak announced its Photo CD system in 1990. Photo CDs allowed digitized photographic images to be stored on a compact disk, which could then be viewed and manipulated on a personal computer.

- In 1991, Kodak introduced its first digital camera, the 1.3 megapixel Kodak DCS-100, which combined a digital back made by Kodak with a camera body produced by Nikon. It was priced at $13 000.

Creating a Digital Strategy: George Fisher and Dan Carp, 1993–2005

By the early 1990s it was clear that Kodak was extended over too many initiatives with too little commitment to any area outside of its traditional imaging business. In 1993, the Kodak board ousted Whitmore and brought in George Fisher, then CEO of Motorola. With a doctorate in applied mathematics and ten years of R&D experience at Bell Labs, Fisher had a scientist's grasp of electronic technology while his experience at Motorola demonstrated an ability to turn new technology into world-beating new products.

From the outset, Fisher's strategic vision for Kodak was as an imaging company: "We are not in the photographic film business or in the electronics business; we are in the picture business."[5] To focus Kodak's efforts on the digital challenge, Fisher's first moves were to spinoff of Eastman Chemical Company and sell most of Kodak's healthcare businesses (other than medical imaging).

Fisher's digital strategy was to create greater coherence among Kodak's many digital imaging projects, in part through creating a single digital projects division headed by newly hired Carl Gustin (previously with Apple Computer and DEC). During his tenure, and continuing through that of his successor, Dan Carp, Kodak developed a digital strategy that comprised the following key themes.

An Incremental Approach

"The future is not some harebrained scheme of the digital information highway or something. It is a step-by-step progression of enhancing photography using digital technology," declared Fisher.[6] This recognition that digital imaging was an evolutionary rather than a revolutionary change would be the key to Kodak's ability to build a strong position in digital technology. If photography was to switch rapidly from the traditional chemical-based technology to a wholly digital technology where customers took digital pictures, downloaded them onto their computers, edited them and transmitted them through the internet to be viewed electronically, then Kodak would face an extremely difficult time. Not only would the new digital value chain make most of Kodak's core competitive advantages redundant (its silver halide technology, its global network of retail outlets and processing facilities)—most of this digital value chain was already in the hands of computer hardware and software companies.

Fortunately for Kodak, during the 1990s digital technology made only selective incursions into traditional photographic imaging. As late as 2000 digital cameras had achieved limited market penetration; the vast majority of photographic images were still captured on traditional film.

Hence, central to Kodak's strategy was a hybrid approach where Kodak introduced those aspects of digital imaging that could offer truly enhanced functionality for users. Thus, in the consumer market, Kodak recognized that image capture would continue to be dominated by traditional film for some time (digital cameras offered inferior resolution compared with conventional photography). However, digital imaging offered immediate potential for image manipulation and transmission.

If consumers continued to use conventional film while seeking the advantages of digitization for editing and emailing their pictures, this offered a valuable opportunity for Kodak's vast retail network. Kodak had installed its first self-service facility for digitizing, editing and printing images from conventional photographs in 1988. In 1994, Kodak launched its Picture Maker, a self-service kiosk located in retail stores where customers could edit and print digital images from a variety of digital inputs, or from digital scans of conventional photo prints. Picture Maker allowed customers to edit their images (zoom, crop, eliminate red-eye and add text) and print them in a variety of formats. George Fisher emphasized the central role of retail kiosks in Kodak's digital strategy:

> Four years ago, when we talked about the possibilities of digital photography, people laughed. Today, the high-tech world is stampeding to get a piece of the action, calling digital imaging perhaps the greatest growth opportunity in the computer world. And it may be. We surely see it as the greatest future enabler for people to truly "Take Pictures. Further."
>
> We start at retail, our distribution stronghold. Here consumers are at the peak moment of satisfaction, when they open their photofinishing envelopes. We believe the widespread photo-retailing infrastructure will continue to be the principal avenue by which people obtain their pictures. Our strategy is to build on and extend this existing market strength which is available to us, and at the same time be prepared to serve the rapidly growing, but relatively small, pure digital market that is developing. Kodak will network its rapidly expanding installed base of Image Magic stations and kiosks, essentially turning these into nodes on a massive, global network. The company will allow retailers to use these workstations to bring digital capability to the average snapshooter, extending the value of these images for the consumers and retailers alike, while creating a lucrative consumable business for Kodak.[7]

Despite the growing ownership of inkjet printers, a very large proportion of consumers continued to use photo-print facilities in retail stores. By the end of 2000, some 30 000 retail locations worldwide offered Picture Maker facilities. By the beginning of 2004, Kodak was the clear leader in self-service digital printing kiosks, with 24 000 installed Kodak Picture Makers in the U.S. and over 55 000 worldwide. The G3 Picture Maker—Kodak's third generation of retail kiosk launched in 2004 could print a picture in as little as five seconds.

Kodak also used digital technology to enhance the services offered by photofinishers. Thus, the Kodak I.Lab system offered a digital infrastructure to photofinishers that digitized every film negative and offered better pictures by fixing common problems in consumer photographs.

Kodak's hybrid approach was also evident in introducing digital enhancement of conventional film. In 1996, Kodak launched its Advantix advanced photo system, which allowed both chemical film images and electronic data to be stored on a single film. The new standard failed to make much impact on the market.

Despite the inferior resolution of digital cameras, Fisher recognized their potential and pushed Kodak to establish itself in this highly competitive market. Kodak's digital cameras addressed both the top end and the bottom end of the market. In January 1994, Kodak launched its DigitalNews Camera, which had been developed in cooperation with Associated Press, was targeted at photojournalists and was priced at $15 000. It also launched the Apple Quicktake computer camera (manufactured by Kodak, marketed by Apple Computer), which, at $75, was the cheapest digital camera available at the time. In March 1995, Kodak introduced the first full-featured digital camera priced at under $1000. During the subsequent six years, Kodak continued to bring out new, more sophisticated digital cameras, including professional cameras developed in conjunction with Canon. By 2000, Kodak offered a wide range of digital cameras. At the top end was its DC4800 camera with 3.1 megapixel resolution; at the other a PalmPix camera that allowed a Palm personal digital assistant to be used as a digital camera.

The Consumer Market: Emphasizing Simplicity and Ease of Use

Fisher advocated different approaches to consumer and commercial markets. While the commercial and professional market offered the test-bed for Kodak's advanced digital technologies, the emphasis in the consumer segment was to maintain Kodak's position as mass-market leader by providing simplicity, quality and value. It was in the consumer market where incremental strategy was most evident; through this it could exploit its brand and distribution strengths. The key was providing an easy pathway for customers from traditional to digital photography.

Kodak continued to be guided by its original vision of "You push the button; we do the rest!" Both Fisher and Carp believed that Kodak's market position in digital imaging should seek to replicate that in traditional imaging: Kodak should be the mass-market leader providing security, reliability and simplicity for customers bewildered by the pace of technological change. This required Kodak to offer a transition path for customers seeking to migrate from traditional to digital imaging. Thus, Kodak would offer an array of services that would allow consumers to digitize conventional photographs, edit digitized images and obtain printed photographs in a variety of formats.

Simplicity and mass-market leadership also implied that Kodak provided the fully integrated set of products and services needed for digital photography. The essential characteristic of the Kodak system would be ease of use. "For Kodak, digital photography is all about ease of use and helping people get prints—in other words, getting the same experience they're used to from their film cameras," Martin Coyne, head of Kodak's Photographic Group, said at the 2002 Kodak Media Forum. He supported his argument with data showing that while 90% of consumers were satisfied with the pictures obtained from traditional photography, for digital photography only between 50% and 70% were satisfied.[8] A systems approach rather than a product approach was based on the recognition that most consumers had neither the time nor the patience to read instructions and to integrate different devices and software. Kodak believed that its integrated system approach would have particular appeal to women who comprised the major part of the consumer market.

The result was Kodak's EasyShare system, launched in 2001. According to Willy Shih, head of digital and applied imaging, EasyShare's intention was to:

> . . . provide consumers with the first easy-to-use digital photography experience . . . Digital photography is more than just about digital cameras. This is just the first step . . . People need to get their pictures to their PCs and then want to share by printing or e-mail. So we developed a system that made the full experience as easy as possible.[9]

The result would be a comprehensive digital system within which consumers could take digital pictures on digital cameras or phone-cameras (or have conventional photographs digitized), could view their images on a variety of devices, and print their digital images at home, at retail kiosks, or through Kodak's online processing service. Figure 7.1 shows Kodak's conceptualization of its EasyShare system.

By 2005, most of the main elements of the EasyShare system were in place:

● Kodak had a broad range of EasyShare digital cameras. Despite a crowded market (by 1998, 45 companies were offering digital cameras) and Japanese dominance in both conventional and digital cameras, Kodak had succeeded in positioning itself among the global big-three. Its EasyShare range resulted in substantial market share gains across the globe.

FIGURE 7.1 Kodak's EasyShare Network: "Your Pictures—Anytime, Anywhere"

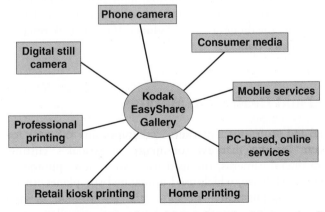

Source: Based upon Bob Brust, "Completing the Kodak Transformation," Presentation, Eastman Kodak Company, September 2005.

- EasyShare software allowed downloading, organization, editing and emailing of images and the ordering of online prints. EasyShare software was bundled with Kodak's cameras as well as being available for downloading for free from Kodak's web site.

- EasyShare camera docks allowed the transfer of digital images from camera to PC at the touch of a button. However, the ability to print photographs without the need for a computer was even more important: EasyShare printer docks enabled photographic prints to be made direct from the camera without the need for downloading to a PC. To provide an integrated offering to consumers, Kodak had begun providing special-purpose printers for producing photographic images. Initially, Kodak sourced inkjet printers from Lexmark. The 2003 EasyShare dock printer represented a major step forward for Kodak: a combined printer and camera dock that offered "one touch simple" thermal-dye printing either with a PC or direct from the camera. In 2002, Kodak acquired Scitex, a leader in continuous-flow inkjet printing, to augment its capabilities in variable data digital printing. Antonio Perez's appointment as COO in 2003 reinforced Kodak's push into printers: "If a company wants to be a leader in digital imaging, it necessarily has to participate in digital output."[10]

- Online digital imaging services. Kodak had been quick to recognize the potential of the internet for allowing consumers to transmit and store their photographs and order prints. According to Willy Shih: "the next killer app . . . is when photography meets the network effect. Or, in other words, when the internet is coupled with digital photography." Kodak's Picture Network was launched in 1997. Consumers could have their conventional photographs digitized by a retail photo store, then uploaded to a personal internet account on Kodak's Picture Network. The following year Kodak launched its online printing service, *PhotoNet*, enabling consumers to upload their digital photo files and order prints of them. Kodak also partnered with AOL to offer *You've Got Pictures*, Kodak providing their printing services and operational support for several of its online photofinishing competitors, including Razorfish. In 2001, Kodak became a leader in online photographic processing when it acquired Ofoto. In addition to online processing, whereby consumers emailed their digital images and received their photographic prints by mail, Ofoto allowed members to build online albums through which family and friends could view and order prints for themselves. In January 2005, Kodak renamed Ofoto "Kodak EasyShare Gallery."

Commercial and Healthcare Markets

The commercial and professional markets were important to Kodak for two reasons. First, they were leading markets for many of Kodak's cutting-edge digital technologies. In digital cameras, the lead users were news photographers and the U.S. Department of Defense, which used unmanned spy-planes for reconnaissance. More generally, the sophisticated needs of the government in satellite imaging, planning military campaigns, weather forecasting, and surveillance activities favored digital technologies for transforming, transmitting, and storing images. In the U.S.

space program, Kodak cameras and imaging equipment accompanied a number of missions, including the Mars probe and the IKONOS Earth-orbiting satellite. In its research activities, Kodak benefitted considerably from Department of Defense and NASA contracts. In both healthcare and in commercial markets, Kodak took a systems approach, seeking to bundle hardware, software and consumables into customer solutions.

In healthcare, medical imaging (especially CT, MRI and ultrasound) required digital technologies for 3D imaging, diagnosis and image storage. In commercial printing, digital imaging provided the basis for a revolution in the publication and printing of newspapers and magazines. Across a wide range of commercial applications ranging from journalism to highway safety to real estate, digital imaging offered huge advantages because of its ability to transmit images (especially through the internet) and link with sophisticated IT management systems for image storage and retrieval. The huge price premium of commercial consumer products (in the case of digital cameras, a professional camera could be up to 100 times that of a basic consumer version; price differentials were similar in color printers) meant that Kodak's R&D was often focused on these leading-edge users in the anticipation of trickle-down to the consumer market.

In commercial printing and publishing (which became the Graphic Communications Group in 2005), Kodak assembled a strong position in commercial scanning, formatting, and printing systems for the publishing, packaging, and data processing industries. This sector comprised NexPress, which supplied a range of high-end color and black-and-white printing machines;[11] Kodak Polychrome Graphics, a leader in graphic communications; Creo Inc., a supplier of pre-press and workflow systems used by commercial printers; Kodak Versamark, a provider of continuous inkjet technology; Encad, a maker of wide-format inkjet printers; and Kodak's Document Products and Services organization, which supplied document scanners, microfilm and support services. Kodak's opportunity was to exploit the transition from traditional offset printing to digital, full-color, variable printing. This opportunity built on two key strengths: first, Kodak's proprietary inkjet technology and, second, its leadership in variable-data printing—printing that required individually customized output (as in personalized sales catalogs or bills).

In the healthcare field, Kodak's market position was similar to that in consumer photography: its strength was in film for X-rays and in related chemicals and accessories. Hence, the encroachment of digital technology offered a major threat. Under Fisher and Carp, Kodak responded by broadening its involvement in medical imaging. Its Ektascan Imagelink system, which enabled medical images to be converted into digital images that could be transmitted via phone between hospitals, was launched in 1995 followed by its Ektascan medical laser printer in 1996. This leadership was extended with the acquisition of Imation's Dry View laser imaging business in 1998. In addition to the printing of medical images, Kodak invested heavily in healthcare information systems, including picture archiving and communications systems (PACS). Kodak also built up a strong, integrated dental imaging business.

In several areas of government service, Kodak used its capabilities in "infoimaging"—the convergence of imaging with information technology to bid on large contracts involving image management and retrieval. Kodak's digital scanning and document management systems were used in national censuses in the U.S., U.K., France, Australia and Brazil. At the German post office, a Kodak team achieved a world record, creating digitized copies of 1.7 million documents in 24 hours.

Hiring, Alliances, and Acquisitions

The traditional Kodak business system was based upon vertical integration and self-sufficiency: at its Rochester base, Kodak developed its own technology, produced its own products and supplied them worldwide through its vast global network. In digital imaging, not only did Kodak lack much of the expertise needed to build a digital imaging business but the pace of technological change was too rapid to rely on in-house development. Hence, as Kodak transformed its capability base from chemical imaging to digital imaging it was forced to look outside for the knowledge it required.

Kodak had traditionally been a lifetime employment company that grew its own senior executives. The arrival of George Fisher from Motorola changed all that. Under Fisher's leadership Kodak launched a major hiring campaign to put in place the executives and technical specialists it needed for its new digital strategy. Key executives who relocated from Silicon Valley to Rochester included Kodak's first head of its digital imaging division, Willy Shih, whose prior experience included Silicon Graphics and IBM. Kodak also brought in senior hires from Xerox, HP, Lexmark, Apple, GE Medical Electronics, Olympus Optical, and Lockheed Martin. Table 7.2 shows the backgrounds of Kodak's top management team.

Fisher's recognition that Kodak's strategy of vertical integration from image capture through to printing photographic images would not work in digital imaging acknowledged that the digital imaging chain already included companies that were well established—sometimes dominant—in particular activities. For example, Adobe Systems dominated image formatting software; HP, Epson, and Canon were leaders in inkjet printers for home use; and Microsoft's control over PC operating systems meant that software for image editing had to be compatible with its Windows system. Willy Shih, head of Kodak's digital imaging products from 1997 to 2003, observed: "We have to pick where we add value and commoditize where we can't."[12] The difficult decision was identifying the activities and product areas where Kodak could add value.

In many cases this meant partnering with companies that were already leaders in digital technologies and hardware and software products. Under Fisher's leadership, Kodak forged a web of joint ventures and strategic alliances. In addition to the already mentioned alliances with Canon, AOL and Heidelberg, Kodak's alliances included:

- Intel Corporation: development and co-marketing of Picture CD; development of digital image storage media and development of an ASP system for archiving and downloading medical images on a pay-per-use basis. Adobe Systems also collaborated with Kodak and Intel in producing software for Picture CD.
- Hewlett-Packard: a primary source of inkjet technology for Kodak, Phogenix Imaging was a joint venture between Kodak and HP to develop high-quality inkjet solutions for micro and mini photo-finishing labs utilizing Kodak's DLS software.[13]
- Microsoft: cooperation to establish standards for Windows-based Picture Transfer Protocols and cooperation in the development of Photo-CDs and development of FlashPix image storage for digital cameras (also with HP).

TABLE 7.2 Eastman Kodak's senior management team, 2005

Name	Position	Joined Kodak	Prior company experience
Corporate officers			
Robert L. Berman	Senior Vice President	1980	Kodak veteran
Charles S. Brown, Jr.	Senior Vice President, Chief Administrative Officer	1973	Kodak veteran
Richard G. Brown, Jr.	Chief Accounting Officer and Controller	2003	Ernst & Young LLP partner,
Robert H. Brust	Chief Financial Officer and Executive Vice President	2000	General Electric, Unisys Corp
Carl E. Gustin, Jr.	Senior Vice President, Chief Marketing Officer	1994	DEC, Apple
Joyce P. Haag	General Counsel and Senior Vice President	1981	Boylan, Brown, Code, Fowler, Vigdor & Wilson LLP
William J. Lloyd	Senior Vice President, Director Inkjet Systems	2003	Inwit, Gemplus, HP
Daniel T. Meek	Senior Vice President, Director Global Manufacturing and Logistics	1973	NYPRO, Verbatim
Antonio M. Perez	Chairman of the Board, Chief Executive Officer	2003	President and CEO of HP
Divisional presidents			
Mary Jane Hellyar	Senior Vice President, President Film and PhotoFinishing Systems Group	1982	Kodak veteran
Philip J. Faraci	Senior Vice President, President Consumer Digital Imaging Group	2004	Phogenix Imaging, Gemplus
James T. Langley	Senior Vice President, President Graphic Communication Group	2003	HP
Kevin J. Hobert	Senior Vice President, President Health Group	2002	General Electric Medical Systems

Sources: Eastman Kodak Annual Report, 2005; www.kodak.com.

- Olympus: sharing digital camera technology; developing common standards for Web-based storage and printing of photographs (each company had over a thousand patents relating to digital cameras and digital photographic systems).
- AOL: Kodak collaborated with AOL to create AOL's *You've Got Pictures* service for uploading, storing and sharing digital photographs.

- Sanyo Electric Co.: joint development of color, active matrix organic electroluminescent (OLED) displays.
- IBM: a manufacturing alliance to produce CMOS image sensors. The first sensors from the alliance were announced in July 2005.

In activities and markets where Kodak believed that a strong proprietary position was essential to its strategy, and in technologies where it needed to complement its own expertise, it used acquisitions. Although Kodak's profits were under pressure for most of the period, its size and balance-sheet strength meant that it was still one of the financially strongest firms in the industry. The bursting of the stock-market bubble in technology stocks in 2000, allowed Kodak to make a number of key acquisitions at for modest outlays. Its major acquisitions over the period are shown in Table 7.3.

TABLE 7.3 Kodak's major acquisitions, 1994–2006

1994	Qualex, Inc.	Provider of photo-finishing services, became key component of Kodak's online photofinishing service
1997	Wang Laboratories	Acquisition of Wang's software unit
1998	PictureVision, Inc.	Provider of PhotoNet online digital imaging services and retail solutions; this service integrated within Kodak's Picture Network business
	Shantou Era Photo Material, Xiamen Fuda Photographic Materials	Kodak strengthens its position in the photographic film market in China
1999	Imation	Kodak acquires Imation's medical imaging business
2000	Lumisys, Inc.	Leading provider of desktop computed radiography systems and x-ray film digitizers
2001	Bell & Howell	Imaging businesses only acquired
	Ofoto, Inc.	Leading online photography service
	Encad, Inc.	Wide-format commercial inkjet printers
2003	Practiceworks	Digital dental imaging and dental practice management software
	Lucky Film Co., Ltd.	Acquires 20% of China's biggest manufacturer of photographic film
	Laser-Pacific Media Corporation	A provider of post-production services for filmmakers
	Algotec Systems Ltd.	Developer of picture archiving systems
	Applied Science Fiction	Digital PIC rapid film processing technology
2004	NexPress	Acquired Heidelberg's 50% of this joint venture, which supplied high-end, on-demand color printing systems and black-and-white variable-data printing systems
	Scitex Digital Printing	A leader in high-speed variable data inkjet printing (renamed Kodak Versamark, Inc.)
	Chinon Industries	Kodak purchases outstanding shares
	National Semiconductor	Kodak acquires National's imaging sensor business
2005	Kodak Polychrome Graphics LLC	Kodak acquires Sun Chemical's 50% stake in the joint venture, which is a leader in graphic communication
	Creo Inc.	Leading supplier of prepress and workflow systems used by commercial printers around the world

Source: Eastman Kodak, 10-K Reports.

Kodak and the Digital Imaging Market in 2006

The digital imaging market—especially the consumer segment—displayed the same features as most other markets that were founded upon digital technologies. Like personal computers, mobile phones, pocket calculators, and DVD players, digital imaging hardware was subject to intense competition, low entry barriers, falling real prices and commoditization. As a result, profit margins on most products were either slim or non-existent.

Digital cameras featured particularly brutal competition. While fierce price competition was restricted to the lower end of the market where Sony, Panasonic, Samsung and other consumer electronics companies were the main players, by 2006 these companies were increasingly moving into the high-price market for digital, single-lens reflex cameras traditionally dominated by Canon and Nikon. Some observers believed that during 2006, the market for digital cameras would begin to decline as more and more consumers relied on their mobile phones for taking digital images.

The situation was similar in printers where about 20 companies—including HP, Canon, Epson, Lexmark, Xerox, Samsung, Brother, Dell, Konica, Fuji, Panasonic, Toshiba, and Apple—supplied inkjet printers. The difference was that, in printers, high margins could be earned on ink cartridges.

For Kodak too, its highest margins were earned on consumables—notably photographic paper. However, in the home market Kodak faced strong competition notably from Xerox, HP, 3M, and Oji, as well as from many minor brands. In supplying photofinishers and commercial printers, Kodak was able to benefit from its leadership in supplying printing hardware. To fight commoditization in printing paper, Kodak pioneered a number of technical advances particularly in inkjet printing paper. Most significant was its Colorlast technology, designed to preserve the fidelity and vibrancy of photographic prints for a hundred years or more. However, across all markets, Kodak was suffering from the growing trend for people to view photographic images and read magazines by electronic display rather than in printed form.

In most other industries based upon digital technology, the primary source of profit was in software rather than hardware. Thus, in PCs, Microsoft earned huge profits from its dominance of operating systems (Windows) and office applications (Microsoft Office). Similarly with Google in internet search. In video games, it was the games developers and publishers rather than the console manufactures who made most money. Software also appeared to be the major source of profit in digital imaging. Thus, in software for creating, manipulating, displaying, and transmitting digital images, Adobe Systems was the major player. During 2005 Adobe earned a return on equity in excess of 30%. In software for editing digital images, programs for basic image manipulation included Microsoft's Picture It, while more comprehensive picture editing and formatting software included Adobe's Photoshop—the leader in this market.

Kodak's software development was primarily focused on the proprietary imaging software included in the systems it supplied to photofinishing lab, retail stores, commercial printers and medical imaging facilities. However, with the launch of its PhotoCD system in 1990 Kodak was heavily involved in developing software for the home market. Kodak's main strengths were in its color management software and its DLS System Management and Enhanced Services Software for managing retail processing and printing operations. In 2003, despite Adobe Systems' domination of the market for image display, formatting, and editing with its Photoshop and Acrobat products, Kodak released its EasyShare software. Adobe quickly followed with Photoshop Album, a $49 derivative of its Photoshop software. Google's introduction of its Picasa free photo-editing software in 2004 was putting additional pressure on prices.

Intense price competition was also a feature of online photosharing and photo-printing services. While Kodak's Easyshare Gallery was the market leader, it competed with a host of other online competitors including: Shutterfly, Snapfish, Walmart Photo Center, FujiFilmNet, Yahoo Photos, and searsphotos.com. As photography increasingly shifted to mobile phones, so Kodak sought to achieve leadership on online photosharing through a mobile phone. In 2003, through collaboration with Nokia and Cingular, Kodak introduced Kodak Mobile Service allowing users to store and organize phone-captured pictures. By 2005, pictures could be uploaded and downloaded by mobile phone to and from Kodak's EasyShare Gallery. Images could also be transmitted by mobile phone to Kodak's retail kiosks for printing.

By the beginning of 2006, it was clear that, under the brand umbrella of EasyShare, Kodak had created a complete digital imaging system for consumers. Kodak was finally a full-system supplier. It was positioned at every stage in the digital imaging chain and, with its EasyShare brand, it was communicating its system capabilities to consumers. Kodak's ability to serve the needs of several types of customer was particularly important. Through its retail network it provided digital scanning, enhancement and storage facilities to consumers who took pictures with conventional film. For consumers with digital cameras it offered editing and printing services both through retail kiosks and online and, with its EasyShare printers, it allowed customers the independence to pursue digital photography without using any of Kodak's retail services.

Kodak's Resources and Capabilities

Digital imaging was a classic "disruptive technology".[14] For traditional photographic companies it was "competence destroying"[15]—the new technological regime meant that many of their resources and capabilities became close to useless. For the camera companies—Nikon, Canon, Olympus and Pentax, for example—digital imaging was not such a threat: digital backs could be added to standard camera architectures; these companies' optical capabilities remained important. In addition, the camera companies had already adopted a good deal of microelectronic technology. For the film companies—Kodak, Fuji Film, Agfa, and Ilford—whose technical capabilities were based on chemical technologies, the threat of digital imaging was much greater. This is why the transition period between traditional and digital imaging was so important for Kodak. So long as the replacement of photographic film was gradual, Kodak could exploit its brand strength and vast distribution system to offer hybrid solutions, while using the time available and its cash flow from film to invest in the resources and capabilities it required for digital imaging. The problem was that many of the companies that Kodak was now competing with in the digital imaging arena had the advantage of well-developed microelectronic expertise: Casio, Ricoh and Hewlett-Packard had entered digital imaging from office electronics and printing,

FIGURE 7.2 Eastman Kodak's "Fundamental Challenges"

Scope of transformation	
FROM	*TO*
Analog technology	Digital technology
Long design cycle	Rapid prototyping
Industrial manufacturing processes	Flexible manufacturing processes
Value based on physical products	Value based on solutions (product + consumables + services)
Mass-produced, large inventories	Just-in-time, just-in-place, customized
High margins, heavy infrastructure	Lower margins, leaner organization

Source: A. Perez, "Creating the New Kodak," J. P. Morgan Technology Conference, May 2005.

while Sony came out of consumer electronics. All these companies possessed different sets of resources and capabilities, with strengths and weaknesses in different areas.

Perez recognized that the challenge of renewing Kodak's resource and capability base was not limited to technology. At J.P. Morgan's Technology Conference in May 2005, Perez emphasized that change also embraced production processes, design, and different sources of value (see Figure 7.2).

In reviewing Kodak's competitive position and its future potential, Perez placed particular attention on the following resources and capabilities:

- brand and distribution;
- technology;
- new product development;
- finances.

Brand and Distribution

Foremost among Kodak's resource strengths were its brand equity and distribution presence. After almost a century of global leadership in the photographic industry, Kodak possessed brand recognition and a worldwide distribution reach that was unrivaled in that industry. Kodak could bring new products to consumers' attention and support these products with one of the world's best known and most widely respected brand names, giving the company a huge advantage in a market where technological change created uncertainty for consumers. Kodak's brand reputation was supported by its massive, worldwide distribution presence primarily through retail photography stores, film processors, and professional photographers. This retail presence was critical to Kodak's entire digital strategy, which was built around providing consumers with a pathway to digital imaging using services offered through retail stores and photo-finishers.

To what extent would Kodak's distribution and brand strengths continue to be a source of competitive advantage in digital imaging? Kodak's retail network was a depreciating asset as consumers' own home-based computer, email, and print capabilities increased. The brand, according to Chief Marketing Officer Carl Gustin, would continue to be Kodak's most valuable asset: "I have always said our brand is almost bulletproof when it comes to images, to memories, to trust, reliability, family values, and more." In studies of digital imaging products, Kodak's brand had ranked either No. 1 or No. 2 in recent years. However, the huge changes in the market might necessitate changes in Kodak's brand strategy. As Gustin remarked:

> Does the Kodak name go everywhere, or is a variance of the Kodak name required? Does the name need some tagline? Multiple taglines? Does it mean the same in the commercial and services sector as it does in the consumer sector? That's all being investigated."[16]

These questions were resolved with the decision to launch the *EasyShare* brand in 2001. Easyshare become Kodak's umbrella sub-brand for its digital consumer products—including hardware (cameras and printers), software (Kodak EasyShare software allows the transfer, enhancement and cataloging of digital images), and services (such as Kodak's online Easyshare Gallery).

In relation to professional, commercial, medical, and government markets, Perez believed that Kodak's brand and reputation as a reliable, financially secure partner capable of providing comprehensive products and support services was a particular strength.

Technology

In technology, Kodak came to digital imaging with some well established strengths. Its huge R&D investments in digital imaging since the early 1980s had created proprietary technologies across a broad front. Despite R&D cutbacks during the late 1990s, Kodak maintained one of the world's biggest research efforts in imaging. At its research labs in the U.S., U.K., France, Japan, China and Australia, Kodak employed more than 5000 engineers and scientists, including more than 600 PhDs. Kodak received 748 U.S. patents in 2003, 724 in 2004 and 575 in 2005. Table 7.4 identifies some of Kodak's principal areas of technological strength.

TABLE 7.4 Kodak's technical capabilities

Area of technology	Kodak capabilities
Color science	Kodak is a leader in the production, control, measurement, specification and visual perception of color, essential to predicting the performance of image-capture devices and imaging systems. Kodak has pioneered colorimetry, measuring and quantifying visual response to a stimulus of light.
Image processing	Includes technologies to control image sharpness, noise and color reproduction. It is used to maximize the information content of images and to compress data for economical storage and rapid transmission. Kodak is a leader in image processing algorithms for automatic color balancing, object and text recognition and image enhancement and manipulation. These are especially important in digital photo-finishing for image enhancement, including adjustments for scene reflectance, lighting conditions, sharpness and a host of other conditions.

TABLE 7.4 *(Continued)*

Area of technology	Kodak capabilities
Imaging systems analysis	Provides techniques to measure the characteristics of imaging systems and components. Predictive system modeling is especially important in Kodak's new product development, where it can predict the impact of individual components on the performance of the entire system.
Sensors	Kodak is a world leader in image sensor technology, with 30 years' experience in the design and manufacture of electronic image sensors—both CCD and CMOS—for use in cameras, camera phones, machine vision products and satellite and medical imaging. The first cameras embodying Kodak/IBM's new generation CMOS sensors were launched in 2007.
Ink technology	Kodak leads in technical understanding of dyes and pigments. It has pioneered *micro-milling technology* (that it originally invented for drug delivery systems). It has advanced knowledge of *humectants* (which keep printhead nozzles from clogging) and *surface tension and viscosity modifiers* (which control ink flows).
Inkjet technology	Innovations in the electronic and thermal control of inkjet heads together with innovation in inks has allowed Kodak to make substantial technological advances in inkjet printing. In commercial printing, Kodak's continuous inkjet technology has permitted the flexibility of inkjet printing to be matched with substantial improvements in resolution and color fidelity. Kodak's EasyShare home printers offered lab-quality photo prints and image editing, without the need for a computer.
Microfluidics	Microfluidics, the study of miniature devices that handle very small quantities of liquids, is relevant to film coating, fluid mixing, chemical sensing and liquid inkjet printing.
Print media	Kodak has unrivaled know-how in applying polymer science and chemical engineering to the materials that receive ink: paper, glass, fabric. Key strengths include specially constructed inkjet media in which layers of organic and/or inorganic polymers are coated onto paper or clear film and multi-layer coated structures of hydrogels, inorganic oxides, and similar substances.
Electronic display technology	Through its joint venture with Sanyo, Kodak pioneered organic light-emitting diode (OLED) technology for self-luminous flat panel displays. Kodak's OLED display panels were used mainly in cameras and other small-screen devices, but Kodak was also working on larger size displays that could be used for digital picture frames.
Software	Under Perez, Kodak greatly increased its investment in software. Its EasyShare software focused on ease of image manipulation, printing, and storage—even without a computer. Kodak's commercial software leads in workflow solutions (Kodak EMS Business Software), scanning software (Perfect Page) and printing software (Kodak Professional Digital Print Production Software). Kodak has particular strengths in control software and printing algorithms that can overcome many of the technical limitations of inkjet printing and optimize color and tone reproduction (e.g. the Kodak One Touch Printing System).

Source: www.kodak.com.

FIGURE 7.3 Kodak's technological position within the digital imaging chain

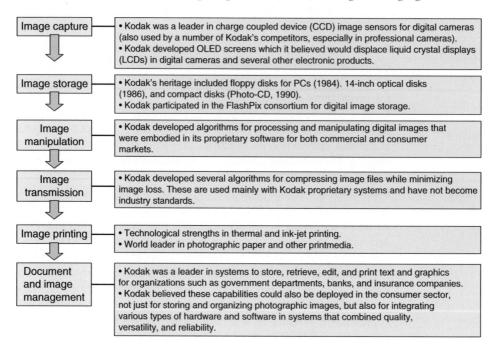

Moreover, its century of innovation and development of photographic images gave Kodak insight and intuition that transcended specific imaging technologies. Central to Kodak's imaging capability was its color-management capability. As *Business Week* observed more than a decade earlier when Fisher joined Kodak:

> The basic know-how of combining electronic image capture and color management has been Kodak's for years. Kodak is a world-beater in electronic sensors, devices that see and capture an image, and has a raft of patents in color thermal printing. It also has the best understanding of color management software, which matches the colors you see on the screen with what's on the printed page.[17]

Kodak used the term "color science" to refer to the production, control, measurement, specification, and visual perception of color; this included "colorimetry," the measurement of color characteristics.

Kodak's technological capabilities meant that it was positioned at each of the principal stages in the digital imaging value chain even though, at most of these stages, it lacked market leadership (see Figure 7.3).

At the image-output level, Kodak believed that consumers would continue to demand printed photographs. In print media, particularly specialty coated papers, Kodak was world leader. During 2000–3, Kodak introduced a number of new inkjet papers embodying new technologies.

New Product Development

Despite Kodak's strengths in basic and applied research and its long history of successful new product launches, Carp was acutely aware of the criticisms that had been leveled at Kodak for its weaknesses in bringing new products to market: Kodak was too slow and its marketers had little understanding of the digital world.

Kodak's product-development process still reflected the company's origins in chemistry. Product development traditionally began with basic research where innovations were exploited through a long and meticulous product-development process before being rolled out onto the world market. One of George Fisher's major initiatives as Kodak chairman and CEO had been to streamline and speed Kodak's cumbersome product development process. In place of Kodak's sequential "phases-and-gates" development process, Fisher transferred approaches that had worked well at Motorola—greater decentralization of new product development and the use of cross-functional development teams to accelerate cycle times. Speed also required collaboration to access the technologies and capabilities of outside companies. Kodak had no problem in establishing collaborative agreements with other companies—its size, brand name and technological strength were sufficient to make it a highly attractive partner for small, technology-intensive firms in digital imaging. The real challenge was for Kodak to overcome a long history of insularity and hierarchical control in order to make its new-found alliances fruitful. Kodak's track record of alliances and joint ventures was mixed. Its Phogenix joint venture with HP to develop digital minilabs for film and image processes was dissolved in May 2003 after three years.[18]

Finances

One of Kodak's key advantages in withstanding the uncertainties and rapid technological changes of the market for digital imaging was its size and financial security. In contrast to the many start-up companies that sought to establish themselves in the sector, Kodak was independent of venture capitalists and the vagaries of the IPO market. In contrast with even some of its large and well established rivals, Kodak had the security of cash flows from its traditional photographic business.

By the beginning of 2004, Eastman Kodak remained a financially strong company but it was no longer the financial powerhouse of yesteryear. Since the late 1990s, debt had risen considerably and retiree healthcare benefits represented a substantial long-term liability. Meanwhile, profitability declined substantially between 2000 and 2003 because of the deterioration of the core photography business and because of the restructuring charges that were becoming a regular feature of Kodak's income statement. As a result, some analysts doubted Kodak's ability to finance its "digital growth strategy," which involved investing some $3 billion in capital expenditures and acquisitions during 2004–6. Tables 7.5 and 7.6 summarize Kodak's recent financial results.

Looking Forward

As he returned to Kodak's headquarters in Rochester, New York, from the Consumer Electronics show in Las Vegas, Antonio Perez reflected on his three years at Kodak—first as COO and then as CEO. For a company that had dominated its traditional market for so long, Kodak's ability to survive the annihilation of its

TABLE 7.5 Eastman Kodak: selected financial data, 2000–5 ($ million)

	2000	2001	2002	2003	2004	2005
From income statement						
Sales	13994	13234	12835	13317	13517	14268
Cost of goods sold	8019	8670	8225	9033	9582	10617
Selling, general, and admin.	2977	2627	2530	2648	2491	2668
R&D costs	784	779	762	781	836	892
Operating earnings	2214	345	793	238	−87	−599
Interest expense	178	219	173	148	168	211
Other income (charges)	96	−18	101	51	161	44
Restructuring and other costs	−44	659	98	484	695	690
Provision for income taxes	725	32	153	−66	−175	689
Net earnings	1407	76	770	265	556	−1362
From balance sheet						
Total current assets	5491	4683	4534	5455	5648	5781
Including:						
Cash and cash equivalents	246	448	569	1250	1255	1665
Receivables	2653	2337	2234	2389	2544	2760
Inventories	1718	1137	1062	1075	1158	1140
Property, plant, and equipment	5919	5659	5420	5094	4512	3778
Other noncurrent assets	1767	2072	3540	4269	3131	3221
Total assets	14212	13362	13494	14818	14737	14921
Total current liabilities	3,275	5,354	5,502	5,307	4,990	5,489
Including:						
Payables	3,403	3,276	3,351	3,707	3,896	4,187
Short-term borrowings	2,058	1,378	1,442	946	469	819
Other liabilities:						
Long-term borrowings	1,166	1,666	1,164	2,302	1,852	2,764
Post-employment liabilities	2,610	2,728	3,412	3,344	3,338	3,476
Other long-term liabilities	671	720	639	601	737	1,225
Total liabilities	10,784	10,468	10,717	11,554	10,917	12,954
Shareholders' equity	3,428	2,894	2,777	3,264	3,820	1,967
Total liabilities (and equity)	14,212	13,362	13,494	14,818	14,737	14,921
From cash flow statement						
Cash flows from operating activities:						
Earnings from continuing operations	1,407	76	770	265	556	−1362
Adjustments for noncash items	−425	1989	1448	1361	590	2542
Net cash provided by operating activities	982	2065	2204	1645	1168	1208
Cash flows from investing activities:						
Additions to properties	−945	−743	−577	−506	−460	−472
Proceeds from sale of businesses/assets	277	0	27	26	24	130
Acquisitions, net of cash acquired	−130	−306	−72	−679	−369	−984
Net cash used in investing activities	−783	−1074	−758	−1267	−120	−1304
Net cash flows from financing activities	−314	−804	−1331	270	−1066	533
Number of employees (thousands)	78	75	70	64	55	51

Source: Eastman Kodak Annual Reports.

TABLE 7.6 Eastman Kodak: results by business segments, 2000–2005 ($ millions)

	2000	2001	2002	2003	2004	2005
Net sales from continuing operations:						
Digital & Film Imaging Systems	10231	9403	9002	9415	9366	8460
Health Group	2220	2262	2274	2431	2686	2655
Graphic Communications Group	1417	1454	1456	967	1343	2990
All other	126	110	103	96	122	163
Consolidated total	13994	13229	12835	12909	13517	14268
Earnings (losses) from continuing operations before interest and taxes						
Digital & Film Imaging Systems	1430	787	771	427	598	362
Health Group	518	323	431	497	452	354
Graphic Communications Group	233	172	192	82	−39	1
All other	−11	−60	−28	−93	−191	−177
Total of segments	2170	1222	1366	913	820	540
Net earnings (losses) from continuing operations:						
Digital & Film Imaging Systems	1034	535	550	370	520	212
Health Group	356	221	313	415	366	196
Graphic Communications Group	90	84	83	35	−8	−9
All other	−2	−38	−23	−95	−163	−98
Total of segments	1478	802	923	725	715	301
Segment total assets:						
Digital & Film Imaging Systems	7100	9225	8798	9129	8458	7070
Health Group	1491	2038	2011	2598	2647	2404
Graphic Communications Group	1045	1438	1405	1011	1638	3543
All other	−92	−16	66	12	98	139
Total of segments	9544	12685	12280	12750	12841	13156

Note: Kodak made several changes in its segment reporting over the period. In 2003, *Photography* became *Digital and Film Imaging Systems*, and *Commercial Imaging* became the *Graphic Communication Group*.

technology was remarkable. For a company to emerge as a leader in a technology that was so radically different from its predecessor was unique. Most of Kodak's competitors in its old photographic business—Agfa, Polaroid, Konica—failed to make the leap; only Fuji Film trumps Kodak in its ability to cross the digital divide—in the period prior to 2005 Fuji grew substantially and was consistently profitable.[19]

From being a near monopolist in silver-halide photographic film, Kodak had emerged as a global leader in digital cameras, online photo storage and processing, light sensors and digital graphic displays. Under his leadership, there was no longer an Old Kodak and New Kodak: the Old Kodak had been buried.

Yet Perez realized that his job was only just beginning. Kodak had successfully crossed over to the other side. It had adopted digital technologies, developed those technologies and introduced a number of highly successful products. But there was no financial return. Kodak continued to bleed cash.

Part of the problem was the restructuring costs that Kodak incurred as it closed plants and shed employees. But this was only part of the story. In the consumer market, Kodak lost money on most hardware products and gave away its software. The commercial and healthcare sectors offered better prospects for margins, but in both of these sectors Kodak was still integrating its multiple acquisitions and building its market presence. Consumables and photofinishing services offered attractive margins, but these too were threatened by the growing tendency for consumers to view their pictures on screens rather than on printed copies.

Kodak's digital strategy had shown considerable awareness of the potential for competitive advantage, most notably in providing customers with integrated solutions, in emphasizing ease of use, and in combining alliances and acquisitions in order to build a presence throughout the digital value chain. The critical issue now was linking these sources of competitive advantage to the generation of profit.

Consumer digital products were unlikely to offer attractive margins—competition was simply too strong. Components offered a better bet: Kodak had strong portfolios of patents protecting its sensor and OLED technologies. However, Perez believed that some of the best opportunities would come from meeting the emerging needs of the consumers of digital images.

Notes

1 "Banishing the Negative: How Kodak is Developing its Blueprint for a Digital Transformation," *Financial Times,* January 26, 2006.
2 "Banishing the Negative: How Kodak is Developing its Blueprint for a Digital Transformation," *Financial Times,* January 26, 2006.
3 "Kodak Zooms in on Software as Industry Focus Shifts to Computers," *Financial Times,* January 9, 2006.
4 "Bill Miller's Kodak Moment," *Fortune,* November 14, 2005.
5 Address to the Academy of Management, Boston, August 1997.
6 "Kodak's New Focus," *Business Week,* January 30, 1995, pp. 62–8.
7 Eastman Kodak Company, "Kodak Leaders Outline Road Ahead to get Kodak 'Back on Track'," press release, November 11, 1997.
8 Eastman Kodak Company, "The Big Picture: Kodak and Digital Photography," www.Kodak.com/US/en/corp/presscenter/presentations/020520mediaforum3.shtml.
9 See www.Kodak.com/US/en/corp/presscenter/presentations/020520mediaforum3.shtml, accessed October 29, 2009.
10 Interview with Antonio Perez, President and COO, Kodak, *PMA Magazine,* February 2004.
11 NexPress was initially a joint venture with Heidelberg; Kodak bought out Heidelberg's share in 2004.
12 "Why Kodak Still Isn't Fixed," *Fortune,* May 11, 1998.
13 Eastman Kodak Company, "Kodak and HP Joint Venture to be Named Phogenix Imaging," press release, August 1, 2000.
14 J. L. Bower and C. M. Christensen, "Disruptive Technologies: Catching the Wave," *Harvard Business Review,* January–February, 1995.
15 M. Tushman, and P. Anderson, "Technological Discontinuities and Organizational Environments," *Administrative Science Quarterly,* 31 (1986): 439–65.
16 Interview with Carl Gustin, Chief Marketing Officer, Kodak, *PMA Magazine* (February 2004).
17 "Kodak's New Focus," *Business Week,* January 30, 1995, pp. 62–8.
18 Jeff Macher and Barak Richman in "Organizational Responses to Discontinuous Innovation: A Case Study Approach," *International Journal of Innovation Management* 8 (2004): 87–114 describe Kodak's joint project with Intel to develop the Picture CD: "Meetings scheduled to discuss the new product suffered from logistical constraints and unsolicited and unnecessary input from neighboring divisions . . . [T]he project's slow start highlighted that the firm's current routines and practices were not capable of developing a new technology for an uncertain, albeit rapidly emerging, market."
19 Fuji Film's operating margin was 2.8% in the year ended March 31, 2006; down from 10.8% four years earlier.

Case 8 Procter & Gamble's Organization 2005 Project*

During the first half of 2000, Procter & Gamble, the world's largest supplier of personal and household products, faced a slumping stock price and a crisis of leadership.

On March 7, 2000, Procter & Gamble announced it would not meet its projected first quarter earnings, and the stock price abruptly fell from $86 to $60 per share. In total, between January, 2000—when the stock peaked at $116—and March 7th, 2000, P&G stock fell 52 per cent. The biggest crisis at

* This case was prepared by Robert M. Grant. It draws upon information contained in three earlier case studies: *P&G Japan: The SK-II Globalization Project* (Harvard Business School Case No. 9-303-003, 2003); *Procter & Gamble: Organization 2005* (Harvard Business School Case No. 9-707-519, 2007); *Procter & Gamble: Organization 2005 and Beyond* (ICFAI Knowledge Center, Case No. 303-102-1 ECCH, 2003).

P&G was not the loss of $85 billion in market capitalization, however: it was the crisis in confidence—particularly leadership confidence—that permeated the organization. In too many of our businesses, best-in-class competitors were on the attack. P&G business units around the world were blaming headquarters for their problems, while headquarters was blaming the business units.

On the day I was announced as the new CEO, P&G's stock fell another four dollars, and after 15 days on the job, it fell another $3.85—which was not much of a confidence builder.[1]

On June 8, 2000, Procter & Gamble's board of directors fired its CEO, Dirk Jager, and appointed A. G. Lafley as his replacement. Lafley had held a series of senior appointments at P&G, most recently as head of Global Beauty Care.

Lafley immediately embarked upon a series of cost-cutting measures and management changes while beginning work on the more fundamental strategic issues that had been undermining P&G's performance. However, there was one key decision that could not wait. In July 1998, P&G had announced Organization 2005—a plan for a complete redesign of P&G's organization that would involve a shift from a structure based primarily upon geographical regions to one based upon global product divisions. The new structure was implemented in July 1999 but, by the time Lafley took over as CEO, P&G was still in the midst of considerable organizational upheaval.

Given the apparent failure of Organization 2005 to deliver either sales growth or improved margins for P&G and its association with Lafley's predecessor, many P&G senior managers favoured its abandonment and a reversion to P&G's previous regional structure. However, undoing the structure that had been in place for less than a year risked creating even greater upheaval at P&G. Moreover, Lafley acknowledged that Organization 2005 had been a response to widely perceived inadequacies in P&G's ability to coordinate across countries and regions.

The Evolution of P&G's Organizational Structure

P&G began making soap and candles in Cincinnati in 1837. During the twentieth century P&G's diversification across a broad range of branded, packaged consumer goods was a result of three key management innovations. The first was its creation of a central research laboratory (1890), which became the source of a flow of new product introductions. Second was its establishment of a market research department (1924). The third was its invention of brand management—an organizational system where individual products were assigned to entrepreneurial brand managers.

In the U.S., P&G's structure evolved, first, into a divisionalized corporation where each product division had its own manufacturing, marketing and sales functions, then into a matrix organization, where the product divisions formed the primary structure but functional heads within each division had "dotted-line" relationships with corporate-level functional heads. Thus, in the laundry division, the director for manufacturing would report first to the vice president of the laundry division and secondarily to the vice-president of manufacturing at the corporate level.

Overseas expansion had been based around the creation of stand-alone national subsidiaries. The basic principle had been established by the first VP of overseas operations, Walter Lingle: "We must tailor our products to meet consumer demands in each nation. But we must create local country subsidiaries whose structures, policies and practices that are as exact a replica of the U.S. Procter & Gamble organization as it is possible to create." During the 1960s and 1970s, P&G's geographical scope and international sales expanded rapidly. However, duplication of functions at the national level was creating considerable inefficiency. Attempts to consolidate functions around regional headquarters included the creation of a European Technical Center at P&G's European headquarters in Brussels in 1963. It conducted research and process engineering and developed products and processes that country managers could choose to adapt to and launch in their own countries.

Although regional headquarters gained increased authority over the national subsidiaries, there was still limited cross-border integration of product policies, new product introductions, or functional activities. Moreover, while the existing structure allowed P&G to adapt its products and marketing to the needs of existing markets, it did not provide much impetus for expanding into new markets. During the 1980s, Asia—Japan in particular—was offering exciting opportunities for P&G and by the end of the 1980s, the breakup of the Soviet Union and opening of Eastern Europe would lead to a massive expansion in P&G's opportunities for entering unsaturated markets.

The Global Matrix

In 1989, P&G introduced a major change in its organization structure. It created a global product structure where each product category was headed by a president who reported directly to the CEO. The country general managers and their regional bosses retained profit-and-loss responsibilities, HR reporting and career management. However, the new global category executive presidents were given direct control over R&D. For each category a VP of R&D was appointed to manage R&D within the product category worldwide. These VPs of R&D reported directly to their global category presidents. The result was a move towards product-category platform technologies that could be applied globally.

The new structure also strengthened P&G's functional organization. Manufacturing, purchasing, engineering and distribution were integrated into a single supply function headed by a senior vice president. This function was intended to facilitate the end-to-end integration of P&G's global product-supply function. Supply-chain integration was particularly important for integrating the manufacturing and distribution facilities of the acquisitions that P&G was making at this time.

This was followed in 1994 by the reorganization of P&G's sales function into a customer business development (CBD) function. A major goal of this strengthened global sales function was to develop closer relationships with P&G's biggest customers. One of the CBD's first initiatives was to open an office in Wal-Mart's home town of Bentonville.

Figure 8.1 shows a partial picture of P&G's structure in 1990. To show how the geographical structure linked to the products structure, Figure 8.1 shows the detailed products organization for P&G Japan.

The new structure resulted in some improvements in global coordination and allowed cross-border consolidation of some activities and facilities. However, these improvements did little to stimulate growth at P&G. Table 8.1 shows key financial

FIGURE 8.1 Procter & Gamble's organizational structure in 1990

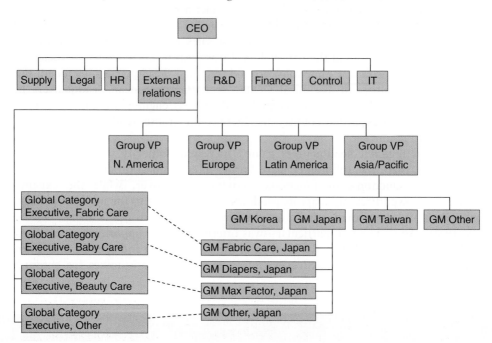

TABLE 8.1 Procter & Gamble: financial data for 1992–2000 (year ended June 30; in $000s except where indicated)

	1992	1993	1994	1995	1996	1997	1998	1999	2000
Net sales	29 362	30 433	30 385	33 482	35 284	35 764	37 154	38 125	39 951
Cost of goods	17 324	17 683	17 338	19 561	20 938	20 510	20 896	21 027	21 018
Gross profit	12 038	12 750	13 047	13 921	14 346	15 254	16 258	17 098	18 933
Total SG&A	9171	9589	9377	9677	9531	9766	10 203	10 845	12 165
Of which: advertising	*2693*	*2973*	*2996*	*3284*	*3254*	*3466*	*3704*	*3639*	*3793*
R&D expense	*861*	*956*	*964*	*1148*	*1399*	*1469*	*1546*	*1726*	*1899*
Operating income	2867	3161	3670	4244	4815	5488	6055	6253	6768
Net income	1872	269	2211	2645	3046	3415	3780	3763	3542
Cash from operation	3025	3338	3649	3568	4158	5882	4885	5544	4675
Cash from investing	(2860)	(1630)	(2008)	(2363)	(2466)	(2068)	(5210)	(2175)	(5345)
Return on equity (%)	23.2	2.9	22.6	25.0	26.0	28.3	30.9	31.2	28.8
Employees ('000)	106	103.5	96.5	99.2	103	106	110	110	110

data for P&G and Table 8.2 shows a breakdown by region. By the time Dirk Jager, P&G's chief operating officer, took over as CEO at the beginning of 1999, the view that P&G was not performing to its full potential had become widespread both within the company and outside. In mid-1999, *The Economist* reported:

Few companies have suffered as much from price competition as Procter & Gamble. Unwilling to lower its prices and unable to distinguish itself as an

TABLE 8.2 Procter & Gamble: Regional financial performance, 1996–1999 (year ended June 30; in $000s).

		North America	Europe, Middle East, Africa	Asia	Latin America	Corporate and other
Net sales	1999	18 977	11 878	3648	2825	797
	1998	18 456	11 835	3453	2640	770
	1997	17 625	11 587	3573	2306	673
	1996	17 230	11 458	3881	2173	542
Net earnings	1999	2710	1214	279	318	(758)
	1998	2474	1092	174	274	(234)
	1997	2253	956	275	256	(325)
	1996	1953	793	273	219	(192)
Identifiable assets	1999	11 390	6286	2793	1577	10 067
	1998	11 063	5998	2499	1519	9887
	1997	10 280	5433	2726	1389	7716
	1996	10 382	5853	2770	1270	7455

innovator, the firm has failed to increase its volumes in the past three quarters and has lost around 10% of its market share in the past five years . . . P&G's problems reflect its risk-averse culture; its willingness to allow individual country managers a veto over R&D, sales and marketing decisions; and its mish-mash of different manufacturing platforms.[2]

Organization 2005

Jager's primary concern was P&G's low growth of sales during the 1990s. The central problem, in his view, was lack of innovation. P&G's expansion had been based upon innovation: synthetic detergents, fluoride toothpaste, disposable diapers. What had happened to P&G's flow of breakthrough innovations? Jager cited the *Always* range of feminine-hygiene products launched in 1982 as P&G's last major new product innovation. Even when new products were introduced, weak coordination among P&G's complex regional and country organizations resulted in slow global rollout. Pampers disposable diapers were a classic example: launched in the U.S. in 1961, Pampers were introduced into Germany in 1973, France in 1978 and the U.K. in 1981. As a result, in international markets, competitors were often able to launch imitative products before P&G.

Jager's response was an ambitious, six-year program of organizational restructuring that he had been working on while COO. Announcing Organization 2005 in 1999, Jager said:

Success is defined first and foremost in terms of growth. Unless a company grows at an acceptable rate—year in, year out—it can't sustain its organization. Success also means growing profitably. Otherwise, it can't produce the resources and capability to invest, to take risks, seizing new opportunities. The program we lay out here today is designed to deliver that growth, at a consistently higher level. Just come back in a couple of years and take a look. I believe that the best way to accelerate growth is to innovate bigger and move faster consistently and across the entire company.[3]

Organization 2005 promised to be one of the biggest upheavals in P&G's history. It involved new processes to boost innovation, plant closures, extensive job losses, and changes in incentives and cultural norms designed to make P&G less risk averse and more responsive. The program had a budget of $1.9 billion.

In his two decades at P&G, Jager had come to regard the organization as bureaucratic, conformist, risk-averse and slow. The goals of greater innovation and responsiveness would require a cultural revolution. By pressuring the organization to increase the rate of new product introductions and speed of rollouts, he hoped to shake up the organization and drive out inertia. Key to a less risk-averse culture was a stronger emphasis on performance. This would be achieved by increasing the importance of performance pay. For senior management, the performance-related variation in annual compensation would change from 20% to 80%. Stock options were extended from the top management team to include middle managers. P&G's complex and tedious budget-setting process was organized into a single integrated business-planning process, built around the agreement of stretch performance targets.

The New Structure

At the heart of Organization 2005 was a fundamental reorientation of P&G's organizational structure. Primary profit responsibility shifted from P&G's four regional organizations to seven global business units (GBUs). The GBUs were given worldwide responsibility for product development, manufacturing and marketing of the products within their categories. The regional organizations were transformed into seven market development organizations whose responsibility was the local implementation of the GBUs' global strategies. Functional services, including accounting, human resources, payroll and IT, were organized into a new global business service unit (GBS). Figure 8.2 shows the new structure.

While the primary strategic mandate of the GBU presidents was developing and rolling out new products, the fact that the GBUs were now responsible for profit and loss meant that they were ultimately responsible for the performance of the whole range of functions within their business. A key objective for the GBU presidents was to increase efficiency through greater cross-border integration. This included standardizing manufacturing processes, simplifying brand portfolios and coordinating marketing activities. For example, the GBU for Baby Care intended to reduce P&G's 12 different diaper-manufacturing processes to one standard production model. By placing emphasis on brands with global potential, P&G identified 300 brands to be closed or sold.

In addition to shifting P&G's primary organizational structure from geographical regions to business divisions, the restructuring also attempted to reduce bureaucracy and enhance accountability by reducing the number of hierarchical levels between the CEO and front line managers. This involved increasing the decision-making authority

FIGURE 8.2 Procter & Gamble's organizational structure in 1999

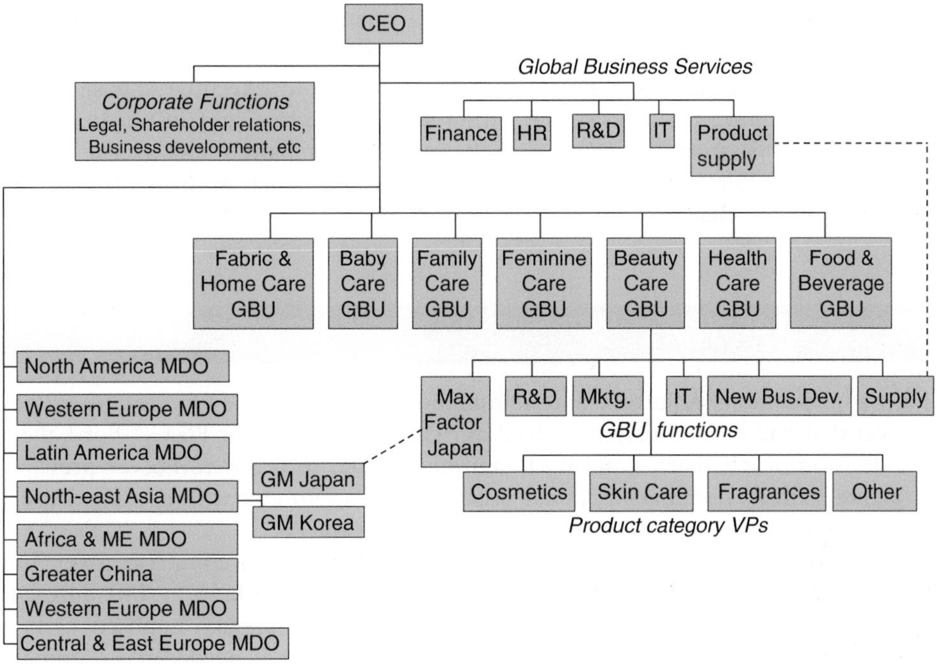

of middle managers. By stripping out much of the hierarchical approval process, it was intended that decision making would become faster and the lag between decisions and their implementation would be reduced.

September 1999 to June 2000

Jager fulfilled his promise to bring far-reaching change to P&G. Where he failed was in delivering the performance improvements that he had targeted. His first year as CEO had gone well—the stock market responded well to his plans for shaking up P&G and even the two quarter-year periods that followed the introduction of Organization 2005—July–December 1999—showed satisfactory sales and profit growth despite the upheaval caused by reorganization. At the end of January 2000, P&G's stock price hit an all-time high. On March 7, 2000, P&G revised its quarterly earnings guidance for the first quarter of 2000: instead of earnings growth of 2%, its earnings would fall by 10% due to higher costs. In fact, earnings for the quarter declined by 18%. The stock market reaction was brutal. On March 7, P&G's stock price fell by 30%; by the end of March it was more than 50% off its peak. On June 8, P&G revised downwards its earnings and sales forecasts for the second quarter of 2000. For a company that had prided itself on the consistency of its performance and achieving its financial targets, this was too much. Jager's credibility in the financial community had been destroyed.

Was Jager's ousting by the board simply a matter of failing in his relations with Wall Street? Two other factors are relevant. First, despite considerable success in increasing P&G's rate of new product introduction, the company's core established brands continued to lose market share. Second, Jager's hard-driving aggressive style generated considerable opposition within P&G's management ranks:

> Jager's resignation also suggests that the 57-year-old executive's push for change may have faced resistance within P&G's culture. The CEO had made clear that his mandate was to shake up the company's risk-averse and bureaucratic culture. And he wasn't afraid to make enemies. Actually, he might have done just that.[4]

Lafley's Decision

Jager's ignominious departure had undoubtedly discredited the Organization 2005 project that had been widely perceived as "Jager's blueprint for P&G." For Lafley, the decision of whether to affirm Organization 2005, to revert to P&G's previous structure with its dominant regional organizations, or to embark upon an entirely new solution would be critical in defining his vision for P&G.

P&G was one of the world's most complex companies. It comprised over 300 brands, thousands of products, and 110 000 employees working in 140 different countries across a broad range of functions. This complexity imposed certain minimal requirements on P&G's organizational structure: it needed to coordinate within each product area, it needed to coordinate within each function and it needed to coordinate within each country. It also needed to coordinate its sales activities in order to meet the needs of multiproduct and multinational customers such as Wal-Mart and Carrefour. While some form of matrix was inevitable, what form should this matrix take? In particular, what should be the responsibilities of each dimension? Until 1999, geographical organization had been paramount. It was responsible for financial control ("profit-and-loss responsibility"), strategic planning and human resource appraisal and control. In 1999 decision-making power had shifted to the business areas. However the case for empowering global product divisions over regional divisions and national subsidiaries was far from clear cut.

The case for global product divisions was based primarily upon the advantages of efficiency and innovation. Global product divisions facilitated cross-border integration and avoiding duplicating functions and facilities by country. Global product divisions allowed pooling research activities around the technologies relevant to different product categories and permitted new products to be rolled out globally in a coordinated way.

Yet, in most of P&G's product markets, national and regional differences between markets remained substantial. Very few of P&G's products were globally standardized (*Pringles* potato chips were among the nearest thing P&G had to a global product). In skin care and cosmetics, household products and most foods, customer preferences were markedly different between countries—and even within countries. Differences in channels of distribution also necessitated nationally differentiated strategies with regard to packaging, product size, marketing, sales, and distribution. In skin care products (see Exhibit 8.1) and in laundry detergents (see Exhibit 8.2) national market differences severely limited the potential for global product strategies.

A key argument in favor of globally standardized products was that the forces of globalization were reducing the national market differences.[5] Yet, as more countries entered the global system of trade and financial transactions—most notably the former communist economies of Russia, China and Eastern Europe—so multinational corporations increasingly sought to develop integrated country-based strategies to develop their businesses within these countries. In the case of P&G, it is notable that the transfer of profit-and-loss responsibility from the regional organizations to the global business units occurred only in the developed countries. For the emerging markets of Eastern Europe, South-east Asia, and Greater China, the regional organizations retained profit-and-loss responsibility. The implication was that, for certain key emerging markets such as China, achieving a coherent country strategy through close cooperation between P&G's different business units took precedence over the need for global coordination within each of these business units.

EXHIBIT 8.1

Organization 2005 in Action: the Case of SK-II

The introduction of Organization 2005 resulted in massive management disruption at P&G. A. G. Lafley, who had only recently been appointed President of the North American regional organization, was appointed President of the new Global Business Unit for Beauty Care. He also retained his North American regional responsibilities as President of the North America Market Development Organization "It was a crazy year," he recalled, "There was so much to build, but beyond the grand design, we were not clear about how it should operate."

Among the large number of initiatives and projects that required his attention, he was attracted towards the case of SK-II, a skin-cleansing product developed by P&G Japan. As part of the management changes ushered in by Organization 2005, Paolo de Cesare, head of P&G's European skin-care business, was promoted to vice president and appointed to head up Max Factor Japan. Under the old structure his primary reporting relationship would have been through P&G Japan to P&G

Asia Pacific. Under the new structure he reported to Lafley's Beauty Care GBU and on a dotted-line basis to the head of the MDO for Northeast Asia. At the Beauty Care GBU, de Cesare became a member of the unit's Global Leadership Team whose primary purpose was to develop global brands. The team was chaired by Lafley and comprised business GMs from three key MDOs together with representatives from R&D, consumer research, product supply, human resources, and finance functions. The Japanese Max Factor organization had become increasingly involved in global product development initiatives in beauty care—partly because of Japanese technical leadership in cosmetics and the extremely high-quality demands of Japanese consumers. The development process sponsored by the global category organizations under P&G's former structure involved using consumer research to identify a worldwide unmet consumer need, assigning a lead research center to developing a technical response to the need, then drawing upon marketing expertise from lead markets to build a new product concept on that technology base. In the case of facial cleansing, consumer researchers found that, despite regional differences, there was widespread dissatisfaction among women with existing products and practices. Chris Bartlett describes the next stages:

> A technology team was assembled at an R&D facility in Cincinnati, drawing on the most qualified technologists from its P&G's labs worldwide. For example, because the average Japanese woman spent 4.5 minutes on her face-cleansing regime compared with 1.7 minutes for the typical American woman, Japanese technologists were sought for their refined expertise in the cleansing processes and their particular understanding of how to develop a product with the rich, creamy lather. Working with a woven substrate technology developed by P&G's paper business, the core technology team found that a 10-micron fiber, when woven into a mesh, was effective in trapping and absorbing dirt and impurities. By impregnating this substrate with a dry-sprayed formula of cleansers and moisturizers activated at different times in the cleansing process, team members felt they could develop a disposable cleansing cloth that would respond to the identified consumer need. After this technology "chassis" had been developed, a technology team in Japan adapted it to allow the cloth to be impregnated with a different cleanser formulation that included the SK-II ingredient, Pitera.[6]

The result of this global initiative was two very different products for two major national markets. The U.S. marketing team developed an Olay version with a one-step routine that combined the benefits of cleansing, conditioning and toning. The Japanese team developed SK-II version positioned as a "foaming massage cloth" that increased skin circulation through a massage while boosting skin clarity due to the microfibers' ability to clean pores and trap dirt. While the Olay Facial Cloth was priced at $7 in the U.S., SK-II Foaming Massage Cloth was priced at the equivalent of $50 in Japan.

A key goal of Organization 2005 was to speed the global rollout of innovative new products. Yet, as Lafley prepared for his meeting with the Beauty Care Global Leadership Team to discuss the introduction of SK-II in other markets (notably Europe and China), it was clear that there were huge differences between national markets that needed to be taken into account. Not only were women's facial cleansing regimes very different between countries but women also gave different emphasis to the different performance characteristics of cleansing products and their willingness to pay for skin-care products varied in a way that could not be explained simply by disposable income. Moreover, countries varied greatly according to the structure of their distribution channels. SK-II was designed for use in Japanese cosmetics retailing, which made extensive use of beauty consultants who could introduce consumers to the products and demonstrate their use. In the U.S., only upmarket department stores and a few specialized cosmetics stores make use of beauty consultants: the U.S. mass market was made up of drugstores and discount stores, which were totally unsuited to the price point or the customer education requirements of SK-II.

Source: This account draws heavily upon *P&G Japan: The SK-II Globalization Project* (Cambridge, MA: Harvard Business School Case No. 9-303-003, 2003).

EXHIBIT 8.2
Global versus Local Brands

For multinational companies supplying branded goods and services to consumers, deciding whether to replace local brands with global brands is an important and difficult strategic issue. Whether the company has internationalized by acquisition or through setting up wholly-owned overseas subsidiaries, most multinationals find themselves with unwieldy brand portfolios that comprise a few global bands together with a number of local brands, many of which make only minor contributions to overall sales. For example, in 1999, just 25% of Unilever's brands contributed over 90% of its sales. As a result, Unilever launched a program to cull its brand portfolio from 1600 to 400 over a five year period.

Global brands offer two types of advantage over local brands:

- differentiation advantages from the superior status of global bands and their appeal to affluent, globally mobile consumers
- cost efficiencies in advertising resulting from scale economies and spillovers across national borders.

Despite these advantages, many companies retain local brands because of the risks of losing market share when migrating customers from a familiar local brand to a global brand.

Different multinationals have adopted different branding strategies. In retail banking, HSBC and Santander have replaced local bank names with the parent's brand; Unicredit and Royal Bank of Scotland have retained most of their local brands. In household and personal products, Procter & Gamble, Unilever, and Colgate-Palmolive have concentrated upon

developing global brands, Henkel has retained national brands where they possessed a strong local identity.

In laundry products, Henkel's different brands exploit national differences in laundry practices. For example, in southern Europe consumers use cooler water than in northern Europe and frequently add bleach to their washes. Packaging practices also vary with northern European consumers preferring compact packages. Henkel markets its leading detergent, Persil, in Germany, France and the Netherlands and uses separate brands for the Spanish and Italian markets. Even with its international brands, Henkel varies product formulation and brand positioning. For example, in France, Persil emphasizes whiteness and stain removal; in the Netherlands Persil is positioned as an environmentally friendly detergent. In Italy, where the preference is for stain-removing ability and blue color, Henkel introduced a brand other than Persil (to allow Persil to fully own the color white in northern Europe). In Spain, the company acquired an existing brand.

Procter & Gamble's moves towards global brands have sometimes encountered local setbacks. In 2000, P&G renamed its popular Fairy laundry detergent in Germany as Dawn. There was no change in the product's formulation, but within a year, P&G's share of the German detergent market had declined drastically.

Source: Draws upon Randall Frost, "Should Global Brands Trash Local Favorites?" BrandHome (March 7, 2005), see http://www.brandchannel.com/features_effect.asp?pf_id=253.

Notes

1 A. G. Lafley, "Getting Procter & Gamble Back on Track," *Rotman Integrative Thinking Seminar*, University of Toronto, April 21, 2003, www.rotman.utoronto.ca/integrativethinking/Lafley.pdf, accessed October 13, 2009.

2 "Procter's Gamble," *The Economist*, June 10, 1999.

3 Quoted in: *Procter & Gamble: Organization 2005 and Beyond* (ICFAI Knowledge Center, Case No. 303-102-1 ECCH, 2003).

4 "What's Driving P&G's Executive Spin Cycle?" *Business Week*, June 8, 2000.

5 This argument was first made by Ted Levitt in "The Globalization of Markets" *Harvard Business Review* (1983): 92–102.

6 C. A. Bartlett, *P&G Japan: The SK-II Globalization Project* (Harvard Business School Case No. 9-303-003, 2003).

Case 9 AirAsia: The World's Lowest Cost Airline*

By 2009, AirAsia had established itself as Asia's most successful low-cost airline. Between January 2002 and March 2009, AirAsia had expanded from two aircraft and 200 000 passenger journeys to 79 aircraft and 11.8 million passengers. Its route network had grown beyond Malaysia to cover 10 South-East Asian countries. In addition to its hub in Kuala Lumpur (KL), Malaysia, it had replicated its system by establishing associated airlines in Thailand and Indonesia.

*Written by Robert M. Grant. The case draws upon a report written by Sara Buchholz, Nadia Fabio, Andrés Ileyassoff, Laurent Mang and Daniele Visentin, *AirAsia—Tales from a Long-haul Low Cost Carrier*, Bocconi University (2009), and from an earlier case by Thomas Lawton and Jonathan Doh, *The Ascendance of AirAsia: Building a Successful Budget Airline in Asia* (Ivey School of Business, Case No. 9B08M054 2008). Used by permission of the authors. © 2010, Robert M. Grant.

FIGURE 9.1 Costs in U.S. cents per available seat kilometer for different low cost airlines

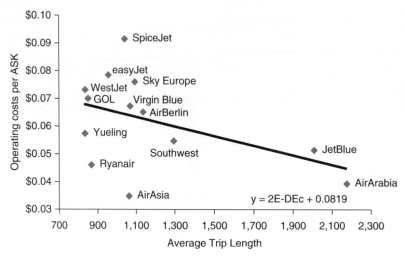

Source: AirAsia Presentation, CLSA Forum, Hong Kong, September 2007

By 2007, UBS research showed that AirAsia was the world's lowest cost airline with costs per available seat kilometer (ASK) significantly below those of Southwest, Jet Blue, Ryanair or Virgin Blue (see Figure 9.1). It was also one of the world's most profitable airlines. In 2008, when very few of the world's airlines made any profit at all, AirAsia earned return on assets of 4%.[1] In 2009 it won the Skytrax Award as "The World's Best Low Cost Airline."

AirAsia had built its business on the low-cost carrier (LCC) model created by Southwest Airlines in the U.S. and replicated throughout the world by a host of imitators. AirAsia had adapted the basic LCC model to the market, geographical and institutional features of South-East Asia while preserving the principal operational features of the strategy. However, in 2007, AirAsia embarked upon a major departure from the LCC model: expansion into long-haul flights by inaugurating routes to Australia and China and then, in 2009, to India and the U.K. The conventional wisdom was that the efficiency of the LCC model was dependent upon short- and medium-distance flights with a single type of aircraft and minimal customer amenities—intercontinental flights required contravening these basic conditions. Very few LCCs had ventured into long-haul; even fewer had made a success of it.

To evaluate AirAsia's potential to expand from being a regional carrier to an international airline would require a careful analysis of the basis of its existing cost advantage and an evaluation of the transferability of these cost advantages to the long-haul market.

The History of AirAsia

The growth of AirAsia is closely associated with the entrepreneurial effort of Tony Fernandes. Son of a Malaysian doctor, Tony was sent to boarding school in Britain with a view to following in his father's footsteps into the medical profession. The son had other ideas and, after an accounting degree at the London School of Economics, went into music publishing, first with Virgin, then Time Warner. He describes his decision to start an airline as follows:

> I was watching the telly in a pub and I saw Stelios [Haji-Ioannou] on air talking about easyJet and running down the national carrier, British Airways. (Sound familiar? Hahaha.) I was intrigued as I didn't know what a low cost carrier was but I always wanted to start an airline that flew long haul with low fares.
>
> So I went to Luton and spent a whole day there. I was amazed how people were flying to Barcelona and Paris for less than 10 pounds. Everything was organized and everyone had a positive attitude. It was then at that point in Luton airport that I decided to start a low cost airline.[2]

He subsequently met with Conor McCarthy, former operations director of Ryanair. The two developed a plan to form a budget airline serving the South-East Asia market.

Seeking the support of the Malaysian government, Prime Minister Mahathir Mohammad encouraged Fernandes to acquire a struggling government-owned airline, AirAsia. With their own capital and support from a group of investors, they acquired AirAsia for 1 Malaysian ringgit (RM)—and assumed debts of RM 40 million (about $11 million). In January 2002, AirAsia was relaunched with just three planes and a business model that McCarthy described as: "a Ryanair operational strategy, a Southwest people strategy, and an easyJet branding strategy."[3]

Fueled by rising prosperity in Malaysia and a large potential market for leisure and business travelers seeking inexpensive domestic transportation, AirAsia's domestic business expanded rapidly. In January 2004, AirAsia began its first international service from KL to Phuket in Thailand; in February 2004 it sought to tap the Singapore market by offering flights from Johor Bahru, just across the border from Singapore, and in 2005 it began flights to Indonesia.

International expansion was fueled by its initial public offering in October 2004, which raised RM 717 million. Airline deregulation across South-East Asia greatly facilitated international expansion. To exploit the market for budget travel in Thailand and Indonesia, AirAsia adopted the novel strategy of establishing joint-venture companies in Thailand (Thai AirAsia) and Indonesia (Indonesia AirAsia) to create new hubs in Bangkok and Jakarta. In both cases, the operations of these companies were contracted out to AirAsia, which received a monthly fee from these associate companies.

From the beginning, Fernandes had set his sights on long-haul travel—guided by the example of his hero, Freddie Laker, the pioneer of low-cost transatlantic air travel. However, this risked his good relations with the Malaysian government because it put AirAsia into direct competition with the national airline, Malaysian Airlines. Hence, Fernandes established a separate company, AirAsia X to develop its long-haul business. AirAsia X is owned 16% by AirAsia (with an option to increase to 30%), 48% by Aero Ventures (co-founded by Tony Fernandes), 16% by Richard Branson's Virgin Group, with the remaining 20% owned by Bahrain-based Manara Consortium and Japan-based Orix Corporation. Operationally, AirAsia and AirAsia X are closely linked.

In 2007, flights began to Australia followed by China. By July 2009, AirAsia X had flights from KL to the Gold Coast, Melbourne and Perth in Australia; Tianjin and Hangzhou in China; and Taipei and London using five Airbus 340s—with three more to be delivered by year end. Planed future routes included Abu Dhabi (October 2009), India (2010) and later Sydney, Seoul and New York. At Abu Dhabi, AirAsia X planned to have a hub that would serve Frankfurt, Cairo, and possibly East Africa too: "You just can't get to East Africa from Asia," observed Fernandes.[4] To support its expansion, AirAsia X ordered 10 Airbus A350s for delivery in 2016.

AirAsia's Strategy and Culture

Strategy

AirAsia described its strategy as follows:

- Safety first: partnering with the world's most renowned maintenance providers and complying with world airline regulations.
- High aircraft utilization: implementing the region's fastest turnaround time at only 25 minutes, assuring lower costs and higher productivity.
- Low fare, no frills: providing guests with the choice of customizing services without compromising on quality and services.
- Streamline operations: making sure that processes are as simple as possible.
- Lean distribution system: offering a wide and innovative range of distribution channels to make booking and traveling easier.
- Point-to-point network: applying the point-to-point network keeps operations simple and costs low.[5]

Prior to its expansion into long haul, AirAsia identified its geographical coverage as encompassing three-and-a-half hours' flying time from its hubs. Fernandes' confidence in his growth strategy rested on the fact that: "This area encompasses a population of about 500 million people. Only a small proportion of this market regularly travels by air. AirAsia believes that certain segments of this market have been under-served historically and that the Group's low fares stimulate travel within these market segments."[6] Its slogan "Now Everyone Can Fly!" encapsulated AirAsia's goal of expanding the market for air travel in Southeast Asia.

To penetrate its target market, AirAsia placed a big emphasis on marketing and brand development. "The brand is positioned to project an image of a safe, reliable low-cost airline that places a high emphasis on customer service while providing an enjoyable flying experience." For an LCC, AirAsia had a comparatively large expenditures on TV, print and internet advertising. AirAsia used its advertising expenditures counter-cyclically: during the SARS outbreak and after the Bali bombings, AirAsia boosted its spending on advertising and marketing. In addition it sought to maximize the amount of press coverage that it received. AirAsia also built its image through co-branding and sponsorship relationships. A sponsorship deal with the AT&T Williams Formula 1 race car team resulted in AirAsia painting one of its A320s in the livery of the a Williams race car. Its sponsorship of Manchester United has resulted in it painting its planes with the portraits of Manchester United players. It also sponsors referees in English Premier League. A cooperative advertising deal with *Time* magazine resulted in an AirAsia plane being painted with the *Time* logo.

Its internet advertising includes banner ads on the Yahoo mobile homepage and a Facebook application for the Citibank-AirAsia credit card with the goal of increasing visibility, encouraging interaction and allowing users to immerse themselves with the AirAsia brand.

This heavy emphasis on brand building has provided AirAsia with a platform for providing services that meet other travelers' needs. AirAsia offers an AA express shuttle bus connecting airports to city centers with seats bookable simultaneously with online booking of plane tickets. Fernandes has also founded Tune Hotels, a chain of no-frills hotels co-branded with Air Asia. Tune Money offers online financial services—again co-branded with AirAsia.

Culture and Management Style

AirAsia's corporate culture and management style reflect Tony Fernandes' own personality:

Mr. Fernandes says that he came to the industry with no preconceptions but found it rigidly compartmentalized and dysfunctional. He wanted AirAsia to reflect his own unstuffy, open, and cheerful personality. He is rarely seen without his baseball cap, open-neck shirt and jeans, and he is proud that the firm's lack of hierarchy (very unusual in Asia) means anyone can rise to do anyone else's job. AirAsia employs pilots who started out as baggage handlers and stewards; for his part, Mr. Fernandes also practices what he preaches. Every month he spends a day as a baggage handler, every two months as cabin crew, every three months as a check-in clerk. He has even established a "culture department" to "pass the message and hold parties".[7]

The share offer prospectus describes AirAsia's culture as follows:

The Group prides itself on building a strong, team-orientated corporate culture. The Group's employees understand and subscribe to the Group's core strategy and actively focus on maintaining low costs and high productivity. AirAsia motivates its employees by awarding bonuses based upon each employee's contribution to AirAsia's productivity, and expects to increase loyalty through its ESOS [employee share ownership scheme] which will be available to all employees. The Group's management encourages open communication which creates a dynamic working environment, and meets all its employees on a quarterly basis to review AirAsia's results and generate new ways to lower costs and increase productivity. Employees . . . frequently communicate directly with AirAsia's senior management and offer suggestions on how AirAsia can increase its efficiency or productivity . . .

In addition to the above, AirAsia:

- inculcates enthusiasm and commitment among staff by sponsoring numerous social events and providing a vibrant and friendly working environment
- strives to be honest and transparent in its relations with third parties . . .

- fosters a non-discriminatory, meritocratic environment where employees are offered opportunities for advancement, regardless of their education, race, gender, religion, nationality or age, and

- emphasizes maintaining a constant quality of service throughout all of AirAsia's operation through bringing together to work on a regular basis employees based in different locations.[8]

AirAsia's Operations

AirAsia's operations strategy comprises the following elements:

- *Aircraft.* In common with other LCCs, AirAsia operates a single type of aircraft, the Airbus A320. (It switched from Boeing 737s in 2005.) A single aircraft type offers economies in purchasing, maintenance, pilot training and aircraft utilization.

- *No-frills flights.* AirAsia offers a single class, which allows more seats per plane. For example, when it was operating its Boeing 737s, these were equipped with 148 seats, compared to 132 for a typical two-class configuration. Customer services are minimal: complimentary meals and drinks are not served on board (but snacks and beverages can be purchased), passengers pay for baggage beyond a low threshold, and there is no baggage transfer between flights—passengers must do this themselves. AirAsia does not use aerobridges for boarding and disembarking passengers—another cost-saving measure. Flights are ticketless and there is no assigned seating. Such simplicity allows quick turnaround of planes, which also permits better utilization of planes and crews.

- *Sales and marketing.* AirAsia engages in direct sales through its web site and call center. As a result, it avoids paying commissions to travel agents.

- *Outsourcing.* AirAsia achieves simplicity and cost economies by outsourcing those activities that can be undertaken more effectively and efficiently by third parties. Thus, most aircraft maintenance is outsourced to third parties, contracts being awarded on the basis of competitive bidding. Most of AirAsia's information technology requirements are also outsourced.

- *Information technology.* AirAsia uses Navitair's *Open Skies* computer reservations system (CRS), which links Web-based sales and inventory system which also links with AirAsia's call center. The CRS is integrated with AirAsia's yield management system (YMS) that prices seats on every flight according to demand. The CRS also allows passengers to print their own boarding passes. In 2006, AirAsia implemented a wireless delivery system which allows customers to book seats, check flight schedules and obtain real time updates on AirAsia's promotions via their mobile phones—an important facility in the Asia-Pacific region because of the high use of mobile phones. While the YMS maximizes revenue by providing trend analysis and optimizing pricing, the APS minimizes operational costs by using the information generated by the YMS to plan and schedule the needed facilities more efficiently. These two IT systems allow Air Asia to reduce costs in logistics and inbound activities. During 2005, AirAsia adopted an ERP (enterprise resource planning) system to support its processes, facilitate month-end financial closing, and speed up reporting and data retrieval.[9] This was superseded by an advanced planning and scheduling system, which optimizes AirAsia's supply chain management and forecasts future resource requirements.

● *Human resource management.* Human resource management has been a priority for AirAsia since its relaunch under Tony Fernandes. A heavy emphasis is given to selecting applicants on the basis of their aptitudes, then creating an environment and a system with develops employees and retains them. Retention rates are exceptionally high for AirAsia which is important, first, as an indicator of motivation and job satisfaction, but also as a cost saving measure: because employees are multi-skilled, training costs per employee tend to be high for AirAsia. Job flexibility at all levels of the company, including administration, is a major source of productivity for AirAsia.

Air Asia: Cost Information

To offer a comparative view of AirAsia's operational efficiency and cost position, Table 9.1 provides operating and financial information on Malaysia's two leading airlines: Malaysian Airline System (MAS) and AirAsia. Although MAS's route network is very different from that of AirAsia's (MAS has a larger proportion of medium- and long-haul routes), it was subject to similar cost conditions as AirAsia.

For the first time since its relaunch in 2002, AirAsia made a loss in 2008. This was the result of Fernandes' decision to unwind AirAsia's futures contracts for jet fuel purchased. When crude oil prices started to tumble during the latter half of 2008, Fernandes believed that AirAsia would be better off taking a loss on its existing contracts in order to benefit from lower fuel prices.

Going Long-haul

Fernandes was aware that expanding from short-haul flights in South-East Asia into flights of more than four hours to China, Australia, Europe and the Middle East required major changes in operating practices and major new investments— primarily in bigger planes. The creation of AirAsia X was intended to facilitate a measure of operational independence for the long-haul flights while also spreading the risks of this venture among several investors. The investors in AirAsia X also contributed valuable expertise: Virgin Group had experience in establishing and operating four airlines (Virgin Atlantic, Virgin Express, Virgin Blue and Virgin USA), and the chairman of Air Ventures was Robert Milton, the former CEO of Air Canada.

Table 9.2 shows the principal differences in AirAsia and AirAsia X's operations and services.

TABLE 9.1 Comparing operational and financial performance between AirAsia and Malaysian Airline System

	AirAsia	MAS
Operating data		
Passengers carried (millions)	11.81	13.76
Available seat kilometers (millions)	18.72	53.38
Revenue passenger kilometers (millions)	13.49	36.18
Seat load factor (%)	75	67.8
Cost per available seat kilometers (sen)	11.66	22.80
Revenue per available seat kilometers (sen)	14.11	20.60
Number of aircraft in fleet December 31, 2008	78	109
Number of employees	3799	19 094
Aircraft utilization (hours per day)	11.8	11.1
Financial data (RM, millions)		
Revenue	2635	15 035
Other operating income	301.8	466.0
Total operating expense	2966	15 198.3
of which:		
—Staff costs	236.8	2179.9
—Depreciation	347.0	327.9
—Fuel costs	1389.8	6531.6
—Maintenance and overall.	345.1	1146.4
—Loss on unwinding derivatives	830.2	—
—Other operating expenses[a]	139.2	5020.0
Operating profit (loss)	(351.7)	305.5
Finance cost (net)	517.5	60.8
Pre-tax profit (loss)	(869.2)	264.7
After-tax profit	(496.6)	245.6
Total assets	9520.0	10 071.6
of which:		
—Aircraft, property, plant and equipment	6594.3	2464.8
—Inventories	20.7	379.7
—Cash	153.8	3,571.7
—Receivables	694.4	2020.1
Debt	6690.8	433.4
Shareholders' equity	1605.5	4197.0

[a] For AirAsia the main components are aircraft lease expenses and loss on foreign exchange. For MAS the main components were: hire of aircraft, sales commissions, landing fees, and rent of buildings.

Kuala Lumpur to London: Price and Cost Comparisons

A comparison of prices and costs allows a clearer picture of AirAsia's ability to compete in the long-haul market—where AirAsia must position itself against some of the world's major airlines. Between KL and London, AirAsia competes with at least six international airlines, among which the closest competitors are Malaysian Airlines, Emirates and British Airways.

TABLE 9.2 AirAsia and AirAsia X compared

	AirAsia	AirAsia X
Concept	Low cost short haul, no-frills	Low cost long haul, no frills
Flying range	Within four hours flying time from departing city	More than four hours flying time from departing city
Aircraft	Airbus A320 with 180 seats	Airbus A330 with more than 330 seats
Seat type	Single seat	Economy seat and Premium (previously known as XL) seat
Seat option	Free seating with Xpress Boarding option	Assigned seating with advance seat request option
In-flight dining	Wide range of light meals and snacks available for purchase onboard the	Pre-ordered full meals available including Asian, Western, vegetarian and kid's meal; light snacks also available for purchase onboard aircraft

TABLE 9.3 Fare comparisons: AirAsia and its competitors between Kuala Lumpur and London

	AirAsia X[a]	Cheapest other airline[b]	AirAsia price advantage	Cheapest other airlines
KL–London round trip	US$433.96[c]	US$683.68	36.5%	1. Gulf Air, 2. Qatar Air 3. Emirates
London-KL round trip	US$433.96[c]	US$530.35	18.2%	1. Emirates, 2. Etihad, 3. Gulf Air

[a] Average fare between September 1 and October 1, 2009.

[b] Average of lowest airline fare on each day between September 1 and October 1, 2009.

[c] Average outbound fare: U.S.$187.87; average inbound fare: U.S.$209.48; meals and baggage charges: U.S.$36.61.

A comparison of economy, round-trip airfares between the two cities is shown in Table 9.3. As Table 9.4 shows, these fare differentials reflect differences in cost between AirAsia and its long-haul competitors. These cost differences do not take account of differences in load factors, which can make a major effect on the average cost per passenger. AirAsia reports that its KL–London flights have a load factor in excess of 90%. For the airlines as a whole, Table 9.5 shows load factors.

The Outlook for Long-haul

There can be little doubt that AirAsia has been remarkably successful in building a budget airline in South-East Asia. Its cost efficiency, growth rate, brand awareness and awards for customer service, airline management and entrepreneurship all pointed to outstanding achievement, not simply in replicating the LCC business model pioneered by Southwest Airlines but adapting that model and augmenting it with innovation, dynamism and marketing flair that derived from Tony Fernandes' personality and leadership style.

TABLE 9.4 Flight operating cost comparison, Kuala Lumpur to London (in U.S.$)

	AirAsia	British Airways	Malaysia Airlines	Emirates	
Aircraft type [a]	Airbus 340-300	Boeing 747-400	Boeing 747-400	Boeing 777-300	
Route	KUL-STN	KUL-LHR	KUL-LHR	KUL-DXB-LHR	
Maximum passenger capacity	286	337	359	360	
				KUL-DXB	DXB-LHR
Flight fuel cost	79 299	159 522	159 522	77 525	80 822
Leasing costs	5952	0	0	0	0
En route navigation charges	7949	12 294	12 294	1435	6613
Terminal navigation arrival charges	419	645	645	0	645
Landing/parking	1100	2200	2200	2200	2200
Departure handling	6000	12 000	12 000	12 000	12 000
Arrival handling	6000	12 000	12 000	12 000	12 000
Segment totals				105 160	114 280
TOTAL cost per flight [b]	106 719	198 661	198 661	219 440	
Average cost per passenger [b]	373.14	589.50	553.37	609.56	

[a] KUL= Kuala Lumpur, STN = London Stansted, LHR = London Heathrow, DXB = Dubai.
[b] Excluding maintenance, depreciation, meal services and crew salaries.

Source: S. Buchholz, N. Fabio, A. Ileyassoff, L. Mang, and D. Visentin, *AirAsia—Tales from a Long-haul Low Cost Carrier* (Bocconi University, 2009). Data based on NewPacs Aviation Tool Software. Used by permission of the authors.

However, its AirAsia X venture presented a whole set of new challenges. AirAsia had successfully transferred several of its competitive advantages from AirAsia to AirAsia X. The low costs associated with fuel-efficient new planes, secondary airports and human resources practices had allowed AirAsia X to become the low cost operator on most of its routes. The AirAsia brand and reputation provided

TABLE 9.5 Difference between airlines in load factors (%)

	2004	2005	2006	2007	2008
AirAsia	77.0	75.0	78.0	80.0	75.5
Emirates	73.4	74.6	75.9	76.2	79.8
British Airways	67.6	69.7	70.0	70.4	71.2
Malaysia Airlines	69.0	71.5	69.8	71.4	67.8

Source: S. Buchholz, N. Fabio, A. Ileyassoff, L. Mang and D. Visentin, *AirAsia—Tales from a Long-haul Low Cost Carrier* (case report, Bocconi University, 2009). Used by permission of the authors.

AirAsia X with credibility and reputation on each new route it inaugurated. By sharing Web-based and telephone flight booking systems along with administrative and operational services between the two airlines, AirAsia X was able to secure cost efficiencies that would not be possible for an independent start-up.

Nevertheless, doubts remained over AirAsia X's ability to compete against established international airlines. Unlike AirAsia, which was attracting a whole new market for domestic and regional air travel, AirAsia X would have to take business away from the established international airlines whose business models offer some key competitive advantages over that of long-haul LCCs. In particular, its dense domestic and regional route networks offer feeds for their intercontinental flights. These complementarities are supported by through-ticketing, baggage transfer, and frequent flyer schemes. Its sources of profit are very different from the LCCs: most of their profit is earned from first class and business class travelers, which allows it to subsidize its economy class fares.

These challenges pointed towards the advantage of closer integration of AirAsia X with AirAsia. AirAsia X's CEO, Azran Osman-Rani, has argued for the operational and financial rationale of merging AirAsia X into AirAsia: "It would be difficult for AirAsia in the future if it did not have trunk routes as (this) is where the traffic volumes come from, so AirAsia needs growth from AirAsia X and the merger allows it to tap growth opportunities in the long-haul markets." Responding to allegations that the real rationale for the merger was to allow AirAsia to finance AirAsia X's losses, Azran said: "Rubbish, we can clearly dispute that. For the first quarter ended March 31, 2009 our net profit was RM 18 million and we are net cash flow positive. We even had a little cash at RM 3million. We are in a very good position and on a much firmer footing and now is an interesting time to talk about a merger."[10]

Notes

1 Operating profit before depreciation, amortization, and interest as a percentage of average total assets.

2 See www.tonyfernandesblog.com, accessed June 3, 2009.

3 Quoted by T. Lawton and J. Doh, *The Ascendance of AirAsia: Building a Successful Budget Airline in Asia* (Ivey School of Business, Case No. 9B08M054, 2008).

4 "AirAsia X to Hub in Abu Dhabi: AirAsia CEO," *Khaleej Times*, August 5, 2009.

5 "Company Profile," http://www.airasia.com/site/my/en/page.jsp;jsessionid=2FE125E6F301CBFA16C86B62ED064A20?name=Company%20Profile&id=75dbf230-ac1e2082-29962900-ae960618.

6 "AirAsia Berhad," *Offering Circular*, October 29, 2004, p. 3.

7 "Cheap, but Not Nasty," *The Economist*, March 19, 2009.

8 "AirAsia Berhad," *Offering Circular*, October 29, 2004, p. 5.

9 C. Cho, S. Hoffman Arian, C. Tjitrahardja and R. Narayanaswamy, *Air Asia—Strategic IT Initiative* (student report, Faculty of Economics and Commerce, University of Melbourne, 2005).

10 "AirAsia X CEO backs Merger with AirAsia Bhd," *The Star Online*, July 23, 2009, http://biz.thestar.com.my/news/story.asp?file=/2009/7/23/business/4369512&sec=business"

Case 10 Harley-Davidson, Inc., July 2008

You've shown us how to be the best. You've been leaders in new technology. You've stuck by the basic American values of hard work and fair play . . . Most of all, you've worked smarter, you've worked better, and you've worked together . . . as you've shown again, America is someplace special. We're on the road to unprecedented prosperity . . . and we'll get there on a Harley.

PRESIDENT RONALD REAGAN, HARLEY-DAVIDSON PLANT, YORK, PA, MAY 6, 1987

The recovery of this company since the 1980s has been truly remarkable. When you were down in the dumps, people were saying American industry was finished, that we couldn't compete in the global economy, that the next century would belong to other countries and other places. Today, you're not just surviving—you're flourishing, with record sales and earnings; and one of the best-managed companies in America.

PRESIDENT BILL CLINTON, HARLEY-DAVIDSON PLANT, YORK, PA, NOVEMBER 10, 1999

I've been impressed by Harley-Davidsons. It's one of America's finest products. And today I add to my impressions about the product the impressions of the workforce . . . I'm impressed by the esprit de corps, I'm impressed by the fact that these people really enjoy what they're doing, I'm impressed by the fact that they're impressed by the product they make.

PRESIDENT GEORGE W. BUSH, HARLEY-DAVIDSON PLANT, YORK, PA, AUGUST 16, 2006

On May 1, 2009, Keith Wandell took over as CEO of Harley-Davidson, Inc. He faced a dramatically different situation from that which had greeted his predecessors. The financial year 2008 had seen Harley's first decline in revenue since 1984 and a sharp decline in motorcycle shipments (see Figure 10.1). After decades of customer waiting lists and insufficient production capacity, Wandell now had to lay off employees and amalgamate plants in order to cut capacity.

The quarterly financial results released on July 16 showed a further deterioration in demand. During the first half of 2009, motorcycle shipments were down by 12.7% and revenue by 15.1% on the year ago period. The credit crunch was also affecting Harley's balance sheet. A large proportion of Harley's sales were financed by loans from its own financial services subsidiary. Unable to securitize its customer loans, Harley was forced to retain more of these loans on its own balance sheet. With rising default rates on consumer credit, Harley was perceived as much more risky than previously.

Wandell viewed these problems as cyclical. Already the credit markets and macroeconomic forecasts were pointing to the U.S. economy bottoming out and then recovering. Moreover, even with sharply reduced profits, Harley was still the world's most profitable motorcycle company in 2008 with a return on average equity of 29%. Wandell was more concerned with the longer term threats to Harley's business.

Harley's long-term profit growth depended on its ability to keep expanding the sales of its high-priced, heavyweight motorcycles. With the U.S. accounting for 69% of Harley's motorcycle revenues and with the U.S. government and U.S. households facing a painful rebuilding of their balance sheets over the next decade, it seemed likely that the demand for luxury leisure products costing between $8000 and $26 000 would continue to be subdued.

The opportunity for Harley to grow its market share at the expanse of rivals was limited by the fact that Harley already accounted for more than 50% of the U.S.

FIGURE 10.1 Annual shipments of motorcycles by Harley-Davidson

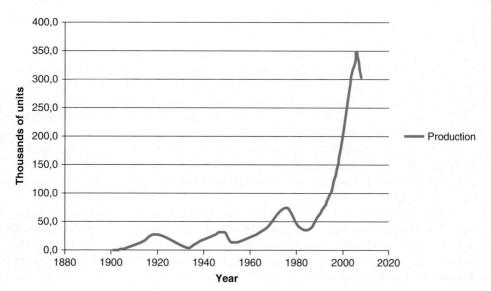

heavyweight motorcycle market. Indeed, Harley's own market might be vulnerable to competition. While no other company could replicate the emotional attachment of riders to the "Harley Experience," there was always the risk that motorcycle riders might seek a different type of experience and become more attracted to the highly engineered sports models produced by European and Japanese manufacturers. Such concerns were fueled by demographic trends. Harley's core market was the baby-boomer generation—and this cohort was moving more towards retirement homes than outdoor sports.

The History of Harley-Davidson

1903–81: From Birth to Maturity

Harley-Davidson, Inc. was founded in 1903 by William Harley and brothers William Davidson, Arthur Davidson, and Walter Davidson. Harley's 1903 model was made in the Davidson family shed and had a three-horsepower engine. In 1909 Harley introduced its first two-cylinder, V-twin engine, featuring the deep, rumbling sound for which Harley motorcycles are renowned. In 1953, the closure of the Indian Motorcycle factory in Springfield, MA, meant that Harley-Davidson was the sole survivor of the 150 U.S. motorcycle producers that had existed in 1910.

The postwar era saw new challenges for Harley-Davidson. Increasing affluence and the rise of youth culture created a growing demand for motorcycles. However, this was satisfied primarily by imports: first the British (by 1959, BSA, Triumph, and Norton took 49% of the U.S. market), then the Japanese. Initially Harley benefitted from the rebirth of motorcycling as a leisure activity, but soon it was facing direct competition: in 1969 Honda introduced its four-cylinder CB750, a huge technical advance on anything produced by Harley or the British. In the same year, Harley-Davidson was acquired by AMF. An expansion of production capacity to 75 000 units a year led to horrendous product quality problems followed by financial losses and a loss of leadership of the U.S. heavyweight motorcycle market.

1981–2008: Rebirth

In 1981, Harley's senior managers, led by Vaughn Beals, organized a leveraged buyout of AMF's Harley-Davidson subsidiary. Harley emerged as an independent, privately owned company, heavily laden with debt. The buyout coincided with a severe recession and soaring interest rates. Harley's sales fell and during 1981 and 1982 it lost a total of $60 million. Only by drastically cutting costs and gaining temporary protection from Japanese import did Harley survive.

At the same time, the management team devoted itself to rebuilding production methods and working practices. Managers visited several Japanese automobile plants and carefully studied Toyota's just-in-time (JIT) system. Less than four months after the buyout, Harley management began a pilot JIT inventory and production-scheduling program called "MAN" (Materials-As-Needed) in its Milwaukee engine plant. The objective was to reduce inventories and costs and improve quality control. Within a year, all Harley's manufacturing operations were being converted to JIT: components and subassemblies were "pulled" through the production system in response to final demand.

With revamped production methods and a new spirit of cooperation between workers and management, Harley increased sales and returned to profitability, allowing it to go public in 1986. With increase investment in new models, plants and its dealership network, Harley's share of the super-heavyweight market (over 850ccs) grew from about 30% in 1986 to over 60% in 1990. The 1990s saw uninterrupted growth in the heavyweight motorcycle market and a continued increase in Harley's market share. The company's biggest challenge was satisfying the surging demand for its products. To overcome this constraint, in 1996, the company announced its Plan 2003 to dramatically increase production capacity during the period preceding Harley's 100th anniversary in 2003. New production plants in Kansas City and York, Pennsylvania, the launching of several new models, and international expansion resulted in sales exceeding 300 000 in 2004 and approaching 342 000 in 2007—a tenfold increase on 1983.

The Heavyweight Motorcycle Market

The heavyweight segment (over 650 cc) was the most rapidly growing part of the world motorcycle market between 1990 and 2007, with the U.S. accounting for a major part of this growth. Sales of heavyweight motorcycles in the major markets of the world almost trebled between 1990 and 2007. North America was the largest market for big bikes, representing 56% of the sales in the major world markets.

In North America, Harley consolidated its market leadership, accounting for almost half of big bike sales. Overseas, however, Harley was unable to replicate this market dominance despite strong sales in a few markets—Harley achieved the remarkable feat of becoming heavyweight market leader in Japan, pushing Honda into second place. In Europe, on the other hand, Harley lagged behind its Japanese competitors and BMW (see Tables 10.1 and 10.2).

TABLE 10.1 Retail sales of heavyweight motorcycles (651+ cc), 2000–8 (in thousands of units)

	2000	2001	2002	2003	2004	2005	2006	2007	2008
North America (total)	365	423	475	495	531	554	579	555	477
Harley-Davidson[a]	163	186	220	238	256	265	282	267	235
Market share (%)	44.6	43.9	46.4	48.1	48.2	47.8	48.6	48.7	49.3
Europe (total)	293	321	332	323	336	351	377	372	384
Harley-Davidson	22	23	24	26	25	30	34	42	45
Market share (%)	7.4	7.1	7.1	8.1	7.3	8.5	9.1	11.3	11.7
Japan/Australia (total)[b]	63	64	64	59	n.a.	n.a.	n.a.	n.a.	n.a.
Harley-Davidson[a,b]	13	14	14	15	10	11	13	23	25
Market share (%)	20.5	21.9	21.2	25.8	n.a.	n.a.	n.a.	n.a.	n.a.

n.a. = not available.

[a] Excludes Buell.

[b] Years 2004–8 include Japan only.

Source: Harley-Davidson 10-K reports.

TABLE 10.2 Market shares in heavyweight motorcycles (651+ cc), 2005–2007 (%)

	North America			Europe		
	2005	2006	2007	2005	2006	2007
Harley-Davidson	47.8	48.6	48.7	8.9	9.1	9.6
Honda	16.6	15.1	14.3	13	14.6	12.3
Kawasaki	6.9	7.1	7.5	12.6	10.7	11.3
Suzuki	12.6	13.1	12.7	13.3	14.8	16.5
Yamaha	9.3	8.8	9.2	15.8	15.5	13.6
BMW	3.3	–	–	17.7	16.5	15.1
Ducati	–	–	–	5.2	5.2	5.9
Triumph	–	–	–	5	5.1	6.5
Other	4.5	7.3	8.3	8.5	8.5	9.2

Source: Harley-Davidson, Annual Reports, 2005, 2007.

The heavyweight motorcycle market comprised three segments:

- *Cruiser motorcycles.* These were "big, noisy, low riding, unapologetically macho cycles,"[1] typically with V-twin, large displacement engines and an upright riding position. Their design reflected the dominance of styling over either comfort or speed. For the urban males (and some females) in congested cities such as Los Angeles, New York, Paris and Tokyo, the cruiser motorcycle was practical transportation but it was primarily a statement of style. The cruiser segment was practically created by Harley and was preeminent in the U.S., representing over half of the heavyweight market. Most of Harley's competitors in this segment had imitated the main features of the traditional Harley design.

- *Touring motorcycles.* These included cruisers specially equipped for longer distance riding and bikes especially designed for comfort over long distances (including the Honda Goldwing and the bigger BMWs). These tourers featured luxuries such as audio systems, two-way intercoms and heaters. While Harley led this segment on the basis of style and image, Honda and BMW had engineered their motorcycles for greater smoothness and comfort over long distances through the use of multi-cylinder, shaft-drive engines, and advanced suspension systems.

- *Performance motorcycles.* These were based on racing bikes, with high-technology, high-revving engines, an emphasis on speed, acceleration and race-track styling; minimal concessions were provided to rider comfort. The segment was the most important in the European and the Asian/Pacific markets, representing 62% and 65% of total heavyweight bike sales, respectively. The segment was dominated by Japanese motorcycle companies, with a significant representation of European specialists such as Ducati and Triumph. Harley entered the performance segment in 1993 through its offshoot, Buell Motorcycles, which it fully acquired in 1998.

Unlike its Japanese competitors, Harley was highly market focused. With the exception of the single-cylinder Buell Blast, Harley's models were not only all heavyweight motorcycles (over 650 ccs engine displacement)—they were concentrated in the narrower super-heavyweight segment (over 850ccs).

Harley-Davidson in 2009

The Brand

Harley's top management team considered the Harley-Davidson image and the loyalty it engendered among its customers to be its greatest assets. Harley-Davidson was an archetype of American style. The famed spread eagle signified not just the brand of one of the world's oldest motorcycle companies, but an entire lifestyle with which it was associated. Harley has been described as "the ultimate biker status symbol . . . a quasi religion, an institution, a way of life."[2] Together with a few other companies—possibly Walt Disney and Levi Strauss—Harley had a unique relationship with American culture. The values that Harley represented—individuality, freedom, and adventure—could be traced back to the cowboy and frontiersman of yesteryear, and before that to the quest that brought people to America in the first place. As the sole surviving American motorcycle company from the pioneering days of the industry, Harley-Davidson represented a tradition of U.S. engineering and manufacturing.

This appeal of the Harley brand was central not just to the company's marketing, but also to its strategy as a whole. The central thrust of the strategy was reinforcing and extending the relationship between the company and its consumers. Harley-Davidson had long recognized that it was not selling motorcycles—it was selling the Harley Experience. Its annual reports made considerable efforts to convey this experience:

A chill sweeps through your body, created by a spontaneous outburst of pure, unadulterated joy. You are surrounded by people from all walks of life and every corner of the globe. They are complete strangers, but you know them like your own family. They were drawn to this place by the same passion—the same dream. And they came here on the same machine. This is one place you can truly be yourself. Because you don't just fit in. You belong.[3]

If the appeal of the Harley motorcycle was the image it conveyed and the lifestyle it represented, then the company had to ensure that the experience matched the image. To increase Harley's involvement in its consumers' riding experience it formed the Harley Owners' Group (HOG) in 1983. Through HOG, the company became involved in organizing social and charity events. Employees, from the CEO down, were encouraged to take an active role in HOG activities. Each year, senior managers typically attended a total of more than 150 shows, rallies, and rides. The bond between the company and its customers is captured in Willie G. Davidson's phrase: "We ride with you." The HOG provided the organizational link for this sense of community: "the feeling of being out there on a Harley-Davidson motorcycle links us like no other experience can. It's made HOG like no other organization in the world . . . The atmosphere is more family reunion than organized meeting."[4] The loyalty of Harley owners was reflected in their repurchase and upgrading of Harley products. More than half of all sales were to customers who had owned a Harley previously, while about 20% were first-time motorcycle buyers.

Since the 1980s, the demographic and socioeconomic profile of Harley customers had shifted substantially: once blue-collar youngsters, Harley owners were middle-aged and middle class:

> The average U.S. retail purchaser of a new Harley-Davidson motorcycle is a married male in his mid to late forties (nearly two-thirds of U.S. retail purchasers of new Harley-Davidson motorcycles are between the ages of 35 and 54) with a median household income of approximately $87,000. Nearly three-quarters of the U.S. retail sales of new Harley-Davidson motorcycles are to buyers with at least one year of education beyond high school and 32% of the buyers have college/graduate degrees. Approximately 12% of U.S. retail motorcycle sales of new Harley-Davidson motorcycles are to female buyers.[5]

The Products

Broadening Harley's market appeal had major implications for product policy and design. Ever since its disastrous foray into small bikes during the AMF years, Harley had recognized that its competitive advantage lay with super-heavyweight bikes. Here it stuck resolutely to the classic styling that had characterized Harleys since its early years. At the heart of the Harley motorcycle was the air-cooled V-twin engine that had been Harley's distinctive feature since 1909. Harley's frames, handlebars, fuel tanks, and seats also reflected traditional designs.

Harley's commitment to traditional design features may be seen as making a virtue out of necessity. Its smaller corporate size and inability to share R&D across cars and bikes (unlike Honda and BMW) limited its ability to invest in technology and new products. As a result, Harley lagged far behind its competitors in the application of automotive technologies: its motorcycles not only looked old-style, much of the technology was old-style. When Harley introduced its new Twin Cam 88 engine in 1998, *Motorcycle* magazine reported:

> Honda comes out with an average of two new (or reworked) motors every year. The other Japanese manufacturers are good for about one. Count on Ducati and BMW to do something every few years. That leaves only Moto Guzzi and Harley . . . The Twin Cam 88 is Harley's first new engine since the Evolution Sportster motor of 1986, and their first new Big Twin motor since the original Evolution, released in 1984.[6]

Harley's engines were representative of the company's overall technological backwardness. Long after Honda had moved to multiple valves per cylinder, overhead camshafts, liquid cooling, and electronic ignition, Harley continued to rely on air-cooled push-rod engines. In suspension systems, braking systems and transmissions too, Harley lagged far behind Honda, Yamaha, and BMW.

Nevertheless, Harley was engaged in constant upgrading—principally incremental refinements to its engines, frames and gearboxes aimed at improving power delivery and reliability, increasing braking power, and reducing vibration. Harley also accessed automotive technology through alliances with other companies, including Porsche AG, Ford, and Gemini Racing Technologies.

Despite being a technological laggard, Harley was very active in new product development and the launching of new models. By 2009, Harley offered 31 Harley-Davidson models and 10 Buell models. Harley's product development efforts had been assisted by doubling the size of its Product Development Center in 2004 and the creation of a Prototyping Lab. Most of Harley's product development efforts were limited to style changes, new paint designs and engineering improvements. However, between 2000 and 2008, Harley had accelerated technological progress and had introduced more radical new product developments. Its V-Rod model introduced in October 2001 featured innovative styling and an all-new liquid-cooled engine. The Buell range also allowed greater scope for Harley's engineers. The 2002 Buell Firebolt featured a new engine, an all-aluminum frame, and the "naked" styling pioneered by Ducati, while the 2006 Ulysses was Harley-Davidson's first ever "adventure sportbike." In 2006, Harley introduced another new engine, the Twin Cam 96, which featured electronic ignition and was teamed with a new six-speed gearbox.

It is notable that between October 2001 and June 2009, Harley made just 90 patent applications to the U.S. Patent Office. Most of these related to peripheral items: a saddlebag mounting system, footpegs, real light assemblies, an adjustable backrest, an LED fuel gauge. By contrast, over the same period, Suzuki made 247 patent applications, Kawasaki 502, Yamaha 2057, and Honda 3971.

Central to Harley's product strategy was the idea that every Harley rider would own a unique, personalized motorcycle as a result of the company offering a wide range of customization opportunities. New bikes allowed multiple options for seats, bars, pegs, controls, and paint jobs, with the potential for augmentation through a range of 7000 accessories and special services such as "Chrome Consulting."

Reconciling product differentiation with scale economies was a continuing challenge for Harley. The solution was to offer a wide range of customization options while standardizing on key components. For example, among the different Harley-Davidson models there were three engine types (Evolution XL, Twin Cam 88, and Revolution), four basic frames, four styles of gas tank and so on.

The Harley product line also covered a wide price range. The Sportster model was positioned as an entry-level bike beginning at $6999, less than one-third of the price of the Ultra Classic Electra Glide, with "custom coloring" at $22 159. Top of the price range was the three-wheeler Tri-Glide at $31 994 (including non-black paint and a reverse gear).

Buell

Buell offered the opportunity for Harley to broaden its appeal to younger riders and those more interested in speed and maneuverability. Founded by ex-Harley engineer Erik Buell, Buell Motor Company developed bikes that used Harley engines and other components but mounted them on a lighter, stiffer frame. Harley acquired complete ownership of Buell in 1998. The lighter weight and superior handling of Buell models were also seen as appealing to the European customers who put greater emphasis on sporty performance. In the U.S., the age of the typical Buell customer was seven years younger than that of Harley buyers and the price was about $10 000

TABLE 10.3 Harley-Davidson shipments 1997–2006 thousands of units

	1998	1999	2000	2001	2002	2003	2004	2005	2006	2007	2008
H-D motorcycle shipments											
—United States	110.9	135.6	158.9	186.9	212.8	237.7	260.6	266.5	273.2	241.5	206.3
—Export	39.9	41.6	45.8	47.5	50.8	53.5	56.7	62.5	76	89.1	97.2
Motorcycle product mix (%)											
—Sportster	22.5	23.6	22.6	21.7	19.4	19.7	22	21.3	18.5	21.8	20.0
—Custom (a)	51.3	49.6	49.3	50.5	53.7	52	48.6	45.2	46.2	43.7	46.4
—Touring	26.2	26.8	28.1	28	26.8	28.4	29.4	33.5	35.4	34.5	33.6
Buell motorcycle shipments	5.5	6.8	6.9	9.9	10.9	10	9.9	11.2	12.5	11.5	13.1
Company total	156.3	184	211.6	244.3	274.5	301.2	327.2	340.2	361.6	330.6	303.5

compared with an average Harley price of $17 500. The Buell Riders Adventure Group (BRAG) was founded to build the same type of community of riders that HOG had done so successfully. The Buell Blast, with its 490 cc single cylinder engine and a price tag of $4595 was a major departure for Harley: it was Harley's first entry into the middleweight motorcycle market since the 1970s. Yet, despite heavy investments in developing and launching new models, there was little overall growth in Buell's unit sales between 2001 and 2006 (see Table 10.3).

Distribution

Upgrading Harley's distribution network was central to its transformation strategy of the 1980s and 1990s. At the time of the buyout, many of Harley's 620 U.S. dealerships were operated by enthusiasts, with erratic opening hours, a poor stock of bikes and spares and indifferent customer service. If Harley was in the business of selling a lifestyle and an experience, then dealers played a pivotal role in delivering that experience. Moreover, if Harley's target market had shifted towards mature, upper income individuals—Harley needed to provide a retail experience commensurate with the expectations of this group.

Harley's dealer development program increased support for dealers while imposing higher standards of pre- and after-sales service, and requiring better dealer facilities. The dealers were obliged to carry a full line of Harley replacement parts and accessories, and to perform service on Harley bikes. Training programs helped dealers to meet the higher service requirements, and encouraged them to recognize and meet the needs of the professional, middle-class clientele that Harley was now courting. Harley pioneered the introduction of new services to customers. These included test ride facilities, rider instruction classes, motorcycle rental, assistance for owners in customizing their bikes through dealer-based design centers and chrome consultants, and insurance services. Close to 85% of Harley dealerships in the U.S. were exclusive—far more than for any other motorcycle manufacturer.

Given the central role of dealers in the relationship between Harley-Davidson and its customers, dealer relations continued to be a strategic priority for Harley. Its retail environments group liaised closely with dealers with a goal of bringing the same retail experience to customers everywhere in the world. Harley-Davidson University was established to "enhance dealer competencies in every area, from customer satisfaction to inventory management, service proficiency, and front-line sales." Dealer relationships were critical to Harley's goal of growing sales of financial services, parts and accessories and general merchandise. Harley believed that the quality and effectiveness of its dealer network was a key determinant of the strong demand for its products.

Other Products

Sales of parts, accessories, and "general merchandise" (clothing and collectibles) represented 20% of total revenue in 2008—much higher than for any other motorcycle company (see Table 10.4). Clothing sales included not just traditional riding apparel, but a wide range of men's, women's and children's leisure apparel.

Only a small proportion of the clothing, collectibles and other products bearing the Harley-Davidson trademark were sold through the Harley dealership network. Most of the "general merchandising" business represented licensing of the Harley-Davidson name and trademarks to third-party manufacturers of clothing, giftware, jewelry, toys and other products. L'Oréal offered a line of Harley-Davidson cologne. To expand sales of licensed products, Harley opened a number of "secondary retail locations," which sold clothing, accessories and giftware but not motorcycles. Harley-Davidson Financial Services was established to supply credit, insurance, and extended warranties to Harley dealers and customers. Between 2000 and 2007 it was Harley's most rapidly growing source of profit, contributing almost 12% of operating profit in 2007. However, the credit crunch hit the business hard. Unable to securitize its customer loans, Harley was forced to retain these loans on its own books, causing a large increase in its current assets. Some analysts believed that this build up of consumer loans had made Harley more reluctant to extend 100% loans to purchasers which was depressing sales volume.

International Expansion

A key part of Harley-Davidson's growth strategy was expanding sales outside of the U.S. A critical issue was the extent to which Harley needed to adapt its products, image, and customer approach to conditions in overseas markets. Harley's image was rooted in American culture—to what extent was Harley's appeal to European and Asian customers rooted in its status as an American icon? "The U.S. and Harley

TABLE 10.4 Harley-Davidson's non-motorcycle sales, 2000-8 ($, millions)

	2000	2001	2002	2003	2004	2005	2006	2007	2008
Parts and accessories	447.9	509.6	629.2	712.8	781.6	815.7	862.3	868.3	858.7
General merchandise	151.4	163.9	231.5	211.4	223.7	247.9	277.5	305.4	313.8
Financial services	140.1	181.5	211.5	279.5	305.3	331.6	384.9	416.2	377.0

are tied together," observed Hugo Wilson of Britain's *Bike* magazine, "the guy who's into Harleys here is also the guy who owns cowboy boots. You get a Harley and you're buying into the U.S. mystique."[7] At the same time, the composition of demand and the customer profiles were different in overseas markets.

Europe was the focal point of Harley's overseas ambitions, simply because it was the second largest heavyweight motorcycle market in the world. Europe was also a huge challenge for Harley. Unlike in the U.S., Harley had never had a major position in Europe—it needed to fight to take market share from the established leaders in the heavy bike segment: BMW, Honda, Kawasaki, and Yamaha. The European motorcycle market differed significantly from the American market in that 70% of the heavyweight motorcycle market was for performance bikes, while touring and cruiser bikes accounted for just 30%. European buyers were knowledgeable and style conscious but their style preferences were different from those of U.S. riders. European roads and riding styles were also different from the U.S. As a result, Harley modified some of its models for the European market. The U.S. Sportster, for example, had a straight handlebar instead of curled buckhorns and a new suspension system to improve cornering. The name was also changed to the "Custom 53." The Harley Softail also received a new look, becoming the "Night Train." As in the U.S., HOG played a critical role in building brand image and customer loyalty. Harley's centenary celebration in Barcelona on June 2003 attracted some 150 000 people—a large proportion were Harley owners from all over Europe.

Central to Harley's international strategy was building its dealer network. Between 2000 and 2008, Harley expanded its overseas dealership network and built a new European headquarters in Oxford, England. In 2008, Harley had 686 dealers in the U.S., 71 in Canada, 383 in Europe (including the Middle East and Africa), 201 in Asia/Pacific and 32 in Latin America.

Between 2006 and 2008, Harley achieved greater success in penetrating international markets. Non-U.S. sales of motorcycles and related products were $1.75 billion in 2008, representing 31% of net revenue of the motorcycles segment—up from 20% in 2006.

In July 2008, Harley extended its European presence when it announced the acquisition of the Italian motorcycle manufacturer, MV Agusta, for $105 million. According to the Harley press release:

> MV Agusta Group has two families of motorcycles: a line of exclusive, premium, high-performance sport motorcycles sold under the MV Agusta brand; and a line of lightweight motorcycles sold under the Cagiva brand. MV Agusta's F4-R motorcycle, powered by a 1078 cc in-line four-cylinder liquid cooled engine, is rated at 190 hp. The company sells its products through about 500 dealers worldwide, the vast majority of them in Europe. In 2007, MVAG shipped 5,819 motorcycles. During 2008 MVAG has significantly slowed production due to financial difficulties.
>
> "Motorcycles are the heart, soul and passion of Harley-Davidson, Buell and MV Agusta," said Harley-Davidson, Inc. Chief Executive Officer Jim Ziemer. "Both have great products and close connections with incredibly devoted customers. The MV Agusta and Cagiva brands are well-known and highly regarded in Europe. They are synonymous with beautiful, premium, Italian performance motorcycles," Ziemer said.[8]

Operations

As already noted, Harley-Davidson development during the 1980s and 1990s focused heavily on upgrading its manufacturing operations. Investment in plant and equipment included the introduction of advanced process technologies and capacity expansion. Particular emphasis was placed on developing manufacturing capabilities through total quality management, just-in-time scheduling, CAD/CAM, and the devolution of responsibility and decision making to the shop floor. Table 10.5 shows Harley's main manufacturing and development facilities.

Despite constant development of its manufacturing facilities and operational capabilities, Harley's low production volumes relative to Honda and the other Japanese manufacturers imposed significant cost disadvantages. A key cost disadvantage was in the purchasing components. Bought-in, customized components accounted for a large proportion of manufacturing costs and Harley lacked the buying power of Honda or BMW. To compensate for lack of bargaining clout, Harley fostered close relations with its key suppliers and placed purchasing managers at senior levels within its management structure. Its supplier advisory council (SAC) promoted collaboration and best practice sharing within the Harley network.[9] Harley's director of purchasing, Garry Berryman, commented: "Through the SAC, we're able to take some of the entrepreneurial aspects of our smaller, privately held suppliers and inject that enthusiasm, spirit, and energy into those that may be larger, publicly held companies. In this way, the SAC serves not only to improve purchasing efficiency, but also provides a forum to share information, ideas, and strategy."[10]

Harley's capacity for efficiency was also limited by its dispersed manufacturing operations: engine manufacture in Milwaukee, Wisconsin; assembly in York, Pennsylvania and Kansas City, Missouri. To cut costs, Harley initiated a program of plant consolidation. The two Milwaukee-area powertrain plants would be combined

TABLE 10.5 Harley-Davidson's main facilities, 2008

Location	Function	Square Feet
Menomonee Falls, WI	Motorcycle powertrain production	881 600
Milwaukee, WI	Corporate Office	515 000
Wauwatosa, WI	Motorcycle powertrain production	430 000
Wauwatosa, WI	Product Development Center	409 000
Franklin, WI	Distribution Center	255 000
Tomahawk, WI	Fiberglass/plastic parts production and painting	211 000
East Troy, WI	Buell motorcycle assembly	40 000
Kansas City, MI	Motorcycle parts fabrication, painting and Dyna, Sportster	450 000
York, PA	Motorcycle parts fabrication, painting, assembling Softail and touring models	1 321 000
Manaus, Brazil	Assembly of models for Brazilian market	82 000
Varese, Italy	MV Agusta and Cagiva motorcycle assembly	1 378 600
Morazzone, Italy	MV Agusta and Cagiva warehouse	446 500
Adelaide, Australia	Motorcycle wheel production	485 000

Source: Harley-Davidson 10-K Report, 2008.

into a single facility and the separate paint and frame operations at York, Pennsylvania, would be merged into a single plant. The measures announced between January and July 2009 would eliminate about 2400 jobs and reduce costs by about $250 million annually.

People and Management

Central to Harley-Davidson's renaissance was the creation of a new relationship between management and employees. Following the management buyout in 1981, Harley's new management team systematically rethought management-employee relationships, employee responsibilities and organizational structure. The result was a transformation in employee commitment and job satisfaction. Harley's employee relations focused on involvement, self-management, open communication and the provision of generous health and leave benefits. Harley's Kansas City assembly plant, opened in 1998, featured a management structure and working methods designed to promote employee commitment and involvement. The plant manager and other administrators worked in a "bullpen area" on the production floor rather than in separate offices. The entire plant was organized into teams. Production was by eight- to 15-member *natural work groups*. Representatives from these formed four *process operating groups* for fabrication, engine production, assembly and painting. Overall plant management was by a 14-member *plant leadership group* comprising the plant manager, union representatives, elected representatives from the process groups, and six staff members.[11]

Harley's belief in the effectiveness of non-hierarchical, team-based structures in fostering motivation and accelerating innovation and learning was evident throughout the company—including the corporate headquarters. "In our new organization," explained Clyde Fessler, VP for Business Development, "the Harley-Davidson Motor Company has been divided into three broad, functional areas called Circles. They are: the Create Demand Circle (CDC), the Produce Product Circle (PPC), and the Provide Support Circle (PSC). Each Circle is composed of the leaders representing the functions within it."[12] Each Circle operated as a team with leadership moving from person to person, depending on the issue being addressed. Overall coordination was provided by the Strategic Leadership Council (SLC), comprising individuals nominated by each of the three Circles.

Competition

Despite Harley's insistence that it was supplying a unique Harley experience rather than competing with other motorcycle manufacturers, the more it took market share from other manufacturers and expanded its product range and geographical scope, the more it came into direct competition with other producers. The clearest indication of direct competition was imitation: Honda, Suzuki, Yamaha and Kawasaki had long been offering V-twin cruisers styled closely along the lines of the classic Harleys, but at lower prices and with more advanced technologies. In competing against Harley, the Japanese manufacturers' key advantage was the scale advantages deriving from vastly greater volume. However, despite their large price premium, Harley-Davidson motorcycles benefitted from a much smaller rate of depreciation than other brands.

FIGURE 10.2 Cruiser motorcycles, 2009 models

Harley-Davidson Fat Boy   Honda Shadow Spirit 750

Yamaha Roadstar   Suzuki Boulevard C50

Kawasaki Vulcan 900   Polaris Victory Kingpin

Harley lacked the diversification of its rivals. Honda, BMW, and Suzuki were important producers of automobiles and more than one-third of Yamaha's turnover came from boats and snowmobiles. These companies could benefit from sharing technology, engineering capabilities and marketing and distribution know-how across their different vehicle divisions. In addition, sheer size conferred greater bargaining power with suppliers.

Imitators also included several domestic companies producing retro-styled cruiser bikes. In recent years Excelsior, Polaris (Victory) and a resuscitated Indian had all entered the U.S. super-heavyweight market, mostly selling at prices exceeding those of Harley (the Indian Vintage Chief cost $35 499).

Figure 10.2 shows competitive product offerings while Table 10.6 shows price comparisons. Appendix 2 gives profiles of several leading competitors.

Meeting the Challenges of Tomorrow

In his July 16, 2009 conference call with analysts, CEO Keith Wandell focused upon the short-term problems that Harley was facing in terms of depressed demand and Harley's responses in terms of cost reduction and production cutbacks. Wandell was confident that Harley would emerge from the 2008–9 recession in strong shape. He

TABLE 10.6 Price comparison of V-twin, cruiser motorcycles, 2009

Manufacturer and model	Engine	Recommended retail price ($)
Harley-Davidson		
Sportster 883 Low	V-twin, air-cooled, 883 cc	6999
Fat Boy	V-twin, air-cooled, 1540 cc	15 999
VRSC V-Rod Muscle	V-twin, liquid-cooled, 1131 cc	17 199
Heritage Softail Classic	V-twin, air-cooled, 1450 cc	17 999
Honda		
Shadow Spirit 750	V-twin, liquid-cooled, OHC, 745 cc	7699
VTX1300C	V-twin, liquid-cooled, OHC, 1312 cc	10 299
VTX1800N	V-twin, liquid-cooled, OHC, 1800 cc	13 699
Suzuki		
Boulevard S50	V-twin, liquid-cooled, OHC, 805 cc	7199
Boulevard C90	V-twin, air-cooled, OHC, 1475 cc	11 299
Boulevard M109R	V-twin, liquid-cooled, 1783 cc	13 799
Kawasaki		
Vulcan 900 Classic	V-twin, 8-valve, OHC	7499
Vulcan 1600 Mean Streak	V-twin, air-cooled, 1552 cc	11 099
Yamaha		
V-Star Custom	V-twin, OHC, air-cooled, push-rod, 649 cc	6290
Road Star	V-twin, OHC, air-cooled, push-rod, 1670 cc	12 390
Polaris		
Victory Kingpin	V-twin, 4-valve per cylinder, 1634 cc	16 399

Source: Web sites of different motorcycle manufacturers.

was particularly encouraged by the fact that Harley's 2009 sales were showing greater resilience that those of its main competitors—as a result Harley's share of the U.S. heavyweight market had jumped from 50% to 58%.

The longer term threats were more troubling. A *New York Times* article headed "Harley, You're Not Getting Any Younger," had painted a gloomy picture of Harley's future market position:

> After riding high for two decades, the company that makes the hulky bikes that devoted riders affectionately call Hogs is sputtering. Harley's core customers are graying baby boomers, whose savings, in many cases, have gone up in smoke in the market downturn. Few are in the mood to shell out up to $20 000 or more for something that is basically a big toy, and the company, in turn, has not captured much of the younger market . . .
>
> Its core customers have grayed, and they are buying new bikes less often. The average age of a Harley rider is 49, up from 42 five years ago. But company executives don't seem outwardly worried by the lackluster growth among those 35 and younger, even as it takes steps to turn them into Harley owners.
>
> They say they're confident that the baby-boom generation has 15 more years of riding life. "They're not about to stop riding because they're getting older," Mr. Richer says. "It would be dumb to walk away from our core customer, the most lucrative customer."

As Harley keeps most of its focus on its aging consumers, rivals like BMW, Honda and Yamaha are attracting younger customers who seem less interested in cruising on what their old man rides. United States sales of light sport bikes, intended for the younger crowd, have increased more than 50% in the last five years, and the Japanese makers have popular cruisers of their own. Harley has roughly 30% of the overall United States motorcycle market, but it accounts for half of the heavyweight bikes sold in America . . .

"Harley understands the baby-boomer consumer incredibly well, in a holistic sense," says Gregory Carpenter, a marketing professor at the Kellogg School of Management at Northwestern. "But to grow and thrive, they must create a deep emotional connection with younger consumers."

A decade ago, Harley executives made a decision that now appears to be a major contributor to its current problems. Determined to appease consumers who were stuck on two-year waiting lists, the company ramped up production. Last year, Harley built more than 303,000 bikes, up from 159,000 in 2000 . . .

Now, with so many Hogs in the marketplace, Harley has an issue involving its brand.

"Traditionally, Harley-Davidson had a very loyal consumer," says Anthony Gikas, senior research analyst at Piper Jaffray. "But those riders lost interest in the brand because everyone has a Harley bike. It's not a club anymore."[13]

Reflecting on these challenges, one Milwaukee blogger asked:

So what does Harley do?

One tack would be to stay focused on what it does best: big bikes. While that strategy may make sense on some fronts (focus on what you know, stay loyal to the brand identity, etc.), that approach will mean greatly reduced growth prospects and could doom it if the current consumer spending environment holds out long term. And meanwhile its core audience just gets older.

Or it could do what people have been saying what it should do for years (and what Harley itself has suggested, intermittently, it may do): Make smaller, more affordable bikes. That's easier than it sounds, as it would force Harley to compete against the Japanese manufacturers on their own turf. But if the market is moving away from Harley, does it have a choice?[14]

Appendix 1   Selected Items from Harley-Davidson Financial Statements, 2000–8 ($, millions)

	2000	2001	2002	2003	2004	2005	2006	2007	2008
Income statement									
Net sales	2906	3407	4091	4624	5015	5342	5801	5727	5594
Gross profit	991	1153	1418	1666	1900	2040	2233	2114	1931
R&D	76	130	140	150	171	179	177.7	186	164
Selling, administrative and engineering expense	513	552	639	684	727	762	846	901	985

(Continued)

	2000	2001	2002	2003	2004	2005	2006	2007	2008
Operating income	515	663	883	1149	1361	1470	1603	1426	1029
Of which:									
Financial services	37	61	104	168	189	192	211	212	83
Interest income	18	17	17	23	23	23	27	22	9
Other income/ (expense)	16	−7	−13	−6	−5	−5	−5		5
Income before taxes	549	673	886	1166	1379	1488	1624	1448	1034
Provision for income taxes	201	236	306	405	490	528	581	514	379
Net income	348	438	580	761	890	960	1043	934	655
Balance sheet									
Assets									
Cash	419	439	281	329	275	141	238	403	594
Finance receivables held for investment[a]	581	921	1139	1391	1656	1943	2101	1575	1378
Accounts receivable, net	98	119	109	112	121	122	143	181	296
Inventories	192	181	218	208	227	221	288	350	401
Total current assets	1297	1665	2067	2729	3683	3145	3551	3467	5378
Property, plant and equipment, net	754	892	1033	1046	1025	1012	1024	1061	1094
Total assets	2436	3118	3861	4923	5483	5255	5532	5657	7829
Liabilities									
Current portion of long-term debt	89	217	383	324	495	205	832	398	0
Accounts payable	170	195	227	224	244	271	763	300	324
Total current liabilities	498	716	990	956	1173	873	1596	1905	2604
Non-current liabilities									
Long-term debt	355	380	380	670	800	1000	870	980	2176
Other long-term liabilities	97	158	123	86	91	82	109	152	175
Postretirement healthcare benefits	81	90	105	127	150	61	201	193	274
Stockholders' equity	1406	1756	2233	2958	3218	3084	2757	3352	3357
Total liabilities and equity	2436	3118	3861	4923	5483	5255	5532	6796	6786
Cash flows									
Operating activities	565	757	546	597	832	961	762	798	−685
Capital expenditures	−204	−290	−324	−227	−214	−198	−220	−242	−232
Total investing activities	−171	−772	−720	−540	−570	177	−35	391	−393
Financing activities	−158	34	80	81	−316	−1272	−637	−1038	1293
Net increase in cash	236	20	−95	137	−54	−134	97	164	191

[a] In addition Harley-Davidson holds financial receivables (mainly loans to customers) for sale. These amounted to $2444 million in 2008, up from $781 million in 2007.

Source: Harley-Davidson 10-K reports (www.harleydavidson.com).

Appendix 2 Comparative Financial Data for Honda, Yamaha, BMW and Harley-Davidson ($, millions, unless otherwise indicated)

	Honda Motor			Yamaha Motor			BMW			Harley-Davidson		
	2006	2007	2008	2006	2007	2008	2006	2007	2008	2006	2007	2008
Revenue	84218	94241	121229	5181	5339	5323	64644	82453	n.a.	5801	5727	5594
Gross profit margin	29.20%	29.10%	28.80%	36.00%	36.00%	37.40%	23.10%	21.80%	n.a.	39.50%	37.90%	33.70%
SGA expense	15015	16988	20080	1631	1652	1671	10215	11737	n.a.	846	901	985
Operating income	7386	7241	9626	234	269	319	5343	6200	n.a.	1603	1426	1029
Net income after tax	4228	4327	5135	273	270	384	3792	4613	n.a.	1043	934	655
Net margin	6.00%	5.30%	5.00%	5.30%	5.10%	7.20%	5.60%	5.90%	n.a.	16.90%	15.20%	11.00%
Op. income/total assets	8.22%	7.08%	7.56%	4.64%	4.95%	6.08%	5.12%	4.73%	n.a.	28.98%	25.20%	13.14%
Total assets	89859	102310	127417	5044	5423	5241	104300	130995	n.a.	5532	5657	7829
Cost of goods sold	59588	66854	86286	n.a.	n.a.	n.a.	49685	64516	n.a.	3742	3817	3958
Inventory turnover	6.76%	6.65%	7.12%	6.80%	6.90%	6.90%	5.54%	5.96%	n.a.	12.99%	10.91%	9.87%
Inventories	8809	10057	12113	756	798	740	8963	10817	n.a.	288.0	349.7	400.9
Total equity	35069	38102	45897	3109	3410	3327	25238	32005	n.a.	2757	3352	3357
Return on equity	12.06%	11.36%	11.19%	8.78%	7.93%	11.53%	15.02%	14.41%	n.a.	37.83%	27.86%	19.50%
Operating cash flow	4901	7689	11382	247	385	361	13167	17360	n.a.	762	798	-685
Cash flow from investing activities	-5718	-9611	-17033	-176	-218	407	-18035	-25387	n.a.	-35	391	-393
R&D expenditure	4354	5352	5703	233	235	241	4160	4363	n.a.	178	186	164
Advertising expenditure	3062	2992	2793	250	256	282	5941	6302	n.a.	70	77	89
Motorcycles shipped (thousands of units)	10271	10369	9320	n.a.	n.a.	n.a.	100	102	n.a.	362	331	303
Employees (thousands)	145	167	179	27	26	25	104	104	n.a.	9	9	9

Source: Company financial reports.

Notes

1 G. Strauss, "Born to be Bikers," *USA Today,* November 5, 1997.
2 M. Ballon, "Born to be Wild," *Inc,* November, 1997, p. 42.
3 Harley-Davidson, Inc. *Annual Report,* 2000.
4 See www.harley-davidson.com/experience/family/hog.
5 Harley-Davidson, Inc. 10-K Report for 2008, p. 8.
6 *Motorcycle,* February, 1998.
7 Quoted in: "Motorcycle Maker Caters to the Continent," *USA Today,* April 22, 1998.
8 "Harley-Davidson to Acquire MV Agusta Group Expanding Presence in Europe," press release, Harley-Davidson, Inc., July 11, 2008.
9 K. R. Fitzgerald, "Harley's Supplier Council Helps Deliver Full Value," *Purchasing,* September 5, 1996.
10 A. Millen Porter, "One Focus, One Supply Base," *Purchasing,* June 5, 1997.
11 S. Roth, "Harley's Goal: Unify Union and Management," *Kansas City Business Journal,* May 16, 1997.
12 C. Fessler, "Rotating Leadership at Harley-Davidson: from Hierarchy to Interdependence," *Strategy and Leadership,* July 17, 1997.
13 "Harley, You're Not Getting Any Younger," *New York Times,* March 21, 2009.
14 See http://brewcitybrawler.typepad.com/brew_city_brawler/2009/01/screw-it-lets-ride-is-not-a-strategy.html, accessed July 25, 2009.

Case 11 Raisio Group and the Benecol Launch*

Case A: The Situation in January 1997

During 1996, Raisio Group, a 57-year-old grain-milling company based in Raisio in the south-west of Finland, emerged from obscurity to become the second most valuable public company in Finland (after Nokia) and the focus of worldwide attention. The launch of Benecol, its cholesterol-lowering margarine, at the end of 1995 had attracted the interest of food processors and supermarket groups

*This case draws upon an earlier case by Michael H. Moffett and Stacey Wolff Howard, *Benecol: Raisio's Global Nutriceutical* (Thunderbird, The American Graduate School of International Management. Case No. A06-99-0004, 1999). I am grateful to Ayan Bhattacharya for assistance in preparing this case. Copyright © 2008 Robert M. Grant.

throughout the world and fueled a surge of investor interest. Demand for the product had outstripped Raisio's capability to produce the active ingredient in Benecol, stanol ester. On the Helsinki stock market, foreign demand pushed Raisio's share price from FIM61 at the beginning of the year to FIM288 at the end (after touching FIM322 during the summer).[1] CEO Matti Salminen commented:

> 1996 will go down in the Raisio Group's history as the "Benecol year"—such was the role of this new cholesterol-reducing margarine in increasing the Group's visibility and raising its profile in all our sectors of operations. Although we have not been able to meet even the domestic demand for Benecol margarine so far, the product is already known worldwide and great expectations are attached to it. The Benecol phenomenon quintupled the value of our shares, increasing the Group's capitalization by billions of Finnish marks.[2]

It was the international prospects for Benecol margarine (and potentially other food products incorporating stanol ester) that had drawn a bevy of stock analysts and portfolio managers to Raisio's headquarters. Not only was the potential market for Benecol considered huge—the U.S. alone was seen as having a multi-billion market potential—but the profit opportunities also appeared excellent. In Finland, Benecol was selling at about six times the price of regular margarine. In addition to being first to market, Raisio had the ability to sustain its market leadership through its patents relating to the production and use of the active ingredient, stanol ester, and recognition of its Benecol brand name.

However, within Raisio a vigorous debate had broken out as to the best strategy for exploiting the vast commercial potential that Raisio's innovation offered. This debate focused around two issues. The first was whether Raisio's emphasis should be on supplying its Benecol margarine or its active ingredient, stanol ester. Despite the phenomenal success of Benecol margarine in Finland, margarine was only one of a number of potential food and drink products to which stanol ester could be added. Several Raisio managers argued that the company could exploit its innovation more widely if it supplied stanol ester to a number of food and drink companies. A second issue concerned the means by which Raisio would exploit the international potential of its innovation. Although Raisio was a significant margarine manufacturer in Finland, it possessed few facilities and limited experience outside its home market. A number of multinational food companies and leading food retailers had approached Raisio expressing interest in licensing agreements, joint ventures and supply agreements—for Benecol margarine, for stanol ester, or for both. Should Raisio license its intellectual property to other firms, create joint-ventures with foreign companies, or should it keep its technology in-house and use it to build a multinational presence for Raisio?

History

The Raisio Group began life in 1939 as Vehnä Oy, a grain-milling company located in the town of Raisio. In 1950, a vegetable oil factory called Oy Kasviöljy-Växtolje Ab was founded next to the milling plant. The two companies cooperated in introducing rapeseed cultivation to Finland. They eventually merged in 1987 to form Raisio Tehtaat Oy Ab.[3] From cereals and vegetable oil, the company expanded into animal feeds, malt production, potato starch and margarine. In the 1960s, production of starch provided the basis for the supply of a number of chemical products, mainly to the paper industry.

During this period Raisio developed a substantial export business. This began with malt exports to Sweden, followed by exports of margarine, pasta and other food products to the Soviet Union and subsequently to Poland. In the St. Petersburg area of Russia and in Estonia, Raisio's Melia-branded products were market leaders in flour, pasta and muesli. Finland's accession to the European Union in 1995 allowed Raisio to expand its sales in other European countries. By 1996, 39% of Raisio's sales were outside of Finland. Raisio's increased international presence included margarine plants in Sweden and Poland and joint-venture plants supplying starch and other products for the paper industry in Sweden, the U.S., France, Germany and Indonesia.

From its earliest days, Raisio had shown considerable entrepreneurial initiative and technical ingenuity. Its first oil-milling plant was constructed by its own employees using spare parts, scrap metal, and innovative improvisation. Raisio's first margarine plant was built partly to stimulate demand for its own rapeseed oil, which was not widely used in margarine production at that time. Raisio also maintained an active program of R&D. Benecol was the result of Raisio's research into plant sterols. Raisio's annual report tells the story:

> The cholesterol-reducing effects of plant sterols were known as early as the 1950s and ever since that time, scientists all over the world have been studying plant sterols and their properties.
>
> In 1972, a project led by Professor Pekka Puska was launched in North Karelia. The purpose of the project, which enjoyed international prestige, was to reduce the high cardiovascular rates in the region.
>
> In 1988, the Department of Pharmacy at the University of Helsinki started cooperation with the Helsinki and Turku Central Hospitals and the Raisio Group aimed at studying the effect of rapeseed oil on blood cholesterol levels. Professor Tatu Miettinen, who had already done extensive research on fat metabolism, suggested research on plant sterols to the Raisio Group.
>
> The following year, R&D Manager Ingmar Wester (of Raisio's Margarine Sub-division) and his research team found a way of turning plant sterol into fat-soluble stanol ester suitable for food production. A patent application was filed in 1991. This started a period of intense research aimed at producing indisputable evidence of the cholesterol-reducing effect of stanol ester. In 1993, the North Karelia project launched a long-range stanol ester study as part of its other clinical research.
>
> The digestive tract receives cholesterol from two sources, i.e. food and the human body itself. Normally, some 50% of the cholesterol that enters the digestive tract is disposed of and the rest is absorbed by the body. Fat-soluble plant stanol was shown as efficiently preventing the absorption of cholesterol. In a diet containing stanol ester, 80% of the cholesterol entering the digestive tract is disposed of and only 20% is absorbed by the body. The plant stanol itself is not absorbed, but disposed of naturally.
>
> The findings of the North Karelia study were published in the New England Journal of Medicine in November 1995. (The article reported that, after a 14-month trial, a daily intake of 25 grams reduces total cholesterol in the

bloodstream by 10% and the level of more harmful LDL cholesterol by 14%.) At the same time the first patents were issued for the production and use of stanol ester.

The first stanol ester product, Benecol margarine, was introduced on the Finnish market. The interest it aroused soon exceeded all expectations both in Finland and internationally. The registered name, Benecol, has since been confirmed as the common name for all products containing stanol ester.

Production of stanol ester began with experimental equipment, which limited the supply. The availability of plant sterol, the raw material, was another limiting factor. All plants contain small amounts of plant sterol, but it can be recovered economically only from plants processed in very large quantities. Since there had been no demand for plant sterols, no investments had been made in separation facilities.[4]

Exhibit 11.1 describes the cholesterol reducing properties of sterols and stanols. The Appendix gives information on Raisio's main patents relating to stanol ester.

Raisio in 1997

At the beginning of 1997, the Raisio Group had annual sales of $866 million and 2594 employees. The group comprised three divisions:

- Foodstuffs (47% of total sales), including the subdivisions: margarine (39% of sales), Melia Ltd (flour, pasta, breakfast cereal, muesli), oil milling, potato processing (mainly frozen French fries), malting, and Foodie Oy (rye products, pea soup, frozen pastry dough, salad dressings).
- Chemicals (34% of sales).
- Animal feeds (19% of sales).

Outside of Finland, Raisio had subsidiaries in Sweden, Estonia, Latvia, the U.K., France, Spain, Germany, Belgium, Poland, Canada, the U.S. and Indonesia. Raisio also had joint ventures in Mexico (49% ownership) and Chile (50%). Figure 11.1 shows Raisio's share price. Table 11.1 shows Raisio's financial performance.

EXHIBIT 11.1

Sterols and stanols

Sterols play a critical role in maintaining cell membranes in both plants and animals. Plant sterols (phytosterols) can reduce the low-density lipoprotein (LDL) in human blood, therefore reducing the risk of coronary heart disease. In plants, more than 40 sterols have been identified, of which sitosterol, stigmasterol and campesterol are the most abundant.

Plant stanols (phytostanols) are similar to sterols and are also found naturally in plants—though in much smaller quantities than sterols.

The effect of plant sterols in lowering human cholesterol levels has been known since the 1950s. Sitosterol has been used as a supplement and as a drug (Cytellin, marketed by Eli Lilly) to lower serum cholesterol levels. However, the use of plant sterols was limited by problems of poor solubility.

An important breakthrough was made by Finnish chemist Ingvar Wester, who hydrogenated plant sterols (derived from tall oil, a byproduct of pine-wood pulp) to produce stanol, then esterified the stanol to produce stanol ester, which is fat-soluble. Unlike sterol ester, stanol ester is not absorbed by the body. Clinical trials in Finland showed that stanol ester reduced total blood serum cholesterol in humans by up to 15%.

Plant sterols can also be produced as a byproduct of vegetable oil processing. One of the final stages of the processing of vegetable oil is deodorization—high-temperature distillation that removes free fatty acids. Sterols can be recovered from the resulting distillate.

Plant sterols themselves have a waxy consistency and a high melting point, creating solubility issues for the food processor. While they are oil-dispersible to some extent in their raw form, the amount required to produce an efficacious effect in a finished product can cause granulation. The answer to this problem is esterification: to make stanols and sterols fat soluble. During 1996, Unilever was working on the esterification of plant sterols. Meanwhile, Archer Daniels Midland was believed to be developing processes that would allow the introduction of sterols into nonfat systems, thus creating entirely new product lines (for example, adding sterols to beverages).

FIGURE 11.1 Raisio's share price (unrestricted shares, Helsinki Stock Exchange)

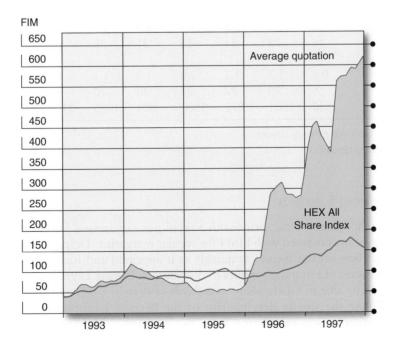

TABLE 11.1 Raisio's financial performance, 1987–1996

	1987	1988	1989	1990	1991	1992	1993	1994	1995	1996
Sales (FIM m)	2011	2184	2487	2557	2315	3070	3549	3518	3224	3928
Change (%)	+9	+9	+14	+3	−9	+33	+16	−1	−8	+22
Exports from Finland (FIM m)	126	106	110	136	172	241	389	358	519	735
International sales (FIM m)	288	16	189	217	279	405	561	568	886	1541
Operating margin (FIM m)	214	247	232	213	316	431	492	428	383	420
Percentage of turnover	10.6	11.3	9.3	8.3	13.6	14.0	13.9	12.2	11.9	10.7
Profit after depreciation (FIM m)	147	167	120	90	185	252	294	230	183	196
Percentage of turnover	7.3	7.6	4.8	3.5	8.0	8.2	8.3	6.5	5.7	5.0
Pre-tax profit[a] (FIM m)	97	98	91	64	63	114	185	35	140	162
Percentage of turnover	4.8	4.5	3.7	2.5	2.7	3.7	5.2	1.0	4.3	4.1
Return on equity (%)	15.5	15.3	5.4	0.1	6.9	10.3	10.3	9.4	6.8	5.8
Return on investment (%)	12.6	13.1	9.0	5.8	10.7	13.7	12.4	10.3	8.5	8.5
Shareholders' equity (FIM m)	670	994	1123	1224	1246	1246	1517	1564	1648	1973
Balance sheet total (FIM m)	1831	2257	2493	2872	2702	3268	3302	3071	3175	3678
Equity ratio (%)	36	44.3	46.0	46.7	47.3	44.3	46.5	51.4	52.1	54.0
Quick ratio	0.8	1.0	0.8	0.8	0.9	0.8	1.0	1.1	0.9	1.1
Current ratio	1.6	1.7	1.6	1.5	1.6	1.5	1.6	1.6	1.6	1.8
Gross investments (FIM m)	101	329	269	462	197	293	174	188	380	387
Percentage of turnover	5.0	15.1	10.8	18.1	8.5	9.5	4.9	5.3	11.8	9.9
R&D expenditure (FIM m)	16	28	31	52	31	35	40	54	54	87
Percentage of turnover	0.8	1.3	1.2	2.0	1.3	1.1	1.1	1.5	1.7	2.2
Direct taxes (FIM m)	5	10	27	25	20	20	47	21	32	64
No. of employees	1538	1581	1877	1987	803	1985	2106	1958	2054	2365

[a] Before appropriations, taxes and minority interest.

Source: Raisio Group annual reports.

The Benecol Launch

Raisio launched Benecol margarine with a retail price of around FIM25 ($4.50) for a 250 g tub—this compared with FIM4 for regular margarine. Despite the high price, the product flew off the shelves as quickly as it appeared and Raisio was forced to institute a system of rationing supplies to distributors. During 1996, Raisio estimated that it was only able to satisfy about two-thirds of domestic demand.

To facilitate the speedy development of the Benecol business, in March 1996 Benecol margarine was transferred from the margarine subdivision to a separate

Benecol unit. The unit was headed by Jukka Kaitaranta, who reported to deputy chief executive and head of the Food Division, Jukka Maki. It was intended that, during 1997, Benecol would become a separate division within Raisio. The Benecol Unit was responsible for developing all aspects of the business. It was responsible for acquiring plant sterol, producing stanol ester, managing international publicity for the project and conducting research.

The key problem was limited supplies of the active ingredient, stanol ester. While plant sterols—the raw material from which stanol ester is produced—are a common byproduct of industries that mass-process vegetable matter, almost no one had the systems in place to collect them. Raisio's primary source of supply of plant stanols was UPM-Kymmene, Europe's biggest pulp and paper company. During 1996, it negotiated increased supplies from UPM-Kymmene and also sought access to sterols from vegetable oil processors. Also in 1996, the Group built its first stanol ester plant, which was located in Raisio, and announced plans for a second plant to bring total stanol ester capacity up to 2000 tonnes a year by January 1998. Mr. Kari Jokinen, chief executive of Raisio's margarine division, estimated that this production of stanol ester would allow the production of 25 million kg of margarine, which could supply a total market of 60 million people.[5] The Benecol Unit also began work on a new 1500 m^2 R&D laboratory at Raisio's main industrial site.

During 1996, Raisio began planning for the international launch of Benecol. Its first overseas market was to be Sweden. The Swedish launch would be facilitated by Raisio's acquisition of a 77.5% stake in Carlshamm Mejeri AB, one of Sweden's main margarine producers, for $44.4 million. However, Raisio's horizons were not limited to Scandinavia—nor even to Europe. Benecol margarine was seen as having a huge international potential. Sales to the U.S. market could be massive, given that Americans spent some $33 billion a year on health foods and slimming products. Some estimates suggested that sales of Benecol margarine could reach $3 billion.

By January 1997, Raisio was being bombarded with requests and proposals from all over the world. Sainsbury's, at the time Britain's leading supermarket chain, requested an own-label version of Benecol margarine.[6] Other food processing companies were interested in purchasing licenses either for Benecol margarine or for Raisio's stanol ester technology, or for both.

Raisio's senior executives recognized that product formulation, marketing strategy and distribution policies would need to be adapted to the requirements of different national markets. Moreover, there were complex national regulations relating to the marketing of food products—especially those that included additives claiming to have health benefits. The Raisio executives were especially interested in an approach from McNeil Consumer Products, a division of the U.S.-based pharmaceutical and consumer products company Johnson & Johnson. McNeil was the world's biggest supplier of over-the-counter medicines and was known by its leading brand-name products such as Tylenol, Imodium, and Motrin. McNeil was headquartered in Fort Washington, Pennsylvania and was able to field a range of relevant resources—not least Johnson & Johnson's worldwide marketing and distribution system.

Competition

In formulating a strategy for the global exploitation of Benecol, Raisio faced a number of uncertainties. One issue that especially concerned Raisio executives was the potential for Benecol to encounter competition. In 1991, Raisio had filed its first patent relating to its process for the production of stanol ester from plant sterols and for its use in reducing cholesterol as an additive to human foods. In 1996, its first U.S. patent relating to stanol ester was issued. In the same year, Raisio filed a broader patent relating to the processing and use of stanol ester (see the Appendix). However, a number of competing products were available for reducing cholesterol. In particular, the cholesterol-reducing properties of naturally available plant sterols were well known. While Raisio believed it owned the only effective means for converting plant sterols into a fat-soluble form, it thought it likely that other processes might offer alternative approaches to the use of plant sterols as a food additive. Tor Bergman, head of chemicals (and soon to be appointed head of the Benecol Division as well) reckoned that Raisio had an 18- to 24-month lead over competitors.

Apart from plant sterols and stanols, a growing array of cholesterol-reducing drugs was available on the market. The major category was statins, which included lovastatin (brand name Mevacor), simvastatin (brand name Zocor), pravastatin (brand name Pravachol), fluvastatin (brand name Lescol) and atorvastatin (brand name Lipitor). Statins worked through slowing down the production of cholesterol by the body and by increasing the liver's ability to remove the LDL-cholesterol already in the blood.

In addition there are a number of natural food products that have the effect of reducing cholesterol within the blood. These include fish oil, garlic, flax seed, dietary fiber, policosanol (fatty alcohols derived from waxes of sugar cane) and guggulipid (an ancient herb from India).

Regulation

Benecol margarine falls into a wide category of products generally referred to as "nutraceuticals" or "functional foods." These are food products or supplements that may have a functional or physiological effect that is beneficial. Nutraceuticals have traditionally included food supplements such as vitamin pills, herbal products and more recently food products with additives that offer particular nutritional benefits—energy-enhancing drinks, vitamin-enriched cereals and the like. Nutraceuticals occupy a middle ground between food and medicines. The regulations relating to them also fall between food regulations and drug regulations. They also vary greatly between countries. Japan was one of the few countries that recognized functional foods as a distinct category and, since 1991, has had a well-developed administrative system for vetting and approving health claims relating to food. Canada, on the other hand, made no distinction between functional foods and drugs in relation to health claims—inevitably, this resulted in a highly restrictive regulatory climate for functional foods. Typically, regulations required that claims regarding the beneficial effects of food products could only be *health* claims (improved health) and not *medicinal* claims (claims relating to the prevention or cure of a disease). The most important markets for Benecol would be the U.S. and European Union. Here the regulations were far from clear cut (see Exhibit 11.2).

The Emerging Strategy

Until the beginning of 1997, Raisio had pursued a largely self-sufficient strategy for the exploitation of its stanol ester technology. It had fabricated stanol ester itself in its own plant using its own technology. Rather than selling the stanol ester to other

EXHIBIT 11.2

Country Regulations Relating to "Functional Foods"

United States

Under the 1990 Nutrition Labeling and Education Act (NLEA), the U.S. Food and Drug Administration allowed health claims in the case of certain well-documented relationships, for example between calcium and osteoporosis and sodium and hypertension.

The 1997 Food and Drug Administration Modernization Act (FDAMA) allowed for two types of health claim:

- Authoritative statement health claims (for example, relating to whole grain foods and risk of heart disease and certain cancers, and potassium and risk of high blood pressure and stroke).

- Qualified claims restricted to dietary supplements—typically in the form of pills, capsules, tablets or liquids, labeled as dietary supplements and not represented or marketed for consumption as a conventional food or sole item of a meal. Such claims could be based on a preponderance of scientific evidence.

In practice this meant three possible paths for gaining approval of a food product offering stated heath benefits:

- As a dietary supplement. This was the simplest path. The applicant had to file notification to the FDA 60 days prior to commercial rollout together with supporting evidence.

- As a food additive. This was a more time-consuming process involving much stronger evidence and a determination by an independent panel of experts assembled by the applicant and reporting to the FDA.

- As a pharmaceutical. Finally, a new food product could be approved as a drug. This process typically required several years.

Canada

The Canadian Food and Drug Act stipulated that all products represented for the cure, treatment, mitigation, prevention, risk reduction, and correction or modification of body structure and function are regulated as a "drug" regardless of the available scientific evidence.

European Union

During the 1990s the EU was in the process of harmonizing legislation among its individual member countries regarding health claims for food products. Regulation No. 258/97 concerning novel foods and novel food ingredients applied to new foods or ingredients that were primary molecular structures, micro-organisms, or were isolated from plants or isolated from animals (but this was not applicable to food additives). Such novel foods were to be assessed by the government of a member state, which would make an initial assessment to determine whether the product met EU standards of safety and accurate labeling and whether an additional assessment was needed.

If neither the Commission nor the Member States raise an objection, and if no additional assessment is required, the Member State informs the applicant that he may place the product on the market . . . Any decision or provision concerning a novel food or food ingredient which is likely to have an effect on public health must be referred to the Scientific Committee for Food.

Fast-track approval was possible for products that were essentially similar to products already on the market but entirely new products required a full assessment by the Scientific Committee for Food. It would appear that Benecol was a new food product (given its first-time use of stanol ester). However, the fact that it had already been marketed in Finland before the EU's regulation had taken effect might provide it with a loophole to avoid full-assessment approval.

Japan

In 1991, Japan became the first global jurisdiction to implement a regulatory system for functional foods. Under the Japanese system, "foods for specific health use" (FOSHU) had a specific regulatory approval process separate from foods fortified with vitamins and minerals and dietary supplements not carrying FOSHU claims. "Foods for specific health use" are defined as "foods in the case of which specified effects contributing to maintain health can be expected based on the available data concerning the relationship

between the foods'/food's contents and health, as well as foods with permitted labeling which indicates the consumer can expect certain health effects upon intake of these particular foods." Approved FOSHU bear a seal of approval from the Japanese Ministry of Health, Labor and Welfare (MHLW) identifying their role in disease prevention and health promotion. To achieve FOSHU status and an approved health claim, companies submit a scientific dossier to MHLW, which includes scientific documentation demonstrating the medical and nutritional basis for the health claim, including the recommended dose of the functional ingredient. The MHLW has established a detailed approval process, which typically takes about one year to complete. Japan was estimated to have the world's second largest functional food market behind the U.S.

Sources: Michael H. Moffett and Stacey Wolff Howard, *Benecol: Raisio's Global Nutraceutical*, (Thunderbird, The American Graduate School of International Management, 1999). Sean A. MacDonald, "A Comparative Analysis of the Regulatory Framework Affecting Functional Food and Functional Food Ingredient Development and Commercialization in Canada, the United States (U.S.), the European Union (E.U.), Japan and Australia/New Zealand," *Agriculture and Agri-Food Canada*, (August, 2004).

food manufacturers for incorporation into their own products, it had followed a strategy of vertical integration. Its stanol ester was used only in its own branded margarine, Benecol, which was produced in its own factories and marketed and distributed through its own sales and distribution system.

If it was to exploit the full potential of its innovation, Raisio would need to draw upon the resources of other companies. Clearly the market for cholesterol-reducing foods was worldwide. Moreover, the potential for using stanol ester in foods was not restricted to margarine. Raisio envisaged its use in a variety of health-food products, including salad dressings, dairy products and snack bars. If Raisio's stanol ester technology was to be exploited effectively throughout the EU, in North America, the Far East, and Australasia, then this would require food-processing facilities, market knowledge, regulatory know-how, and distribution facilities, the provision of which was quite beyond Raisio's ability. Time was a critical issue. Raisio patents related to its own process of producing stanol ester and incorporating it within food products. While Raisio's technology and the patent protection it had received bought it a few years' lead-time, it was likely that other companies would find alternative approaches to the use of plant sterols as a cholesterol-reducing food additive.

In Johnson & Johnson, Raisio had a potential partner that had the capabilities needed to introduce Benecol margarine—and other Benecol products—to the world market. Johnson & Johnson possessed global manufacturing, marketing, and distribution capabilities, together with extensive experience in the food and drug approval procedures of the U.S., Europe and most other countries. It was widely considered to be one of the most effective health product-marketing companies in the world, with an outstanding reputation for quality and social responsibility, a global sales and distribution reach, and vast experience in guiding products through government regulations relating to foods and drugs. It viewed nutraceuticals as an important strand of its growth strategy. Its first nutraceutical was Lactaid for people unable to digest lactose. Lactaid was sold in caplets and as lactose-reduced milk and lactose-free foods. It also supplied sucralose, a low-calorie sweetener that had been approved by the U.S. Food and Drug Administration and was sold in nearly 30 countries.

At the same time, there were voices within Raisio that saw risks in an exclusive relationship with Johnson & Johnson. If stanol ester was a potential additive to a wide range of products, did it make sense for Raisio to become identified with a single product—margarine—and was it desirable for Raisio to link its fortunes with a single partner? An alternative approach for Raisio would be to focus on the supply of its key ingredient, stanol ester. At one meeting of Raisio's executive committee, the case of Monsanto and NutraSweet was discussed. It was noted that following the development of NutraSweet (the branded name for aspartame), Monsanto did not forward integrate into the production of diet foods and beverages, but became a supplier of NutraSweet to a wide range of different beverage suppliers and food processors.

In relation to the production and supply of stanol ester, Raisio also faced some critical strategic choices. The crucial problem in 1996 appeared to be limited capacity for producing stanol ester. Even with a new plant planned for 1997, Raisio would still be unable to supply the potential market for Benecol margarine in Finland and nearby markets. If, as anticipated, the demand for Benecol products was to be worldwide, it would need to produce stanol ester in all regions where Benecol products were manufactured and marketed. Thus, even if Raisio agreed a licensing agreement with Johnson & Johnson to produce and market Benecol products, Raisio would need to specify the terms under which stanol ester would be supplied. All Raisio's sterol requirements were supplied by the pulp and paper group, UPM-Kymmene. Raisio had cooperated closely with UPM-Kymmene in developing the technology for separating plant sterols during wood pulp processing. To ensure access to adequate supplies of plant sterols for its stanol ester production, Raisio would need to collaborate closely with the processors of forest and agricultural products. Raisio was considering forming a joint venture with UPM-Kymmene specifically for the extraction and supply of plant sterols. Irrespective of whether the global licensing deal with J&J for the production and distribution of Benecol products went ahead, Raisio faced critical decisions with regard to the production of stanol ester and the supply of plant sterols. Should it keep its production of stanol ester in-house, or should it license this technology also?

Case B: Developments 1997–2000

The Agreement with Johnson & Johnson

During 1997, negotiations between Raisio Group and Johnson & Johnson's McNeil subsidiary progressed to the point where an agreement was signed between the two companies. Raisio's 1997 annual report outlined the deal:

> In July 1997, the Raisio Group signed a cooperation agreement with the American McNeil Consumer Products Company, which is part of the Johnson & Johnson Group. The contract gives McNeil the sole right to use the Benecol trademark and patents on the U.S., Canadian, and Mexican markets. The Raisio Group retains the right to supply the stanol ester required for the products. McNeil aims to introduce the first products during 1998. Raisio received a lump payment for assignment of these license rights and will receive remunerations related to operative development and royalties for the sales of Benecol products and for deliveries of stanol ester.
>
> Johnson & Johnson is the world's biggest and most versatile producer of health-related products. Its turnover totaled U.S.$21.6 billion in 1996 and it has 170 operative companies in 50 countries.
>
> In November a new letter of intent was signed, which will extend cooperation with Johnson & Johnson to global dimensions. Europe and Japan will take their places by the side of the United States as the chief Benecol markets. The agreement also includes a plan to strengthen the position of the Benecol brand by cooperating with other companies producing strong brands that fit in with the Benecol product family. The letter of intent leads to a final agreement on March 2, 1998.
>
> These agreements confirm the principle that the Raisio Group will keep the entire production of stanol ester in its own hands and will develop Benecol production and marketing in Finland and neighboring areas. Global marketing will be carried out with a strong and skilled cooperation partner.[7]

Expectations for Benecol were high. Raisio's consultants estimated total worldwide sales of nutraceuticals at $35 billion a year, excluding supplements (such as vitamins and minerals). Of these, functional foods comprised about one-third ($10–12 billion) with an annual growth of 25–35%. If consumer reaction to Benecol in other industrialized nations was anything like that in Finland, Benecol promised to be a blockbuster. By the beginning of 1998, Raisio's share price exceeded EUR12—up 1200% over three years.

The agreement would involve close cooperation between Raisio and Johnson & Johnson. Not only would Raisio be supplying J&J with stanol ester—the agreement also provided for the two companies to coordinate medical and clinical research and marketing and cooperate in product development on a project-by-project basis.

Putting together the partnership with J&J was the dominant priority of Raisio's top management during the first half of 1997. As a result, several other initiatives were put on hold. Raisio's 1997 annual report noted that: "The introduction of Benecol products was delayed on the Finnish market because of the extensive license negotiations at group level and the need to adopt a common approach on all markets."[8]

Stanol Ester Production

Given the optimism for worldwide sales of Benecol and Raisio's current inability to meet home demand because of a shortage of stanol ester, the worldwide launch of Benecol margarine depended critically on expanding the production of stanol ester.

The first priority was increasing Raisio's purchases of plant sterol. Raisio's 1997 annual report described the quest:

> The plant sterol needed to produce stanol ester has from the very beginning been supplied by Kaukus Oy, part of the UPM-Kymmene Group. Kaukas separates the sterol during the pulp cooking process and is a pioneer in sterol separation techniques.
>
> In April 1997, Raisio and UPM-Kymmene set up a joint venture called Sterol Technologies Ltd. Raisio's holding is 65%. The company develops sterol separation methods and markets them to the forest industry. In October 1997, Sterol Technologies began to build an experimental sterol recovery unit at the Kaukas mill, which is scheduled for completion in March 1998.
>
> An agreement has been made with the French company Les Derives Raisiniques et Terpeniques to achieve a major increase in its sterol production. The new plant covered by the agreement should go on stream in 1999. The entire additional capacity has been reserved for Raisio Benecol.
>
> In August, a letter of intent was signed with the American Westvaco Corporation on cooperation in studying ways of producing plant sterol in America. The aim is to build a sterol production plant in South Carolina to go on stream in 2000.
>
> In November, an agreement was signed with the Chilean company Harting S.A. on establishing a joint venture called Detsa S.A. in Chile. Raisio's holding is 49%. Detsa will build a sterol plant and Sterol Technologies will be responsible for the technology.
>
> When the Detsa plant is completed in 1999, Raisio Benecol will have close to 400 tonnes of raw sterol a year at its disposal. Refined into stanol ester, this amount will satisfy the daily needs of 4 million people. If the percentage of population accounted for by users of Benecol settles at the same level as in Finland, this amount will be sufficient to supply markets comprising close on 200 million consumers.[9]

Raisio had been operating a prototype stanol ester plant at its headquarters since 1996. It had planned to build an adjoining unit to expand stanol ester production. However, following the J&J deal Raisio decided that the priority was to begin stanol ester production in America. Hence, in June 1997, Raisio began construction of a stanol ester plant at Charleston, South Carolina.

The International Launch

United States

During 1998, J&J planned for the launch of Benecol margarine both in the U.S. and Europe. After considerable analysis and discussion, J&J decided that, for the purposes of meeting the FDA regulations, it would introduce Benecol spreads to the U.S. market as a dietary supplement. As Exhibit 11.2 explains, this would involve the least delay and would allow J&J to promote Benecol's cholesterol-reducing benefits.

However, in October 1998, a letter from the FDA torpedoed the U.S. launch:

> The purpose of this letter is to inform you that marketing the product with the prototype label . . . would be illegal under the Federal Food, Drug and Cosmetic Act . . . The label for the Benecol spread, through the statement that the product replaces butter or margarine, vignettes picturing the product in common butter or margarine uses, statements promoting the texture and flavor of the product, and statements such as ". . . helps you manage your cholesterol naturally through the food you eat," represents this product for use as a conventional food. Therefore, the product is not a dietary supplement.

As a food with an additive that had not been approved as safe, Benecol margarine was subject to FDA regulation and J&J would have to embark on the protracted process of submitting evidence of stanol ester's safety and efficacy.

Johnson & Johnson halted the U.S. launch of Benecol and decided that it would introduce the product as a food product without any explicit health claims. By early 1999 Benecol received "Generally Recognized As Safe" (GRAS) status from a panel of independent experts that allowed Benecol to be launched in May 1999.

Europe

In Europe, J&J avoided the regulatory tussles that had delayed the U.S. launch of Benecol, principally because the 1995 introduction into Finland had predated the new EU regulations. Nevertheless, the European launch still needed to take account of different national regulations and Benecol's formulation also needed to be adapted to different national preferences. In March 1999, Benecol was launched in the U.K., and in Belgium, the Netherlands, and Luxemburg in September. The European launch comprised four products: regular and low-fat Benecol spread (margarine) and a natural and a herb cheese spread. In the fall of 2000, Benecol products were launched in Sweden and Denmark.

Competition

Unilever

The delays to Benecol's international launch eliminated Raisio's first-mover advantage in cholesterol-reducing margarine. Almost simultaneous with Benecol's U.S. debut, Unilever launched its rival product, Take Control, which contained sterol esters derived from vegetable oil. Because Take Control's sterol esters were simpler and less expensive to prepare than Raisio's stanol ester (it did not require a complex hydrogenation process), the Unilever product could be sold at a lower price. Initially, Raisio and J&J were not overly concerned at the price differential, in the belief that stanol ester was more effective than sterol ester in cholesterol reduction. However, some new research suggested that the differential was probably very small.

In September 2000, Raisio and J&J received some rare good news from the FDA. After a careful review of the evidence, the FDA had determined that J&J could issue explicit health claims for the effects of stanol ester within Benecol margarine in reducing coronary heart disease. The only downside was that the ruling gave equal rights to Unilever for its sterol ester ingredient.

Despite overcoming the regulatory hurdles, the market reaction to Benecol was disappointing. Johnson & Johnson spent $49 million on advertising Benecol within the U.S., but U.S. retail sales for Benecol between May and December 1999 reached just $17 million. Another estimate put U.S. sales between May 1999 and August 2000 at $42 million.

Unilever's initial launch met similar results. During 1999 it was estimated that Take Control was supported by $15 million in advertising only to generate $13 million in sales. By January 2000, Take Control had gained 1.6% of the U.S. margarine market, with Benecol holding 1.2%. In response to this poor consumer response, J&J shifted the emphasis of its marketing strategy from consumer advertising to providing information to U.S. doctors on the health benefits of Benecol.

In Europe, J&J was able to enter the market for cholesterol-reducing margarine before Unilever in most countries. Unilever launched its sterol ester margarine as "Pro-activ"—an extension to its existing Flora and Becel ranges of low saturated fat margarines. In the U.K., Unilever's Flora Pro-activ was launched early in 2000—nine months after Benecol. Yet, Unilever's superior sales and distribution for grocery products and its lower price (Benecol retailed at £2.49 per 250 g pack compared with Flora Pro-activ at £1.99) meant that Unilever soon had twice the market share of Benecol. Market observers also noted that Unilever's marketing was more effective than J&J's:

> The brand is backed by the Flora Project, a nutrition marketing effort that educates people about heart disease prevention including diet, smoking cessation, lifestyle habits and exercise. Flora sponsors the London marathon, as well as other sporting events. Before Pro-activ came onto the market, tubs of regular Flora already bore the words, "as part of a healthy diet helps lower cholesterol," a statement scientifically backed by Unilever. Moreover, the Flora name had a massive "share of mind"—from the 1980s until the mid-1990s, the Flora brand accounted for 60% of media spending in the spreads category. Because Flora was associated in consumers' minds for 30 years with heart health—and with good taste—it was logical to leverage the Flora brand assets.
>
> The London Flora marathon seamlessly became the London Flora Pro-activ marathon. There is little company communication about the ingredient—the words "plant sterols" are mentioned only on about page six of the information leaflet. But that is as it should be—Unilever is selling the benefits of Flora, a known and trusted food brand; it is not selling plant sterols, specifically.
>
> In contrast, rival Johnson & Johnson's McNeil Consumer Products group had no pre-existing supermarket brand to extend when it launched the cholesterol-lowering spread, Benecol, in Finland in late 1995 (then owned by Raisio). Benecol, therefore, started out with zero brand equity in the U.K. By the time Pro-activ joined it on the market, Benecol had garnered $30 million in sales—no small achievement for an entirely new brand—and it held a 0.5 per cent volume share and 2.5 per cent value share.
>
> As the brand creator, Benecol had to set the price point, which it did at seven times the price of regular spreads. In response, Unilever added to Pro-activ's competitive advantage by bringing it to market 25 per cent cheaper than Benecol.
>
> Add to these factors the massive brand equity of the Flora name, and it is no surprise that Flora Pro-activ is now outselling Benecol in the U.K. by a factor of almost three-to-one.[10]

Other Competitors

Unilever was not the only company interested in the market for stanol and sterol esters. By 2000, some of Raisio's worst fears were being realized. Several companies had either entered the market for cholesterol-reducing nutraceuticals, or had announced their intention to enter:

- *Forbes Medi-Tech and Novartis.* In April 1999, the Swiss pharmaceutical company Novartis signed a five-year agreement with Canadian biotechnology company Forbes Medi-Tech to license Phytrol—a plant sterol-based ingredient with similar cholesterol-reducing properties to stanol ester. Novartis would become responsible for clinical trials, regulatory submissions, and commercialization of end products. Phytrol (marketed also as Reducol) received FDA "Generally Recognized As Safe" approval in May 2000.[11] In 2000, Novartis announced a joint venture with Quaker Oats to form Altus Foods, which would manufacture healthy foods containing Phytrol. Novartis launched a number of products including breakfast cereals and cereal bars under the Aviva brand name. However, market response was, at best, tepid. In the U.K., the Aviva range was withdrawn six months after the launch.

- *Paulig.* In July 1999, Finland's Paulig (a company known for its coffee and spice operations) announced its own plant sterol ingredient, Teriaka, derived from maize, soy and pine trees. Because its manufacture utilizes normal processing technology and does not require chemical synthesis or high temperatures/pressures, it was believed that it could gain quick approval under the EU's Novel Foods Regulations.

- *Procter & Gamble* introduced a line of cooking oils containing sterol esters under the brand name CookSmart.

- *Archer Daniels Midland* developed a patent-pending sterol ingredient that is dispersible in liquids, allowing sterols to be added to beverages, milk products, and other water-based and non-fat products.

- *Monsanto* in 2000 received a patent on a "phytosterol protein complex" composed of sterols, proteins, and edible oil. The product claimed to enhance the cholesterol-reducing effects of sterols.

Mounting Crisis

During 2000, Raisio was incurring rapidly increasing losses from its Benecol Division. During the first half of 2000, it reported losses of €44.0 million, mostly resulting from a non-recurring charge of €38.0 million. This compared with a profit that totaled €11.2 million during the corresponding period in 1999 (although this resulted entirely from a one-time payment under the agreement with J&J). Between the first half of 1999 and first half of 2000, revenues for the first six months of Raisio's Benecol Division were down from €47 million to €16 million, reflecting the end of payments from J&J and sharply reduced sales of stanol ester to J&J. Tables 11.2 and 11.3 show Raisio's financial performance between 1996 and 2000.

The company's report for the first half of 2000 analyzed the problems:

The development of the Group's Benecol business derives from a vision dating back to 1996–7 which predicted a rapid and impressive rise in Benecol

TABLE 11.2 Raisio Group financial indicators, 1996–2000

	1996	1997	1998	1999	2000
Sales and operations					
Turnover (€m)	661	858	833	763	800
Change (%)	+22	+30	−3	−8	+5
Exports from Finland (€m)	124	135	178	145	131
Total international turnover (€m)	259	423	421	374	399
Percentage of turnover	39.2	49.3	50.5	49.0	49.9
Gross investments (€m)	65	73	75	61	49
R&D expenditure (€m)	15	17	18	16	18
Percentage of turnover	2.2	1.9	2.1	2.1	2.3
Average personnel	2365	2817	2904	2897	2775
Profitability					
Operating result (€m)	33	41	52	16	−32
% of turnover	5.0	4.8	6.3	2.1	−4.0
Result before extraordinary items (€m)	28	35	42	6	−47
Result before taxes and minority interest (€m)	27	20	39	−2	−47
Percentage of turnover	4.1	2.3	4.7	−0.3	−5.8
Return on equity (ROE) (%)	4.5	7.8	9.2	0.4	−14.9
Return on investment (ROI) (%)	9.2	10.1	11.1	4.0	−4.2
Financial and economical position					
Shareholders' equity (€m)	291	298	317	304	260
Net interest-bearing liabilities (€m)	119	143	174	233	251
Balance sheet total (€m)	619	643	690	744	750
Equity ratio (%)	47.3	46.6	46.0	41.0	34.7
Quick ratio	1.1	0.8	0.7	0.6	0.7
Current ratio	1.8	1.5	1.2	1.2	1.2
Cash flow from business operations	43	60	47	6	16

Source: Raisio Group 2000 Annual Report.

TABLE 11.3 Raisio Group divisional performance, 1997–2000 (millions of euros)

		1997	1998	1999	2000
Benecol	Turnover	16	48	52	23
	Operating profit	n.a.	n.a.	7.5	−45.6
Margarine	Turnover	282	235	200	204
	Operating profit	n.a.	n.a.	79.5	78.0
Grain	Turnover	287	274	235	244
	Operating profit	n.a.	n.a.	0.8	0.7
Chemicals	Turnover	278	277	299	347
	Operating profit	n.a.	n.a.	20.3	11.9

n.a. = not available.
Source: Raisio Group annual reports, 1998–2000.

products containing stanol ester into global functional foods. This vision was based on Raisio and McNeil's joint assessment and on market and need analyses by leading international consultants.

Raisio then made safeguarding long-term availability of the main raw material in Benecol products—sterol—its strategic goal. Action aimed at large-scale procurement of sterol was therefore taken immediately on both the plant and the wood sterol markets. Plant sterols were acquired under long-term purchasing agreements, as world supply was limited and indeed inadequate for the targets then set for Benecol operations.

The limited nature of plant sterol production thus faced Raisio with a strategic challenge, in view of which several projects were launched aimed at developing more wood sterol separation. The biggest are a tall oil and sterol separation project in Chile (Detsa) and the Westerol project planned for North America. Supplies of wood sterol were also ensured through various contracting and financing arrangements.

Since the launch in Finland in 1995, however, Benecol products have actually reached the market only in the U.S.A., U.K., Ireland and the Benelux countries, and mainly only in the second half of 1999, and in Sweden and Denmark this autumn. Market penetration has thus been slower than expected, partly due to regulatory obstacles. Current experience suggests that the expectations concerning cholesterol-reducing foods on which Raisio's plans were based were overly optimistic. So far, less than 20% of the targets have been achieved.

As a result of its high expectations and targets, Raisio has tied up substantial resources in both wood sterol projects and sterol and stanol stocks. In today's market situation, however, the company has had to review and reassess its sterol strategy and the preconditions for completing ongoing projects, as well as the value of the sterols and stanols already procured.

To stem the losses, Raisio renegotiated several of its long-term sterol purchase agreements, withdrew from its sterol separation joint venture in Chile and suspended its Solexin plant sterol project in New Zealand. Other sterol separation projects were to be reviewed on a case-by-case basis. Inventories of sterol and stanol were revalued at current market prices and several of the fixed assets involved written down.

The central problem, Raisio believed, lay with the agreement with J&J. Johnson & Johnson's worldwide license meant that Raisio was completely dependent on J&J's commitment to Benecol and the success of J&J's marketing strategy. Observing Unilever's ability to push Benecol into second place in the U.S. and Europe, many at Raisio believed that the company had backed the wrong horse. Despite J&J's expertise with FDA regulations and healthcare, and its massive R&D budget, in terms of marketing food products and selling to supermarkets, J&J like other big pharmaceutical companies had limited expertise and channel power in branded, packaged foods.

During 2000, Raisio's share price was in free fall. By October 2000, Raisio's shares had lost 85% of their value compared with the peak in mid-1998 (see Figure 11.2). CEO Tor Bergman, who, as head of Raisio's Chemical Division and head of the Benecol Division, had been the primary architect of the Benecol strategy, was the main casualty of the collapse. He left Raisio in August 2000 and was replaced as CEO by Lasse Kurkilahti. The new CEO's review of 2000 was in

FIGURE 11.2 Raisio Group plc, price of unrestricted shares (Helsinki Stock Exchange).

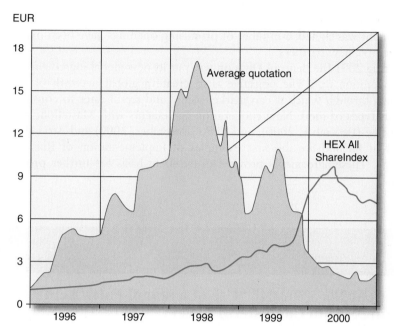

Note: Figures 11.1 and 11.2 are not directly comparable because of a 10:1 share split in June 1998. Figure 11.2 shows Raisio's share price adjusted for the share split.

sharp contrast to the optimistic tone of previous communications to shareholders. After acknowledging 2000 to be "the worst in the past ten years," he went on to outline the challenge of Raisio competing internationally:

> Earlier, Raisio competed with Finnish and Nordic companies; now, its competitors are European or global players . . . The diversified enterprises that formed during the '80s in a closed economy will not survive in today's open economy, where a business's only hope lies in being competitive. The Raisio Group has to focus its resources on the fewer fields.[12]

Benecol would occupy a prominent position among these "fewer fields." However, to succeed, the Division needed a new strategy. The starting point was a new relationship with J&J. By December 2000, a new agreement was reached:

> . . . This gives the Benecol Division the opportunity to implement a global strategy concentrating on functional food ingredients—that is, stanol and sterol ester—in certain clinical areas. The new agreement covers two main aspects of the Benecol stanol ester business. The companies agreed that McNeil would concentrate on markets in North America, the EU (excluding Finland, Sweden and Denmark), Japan and China. Raisio's market area, in turn, comprises Scandinavia, the Baltic region, the former East European countries, the Near East, Latin America, the Far East and Oceania. The two

companies also agreed on a new market-driven delivery agreement for Benecol ingredients. Further, Raisio acquired global rights to sell and market sterol ester. Both companies may agree independently to involve third parties in their market areas in order to expand the product range. Since the agreement was signed, a number of promising openings have been made with prospective new partners . . .

During 2001 the Benecol Division will put its new global ingredient strategy into operation . . . The objective is to create a global network of business partners through which it can market stanol and sterol ester to consumers in various types of food. New cooperation agreements with Mastellone Hnos in Argentine (December, 2000), and Valio (December, 2000) and Atria (January, 2001) in Finland are the first examples of implementation of Raisio's new strategy. These agreements provide an excellent basis for further progress in 2001.[13]

Appendix: Raisio's Principal Patents Relating to Stanol Ester

U.S. Patent No. 5,502,045 "Use of a Stanol Fatty Acid Ester for Reducing Serum Cholesterol Level"

Inventors: Tatu Miettinen, Hannu Vanhanen, Ingmar Wester.

Assignee: Raision Tehtaat Oy AB

Filed: November 22, 1993

Awarded: March 26, 1996

Abstract

The invention relates to a substance which lowers cholesterol levels in serum and which is a .beta.-sitostanol fatty acid ester or fatty acid ester mixture, and to a method for preparing the same. The substance can be used as such or added to a food.

Claims

We claim:

1 The method of reducing the absorption of cholesterol into the bloodstream comprising orally introducing into the body an effective amount of a substance containing a .beta.-sitostanol fatty acid ester prepared by the interesterification of .beta.-sitostanol with a fatty acid ester containing between 2 and 22 carbon atoms in the presence of an interesterification catalyst.

2 The method according to claim 1, wherein the interesterification of .beta.-sitostanol is carried out in a solvent free food grade process.

3 The method according to claim 2, wherein the interesterification occurs at a temperature of approximately 90 degree-120 degree C and a vacuum of approximately 5–15 mmHg.

4 The method according to claim 3, wherein the catalyst is sodium ethylate.

5 The method of claim 1, wherein the fatty acid ester comprises a mixture of fatty acid esters.

6 The method according to claim 1, wherein the .beta.-sitostanol is prepared by hydrogenation of a commercial .beta.-sitosterol mixture.

7 The method according to claim 1, wherein the interesterification is carried out in the presence of a stoichiometric excess of the fatty acid ester.

8 The method according to claim 1, wherein an effective amount of the substance is between about 0.2 and about 20 grams per day.

Extract from "Description" Section
. . . The present invention relates to the use of a sterol of an entirely different type for lowering the cholesterol level in serum. What is involved is fatty acid esters of alpha-saturated sterols, especially sitostanol fatty acid esters (sitostanol = 24-ethyl-5.alpha. -cholestane-3.beta.-ol), which have been observed to lower cholesterol levels in serum with particular efficacy. The said esters can be prepared or used as such, or they can be added to foods, especially to the fatty part of a food. The sitostanol fatty acid ester mixture is prepared by hardening a commercial .beta.-sitosterol mixture (sitosterol = 24-ethyl-5-cholestene-3.beta.-ol). .beta.-sitostanol can be prepared by a prior-known cholesterol hardening technique by hardening .beta.-sitosterol by means of a Pd/C catalyst in an organic solvent . . . This mixture has the approval of the FDA (Cytellin, Eli Lilly). A hardening degree of over 99% is achieved in the reaction. The catalyst used in the hardening is removed by means of a membrane filter, and the obtained sitostanol is crystallized, washed and dried. In accordance with the invention, the .beta.-sitostanol mixture, which contains campestanol approx. 6%, is esterified with different fatty acid ester mixtures by a commonly known chemical interesterification technique . . . A methyl ester mixture of the fatty acids of any vegetable oil can be used in the reaction. One example is a mixture of rapeseed oil and methyl ester, but any fatty acids which contain approx. 2 to 22 carbon atoms are usable. The method according to the invention for the preparation of stanol fatty acid esters deviates advantageously from the previously patented methods in that no substances other than free stanol, a fatty acid ester or a fatty acid ester mixture, and a catalyst are used in the esterification reaction. The catalyst used may be any known interesterification catalyst, such as Na-ethylate.

U.S. Patent No. 5,958,913 "Substance for Lowering High Cholesterol Level in Serum and Methods for Preparing and Using the Same"

Inventors: Tatu Miettinen, Hannu Vanhanen, Ingmar Wester.
Assignee: Raisio Benecol Ltd.
Filed: November 5, 1996
Awarded: September 28, 1999

Abstract
The invention relates to a substance which lowers LDL cholesterol levels in serum and which is fat soluble .beta.-sitostanol fatty acid ester, and to a method for preparing and using the same. The substance can be taken orally as a food additive,

food substitute or supplement. A daily consumption of the .beta.-sitostanol ester in an amount between about 0.2 and about 20 grams per day has been shown to reduce the absorption of biliary and endogenic cholesterol.

Claims

What is claimed is:

1 A food composition suitable for reducing blood serum cholesterol levels or reducing absorption of cholesterol from the intestines into the bloodstream, the food composition comprising a nutritional substance and a blood serum cholesterol level reducing or cholesterol absorption reducing effective amount of a sterol component comprising at least one 5.alpha.-saturated sterol fatty acid ester.

2 The food composition as claimed in claim 1, wherein the sterol component comprises .beta.-sitostanol fatty acid ester.

3 The food composition as claimed in claim 1, wherein the fatty acid contains about 2 to 22 carbon atoms.

4 The food composition as claimed in claim 2, wherein the fatty acid contains about 2 to 22 carbon atoms.

5 The food composition as claimed in claim 1, wherein the 5.alpha.-saturated sterol fatty acid ester is produced by esterifying the alpha-saturated sterol and a fatty acid ester in a solvent-free food grade process.

6 The food composition as claimed in claim 2, wherein the .beta.-sitostanol fatty acid ester is produced by esterifying .beta.-sitostanol and a fatty acid ester in a solvent-free food grade process.

7 The food composition as claimed in claim 5, wherein the esterifying step is conducted in the presence of an esterification catalyst.

8 The food composition as claimed in claim 6, wherein the esterifying step is conducted in the presence of an esterification catalyst.

9 The food composition as claimed in claim 7, wherein the esterification catalyst comprises sodium ethylate.

10 The food composition as claimed in claim 8, wherein the esterification catalyst comprises sodium ethylate.

11 The food composition as claimed in claim 5, wherein the esterifying step is conducted at a temperature of about 90–120 degree C under a vacuum of about 5–15 mmHg.

12 The food composition as claimed in claim 6, wherein the esterifying step is conducted at a temperature of about 90–120 degree C under a vacuum of about 5–15 mmHg.

13 The food composition as claimed in claim 5, wherein the esterifying step is conducted without the presence of additional interesterifiable lipids.

14 The food composition as claimed in claim 6, wherein the esterifying step is conducted without the presence of additional interesterifiable lipids.

15 The food composition as claimed in claim 1, wherein the nutritional substance comprises a member selected from the group consisting of

cooking oil, margarine, butter, mayonnaise, salad dressing and shortening.

16 The food composition as claimed in claim 2, wherein the nutritional substance comprises a member selected from the group consisting of cooking oil, margarine, butter, mayonnaise, salad dressing and shortening.

17 A method for reducing the cholesterol level in blood serum of a subject in need thereof, comprising orally administering to the subject the food composition as claimed in claim 1, wherein the sterol component is present in a blood serum cholesterol level reducing effective amount.

18 A method for reducing the cholesterol level in blood serum of a subject in need thereof, comprising orally administering to the subject the food composition as claimed in claim 2, wherein the sterol component is present in a blood serum cholesterol level reducing effective amount.

19 The method as claimed in claim 17, wherein about 0.2 to 20 grams per day of the sterol component are orally administered.

20 The method as claimed in claim 18, wherein about 0.2 to 20 grams per day of the sterol component are orally administered.

21 A method for reducing the absorption of cholesterol from the intestines into the bloodstream of a subject in need thereof, comprising orally administering to the subject the food composition as claimed in claim 1, wherein the sterol component is present in a cholesterol absorption reducing effective amount.

22 A method for reducing the absorption of cholesterol from the intestines into the bloodstream of a subject in need thereof, comprising orally administering to the subject the food composition as claimed in claim 2, wherein the sterol component is present in a cholesterol absorption reducing effective amount.

23 The method as claimed in claim 21, wherein about 0.2 to 20 grams per day of the sterol component are orally administered.

24 The method as claimed in claim 22, wherein about 0.2 to 20 grams per day of the sterol component are orally administered.

Brief Description of the Invention

The present invention relates to a sterol of an entirely different type for lowering the cholesterol levels in blood serum. The substance comprises a fatty acid ester of alpha saturated sterols, especially sitostanol fatty acid esters, which have been observed to lower cholesterol levels in serum with particular efficacy.

The present invention includes a method of reducing the absorption of cholesterol into the bloodstream from the digestive tract by orally introducing into the body an effective amount of a fatty acid ester of a beta-sitostanol. More preferably, the invention further includes orally introducing between about 0.2 and about 20 grams per day of beta-sitostanol fatty acid ester into the body. The ester is introduced either as a food additive, a food substitute or a food supplement. When used as a food additive, the fatty acid ester of the beta-sitostanol may be added to food products such as cooking oils, margarines, butter, mayonnaise, salad dressings, shortenings, and other foods having an essential fat component.

Notes

1 FIM = Finnish marks. The average exchange rate during 1996 was U.S.$1 = FIM4.54.

2 Raisio Group, "Chief Executive's Review," Annual Report, 1996, p. 3.

3 The company was renamed Raisio Group plc in September 1997. Throughout this case we shall refer to the company as "Raisio Group."

4 Raisio Group, Annual Report, 1997, p. 38.

5 "Market Split over 'Miracle' Margarine," *Financial Times*, October 25, 1996, p. 26.

6 "Wonder spread from Finland," *The Grocer*, May 18, 1996, p. 9.

7 Raisio Group, Annual Report, 1997, p. 39.

8 Raisio Group, Annual Report, 1997, p. 39.

9 Raisio Group, Annual Report, 1997, p. 40.

10 J. Mellentin, "Trusted Brands Sell Healthy Hearts," *Functional Foods and Nutraceuticals*, June 2002.

11 See http://resources.bnet.com/topic/cholesterol+ and+fda.html, accessed 29 October, 2009.

12 Raisio Group, Annual Report, 2000, p. 5.

13 Raisio Group, Annual Report, 2000, p. 19.

Case 12 Rivalry in Video Games

By summer 2009 the world video games industry had entered a new and unusual stage of its development. Between 1995 and 2006 the industry had been dominated by Sony, whose PlayStation had accounted for well over half of world console sales during the previous two product generations. However, in the new generation of video game consoles—the seventh since the industry's origins at the beginning of the 1970s—an entirely new situation had emerged. What was once believed to be a winner-take-all market was now a three-way battle between Sony, Microsoft and Nintendo with unusually small differences between them in market share.[1]

In terms of unit sales, Nintendo's Wii was the outright winner in all three of the world's major markets (see Table 12.1). However, in revenue terms, market shares were almost equal, reflecting the fact that the PS3 ($399 in the U.S.) was considerably more expensive than either the Xbox 360 ($199 in the U.S.) or the Wii ($149 in the

TABLE 12.1 Cumulative sales of leading models of video game console in major markets to March 31, 2009

Console	Japan	U.S.	Europe
Nintendo Wii (million)	8.1	20	15
Microsoft Xbox 360 (million)	1.0	14	9
Sony PlayStation 3 (million)	3.0	7	9

Sources: Estimates based on information from http://en.wikipedia.org/wiki/Seventh-generation_video
_game_console; Forrester Research.

U.S.). The emergence of Nintendo as the new market leader after several years of lagging as a weak third to Sony and Microsoft was a major reversal of fortune. Many observers had written off Nintendo as a serious contender—it seemed to lack the financial or technological muscle to compete against Sony or Microsoft.

As Sony and Microsoft's product development teams prepared for the next generation of competition—both companies were rumored to be planning the launch of new consoles in 2012—the unexpected success of Nintendo's Wii had created considerable confusion for their video game strategies.

The Nintendo Wii had challenged several deeply entrenched assumptions about the video game industry. The evolutionary trajectory of the video game console had been perceived to be towards greater multifunctionality. One of the reasons that Sony and Microsoft had placed so much emphasis on their video game businesses and devoted so many resources to them was because they viewed the video game console as a general-purpose home entertainment device and a mechanism for linking with the internet. As a result, both Sony and Microsoft viewed video game consoles not just as important products in their own right but as critical components of their strategies for building strength within the fast-moving market for home entertainment. For example, Sony had used the PS3 as its standard bearer in its standards battle with Toshiba over technical standards for high-definition video disks. Wii had severely dented this logic—it was a dedicated gaming machine with few of the general entertainment features of PS3 or Xbox 360.

Wii's success also pointed to a major shift in the market for video gaming. The conventional wisdom of the industry had been that the video games market was concentrated among males aged between 11 and 30 and in order to access this demographic group the console makers needed to court "hardcore gamers" when developing and launching new models. The way to attract these sophisticated, intensive consumers was through hardware with immense processing power and brilliant graphics and games that combined cinematic-quality and graphic realism with strong characters and complex storylines. Yet, Wii's main market was among casual gamers. Compared to PS3 and Xbox 360 it was seriously underpowered in terms of both processing speed and graphics. The appeal of its games was the speed with which they could be learned rather than their sophistication.

In developing their video game strategies and their next-generation consoles, a critical issue for Sony and Microsoft was whether Wii was an outlier. If it was, the two companies could continue with the strategic logic that had guided their efforts since the beginning of the twenty-first century. If it was not, then Sony and Microsoft had better imitate the key elements of the Wii strategy. The stakes were high. In recent years the world market for video game hardware and software was about $25 billion. The fact

FIGURE 12.1 Worldwide unit sales of video game consoles by product generation

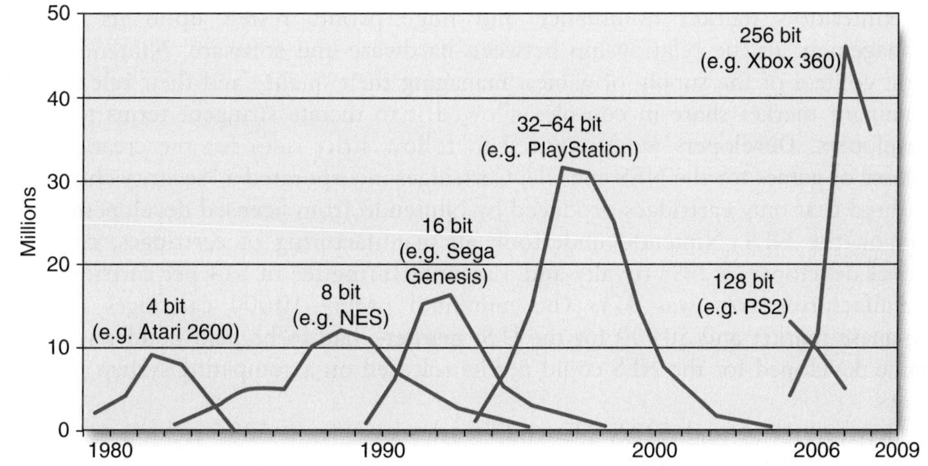

that every new generation of consoles had surpassed the sales of its predecessor (see Figure 12.1), reinforced both firms' interest in capturing market leadership in the future.

History of the Video Game Industry, 1972–2007

Atari and First and Second Generation Consoles: 1972–1985

The home video games market emerged during the late 1970s as an extension of arcade video games. The first generation of home video consoles were dedicated machines that embodied a single game. One of the first of these was *Pong*, created by Nolan Bushnell in 1972. He formed Atari to market this game player. In 1976 Atari was acquired by Warner Communications, Inc.

The second generation of players featured 4-bit processors and interchangeable cartridges. Bushnell designed the Atari 2600 home video game console, which, following the release of *Space Invaders* (1979) and *Pac-Man* (1981), unleashed a craze for video games. By 1982 Atari held almost 80% of the video game market.

Atari was unable to prevent independent software developers from marketing games for the Atari 2600. During 1982, 20 new suppliers of Atari-compatible consoles entered the market and 350 new game titles were released in that year. Declining sales of consoles and oversupply of games caused video game sales to decline from $3 billion in 1982 to $100 million in 1985, resulting in massive losses for Warner.

Nintendo and Third Generation Consoles: 1986–1991

In 1983, Nintendo, the leading Japanese supplier of arcade video games, released its 8-bit Famicom home video system. The U.S. launch of Famicom—renamed the Nintendo Entertainment System (NES)—in fall 1985 was a huge success, selling over a million units during the first year. Nintendo Entertainment System's sales were driven by a series of games created by legendary games developer Sigeru Miyamota: *Donkey Kong, Legend of Zelda* and *Super Mario Brothers* (which eventually sold 40 million copies worldwide). By 1988, Nintendo had an 80% market share of the $2.3 billion U.S. video games industry.

Nintendo's market dominance and huge profits rested upon its careful management of the relationship between hardware and software. Nintendo kept tight control of the supply of games, managing their quality and their releases. Its dominant market share in consoles allowed it to dictate stringent terms to game developers. Developers were required to follow strict rules for the creation and release of games for the NES console. Cartridges incorporated a "security chip" that ensured that only cartridges produced by Nintendo from licensed developers could run on the NES. Nintendo undertook all manufacturing of cartridges, charging games developers a 20% royalty and a manufacturing fee of $14 per cartridge (the manufacturing cost was $7). The minimum order—10 000 cartridges for the Japanese market and 50 000 for the U.S. market—had to be paid in advance. Any game developed for the NES could not be released on a competing system for two years.

Between 1984 and 1992, Nintendo's sales rose from $286 million to $4417 million. By 1990, one-third of U.S. and Japanese households owned an NES and in both countries its share of the home video console market exceeded 90%. Nintendo's return on equity over the period was 23.1%, while its stock market value exceeded that of both Sony and Nissan during most of 1990–1.

Sega and Fourth Generation Consoles: 1992–5

Sega's origins, like Atari and Nintendo, were in arcade games machines. Sega launched its 16-bit Genesis home video system in Japan in October 1988 and in the U.S. in September 1989. Despite graphics and sound that were superior to Nintendo's 8-bit system, sales of Genesis were initially sluggish until the introduction of *Sonic the Hedgehog* in June 1991. With strong support from independent games developers, 130 software titles were available for the Genesis by September 1991.

Nintendo launched its 16-bit machine, the Nintendo Super-NES, in September 1991. Its huge installed base, brand awareness, and distribution strength, allowed it to maintain its leadership in Japan. However, in the U.S. and Europe, Sega's bigger library of 16-bit titles (320, compared with 130 for Nintendo by January 1993) allowed it to split the market with Nintendo.

Sony PlayStation and Fifth Generation Consoles: 1995–8

The new generation of 32-bit consoles was initiated by Sega with the launch of its Saturn console in November 1994. A month later Sony introduced its PlayStation console—the result of a six-year development effort led by Sony's video games guru, Ken Kutaragi. Both PlayStation and Saturn used CD-ROMs rather than cartridges. However, PlayStation was launched with an impressive number of new game titles—the result of courting top games developers, financing game development and providing comprehensive software development tools. Sony also entered with a powerful array of resources: a strong brand reputation, global distribution capability and content from its movie division. Its launch of PlayStation was well-orchestrated and supported by a massive advertising budget—prelaunch promotion included a number of cryptic and ambiguous advertisements that created strong interest within the gamer community. Sega ill-coordinated its Saturn system—few game titles, haphazard distribution and a shortage of manufacturing capacity meant that Sony was able to overtake Sega's early lead.

Meanwhile, Nintendo attempted to recapture market leadership by leapfrogging Sony in technology. The N-64 system—launched in Japan in June 1996, in the U.S. in September 1996 and in Europe in the spring of 1997—used a 64-bit processor and came with several highly popular new games, including *Super Mario 64*. Although the N-64 had a big price advantage over PlayStation ($199 compared to $299) it retained cartridge storage of games. The production of cartridges involved higher fixed costs and did not allow the flexibility to quickly produce and distribute additional copies of hit games.

The result was that Sony pursued a different software strategy from Nintendo. While Nintendo concentrated on a smaller number of big-selling games (the average N-64 title sold over 400,000 units in 1997), Sony went for a much bigger library of games (over 300 titles at any point of time) many of which targeted minority preferences (the average PlayStation game sold 69 000 copies). The outcome was leadership for the PlayStation in all the world's major markets.

The Sixth Generation: Sony versus Microsoft, 1999–2005

The 128-bit generation of video game consoles was inaugurated by Sega's launch of its Dreamcast console in November 1998. It most innovative feature was the capacity for internet connectivity which allowed interactive games playing. Despite a successful initial launch—900 000 units were sold in Japan and 1.5 million in the U.S. during its first three months of their respective launches—Dreamcast failed to deliver a knockout blow to Sony's market leadership. The advantages of 128-bit over 64-bit technology were marginal and standard internet connections did not support fast-action interactive play. Sega attracted limited support from independent developers and failed to find a killer app for its Dreamcast.

On March 4, 2000, Sony launched PlayStation 2 (PS2) in Japan. Although 17 months behind Dreamcast, Sony's periodic leakage of information about PS2 had supported intense pre-release interest in PS2 and had continually undermined Sega's efforts to popularize Dreamcast. Kutaragi's brief had been to design a games machine with performance that exceeded any PC and with graphics processing power ten times that of the original PlayStation. With cinematic-style graphics, a DVD player and the potential for internet connectivity, PS2 aspired to be a multifunctional tool for accessing the internet, offering online games, e-commerce, email, and playing music and videos. According to Kazuo Hirai, president of Sony U.S.: "PlayStation 2 is not the future of video games entertainment, it is the future of entertainment, period."

Yet, despite billions of dollars spent on product development, new manufacturing plants and a massive worldwide advertising campaign, PS2's launch was marred by a shortage of key components—notably the graphics synthesizer (made by Sony) and the "Emotion Engine" microprocessor (made by Toshiba)—resulting in a shortage of PS2s for the critical U.S. Christmas shopping period. There was also a lack of software. The power and sophistication of PS2, together with its technical quirks, created complex problems for developers—most PS2 launch titles were revisions of earlier titles.

For all the massive resources that Sony brought to the battleground for the new generation, success was far from assured—in November 2001 the industry's competitive landscape was transformed by the entry of Microsoft. The software giant's entry was seen as symbolizing the potential of video games consoles. Once viewed as children's toys, games consoles were emerging as the primary tool for electronic entertainment, with the ability to offer movies, music and many of the communications functions currently performed by PCs.

The Xbox was a technology breakthrough: "Arguably the most powerful games console ever made, developed after consultation with more than 5000 gamers and games creators, it has a staggering array of features: an internal hard disk with a 733MHz processor, 64MB of memory, a DVD player, Dolby Digital 5.1 Surround Sound and an Ethernet port that makes it the only game console that's internet-ready and broadband-enabled."[2] Yet, with successive generations of consoles, technological capabilities were becoming less and less a distinguishing factor and the critical differentiator—software—was a problem for Microsoft. Xbox was launched with 19 games available, compared with 200 for PS2.

Despite a successful U.S. launch with 1.5 million sold in the six-week Christmas shopping period, Japan proved to be a difficult market for Xbox—not only were launch sales disappointing but Xbox's reputation was damaged by complaints that it caused scratching of CDs and DVDs. Microsoft's ability to establish itself in a strong second place to Sony rested on three factors: Microsoft's formidable reputation in IT, its launch of blockbuster games *Halo* and *Halo2*, and Xbox's online capabilities. In November 2002, Microsoft launched its Xbox Live online gaming service with interactive gaming and direct downloading of new games. A few days after the launch of Xbox, Nintendo joined the fray with its GameCube console.

The major casualties of the intense competition between Sony and Microsoft were Sega and Nintendo. Despite massive price cutting, Dreamcast sales went into sharp decline even before Microsoft's entry. At the end of 2000, Sega announced its withdrawal from video games hardware to focus on software. Meanwhile Nintendo was trailing both Sony and Microsoft in sales. By December 2006, Sony had sold around 111 million PS2s, compared to 24 million Xboxes, 21 million GameCubes and over 10 million Dreamcasts.

The Seventh Generation: Nintendo Bounces Back

The next round of competition in video game consoles—the seventh generation—featured the three survivors from the previous round: Sony, Microsoft and Nintendo. However, both Sony and Microsoft believed that the market was tending towards a duopoly. Nintendo had neither the financial nor the technological resources to match those of Sony and Microsoft. Yet, these new round of competition would feature some major changes in the competitive dynamics of the video game industry and some surprising reversals of fortune.

Microsoft Xbox 360

The first of the seventh generation video game consoles was Microsoft's Xbox 360 released on November 25, 2005. Xbox 360 was the first major console with a near simultaneous global launch as opposed to a phased rollout. The Japanese launch occurred just two weeks after the North American launch. The launch also features a major shift in the market positioning of Xbox. Compared with the original Xbox, which emphasized processing power and focused on hardcore gamers, Xbox 360's positioning eschewed technology in favor of versatility, design and coolness. The Xbox 360 strategy emphasized the hardware's multifunctionality for home entertainment and Microsoft's strong online presence. Through Xbox Live, users could purchase and download video games, in-game extras such as weapons and costumes, and movies and TV shows—including high-definition TV shows.

Sony PS3

Meanwhile, Sony's launch of its PS3 was dogged with multiple delays. Most of the problems related to the technological ambitiousness of the hardware. PS3's revolutionary multicore cell processor, developed jointly with IBM and Toshiba, proved difficult and expensive to manufacture—it was estimated that each cell processor cost Sony $230 per unit. Even more problematic was the delayed Blu-ray DVD drive, the initial production of which was believed to cost about $350 per unit. Merrill Lynch estimated that the total cost of the components for the PS3 could amount to $900 per unit.[3]

The Blu-ray drive was a central element of Sony's strategy. It was engaged in a fierce standards battle with Toshiba over the technical format of the next generation of high definition DVDs. PS3 was to be a key product in gaining market acceptance of Blu-ray.

Software was another problem for PS3. The complexity and power of the hardware extended the potential and the cost of games written for PS3. Software development costs were estimated at four or five times those of PS2. To encourage developers to write for PS3, Sony was obliged to cut its royalties. At its initial launch, Sony had 15 titles available for PS3, although few made full use of PS3's technical capabilities. The most popular of the new games was *Resistance: Fall of Man.*

PS3's launch in Japan on November 11, 2006 and in North America on November 17 was marred by lack of product. Following both launches, PS3s were selling on online auction sites in Japan and the U.S. at a substantial premium to their retail list prices. The European and Australian launches were set for March 23, 2007. One of the results of product shortage was continuing strength of Sony's PS2. During the critical month of December 2006, Americans bought 1.4 million PS2s, outselling PS3 (491 000 units), Xbox 360 (1.1 million units) and Nintendo Wii (604 000 units).

Nintendo Wii

One of the biggest surprises of the new round of competition was the strong initial showing of Nintendo's Wii. Technologically, the Nintendo Wii lacked the advanced features of either the Xbox 360 or PS3; its primary innovative feature was its remote wand-like controller that was sensitive to a range of hand movements. As a result, Nintendo claimed that its Wii was more intuitive than other consoles and could be learned more easily. This linked with a marketing strategy that aimed to recruit new games players and targeted a very broad demographic—including older consumers. Wii was launched in North America on November 19, 2006, on December 2 in Japan and December 8 in Europe. The launch was accompanied by 16 new games for Wii—of which several were new versions of existing franchises (for example, *Legend of Zelda: Twilight Princess)*. Nintendo also mounted its biggest ever advertising campaign.

Table 12.2 compares the rival seventh generation consoles. Table 12.3 shows unit sales of leading video game consoles across the different product generations.

TABLE 12.2 Comparison of seventh-generation games consoles

Console	Hardware	Connectivity	DVD	Games	Price (December 2006)
Sony PS3	Cell Broadband Engine 550 MHz RSK GPU HDTV-capable	*20 GB version:* Bluetooth 2.0, an ethernet port and four USB docks. *60 GB version:* Compact flash, SD and memory stick duo, WiFi.	Integrated Blu-Ray player. Backwards compatible with DVD	50 titles available at end of 2006	*20GB version:* $499 *60GB version:* $599
Microsoft Xbox360	IBM Xenon, Power-PC CPU 500MHz ATI custom GPU HDTV-capable	Option to purchase WiFi adapter. *Core version:* Three USB docks, ethernet port *20GB version:* Wireless controllers	DVD player. Additional HD-DVD drive available for $199	130 titles at end of 2006 (of which 65 allow interactive play through Xbox Live). Backwards compatible	*Core version:* $299 *20 GB version:* $399
Nintendo Wii	IBM Broadway Power-PC CPU GPU developed with ATI EDTV video output	Bluetooth, two USB docks, SD slot, internet via IEEE 802.11 or a Wii LAN adaptor	No current DVD playback. Plans to launch integrated DVD version in Japan in 2007	c. 30 titles at time of launch. Backwards compatible with GameCube	$250

TABLE 12.3 Worldwide sales of video game consoles by platform (millions)

	Second generation	Third generation	Fourth generation	Fifth generation	Sixth generation	Seventh generation (to end-March 2009)
Nintendo	–	NES: 60	Super NES: 49	N-64: 32.9	GameCube: 21.2	Wii: 50.4
Sega	–	Master System: 13	MegaDrive/ Genesis: 29	Saturn: 9.3	Dreamcast: 10.6	–
Sony	–	–	–	PlayStation:100	PS2: 140	PS3: 26.7
Microsoft	–	–	–	–	Xbox: 24.0	Xbox 360: 30.2
Others	Atari 2600, Fairfield Channel F, Magnavox Odyssey	Atari 7800: <0.3	NEC TurboGrafx: 11	3DO: 1.2		

Source: Various newspaper articles.

The Video Games Industry in 2009

The Video Games Market

During 2009, the world video games industry was experiencing contraction after consumer expenditures hit a peak in 2007 and 2008. Unit sales for all three leading consoles were down sharply—partly as a result of market saturation and partly as a result of global recession. Sales of games had contracted too—refuting the widely held assumption that video games were recession-proof. In the U.S. the decline in consumer expenditure was especially severe (see Figure 12.2).

However, most observers believed that the recent slump was cyclical rather than an indicator of a longer term decline. As a form of entertainment, video game playing was continuing to grow. In the U.S. over 40% of households owned video game consoles and annual expenditures on consoles and games exceeded cinema box office receipts. Although prices on consoles had been cut during 2008 and 2009, video games consoles had not suffered the same decline in prices that had afflicted computers.

Central to the long-term expansion of the video games market was a broadening of the consumer base. Not only was video game playing expanding from Japan, North America and Western Europe to most of the world—its demographic appeal was broadening. Once the preserve of teenage boys, by 2008, the majority of the age group 18–44 were video games players and even among the 55–64 age group, 24% played video games. Female participation had also increased strongly. While children who grew up playing video games continue to do so as adults, game preferences changed greatly with age. Adolescents were more concerned with what

FIGURE 12.2 Worldwide consumer expenditure on video game hardware and software, 1990–2009

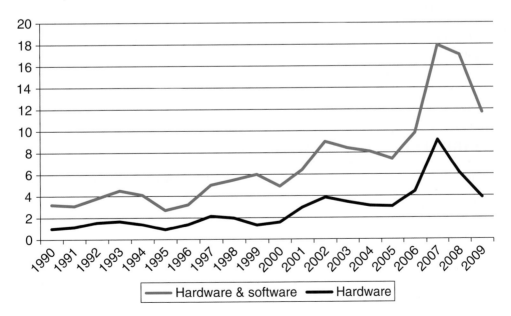

was "in" and "hot." The adult market comprises numerous niches, each with an interest in a different type of game. Adults like titles that fit in with their lifestyle and interests. Sports-based games were very popular among adult males. However, in terms of intensity of game playing, teenage boys remained clear leaders: U.S. males between the ages of 12 and 17 with a video game console in their home devoted an average of 14 hours a week to game playing. Females in the same age bracket played an average of 4 hours a week. The popularity of Nintendo's Wii had contributed substantially to the growth of video gaming among adults and females.

The growth of video games playing had opened up an entirely new source of revenue for video games publishers: advertising. Product placement within video games generated advertising revenues of $56 million in 2005 in the U.S. alone. Both Microsoft and Google acquired advertising agencies specializing in video game advertisement placement.

Software

Each video game console supplier ("platform provider") licensed third-party software companies to develop and distribute games for its system. Two types of company were involved in video games software: video games; publishers, which were responsible for financing, manufacturing, marketing and distributing video games, and video game developers, which developed the software. Video game publishing was increasingly dominated by a few large companies—the most prominent being Electronic Arts (see Table 12.4). Typically, the software publisher submitted a proposal or a prototype to the console maker for evaluation and approval. The licensing agreement between the software company and the hardware provider gave the console maker the right to approve game content and control over release timing, and provided for a royalty payment from the software company. Game developers were paid a royalty, typically between 5% and 15%, based on the publishers' revenues from the game.

Escalating game development costs were a result of the demand for multifeatured, 3-D, cinematic-quality games made possible by increasingly powerful consoles. Atari's *Pac-Man* released in 1982 was created by a single developer and cost about $100 000. *Halo 2* released for the Xbox in 2004 involved 190 developers and cost $40 million. By late 2006, *Halo 2* had sold 8 million copies at $50 each. For the new generation of consoles, most games cost more than $12 million to develop. In terms of both costs and revenue patterns, video games closely resembled movies, with

TABLE 12.4 Share of U.S. video games market by publisher, 2006

Publisher	Market share by value (%)
Electronic Arts	19.8
Konami	9.8
Take-Two Interactive	9.9
Activision	8.8
Others	52.7

Source: From www.researchandmarkets.com/reports/354861/video_game_industry.htm.

TABLE 12.5 Top-selling console games in the U.S., 2008 (by units sold)

Title/platform	Publisher	Release date	Units sold (000s)	Av. retail price ($)
Wii Play (Wii)	Nintendo	Dec. '06	5280	50
Mario Kart Wii (Wii)	Nintendo	Apr. '08	5000	50
Wii Fit (Wii)	Nintendo	May. '08	4530	90
Super Smash Bros. Brawl (Wii)	Nintendo	Mar. '08	4170	50
Grand Theft Auto IV (Xbox 360)	Rockstar Games	Apr. '08	3290	40
Call of Duty: World at War (Xbox 360)	Activision	Nov. '08	2750	60
Gears of War 2 (Xbox 360)	Microsoft	Nov. '08	2310	40
Grand Theft Auto IV (PS3)	Rockstar Games	Apr. '08	1890	40
Madden NFL 09 (XBox 360)	Electronic Arts	Aug. '08	1870	30
Mario Kart DS (DS)	Nintendo	Nov. '05	1650	40

similar success rates—a mere few became money-spinning blockbusters. Table 12.5 shows the top selling titles of 2008. Like movies too, creating a brand franchise through a succession of sequels had become a key competitive strategy. Rising development costs were a key factor causing consolidation among publishers.

As the power of the publishers had grown and the costs of development had risen, so exclusivity ties had disappeared from most licensing contracts—most leading games titles were cross-platform. For example, several titles that were once PS3 exclusives have been released simultaneously on Xbox 360. These include *Grand Theft Auto IV*, *Final Fantasy XIII*, *Virtual Fighter*, and *Devil May Cry*. Wii has several exclusive titles, most of which were developed by Nintendo.

The development of video games required a blend of technology and creative talent. The development process included game development and design, prototyping, programming, art, computer graphic design, animation, sound engineering, technical writing, editorial review and quality assurance. It took 18 to 36 months to complete a new title based on a new platform. To "port" an existing title to a different platform took up to 9 months. Many games were based on characters and themes that were either owned by the game developer or licensed from third parties. The licensing fees paid by software publishers for exclusive rights to the intellectual property of media companies and sports organizations grew substantially between 1998 and 2002. Securing the license to produce a game based on a hit movie (for example, *Harry Potter)* could cost several million dollars. In the sports market, licenses paid to sports leagues (NFL, NHL, MLB, NBA, FIFA) typically involved an upfront payment, plus a royalty of 5% to 15% of the wholesale price for each unit sold.

Not only did software sales exceed hardware sales—software was responsible for virtually all of the industry's profit. The console makers followed a "razors and blades" business model: the consoles were sold at a loss; profits were recouped on software sales—both games developed internally and royalties received from third-party games publishers. The result was strongly cyclical earnings for the platform providers: the launch of a new console would result in massive cash outflows; only with a substantial installed base would the platform provider begin to recoup the investment made.

The Console Suppliers

For the console makers, 2009 was a troubling year. Sony and Microsoft had achieved revenues that were not far behind Nintendo but both were still losing money on their video game businesses. During the first two years of product launch, losses were to be expected—but Xbox 360 had been on the market for almost four years and PS3 for almost three years. Most observers believed that these losses were primarily the result of the costs associated with the technologically advanced specifications of the two consoles. This was particularly the case with PS3. By contrast, as a result of its inexpensive components, Nintendo had been earning a contribution from its Wii from the outset.

Moreover, profits from software were failing to fill the gap. Only 3.8 PS3 games per console were sold in the U.S. by March 2008 and 3.5 Wii games per console. By contrast, each Xbox 360 user bought an average of 7.5 games. This pointed towards the emergence of Xbox as the preferred platform both for serious game players and for games developers.

For Sony, the losses associated with PS3 pointed to the challenges of designing a console that would be a favorite among game players while also establishing the video game console as a general home entertainment device. The decision to incorporate a Blu-ray DVD player in PS3 had little to do its ability to offer a superior video gaming experience—there were few games that exploited its functionality and few consumers had HDTV.

As the three leading console providers looked towards the future, two issues preoccupied them. First, what factors would determine which of them would emerge as a leader in the competitive battle for the next generation of video game consoles? Second, as the games developers and publishers grew in size and strength, had the console makers lost the capacity to dictate industry evolution and with it the capacity to reap profits?

Appendix: Financial Data on the Console Manufacturers

Nintendo

(Yen, billions)

	1998	1999	2000	2001	2002	2003	2004	2005	2006	2007	2008
Total sales	534	573	531	463	554	504	514	515	509	966	1672
Operating income	172	156	145	85	119	100	110	113	91	226	487
Net income	84	86	56	97	106	67	33	87	98	174	257
Op. income/Av. total assets (%)	10.6	9.9	6.1	9.7	9.5	8.9	10.5	9.7	7.9	19.5	27.0
Return on av. equity (%)	14.0	12.9	7.7	12.2	12.0	7.4	3.7	9.6	10.4	16.8	11.0

Sony

(Yen, billions)

	1998	1999	2000	2001	2002	2003	2004	2005	2006	2007	2008
Sales *of which:*	6761	6804	6687	7315	7578	7474	7496	7160	7475	1016	1284
Games	700	760	631	661	1004	936	754	703	918	974	1219

Sony
(Yen, billions)

	1998	1999	2000	2001	2002	2003	2004	2005	2006	2007	2008
Operating income *of which:*	526	348	141	225	135	185	99	114	191	71	374
Games	117	137	77	(51)	84	113	68	43	9	(232)	(124)
Net income (loss)	222	179	122	17	15	116	89	164	124	126	369
Op. income/Av. total assets (%)	6.7	5.5	3.7	3.1	1.7	2.2	1.1	1.2	1.9	0.6	2.9
Return on av. equity (%)	13.2	9.8	6.1	0.1	0.1	4.8	3.6	6.3	4.1	3.94	(3.08)

Microsoft
($, millions)

	2000	2001	2002	2003	2004	2005	2006	2007	2008
Sales *of which:*	22 956	25 296	28 365	32 187	36 835	39 788	44 282	51 122	60 420
Home & entertainment	n.a.	n.a.	2453	2748	2731	3110	4292	6069	8140
Operating income *of which:*	11 006	11 720	11 910	13 217	9034	14 561	16 472	18 524	22 492
Home and entertainment	n.a.	n.a.	(847)	(924)	(1011)	(451)	(1283)	426	(1969)
Net income	9421	7346	7829	9993	8168	12 254	12 599	14 065	17 681
Op. income/Av. total assets (%)	24.4	21.2	18.8	17.9	10.3	17.6	23.6	29.3	30.9
Return on av. equity (%)	26.9	16.6	15.7	17.6	11.7	19.9	28.6	16.45	42.47

n.a. = not available.

Notes

1 Successive generations of video game consoles have conventionally been designated according to processor bit size. In practice, bit size is a poor indicator of processing power. Beyond 32 bits, bit size has little to do with console performance—processor clock speed is much more important.

2 "Out of the Box at Last," *Financial Times* (Creative Business section), November 20, 2001.

3 "Delays likely for Sony's PlayStation 3," *Financial Times,* February 20, 2006.

Case 13 DVD War of 2005–8: Blu-ray versus HD-DVD

On Tuesday February 19, 2008, Toshiba announced that it would stop manufacturing HD-DVD DVD discs and players. The announcement marked the end of the battle between Toshiba and Sony to establish the format standard for the next generation of digital versatile discs (DVDs).[1]

In the history of standards wars, the HDV format war was surprisingly short. The coalescing of technological development of next-generation DVDs around two competing formats can be traced to 2002. However, open warfare did not commence until summer 2005 when attempts to reach agreement on a single standard finally broke down. Products featuring the new technologies did not appear until April 2006 in the case of HD-DVD and June 2006 in the case of Blu-ray. Yet, after a mere 19 months during which products based upon one or other of the two formats competed for market supremacy, it was all over. Over a period of few weeks, Toshiba's position crumbled and Sony emerged victorious.

The Technology

The optical disc was invented in 1958 by David Paul Gregg whose patent was registered in 1961. The first commercial product using the technology was the laserdisc system launched by Philips and MCA in 1978. However, optical discs were superseded by video cassettes.

The breakthrough for optical discs was Philips and Sony Corporation's development of the compact disc in 1983, which became the dominant medium for audio recordings. The CD was followed by the DVD which was introduced into Japan in 1996, the U.S. in 1997, and Europe in 1998. The successful launch of the DVD was the result of an industry-wide forum that forced the proponents of different formats to agree a common technological standard. This industry group became the DVD Forum.

The impetus for developing a high-definition DVD came from the emergence of high-definition television (HDTV) during the 1990s. With HDTV seen as the next wave in consumer electronics there came the need for a storage medium capable of holding high definition images. The distinctive feature of both HD-DVD and Blu-ray formats was the use of short-wavelength blue-laser technology instead of the red lasers used in earlier generations. Blue lasers allowed a vast increase in the amount of data that could be stored on a standard 12 centimeter disc.

The key difference between HD-DVD and Blu-ray was in the thickness of the DVD's protective plastic layer: the HD-DVD retained the 0.6 mm thickness common to conventional DVDs; Blu-ray featured a 0.1 mm coating. The result was that a dual-layer Blu-ray DVD could hold 50GB (gigabytes) of data, compared to 30GB for a dual-layer HD-DVD. This compared to 8.5GB for a conventional DVD.

For content owners—film studios in particular—Blu-ray had an additional advantage. While both formats incorporated the new AACS (Advanced Access Content System) anti-piracy device, Blu-ray included an additional layer of protection. Microsoft was concerned that the additional protection provided by Blu-ray restricted the ability of PC users to integrate video images with other computer functions. In July 2005, Bill Gates argued that the Blu-ray standard had to change to "work more smoothly with personal computers."

Blu-ray's technical refinements came at some cost. HD-DVDs could be manufactured by modifying the production line used for making ordinary DVDs: "It is a simple and low-cost step to go from manufacturing standard DVDs to producing HD-DVDs," said Mark Knox, a Toshiba spokesman. "The changes [for a factory] cost less than $150,000."[2] Blu-ray discs required major changes in manufacturing processes and manufacturing equipment. The implication was that for content owners and consumers, Blu-ray discs would be more costly.

Neither format could be played on existing DVD players. Moreover, HD-DVD players could not play Blu-ray discs and vice-versa. Hence, movie studios and video games publishers faced the prospect of having to stock media in three formats: HD-DVD, Blu-ray and conventional DVDs. Both HD-DVD and Blu-ray players were backward compatible— they could play conventional DVDs.

As far as economizing on the number of formats that content producers needed to manufacture and distributors needed to stock, one of the advantages envisaged by the HD-DVD camp was the ability to produce an HD-DVD disc of a game or movie that also included a standard DVD version of the content. In September 2006, Toshiba announced: "Toshiba, in collaboration with disc manufacturer Memory Tech Japan, has successfully combined a HD-DVD and DVD to a single 3-layer, twin-format disc. The resulting disc conforms to DVD standards so it can be played on DVD players, and also on HD-DVD players."[3]

Moreover, the benefits of Blu-ray's greater storage capacity were not readily apparent at the time. Existing high-definition formats for full-length movies could be easily accommodated on both types of disc. Blu-ray's ability to "to fit an entire season of a television series" on a single disc, and "offer multiple versions of the same film" seemed marginal benefits to most consumers. The case for Blu-ray over HD-DVD seemed to rest primarily on its potential for accommodating future developments in video entertainment: "You open up a whole new spectrum of creative possibilities," says Tim Baxter, senior vice-president of strategic marketing at Sony Corp. of America. "This format is about gearing up for this holiday season and the next 10 years."[4]

Building Bandwagons

In February 2002 the Blu-ray Disc Association was formed with founder members Hitachi, Panasonic, Pioneer, Philips, Samsung, Sharp, Sony, and Thomson. It was soon joined by Dell Computer, Mitsubishi and TDK.[30] The HD-DVD Promotion Group comprised Toshiba, NEC, Sanyo, Microsoft, Kenwood, Intel, Venturer Electronics and Memory-Tech Corporation. Some companies were members of both groups. These included Hewlett Packard (HP), LG, Acer, Asus, Lite-On, Onkyo, Meridian and Alpine.

Blu-ray was the favorite among the leading film studios: Disney, Fox, Lions Gate, MGM, and of course Sony Pictures had aligned with Blu-ray, while Universal was the only major studio that joined the HD-DVD camp. Paramount (including subsidiaries Nickelodeon Movies, MTV Films, DreamWorks Pictures and DreamWorks Animation) and Warner Bros. supported both standards.

Product Roll-out

Even while both camps were developing products incorporating the two incompatible standards, attempts to avoid a costly format war continued. However, on August 22, 2005, the Blu-ray Disc Association and DVD Forum announced that the negotiations to unify their standards had failed. From then on the race was on to bring discs and hardware to market as quickly as possible in order to build market share leadership.

HD-DVD was first to market with the Toshiba HD-A1 launched in the U.S. on April 18, 2006 at a retail price of $499. The Samsung BD-P1000 was the first Blu-ray disc player. It was launched at the end of June 2006 at a retail price of $999.

In April 2006, Universal and Warner Brothers both began releasing HD-DVDs of existing movies at prices of between $29 and $35. Sony Pictures was first to release movies on Blu-ray—with an initial release of 8 movies at $28.95 to coincide with the launch of the Samsung BD-P1000. However, the early Blu-ray movies suffered from major quality problems. Several movies suffered from poor film-to-disc transfers and until October 2006 only single-layer recording was possible on Blu-ray discs which limited their capacity to 25 gigabytes.[5]

The other two major hardware products incorporating the new-generation DVD drives were personal computers and video game consoles. Both Toshiba and Sony were major players in personal computers. Toshiba released an HD-DVD-compatible notebook, the Qosmio G35-AV650.

In May 2006, Sony launched a Vaio notebook with a Blu-ray drive. By the end of 2006, NEC and HP had introduced notebooks with HD-DVDs, while Dell joined Sony in adding Blu-ray to one of its notebook models.

In video game consoles, the market leaders were Sony with its PlayStation and Microsoft with its Xbox. The battle for the next generation of consoles began with Microsoft's launch of its Xbox 360 in November 2005. The Xbox 360 came with a standard DVD drive. In November 2006, Microsoft launched a HD-DVD drive as a separate plug-in unit for its Xbox 360 priced at $200 in the U.S. and £130 in the U.K. Microsoft's unwillingness to include a built-in HD-DVD player was a result of, first, the lack of games developed to exploit HD-DVD capabilities and, second, its belief that online access to games would displace DVD distributed games within a few years.

For Sony, its new PS3 video game console formed a central component of its Blu-ray strategy. Sony's decision to launch its PS3 with a Blu-ray disc player was widely viewed as a strategic blunder. It delayed the launch of the PS3 giving Microsoft lead time of over a year in the new generation of consoles. It also greatly increased the cost. The cost and complexity of developing games that utilized the technical potential of Blu-ray meant that very few new high-definition games were available at launch. Launched at a price of $499 in the U.S., PS3 was seen as something of a desperate gamble by Sony, faced with the market momentum of Xbox 360 and the low-cost challenge of the Nintendo Wii. At $499 it was estimated that Sony would lose over $200 on every unit sold.

Video games developers and publishers were slower than the movie studios to sign up for one or other of the rival formats. However, on January 7, 2007, Sony received a major boost when Electronic Arts (the world's biggest games software company) and Vivendi Universal Games joined the Blu-ray association.

Distributors bore considerable cost burdens because of the standards war. The leading retailers (including Wal-Mart, Target and Best Buy) and movie distributors such as Blockbuster and Netflix felt obliged to carry both formats.

Shifting Alliances

The central battle was for the support of the movie studios. Despite the initial preference of the majority of the major studios for Blu-ray, financial and other incentives resulted in several defections. Early in 2005, Warner Brothers and Paramount had backed HD-DVD, but in October 2005 both announced support for both formats. However, in August 2007, Paramount and DreamWorks Animation SKG dropped Blu-ray and announced that their high-definition movies would be released exclusively on HD-DVD. The studios mentioned cost and technical advantages but most observers believed that the offer from Toshiba of $150 million in cash and promotional guarantees were a bigger factor. Sony's CEO, Sir Howard

Stringer, was particularly active in using his Hollywood connections to build support for Blu-ray among the studios.

Growing frustration with dual formats resulted in several distributors abandoning HD-DVD. In June 2007, Blockbuster, the largest U.S. movie rental company, adopted Blu-ray exclusively after test-marketing both formats and finding that over 70% of high definition rentals were Blu-ray discs. In July 2007, Target Corporation began carrying only Blu-ray standalone players in its stores.

During 2007, sales of Blu-ray decisively overtook sales of HD-DVD in both hardware and software, with PS3 providing a particularly strong boost for Blu-ray. Home Media Research estimated that for 2007 as a whole, Blu-ray outsold HD-DVD players by three to one in the U.S., 10 to one in Europe, and 100 to one in Japan.

A critical event in the battle was Warner Brothers' announcement on January 4, 2008 that it would drop support for HD-DVD from June 2008. The significance of Warner's move was that it was the biggest player in DVD movies. Toshiba responded by cutting the price of its HD-DVD players by up to 50%; however, there was little it could do to prevent the chain reaction that followed the Warner announcement. In January 2008, U.K. retailer Woolworths said it would stock only Blu-ray discs from March 2008. On February 11, 2008, Best Buy began recommending Blu-ray as the customer's digital format choice. Then, on February 15, 2008 Wal-Mart, the largest DVD retailer in the U.S., announced that it would discontinue HD-DVD products from June 2008. Also in February, Netflix, the largest online video rental service, began phasing out its HD-DVD inventory.

On February 19, 2008, Universal Studios—the only studio to have consistently supported HD-DVD from the outset—defected to Blu-ray. On the same day, Toshiba announced it would cease developing, manufacturing and marketing HD-DVD players and recorders. The next day Paramount, the remaining supporter of HD-DVD, announced its move to Blu-Ray.

Even before Toshiba's announcement the fate of HD-DVD was clear. On February 16, 2008, the *New York Times* published its obituary:

> HD-DVD, the beloved format of Toshiba and three Hollywood studios, died Friday after a brief illness. The cause of death was determined to be the decision by Wal-Mart to stock only high-definition DVDs and players using the Blu-ray format.
>
> There are no funeral plans . . .[6]

Costs and Benefits

No reliable data is available concerning the costs and benefits of the DVD war to the main participants. Clearly Toshiba was the chief loser in financial terms. The Nikkei business daily reported that for its financial year ending March 31, 2008, Toshiba was likely to book a 100 billion yen loss ($986 million) relating to the termination of its HD-DVD project.[7] However, most observers believed that the full cost—including R&D expenditures, incentive payments to partners, forced price reductions on hardware and inventory write-offs—would be much greater.

To what extent was Sony a winner? Its costs included not only the massive R&D expenditures on Blu-ray but also the costs of supporting its alliance partners, price cuts in hardware and software and the significant costs of delaying the launch of PS3 until Blu-ray was ready. Moreover, the revenues generated by Sony's Blu-ray technology would be limited, first, by Sony's offer of highly favorable licensing terms in order to attract supporters to the Blu-ray camp and, second, by the likelihood that the commercial life of Blu-ray would be short. Professor Pai-Ling Yin of MIT's Sloan School of Management argues:

. . . technology markets are characterized by waves of innovation, where the latest and greatest of last year is replaced by the latest and greatest of next year. Joseph Schumpeter described this pattern as "the perennial gale of creative destruction." Blu-ray and HD-DVD are simply the next generation of discs, replacing the standard DVD of the last generation. Thus, there is but a limited amount of time (until the appearance of the next generation technology) for the firms and the technology of this generation to reap the rewards of being the shiny new item on the block.[8]

By failing to agree on a common standard, the time available to exploit the current generation of media storage technology before it is rendered obsolete was greatly reduced: "The reality is that relative to the sales that could have been garnered from faster and higher volumes of DVD players had Sony & Toshiba been able to come to some agreement, both firms have lost."[9]

Notes

1 The correct interpretation of the DVD acronym is a matter of dispute. The two most common are "digital versatile disc" and "digital video disc."

2 "Format Wars: Everyone Could End Up Losing," *Financial Times*, April 3, 2006.

3 See http://news.digitaltrends.com/news-article/11271/three-layer-disc-combines-dvd-hd-dvd, accessed October 17, 2009.

4 "Format Wars: Everyone Could End Up Losing," *Financial Times*, April 3, 2006.

5 "Two years of battle between HD-DVD and Blu-ray: a retrospective," www.engadgethd.com/2008/02/20/two-years-of-battle-between-hd-dvd-and-blu-ray-a-retrospective/, accessed November 12, 2008.

6 "Taps for HD-DVD as Wal-Mart Backs Blu-ray," *New York Times*, February 16, 2008.

7 "The Fall of HD-DVD Will Cost Toshiba $986 Million," March 17, 2008, www.dailytech.com/article.aspx?newsid=11069, accessed October 17, 2009.

8 "What Are the Lessons of the Blu-ray/HD-DVD Battle?" A Freakonomics Quorum, March 4, 2008, http://freakonomics.blogs.nytimes.com/2008/03/04/what-are-the-lessons-of-the-blu-rayhd-dvd-battle-a-freakonomics-quorum/, accessed November 12, 2008.

9 "What Are the Lessons of the Blu-ray/HD-DVD Battle?" A Freakonomics Quorum, March 4, 2008, http://freakonomics.blogs.nytimes.com/2008/03/04/what-are-the-lessons-of-the-blu-rayhd-dvd-battle-a-freakonomics-quorum/, accessed November 12, 2008.

Case 14 *New York Times*

Troubled Times for the "Good Gray Lady"

The early months of 2009 were a difficult period for the New York Times Company (NYT), publisher of the *New York Times* and *Boston Globe* and the owner of a number of regional titles as well as several nonprint media businesses. In common with other U.S. newspaper publishers, the NYT was suffering from the cyclical problem of cutbacks in advertising budgets and the long-term problem of declining readership as newspapers increasingly lost ground to online sources of information.

During January and February, the company was subject to repeated speculation concerning its ability to meet its financial obligations—in particular, the refinancing of a $400 million line of credit due to expire in May. In January the

TABLE 14.1 New York Times Company, Inc.: selected financial data ($000s, except where indicated)

	2008	2007	2006	2005	2004
Revenues	2 948 856	3 195 077	3 289 903	3 231 128	3 159 412
Operating costs	2 791 613	2 928 070	2 996 081	2 911 578	2 696 799
Impairment of assets	197 879	11 000	814 433	–	–
Gain on sale of assets	–	(28 578)	–	122 946	–
Operating (loss)/profit	(40 636)	227 429	(520 611)	442 496	462 613
Interest expense, net	47 790	39 842	50 651	49 168	41 760
Income from continuing operations	(66 139)	108 939	(568 171)	243 313	264 985
Discontinued operations – Broadcast Media Group	8300	99 765	24 728	15 687	22 646
Net income	(57 839)	208 704	(543 443)	253 473	287 631
Property, plant and equipment	1 353 619	1 468 013	1 375 365	1 401 368	1 308 903
Total assets	3 401 680	3 473 092	3 855 928	4 564 078	3 994 555
Total debt	1 059 375	1 034 979	1 445 928	1 396 380	1 058 847
Stockholders' equity	503 963	978 200	819 842	1 450 826	1 354 361
Return on average stockholders' equity (%)	−8	23	−48	18	21
Total debt to total capitalization (%)	68	51	64	49	44
Operating profit/revenues (%)	−1	7	−16	14	15
Current assets to current liabilities	0.60	0.68	0.91	0.95	0.84
Employees (full-time equivalent)	9346	10 231	11 585	11 965	12 300

Source: New York Times Company, Inc., 10-K Report, 2008.

company bought itself breathing space with a $250 million loan at 14% interest from the Mexican billionaire, Carlos Slim. In February it eliminated its dividend for the year.

The annual results for 2008 showed revenues contracting at a faster pace than the company could cut costs. Once impairment charges were taken into account (mainly relating to write-downs of goodwill and the masthead values), NYT made a net loss of almost $58 million (see Table 14.1).

The NYT's share price reflected the general pessimism concerning the company's prospects. In September 2008, its shares had been trading at above $14. On February 20, 2009, they closed at $3.44. At the shareholder's annual meeting on April 29, 2009, Board Chairman Arthur Sulzberger Jr. addressed the company's problems and the board's strategy for dealing with them:

> In our remarks this morning, both Janet Robinson, president and CEO of The New York Times Company, and I will talk about the actions we and our colleagues are taking to steer our organization through the current financial downturn, advertising decline and technological fragmentation—which, collectively, are having a brutal effect on all in the media business.
>
> As you will hear and see this morning, The New York Times Company is no exception. As the Times Company's board of directors and senior management

continue to lead our enterprise through this uncertain era, we are guided by four underlying premises:

- First, quality will remain the distinguishing feature of all that we have to offer;
- Second, business will continue to be difficult, but we are absolutely committed to creating greater shareholder value;
- Third, there is no one single solution that will return us to revenue growth;
- And fourth, we will aggressively go where our new thinking and analysis take us.

Let me expand on these last two thoughts: we recognize that the answers for national and international media outlets such as the *New York Times* and the *International Herald Tribune* will be different than those for our local papers such as the *Sarasota Herald-Tribune* and the *Wilmington Star-News*. And, of course, About.com faces yet a different set of issues and solutions.

Of all our properties, the *Boston Globe* has been most dramatically affected by the secular and cyclical forces that are roiling the entire media industry. We have responded by consolidating printing facilities, raising circulation prices and reducing headcount. But more needs to be done to align the *Globe*'s costs and revenues . . .

We know that there are considerable challenges before us, but past experience teaches us that the outcome will be determined by our ability to adhere to the formula that has successfully driven this Company for so long. That formula can be summed up in this thought: quality journalism attracts a quality audience which, in turn, attracts quality advertisers.

It is this idea, expressed various ways over numerous decades, which has seen The New York Times Company through previous grim economic periods and has enabled *The Times* to emerge as the world's most powerful journalistic voice. Our quality journalism is the fundamental asset our shareholders have. And just three days ago that quality was again recognized as five Pulitzer Prizes were awarded to the men and women of *The New York Times* . . .

Now let me turn to a basic question that I am repeatedly asked: Can quality journalism exist in this new economic environment?

Let me rephrase that question with the one we ask ourselves: How can we enhance our digital revenue sufficiently so that we have the financial foundation necessary to support our news gathering operations, be they at *The New York Times*, the *Boston Globe* or any of our regional news outlets?

At The New York Times Company, we are focusing on three key levers to achieve this essential goal: attracting more users, deepening their engagement and then earning revenue from their usage. To do all this effectively has and will continue to require our making bets on how this new medium will evolve and then making investments in that vision. This is certainly not an easy task, but our insights into human behavior and digital evolution are helping to guide us.

Throughout 2008 and the first months of 2009, we have continued to create a new form of web journalism that is both informative and compelling. Our goal is to respond to our audiences' demand for interactivity, community and multimedia, as well as news and information on an increasingly wide range of topics. We are aggressively responding to our readers' desire to do something with our content. Our readers want to share it, or blog it, or comment on it. They want to use our journalism as raw material for what they make . . .

Our strategy is rooted in the fundamental premise that we must be OF the internet, not ON it, requiring all of us to move from merely publishing our content on the web to becoming full web publishers.

Presently, we are doing this with an increasing battery of online initiatives, but we are not yet bringing in the revenue we will need in the long-term. We are currently examining a vast array of tactics and options that will enable us to adapt financially to the new realities of our business. As we chart our course toward a sustainable digital future, we have come to recognize with increasing clarity that online success will require substantial re-conceptualization, thoughtful execution, and a great willingness to take full advantage of the web, an amazing laboratory for entrepreneurs, technologists and, of course, journalists.

While we have talked a lot about our Company's online efforts, I am sure that some shareholders wonder whether all this web activity portends the end of print.

Of course not! . . . [A]pproximately 88% of our Company's revenues come from print. There are currently more than 830 000 readers who have subscribed to *The New York Times* for two years or more, what we call loyalists. This is up from 650 000 in the year 2000. Across the Company, circulation revenues made up 38% of our total in the first quarter, significantly higher than others in the industry and a sizeable and stable base. As other newspapers cut back on international and national coverage or, in some sad cases, cease operations, we believe there will be opportunities for *The Times* in print to fill this void, resulting in increased revenue from circulation, news services and other products.[1]

Sulzberger closed his presentation by reminding shareholders of the consistency and steadfastness of the NYT's long-term strategy:

The path to our digital future is not a new one. Let me repeat something I said to my colleagues a decade ago, at my 1999 annual speech to the staff:

"At the heart of this presentation are plans for ensuring that, a decade from now and a century from now, *The New York Times* will still be the leader in its field of quality journalism, regardless of how it is distributed. These plans entail our moving from a strategy focused on the specific products we produce to one built around our audience—*a quality audience strategy*. Our goal is to know our audience better than anyone else; to meet their informational and transactional needs—by ourselves where we can; in partnership with others when necessary; and to serve them in print and digitally, continuously and on-demand."

Ten years later, we have done this and much more with the tools and platforms that are now at our disposal. We understand this audience and they come to us in what once would have been unimaginable numbers. Now, because of secular and cyclical changes that are transforming our marketplace, we are in the process of fundamentally re-conceptualizing our relationship with that audience.

What does this mean?

Specifically we are in the process of rethinking the value of what we are offering. As you will hear in the months ahead, we will be:

- Engaging in a thoughtful analysis of brand loyalty and circulation revenue.
- Exploring a new online financial strategy.

- Leveraging the added value we bring to advertisers in terms of brand, technology and thought leadership.
- And thinking about how mobiles, e-readers and social networking can be brought more deeply into the equation.

Fundamentally, we are taking an increasingly deeper look at the role that quality journalism plays in the twenty-first century. We will be determining how best to take what we know, and create a more effective business model. Of course, this search for long-term financial stability is taking place throughout the media industry and each enterprise will have its own answers.

At The New York Times Company, our new relationship with our audience will be guided by our cornerstone belief that world class news, opinion, photography, videography and blogging will grow in value as the interconnection between what happens in the world and the lives of our readers becomes more personal, immediate and direct.

This is why we unequivocally believe in our future.[2]

Sulzberger's faith in the future of the NYT was not widely shared. Skeptics pointed to the decline in newspaper circulation, the sharp decline in newspaper readership among the young, the shift of advertising from print media to online and the failure of the major newspapers to establish a viable business model for their online publishing. There were also concerns regarding the financial acumen of the family-controlled board of directors. In 2006, NYT's board rejected a bid led by former General Electric chairman, Jack Welch, to buy the *Boston Globe* for $600 million. The *Globe* had subsequently become the NYT's biggest cash drain. In 2007, NYT moved into a new $500 million headquarters in midtown Manhattan. Between 1997 and 2004 the company spent $3 billion on stock repurchases at an average price of $37. Some shareholders viewed Chairman Sulzberger, the great-grandson of the newspaper's founder, as part of the problem rather than its solution. However, with NYT's dual-class share structure, the Sulzberger family had been able to dominate the board ever since the NYT had gone public in 1969. Media tycoon, Rupert Murdoch, has referred to the *New York Times* as "his favorite train wreck" and puts the blame firmly on the shoulders of Arnold Sulzberger, who he blamed for loosening *The Times'* links with New York in his urge to make *The Times* a national newspaper.[3]

The New York Times Company in 2009

The Business

The NYT comprises two business segments:

- The News Media Group, which consists of:
  - The New York Times Media Group, which includes *The Times*, NYTimes.com, the *International Herald Tribune* and a New York City radio station, WQXR-FM;
  - The New England Media Group, which includes the *Boston Globe* (the *Globe*), Boston.com, the *Worcester Telegram and Gazette* and related web sites;

- The Regional Media Group, which includes 15 daily newspapers in Alabama, California, Florida, Louisiana and the Carolinas, plus other print publications.
- The About Group, which consists of the web sites of About.com, ConsumerSearch.com, UCompareHealthCare.com and Caloriecount.about.com.

In addition NYT owns equity interests in a Canadian newsprint company, a paper maker in Maine and Metro Boston (a free daily newspaper), 18% of the Boston Red Sox and Fenway Park stadium, 80% of New England Sports Network (the regional cable sports network), and 50% of Roush Fenway Racing, a leading NASCAR team.

The News Media Group comprised by far the largest part of the company's operations. However, shrinking advertising revenues, declining circulation and increasing competition from free newspapers and nonprint sources of news had placed major pressures on margins. Table 14.2 shows results for NYT's two business segments. Table 14.3 shows circulation for NYT's three major newspaper titles, while Table 14.4 shows traffic to NYT's web sites.

Within the News Media Group, *The Times* was the company's jewel. It is the only general daily newspaper to be distributed in all 50 states of the U.S. In terms of journalistic reputation it is unsurpassed. By 2009, its tally of Pulitzer prizes was 101— more than double that of any other newspaper. Its columnists include Nicholas Krista, Thomas Friedman and Nobel Prize-winning economist, Paul Kurgan. The company has attributed its ability to raise the cover price of *The Times* (up from $1 to $2 between July 2007 and May 2009) to the appeal of its quality journalism.

Web revenues were almost wholly generated by advertising while newspaper revenues were primarily dependent upon advertising. Hence, as Table 14.5 shows, the great majority of NYT revenues were provided by advertisers.

TABLE 14.2 New York Times Company: segment results ($000s)

	2008	2007	2006
Revenues			
News Media Group	2 833 561	3 092 394	3 209 704
About Group	115 295	102 683	80 199
Total	2 948 856	3 195 077	3 289 903
Operating profit			
News Media Group	(30 392)	248 567	(497 276)
About Group	39 390	34 703	30 819
Corporate	(49 634)	(55 841)	(54 154)
Total	(40 636)	227 429	(520 611)
Net income/(loss) from joint ventures	17 062	(2618)	19 340
Interest expense, net	47 790	39 842	50 651
(Loss)/income from continuing operations before income taxes and minority interest	(71 364)	184 969	(551 922)

Source: New York Times Company, Inc. 10-K Report, 2008.

TABLE 14.3 Average daily circulation of New York Times Company newspapers (000s of copies)

	2008	2007
New York Times (Monday–Friday)	1033.8	1066.6
New York Times (Sunday)	1451.3	1529.7
International Herald Tribune	240.3	241.6
Boston Globe (Monday–Friday)	323.9	364.6
Boston Globe (Sunday)	500.0	544.1

Source: New York Times Company, Inc., 10-K Report, 2008.

TABLE 14.4 New York Times Company principal web sites, 2008

	Average monthly U.S. visits 2008 (millions)	Content	Revenue source
NYTimes.com	19.5	*New York Times* web sites	Advertising
IHT.com	6.3*	International Herald Tribune web site	Advertising
Boston.com	5.2	*Boston Globe* web site	Advertising
About.com	39.0	Information on over 70 000 topics prepared by 770 advisers	Advertising
ConsumerSearch.com	n.a.	Expert and user-generated consumer product reviews	Advertising
UCompareHealthCare.com	n.a.	Information on the quality of certain healthcare services	Advertising
Caloriecount.about.com	n.a.	Weight management tools, social support and nutritional information	Advertising

*Worldwide visitors

Source: New York Times Company, Inc., 10-K Report, 2008.

Cost Cutting

The principal response by NYT management to shrinking revenues had been to cut costs. In her presentation to shareholders at the 2009 Annual General Meeting, CEO Janet Robinson identified five areas of cost savings:

- Consolidation of operations. The *Times* had consolidated two of its New York printing plants into a single facility, saving $30 million annually. The *Globe* would do the same with its two printing plants, saving about $18 million annually.
- Closure of businesses that did not meet their financial targets. In early 2009, NYT closed City & Suburban, its retail and news-stand distribution business in the New York area. This would improve operating profit by an estimated $27 million annually.

TABLE 14.5 New York Times Company: principal revenue and cost components ($000s)

	2008	2007	2006
Total revenues	2 948 856	3 195 077	3 289 903
of which:			
—Advertising	1 779 699	2 047 468	2 153 936
—Circulation	910 154	889 882	889 722
—Other	259 003	257 727	246 245
Total production costs	1 315 120	1 341 096	1 435 456
of which:			
—Raw materials	250 843	259 977	330 833
—Wages and benefits	622 692	646 824	665 304
—Other	441 585	434 295	439 319
Selling, general and administrative costs	1 332 084	1 397 413	1 398 294
Depreciation and amortization	144 409	189 561	162 331
Total operating costs	2 791 613	2 928 070	2 996 081

Source: New York Times Company, Inc., 10-K Report, 2008.

- Streamlining the organization—principally through outsourcing functions such as advertising service, circulation telemarketing, customer service and financial back-office functions. At some of the smaller newspapers, printing would be outsourced.
- Reducing the resources devoted to marginal areas of circulation.
- Reducing newsprint consumption and production costs by eliminating some newspaper sections (e.g. magazines and TV guides) and reducing the page size of *The Times*.[4]

Asset Sales

The New York Times Company has divested a number of non-core businesses. In 2007 it sold its nine local television stations; in 2008 it sold Alabama-based *Times Daily*. In 2009, it was negotiating to sell its 18% stake in New England Sports Ventures (owner of the Boston Red Sox and Fenway Park) and its 80% holding in New England Sports Network (a cable TV network).

The Quest for a New Business Model

Arnold Sulzberger's notion of the NYT providing "quality journalism, regardless of how it is distributed" was appealing to many who perceived that NYT's core competence was journalism, yet its primary distribution medium—printed newspapers—was in long-term decline. Sulzberger's vision also lacked a well-articulated business model.

Amidst the carnage of the U.S. newspaper industry, profitable titles tend to be those where costs have been slashed by radical outsourcing and those that have been able to establish strong differentiation through strongly focusing upon local needs.

Where all newspapers have experienced difficulty is in establishing a viable business model for their online editions and establishing a synergistic relationship between their web and print editions. In the case of NYTimes.com, fees were initially collected from international users then, in 1997, the online edition became free in an effort to increase the online audience. In 2005, NYTimes.com moved to a mixed model—TimesSelect charged a fee for premium content and access to *The Times'* online archives. By 2007, the desire to build advertising revenues resulted in NYTimes.com providing free access. By 2009, the company was once again evaluating the best approach to charging for content.

Creating a viable online business model for a newspaper represents a challenge that has yet to be met. Rick Wartzman, Director of the Drucker Institute, has proposed an online-only solution: "The web needs to be embraced much more fully than most papers have done. This means no more tentative, halfway initiatives. Dead-tree editions must immediately yield to all-internet operations. The presses need to stop forever, with the delivery trucks shunted off to the scrapyard." As an example, he proposed that if the *Los Angeles Times* went online only it could operate with a staff of 275 and earn a net margin of 10%.[5] The *Huffington Post* has been viewed as a model for an online newspaper.

The central debate over online newspapers has been between advocates of "charging-for-content" and those that see the advertising-only approach as the only viable business model. Eric Schmidt, CEO of Google, comes down firmly on the side of free content and revenues for advertising. Only where content is unique, he argues, will users be willing to pay. For the great majority of news, there is no alternative to providing it free because it is available from so many online sources. The opportunity for online newspapers was to offer targeted advertising—that's where he sees Google as being an essential partner for the newspaper companies. In terms of the design of online newspapers, he suggested that critical features for an online newspaper were, first, it should remember which stories each reader had read so that content could be customized and, second, it should allow the reader to go deeper into topics in which he/she was interested.[6]

However, the discussion of business models for online newspaper content raised the question of what the traditional business model was for print newspapers? The history of the newspaper industry in the U.S. and in other countries of the world, suggested that profit typically took a second place behind political influence and ego projection among most newspaper proprietors. The attraction of newspaper ownership to already rich individuals could mean that a newspaper could be financially viable even if its costs exceeded its revenues. The attraction of *The Times* to the rich and famous was indicated by the presence of a number of potential suitors—in addition to Rupert Murdoch and Carlos Slim, Hollywood and record mogul David Geffen had expressed interest in taking a stake in it.

A key issue was whether the financial problems of the newspapers would stretch the willingness to pay of potential "rich daddies." The *Financial Times* warned that:

> Even wealthy patrons have reason to be wary, however. Sam Zell, the highest profile recent new entrant into the newspaper business, saw his $8.2bn purchase of the Tribune Company end last month in the bankruptcy courts. Having long

been seen as useful assets for burnishing their proprietors' reputations, newspapers now pose as much risk of tarnishing their owners' names.[7]

A major reason why the financial plight of the newspaper industry has attracted so much attention and concern is that newspapers have been regarded as a valuable public service—the "fourth estate" that can shine the light of public exposure on the wrongdoings of politicians and powerful individuals. If a free press is a central component of a democratic state, then an alternative business model might be that of a charity. Penelope Muse Abernathy of the University of North Carolina, has proposed four options for newspaper funding: establishing an endowment that funds a paper's news department; charitable support for some aspects of the paper's coverage, such as foreign or cultural coverage; purchase of the paper by a university or other educational institution; and sale to an angel investor who would run the paper as a "low-profit limited liability corporation."[8]

Non-profit organizations are also entering the field of journalism. ProPublica, led by Paul Steiger, a former senior editor at the *Wall Street Journal*, funds investigative journalism from charitable endowments. It then makes its stories available to *The Times* and other newspapers. *The Times* also collaborates with Spot.Us, a web site on which journalists can post story ideas they wish to pursue and what it will cost them to do it, raising the money from the public $20 at a time.[9]

Notes

1 The New York Times Company 2009 Annual Meeting of Stockholders, April 23, 2009.
2 The New York Times Company 2009 Annual Meeting of Stockholders, April 23, 2009.
3 "Feeling the Pinch," *The Economist*, December 4, 2008. "All the News that's Free to Print," *The Economist*, July 21, 2009.
4 The New York Times Company 2009 Annual Meeting of Stockholders, April 23, 2009.
5 "Out with the Dead Wood for Newspapers," *Business Week*, March 10, 2009.
6 "View from the Top: Eric Schmidt of Google," *Financial Times*, May 21, 2009.
7 "Playthings for Rich Men could be Unsafe Toys," *Financial Times*, January 21, 2009.
8 Penelope Muse Abernathy, "A Nonprofit Model for The New York Times?" Duke Conference on Nonprofit Media, May 4–5, 2009.
9 "All the News that's Free to Print," *Economist*, July 21, 2009.

Case 15 Eni SpA: Building an International Energy Major

May 2009 marked the beginning of Paolo Scaroni's fifth year as CEO of the Italian energy giant, Eni. Under his leadership, production of hydrocarbons had grown by 11% (most other oil and gas majors had experienced declining output), sales had risen by 86% (in euros) and operating income by 50% (in euros). Eni's market capitalization had declined from €69 billion to €57 billion—nevertheless, Eni had outperformed the market indices on all three of the stock markets where its shares were listed (Milan, London and New York). Moreover, Eni remained Italy's most valuable company with a market capitalization that was almost double that of second-placed ENEL (where Scaroni had been CEO prior to coming to Eni).

The change in leadership had not resulted in any major shifts in strategy for Eni. Scaroni had continued the two main strategic thrusts of his predecessor, Vittorio Mincato:

- A heavy emphasis on upstream investment with the organic growth of Eni's oil and gas reserves supplemented by selective acquisitions.
- A commitment to developing a vertically integrated natural gas business, which was built around linking Eni's gas production in north and west Africa with its downstream gas business in Europe through developing pipelines and liquefied natural gas (LNG), collaborating with Gazprom (the Russian gas giant), extending Eni's downstream gas business into other European countries and developing Eni's power-generation business.

However, in pursuing this strategy, Scaroni was forced to navigate an exceptionally turbulent environment. During his four years at Eni, oil prices had oscillated between $32 and $148 a barrel, European refining margins had widened then shrunk rapidly, and relations with producer governments had become contentious as a result of nationalism, Middle East conflict, and producer countries demanding a bigger share of production and profit from their hydrocarbon resources. In Venezuela and Kazakhstan, Eni had been forced into major concessions by the host governments.

Looking ahead, Eni remained committed to its strategy of growth—both upstream in oil and gas production and downstream in the European gas market. However, a number of uncertainties clouded Eni's future.

Its most immediate problem was the global recession that had reduced the demand for oil, gas and power and had resulted in sharp reductions in energy prices. In its first-quarter results for 2009, Eni had reported a decline in net profit of 43% compared with the first quarter of 2008.

However, the greatest uncertainties related to Eni's future over the long term. Oil and gas reserves were becoming increasingly difficult to find. Exploration in increasingly remote and geologically complex locations was causing finding and lifting costs to rise rapidly. The fragile geopolitical state of the world greatly increased investment risks. Because of its upstream activities in Kazakhstan, Russia, Iran, Libya, Algeria, Nigeria, Congo and Angola, Eni was viewed as especially vulnerable to political instability.

The threats to Eni's vertically integrated natural gas strategy were not all at the upstream level. National gas giants such as Eni and Gaz de France were viewed by the European Commission as critical obstacles to its program of liberalizing Europe's gas market. The Commission was particularly concerned at the monopoly power that resulted from the ownership of the gas-distribution infrastructure. As a result Eni had been required to separate its domestic pipeline and gas-storage assets into a separate company, Snam Rete Gas. The Commission was concerned that Eni's international pipelines represented a barrier for competitors.

The growing problem of global warming was an emerging threat to the oil and gas industry. Although the global recession had shifted attention away from climate issues, there was increasing awareness that the global warming may have reached "tipping point", where the forces driving climate change accelerate and become irreversible.

The History of Eni

Mattei and the Creation of Eni, 1926–62[1]

In 1926, Italian Prime Minister Benito Mussolini established Agip (Azienda Generali Italiana Petroli) as a state-owned oil company.[2] At the end of the Second World War, Enrico Mattei, a former partisan, was appointed head of Agip and instructed to dismantle this relic of fascist economic intervention. Contrary to instructions, Mattei renewed Agip's exploration efforts and, in 1948, discovered a substantial gas field in northern Italy's Po Valley. In 1949, Mattei also took over the management of SNAM, the Italian gas distribution company. With the opportunity to create a national energy system based upon the newly found gas reserves, pipelines were laid at a frantic rate. "Mattei built the pipelines first and negotiated afterwards . . . He simply ignored private and public rights and the law . . . Much of the work was done at night on the theory that by morning the work would be so far along that there would not be very much that anybody could do about it."[3]

On February 10, 1953, the government merged Agip, SNAM and other state-owned energy activities to form Ente Nazionale Idrocarburi (Eni) with the task of "promoting and undertaking initiatives of national interest in the fields of hydrocarbons and natural gases." Mattei was appointed its first chairman and chief executive. Eni's 36 subsidiaries extended well beyond oil and gas to include engineering services, chemicals, soap and real estate.

Under Mattei's leadership, Eni became committed to building an integrated, international oil and gas company that would ensure the independence of Italy's energy supplies and make a substantial contribution to Italy's postwar economic regeneration. Mattei soon established himself as a national hero: "He embodied great visions for postwar Italy—antifascism, the resurrection and rebuilding of the nation, and the emergence of the 'new man' who had made it himself, without the old boy network."[4]

Mattei's daring and resourcefulness was especially evident in Eni's international growth. The international oil majors—which Mattei referred to as the "Seven Sisters" because of their collusive tendencies—had tied up most of the world's known sources of oil in the Middle East and Latin America. The production-sharing agreement that Mattei signed with the Shah of Iran in 1957 marked the beginning of a fundamental shift of power from the oil majors to producer governments and established Eni as the *enfant terrible* of the oil business. The Iranian agreement was revolutionary. It created a jointly owned exploration and production company headed by an Iranian chairman and with the proceeds shared between Eni and the Iranian National Oil Company. The "Mattei formula" was the basis on which Eni extended its upstream interests to Libya, Egypt, Tunisia and Algeria between 1958 and 1960. Mattei also concluded a barter deal for crude oil from the Soviet Union. By 1960, Italy was the Soviet Union's biggest oil customer after China.

All the time Mattei was building political support within Italy. This typically involved Eni in politically motivated investments, especially in acquiring struggling companies. By 1962, Eni was "engaged in industries as various as motels, highways, chemicals, soap, fertilizers, synthetic rubber, machinery, instruments, textiles, electrical generation and distribution, contract research, engineering and construction, publishing, nuclear power, steel pipe, cement, investment banking, and even education, to mention only a few."[5]

Eni under State Control, 1962–92[6]

Mattei died in a plane crash on October 27, 1962 at the age of 56. He left a sprawling corporate empire whose strategy had been Mattei's own vision and whose integrating force had been Mattei's charisma and personal authority. At the time of his death, Mattei was president not just of Eni but also of its main operating companies.[7] Without Mattei's leadership, power shifted to the politicians; increasingly Eni became an instrument of government economic, industrial and employment policies.[8] After 1975, the chairman of Eni lost direct control of its operating companies—their chief executives were appointed by government on the basis of political considerations. Nevertheless, Eni continued to expand its oil and gas interests. Major initiatives included the purchase of natural gas from the Soviet Union (which involved Eni building a pipeline from the Austrian-Czechoslovak border to Italy), the Trans-Med Pipeline from Algeria and Tunisia to Italy, and offshore projects in West Africa, Congo and Angola. But financial performance remained weak—Eni earned significant profits only during 1988–90 (see Table 15.1).

The Bernabè Era: Privatization and Transformation, 1992–8

By 1992 the Italian government was facing pressure from the European Commission and the new European Monetary Union to cut the public-sector deficit and free up industry from state intervention. In June 1992, reformist Prime Minister Giuliano Amato announced the first steps in granting Eni greater autonomy—Eni became a joint-stock company and its relations with government were transferred to the Treasury. At the same time, Franco Bernabè, a 44-year-old economist, was appointed CEO. Although lacking line-management experience, Bernabè possessed a clear vision of Eni's future as a privatized, integrated energy company, shorn of its various diversified businesses.[9]

Bernabè's opportunity for leading a radical transformation of Eni came with the corruption scandal that swept Italy in 1993. During March 1993, Eni's chairman Gabriele Cagliari and several senior Eni board members and executives were arrested on corruption charges.[10] In the following three months Bernabè led a comprehensive restructuring of management. The boards of Eni and its main subsidiaries were forced to resign and some 250 new board members were appointed.[11]

Bernabè's corporate strategy was "to reduce Eni from being a loose conglomerate to concentrate on its core activity of energy."[12] The sale of Nuovo Pigone (a turbine manufacturer) was followed by halving capacity at EniChem—Eni's troubled chemicals business. During 1993, Bernabè's first whole year as chief executive, 73 Eni businesses were closed or sold and employment was cut by 15 000. Cost savings and asset sales resulted in a profit of almost $2 billion in 1994.[13]

Eni's initial public offering of 15% of its total equity on November 21, 1995 raised €3.3 billion for the Italian treasury and on November 28, Eni shares commenced trading in Milan, London, and New York. After more than 40 years of looking to politicians in Rome for guidance, Eni's top management had to adjust to a new set of masters—the investment community in the world's financial capitals.

Commitment to shareholder value provided impetus for further refocusing: "Eni's strategy is to focus on businesses and geographical areas where, through size, technology, or cost structure, it has a leading market position. To this end, Eni intends to implement dynamic management of its portfolio through acquisitions, joint

TABLE 15.1 Eni's sales, profits, employment and production, 1985–2008

	1985	1986	1987	1988	1989	1990	1991	1992	1993	1994	1995	1996
Sales ($m)	24328	22557	24464	25220	27105	41764	34594	38659	33595	30670	35335	37973
Net income ($m)	406	42	544	1006	1176	1697	684	−768	154	1977	2704	2930
Employees (000s)	129	130	119	116	136	131	131	126	109	92	86	83
Oil and gas produced (000s boe/day)	371	384	443	490	538	590	618	860	901	941	982	984

	1997	1998	1999	2000	2001	2002	2003	2004	2005	2006	2007	2008
Sales ($m)	34323	33177	31225	46000	43607	51379	59322	72394	91423	108492	119541	158978
Net income ($m)	2980	2891	3019	5671	7333	4816	6323	9020	10897	11613	13715	14050
Employees (000s)	80	79	72	70	71	81	77	71	72	73	75	78
Oil and gas produced (000s boe/day)	1021	1038	1064	1187	1369	1472	1562	1624	1737	1770	1736	1797

Source: Eni annual reports for various years.

ventures, and divestments. Eni also intends to outsource non-strategic activities."[14] Capital investment became increasingly concentrated upon upstream activities. In refining and marketing and petrochemicals, costs were reduced and assets sold.

The results were striking. Between 1992 and 1998, Bernabè halved Eni's debt, turned a loss into a substantial profit and reduced employment by 46 000. However, 1998 was to be Bernabè's last year at Eni: his success had made him prime candidate to lead the turnaround of another newly privatized giant—Telecom Italia.

The Mincato Era 1998–2005: From Restructuring to Growth

Vittorio Mincato brought a different background and a different style of management to Eni. Twelve years Bernabè's senior, Mincato had already spent 42 years at Eni—including 15 years as chairman of EniChem where he had pioneered turnaround and restructuring.

If Bernabè's strategy was to focus on Eni's core energy businesses, Mincato's was to grow them. In the 1999 annual report, Mincato outlined the strategy he intended to pursue:

> The four-year plan approved at the end of 1999 derives from a new strategic vision that features, on one side, an aggressive growth option in upstream activities and, on the other, a customer-oriented approach in the energy markets.
>
> For the upstream sector we devised a plan calling for 50% growth in hydrocarbon production by 2003. Such an objective will be made up of two components. The first is represented by ordinary growth . . . the second component of growth is related to mergers and acquisitions . . .
>
> In the natural gas sector, Eni has been active at three levels. First, it followed an internationalization strategy in downstream activities with the aim of selling at least 10 billion cubic meters of natural gas per year by 2003 in foreign growth markets . . . Second, with the creation of EniPower, Eni started to restructure its activities in the electricity sector, an area which represents a necessary step to strengthen its position in the gas chain, in view of the fact that most of the growth in demand for natural gas in Europe will come from the expansion of combined cycle electricity production.
>
> To support the opening up of the natural gas market in Italy, we started to restructure our activities at Snam, separating . . . transport activities from supply and sale.
>
> The scope of the changes affecting our industry will require on our part the achievement of strong efficiency improvements. For this reason, plans to cut costs have been revised, raising to €1 billion (an increase of €250 million) the amount of savings that Eni plans to achieve through cost cutting by 2003 . . . While costs will be cut across all sectors, strong measures will be taken in the Petrochemical sector—whose weight in terms of net capital will decline to 7% by 2003.[15]

By the time he retired in 2005, Mincato had won plaudits from the investment community and from industry insiders both for the clarity of Eni's strategy and the effectiveness of its execution. Upstream, Eni extended its exploration activities in Kazakhstan (where Eni took over operatorship of the huge Kashagan oilfield), West Africa, Iran and the Gulf of Mexico. In addition it acquired British Borneo in

May 2000 for €1.3 billion, LASMO in December 2000 for €4.1 billion and Fortum's Norwegian oil and gas assets in November 2002 for $1.1 billion.

In its natural gas business, Eni embarked on several major projects to link gas production with markets. The biggest and most ambitious was the Blue Stream project, a 50–50 joint venture with the Russian gas giant, Gazprom, to build a gas pipeline under the Black Sea from Russia to Turkey. This was followed by the Greenstream pipeline from the Libya to Italy. Both projects were undertaken by Eni's affiliate, Saipem.

Outside of Italy, Eni acquired several gas distribution companies including major stakes in Spain's Union Fenosa Gas (50%), GVS in Germany (50%) and Galp Energia in Portugal (33%). Eni also entered the downstream gas markets of Hungary, Greece and Croatia. Within Italy, Eni began investing heavily in power generation.

Downstream, Eni pursued rationalization and cost reduction in both refining and distribution. Between 1999 and 2005, refining capacity was cut from 664 000 to 524 000 barrels per day and the number of retail service stations was halved. Eni's chemical business was consolidated into a separate company, Polimeri Europa.

Internally, Mincato sought to make Eni a more integrated corporation. Between 2000 and 2004, Mincato transformed Eni from a holding company into a multidivisional corporation. The main subsidiaries companies, which had operated with their own boards of directors and chief executives, were reorganized into three divisions: exploration and production, gas and power, and refining and marketing. A key aspect of integration was a company-wide human resources strategy that emphasized training, appraisal and career planning over traditional "personnel" activities.

To forge a clearer identity and image for Eni, the slogan "Eni's Way" was adopted as the company's tag line in advertising and corporate communication. The key themes that "Eni's Way" embraced were technological strength, originality, spirit of adventure, and social and environmental responsibility.

Eni's Strategy under Scaroni's Leadership, 2005–9

Prior to his appointment as CEO of Eni, Paolo Scaroni had been CEO of Enel, Italy's largest electricity supplier, and CEO of Pilkington, the British glass company. He was a graduate of Bocconi University and held an MBA from Columbia University. His appointment as CEO of Eni had been greeted initially by dismay from some outside observers:

> Corporate governance [in Italy] continues to suffer big reverses, none bigger than the ousting last week by the government of Vittorio Mincato, the boss of Eni, the world's sixth-largest oil and gas company. Not only was this talented and apolitical manager replaced by somebody who knows nothing of the industry (Paolo Scaroni, boss of Enel, Italy's electrical utility); but also that ignorance is now shared by Eni's entire board.[16]

During the following 12 months, Scaroni allayed these early fears by his effectiveness in communicating with the investment community and in his leadership of Eni's international initiatives—particularly in relation to producer countries. From the outset, Scaroni made it clear that he would not deviate substantially from the strategy put in place by Mincato. In an interview with the *Financial Times* he committed Eni to a ten year strategy of turning Eni into one of world's oil and gas majors: "This is my vision, and it's shared within the company. Eni has moved from a small company to being close to becoming a major. It's closer than it was five years ago. We will use our unique features to build a long-term growth strategy." This growth would be achieved organically: "I do not see a climate for acquisitions today. If there is a target, then everybody would be in a position to get it because everyone has the money for it. In the game of cash, we are not the richest."

Achieving growth would require Eni to draw upon its unique strengths, such as its long experience of politically sensitive, oil-producing states, where it was seen as an even-handed player: "We want to use the dimensions of our company and the dimensions of our country as a positive." Unlike his previous position at Enel, his job at Eni did not require extensive restructuring: "At Eni the strategy is solid and good. If it isn't broken, don't fix it."[17]

Upstream Growth

Annual capital expenditure more than doubled between 2005 and 2008 with more than two-thirds going into exploration and production. Eni's principal upstream initiatives included the following:

- In Kazakhstan, Eni's giant Kashogan oilfield with upward of 15 billion barrels of oil was the world's biggest oil find in 30 years. Eni held an 18.5% stake and was the field's operator. It was Eni's biggest upstream project. However, it was also Scaroni's biggest challenge. As the oil price rose during 2006–8 and development suffered from recurrent cost overruns (the estimate of the total project cost rose from an initial $57 billion to $136 billion) and delays (the date for first oil production was pushed back from 2005 to 2013). The relationship with the Kazak government was the number one item on Scaroni's agenda during his first four years at Eni. The Kazak government complained about Eni's mismanagement of the project, while Eni referred to the technical, geological and logistical complexities of the project and the world shortage of engineers, geologists and technicians. A new agreement, signed in October 2008, reduced the share of Eni and its partners in the project and provided for a joint operating company to replace Eni as the developer of the field.

- In Russia, Eni built upon its historical relationship as one of biggest customers for Soviet gas, to broaden its relationship with Gazprom. In April 2007, Eni acquired equity stakes in four Russian oil companies, including 20% of Gazprom's oil business, for €3 billion. However, Gazprom retained an option to repurchase these assets which it exercised in April 2009.[18] In November 2007, it formed a joint venture with Gazprom to build South Stream—a pipeline to ship gas from Central Asia to Southern Europe.

- In Congo, Eni negotiated an agreement with the Republic of Congo that some observers hailed as a model for the future oil company relations with host governments. The May 2008 agreement involved Eni investing $3 billion in a variety of projects. In addition to onshore and offshore exploration and production (E&P) projects, Eni will build two power plants that will use associated gas from Eni's M'Boundi oil field. The project includes distribution infrastructure and will provide 80% of Congo's electricity needs. In addition, Eni will develop a palm oil plantation to produce biofuels. The Eni Foundation is funding local health clinics and a program of vaccination of children.

- In Libya, Eni built on its status as Libya's longest partner in oil production and biggest buyer of Libyan oil by extending its concession for a further 25 years and agreeing with the Libyan government to sell it a 10% equity stake in Eni.[19]
- Some of Eni's most important new upstream initiatives concerned the development of its LNG business. This was strategically important for Eni. Hitherto, Eni's vertically integrated natural gas business had been built around the use of pipelines to link sources of gas in North Africa and Russia to its large domestic market in Italy. With LNG, Eni could extend geographically both its production and marketing of gas. LNG projects included Egypt, Algeria, Nigeria, Angola, and Indonesia. In Qatar, Eni's agreements to purchase LNG provided the basis for an alliance with Qatar Petroleum to pursue gas and oil exploration projects in Africa and the Mediterranean region.

Table 15.2 shows Eni's geographical distribution of production and reserves.

A key feature of Eni's upstream strategy is a focus on countries that are conventionally viewed as difficult places to do business. According to petro-politics expert, Steve LeVine: "Italy's Eni continues to pioneer a successful path to survival in Big Oil's treacherous new world—get in bed, don't compete with the world's state-owned oil companies . . . It has grown into a hugely successful heir to the Seven Sisters, the most successful of the West's Big Oil companies at finding comfort with the world's autocrats. Where its brethren bicker with Hugo Chavez and Vladimir Putin, Eni has found a comfortable embrace."[20]

Scaroni's response to accusations of being opportunistic and unprincipled was matter-of-fact: "We deal with countries that have gas. If Switzerland had gas, we would deal with Switzerland." At the root of Eni's flexible, innovative approach to

TABLE 15.2 Eni's hydrocarbon production and reserves by geographical region (thousands of barrels of oil equivalent per day)

	Italy	North Sea	North Africa	West Africa	Rest of world	World
Production						
2008	199	237	645	335	381	1797
2007	212	261	594	327	342	1736
2006	238	282	555	372	323	1770
2005	261	283	480	343	370	1737
2004	271	308	380	316	349	1624
2003	300	345	351	260	306	1562
2002	316	308	354	238	256	1472
2001	308	288	317	233	223	1369
2000	333	168	306	225	155	1187
1999	358	154	269	206	77	1064
1998	394	156	236	196	56	1038
1997	404	155	229	180	54	1021
Reserves						
2008	681	510	1922	1146	1983	6242

Source: Eni annual reports for various years.

relationships with producer countries was acceptance of a changed balance of power between producer countries and the Western oil and gas companies: "The fact is, the oil is theirs . . . If you are looked at as a partner, you are allowed to exploit their oil; if not, you are pushed aside."[21]

Eni also continued to increase its oil and gas reserves through selective acquisitions—both of particular assets and of entire companies. In addition to its Russian investments, Eni purchased:

- Maurel and Prom's assets in Congo for $1.4 billion (February 2007);
- a Gulf of Mexico oilfield from Dominion Resources for $4.8 billion (April 2007);
- Burren Energy Plc, whose principal assets were gas fields in Turkmenistan for €2.36 billion (January 2008);
- First Calgary Petroleum Ltd (with upstream assets in Algeria) for €0.7 billion (November 2008).

The strategic plan invented by Scaroni in February 2009 committed Eni to continuing its steady growth in hydrocarbon production (see Appendix 4).

Downstream: Building the European Gas Business

Unlike most other oil and gas majors, the oil refining and the marketing of oil products was a comparatively minor part of Eni's downstream business, accounting for a mere 11% of Eni's total assets. Refining and marketing were heavily focused on Italy, which accounted for 70% of its sales of oil products, representing almost 31% of the Italian market in 2008. Outside of Italy, Eni's main markets for oil products were Austria, Hungary, Slovakia, Switzerland and Germany. Nowhere did it have a maximum market share of more than 12%. Under Scaroni, Eni continued to shrink its refining capacity and reduce its number of retail outlets. It also reduced the geographical scope of its refining and marketing activities—earlier withdrawals from Africa and northern Europe were followed by the sale of its downstream businesses in Spain and Portugal.

In gas, Scaroni continued to pursue expansion of Eni's European gas presence—in part to compensate for the undermining of its dominance of the Italian market by the EU's attempt to promote a competitive European gas market. In France, Eni bought a 27.8% stake in Altergaz in 2007. In Belgium, Eni bought 57% of gas operator Distrigas NV. In Russia Eni contracted to supply gas to a Russian electricity generator, making Eni the first European company to enter the Russian downstream gas market.

Scaroni regarded Eni's vertical integration as its key competitive advantage in the European gas market:

Eni has a very distinctive way of dealing with the gas in Europe. We are both upstream with our E&P division, and downstream in distribution, transport and sales. Just to give you an idea of how integrated these two divisions are, 35% of our equity gas is sold through our Gas & Power division, so we are already where most of our competitors in the midstream and downstream business of gas would like to be: integrated upstream, and generating our sales from our own equity gas. . . Then of course we have a wide portfolio of sourcing of gas, which goes from Algeria to Libya, Poland, Norway, and of course, Russia.

To summarize, we combine a strong upstream position in gas, with an extensive and well balanced infrastructure, a strong marketing position in Italy and in Europe. There is no other player that has such a privileged position in the European market—I hope we will demonstrate to you that for each segment of our business— and we have exciting opportunities for growth.

According to Marco Alvera, in charge of gas supplies, Eni's vertical integration in gas offered five main advantages:

Our gas, be it equity or contracted, comes from ten different countries. This gives us considerable diversity and security of supply. Second, we can leverage on a growing integrated LNG business. Third, we have attractive contractual structures and terms. Fourth, we have access to a very large set of transportation and storage assets across Europe from north to south and east to west. Finally, we have significant commercial flexibility that allows us to vary, on a daily basis, the amounts of gas produced or drawn from each of our contracts. Let's look at these points one by one.[22]

On the fourth of these points, Alvera pointed to the key role of Eni's transportation infrastructure:

We have direct access to every key gas consuming or producing country around Europe. It gives us an ideal position to support the growth of our non-Italian business. Historically, our transport and significant storage have been developed to bring gas into fixed ebb and flows, where into Italy the model was Italian-centric. They pumped gas into Northern Europe, or Eastern or Western Europe. All we need to do is simply take the gas that's transiting through those regions, on its way to Italy, and stop it exactly where we need it. If we add our ability to complement this with an LNG strategy, and with swap agreements, this effectively means that we can have gas in all our markets in Europe, or all target markets, at no additional costs. This is pretty unique.

This gives us a unique flexibility that we can really sum up in three points. We have strong structural flexibility in our gas contracts, as well as the necessary transport infrastructure to use it. The difference between the maximum quantities we can take from our contracts and the minimum quantities that we must draw from these contracts is 14 billion cubic meters per year. To put this into perspective, this is almost 3% of total European gas demand.

Second, thanks to our presence in most downstream, midstream and upstream markets around Europe, we have a broad and deep understanding of our industry, and finally, of course, we can leverage a unique set of relationships, which in some cases date back 50 years, and our engagements with the broad sets of really strategic partners.

Summing up, I would say that no other operator in the European gas market can claim to have the same scale and asset backed flexibility as Eni's Gas and Power division. Enhancing our optimization capabilities, as we continue our transition from former state monopoly in Italy to a true European leader in the gas market, will further push us even further into a league of our own.

The key obstacle to Eni's vertically integrated gas strategy was the European Union's goal of a competitive European gas market. European directives on competition in natural gas required Eni to limit its share of the Italian downstream gas market to 50% and vest its gas storage and gas transportation assets into separate, regulated companies.

Eni's response was to transfer all its regulated gas businesses to a separate company. In 2001, Snam Rete Gas was created to own and manage Eni's primary (high pressure) gas distribution system. In 2008, Eni sold its gas storage company, Stogit and Italgas, to Snam Rete Gas for a total of €4.8 billion.

Eni's vertical chains for oil and gas are shown in Figure 15.1. It is interesting to note that, despite Eni's commitment to international expansion in both upstream and downstream gas, its sales and assets were still heavily concentrated in Italy (see Figures 15.2 and 15.3).

FIGURE 15.1 Eni's vertical chains in oil and gas

OIL (millions of tonnes)

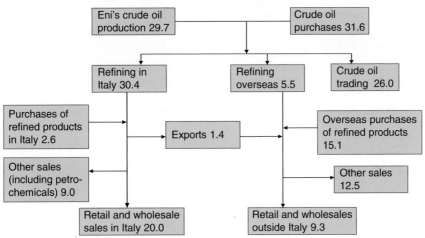

NATURAL GAS (billion cubic meters)

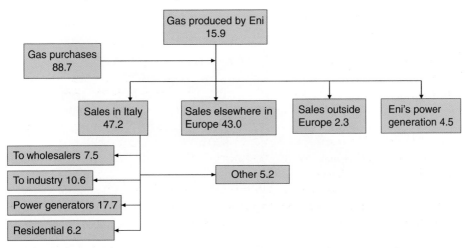

Source: Eni Fact Book 2008, www.eni.it/attachments/publications/reports/reports-2009/fact_book_2008. pdf, accessed October 29, 2009.

FIGURE 15.2 Eni's sales by geographic area ($ millions)

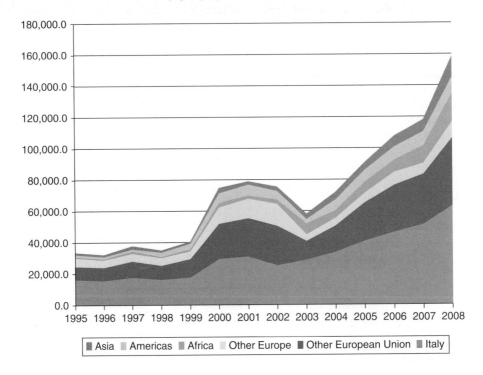

FIGURE 15.3 Eni's assets by geographic area ($ millions)

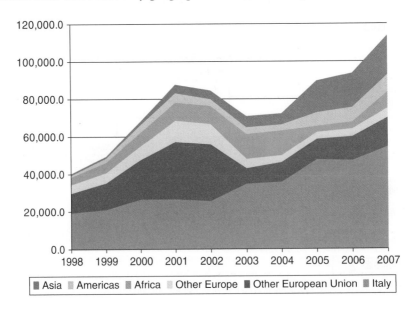

The Petroleum Sector in 2009

The petroleum sector comprises two major segments: *upstream,* comprising exploration and production, and *downstream.* Downstream is further divided into the refining and marketing of oil products and the distribution and marketing of natural gas. Between upstream and downstream are mid-stream activities comprising the transportation of oil and gas (pipeline and marine) and trading.

The Companies

The petroleum sector features three main types of company:

- *The oil and gas majors* are characterized by their age, size, international scope, and vertical integration. They are among the oldest and largest companies in the industry. Between 1998 and 2002 a wave of mergers and acquisitions resulted in the emergence of an elite group of "super majors" comprising Exxon Mobil, BP, Royal Dutch Shell, ChevronTexaco, ConocoPhillips and Total (see Table 15.3). Some of the majors are also major petrochemical producers (for example, Exxon Mobil, Royal Dutch Shell, Total).

TABLE 15.3 Major mergers and acquisitions in the oil and gas industry[a]

Major oil companies in 1995	Revenues in 1995 ($ bn)	Date merged	Major oil companies in 2008	Revenues in 2008 ($ bn)
Exxon	124		**Exxon Mobil Corp.**	425
Mobil	75	1999		
Royal Dutch/Shell Group	110		**Royal Dutch Shell**	458
Enterprise Oil	1	2002		
British Petroleum	56		**BP**	361
Amoco	28	1998		
Arco	16	2000		
Chevron	31	2001	**Chevron**	255
Texaco	36	2001		
Total	28		**Total**	223
PetroFina	n.a.	1999		
Elf Aquitaine	n.a.	2000		
Conoco	15		**ConocoPhillips**	225
Philips Petroleum	13	2002		
Tosco	n.a.	2001		
Eni	36		**Eni**	158
Repsol	21		**Repsol YPF**	68
YPF	5	1999		

[a]Only includes acquisitions of companies with revenues exceeding $1 billion.

234 CASE 15 ENI SpA

Others divested most of their chemical activities (BP, Chevron). The real economic benefits from these mergers and acquisitions remain unclear. There are advantages to spreading risks across a portfolio of major upstream projects. Pursuing multiple projects also offers potential for innovation and learning. However, there was little evidence that scale economies offered significant advantages to "super majors" over mere "majors."

- *The national oil companies (NOCs)* are the state-owned monopolies created by producer governments to manage their countries' petroleum reserves. In terms of production and reserves, the NOCs dominate the ranks of the leading petroleum companies (see Table 15.4). Most were created between the mid 1960s and the early 1980s by nationalizing the oil assets of the majors. During 2000–8, the relationship between the majors and the NOCs shifted substantially. Rising crude prices and growing nationalism among oil producing countries resulted in increasing desire by the NOCs for greater control over the countries' hydrocarbon resources and bigger shares of production and revenues. In Venezuela, Bolivia and Russia, foreign oil companies were forced to transfer upstream assets to the national government or to local companies. Elsewhere higher taxes were imposed and participation agreements renegotiated. Increasingly the NOCs have become direct competitors of the majors. Some, such as Petrobras and CNOOC, have become important international players. Others such as Saudi Aramco, Kuwait Petroleum and PDVSA have established large downstream (and petrochemical) businesses, which have depressed margins in refining and bulk chemicals. With the help of oil service companies such as Halliburton and Schlumberger, the NOCs have access to modern technologies and have become less dependent upon the majors.

- *Independents.* At all vertical levels, specialist companies play an important role. In exploration and production, companies such as Devon Energy, Anadarko, Cairn Resources, and Woodside Petroleum are important players, especially in exploring frontier regions. Their operational and financial success contradicts the arguments of the majors that huge size is an essential requirement in the petroleum industry. In refining, independent refiners such as Valero in the U.S. have grown as the majors have sold off downstream assets. (Appendix 3 lists the world's largest oil and gas companies with publicly traded shares.)

Vertical Integration Strategies

A key feature of the strategies of majors has been vertical integration throughout the value chain from exploration through to retailing gasoline and other refined products. The basis for vertical integration was the need for downstream outlets for a company's upstream production. In the case of oil, the development of a global infrastructure of transportation and storage, competitive markets for both crude and refined products, and the presence of specialist companies at every stage of the value chain has reduced (if not eliminated) the advantages of vertical integration. In response, the majors have dismantled their vertical integrated structures. This has involved dissolving close operational linkages between upstream and downstream and withdrawing from some vertical stages—for example outsourcing oilfield services, marine transportation, IT—and selling off chemical plants. Nevertheless, all the majors maintained their presence in exploration, production, refining, and

TABLE 15.4 *Petroleum Intelligence Weekly's* top 40 petroleum companies

Rank 2005	Rank 2004	PIW Index	Company	Country	State Ownership (%)
1	1	30	Saudi Aramco	Saudi Arabia	100
2	2	36	Exxon Mobil	U.S.	0
3	4	39	NIOC	Iran	100
4	3	44	PDV	Venezuela	100
5	5	48	BP	U.K.	0
6	6	59	Royal Dutch Shell	U.K./Netherlands	0
7	9	68	PetroChina	China	90
8	8	78	Chevron	U.S.	0
8	7	78	Total	France	0
10	9	83	Pemex	Mexico	100
11	11	94	ConocoPhillips	U.S.	0
12	12	96	Sonatrach	Algeria	100
13	13	100	KPC	Kuwait	100
14	14	106	Petrobras	Brazil	32
15	24	108	Gazprom	Russia	50
16	19	130	Lukoil	Russia	0
17	16	132	Adnoc	UAE	100
18	17	134	Eni	Italy	0
19	18	137	Petronas	Malaysia	100
20	21	143	NNPC	Nigeria	100
21	20	152	Repsol YPF	Spain	0
22	25	156	LibyaNOC	Libya	100
23	22	168	INOC	Iraq	100
24	23	183	EGPC	Egypt	100
24	26	183	QP	Qatar	100
26	31	185	Rosneft	Russia	75
26	27	185	Surgutneftegas	Russia	—
28	28	189	Sinopec	China	55
29	30	191	Statoil	Norway	71
30	32	224	ONGC	India	74
31	33	241	Marathon	U.S.	0
32	29	242	Yukos	Russia	—
33	15	253	Pertamina	Indonesia	100
34	37	277	SPC	Syria	100
35	34	283	PDO	Oman	60
36	50	292	OMV	Austria	32
36	36	292	Socar	Azerbaijan	100
38	41	298	TNK-BP	Russia	0
39	40	303	EnCana	Canada	0
40	35	310	Ecopetrol	Colombia	100

Note: The *Petroleum Intelligence Weekly* ranking uses a combination of output and financial measures.

marketing—even if the emphasis was increasingly on the upstream businesses and little attempt was made to ensure close upstream-downstream coordination.

In gas the situation is different. The physical difficulties of transporting and storing gas have meant that monetizing gas reserves requires dedicated investments in transportation, liquefaction, and storage that can link production to consumption. However, unlike oil, most of the majors lack a historical presence in the downstream gas business. Increasingly the majors have forward integrated into the downstream gas sector, either directly or through alliances and long-term contracts with gas marketing companies. In an effort to exploit gas fields that are far from major markets, LNG has been a critical area of investment for most of the majors.

The desire for vertical integration in gas was also a powerful incentive for entering electricity generation. By 2005, Exxon Mobil owned 3700 MW of generating capacity and had invested $2 billion in electricity production.

For all the majors, gas was a key priority during the first decade of the twenty-first century. Once regarded as a worthless impediment that was flared, the world demand for gas was growing at twice the rate as that of oil. By 2008 gas consumption (in terms of oil equivalency) was almost 80% that of oil. If the twentieth century was the "age of oil," the first half of the twenty-first century has been declared the "era of gas" by some observers.

Technology and Knowledge Management

The quest for reserves has taken the petroleum majors to the Arctic and the depths of the ocean. It has encouraged the companies to develop enhanced recovery techniques in order to extend the lives of mature fields. It has resulted in the production of synthetic crudes from sulfur-heavy petroleum, from coal and from tar sands and oilshale. Gas-to-liquids technologies are being deployed to produce gasoline from natural gas.

The result has been increased dependence upon technology. Nevertheless, investments in R&D by the majors have been modest (less than 0.3% of revenues in recent years). Increasingly the majors have outsourced technology-intensive activities to other companies. Upstream, the technological leaders in directional drilling, 4-D seismic modeling, and "intelligent oilfield" management were the oil service companies, Schlumberger in particular.

However, the knowledge requirements of the petroleum business extended beyond technology. The technical, logistical, political and financial complexities of the business meant that a critical driver of competitive advantage was the ability to learn from experience and transfer that learning throughout the company. By the early years of the new century, all the leading oil and gas companies had adopted some form of knowledge management to increase the efficiency of their knowledge capture, storage and utilization. Many of the new knowledge management systems relied heavily on Web-based technology, distributed computing, and digital wireless communication to enhance the speed and quality of decision making.

What Drives Profitability in the Petroleum Sector?

Exploration and Production

The oil price rise of 2002–8 had reinforced the industry's conventional wisdom that upstream provides the primary source of profit for the energy industry. As Table 15.5 shows, upstream was substantially more profitable for the majors than downstream or chemicals. Although upstream activities accounted for only one-fifth

CASE 15   ENI SpA   **237**

TABLE 15.5 Profitability differences between the majors' business segments, 2006–8 (%)

	Exploration and production		Refining and marketing		Gas and power		Chemicals		Corporate and other	
	ROA 2006–8	Share of total assets 2008	ROA 2006–8	Share of total assets 2008	ROA 2006–8	Share of total assets 2008	ROA 2006–2008	Share of total assets 2008	ROA 2006–2008	Share of assets total 2008
Exxon Mobil	28.45	46.83	13.37	25.60	n.a.	n.a.	19.47	8.84	−0.65	18.73
Royal Dutch Shell	20.40	37.70	7.38	28.51	6.03	17.41	5.32	5.46	4.47	6.86
BP	24.87	59.88	3.53	33.00	n.a.	n.a.	n.a.	n.a.	−6.16	8.36
ChevronTexaco	18.22	58.20	9.26	27.43	n.a.	n.a.	10.90	2.56	−5.55	11.81
Eni	20.99	42.53	4.15	11.22	10.82	32.30	−1.38	2.66	−29.60	0.80
Total	32.96	53.91	14.32	24.87	n.a.	n.a.	6.84	11.89	6.47	9.33
Repsol	19.07	34.27	11.22	34.40	14.97	10.23	10.09	5.68	−3.65	15.41

Note: ROA has been calculated as follows:

For Exxon Mobil: earnings after income taxes/segment assets.

For Royal Dutch Shell: earnings for the period/segment assets.

For BP: profit before interest/segment assets.

For ChevronTexaco: segment earnings/segment assets.

For Eni: adjusted net profit/segment assets.

For Total: net operating income/capital employed.

For Repsol: segment operating profit/segment assets.

Source: Company annual reports.

TABLE 15.6 Oil and gas production and reserves by country, 1991 and 2007

	Oil production (000 barrels/day)		Gas production (bn cubic meters/day)		Oil reserves (bn barrels)	Gas reserves (trillion cu. meters)
	2007	*1991*	*2007*	*1991*	*2007*	*2007*
Saudi Arabia	10413	8820	75.9	35	264.2	7.17
U.S.	6879	9076	545.9	510	29.4	5.98
Russia	9978	9326	607.4	600	79.4	44.65
Iran	4404	3500	111.9	26	138.4	27.80
Mexico	3477	3126	46.2	28	12.2	0.37
Venezuela	2613	2501	28.5	22	87.0	5.15
Norway	2556	1923	89.7	27	8.2	2.96
China	3743	2828	69.3	15	15.5	1.88
Canada	3309	1980	183.7	105	27.7	1.63
U.K.	1636	1919	72.4	51	3.6	0.41
U.A.E.	2915	2639	49.2	24	97.8	6.09
Iraq	2145	279		–	115.0	3.17
Kuwait	2626	185	12.6	1	101.5	1.78
Nigeria	2356	1890	28.4	4	36.2	5.30
Algeria	2000	1351	83.2	53	12.3	4.52

Source: BP Statistical Review of World Energy, 2008.

of revenues for large oil firms, they contributed over two-thirds of overall profits during 2004–8. The reasons why upstream has been so profitable are not altogether clear. The structure of the industry—many producers and a commodity product—does not appear particularly attractive. However, one key structural influence is the role of the Organization of Petroleum Exporting Countries (OPEC), which accounts for over half of world oil production and maintains prices through setting production quotas for its members. When OPEC's discipline over oil production disintegrates, prices drop—sometimes catastrophically (as in 1986 and at the end of 1998). However, the massive rise in oil prices (and upstream profits) during 2002–8 was mainly the result of capacity shortage in the face of rising demand from China and India. As Table 15.6 shows, the problem is not a lack of reserves (except in the U.S. and Europe where reserves are becoming exhausted; the problem is limits on production due to underinvestment (Russia, Iran, Libya), internal unrest (Iraq, Nigeria) and poor management (Venezuela, Mexico).

The high prices of 2006–8, combined with restricted access to existing reserves, caused the companies to move increasingly to deep water exploration and nonconventional oils (tarsands, oil shale). The result has been rapidly increasing finding and lifting costs (see Table 15.7).

The desire to control rising upstream costs has encouraged the oil and gas companies to outsource more and more of their E&P activities. Drilling, seismic surveys, rig design, platform construction and oilfield maintenance are increasingly undertaken by oilfield service companies. As these companies have developed proprietary technologies, deepened their experience and grown through mergers and

TABLE 15.7 U.S. energy companies' finding costs by region, 1993–2007 (2007 dollars/barrel of oil equivalent)

	U.S. onshore	U.S. offshore	Canada	OECD Europe	Africa	Middle East	Other Eastern hemisphere	Other, Western hemisphere	Worldwide
1993–1995	4.53	4.58	6.35	5.25	3.32	3.23	5.51	2.66	4.65
1998–2000	5.21	10.52	7.18	7.85	2.93	5.92	7.88	4.59	6.14
2001–2003	9.16	10.24	12.26	9.86	5.79	6.22	4.05	3.98	7.35
2004–2006	11.54	65.49	19.89	23.41	26.36	5.41	13.03	43.87	17.65
2005–2007	13.38	49.54	17.01	31.58	38.24	4.77	20.56	30.30	18.49

Source: Energy Information Administration, U.S. Department of Energy.

TABLE 15.8 Capital investment by business sector among the majors, 2003–7

	Average annual capital expenditure ($ million)	Exploration and production (%)	Refining and marketing (%)	Chemicals (%)	Gas and power (%)	Corporate and other (%)
Exxon Mobil	16.975	78.2	14.7	4.0	2.6[a]	0.5
Royal Dutch/Shell	16400	68.0	17.8	3.2	9.3	1.7
BP	17900	69.3	17.0	—	3.3	6.0
TotalFinaElf	12193	72.3	17.4[b]	9.9	—	0.4
Chevron Texaco	10800	77.0	17.6	1.6	—	3.8[c]
Conoco Phillips	11425	57.9	16.2	—	—	25.9[d]
Eni	9611	65.7	8.6	1.5	17.6	6.8[e]

Notes:

[a] Coal and Power; downstream gas included in refining and marketing.

[b] Includes downstream gas.

[c] Includes Power.

[d] Major item was investment in Lukoil.

[e] Includes engineering and construction.

Source: Company annual reports.

acquisitions, so sector leaders such as Schlumberger, Baker Hughes, Halliburton and Diamond Offshore Drilling have emerged as powerful players within the petroleum industry.

The attractive rates of return earned in the upstream sector have meant that capital investment by the integrated majors has become increasingly focused upon the upstream sector. Between 2000 and 2008, the leading majors invested between three and four times as much upstream as downstream (see Table 15.8). During previous decades, capital investment was split more evenly between upstream and downstream.

Refining and Marketing   In oil, downstream businesses include refining and the wholesale and retail marketing and distribution of refined oil products. The main refined products in order of importance are: gasoline, diesel fuel, aviation fuel, heating oil, liquefied petroleum gas (LPG) and petrochemical feedstocks (e.g. naphtha). Historically, downstream has been less profitable than upstream (see Table 15.9). Both refining and retail distribution have been subject to intense competitive pressure as a result of excess capacity.

During 2004–6, refining margins increased sharply. Mergers between companies and the impact of environmental regulations reduced excess capacity; in the U.S. refinery shutdowns created a temporary squeeze. However, recession, increased fuel efficiency, and new refining capacity in Asia and the Middle East caused profitability to fall during 2007–8. In retailing, profitability was dismal due to excess capacity and new entry by supermarket chains into gasoline distribution (especially in France and the U.K.).

TABLE 15.9 Return on investment by line of business for U.S. petroleum companies, 1980–2007 (%)

	1980–4	1985–9	1990–4	1995–9	2000–3	2004–7
U.S. oil and gas production	15.40	4.00	5.80	10.10	14.40	18.99
U.S. refining and marketing	5.10	8.00	2.70	5.70	7.90	22.33
Foreign oil and gas production	19.30	12.20	9.10	12.40	12.90	21.48
Foreign refining and marketing	10.40	6.80	10.10	7.00	6.20	19.73
Nuclear, nonconventional, and coal	5.50	4.70	2.90	6.10	3.70	16.02

Source: Energy Information Administration, U.S. Department of Energy.

Downstream Gas and Power   Among the petroleum majors, Eni was unusual in being established on natural gas rather than oil. For most of the majors, oil had been their dominant interest and, as a result, few had pursued the same strategy of vertical integration that they had in oil. As the result, in most countries the gas chain was more fragmented than the oil chain with exploration and production undertaken by the petroleum companies and distribution traditionally undertaken by state-owned or state-regulated utilities. As demand for natural gas increased during the 1980s and 1990s, the petroleum majors reoriented their upstream activities towards gas. However, gas reserves were valueless unless they could be brought to market. Hence all the majors developed interests in the transportation and downstream distribution of gas. Regulation of downstream gas markets and privatization of publicly owned gas utilities created the opportunities that the petroleum majors needed to increase their presence in gas marketing and distribution. Similar deregulation in electricity generation and market produced further opportunities for the majors. Not only could they enter the electricity business directly—they could also seek to supply natural gas to independent power producers.

Although downstream gas and power offered growth opportunities for the petroleum majors, these activities typically did not offer rates of return comparable with their upstream businesses. The newly liberalized gas and electricity markets attracted entrants from a number of different sectors and were fiercely competitive. Moreover, the oil majors were relative newcomers to these markets compared with the traditional utilities. Fierce competition coupled with overinvestment could decimate profitability. During 2002, wholesale prices for electricity plunged in the U.S. and U.K. forcing a number of power producers into acute financial difficulty.

Chemicals   The petrochemical sector displayed many of the same structural features as oil refining: capital-intensive processes producing commodity products, many competitors, and a continual tendency for excess capacity (much of it resulting from new investment by Asian and Middle East producers) to drive down prices and margins. Competitive advantage in chemicals depended upon scale economies, technological advantages (such as patented products and processes) and low costs of feedstock. Among the oil and gas majors there were two distinct views about chemicals. Some, like Eni, saw chemicals as a fundamentally unattractive industry and believed that chemical plants were better run by chemical companies. Others (including Exxon, Shell, and Total) viewed chemicals as part of their core business and believed that integration between refining and petrochemicals offered them a cost advantage.

The Outlook for Eni in 2009

The steady evolution of Eni's strategy under its past three CEOs, Bernabè, Mincato, and Scaroni, had provided stability and a clear sense of identity and direction within the Group. Eni was an international energy major with a strong focus on E&P and a commitment to being Europe's leading supplier of natural gas. Upstream it was focused on the core areas of the Caspian Sea and Africa; downstream upon Italy and nearby European countries. Its technically strong engineering and oil services sector allowed it to link the two. Its emphasis on organic growth, capital discipline and shareholder returns had done much to build its reputation within the industry and the international financial community. Looking ahead, its emphasis upon natural gas and its proven ability to work effectively as a valued partner in politically challenging producer countries positioned it well for the future.

Yet, for all Eni's solid achievement, Scaroni was aware that Eni's outstanding performance had taken place under very favorable external circumstances. The next five years posed uncertainties both for the industry and for Eni. Almost certainly maintaining production growth, increasing profits and creating value for shareholders would be more difficult in the future than in the past. By 2006, Eni had divested most of its noncore businesses and eliminated most of the inefficiencies that it had inherited from its state-owned past. Increasing profits in the future would require pursuing profitable growth opportunities, more effective exploitation of existing competitive advantage and building new sources of competitive advantage.

Upstream, Eni—along with the other majors—faced the risk of growing marginalization as the producer countries sought a bigger share of the value from their oil and gas reserves and their national oil companies extended their ambitions to expand downstream and internationally. Despite being among the world's biggest companies, the oil and gas majors were far from being the biggest players in the industry in terms of oil and gas reserves (see Appendix 3). Moreover, they were high-cost producers compared with many of the national oil companies. So far the increased assertiveness of many producer governments had allowed Eni to position itself as a collaborative partner. However, Eni's difficulties in Kazakhstan pointed to the conflicts between petroleum majors and host governments that characterized the oil business. Ongoing tensions between the EU and Russia provided an awkward context for Eni's closer relationships with Gazprom.

Even without these threats, fulfilling Eni's potential would require developing the responsiveness and coordination that it needed to combine technology, physical assets, expertise, and human ingenuity to exploit the opportunities constantly emerging in the world's fast-changing energy markets. Despite the transformation of Eni from a loose-knit holding company to a more tightly integrated divisional corporation, it still faced internal challenges to the successful execution of its strategy. A key challenge was internationalization. Downstream, Eni was heavily dependent on the Italian market (see Figure 15.1) and, overall, Italy accounted for almost half of Eni's sales and assets

TABLE 15.10 Valuation multiples for petroleum majors (28 April 2009)

	Price/earnings ratio	Price/book ratio	Price/sales ratio	Price/cash flow
Exxon Mobil Corp.	7.38	2.83	0.67	5.36
British Petroleum plc	8.17	1.31	0.63	4.77
ChevronTexaco Corp.	5.44	1.48	0.47	4.32
TotalFinaElf S.A.	5.59	1.76	0.53	5.11
Royal Dutch Petroleum Co.	6.96	1.70	0.32	4.23
Eni SpA	3.77	1.35	0.56	3.56
Repsol YPF, S.A.	3.65	0.87	0.30	n.a.
ConocoPhillips	negative	1.08	0.24	2.62
Industry median	7.50	1.08	0.24	3.30

Source: Hoover's Online (www.hoovers.com); *Financial Times*.

(see Figure 15.2 and 15.3). The strong domestic orientation was reflected in Eni's culture and personnel—there were very few non-Italians among the ranks of senior managers.

The second internal challenge was that of integration. Eni's large downstream gas business offered a market for its upstream gas production, and its internal engineering and construction capabilities provided the means to link the two. Eni's ability to pursue vertical integration in gas represented a significant source of competitive advantage for the company. However, to realize this potential required effective collaboration between Eni's different divisions and subsidiaries. Despite the creation of a divisional corporation, effective coordination in exploiting overseas opportunities increasingly required close, flexible coordination across Eni's traditionally independently-minded businesses.

Finally, the issue of size remained an open question. Eni's commitment to organic growth had been applauded by investment analysts. However, investment projects in the industry were growing steadily in complexity and cost. Did Eni have the necessary size to play with the big boys and the diversity of locations and projects to spread technical and political risks? For all Eni's ability to generate strong shareholder returns, Scaroni continued to be dismayed by the stock market's lack of appreciation for Eni's investment qualities. Eni's valuation ratios remained below those of its peers in the international petroleum industry (see Table 15.10).

Appendix 1: Eni SpA: Selected Financial data, 2002–8

Income statement (U.S.$ millions)	2002	2003	2004	2005	2006	2007	2008
Revenue	51 379	59 322	73 063	92 412	109 479	120 674	160 024
Cost of goods sold	33 440	39 132	47 550	60 223	72 437	79 705	112 320
Gross profit	17 939	20 190	25 513	32 189	37 041	40 968	47 704

(Continued)

Income statement (U.S.$ millions)	2002	2003	2004	2005	2006	2007	2008
Gross profit margin	34.9%	34.0%	34.9%	34.8%	33.8%	33.9%	29.8%
SG&A expense	3253	3584	4024	4155	4599	5206	5886
Depreciation and amortization	5771	5831	6028	7168	8090	9913	14428
Operating income	8915	10774	15375	20865	24352	25849	27402
Operating margin	17.4%	18.2%	21.0%	22.6%	22.2%	21.4%	17.1%
Nonoperating income	45	19	3210	3882	5206	6103	11738
Nonoperating expenses	206	7	3404	4336	5003	6239	12051
Income before taxes	8664	10580	16198	21545	25693	27438	28298
Income taxes	3279	3669	5770	10079	13316	12630	14247
Net income after taxes	4816	6323	9781	11466	12377	14808	14050
Net profit margin	9.4%	10.7%	13.4%	12.4%	11.3%	12.3%	8.8%
ROACE	13.7%	15.6%	16.6%	19.5%	20.0%	20.5%	15.7%

Balance sheet (U.S.$ millions)	Dec 02	Dec 03	Dec 04	Dec 05	Dec 06	Dec 07	Dec 08
Cash	3423	4113	1244	1653	5021	2896	2850
Trade and other receivables	14186	17043	17030	22198	23687	28326	32666
Inventories	3355	4031	3530	4418	5988	7534	8941
Other current assets	1868	2244	3135	3018	3131	7569	10121
Total current assets	22832	27431	24939	31288	37826	46325	54578
Net fixed assets	35327	42443	50327	55816	55833	68688	86958
Other noncurrent assets	10840	13024	15072	16870	17614	23987	29851
Total assets	69000	82898	90338	103974	111273	139000	171387
Accounts payable	5806	6975	7238	10131	13265	15196	18507
Short-term debt	8273	9939	5146	5719	4284	10635	10155
Other current liabilities	8560	10285	10696	12029	12374	15602	23304
Total current liabilities	22639	27199	23080	27879	29924	41433	51966
Long-term debt	6868	8251	9433	9490	9335	15522	20476
Other noncurrent liabilities	9766	11734	13755	17976	20103	23317	27636
Total liabilities	39274	43783	46268	55345	59362	80272	100078
Minority interest	2196	2638	3926	2913	2734	3341	5989
Total shareholders' equity	27530	35714	44070	48629	51911	58728	71310

Cash flow statement	2002	2003	2004	2005	2006	2007	2008
Net operating cash flow	11091	12257	15500	18521	21421	21258	32047

Appendix 2: Eni's Operating Performance, 1999–2008

Exploration and production	1999	2000	2001	2002	2003	2004	2005	2006	2007	2008
Proved hydrocarbon reserves (mmboe)	5534	6008	6929	7030	7272	7218	6837	6436	6370	6600
Reserve life index (years)	14.0	14.0	13.7	13.2	12.7	12.1	10.8	10.0	10.0	10.0

Exploration and production	1999	2000	2001	2002	2003	2004	2005	2006	2007	2008
Hydrocarbon production (kboe/d)	1064	1187	1369	1472	1562	1624	1737	1770	1736	1797
Gas and power										
Worldwide gas sales (bcm)	63.08	65.50	67.10	68.54	78.33	87.03	94.21	98.10	98.96	104.23
Electricity sold (TWh)	0	4.77	6.55	6.74	8.65	16.95	27.56	31.03	33.19	29.93
Refining and marketing										
Refinery throughput (mm tonnes)	40.65	41.27	39.99	37.73	35.43	37.69	38.79	38.04	37.15	35.84
Refinery capacity (kbbl/d)	664	664	664	504	504	504	524	534	544	544
Sales of refined products (mmtonnes)	51.82	53.46	53.24	52.24	50.43	53.54	51.63	51.13	50.14	50.68
Retail sales (mmtonnes)	14.21	13.92	14.11	13.71	14.01	14.40	13.72	12.48	12.65	12.67
Service stations at year end (units)	12489	12085	11707	10762	10647	9140	6282	6294	6441	5956
Average service station throughput (kliters/year)	1543	1555	1621	1674	1771	1970	1926	2470	2486	2502
Engineering and construction										
Orders acquired (€ million)	2600	4726	3716	7852	5876	5784	8395	11172	11845	13860
Order backlog (€ million)	4439	6638	6937	10065	9405	8521	10122	13191	15390	19105

Appendix 3: Oil and Gas Companies among the Forbes Global 2000, April 2009 ($ bn)

Rank	Company	Country	Sales ($bn)	Profits ($bn)	Assets ($bn)	Market value ($bn)
2	Royal Dutch Shell	Netherlands	458.36	26.28	278.44	135.10
4	ExxonMobil	U.S.	425.70	45.22	228.05	335.54
5	BP	U.K.	361.14	21.16	228.24	119.70
9	Chevron	U.S.	255.11	23.93	161.17	121.70
11	Total	France	223.15	14.74	164.66	112.90

(Continued)

Rank	Company	Country	Sales ($bn)	Profits ($bn)	Assets ($bn)	Market value ($bn)
13	Gazprom	Russia	97.29	26.78	276.81	74.55
14	PetroChina	China	114.32	19.94	145.14	270.56
18	ENI	Italy	158.32	12.91	139.80	80.68
25	Petrobras	Brazil	92.08	14.12	120.68	110.97
33	Sinopec-China Petroleum	China	154.28	7.43	100.41	93.50
53	StatoilHydro	Norway	93.38	6.20	82.42	53.30
64	Rosneft	Russia	46.99	11.12	77.40	34.07
76	Lukoil	Russia	66.86	9.51	59.14	26.62
101	Repsol-YPF	Spain	68.48^E	3.95	68.79	18.95
121	Reliance Industries	India	34.03	4.87	43.61	35.95
124	EnCana	Canada	30.06	5.94	47.25	29.69
132	Occidental Petroleum	U.S.	24.48	6.86	41.54	42.03
135	Marathon Oil	U.S.	70.25	3.53	42.69	16.47
145	Schlumberger	Netherlands	27.56	5.43	31.99	45.52
152	Oil & Natural Gas	India	24.04	4.95	35.35	28.91
163	BG Group	U.K.	18.34	4.56	35.83	48.10
168	Surgutneftegas	Russia	24.25	3.61	40.29	19.65
193	Hess	United States	41.09	2.36	28.59	17.84
199	Anadarko Petroleum	U.S.	15.72	3.26	48.92	16.07
207	Indian Oil	India	51.66	1.97	33.64	10.20
211	TNK-BP Holding	Russia	36.25	5.94	27.94	9.45
230	Ecopetrol	Colombia	15.42	5.29	22.16	33.38
231	Transocean	Switzerland	12.67	4.20	35.17	19.11
233	Nippon Oil	Japan	65.46	1.49	45.98	7.05
234	Suncor Energy	Canada	24.37	1.73	26.35	19.51
244	PTT Public Company	Thailand	57.08	1.47	25.21	12.18
246	Cnooc	China	11.97	4.12	24.62	39.17
249	Husky Energy	Canada	20.01	3.04	21.48	18.21
251	Canadian Natural Res	Canada	11.47	4.04	34.55	17.44
271	OMV Group	Austria	35.57	1.91	29.52	7.91
273	Petro-Canada	Canada	22.51	2.54	24.61	10.72
305	Sasol	South Africa	16.62	2.87	17.71	15.98
322	Formosa Petrochemical	Taiwan	21.62	2.15	15.15	15.22
325	XTO Energy	U.S.	7.70	1.91	38.25	18.35
346	National Oilwell Varco	U.S.	13.43	1.95	21.48	11.16
365	Halliburton	U.S.	18.28	1.54	14.39	14.63
366	Inpex	Japan	12.05	1.74	17.96	16.34
372	Apache	U.S.	12.39	0.71	29.19	19.78
380	ConocoPhillips	U.S.	225.42	-17.00	142.87	55.29
394	SK Holdings	South Korea	69.66	1.48	61.16	2.62
395	Cepsa	Spain	25.85	1.02	13.90	12.68
405	Chesapeake Energy	U.S.	11.63	0.72	38.44	9.77
414	Enbridge	Canada	13.07	1.08	20.01	11.20
434	Murphy Oil	U.S.	27.51	1.74	11.15	7.97

Appendix 4: Eni 2009–12 Strategic Plan and Targets

London, 13 February 2009—Paolo Scaroni, CEO of Eni, today presented the company's 2009–12 strategic plan to the financial community.

In spite of the uncertain and volatile energy markets, Eni confirms its strategy of delivering hydrocarbon production and reserve growth, based on a solid portfolio of quality projects. Eni will also strengthen its leadership in the European gas market and maintain a dividend yield amongst the highest in the sector.

Exploration and Production

Eni confirms its strategy of delivering production growth, with an average annual rate of 3.5% for the 2009–12 period. This growth strategy is based on organic development plans carried out with a reserve replacement ratio of 130%. Beyond the four-year plan, Eni expects to maintain robust production growth with an average annual growth rate of 3% up to 2015.

In 2012, hydrocarbon production will exceed 2 million boe/day, based on a $55 per barrel price scenario. In 2009, hydrocarbon production will exceed 1.8 million boe/day, based on a $43 per barrel price scenario.

Production growth will be focused on three main strategic areas: Africa, OECD countries and Central Asia/Russia. More than 90% of production and investments to 2012 will be concentrated in these areas.

Eni will maintain a steady growth, even in lower oil price conditions, thanks to its focus on conventional activities and to the quality of its portfolio, which is located largely in low cost production areas and is based upon giant projects with economy of scale benefits.

In the next four years, more than 0.5 million boe/day of new production will come on stream, 85% of which is related to projects that will be profitable even under an oil price scenario below $45 per barrel.

Gas and Power

Eni will strengthen its leading position in the European gas market, where it holds a unique competitive position, thanks to diversification and the size of its large supply contracts as well as to a vast infrastructure system and customer base.

Despite the lower growth we expect in the European gas markets, Eni will grow its international gas sales by an average 7% a year, thanks also to the contribution of Distrigas. This growth will enable the company to reach total gas sales of 124 billion cubic meters by 2012.

Beyond continuing to grow its market share in core European countries, Eni will increase sales in the U.S., thanks to the monetization of the gas produced in the Gulf of Mexico.

In the four-year plan Eni, thanks to the growth in regulated activities and its expansion in international markets, will achieve in G&P a total pro-forma adjusted EBITDA of €20 billion, 1 billion higher than the target set in the previous plan.

Refining and Marketing

Eni's strategy in the R&M sector focuses on the selective strengthening of its refining system, the improvement of quality standards of its marketing activities and the widespread increase in operating efficiency, targeting an improvement of €400 million in EBIT by 2012 excluding scenario effects.

In refining, Eni plans to increase the complexity and the yield in medium distillates, exploiting proprietary technologies.

In marketing, Eni's target is to consolidate its leadership in the Italian market, increasing its market share to 32% by 2012, through loyalty programs and the broadening of nonoil products sales.

Investment Plan and Efficiency Program

In the 2009–12 plan, Eni will invest €48.8 billion, slightly less than in the 2008–11 plan. Investments in exploration and production are estimated at €34 billion and will sustain the production growth over the next four years and beyond.

With regard to the efficiency, Eni doubled the program launched in 2006, after having achieved almost 1 billion in cost reductions by the end of 2008. The new plan will enable Eni to double costs reduction to about €2 billion by 2012, both in real terms and versus the 2005 baseline.

Source: Eni 2009–12 Strategic Plan and Targets, www.eni.it/en_IT/attachments/media/press-release/2009/02/eni-2009-2012-strategic-plan-and-targets.pdf, accessed October 29, 2009.

Notes

1 We refer throughout the case to "Eni." For most of its history, the company's full name was Ente Nazionale Idrocarburi, but was known by its acronym, ENI. In August 1992, the company's name was changed to Eni SpA.

2 In common with other European governments, Italy recognized the growing strategic importance of oil and wished to avoid dependence upon foreign-owned multinationals for its fuel supplies. The British government had purchased a controlling interest in BP in 1914 and France had established the Compagnie Française des Pétroles (Total) in 1924.

3 D. Votaw, *The Six-Legged Dog: Mattei and ENI—A Study in Power,* University of California Press, Berkeley, CA, 1964, p. 15.

4 Daniel Yergin, *The Prize,* Simon & Shuster, New York, 1992, p. 502.

5 Daniel Yergin, *The Prize,* Simon & Shuster, New York, 1992, p. 23.

6 Section sourced from company report, "L'Eni di Fronte a un Bivio," Eni S.p.A, 2002.

7 D. Votaw, *The Six-Legged Dog: Mattei and ENI—A Study in Power,* University of California Press, Berkeley, CA, 1964, p. 71.

8 "L'Eni di Fronte a un Bivio," Eni S.p.A, 2002, p. 5.

9 *Franco Bernabè at Eni* (Harvard Business School Case 9-498-034, April 7, 1998).

10 Chairman Gabriele Cagliari later committed suicide in prison.

11 "L'Eni di Fronte a un Bivio," Eni S.p.A, 2002, p. 11.

12 "Eni Savors the Taste of Freedom", *Financial Times,* June 9, 1994.

13 ENI SpA, Securities and Exchange Commission, Form 20F, 1996.

14 Securities and Exchange Commission, *ENI S.p.A., 20-F for 1996,* p. 3.

15 "Letter to Shareholders," Eni, Annual Report, 1999, pp. 4–5.

16 "Italy: The Real Sick Man of Europe," *The Economist,* May 19, 2005.

17 "Eni's New Chief Intends to become a Big Player," *Financial Times,* September 22, 2005.

18 Lex column, "Gazprom/Eni," *Financial Times,* April 7, 2009.

19 "Rome's Colonial Past key to Libya's Eni Stake," *Financial Times,* December 9, 2008.

20 See http://oilandglory.com/labels/ENI.html, accessed October 19, 2009.

21 "How Italy's ENI Vastly Boosted Oil Output," *Business Week,* April 20, 2009.

22 Eni S.p.A. Gas seminar conference call, December 1, 2006.

Case 16 American Apparel: Vertically Integrated in Downtown L.A.*

December 2008 marked the end of American Apparel's first year as a public company. On December 19, 2007, its shares had begun trading on the American Stock Exchange under the symbol APP. The year 2008 had been eventful for the Los Angeles-based T-shirt and casual clothing company. Fueled by capital from its public listing, it had embarked upon a new phase of expansion: over 80 new stores were opened—including first-time entry into Spain, Brazil, China and Australia—and sales grew by 62% over 2007. Its status as "one of the hottest brands around" was

* © 2010 R.M. Grant, S.J.J. McGuire, E.A. Drost. This case was written by Robert M. Grant, Ellen A. Drost and Stephen J. J. McGuire. It draws upon an earlier case by Ellen A. Drost, Stephen McGuire, Christina Eaves, Lisa Tousant, Sandy Johnson, Sheridan Mascarenhas and William Drescher. Reproduced with permission.

confirmed by its second place (after Nike) in the *Cassandra Report*'s listing of "Top Trendsetter Brands of 2008"—beating Apple (third place). Chief executive Dov Charney was named "Retailer of the Year" in the 2008 Annual Michael Awards.

This success was achieved despite a strategy that defied the conventional wisdom of the "rag trade." In mass-market fashion apparel, outsourcing production to low-wage countries was viewed as the only viable strategy. Yet American Apparel had built a highly profitable business following a vertically integrated model with production concentrated in Los Angeles. American Apparel believed that the higher costs of manufacturing in the U.S. could be offset by the price premium from superior quality, styling, and image, and by the advantages of speed to market. Critical to these advantages were American Apparel's tight linkage between design, manufacture, marketing, and retailing. It was not just the labor costs of producing in California rather than in China that boosted American Apparel's manufacturing costs. Its cost base was further elevated by paying employees premium wage rates and offering benefits that were unheard of in the dog-eat-dog world of garment manufacture. Employee benefits included health care, retirement pensions and a variety of employee amenities.

The source of American Apparel's distinctiveness was its founder and chief executive, Dov Charney. Charney was a self-proclaimed hustler whose lifestyle and management style generated controversy that most publicly traded companies eschewed. Charney's open and frank attitude about progressive social issues and sex stirred up media feeding frenzies from fashion magazines to nationally syndicated television. While the provocative photos he selected for American Apparel's ad campaigns were praised for their ability to grab people's attention, much of the publicity he garnered was highly critical. In the media and on the Web, he was portrayed as an exhibitionist and sexual predator. Even in taking American Apparel public, Charney succeeded in being nonconformist and innovative. Rather than launch an initial public offering (IPO) underwritten by a leading investment bank, American Apparel chose to be acquired by Endeavor Acquisition Corp—a "special purpose acquisition corporation" (otherwise known as a "blank check company")—a listed company set up specifically to acquire other companies. Observers noted that the deal "allowed Mr. Charney to go public without the scrutiny that attends most stockmarket listings."[1]

Looking ahead, Charney believed that American Apparel faced tremendous future growth potential. He saw American Apparel as operating in an "attractive, underserved market segment with large potential." This potential related both to cities and countries where American Apparel was not yet present and customer segments other than American Apparel's core "metropolitan, young adult segment." The long-term goals he outlined included unit growth of 20% annually, an operating margin of 15% and growth of earnings per share of 20%–25%.[2]

These ambitious growth targets presented new challenges for American Apparel. As it grew in size and its retail stores spanned more of the globe, doubts were raised about the scalability of its business model. Expanding output had already forced American Apparel to acquire new plants in Los Angeles. International expansion meant longer supply chains and increased logistical complexity. The impressive growth in same-store sales had been achieved through expanding its product range—American Apparel had expanded from T-shirts and knitted cotton garments into a wide range of clothing and accessories. The increasing product range added further complexity to purchasing, manufacturing and distribution. Overall, American Apparel's tightly coordinated, vertically integrated business model was being stretched in multiple directions. In addition to the challenges of growing size and scope, Charney also had to come to terms with American Apparel's new status as a public company. This raised questions about his personality and management style. To what extent would increased regulation and financial market scrutiny require a more conventional approach to leadership?

The T-Shirt Business

T-shirts—like denim jeans—are quintessentially American clothing products. About 1.4 billion cotton T-shirts are sold in North America annually with a retail value of about $20 billion. Originally underwear garments, T-shirts are the most common summer outerwear garment for weekend Americans. The designs and words they carry are important statements of personal identity indicating affiliation with a sports team, college, political movement, religion, charity or specific social event. Yet despite the T-shirt's place in American culture, the vast majority are imported—with China, Mexico and Central America the major source. Many imports are by U.S. manufacturing firms such as Gildan Activewear, Hanesbrands and Delta Apparel that have plants in Mexico, Latin America and the Caribbean. A high proportion of imported T-shirts are made from cotton grown in the U.S. and knitted into fabric in China. (The U.S. is the world's largest exporter of cotton fiber.)[3] The average import price of a T-shirt was $1.51 in December 2005.[4] Despite import protection, the U.S. garment industry as a whole had shrunk dramatically. When the quota system known as the Multifiber Agreement was created in 1974, 1.4 million Americans worked in the garment industry. By the time it was abolished in 2006, the total was down to 270 000.

The U.S. T-shirt market features a wide range of suppliers. At the wholesale level, blank T-shirts are sold by major suppliers (such as Gildan Activewear, Hanesbrands, Russell Athletic and Fruit of the Loom) to screen printers that add their own designs or corporate and club logos. At the retail level, many different types of retailer compete—independent specialty stores, department stores, and chains such as Gap, Urban Outfitters, H&M, American Eagle, and Forever 21. The price dispersion is wide: at Sears, a basic T-shirt retails at $6.99, while at Nordstrom, a Versace limited edition T-shirt costs $225. Table 16.1 shows some leading suppliers of casual clothing.

Dov Charney and the Development of American Apparel

Dov Charney's character could be described as brilliant to boisterous, clever to crass, and daring to democratic. The native Canadian had a passion for T-shirts and capitalism. Charney believed that "nationalism is over" and "there was something special about the 'can do' spirit of the U.S.A."[5]

Charney's entrepreneurial interest in the garment business was first demonstrated at age 16, when he purchased American-made T-shirts from K-Mart in the U.S. and then drove them to Canada in a U-Haul truck. He sold them outside the old Montreal Forum at concerts.[6] During his senior year at Tufts University, he dropped out, borrowed $10 000 from his father, moved to South Carolina, and started his T-shirt business: "Heavy, The American Apparel Company." He was successful with a line of form-fitting women's T-shirts before going bust when its main contract manufacturer closed down production.[7]

TABLE 16.1 Sales and profits of leading fashion apparel companies, 2009

	Sales ($ bn)	Net income ($ bn)	Return on assets (%)
Gap (U.S.)	14.53	0.97	12.3
Inditex (Spain)	14.00	1.86	18.0
Hennes & Mauritz (Sweden)	10.91	1.88	30.5
VF (U.S.)	7.64	0.60	9.3
Next (U.K.)	6.62	0.70	21.6
Ross Stores (U.S.)	6.40	0.30	12.1
Esprit Holdings (China)	4.77	0.83	30.3
Hannesbrands (U.S.)	4.25	0.13	2.0
Abercrombie & Fitch (U.S.)	3.54	0.27	5.9
J. Crew (U.S.)	1.43	0.05	7.6
Gilden Activewear (U.S.)	1.25	0.14	7.9
American Apparel (U.S.)	0.55	0.01	4.2

Source: www.hoovers.com and company annual reports.

Charney moved to California where in 1998 he met Sam Lim, an owner of a cutting-and-sewing facility located under a freeway in Los Angeles.[8] Charney went into business with Sam Lim and Sam Kim, both Korean. Together they formed a company named "Two Koreans and a Jew."[9] Eventually Sam Kim sold his stake in the partnership and Charney and Lim went on to develop the business into American Apparel.

Charney established American Apparel as a T-shirt manufacturer that was integrated from knitting, through cutting and sewing, to dyeing and finishing. Initially, the main customers were private-label apparel companies who printed their own logos and retailed the products. Recognizing that this was a cut-throat market, Charney shifted focus to specialty screenprinters: "Your client is always looking to make it cheaper. There's no loyalty . . . And there is so much supply, from all corners of the world that it doesn't make it feasible to focus in that one area. So we de-emphasized private label packages and we're focusing on our brands for the imprintable T-shirt industry that services the specialty industry."[10]

American Apparel's main competitors were the blank T-shirt giants Hanes and Fruit of the Loom. American Apparel differentiated itself by focusing on quality and design. In contrast to the standard loose-fitting, heavy-knit T-shirts, American Apparel offered tightly-fitting women's and men's T-shirts with finer thread and a closer knit. In October 2003, American Apparel opened its first retail store. Charney viewed the Los Angeles store more as an experiment than a new business: "It's supposed to be a place for some of the intellectuals of the company and customers to hang out . . . It's not a money-maker—let's put it that way."[11] The Los Angeles store was quickly followed by others in New York and Montreal. By the end of 2004, American Apparel operated 34 stores in North America and three in the U.K. Charney then committed totally to developing the business. As late as 2005, as CEO of American Apparel, he drew a salary of less than $100 000: long-term development of the company took priority over his personal enrichment. "We need to dig in deeper, to penetrate the market we're in right now . . . We're building our foundation right now. We want to be the best at what we do, and once we are . . . once we're strong, then we can take on the world."[12]

Charney's Controversial Image

Dov Charney's key fashion innovation was in turning T-shirts into garments that enhanced the sexual attractiveness of the wearer. However, sexuality played a wider role in the success of American Apparel. In addition to its sexually provocative advertising, the company had a culture that acknowledged the sexual drives of its customers and its employees and embraced sexual conduct and sexual content as part of openness and creativity. If American Apparel's key product differentiation was the sex appeal of its fashion garments, then sexual openness within the company might enhance its ability to design and market these products.

Charney's own contribution to this culture included his wearing solely his American Apparel underwear while in the office and sexual relationships with his employees. "I'm not saying I want to screw all the girls at work," stated Charney, "but if I fall in love at work it's going to be beautiful and sexual."[13] Between 2005 and 2007, American Apparel faced four sexual harassment lawsuits, three of which were dropped after confidential settlements were reached. The fourth resulted in a wider investigation by the Los Angeles office of the Equal Employment Opportunity Commission into sexual harassment at American Apparel.[14] Charney attributed the lawsuits to disgruntled employees seeking personal gain by exploiting California's litigious culture.[15]

As a result of the lawsuits, American Apparel required employees to sign a document that declared:

> American Apparel is in the business of designing and manufacturing sexually charged T-shirts and intimate apparel, and uses sexually charged visual and oral communications in its marketing and sales activities. Employees working in the design, sales, marketing and other creative areas of the company will come into contact with sexually charged language and visual images. This is a part of the job for employees working in these areas.[16]

American Apparel in 2009

By the beginning of 2009, American Apparel had grown to be one of the leading suppliers of T-shirts to the U.S. market—both blank T-shirts sold to screen printers and final products supplied under its own brand through its own retail stores. Despite a tiny share of the overall U.S. garment industry (about one-half of one percent), it was one of the biggest garment manufacturers in the U.S. This reflected the fact that it was one of the few U.S. garment manufacturers that produced at home: most fashion clothing companies concentrated on design, marketing and distribution, with manufacturing outsourced and offshored. American Apparel's Los Angeles headquarters was the biggest cut-and-sew production facility in the U.S.

The distinctive feature of American Apparel was its high level of vertical integration: not only did it undertake most stages of production at its Los Angeles headquarters, it performed its own design, marketing and advertising, and owned and operated all its retail stores, even its overseas stores. Table 16.2 shows financial information for the company.

TABLE 16.2 Selected financial data, 2005–8 ($ million)

	2008	2007	2006	2005
Selected items from operating statement				
Net sales	545.1	387.0	264.7	188.1
Cost of sales	245.9	171.6	138.4	101.0
Gross profit	299.2	215.5	126.3	87.1
Operating expenses	263.1	184.40	135.1	76.8
of which:				
Selling	168.5	115.6	84.0	45.8
Warehouse and distribution	15.6	10.7	6.7	4.2
General and administrative	78.9	58.1	36.8	26.9
Income from operations	36.1	31.1	9.3	10.2
Interest expense	13.9	17.5	10.8	6.3
Income before income taxes	21.4	15.3	(0.3)	4.0
Income tax provision	7.3	(0.2)	1.3	0.4
Net (loss) income	14.1	15.5	(1.6)	3.6
Selected balance sheet items				
Current assets	187.0	152.8	97.0	85.8
of which:				
Inventories	148.2	106.4	76.5	67.5
Total assets	333.0	233.4	163.1	124.2
Current liabilities	74.3	150.7	59.8	44.9
of which:				
Overdraft and current bank debt	3.8	102.8	6.2	9.3
Accounts payable	26.3	21.9	30.1	18.3
Long-term debt	100.0	0.6	52.7	43.0
Total liabilities	196.6	171.5	136 455	110 280
Stockholders' equity	136.4	171.5	11.7	13.9
Cash flows				
Net cash from operating activities	21.2	(5.4)	7.7	(1,1)
Net cash used in investing activities	(72.2)	(23.8)	(16.9)	(15.9)
Net cash provided by financing activities	41.2	44.5	10.6	17.4

Source: American Apparel, 10-K reports.

Product Development and Design

Recreating the T-shirt as a fashion garment was fundamental to American Apparel's business concept. This involved careful attention to fit, texture, shape-retention and color. "We've fashionized and brought fashion to the commodity setting," Charney explained, arguing that his main achievement was "feminizing the blank T-shirt industry"[17] Previously, T-shirts were "bulky, one-size-fits-all" garments that were not gender specific. The company explained that:

> American Apparel's design vision and aesthetic are intended to appeal to young, metropolitan adults by providing them with a core line of iconic, timeless styles offered year-round in a wide variety of colors at reasonable

prices. Since its founding, American Apparel has operated with the belief that there is a large potential market among young adults for well-designed, high-quality fashion essentials.[18]

American Apparel employed an in-house team of designers at its Los Angeles headquarters. The team was led by Dov Charney, who personally approved all new garment designs. Charney personally hired each member of the product-development department, searching for designers he felt had the "eye for what's next."[19] The team didn't read fashion magazines and paid little attention to catwalk fashion trends. The team took its inspiration from classic styles of the past, as well as to emerging style trends among young adults living in metropolitan cities such as Los Angeles, London and New York. Its clothing was reminiscent of 1970s urban apparel and represented a retro urban chic style. Designers often went to vintage clothing stores to find inspirations for new designs.

By 2009, the company had expanded its product range well beyond the T-shirt. It offered over 20 000 stock keeping units (SKUs) including fabric shirts, dresses, denim jeans, sweaters, jackets, swimwear, babywear, and a variety of accessories including bags, hats, scarves, sunglasses and other products—even sweaters for dogs. American Apparel intended to continue to introduce new merchandise to complement its existing products and draw new customers.

Manufacturing

American Apparel's headquarters and main manufacturing facility was the former Southern Pacific Railroad depot in downtown Los Angeles comprising 800 000 square feet of floorspace. Dying and finishing were at a separate facility in Hawthorne, California. Despite three-shift working, capacity shortage at its Los Angeles facility resulted in American Apparel expanding production to newly acquired plants in South Gate, California and Garden Grove, California in 2008. It described its production operations as follows:

> American Apparel purchases yarn which is sent to knitters to be knit into "greige" fabric, which is fabric that is not dyed or processed. The Company currently conducts a portion of its knitting operations in-house at its knitting facilities in Los Angeles and Garden Grove, California. The Company operates circular and flat knitting machines, producing jersey, piqué, fleece and ribbing using cotton and cotton/polyester yarns. The Company also utilizes third-party commission knitters. The Company's knitting facilities knit approximately 80% of the total fabric used in American Apparel's garments, and employed a staff of approximately 100 people, as of December 31, 2008.
>
> Knitted greige fabric produced at the Los Angeles and Garden Grove facilities or other commission knitters is batched for bleaching and dyeing and transported to the Company's dyeing and finishing facilities, or other commission dye houses. In some cases, dyed fabric is transferred to subcontractors for fabric laundering. The Company's dyeing and finishing facilities in the Los Angeles metropolitan area dye approximately 80% of the total fabric used in American Apparel's garments, and employed a staff of approximately 900 people, as of December 31, 2008.

Most fabric is shipped to the Company's primary manufacturing facility in downtown Los Angeles where it is inspected and then cut on manual and automated cutting tables, and subsequently sewn into finished garments. Some fabric is purchased directly from third parties, along with all trims. Garments are sewn by teams of sewing operators typically ranging from five to 15 operators, depending on the complexity of a particular garment. Each sewing operator performs a different sewing operation on a garment before passing it to the next operator. Sewing operators are compensated on a modified piece-rate basis. Quality control personnel inspect finished garments for defects and reject any defective product. American Apparel also manufactures some hosiery in-house at this facility, where it does knitting, inspection, and packing, and uses off-site contractors for washing and boarding. Approximately 3,900 employees were directly involved in the cutting, sewing, and hosiery operations at the downtown Los Angeles facility as of December 31, 2008.

American Apparel purchases yarn, certain fabrics and other raw materials from a variety of vendors over time. American Apparel does not have any major suppliers of raw materials that it relies on exclusively to support its production operations. The inputs that American Apparel uses are produced competitively by a large number of potential suppliers. Since the inputs are commodity in nature, American Apparel believes that it could easily source its inputs from other vendors if its current suppliers were not able to meet its needs.[20]

According to Marty Bailey, Vice President of Operations, "In order for us to be successful, we have to make a good product. . . . [I]f your product is no good, you can count out repeat business. A turd is still a turd no matter how you market or package it."[21] Bailey believed that American Apparel's success was based on four factors: implementing sound quality control, being committed to quick turnaround using lean production, having a specific target market, and careful oversight of manufacturing operations. Bailey continued, "Anytime that you can have your arms around your business, you're in good shape. We are a domestic company and have visibility. We can make commitments to our customers that other people can't."[22]

Workers were organized by the type of garment produced, in modular manufacturing teams. Members rotated positions regularly to alleviate stress and boredom. An average shift included 100 sewing teams. Quality-control supervisors stood across the aisle from the sewing teams and carefully measured and inspected one out of every 24 garments to ensure size and quality consistency.[23] Piece workers spent 11 to 13 seconds per person per piece of garment; the average garment required 140 seconds to manufacture. About 250 000 garments were produced each day and 1.25 million each week. To minimize fatigue and stress, each shift was interrupted by a five-minute stretch or aerobic exercise session accompanied by loud pop music.

An employee's occupation was indicated by attire. Piece workers wore casual clothes of jeans and t-shirts. Supervisors, mechanics, cleaners, and cutters wore t-shirts of a particular color with their position labeled in both English and Spanish on the front. Quality control supervisors wore purple shirts, line supervisors blue shirts, and mechanics red shirts.

Retail and Wholesale Distribution

At the beginning of 2009, American Apparel owned and operated 260 retail stores in 19 countries (see Table 16.3). These were served by distribution centers in Los Angeles, Montreal, and Neuss (Germany). It described its retail operations as follows:

> American Apparel's retail operations principally target young adults aged 20 to 32 through its unique assortment of fashionable clothing and accessories and its compelling in-store experience. American Apparel has established a reputation with its customers, who are culturally sophisticated, creative, and independent-minded. The product offering includes women's and men's basic apparel and accessories, as well as new lines for children and pets. Stores average approximately 2500–3000 square feet of selling space. American Apparel's stores are located in large metropolitan areas, emerging neighborhoods, and select university communities.[24]

American Apparel favored locations away from traditional high streets using nontraditional retail buildings with unique environments. Store selection and design was undertaken by Jordan Parnass of Jordan Parnass Digital Architecture (JPDA), a lifelong friend of Dov Charney. Location scouts searched cities for areas that were populated by artists and musicians and for the hangouts of young adults. Once an ideal location for a store was spotted, designers from JPDA researched the "regional flavor" and developed design concepts that incorporated this regional flavor together with the characteristics of the building's structure.[25] Examples of some unique storefronts included a movie theater marquee that was installed with colored fluorescent triangle lights, and a former auto-garage.[26]

American Apparel's wholesale business sold to about a dozen authorized distributors and over 10 000 screen printers. The latter printed blank products with corporate logos, brands and other images. Wholesale customers were served by a call center at its Los Angeles headquarters. The company prided itself on fast turnaround of orders: orders received before 4:30 pm were shipped the same day.

American Apparel operated online retail sales through its www.americanapparel. com web site. The web site further broadened American Apparel's range of offerings to include shoes, pens, Swiss army knives, audio CDs and even a video described as "the perfect merger of classic pornographic excellence and modern motion."[27]

Tables 16.4 and 16.5 show American Apparel's sales, profits and assets by distribution channel and by geography.

TABLE 16.3 American Apparel's retail outlets

Number of retail stores	Dec. 31, 2008	Dec. 31, 2007	Dec. 31, 2006	Dec. 31, 2005	Dec. 31, 2004
U.S.	148	105	93	66	25
Canada	37	30	26	20	9
International	75	47	30	18	3

Source: American Apparel, 10-K Report for 2008.

TABLE 16.4 American Apparel's financial results by business segment ($ million)

	2008	2007	2006
U.S. wholesale			
Sales	162.7	144.5	127.8
Gross profit	46.9	40.1	31.7
Operating income[a]	21.0	19.7	14.2
Identifiable assets	178.1	125.4	n.a.
Capital expenditure	7.1	5.3	4.3
U.S. retail			
Sales	168.7	115.6	80.2
Gross profit	127.9	88.8	63.0
Operating income[a]	33.5	24.8	11.5
Identifiable assets	98.9	60.0	n.a.
Capital expenditure	30.9	9.3	8.6
Canada			
Sales	67.3	42.4	30.6
Gross profit	40.1	27.1	19.2
Operating income[a]	10.8	1.5	3.5
Identifiable assets	17.1	16.5	n.a.
Capital expenditure	4.7	2.0	1.7
International			
Sales	146.4	84.5	46.4
Gross profit	84.2	59.4	31.7
Operating income[a]	8.0	14.8	4.7
Identifiable assets	38.9	31.5	n.a.
Capital expenditure	18.3	7.1	2.4

[a] Before corporate expense, interest, other income, and foreign currency adjustment

Source: American Apparel, 10-K Report for 2008.

TABLE 16.5 Geographical distribution of sales and fixed assets, 2007 and 2008 ($ million)

	2008	2007
Net sales by location of customer		
United States	331.3	206.1
Canada	67.3	42.4
Europe (excluding U.K.)	74.3	45.1
United Kingdom	35.7	17.6
Japan	14.9	9.8
Korea	10.5	9.2
Other foreign countries	11.1	2.8
Total Consolidated Net Sales	545.1	387.0
Property and equipment, at Dec. 31		
United States	79.3	44.0
Canada	7.3	6.6

	2008	2007
Europe (excluding U.K.)	12.7	7.3
United Kingdom	6.4	4.6
Japan	3.3	1,6
Korea	0.7	0.5
Other foreign countries	2.8	0.2
Total Consolidated	112.4	64.9
Total property and equipment		48 532

Source: American Apparel, 10-K Report for 2008.

Employee Relations: A "Sweat-Shop" Free Environment

American Apparel offered year-round employment and rates of pay where even the lowest paid workers earned around double the minimum wage. Piece-workers started out at $8 an hour and could earn up to $25 an hour based on their productivity. Workers were offered subsidized healthcare for themselves and their families, subsidized lunches (25% paid by American Apparel), free parking, bus passes and low-cost auto insurance. There were five on-site massage therapists who provided regular services for all employees. Yoga classes were also available, along with a health-and-wellness specialist who provided counseling. Workers could take bathroom breaks at any time and use their cell phones for quick personal calls during working hours. Other employee benefits included subsidized public transportation and a bicycle-lending program in which a bicycle, helmet and chain were provided.

Workers received training to improve their job and management skills. American Apparel also offered English and math lessons, classes in human relations and teamwork, and monthly supervisor and management training. The human resources department also assisted employees in gaining the tax benefits available to them and opening bank accounts by inviting a bank to the factory.

Despite a campaign by a garment workers union, American Apparel employees had not elected to form a union. Charney felt that they had no reason to do so. He commented on the failed unionizing campaign:

> The union issue is something that's brought here from a New York-based union. It's a lot of smoke and mirrors. There's not one cut and sew factory in this city that unionized. If the workers wanted a union, they'd have one . . . There's got to be a reason to take on management. There's got to be a reason to say, they're not treating us well enough, we need to rise up and put a gun in management's face.[28]

As noted by *The Economist*:

> The benefits he provides are expensive: subsidizing health insurance costs his firm $4m–5m a year; subsidizing meals costs another $500 000. Even so, Mr. Charney says he has no plans to scale back these benefits. He considers his contented workers the reason for his success. Treating them well means they are less likely to leave, for one thing, which saves money. "American Apparel is not an altruistic company," says Mr. Charney. "I believe in capitalism and self-interest. Self-interest can involve being generous with others."[29]

Marketing and Advertising

American Apparel developed all of its marketing and advertising in-house. The photographs used in advertising and promotion were often taken by Charney and other amateur photographers. Models were all amateurs who posed without makeup or fancy hair-dos. Many were employees, customers, friends, or just women whom Charney wanted to photograph:

> [T]he models in American Apparel's print ads challenge conventional notions of beauty. Before the ballyhooed Dove soap campaign, Charney embraced the notion of "real" advertising, photographing young ethnic and mixed-race men and women with asymmetrical features, imperfect bodies, blemished skin and visible sweat stains on the clothes they are modeling — the kind of artsy, latter-day-bohemian, indie-culture-affiliated young adults who live and shop in the neighborhoods where American Apparel stores are located.
>
> The ads are also highly suggestive and not just because they are showcasing underwear or clingy knits. They depict young men and women in bed or in the shower; if they are casually lounging on a sofa or sitting on the floor, then their legs happen to be spread; frequently they are wearing a single item of clothing but are otherwise undressed; a couple of the young women appear to be in a heightened state of pleasure. These pictures have a flashbulb-lighted, lo-fi sultriness to them; they look less like ads than photos you'd see posted on someone's Myspace page . . . These aren't ads that you'll see on the side of a bus or in famous magazines. American Apparel places advertising in the blogosphere, linking from pop-culture sites like Gawker.com to photo essays and copy on its own web site; on the back pages of alternative newspapers like The Village Voice, L.A. Weekly or The Onion; in slightly obscure art-hipster publications like Purple Fashion and Fantastic Man; and in the profane, anti-P.C. lifestyle magazine Vice, whose louche tastes and attitudes run in close concert with Charney's.[30]

American Apparel's use of internet marketing reached beyond its extensive online catalog and web site. In June 2006, it partnered with Linden Lab to become "the first real life company to open a store in the virtual world of 'Second Life.'"[31] Second Life was an online 3-D virtual world where visitors created alter egos called "avatars." Patrons purchased virtual versions of American Apparel clothing for their avatars for token sums.

Social and Environmental Responsibility

American Apparel took an activist stance on social and political issues and infused social responsibility into its operating practices. The company offered employment to people on the fringes of mainstream society. For example, it hired employees from Homeboy Industries, an organization that assisted at-risk youths and former gang members. An immigrant himself, Charney was active in the Los Angeles immigrant community and was a prominent supporter of free trade and immigrant rights. On May 1, 2006, Charney gave the company's Los Angeles employees a paid day off, a T-shirt with a pro-immigration message, and encouraged them to join a demonstration being held in Los Angeles to protest lack of immigrant rights. American Apparel also supports several international causes, and has used its "Made in USA" and "Sweatshop Free" credentials as part of its advertising messages.

American Apparel also emphasized environmentally friendly manufacturing and clothing. Because most cotton was grown with a very heavy use of insecticides and other pollutants, in 2004 American Apparel introduced its *Sustainable Edition* line made from 100% organic cotton. American Apparel recycled 1 million pounds of fabric scraps annually. Charney remarked: "Actually, the reason we started a panty line was to use all our excessive scraps."[32]

Speed-to-Market

The fundamental performance attribute of American Apparel's business system was its speed and flexibility:

> The Company's vertically integrated business model, with manufacturing and various other elements of the Company's business processes centered in downtown Los Angeles, allows the Company to play a role in originating and defining new and innovative trends in fashion, while enabling the Company to quickly respond to market and customer demand for classic styles and new products. For the Company's wholesale operations, being able to fulfill large orders with quick turn-around allows American Apparel to capture business. The ability to respond to the market quickly means that the Company's retail operations can deliver on-trend apparel in a timely manner, adhere to a policy of not discounting product at retail stores and maximize sales on popular styles by replenishing product that would have otherwise sold out.[33]

From design concept to the American Apparel store rack, a garment took as little as two weeks. Within a day, a designer could come up with an idea, design a garment, create a pattern, cut and have it sewn together. By the evening, the garment could be photographed on a model and emailed for Charney's immediate opinion. If the garment was approved by Charney, then it would be prepared for testing in a few American Apparel retail stores.[34] Customer purchases were tracked and analyzed, and if the product were successful, it would be put into full production for shipping to the rest of American Apparel's retail locations.[35]

Figure 16.1 depicts American Apparel's vertically integrated business system.

The Future

In its presentation to investors in April 2009, American Apparel outlined its long-term goal of becoming "the #1 destination for basic apparel—the first name that consumers think of for T-shirts, sweatpants, underwear, socks, etc." Achieving that goal would require American Apparel to seize the opportunities available for growth and internal development. The opportunities it identified included:

- grow the store base
- expand in underpenetrated urban markets in the U.S., Canada and internationally

FIGURE 16.1 American Apparel's vertically integrated business system

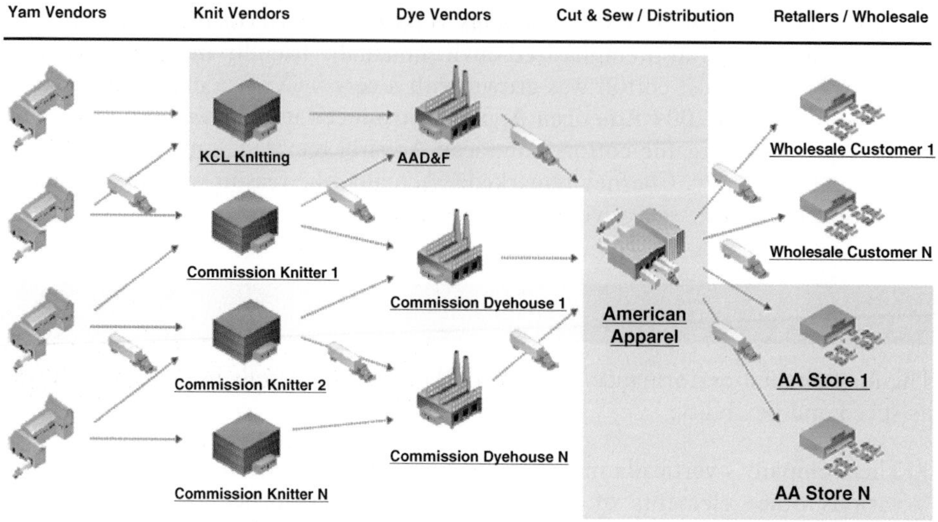

Source: American Apparel, Investors' Presentation (March 2009).

- enter new markets
- improve production efficiency with better supply-chain management and materials resource planning with enterprise resource planning (ERP)
- produce the right SKUs in the right quantities
- improve merchandise allocation in the stores
- improve store productivity by capturing more sales and increasing inventory turns
- add categories to provide customers with a more complete product assortment of basics (jackets, bottoms, wovens, etc.)
- improve store productivity by increasing customer visits, transactions, and average unit revenue
- improve execution through key management hires
- expand brand awareness and reach beyond young metropolitan adults.[36]

During 2009, however, American Apparel's primary emphasis would be efficiency and effectiveness rather than growth. It forecast that only 25 new stores would be opened in 2009 and sales growth would slow to between 5% and 10%. Efforts to improve production efficiency and logistical effectiveness included the implementation of an ERP system and improvements in financial management through implementing the Hyperion Financial Management system and hiring senior finance executives. Improving financial management had become a priority because of "material weaknesses" in American Apparel's financial reporting system identified by its auditors.

American Apparel has shown a remarkable capacity to adapt to change and seize new opportunities. It grew from being a local, wholesale supplier of T-shirts to a multinational corporation vertically integrated from the purchase of cotton yarn to the retailing of garments. Nevertheless, in many respects it is still a medium-sized entrepreneurial company where the founder is engaged in activities that ranges from the approval of new designs, to taking advertising photographs, to selecting sites for new retail stores. Will expansion necessitate a fundamentally different management structure for American Apparel and can its Los Angeles-based production system serve an increasingly global retail network? As American Apparel enhances its profile, will it attract increasing numbers of imitators? Can American Apparel continue to charge the same premium prices for its stylish, socially-responsible, "Made in USA" garments? Dov Charney once described his dream for American Apparel as becoming the "Starbucks of the garment industry." Given Starbucks' forced retrenchment after overexpansion, this is perhaps no longer such an appealing vision.

Notes

1 "American Apparel's Unusual Flotation is Typical of Dov Charney, its Founder," *The Economist,* January 4, 2007.

2 American Apparel, Investor Presentation June 2009, Piper Jaffray Consumer Conference, June 9, 2009, http://investors.americanapparel.net/events.cfm, accessed October 29, 2009.

3 P. Rivoli, *The Travels of a T-Shirt in the Global Economy: An Economist Examines the Markets, Power, and Politics of World Trade,* 2nd edn, John Wiley & Sons, Ltd, Chichester, 2009.

4 "T-shirt Prices are Falling," Trade Fact of the Week, Progressive Policy Institute, February 15, 2006, http://www.ppionline.org/ppi_ci.cfm?contentid=253748 &knlgAreaID=108&subsecid=900003, accessed October 29, 2009.

5 D. Charney, interview, "Charlie Rose," KQED9 (TV broadcasting station), July, 2006.

6 D. Charney, interview, "The New Rich," *20/20,* ABC, 2006; M. Mendelssohn, "Sweatshop-Free Zone," *The Gazette,* May 23, 2004.

7 D. Charney, interview, "The New Rich," *20/20,* ABC (2006); M. Silcott, "Dov Charney, 32, Senior Partner, American Apparel," *The Counselor,* April, 2001.

8 J. Elwain, "American Apparel Takes on the T-Shirt," *Bobbin Magazine,* May, 2001.

9 A. A. Nieder, "The Branding of Blank Tees," http://americanapparel.net/presscenter/articles/20000818 caapparelnews.html, accessed August 18, 2008.

10 J. Elwain, "American Apparel Takes on the T-Shirt," *Bobbin Magazine,* May, 2001.

11 C. M. Chensvold, "American Apparel Opens Three Retail Stores," *California Apparel News,* October 31, 2003)

12 J. Elwain, "American Apparel Takes on the T-Shirt," *Bobbin Magazine,* May, 2001.

13 J. Mankiewicz "Sexy Marketing or Sexual Harassment?," NBC Dateline, http://www.msnbc.msn.com/id/ 14082498/, accessed July 28, 2006.

14 American Apparel, 10-K Report for 2008, 2009, p. 31.

15 "Living on the Edge at American Apparel," *Business Week,* July 27, 2007.

16 "And You Thought Abercrombie & Fitch Was Pushing It," *New York Times,* April 23, 2006.

17 D. Charney, Interview, "Worldwide," Chicago Public Radio, November 13, 2003.

18 American Apparel, 10-K Report for 2008, 2009, p. 2.

19 D. Charney, interview, "Charlie Rose," KQED9, July 2006.

20 American Apparel, 10-K Report for 2008, 2009, p. 5.

21 H. Aquirre, "Go Team," *The Manufacturer,* June, 2004.

22 H. Aquirre, "Go Team," *The Manufacturer,* June, 2004.

23 A. Lopez, interview by case authors, April 2007.

24 American Apparel, 10-K Report for 2008, 2009, p. 5.

25 A. DiNardo, "The Anti-Brand," *Visual Store,* December 4, 2006.

26 A. DiNardo, "The Anti-Brand," *Visual Store,* December 4, 2006.

27 See http://store.americanapparel.net/sexctydvd.html, accessed July 2009.

28 "The Apprenticeship of Dov Charney," CBC Radio, March 20, 2005.

29 "American Apparel's Unusual Flotation is Typical of Dov Charney, Its Founder," *The Economist,* January 4, 2007.

30 J. Wolf, "And You Thought Abercrombie & Fitch Was Pushing It?" *New York Times Magazine,* April 23, 2006.

31 "American Apparel's Virtual Clothes," *Business Week,* June 27, 2006.

32 "American Apparel to Recycle over One Million Pounds of Cotton Cutting per Year," *American Apparel Media Advisory,* August 13, 2002.

33 American Apparel, 10-K Report for 2008, 2009, p. 3.

34 A. Lopez, interview by case authors, April 2007.

35 D. Charney, interview, "Charlie Rose", KQED9, July, 2006.

36 American Apparel, Investor Presentation June 2009, Piper Jaffray Consumer Conference, June 9, 2009, http://investors.americanapparel.net/events.cfm, accessed October 29, 2009.

Case 17 Outback Steakhouse: Going International*

By 1995, Outback Steakhouse was one of the fastest growing and most acclaimed restaurant chains in North America. Astute positioning within the intensely competitive U.S. restaurant business, high quality of food and service, and a relaxed ambiance that echoed its Australian theme propelled the chain's spectacular growth (see Table 17.1).

*By Marilyn L. Taylor and Robert M. Grant. This case is an abridged version of an earlier case "Outback Steakhouse Goes International" by Marilyn L. Taylor, George M. Puia, Krishnan Ramaya and Madelyn Gengelbach (used by permission of the authors). It has been augmented with material from company reports and from "A Stake in the Business," by Chris T. Sullivan, *Harvard Business Review*, September 2005, pp. 57–64. Copyright (c) 2008 Marilyn L. Taylor and Robert M. Grant.

TABLE 17.1 Outback Steakhouse, Inc.: growth and profitability, 1990–5

	Revenue ($ m)	Net income ($ m)	Return on average equity (%)	Company-owned restaurants	Franchised and JV restaurants	Total restaurants
1990	34	2.3	41.2	23	0	23
1991	91	6.1	34.4	49	0	49
1992	189	14.8	23.6	81	4	85
1993	310	25.2	22.2	124	24	148
1994	516	43.4	27.4	164	50	214
1995	734	61.3	27.0	262	58	320[a]

[a]Of these, 297 were Outback Steakhouses and 23 were Carrabba's Italian Grills.

Chairman and co-founder Chris Sullivan believed that at the current rate of growth (around 70 new restaurants each year), Outback would be facing market saturation within five years. Outback's growth opportunities were either to diversify into alternative restaurant concepts (it had already started its Carrabba's Italian Grill restaurants) or to expand internationally.

We can do 500–600 [Outback] restaurants, and possibly more over the next five years . . . [however] the world is becoming one big market, and we want to be in place so we don't miss that opportunity. There are some problems, some challenges with it, but at this point there have been some casual restaurant chains that have gone [outside the U.S.] and their average unit sales are way, way above the sales level they enjoyed in the United States. So the potential is there. Obviously, there are some distribution issues to work out, things like that, but we are real excited about the future internationally. That will give us some potential outside the United States to continue to grow as well.[1]

In late 1994, Hugh Connerty was appointed President of Outback International to lead the company's overseas expansion. Connerty had considerable experience in the restaurant business and had been Outback's most successful franchisee, developing a number of Outback restaurants in northern Florida and southern Georgia. Connerty grasped the opportunity enthusiastically:

We have had hundreds of franchise requests from all over the world. [So] it took about two seconds for me to make that decision [to become President of Outback International] . . . I've met with and talked to other executives who have international divisions. All of them have the same story. At some point in time a light goes on and they say, "Gee we have a great product. Where do we start?" I have traveled quite a bit on holiday. The world is not as big as you think it is. Most companies who have gone global have not used any set strategy.[2]

Connerty's challenges were to decide in which countries to locate; whether to franchise, directly manage, or joint venture; how the Outback restaurant concept should be adapted to overseas markets and what pace of expansion to target.

Outback's Strategy

Outback was founded by Chris Sullivan, Bob Basham and Tim Gannon. The three had met as management trainees at the Steak and Ale restaurant chain. Although red meat consumption was declining, they believed that this was primarily the result of less meat being consumed at home: steakhouses remained extremely popular. They saw an untapped opportunity for serving quality steaks at an affordable price—filling the gap between high-priced and budget steakhouses. Using an Australian theme associated with the outdoors and adventure, Outback positioned itself as a place providing not only excellent food but also a cheerful, fun and comfortable experience. The company explained its strategy as follows:

The Company believes that it differentiates its Outback Steakhouse restaurants by:

- emphasizing consistently high-quality ingredients and preparation of a limited number of menu items that appeal to a broad array of tastes;

- featuring generous portions at moderate prices;

- attracting a diverse mix of customers through a casual dining atmosphere emphasizing highly attentive service;

- hiring and retaining experienced restaurant management by providing general managers the opportunity to purchase a 10% interest in the restaurants they manage; and

- limiting service to dinner (generally from 4:30 p.m. to 11:00 p.m.), which reduces the hours of restaurant management and employees.[3]

Quality of food was central to the chain's differentiation. This began with the raw materials. Outback viewed suppliers as "partners" and was committed to work with them to ensure quality and develop long-term relationships. Outback's food costs were among the highest in the industry—not just in terms of ingredients but also in preparation, with most items prepared from scratch within each restaurant. For example, Outback's croutons were made daily on site with 17 different seasonings and cut into irregular shapes to indicate that they were handmade.

The emphasis on quality extended to service. Among Outback's "principles and beliefs" was "No rules, just right"—employees will do whatever is needed to meet the needs and preferences of customers.

Inevitably, this emphasis on quality and service meant working practices that at other restaurant chains would be regarded as inefficient. Chairman Chris Sullivan explained that Outback had a different management model:

There are three kinds of turnover in the restaurant business—customer, employee and table. Most restaurant chains worry about the first, resign themselves to the second, and encourage the third. At Outback it's not as straightforward as that; we believe that all three are integrally related. Specifically, our management model and approach reflect the importance we place on fighting employee turnover. One of our catchphrases is "fully staffed, fully trained." You can't be either of those things if a restaurant is a revolving door. Besides, customers like to see a familiar face.

Restaurant work can be stressful. The better the staffers, the more intent they will be on doing things right—and the more frustrated they will become with the facilities and tools they've been given if they get in the way, whether the problem is dull knives or not enough burners . . . Bob Basham insisted on making all of our kitchens at least 2500 square feet and keeping lots of cool air flowing through them. The kitchens occupy half of the typical Outback restaurant's floor plan space that other restaurants allocate to revenue-producing tables. But we wanted to offer a bigger menu than the typical casual restaurant did in the 1980s, so we knew we would have to give the cooks and prep people the space to pull it off.

Likewise, we never assign our servers to cover more than three tables; the industry standard is five or six . . . A wide range of customers choose to dine with us on a variety of occasions . . . It has to be the customer who sets the pace for the meal, not the server or the kitchen staff. But for that to happen our servers need time to figure out the mood and expectations of a given table on a given evening, and the kitchen has to be well enough staffed and equipped to turn around orders without delay . . .

We think that employees who are not overstressed stay in their jobs longer than those who are; that employees who stay have time to master their jobs, become familiar with their regular customers' preferences, and learn to operate as teams; that the combination of mastery, memory, and calm is more likely to afford customers themselves a relaxing, enjoyable experience; and that diners who are not hustled through their meals are more likely to come back. In short, low employee turnover leads to well-paced table turnover, which ultimately leads to low customer turnover.[4]

This model linked closely with two other distinctive features of Outback's strategy. First, Outback served only dinner. According to Sullivan, the conventional wisdom that restaurants needed to be open for lunch and dinner in order to make efficient use of capital ignored the hidden costs of longer hours of opening. These included the costs associated with extra hiring and employee turnover, the disruptive effects of shift changes and the fact that employees who worked lunchtime would be tired in the evening—the time when they needed to be at their freshest. Similarly for the food—with preparation of food brought forward to the morning, it would lose its freshness by the evening.

Second, Outback located in residential areas rather than downtown. This reinforced the merits of evening-only opening, kept rents low and encouraged customer and employee loyalty. As Sullivan explained: "The suburbs are our outback."

Outback's management and ownership structure was also unusual. Each of Outback's directly owned restaurants was a separate partnership where Outback Steakhouse, Inc. was the general partner with an ownership of between 71% and 90%. Each restaurant was headed by a "managing partner" while between 10 and 20 restaurants within an area were overseen by a regional manager who is called a "joint venture partner" or "JVP." Sullivan explained the relationship as follows:

The terms "managing partner" and "joint venture partner" aren't symptoms of title inflation. They straightforwardly describe people's roles and relationships to the organization. All managing partners, most of whom start as hourly employees, must invest $25 000 of their own money—not because Outback needs the capital, but because their financial contributions make them committed investors in the business they'll be running. They must also sign a five-year contract, and they are granted roughly 1000 shares of restricted stock, which vest only at the end of their contracts. In return, managing partners can keep 10% of the cash flow their restaurants generate each year. The idea is to ensure that at the end of five years each of them will have stock worth around $100 000 . . . At the end of five years, successful managers are encouraged to sign up with the same restaurant or to manage a different one . . .

Outback's JVPs, who number around 60, must invest $50 000, which entitles them to 10% of cash flow of all the restaurants they oversee after the partners have received their 10%. Whereas the managing partners focus on operations and community relations, the Japes focus on monitoring performance, finding and developing new locations, and identifying and developing new managers, managing partners, and Japes like themselves. The Japes are the only management layer between the six operations executives at headquarters and the managing partners at the individual restaurants.[5]

Initially, Outback intended its restaurants all to be directly owned and managed. However, in 1990, requests for franchising led to Outback agreeing to franchise to well-known acquaintances of the founders. Outback was very careful in its choice of franchisees to ensure that all were fully committed to Outback's principles and beliefs.

Management of hourly employees was very different from most other restaurant chains. One executive described Outback's approach as: "Tough on results, but kind with people." Employee selection was rigorous and included aptitude tests, psychological profiles and interviews with at least two managers. The goal was to create an entrepreneurial climate that emphasized learning and personal growth. All employees were eligible for the company's stock ownership plan and health insurance was made available to all employees.

Part of the culture of "no rules" and commitment to quality and service is a constant drive for innovation and improvement:

> Almost all our innovations bubble up from the individual restaurant, often originating with our servers or kitchen staffers. They'll suggest an idea to the restaurant manager who will try it on an experimental basis. If the recommended menu or process change clicks, the managing partner communicates the idea to his or her JVP . . . If the suggested change meets company standards, videos and other materials showing how to implement it are distributed to other JVPs. Each is free to take it or not.[6]

During 1993, Outback formed a joint venture with Houston-based Carrabba's Italian Grill. In January 1995, Outback acquired the rights to develop Carrabba's nationally. Carrabba's Grills were run with almost identical operating and management practices and ownership structure to Outback Steakhouses.

Preparing for International Expansion

Hugh Connerty, Outback's head of International, outlined his approach to international expansion as follows:

> We have built Outback one restaurant at a time . . . There are some principles and beliefs we live by. It almost sounds cultish. We want International to be an opportunity for our suppliers. We feel strongly about the relationships with our

suppliers. We have never changed suppliers. We have an undying commitment to them and in exchange we want them to have an undying commitment to us. They have to prove they can build plants [abroad].

I think it would be foolish of us to think that we are going to go around the world buying property and understanding the laws in every country, the culture in every single country. So the approach that we are going to take is that we will franchise the international operation with company-owned stores here and franchises there so that will allow us to focus on what I believe is our pure strength, a support operation.[7]

Connerty believed that his experience in developing Outback franchises in the U.S. would provide the guidelines for overseas expansion:

Every one of the franchisees lives in their areas. I lived in the area I franchised. I had relationships that helped with getting permits. That isn't any different than the rest of the world. The loyalties of individuals that live in their respective areas [will be important]. We will do the franchises one by one. The biggest decision we have to make is how we pick that franchise partner. That is what we will concentrate on. We are going to select a person who has synergy with us, who thinks like us, who believes in the principles and beliefs.

Trust is foremost and sacred. The trust between [Outback] and the individual franchisees is not to be violated. The company grants franchises one at a time. It takes a lot of trust to invest millions of dollars without any assurance that you will be able to build another one.[8]

As for the geographical pattern of expansion, Connerty's initial thoughts were to begin close to home then tackle Latin America and the Far East:

The first year will be Canada. Then we'll go to Hawaii. Then we'll go to South America and then develop our relationships in the Far East, Korea, Japan . . . the Orient. The second year we'll begin a relationship in Great Britain and from there a natural progression throughout Europe. But we view it as a very long-term project. I have learned that people [in other countries] think very different than Americans.[9]

Overseas Expansion by U.S. Restaurant Chains

The international market offered substantial growth opportunities for U.S. restaurant chains. For fast-food franchise chains—notably McDonald's, Burger King and Kentucky Fried Chicken—international sales accounted for up to one-half of total sales, although for many "international" was limited to Canada and Puerto Rico. Among "casual dining" chains—such as Denny's, Applebee's, T. G. I. Friday's, and Tony Roma's—relatively few had ventured beyond North America. Table 17.2 shows the international presence of leading U.S. restaurant franchise chains.

The attraction of overseas markets was that their restaurants markets were typically less saturated than those of the U.S. and most of the local competition was independent, family owned restaurants rather than large chains. In overseas markets it was anticipated

TABLE 17.2 The ten largest U.S. restaurant franchise chains, 1994

	Total sales ($m)	International sales ($m)	Total outlets	International outlets
McDonald's	25 986	11 046	15 205	5461
Burger King	7500	1400	7684	1357
KFC	7100	3600	9407	4258
Taco Bell	4290	130	5614	162
Wendy's	4277	390	4411	413
Hardee's	3491	63	3516	72
Dairy Queen	3170	300	3516	628
Domino's	2500	415	5079	840
Subway	2500	265	179	8450
Little Caesars	2000	70	4855	155

Source: "Top 50 Franchises," *Restaurant Business,* November 1, 1995, pp. 35–41.

that market trends would follow those of the U.S.: in particular, that greater affluence and a declining role of family life would result in increased eating away from home.

It was notable that, in overseas markets, not only had success been achieved principally by fast food chains but most of the leaders were subsidiaries of large multinationals with many decades of international experience. For example, KFC, Taco Bell and Pizza Hut were subsidiaries of PepsiCo.; Burger King was a subsidiary of British conglomerate Grand Metropolitan.

A key impetus to overseas expansion was maturing of the U.S. market. By 1994 there were over 3000 franchisers in the U.S., operating close to 600 000 franchised outlets. Not only was competition intense, but growth was slowing. Sales per store were growing at 3% during the early 1990s.

However, overseas markets also represented a substantial management challenge. Among the problems that other restaurant chains had encountered were the following:

- *Market demand.* The extent to which market demand existed for a particular type of restaurant depended on levels of disposable income, urbanization, demographics and a host of other social, economic, and lifestyle factors. Most critical to a specific company were national preferences with regard to cuisine and dining conventions. Even McDonald's, whose name had become synonymous with global standardization, adapted substantially to local differences: "Croque McDos" in France, rice burgers in Hong Kong, "McArabia Koftas" in Saudi Arabia, kosher outlets in Israel, no beef or pork products in India.

- *Cultural and social factors* are critical influences on customer preferences with regard to menus, restaurant facilities and overall ambiance; they are also important with regard to employee management practices and entrepreneurial potential.

- *Infrastructure.* Proper means of transportation and communication, basic utilities such as power and water, and locally available supplies were important elements in the decision to introduce a particular restaurant concept. A restaurant must have the ability to get resources to its location. Easy access to the raw materials for food preparation, equipment for manufacture of food served, and mobility for employees and customers were essential.

- *Raw material supplies.* Overseas restaurant chains needed local supplies of food and drink. The U.S. International Trade Commission noted that: "International franchisers frequently encounter problems finding supplies in sufficient quantity, of consistent quality, and at stable prices. Physical distance also can adversely affect a franchise concept and arrangement. Long distances create communication and transportation problems, which may complicate the process of sourcing supplies, overseeing operations, or providing quality management services to franchisees."[10] While a franchise chain could develop its own supply chain—for example, McDonald's when it entered the Soviet Union—the investment of management time and money could be substantial.

- *Regulations and trade restrictions.* Import restrictions are relatively unimportant in the restaurant business given that most food products are locally sourced. However, some countries have made the import of restaurant equipment difficult and expensive. Restrictions on foreign direct investment are of major significance only in emerging market countries. Far more challenging are national regulations relating to food standards, business licensing, and business contracts. Establishing new businesses in most countries involves far more regulation than within the U.S. Franchise agreements are an especially difficult area because they involve complex contractual agreements between franchisor and franchisee regarding trademark licensing, royalty payments, requirements for quality control and quality monitoring. Despite the provisions of the Uruguay Round's General Agreement on Trade in Services, most countries failed to make public their restrictions on franchising. In some countries some usual terms of franchise agreements have been viewed as restraints on commerce. Employment law was also important—particularly with regard to restrictions on employers' ability to dismiss or lay off employees and requirements for union recognition and national collective bargaining arrangements over wages and work conditions.

Notes

1   M. L. Taylor, G. M. Puia, K. Ramaya and M. Gengelback, "Outback Steakhouse Goes International," in A. A. Thompson and A. J. Strickland, *Strategic Management: Concepts and Cases,* 11th edn, McGraw-Hill, New York, 1999, pp. C296–7.

2   M. L. Taylor, G. M. Puia, K. Ramaya and M. Gengelback, "Outback Steakhouse Goes International," in A. A. Thompson and A. J. Strickland, *Strategic Management: Concepts and Cases,* 11th edn, McGraw-Hill, New York, 1999, p. C291.

3   Outback Steakhouse, Inc., 10K Report, 1996.

4   Chris T. Sullivan, "A Stake in the Business," *Harvard Business Review,* September, 2005, pp. 57–64.

5   Chris T. Sullivan, "A Stake in the Business," *Harvard Business Review,* September, 2005, pp. 59–60.

6   Chris T. Sullivan, "A Stake in the Business," *Harvard Business Review,* September, 2005, p. 58.

7   M. L. Taylor, G. M. Puia, K. Ramaya and M. Gengelback, "Outback Steakhouse Goes International," in A. A. Thompson and A. J. Strickland, *Strategic Management: Concepts and Cases,* 11th edn, McGraw-Hill, New York, 1999, p. C297.

8   M. L. Taylor, G. M. Puia, K. Ramaya and M. Gengelback, "Outback Steakhouse Goes International," in A. A. Thompson and A. J. Strickland, *Strategic Management: Concepts and Cases,* 11th edn, McGraw-Hill, New York, 1999, p. C297.

9   M. L. Taylor, G. M. Puia, K. Ramaya and M. Gengelback, "Outback Steakhouse Goes International," in A. A. Thompson and A. J. Strickland, *Strategic Management: Concepts and Cases,* 11 edn, McGraw-Hill, New York, 1999, p. C299.

10 U.S. International Trade Commission, *Industry and Trade Summary: Franchising,* Washington, DC, 1995, pp. 15–16.

Case 18 Euro Disney: From Dream to Nightmare*

At the press conference announcing Euro Disneyland SCA's financial results for the year ended September 30, 1994, CEO Philippe Bourguignon summed up the year in succinct terms: "The best thing about 1994 is that it's over."

In fact, the results for the year were better than many of Euro Disneyland's long-suffering shareholders had predicted. Although revenues were down 15%—the result of falling visitor numbers caused by widespread expectations that the park would be closed down—costs had been cut by 12%, resulting in a similar operating profit to that of the previous year. The bottom line still showed a substantial loss (net after-tax loss was FF1.8 billion); however, this was a big improvement on the previous year (FF5.33 billion loss). Tables 18.1 and 18.2 show details of the financial performance.

TABLE 18.1 Euro Disneyland SCA: financial performance 1993–4; operating revenue and expenditure (millions of French francs)

	1994	1993
Revenue:		
Theme park	2212	2594
Hotels	1613	1721
Other	322	559
Construction sales	114	851
Total revenue	4261	5725
Direct costs/expenses:		
Park and hotels	(2961)	(3382)
Construction sales	(114)	(846)
Operating income	1186	1497
Depreciation	(291)	(227)
Lease rental expense	(889)	(1712)
Royalties	–	(262)
General and administration	(854)	(1113)
Financial income	538	719
Financial expenses	(972)	(615)
Loss	(1282)	(1713)
Exceptional loss, net	(515)	(3624)
Net loss	(1797)	(5337)
Employees (cast members)		
Number	11 865	10 172
Annual Cost (FF, millions)	2108	1892

Bourguignon was decidedly upbeat regarding the future. Following the FF13 billion restructuring agreed with creditor banks in June, Euro Disney was now on a much firmer financial footing. As a result of the restructuring, Euro Disneyland SCA was left with equity of about FF5.5 billion and total borrowings of FF15.9 billion—down by a quarter from the previous year. With the threat of closure lifted, Euro Disney was now in a much better position to attract visitors and corporate partners.

Efforts to boost attendance figures included a new advertising campaign, a new FF600 million attraction (Space Mountain), which was due to open in June 1996, and changing the park's name from Euro Disneyland to Disneyland Paris.

Moreover, Euro Disney had made a number of operational improvements. Mr. Bourguignon reported that queuing times had been cut by 45% during the year through new attractions and the redesign of existing ones; hotel occupancy rates had risen from 55% in the previous year to 60% and managers were to be given greater incentives. The net result, claimed Bourguignon, was that the company would break even during 1996.

The stock market responded positively to the results. In London, the shares of Euro Disneyland SCA rose 13p to 96p. However, this did not take the shares much above their all-time low. On November 6, 1989, the first day of trading after the Euro Disneyland initial public offering, the shares had traded at 880p. Since then, Euro

TABLE 18.2 Euro Disneyland SCA: financial statements 1992–4 (under U.S. GAAP)

Balance sheet

	1994	1993	1992
Cash and investments	289	211	479
Receivables	227	268	459
Fixed assets, net	3791	3704	4346
Other assets	137	214	873
Total assets	4444	4397	6157
Accounts payable and other liabilities	560	647	797
Borrowings	3051	3683	3,960
Stockholders' equity	833	67	1,400
Total liabilities and stockholders' equity	4444	4397	6157

Statement of operations

	1994	1993	1992
Revenues	751	873	738
Costs and expenses	1198	1114	808
Net interest expense	280	287	95
Loss before income taxes and cumulative effect of accounting change	(727)	(528)	(165)
Income tax benefit	–	–	30
Loss before cumulative effect of accounting change	(727)	(528)	(135)
Cumulative effect of change in accounting for pre-opening costs	–	(578)	–
Net loss	(727)	(1106)	(135)

Source: Walt Disney Company, 10-K Report, 1994.

Disneyland stock had been on a near-continuous downward trend (see Figure 18.1). The *Financial Times'* Lex column was also unenthusiastic:

> Still beset by high costs and low attendances, Euro Disney will find it hard to hit its target of break-even by the end of September 1996. Costs in the year were reduced by FF500m by introducing more flexible labor agreements (more part-timers, increased job sharing and the use of more students in the peak season) as well as outsourcing contracts in the hotel operation. But the company admits that the lion's share of cost reductions has now been realized. Now it hopes attendances are rising . . . Getting people to spend more once they are at the park might be more difficult. Euro Disney is pinning its hopes on economic recovery in Europe. It'll have to start paying interest, management fees and royalties again in five years' time. Management will not say whether it'll be able to cope then.[1]

Returning to his office at the end of the press conference, Bourguignon sighed. Since taking over from the previous chief executive, Robert Fitzpatrick, in 1993, the 46-year-old had been engaged in a continuing battle to ensure the survival of Euro Disney. Now that survival was no longer an issue, Bourguignon now faced his next

FIGURE 18.1 Euro Disneyland's share price in Paris, 1991–4 (in French francs)

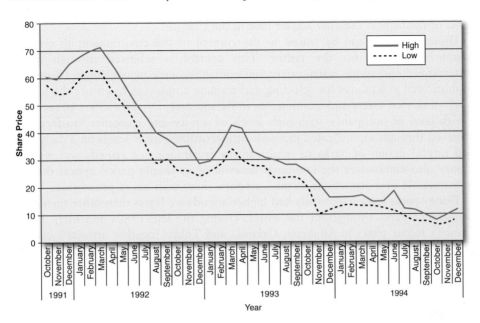

challenge: could Euro Disneyland ever become profitable—especially once Euro Disney had to resume paying licensing and management fees (amounting to some FF500 million a year) to Walt Disney Co. after 1998?

Disney Theme Parks

Walt Disney pioneered the theme park concept. His goal was to create a unique entertainment experience that combined fantasy and history, adventure, and learning in which the guest would be a participant, as well as a spectator. Current Disney-designed theme parks in California, Florida, Japan, and France are divided into distinct lands. All the parks include a number of similar lands with identical attractions. These include Main Street, Frontierland, Tomorrowland, Fantasyland and Adventureland. The objective is to immerse the guest in the atmosphere of the particular land. The theme of each land is reflected in the types of rides and attractions, the costumes of employees, the architectural style of the buildings, and even the food and souvenirs sold within the boundaries of the particular land. Rather than presenting a random collection of roller coasters, carousels and other rides, the Disney parks create an all-embracing experience which envelops the guest in carefully designed, tightly managed fantasy experience such as space flight, a Caribbean pirate attack, a flying ride with Peter Pan, or a race down the Matterhorn in a bob-sleigh.

Disney theme parks benefit from the talent and expertise of the Walt Disney "family" of businesses. Parks are designed by the engineers and architects of a wholly owned subsidiary—WED Enterprises. The themes for the attractions and characters that are featured in them often have their origins in cartoons and live action movies produced by Disney's studios. The parks also benefit from management and merchandising techniques developed over many years at Disney. These techniques have led to tremendous successes. In merchandising, Disney retail stores achieved some of the highest sales per square foot in the U.S.

Disney's success can be traced to the control of the environment to create a unique experience for the visitor. This control is achieved through highly systematized operations management and human resource management. Disney has sophisticated procedures for selecting and training employees to ensure the highest levels of service, safety and maintenance in the industry. Disney's ability to reconcile a high level of occupancy with high levels of service and customer satisfaction is achieved through sophisticated methods of forecasting visitor levels on a daily basis and careful design of parks to minimize the frustrations of crowds and waiting. Disney also emphasizes the continual renewal of its theme parks' appeal through investment in new attractions. It then supports these with heavy promotion.

Disney parks have historically had higher attendance levels than other theme and amusement parks throughout the world. During the late 1980s and early 1990s, Disney's theme parks in Anaheim, Orlando and Tokyo together attracted over 50 million guest visits annually.

Disney's U.S. Parks

The Los Angeles Disneyland theme park was finally opened in July of 1955 on 160 acres of land in Anaheim in California's Orange County. The success of Disneyland created a real estate boom in Anaheim, resulting in Disneyland being surrounded by a ring of hotels, motels, restaurants and other businesses.

For his next theme park project, Walt Disney aimed for undiluted control over the business and its revenue stream. Walt Disney World Resort opened in 1971 on a huge tract of 29 000 acres that Walt acquired outside of Orlando, Florida. Walt Disney World eventually comprised three separate theme parks: the original Magic Kingdom, the Experimental Prototype Community of Tomorrow (EPCOT) Center that opened in 1982 and hosted two themes—*Future World* and *World Showcase*— and Disney-MGM Studios, which opened in 1989.

The experience of creating a theme park as a destination resort represented a major development in Disney's conception of a theme park and was influential in its expansion plans into Europe. The huge site allowed Disney to broaden the scope of its theme park activities to create themed hotels, offer golf courses and other sports, convention facilities, night clubs, a range of retail stores, and even residential housing. The complementary coupling of a theme park with resort facilities that could even host commercial activities (conferences, a technology park) became central to Disney's theme park strategy.

By 1990, Walt Disney World had become the largest center of hotel capacity in the U.S., with approximately 70 000 rooms, of which almost 10% were owned and operated by Disney. Even though the room rates charged by Disney were considerably higher than other hotels in the vicinity, they achieved a remarkable occupancy rate of 94% during the late 1980s.

Tokyo Disneyland

Tokyo Disneyland, which opened in 1983, was a major departure for Walt Disney Company. The Oriental Land Company Limited (OLCL), a Japanese development company, had approached Disney with a proposal to open a Disneyland in Japan. Disney's top management regarded a Disney theme park in another country with a different climate and a different culture as a risky venture. Disney insisted on a deal that would leave OLCL with all the risk: the park would be owned and operated by OLCL while Disney would receive royalties of 10% on the admissions revenues and 5% on receipts from food, beverages and souvenirs. These royalties represented licensing fees for Disney's trademarks and intellectual property, engineering designs for rides and ongoing technical assistance. Despite the challenges of limited space and cold winter weather, Tokyo Disneyland was a huge success. By the late 1980s it was drawing 15 million visitors a year—more than any other Disney park.[2] By 1989, Disney's royalties from Tokyo Disneyland had risen to $573 million—greater than the operating income received from Disney's U.S. theme parks.

Planning and Development

Beginnings of Euro Disneyland

The success of Tokyo Disneyland was clear evidence to Disney's top management of the international potential for Disney's theme parks. Europe was considered the obvious location for the next Disney park. Europe had always been a strong market for Disney movies and there was a strong European demand for toys, books, and comics that featured Disney characters—European consumers generated about one-quarter of revenues from Disney licensed consumer products. The popularity of Disney theme parks with Europeans was evident from the 2 million European visitors to Disneyland and Walt Disney World each year. Moreover, Western Europe possessed a population and affluence capable of supporting a major Disney theme park.

In 1984, Disney management made the decision to commit to development of a European theme park and commenced feasibility planning and site selection. In assessing alternative locations, the following criteria were applied:

- proximity to a high-density population zone with a relatively high level of disposable income;
- ability to draw upon a substantial local tourist population, availability of qualified labor and readily accessible transportation;
- availability of sufficient land to permit expansion of the project to meet increasing demand;
- provision of necessary infrastructure, such as water and electricity.

Two locations quickly emerged as front-runners: Barcelona and Paris. While Barcelona had the advantages of a better year-round climate, Paris offered key economic and infrastructure advantages, together with strong backing from the French government. Disney's interest in a European theme park corresponded with the French government's plans to develop the Marne-la-Vallée area east of Paris. The result was rapid progress of Disney's formal negotiations with the range of local government authorities and public bodies whose cooperation and agreement were essential for a project of this scale. The proposed site's demographic characteristics offered the right set of conditions for a successful theme park. The park rested on a

4500 acre site 32 km east of Paris, providing proximity to a metropolitan area and room for expansion; the high population of the greater Paris area (over 10 million) and Europe (over 330 million) provided a large consumer market and existing and planned transportation equipped the park with access to vital infrastructure. Paris was already a major tourist destination with excellent air, road and rail links with the rest of Europe.

On March 24, 1987, the Walt Disney Company entered into the Agreement on the Creation and the Operation of Euro Disneyland in France (the "Master Agreement") with the Republic of France, the Region of Ile-de-France, the Department of Seine-et-Marne, the Etablissement Public d'Aménagement de la Ville Nouvelle de Marne-la-Vallée, and the Régie Autonome des Transports Parisiens. This was followed by incorporation of Euro Disneyland SCA (the "Company") and the conclusion of an agreement with the SNCF (the French national railway company) to provide TGV (the French high-speed train) service to Euro Disneyland beginning in June 1994. The agreement involved commitments by Disney to establish Euro Disneyland as a French corporation, to develop a major international theme park, and to create 30 000 jobs in the process. The French authorities committed to provide land and infrastructure over the project's 30-year development period ending in 2017. The real estate deal involved Disney acquiring 1700 hectares (approximately 4300 acres)[3] of agricultural land at Marne-la-Vallée. In addition, a further 243 hectares were reserved for public facilities and infrastructure. The purchase price for the land included the raw land price (FF11.1 per square meter or approximately $8360 per acre), direct and indirect secondary infrastructure costs, and certain financing and overhead expenses of the French authorities. The area of the total site was equivalent to one-fifth of the area of the city of Paris. The land for the first phase of the development was purchased outright by Euro Disneyland SCA, with purchase options on the remaining land. Euro Disneyland SCA also had the right to sell land to third parties, as long as the development plans of any purchasers were approved by the French planning authority.

The agreement provided for motorway links to Paris, Strasbourg and the two international airports serving Paris—Charles de Gaulle and Orly, while the planned extension of the RER (the express commuter rail network) would allow visitors to reach the Magic Kingdom from the center of Paris within 40 minutes. Euro Disney[4] would also be linked to France's TGV system, with its own station serving the park. This would also give a rail service from Britain through the Channel Tunnel. In addition to infrastructure, the French government's financial inducements included FF4.8 billion in loans and a favorable tax rate (34%). The total package of incentives added up to roughly FF6.0 billion.[5]

The Market: Demand and Competition

A key factor attracting Disney to Paris was market potential. The greater Paris metropolis has a population of over 10 million. Roughly 16 million people lived within a 160 km radius of the proposed site; within a 320 km radius were 41 million people; and within a 480 km radius were 109 million people. The transportation links of Paris facilitated access to this huge market. As a result, Euro Disneyland would be capable of achieving a high level of capacity utilization, even with much lower market penetration rates than those achieved by Disney's California and

Florida theme parks. European vacation patterns were also seen as conducive to visits—Europeans received substantially more vacation time than U.S. workers and, in addition to their summer vacation, European families frequently took shorter vacations throughout the year. Estimates of numbers of visitors to Euro Disney and their expenditures were made by consultants Arthur D. Little as part of their financial projections for Euro Disneyland SCA (see Appendix 1).

The ability of Euro Disney to achieve its visitor targets would depend not only on the size of the market but also upon the relative attractiveness and number of competing tourist destinations. Although Disney viewed its theme parks as unique in terms of the quality and intensity of the entertainment experience that it offered, the company also recognized that, ultimately, a wide range of family vacation and entertainment experiences compete for household disposable income. Although there were very few large-scale theme parks in Europe to compete directly with Euro Disneyland (most of the world's major theme parks were located in the U.S.) there were a number of family entertainment destinations within Europe that would be potential competitors (see Table 18.3). Moreover, European cities—such as London, Paris, Rome, Prague, Barcelona, and many others—offered a richness and variety of cultural and historical experiences that few U.S. cities could match and represented an alternative to Euro Disney for short family vacations. Furthermore, there was a host of traditional forms of family entertainment in Europe, including fairs, carnivals and festivals, some of which were small and local while others—such as the Munich Bierfest, the Pamplona bull-running festival, the Edinburgh cultural festival, and the Dutch tulip festivals—were major events attracting large numbers of international visitors.

Disney's plans for Euro Disneyland created its own competitors. Within two years of Disney's announcement to build Euro Disney, three French theme parks—Mirapolis, Futuroscope and Zygofolis—had opened in an attempt to pre-empt Disney's entry into the market. By the summer of 1989, two more theme

TABLE 18.3 Attendance at major theme parks

	Estimated attendance in 1988 (millions of guest visits)
Sea World—*Florida*	4.6
Tivoli Gardens—*Denmark*	4.5
Universal Studios Tour—*California*	4.2
Knott's Berry Farm—*California*	4.0
Busch Gardens—*Florida*	3.7
Sea World—*California*	3.4
Six Flags Magic Mountain—*California*	3.1
King's Island—*Ohio*	3.0
Liseberg—*Sweden*	2.8
Alton Towers—*United Kingdom*	2.3
De Efteling—*The Netherlands*	2.3
Phantasialand—*West Germany*	2.2

Source: Euro Disneyland SCA Abridged Offering Circular.

parks—Asterix and Big Bang Schtroumph—opened their gates. However, with aggregate annual losses of about $43 million on a total investment of over $600 million, these parks were considered financial disasters.[6]

The Development Plan

Euro Disney's Development Program provided for a theme park, based closely on the themes and concepts of Disney's U.S. theme parks. It would be the largest theme park and resort development in Europe. The plan established two stages for the project.

Phase 1 Phase 1, the major part of the overall project, was subdivided into two sections. Phase 1A comprised the Magic Kingdom theme park, the Magic Kingdom Hotel (which would serve as the entrance area to the theme park) and a camping ground. These were to be completed at a budgeted cost of FF14.9 billion. Of the 570 acres allocated for Phase 1, Phase 1A would utilize 240 acres. The rest of the land would be developed in Phase 1B to accommodate five additional hotels, an entertainment, restaurant and shopping complex, and sports facilities with an 18-hole championship golf course. Phase 1A also provided for the French government to construct two junctions with the nearby motorway, main access roads to the park, a drinking-water supply and distribution system, storm drainage, sewers, solid waste treatment, and telecommunications networks. The cost of the additional infrastructure, including links with the RER and the TGV, was to be financed by Euro Disneyland SCA.

The Magic Kingdom theme park was to include five themed lands: Main Street USA, the gateway to the park; Frontierland, a reproduction of wooden streets typical of a mid-nineteenth-century frontier town; tropical Adventure Land, the most exotic of the park settings; Fantasyland, with attractions drawn from well-known Disney stories; and Discoveryland, which, through the sophisticated use of technology, illustrates the past and the future. Each offers appropriately themed restaurants and shopping facilities.

To permit year-round operation, Euro Disney included adaptations designed to make attendance less dependent on the weather, with more interconnected covered areas than at other Disney parks. Many modifications to the themes, architecture and dining facilities were made to tailor the park to the European market. For example, while French is the first language of the park, universal signposting is used wherever possible to aid non-French-speaking visitors, and many attractions are identified by visual cues.

Phase 2 Phase 2 of the Long-Term Development Strategy extended to 2011. It envisioned a second theme park (Disney-MGM Studios) on a site adjacent to the Magic Kingdom; 15 additional hotels, which would increase the number of rooms available by 13 000; a water recreation area and second golf course and residential and commercial development. This phase was left flexible to accommodate the policies of the French authorities, economic and market conditions, participant needs, and visitor preferences.

Construction Disney exercised close control over the design and construction of Phase 1A of Euro Disney. Lehrer McGovern Bovis, Inc. (LMB), an independent construction management firm with international experience in the management of large-scale construction projects, was the main contractor. It reported to Euro Disneyland Imagineering SARL (EDLI), a French subsidiary of Disney, which had overall responsibility for designing and constructing Phases 1 and 2 of the theme park. Also reporting to EDLI were separate Disney companies responsible for design (conceptual and otherwise), engineering, and the development and equipping of attractions.

Participants As with other Disney theme parks, at Euro Disneyland "participants" played an important role in financial and in marketing terms. Participants are companies or organizations that enter into long-term marketing agreements with the company. Typically, these relationships represent a ten-year commitment and physically tie the participant to the Magic Kingdom, where it hosts or presents one or more of the theme park's attractions, restaurants, or other facilities. Relationships with participants may also involve marketing activities featuring the association between the participant and the company. Each participant pays an individually negotiated annual fee, which may contribute to the financing of a particular attraction or facility.

Initial participants at Euro Disneyland included Kodak, Banque Nationale de Paris, Renault, and Europcar.

Financial and Management Structure

For Euro Disneyland, Disney chose a unique financial and management structure. Rather than a pure franchise operation similar to Tokyo Disneyland, Disney chose to retain management and operational control of the park while allowing European investors to take majority ownership and European banks to provide most of the debt financing. The relationship between Walt Disney Company and Euro Disneyland is depicted in Figure 18.2.

Euro Disneyland SCA

Euro Disneyland SCA was formed to build and own Euro Disneyland. The company was a *société en commandite par actions*—the French equivalent of a limited partnership. The company was governed by a supervisory board elected by the shareholders and chaired by Jean Taittinger, the Chairman and Chief Executive of Société du Louvre and Banque du Louvre. Disney took a 49% stake in Euro Disneyland SCA; the remaining 51% of equity was floated through an initial public offering underwritten by three investment banks. The shares were listed on the Paris and London stock markets. Although Disney held 49% of Euro Disneyland SCA equity it contributed only 13% of its equity book value (FF273 million net of incentives received). The difference was "granted" to the company, both as a goodwill "gesture" in recognition of Disney's reputation and credibility in the investment community and as compensation for Disney's assumed risk in the undertaking.

The Management Company

Euro Disneyland SCA was managed by a separate management company, Euro Disneyland SA (the "management company"), a wholly owned subsidiary of Disney.

FIGURE 18.2 The financial and management relationship between Walt Disney and Euro Disneyland

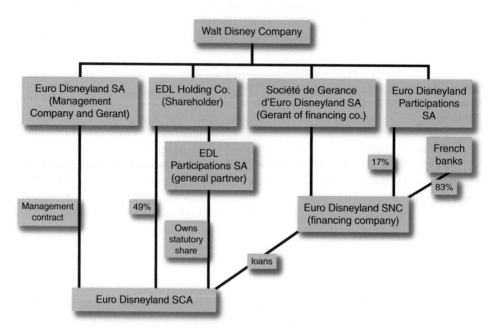

The management company, or *gerant*, was responsible under French law for managing Euro Disneyland SCA and its affairs in the company's best interests. In turn, the management company agreed that the provision of management services to the company would be its exclusive business. Under the Articles of Association, the management company was entitled to annual fees consisting of a base fee and management incentive fees. The base fee in any year was set at 3% of the company's total revenues, and increased to 6% after five years of operation, or after the company had satisfied certain financial targets. On top of the base fee, the management company was entitled to incentive fees based on Euro Disneyland SCA's pretax cash flow. These incentives increased in stages up to a possible maximum of 50% of Euro Disneyland SCA's net profit. The management company also received 35% of pre-tax gains on the sales of hotels. Euro Disneyland SCA was also obligated to reimburse the management company for all its direct and indirect expenses incurred in its management role. The management contract was for five years.

The Shareholding Company and General Partner

Disney's shareholding in Euro Disneyland SCA was held by EDL Holding, a wholly owned subsidiary of Disney. This shareholding company also owned EDL Participations SA, which held the key role of "general partner" in Euro Disneyland SCA—it assumed unlimited liability for the debts and liabilities of Euro Disneyland SCA. As general partner, EDL Participations SA was entitled to a distribution each year equal to 0.5% of Euro Disneyland SCA's net after-tax profits.

The Financing Company

Euro Disneyland SNC was formed to buy the park facilities from Euro Disneyland SCA at book value plus development costs, then lease them back to Euro Disneyland SCA. Euro Disneyland SNC was owned 17% by Disney and 83% by French corporations. The rationale was to allow French corporations to take advantage of the tax benefits of Euro Disneyland's early years of projected losses. Once again, Euro Disneyland SNC was to be managed by a Disney subsidiary and Disney would act as its general partner with full debt default liability.

The License Agreement

Under the License Agreement, Walt Disney Company granted to Euro Disneyland SCA a license to use any present or future Disney intellectual and industrial property rights incorporated in Disney's attractions and facilities and made available to the Company for Euro Disney. These included the Walt Disney name, the Disney characters, and the proprietary technology in theme park attractions. Disney was to receive royalties as follows:

- 10% of gross revenues (net of TVA, the French value-added tax, and similar taxes) from rides, admissions and certain related fees (such as parking, tour guide, and similar services) at all theme parks and other attractions (including the Magic Kingdom and any future theme park);
- 5% of gross revenues (net of TVA and similar taxes) from merchandise, food, and beverage sales in or adjacent to any theme park or other attraction or in any other facility (other than the Magic Kingdom Hotel) whose overall design concept is based predominantly on a Disney theme;
- 10% of all fees due from participants;
- 5% of all gross revenues (net of TVA and similar taxes) from room rates and related charges at Disney-themed accommodations (excluding the Magic Kingdom Hotel).

Cultural Issues

Euro Disneyland presented huge challenges for Disney. Climate was a major problem. The long gray winter of northern France created complex design problems that were absent from Disney's sun-drenched California and Florida parks. However, the challenges posed by adverse weather conditions were mainly technical and amenable to careful analysis. The issues of culture were much less tractable.

While the success of Tokyo Disneyland was a major factor behind the decision to create Euro Disney, the cultural challenges of France were very different from those of Japan. Tokyo Disneyland had been conceived, built, and operated on a wave of popular Japanese acclaim. As a result, Tokyo Disneyland had made very few concessions to Japanese culture. Although, at first, Disney wanted to adapt some of the attractions to the Japanese context (for example, Samurai-Land instead of Frontierland), their Japanese partners strongly resisted efforts to "localize" Disneyland, arguing that the park would attract more Japanese people if it were built as a perfect replica of U.S. Disneyland. They emphasized that Disney's cartoon characters were very familiar to the Japanese people and that visitors would want "the real thing." As a result, only minor changes were made, such as the addition of Cinderella's Castle and the Mickey Mouse Theater.

After the enthusiasm with which the Japanese greeted Disney's entry, the response of the French could not have been more different. France presented a very different situation. French intellectuals had long shown antagonism towards American popular culture and they were supported by widespread nationalistic sentiment that saw the French language and French culture as threatened by the global hegemony of the English language. At the political level too, France had been the most independent of the western European powers in terms of its independent foreign policy and unwillingness to accept U.S. leadership in world affairs. The announcement of the Euro Disneyland project was greeted by howls of outrage from the French media and from the intelligentsia who viewed the park as "a cultural Chernobyl," "a dangerous step towards world homogenization," "a horror made of cardboard, plastic, and appalling colors, a construction of hardened chewing gum and idiotic folklore taken straight out of the comic books written for obese Americans."[7] Euro Disney quickly became a lightning rod for a variety of anti-American issues. For example, shortly after opening, Euro Disney was blockaded by farmers protesting U.S. farm policies.

The design of the park incorporated many adaptations of French and European culture. Disney emphasized the European heritage of many of Disney's characters and storylines (referred to by Chairman Michael Eisner as "European folklore with a Kansas twist"). Some attractions featured European adaptations: Cinderella lived in a French inn and Snow White's home was in a Bavarian village. Other attractions were unique to Euro Disney: Discoveryland (which substituted for Tomorrowland at other Disney parks) was based on themes from Jules Verne and Leonardo da Vinci; "Visionarium" was a 360-degree movie theater showcasing French culture; an Alice-in-Wonderland attraction was surrounded by a 5000 sq. ft. hedge maze. Designing and constructing these European-themed attractions added substantially to the cost of Euro Disneyland.

Some "American" themed attractions were adapted on the basis of market research findings. For example, the finding that European visitors to Disney's U.S. parks responded positively to themes embodying the American West encouraged Disney to redesign several attractions around a Wild West theme—including a mining town setting for one ride, a "Davy Crockett" themed campground, and hotels named the "Cheyenne," "Santa Fe" and "Sequoia Lodge."

Other adaptations were made to cater to European social behavior and culinary tastes. Concern over European aversion to queuing resulted in the provision of video screens, movies and other entertainment for guests waiting in line. Disney's no-alcohol policy was adjusted by allowing wine and beer to be served at Feastival Disney, an entertainment complex just outside the theme park. In the restaurant facilities, greater emphasis was placed on sit-down dining and much less on fast food. At a seminar at UCLA in 1990, Robert Fitzpatrick placed a major emphasis on the Company's determination to provide the highest standards of quality at Euro Disney. This was evident both in the cuisine and in the furnishings and service standards of the hotels. In both areas, Fitzpatrick argued, quality was well in excess of the standards at Disney's U.S. parks.

Human relations management posed further cultural challenges. Central to the Disney theme park experience was the way in which "cast members" interacted with the guests. Disney was famous for its meticulous approach to recruitment, its commitment to employee training and the maintenance of rigorous standards of employee conduct. For example, Disney's employee handbook spelled out a strict code with respect to dress and appearance, including:

- above average height and below average weight;
- pleasant appearance (straight teeth, no facial blemishes);
- conservative grooming standards (facial hair and long hair is banned);
- very modest make-up, very limited jewelry (for example, no more than one ring on each hand);
- employees were required to wear specific types and colors of underwear; only neutral colors of pantyhose were allowed.[8]

Training embraced general principles and specific knowledge and behaviors. For example, employees were instructed that their behavior on the job should be governed by three major rules: "First, we practice a friendly smile. Second, we use only friendly phrases. Third, we are not stuffy."

To what extent could locally recruited employees provide the level, quality and consistency of service at Euro Disney that would match that of other Disney theme parks, and to what extent could Disney simply transplant its U.S. human resource management practices? Euro Disney's selection and training were closely modeled on Disney's U.S. approach. A Euro Disney branch of Disney University was opened and recruitment of 10 000 employees began in September 1991. Selection criteria were "applicant friendliness, warmth, and liking of people." The rules for job applicants were spelled out in a video presentation and in the employee handbook, "The Euro Disney Look." The rules went far beyond weight and height requirements, describing the length of the men's hair, beard and mustache requirements, tattoo coverage requirements and hair color specifications (for example, hair had to be of a natural-looking color, without frosting or streaking). Only moderate use of cosmetics was allowed. Women could wear one earring in each ear with the earrings' diameter not to exceed three-quarters of an inch.[9] The goal was a nationality mix that would match that of Euro Disney's customers, about 45% of whom were French. However, in response to local pressure and the greater availability of local applicants, some 70% of employees were French. At the management level, Disney relied on importing about 200 managers from other Disney parks and training 270 locally recruited managers (this involved training at Disney's other theme parks).

Disney's recruiting practices and employee policies produced a storm of protest. French labor unions started protesting from the moment that Euro Disney started interviewing applicants. Representatives of the General Confederation of Labor handed out leaflets in front of Euro Disney's HQ warning applicants that the Disney hiring practices represented "an attack on individual freedom." Many of Disney's normal U.S. hiring and employment practices contravened French law. Workforce flexibility was limited by the restrictions on terminating employees with more than two years with the company and the high severance payments involved. There were also legal limits over the recruitment and dismissal of seasonal workers. As for Disney's dress and personal grooming codes, French law prohibited an employer from restricting "individual and collective freedoms" unless the restrictions could be justified by the "nature of the objective to be accomplished and were proportional to that end." Since Disney estimated that no more than 700 employees would be involved in "theatrical actions," dress code limitations could only be imposed on those employees, not on those who would only be "back stage."

The First Year

Euro Disney's opening on April 12, 1992 combined both fanfare and protest. An extravagant opening ceremony involved some of the world's leading entertainers and was televised in 22 countries. Michael Eisner proclaimed Euro Disney to be "one of the greatest man-made attractions in the world" while the French Prime Minister described the park as an "incredible achievement which transcends national frontiers . . . We are deeply attached to the links of friendship between our continent and yours. Euro Disney is one of the symbols of this transatlantic friendship." However, the opening was marred by a demonstration of local residents, a train strike affecting lines leading to the park and a terrorist bomb threat. By the end of the first day, park attendance had been way below capacity and only one-half of the anticipated number.

The park ran into early teething problems. Design problems ranged from insufficient breakfast facilities to an absence of toilet facilities for bus drivers and a shortage of employee accommodation. During the first nine weeks of operation, 1000 employees left Euro Disney, about one-half voluntarily. Long hours and hectic work pace were the main reasons given for leaving. Nevertheless, visitor reactions were mainly highly positive. Negative comments related to frustration with long periods of waiting in line and the high cost of admission, food and souvenirs. Some voiced concern over the multinational, multicultural flavor of Euro Disney: "They haven't yet figured out whether it's going to be an American park, a French park, or a European park . . . Differences in waiting line behavior is striking. For instance, Scandinavians appear quite content to wait for rides, whereas some of the southern Europeans seem to have made an Olympic event out of getting to the ticker tape first." Some visitors had difficulty envisaging Disney within a European context: "Disney is very much an American culture. Florida is the true Disney World, the true feeling of Disney, what Disney is trying to project. Americans are part of that, the French aren't."[10]

Start-up difficulties were normal in the theme park business—all major theme parks, including those of Disney, experienced some teething problems during the period of initial operation. Universal Studios in Florida had a disastrous first few months but subsequently rebounded. With 30 000 visitors daily during the summer of 1992, it seemed that Euro Disney might reach its projected target of 11 million visitors annually. However, it was soon clear that, despite good visitor numbers during the summer, Euro Disney's profitability would fall far below expectations. There was a larger number of day visitors and fewer period visits than had been anticipated. As a result, Euro Disney cut hotel rates by up to 25%. Moreover, average visitor expenditure on beverages, food and gifts was 12% less than the $33 per day that had been anticipated. Part of the problem was the economic situation—during 1992, most of Western Europe was mired in one of the worst economic downturns since the Second World War. The depressed state of the French real estate market also prevented Euro Disney from boosting revenues through land sales.

By the end of Euro Disney's first full financial year, the extent of the financial underperformance was becoming clear. Even with exceptional items, the company lost over FF1.7 billion. In terms of U.S. GAAP, Euro Disneyland's pretax loss was over half a billion dollars. Top-line performance was a key problem. Instead of the 11 million visitors forecast, Euro Disney attracted 9.8 million visitors during its first full year. Equally serious was the fact that average visitor spending was below target, and much lower than at Disney's U.S. and Japanese parks. Fewer visitors than projected were staying in Disney theme hotels, deterred by room rates that were much higher than in comparable hotels in Paris. Hotel occupancy rates were below 50% in contrast to the 60% figure projected. On the cost side, Disney's emphasis on quality had boosted both construction and operating costs, while higher than anticipated debt together with rising interest rates caused interest charges to spiral upward. Labor costs amounted to a huge 24% of sales, rather than the forecasted level of 13% of sales. Much of the cost overruns could be attributed to Disney's belief that "Lacoste and Polo loving" Europeans would not tolerate anything unsophisticated or cheap. For example, in the U.S., "The Walt" restaurant had wallpaper but at Euro Disney the walls were covered in Moroccan leather. Yet, when it came to trading off sophistication for lower prices, most Euro Disney customers opted for the latter.

For Walt Disney Company, the financial returns were better than they were for Euro Disneyland's other shareholders. During 1992 and 1993, Disney's 49% share of Euro Disneyland's losses was offset by royalties from its licensing agreement. These amounted to $36.3 million in 1993 and $32.9 million in 1992; however, Disney agreed to defer its management fees for 1992 and 1993.

Restructuring

During the winter of 1993/4, Euro Disney visitor numbers plummeted. Despite the French franc falling against the U.S. dollar, many Europeans found that Disneyland Florida was not only a more attractive destination during the winter months but it was also cheaper. "It's cheaper to go on a two-week holiday in Florida than to come to Euro Disney for five days," remarked one British traveler with a family of four. With low transatlantic fares, European visitors to Walt Disney World in Orlando increased sharply during 1992 and 1993. By early 1994, Euro Disney was in crisis. Faced with mounting losses, rising debt and doubts about the company's capacity to cover its interest payments, rumors were rife that the park would be forced to close.

The financial restructuring package agreed between Euro Disneyland and its creditors in June 1994 involved the following measures:

- A $1.1 billion rights offering of which Disney agreed to take up 41%.
- The provision by Disney of $255 million in lease financing at an interest rate of 1%.
- The cancellation by Disney of $210 million in receivables from Euro Disneyland.
- The agreement by Disney to waive royalties and management fees for five years.

- The agreement that Disney would receive warrants for the purchase of 28 million Euro Disneyland shares and would receive a development fee of $225 million once the second phase of the development project was launched. Euro Disneyland's lenders agreed to underwrite 51% of the Euro Disney rights offering, to forgive certain interest charges until September 2003 and to defer all principal payments for three years. In return, Euro Disneyland issued the lenders ten-year warrants for the purchase of up to 40 million shares of Euro Disneyland stock.

In a separate agreement, Disney agreed to sell 75 million shares, equivalent to 10% of Euro Disneyland's total shareholding, to Prince Alwaleed Bin Talal Bin Abdulaziz Al Saud. The sale reduced Disney's shareholding in Euro Disneyland to 39%.

Looking Ahead

While the restructuring package had staved off disaster for the time being, the traumas of the past year made Bourguignon cautious about the future. Despite heavy advertising, the addition of new attractions and the fine-tuning of Disney's image, customer service, and offering of food, drinks, and souvenirs, Euro Disney had yet to reach the initial forecast of 11 million visitors annually. Significant cost reductions had been achieved; however, the scope for further cost reductions was limited if Euro Disney was to maintain Disney's standards of customer service excellence. While Bourguignon was convinced that the company would be generating operating profits by 1995, such profits would be the result of Disney's agreement to forgo its royalties and management fees. Once these were reinstated, Euro Disney's costs would increase by about FF500 million annually.

Bourguignon believed that many of the problems that had dogged Euro Disney from the beginning had been resolved. In particular, the renaming of the park as Disneyland Paris had helped alleviate ambiguity and conflict over the park's identity. Disneyland Paris was to be a Disney theme park located close to Paris. Dropping the "Euro" prefix released the company from the public's mistrust of all things Euro and helped the park to avoid the debate over what European culture and European identity actually meant. Moreover, the new name firmly associated Euro Disney with the romantic connotations of the city of Paris. In terms of the need to differentiate Euro Disney from Disney's other theme parks, the experience of the past two years suggested that Euro Disney's expensive adaptations to meet European tastes and European culture were not greatly appreciated by customers. For the most part, visitors were delighted by the same rides as existed in Disney's U.S. parks and generally preferred fast food over fine dining.

Over the next six months, Bourguignon recognized that key decisions needed to be taken:

- To what extent should Euro Disney cut admission prices in order to boost attendance? An internal study had estimated that a 20% reduction in admission prices would boost attendance by about 800 000 visitors; however, the net result would still be a reduction in total revenues of about 5%.

- The problems of insufficient demand related primarily to the winter months. In previous winters some senior managers had argued for the closure of the park. However, so long as most of Euro Disney's employees were permanent staff, such a closure would do little to reduce total costs.

- Bourguignon had already deferred Phase 2 of the development plan— construction of a Disney-MGM Studios theme park. The other members of his senior management team were urging him to go ahead with this phase of development. Only with a second theme park, they believed, would Euro Disney's goal of becoming a major destination resort become realized. However, Bourguignon was acutely aware of Euro Disney's still precarious financial situation. With net equity of about FF5.5 billion and total borrowings of FF15.9 billion, Euro Disney was not well placed to begin the large-scale capital expenditures that Phase 2 would involve.

As Bourguignon arranged the papers on his desk at the end of a long day, he reflected on his success at pulling off the rescue plan and the continuing uphill struggle to realize the ambitions that had driven the project in the early days. The wartime words of Winston Churchill summed up the situation well: "This is not the end. It is not the beginning of the end. It is the end of the beginning."

Appendix 1: Euro Disneyland SCA's Financial Model

The company has prepared a financial model, based on the principal assumptions described below, which projects revenues, expenses, profits, cash flows, and dividends of the company for 12-month periods beginning 1 April, 1992 and ending 31 March, 2017 as summarized in Table 18.4. Although the company's accounting year end is 30 September, years beginning 1 April have been used for the projections in order to represent whole operating years from the projected date of opening of the Magic Kingdom. The projections contained in the model do not constitute a forecast of the actual revenues, expenses, profits, cash flows or dividends of the company. The model assumes that the company will complete Phase 1 as described in this document and will develop the remaining elements of Euro Disneyland according to the long-term development strategy. As discussed above, the company retains the flexibility to change the long-term development strategy and the designs for Phase 1B in response to future conditions. Table 18.5 summarizes the principal components of the development plan.

TABLE 18.4 Euro Disneyland SCA: projected revenues and profits (FF millions)

1992–6 12 months commencing April 1	1992	1993	1994	1995	1996
Revenues					
Magic Kingdom	4246	4657	5384	5835	6415
Second theme park	0	0	0	0	3128
Resort and property development	1236	2144	3520	5077	6386
Total revenues	5482	6801	8904	10930	15929
Profit before taxation	351	620	870	1,676	1,941

(Continued)

TABLE 18.4 *(Continued)*

1992–6 12 months commencing April 1	1992	1993	1994	1995	1996
Net profit	204	360	504	972	1121
Dividends payable	275	425	625	900	1100
Tax credit or payment	0	138	213	313	450
Total return	275	563	838	1,213	1550
Per share (FF)	1.6	3.3	4.9	7.1	9.1

Later years: 12 months commencing April 1	2001	2006	2011	2016
Revenues				
Magic Kingdom	9730	13 055	18 181	24 118
Second theme park	4565	6656	9313	12 954
Resort and property development	8133	9498	8979	5923
Total revenues	22 428	29 209	36 473	42 995
Profit before taxation	3034	4375	6539	9951
Net profit	1760	2538	3793	5771
Dividends payable	1750	2524	3379	5719
Tax credit or payment	536	865	1908	2373
Total return	2286	3389	5287	8092
Per share (FF)	13.4	19.9	31.1	47.6

Source: Euro Disneyland SCA Abridged Offering Circular.

TABLE 18.5 Planned development of Euro Disneyland

	Phase 1A	Phase 1B	Long-term development	Total
Theme parks	1	–	1	2
Hotel capacity (rooms)	500	4700	13 000	18 200
Camping ground (campsite plots)	595	–	1505	2100
Entertainment center (sq. meters)	–	22 000	38 000	60 000
Offices (sq. meters)	–	30 000	670 000	700 000
Corporate park (sq. meters)	–	50 000	700 000	750 000
Golf courses	–	1	1	2
Single-family homes	–	570	1930	2500
Retail shopping center (sq. meters)	–	–	95 000	95 000
Water recreation area	–	–	1	1
Multi-family residence	–	–	3000	3000
Time-share units	–	–	2400	2400

Source: Euro Disneyland SCA Abridged Offering Circular.

The model is based on other assumptions developed by the company in light of Disney's experience with existing theme parks and resorts, after taking into account analyses of local market conditions and an assessment of likely future economic, market, and other factors. The major assumptions have been reviewed by Arthur D. Little International, Inc. ("ADL"), the independent consultancy firm retained by the Company to test and verify their reasonableness. Set out at the end of "The financial model" is a letter from ADL regarding its reports. While the Company believes that the assumptions underlying the model are reasonable, there is no certainty that the projected performance of the company outlined below will be achieved.

Principal Assumptions and Rationale Underlying the Financial Model

Theme Park Attendance

To project the number of visitors expected to visit the Euro Disneyland theme parks, several internal and external studies were commissioned. The most recent of these studies was undertaken by ADL in 1989 to verify and confirm the methods and assumptions used in the previous studies and to make its own estimates of attendance.

The Magic Kingdom The model assumes that the Magic Kingdom will be constructed as described in this document and that it will open and be fully operational by April 1992.

Summary figures for assumed attendance at the Magic Kingdom are shown in the table below. Attendance is measured in terms of the total numbers of daily guest visits per annum. For example, a visitor who enters a theme park on three separate days will count as three daily guest visits.

	1992	1996	2001	2011
Magic Kingdom (in millions of persons)	11.0	13.3	15.2	16.2

The assumed attendance of 11 million for the first full year of operation of the Magic Kingdom is in line with the average attendance achieved in the first year of operation of the Magic Kingdom theme parks in Florida and Japan and is below the range of potential initial attendance estimated to be between 11.7 and 17.8 million in the attendance study conducted by ADL. Depending on its seasonal distribution, the higher end of the range could require acceleration of the attraction investment program. Arthur D. Little concluded that the attendance target of 11 million can be achieved if the development program envisaged for Phase 1A is accomplished and a well-conceived marketing campaign tailored to European patterns is carried out to support the opening of the Magic Kingdom.

Attendance at the Magic Kingdom is assumed to grow over the period covered by the financial model at an average compound rate of 2% per annum. This growth rate compares with an average growth rate of 3.8% per annum for the three Magic Kingdom theme parks in California, Florida and Japan.

The assumed growth rate, which is higher in early years, consists of a basic growth rate, adjusted for the effect of the addition of new attractions every two to three years and for the effect of the opening of a second theme park. The overall assumed growth rate is broken down as follows:

Years	2–5	6–10	11–20	20+
Annual growth (%)	4.9	2.7	0.6	0.0

The method used by ADL involved three steps: first, individual target markets were identified by distance and population: second, penetration rates (the percentage of the total population in a target market which visits the theme park) were estimated for each target market; and third, the average number of annual visits per guest from each target market was estimated.

Arthur D. Little noted that a number of factors, including the following, contribute to the high attendance levels at Disney-designed theme parks:

- The design and scope of a Magic Kingdom theme park are such that a complete visit requires more than one full day. This means that visitors are likely either to extend their stay or to return at a future date.
- The quality and capacity available at Disney hotels allow the demand for longer stays to be satisfied.
- The level of recognition of the Disney name and the quality of the experience make Disney theme parks popular holiday destination resorts.

In the opinion of ADL these factors distinguish Disney-designed theme parks from existing theme parks and amusement parks in Europe, which are much smaller and are basically designed for single-day visits. Accordingly, in determining potential penetration rates and the number of annual visits per guest to derive projected attendance levels at Euro Disneyland, ADL relied largely on the experience at Disney-designed theme parks.

Arthur D. Little concluded that because of the large number of people living within a convenient traveling distance of Euro Disneyland, the assumed attendance figures in the model could be achieved with market penetration rates at or below those experienced at other Disney-designed theme parks.

The company believes that these factors will exist at Euro Disneyland and will support the assumed penetration rates and attendance levels, which are consistent with those experienced at Disney-designed theme parks. The company also believes that the location of the site at the center of an area of high population density with well-developed transport links will enable Euro Disneyland to draw visitors from both local and more distant markets.

Second Theme Park The model assumes that a second theme park will be completed and will open to the public in the spring of 1996. Summary figures for assumed attendance at the second theme park are as follows:

	1992	1996	2001	2011
Second theme park (in millions)	–	8.0	8.8	10.1

Attendance at the second theme park is assumed to grow at an average compound rate of 2% per annum over the first ten years, and 1% per annum for the next ten years until 2016. These assumptions are primarily based on Disney's experience of opening a second theme park at Walt Disney World, where EPCOT Center drew attendance of over 11 million guest visits in its first year of operation.

Per Capita Spending Theme parks derive their revenues principally from admission charges, sales of food and beverages consumed by visitors while at the park and from sales of merchandise available at the park's shopping facilities. Revenues from these sources are measured in terms of *per capita* expenditure, which is the average sum spent per daily guest visit.

The company has assumed *per capita* expenditure figures separately for the two theme parks under the four categories below:

	Magic Kingdom		Second theme park	
	Amount in 1988 FF[a]	Annual growth rate (%)	Amount in 1988 FF[a]	Annual growth rate (%)
Admissions	137.6	6.5	137.6	6.5
Food and beverage	56.7	5.0	53.2	5.0
Merchandise	74.9	5.0	46.5	5.0
Parking and other	5.2	5.0	5.2	5.0

[a]Excluding value-added tax.

The assumed real growth rate of admission prices of 1.5% per annum is less than the average 2.6% experienced at the Disney theme parks since 1972.

The *per capita* spending assumptions are based on experience in theme parks designed by Disney, adjusted for local conditions. A separate report on *per capita* spending was undertaken by ADL. To evaluate the reasonableness of the assumed admission prices, ADL reviewed the admission prices charged in Paris for major attractions which could be considered competitive in terms of entertainment value and also the prices charged by European theme and amusement parks. These reviews showed that the assumed admission prices for Euro Disneyland, although higher than those charged at other European theme and amusement parks, (i) could be considered low when related to prices charged in the Paris region for quality adult-oriented entertainment, and (ii) appeared in line with prices charged for other family-oriented attractions. Arthur D. Little concluded that the company's assumed admission prices were justified, having regard for the destination resort features of Euro Disneyland and the high quality of its entertainment.

To evaluate the reasonableness of the assumed prices for food and beverages at Euro Disneyland, ADL analyzed the prices paid by residents of, and tourists to, Paris in those areas that were particularly attractive to visitors. They also examined food and beverage prices at other European theme and amusement parks and reviewed typical food and beverage expenditure patterns in France as compared with the U.S. They concluded that Euro Disneyland's assumptions concerning food and beverage expenditure were reasonable.

Arthur D. Little determined, in the case of assumed merchandise sales, that there was no comparable experience in the Paris region of small, high-intensity retail shops, exposed to a high volume of visitor traffic, as are found at Disney-designed theme parks. They concluded that it was reasonable to forecast Euro Disneyland's retail sales revenue on the basis of that at other Disney theme parks.

Revenues Total revenues projected in the financial model for the two theme parks are summarized in the table below (in FF millions):

	1992	1996	2001	2011
Magic Kingdom				
Admissions and parking	1909	2981	4664	9314
Food, beverage and merchandise	1759	2692	4065	7401
Participant fees and other	229	303	417	421
Second theme park				
Admissions and parking	–	1788	2697	5794
Food, beverage and merchandise	–	1178	1660	3107
Participant fees and other	–	162	208	412

The first two categories of projected revenues are based on the attendance and *per capita* spending assumptions described above. Projected participant fees are based on the assumption that approximately ten participant contracts will have been signed by the opening of the Magic Kingdom. Four contracts have been signed, each with a term of at least ten years.

Operating expenses The principal operating expense assumptions are based on the following estimates. Labor costs (including related taxes) have been estimated on the basis of experience at Disney parks, adjusted to the conditions of the French labor market. They include a premium on operating labor rates of approximately 10% over the market average, intended to attract high-quality personnel. On this basis, it has been assumed that gross operating labor costs will be FF424 million for the Magic Kingdom and FF232 million for the second theme park (measured in 1988 French francs) in the respective opening years of these parks and that they will increase at the rate of inflation, taking into account increased employment associated with higher attendance levels. Cost of sales has been estimated on the basis of experience at Disney parks, adjusted to reflect factors specific to Euro Disneyland. The assumptions are:

Cost of sales (% of revenue)	
Magic Kingdom	
Merchandise	40–43[a]
Food and beverage	31
Second theme park	
Merchandise	41.5
Food and beverage	31

[a]Declining from 43% in 1992 to 40% in 1996 and thereafter.

Other operating expenses have similarly been based on Disney experience, adjusted to reflect local market conditions. Individually they are assumed to be as follows:

- Maintenance expenses:
  - Magic Kingdom: 6% of revenues;
  - Second theme park: 6.5% of revenues;

- General and administrative expenses (which include marketing, legal, finance and data processing):
  - Magic Kingdom: 14% of revenues;
  - Second theme park: 16% of revenues;
- Property and business taxes, which have been estimated according to the French tax regime:
  - the base management fee.

Operating Income Operating income is the difference between revenues and operating expenses but before royalties, financing costs and interest income, depreciation and amortization, lease expense, management incentive fees, and income taxes. The summary table below shows the operating income projected by the financial model for the two theme parks:

	1992	1996	2001	2011
Magic Kingdom (in FF millions)	1603	2773	4226	8006
Second theme park (in FF millions)	–	1334	1921	4293
Total	1603	4107	6147	12 299

Cost of Construction The cost of construction of the Magic Kingdom is assumed to be FF9.5 billion and the total cost of Phase 1A is assumed to be FF14.9 billion, in accordance with the estimated cost for Phase 1A. The construction cost of the second theme park has been assumed to be FF5.9 billion, with construction and related expenditures being incurred equally in 1994 and 1995. The construction cost of the second theme park has been estimated on the basis of Disney's direct experience of recent theme park construction, notably in completing the Disney-MGM Studios Theme Park within Walt Disney World. The construction cost of that theme park was then adjusted for capacity considerations, inflation, and the construction cost differential between Florida and the Paris region.

Table 18.6 summarizes Walt Disney Company's financial results during 1984–8.

TABLE 18.6 Summary of Walt Disney Company financial results, 1984–8 (U.S.$ millions)

	1984	1985	1986	1987	1988
Revenue					
Theme parks and resorts	1097.4	1257.5	1523.9	1834.2	2042.0
Filmed entertainment	244.5	320.0	511.7	875.6	1149.2
Consumer products	109.7	122.6	130.2	167.0	247.0
Operating income					
Theme parks and resorts	185.7	255.7	403.7	548.9	564.8
Filmed entertainment	2.2	33.7	51.6	130.6	186.3
Consumer products	53.9	56.3	72.4	97.3	133.7
Net income	97.8	173.5	247.3	444.7	522.0

Source: The Walt Disney Company, annual reports.

Appendix 2: Excerpt from Walt Disney 1994 Annual Report

Investment in Euro Disney

1994 vs. 1993 The Company's investment in Euro Disney resulted in a loss of $110.4 million in 1994. The loss consisted of a $52.8 million charge recognized in the third quarter as a result of the Company's participation in the Euro Disney financial restructuring and the Company's equity share of fourth quarter operating results. The prior year's loss reflected the Company's equity share of Euro Disney's operating results and a $350.0 million charge to fully reserve receivables and a funding commitment to Euro Disney, partially offset by royalties and gain amortization related to the investment. The funding commitment was intended to help support Euro Disney for a limited period, while Euro Disney pursued a financial restructuring.

A proposed restructuring plan for Euro Disney was announced in March 1994. During the third quarter of 1994, the Company entered into agreements with Euro Disney and the Euro Disney lenders participating in the restructuring (the "Lenders") to provide certain debt, equity and lease financing to Euro Disney.

Under the restructuring agreements, which specify amounts denominated in French francs, the Company committed to increase its equity investment in Euro Disney by subscribing for 49% of a $1.1 billion rights offering of new shares; to provide long-term lease financing at a 1% interest rate for approximately $255 million of theme park assets; and to subscribe, in part through an offset against fully reserved advances previously made to Euro Disney under the Company's funding commitment, for securities reimbursable in shares with a face value of approximately $180 million and a 1% coupon. In addition, the Company agreed to cancel fully reserved receivables from Euro Disney of approximately $210 million, to waive royalties and base management fees for a period of five years and to reduce such amounts for specified periods thereafter, and to modify the method by which management incentive fees will be calculated. During the fourth quarter of 1994, the financial restructuring was completed and the Company funded its commitments.

In addition to the commitments described above, the Company agreed to arrange for the provision of a ten-year unsecured standby credit facility of approximately $210 million on request, bearing interest at PIBOR. As of September 30, 1994, Euro Disney had not requested that the Company establish this facility.

As part of the restructuring, the Company received ten-year warrants for the purchase of up to 27.8 million shares of Euro Disney at a price of FF40 per share. The terms of the restructuring also provide that, in the event that Euro Disney decides to launch the second phase of the development of its theme park and resort complex, and commitments for the necessary financing have been obtained, the Company will be entitled to a development fee of approximately $225 million. On receipt of the development fee, the Company's entitlement to purchase Euro Disney shares by exercise of the warrants described above will be reduced to 15 million shares.

In connection with the restructuring, Euro Disney Associes SNC ("Disney SNC"), an indirect wholly owned affiliate of the Company, entered into a lease arrangement (the "Lease") with the entity (the "Park Financing Company"), which financed substantially all of the Disneyland Paris theme park assets, and then entered into a sublease agreement (the "Sublease") with Euro Disney. Under the

Lease, which replaced an existing lease between Euro Disney and the Park Financing Company, Disney SNC leased the theme park assets of the Park Financing Company for a noncancelable term of 12 years. Aggregate lease rentals of FF10.5 billion ($2.0 billion) receivable from Euro Disney under the Sublease, which has a 12-year term, will approximate the amounts payable by Disney SNC under the Lease.

At the conclusion of the Sublease term, Euro Disney will have the option to assume Disney SNC's rights and obligations under the Lease. If Euro Disney does not exercise its option, Disney SNC may continue to lease the assets, with an ongoing option to purchase them for an amount approximating the balance of the Park Financing Company's outstanding debt. Alternatively, Disney SNC may terminate the Lease, in which case Disney SNC would pay the Park Financing Company an amount equal to 75% of its then-outstanding debt, estimated to be $1.4 billion; Disney SNC could then sell or lease the assets on behalf of the Park Financing Company to satisfy the remaining debt, with any excess proceeds payable to Disney SNC.

As part of the overall restructuring, the Lenders agreed to underwrite 51% of the Euro Disney rights offering, to forgive certain interest charges for the period from April 1, 1994 to September 30, 2003, having a present value of approximately $300 million, and to defer all principal payments until three years later than originally scheduled. As consideration for their participation in the financial restructuring, Euro Disney issued to the Lenders ten-year warrants for the purchase of up to 40 million shares of Euro Disney stock at a price of FF40 per share.

Euro Disney has reported that it expects to incur a loss in 1995, which will have a negative impact on the Company's results. The impact on the Company's earnings, however, will be reduced as a result of the sale by the Company in October 1994 of approximately 75 million shares, or 20% of its investment in Euro Disney, to Prince Alwaleed Bin Talal Bin Abdulaziz Al Saud. The sale will reduce the Company's ownership interest in Euro Disney to approximately 39%. Beginning in 1995, the Company will record its equity share of Euro Disney's operating results based on its reduced ownership interest. The Company has agreed, so long as any obligations to the Lenders are outstanding, to maintain ownership of at least 34% of the outstanding common stock of Euro Disney until June 1999, at least 25% for the subsequent five years, and at least 16.67% for an additional term thereafter.

1993 vs. 1992 The Company's investment in Euro Disney resulted in a loss of $514.7 million in 1993, including the charge referred to below, after being partially offset by royalties and gain amortization related to the investment. The operating results of Euro Disney were lower than expected, due in part to the European recession, which affected Euro Disney's largest markets.

During 1993, Euro Disney, its principal lenders and the Company began exploring a financial restructuring for Euro Disney. The Company agreed to help fund Euro Disney for a limited period, to afford Euro Disney time to pursue the financial restructuring. The operating results for the fourth quarter and the year, and the need for a financial restructuring, created uncertainty regarding the Company's ability to collect its current receivables and to meet the funding commitment to Euro Disney. Consequently, the Company recorded a charge of $350.0 million in the fourth quarter to fully reserve its current receivables and funding commitment.

In 1992, the Company's investment in Euro Disney contributed income of $11.2 million. Although Euro Disney incurred a loss in 1992, the Company's 49% share of the net loss was offset by royalties and gain amortization related to the investment.

Source: Walt Disney Annual Report, 1994.

Notes

1 "Euro Disney," *Financial Times*, October 30, 1996.
2 "Disney Goes to Tokyo," in D. Ancona, T. Kochan, M. Scully, J. Van Maanen and E. Westney, *Organizational Behavior and Processes*, Southwestern College Publishing, Cincinnati, OH, 1999, pp. M-10, 25.
3 The conversion factors used in the case are: 1 hectare = 2.47 acres, and 1 acre = 4,047 square meters. The U.S. dollar/French franc exchange rates at the beginning of each year were: 1987 6.35, 1988 5.36, 1989 6.03, 1990 5.84, 1991 5.08, 1992 5.22, 1993 5.59, 1994 5.93.
4 "Euro Disney" is used to refer to the Euro Disneyland theme park: "Euro Disneyland SCA" or "the company" refers to the company that owns Euro Disney.
5 J. D. Finnerty, "Case Study: The Euro Disneyland Project" in *Project Financing: Asset-based Financial Engineering*, John Wiley & Sons, Inc., New York, 1995, pp. 338–50.
6 "No magic in these kingdoms," *Los Angeles Times*, December 15, 1989.
7 "Disneyland Goes to Europe," in D. Ancona, T. Kochan, M. Scully, J. Van Maanen and E. Westney, *Organizational Behavior and Processes*, Southwestern College Publishing, Cincinnati, OH, 1999, pp. 38–9.
8 "Disneyland Goes to Europe," in D. Ancona, T. Kochan, M. Scully, J. Van Maanen and E. Westney, *Organizational Behavior and Processes*, Southwestern College Publishing, Cincinnati, OH, 1999, p. 15.
9 From J. Neher, "France Amazed, Amused by Disney Dress Code," *New York Times*, October 5, 1995.
10 *Euro Disney: the First 100 Days* (Harvard Business School Case No. 9-693-013, 1993), p. 14.

Case 19   Vodafone: Rethinking the International Strategy

May 2009

On May 19, 2009, Vittorio Colao, Vodafone's CEO, presented the group's results for the year ended March 31, 2009. Despite Colao's emphasis on Vodafone's increases in revenue, adjusted operating profit and free cash flow (see Table 19.1), the results left analysts unimpressed. The reported gains were wholly the result of foreign exchange movements (the euro had appreciated significantly against the British pound during the year); underlying revenues had contracted by 0.4%. Once "impairment charges" (mainly asset write-downs in Spain) had been taken into account, net profit was down by more than a half. Vodafone's shares closed down almost 4% on the day. For Vodafone's long-suffering shareholders, the results raised further questions about how the world's leading wireless telecommunications operator would generate attractive profits from its extensive global empire.

Colao's appointment in July 2008 marked a new phase in the strategy embarked upon by his predecessor Arun Sarin. Under Sarin's leadership, Vodafone's strategic priority had shifted from growth to consolidation. Under Vittorio Colao, this emphasis shifted even more strongly from top-line growth and bold strategic initiatives to the more mundane tasks of cutting costs and improving efficiency. In November 2008, Colao outlined his strategy for Vodafone. The *Financial Times* reported:

> Vittorio Colao compared himself to a ship's captain as the Vodafone chief executive set a new course for the world's largest mobile phone operator by revenue.
>
> Mr Colao's strategy, unveiled yesterday at his first public presentation since becoming chief executive in July, involved bigger than expected changes to the direction taken by Arun Sarin, his predecessor, in 2006.
>
> But the scale of the changes points to the challenges confronting the Italian-born Mr Colao: a potent mix of economic, competitive and regulatory pressures.
>
> "It's a bit like sailing, you know," said Mr Colao, a former McKinsey partner, when asked how much his strategy had in common with Mr Sarin's legacy. "Every new captain takes the boat from where the boat was, and suddenly the wind changes and the sea changes, and you have three sailors who are sick."

TABLE 19.1 Vodafone Group plc: financial highlights 2005–9 (£ millions, except where indicated)

(Year ended 31 March)	2009	2008	2007	2006	2005
Consolidated income statement data					
Revenue	41017	35478	31104	29350	26678
Operating (loss)/profit	5857	10047	(1564)	(14084)	7878
Adjusted operating profit [a]	11757	10075	9531	9399	8353
(Loss)/profit before taxation	4189	9001	(2383)	(14853)	7285
Net (loss)/profit for the financial year	3080	6756	(5297)	(21821)	6518
Consolidated cash flow data					
Net cash flows from operating activities	12213	10474	10328	10190	9240
Net cash flows from investing activities	(6834)	(8544)	3865	(6654)	(4122)
Free cash flow [b]	4987	5540	6127	6418	6592
Consolidated balance sheet data					
Total assets	152699	127270	109617	126738	147197
Shareholders' equity	86162	78043	67067	85425	113800
Total liabilities	67922	50799	42324	41426	33549
Profit ratios					
Operating profit/total assets (%)	3.8	8.0	(1.4)	(11.1)	5.4
Return on equity [c] (%)	3.6	8.7	(7.8)	(23.6)	5.9

[a] Excludes non-operating income of associates, impairment losses and other income and expense.

[b] Free cash flow measures cash available for reinvestment, shareholder returns or debt reduction. It is calculated by subtracting expenditures on fixed assets from operating cash flow.

[c] After tax (loss)/profit as a percentage of shareholders' equity.

The most tangible element of his strategy is to focus on improving Vodafone's bottom line performance. He wants to reduce costs by £1bn by 2010–11 and does not rule out going further if the global recession is deep. The promised savings are centered on Vodafone's core European businesses, which are mature operations given that most people own a mobile phone.

But there will be a revenue-boosting element to the strategy, too. This will be led by a push to persuade more consumers to buy mobiles that are capable of connecting to the internet. Mr Colao also wants to intensify Vodafone's efforts to sell telecoms services to companies.

An even sharper focus on making the most of Vodafone's existing businesses in emerging markets is also central to Mr Colao's thinking. Vodafone believes its expansion into developing countries, which began in 2005 and last year involved the $10.9bn (£7.1bn) purchase of a controlling stake in Indian mobile operator Hutchison Essar, may well be close to accomplished.

Mr Colao is reserving the right to do further deals in developing countries, but says there are few large markets that interest him. Across the board, he will take a relatively conservative approach to future deals, in line with a pledge to be more disciplined on capital management.

Vodafone supports consolidation in its existing markets, notably Europe, because of concerns that too many mobile operators are slugging it out. Mr Colao said Vodafone might buy rival operators, although he stressed any significant acquisition would likely be funded through disposals. He declined to specify the nature of any disposals, but signaled there would be no exit from Vodafone's core European businesses in Germany, Italy, Spain and the U.K. Mr Colao also signaled that, like his predecessor, he wants to retain Vodafone's 45% stake in Verizon Wireless, the second-largest U.S. mobile operator.

The capital discipline that Mr Colao talked about yesterday also involves a greater focus on free cash flow—loosely defined as operating cash flow minus capital spending. Vodafone is targeting £5bn–£6bn of annual free cash flow and its future performance guidance is likely to focus on this measure.[1]

In his May 19, 2009 presentation, Colao acknowledged the weakness of user demand—primarily a result of the recession—and continuing pressure on margins as a result of intensifying competition. He announced an acceleration in Vodafone's cost-cutting program.

Most commentators applauded Vodafone's commitment to cost cutting—"After years of acquisition-fuelled growth, a focus on the more mundane matter of efficiency is just what the world's biggest mobile operator needs"[2]—but there was also a concern that cost cutting might not be enough to restore Vodafone's fortunes given growing maturity and commoditization of Vodafone's principal markets. The most distinctive feature of Vodafone's competitive positioning within wireless communication services was its international spread—with 302 million mobile customers and a presence in 52 countries of the world, Vodafone offered a global presence that was unmatched in the industry (see Tables 19.2 and 19.3). A critical issue for Colao was how far Vodafone could better exploit its global presence through closer cross-border integration of its functions and operations and whether Vodafone should regard itself as a portfolio of largely independent national operators sharing a common brand and a common approach to business.

TABLE 19.2 Vodafone's global reach, March 2009

Country	(%)	Ownership customers[a] (000s)	Country	(%)	Ownership customers[a] (000s)
Subsidiaries			Turkey	100.0	15481
Germany	100.0	35471	Egypt	54.9	10405
Italy	76.9	22914	Kenya	40.0	5345
Spain	100.0	16910	South Africa	50.0	30149
U.K.	100.0	18716	Australia	100.0	3970
Albania	99.9	1395	Fiji	49.0	339
Greece	99.9	5899	New Zealand	100.0	2502
Ireland	100.0	2175	**Associates and investments**		
Malta	100.0	201			
Netherlands	100.0	4618	U.S.	45.0	38948[b]
Portugal	100.0	5639	China	3.2	15324
Czech Republic	100.0	2909	France	44.0	8620
Hungary	100.0	2562	India	51.6	46065
Poland	24.4	3555			
Romania	100.0	9588			

Partner agreements[c]

Country	Operator	Country	Operator
Afghanistan	Roshan	Latvia	Bité
Armenia	MTS	Lithuania	Bité
Austria	A1	Luxembourg	Tango
Bahrain	Zain	Macedonia	VIP operator
Belgium	Proximus	Malaysia	Celcom
Bulgaria	Mobiltel	Nor way	TDC
Caribbean	Digicel	Panama	Digicel
Chile	Entel	Russia	MTS
Croatia	VIPnet	Serbia	VIP mobile
Cyprus	Cytamobile-Vodafone	Singapore	M1
Denmark	TDC	Slovenia	Si.mobile-Vodafone
Estonia	Elisa	Sri Lanka	Dialog
Faroe Islands	Vodafone Iceland	Sweden	TDC
Finland	Elisa	Switzerland	Swisscom
Guernsey	Airtel-Vodafone	Thailand	DTAC
Honduras	Digicel	Turkmenistan	MTS
Hong Kong	SmarTone-Vodafone	Ukraine	MTS
Iceland	Vodafone Iceland	United Arab Emirates	Du
Japan	SoftBank	Uzbekistan	MTS
Jersey	Airtel-Vodafone		

[a] Total number of customers of the country subsidiary or associate.
[b] *These amounts are not included in related group totals as Verizon Wireless is an associated undertaking.*
[c] Partnerships in Latin America are through America Móvil.

Source: Vodafone Group plc, Annual Report 2009.

TABLE 19.3 Vodafone's customer base by country, 2005–8 (customers at year end)

	2008 000s	2007 000s	2006 000s	2005 000s	Prepaid customers (%)
Germany	35 471	33 920	30 622	29 165	54.4
Italy	22 914	22 791	20 129	18 208	92.1
Spain	16 910	15 810	14 464	12 923	45.9
U.K.	18 716	18 447	16 939	16 325	60.6
Albania	1395	1127	920	749	96.9
Greece	5889	5438	4961	4438	68.5
Ireland	2175	2265	2178	2047	74.0
Malta	201	201	188	177	89.9
Netherlands	4618	4038	3817	3981	46.9
Portugal	5639	5111	4618	4119	79.5
Sweden	–	–	–	1573	
Czech Republic	2909	2658	2413	2142	n.a.
Romania	9588	8808	7717	6132	n.a.
Hungary	2562	2304	2134	2038	n.a.
Turkey	15 481	16 116	12 748	–	n.a.
Poland	3555	2638	2355	1774	n.a.
Egypt	10 405	13 333	8704	6125	92.7
Kenya	5345	3698	2134	1395	98.3
South Africa	16 521	16 521	14 103	7524	89.3
India	46 065	39 865	3197	1633	87.2
Australia	3970	3573	3278	3126	73.5
New Zealand	2502	2309	2200	2024	76.4
Fiji	339	186	135	95	95.2
	6811	6068	5613	5245	75.7
Group	**327 181**	**221 157**	**159 954**	**127 713**	**74.9**
Associates					
United States	38 948	29 568	26 230	22 785	5.4
Other	25 194	22 784	17 714	17 780	76.4
Proportionate customers	**391 323**	**252 301**	**198 584**	**164 549**	**68.9**

Building the World's Leading Wireless Communications Provider, 1984–2003

Vodafone was originally Racal Telecom Limited, formed in 1984 as a subsidiary of Racal Electronics Plc—a British-based defense and electronics company. It was established to exploit the opportunities made available by the new cellular technology for wireless communication. In 1983, Racal and Cellnet (a subsidiary of British Telecom) won licenses to supply cellular wireless communication in Britain. In 1988, 20% of Vodafone's equity was sold to the public. In 1991, the Vodafone Group was fully demerged from Racal.

Under CEO Gerald Whent, Vodafone steadily expanded its international reach primarily through minority equity stakes in other wireless telecom companies and by establishing joint ventures to bid for licenses and develop new wireless businesses. The appointment of Chris Gent as CEO in 1997 marked a new era in Vodafone's development. With the goal of becoming the world's leading mobile communications companies and fueled by an escalating share price, Vodafone embarked upon a rapid succession of acquisitions. The acquisitions of Airtouch in the U.S., Mannesmann in Germany and Japan Telecom were three huge takeovers that established Vodafone as the world's largest wireless telecom company in terms of number of customers. Table 19.4 lists milestones in Vodafone's expansion.

TABLE 19.4 Vodafone's international acquisitions and divestments, 1989–2009

Year	Company	Country	Subscribers	Notes
1989	Telecel	Malta	n.a.	Joint venture with TeleMalta. Vodafone owns 80%
1990	SFR	France	60 000	4% of equity acquired by Vodafone
1991	AB Nordic Tel	Sweden, Denmark	n.a.	10% of equity acquired by Vodafone
1991	Pacific Link Communication Ltd	Hong Kong	42 000	30% of equity acquired by Vodafone
1993	Vodacom	S. Africa	n.a.	Joint venture established, Vodafone owns 35%
1993	Panafon	Greece	n.a.	Joint venture established, Vodafone owns 45%
1996	Talkland	U.K.	400 000	Vodafone acquired outstanding two-thirds equity of the service provider for £30.6m.
1996	Peoples Phone	U.K.	n.a.	Retailer /reseller with 181 stores acquired for £77 million
1996	Astec Communications	U.K.	n.a.	Service provider with 21 stores acquired for £77 million
1998	Misrfone	Egypt	n.a.	Misrfone consortium (Vodafone owns 30%) wins license to build Egypt's second mobile network
1998	Bell South New Zealand	New Zealand	138 000	Acquired and renamed Vodafone New Zealand
1999	Airtouch Communications, Inc.	U.S.	3.2 million	$62 billion merger to create Vodafone Airtouch. Included 1m. subscribers in Germany, Italy (Omnitel), Poland, Japan, and India
2000	Verizon Wireless	U.S.	n.a.	Joint venture formed from U.S. wireless assets of Vodafone and Bell Atlantic
2000	Mannesmann	Germany	9.5 million	Acquired for £112 billion

TABLE 19.4 (*Continued*)

Year	Company	Country	Subscribers	Notes
2001	Eircell	Ireland	1.2 million	Acquired for €5 million, rebranded Vodafone Ireland
2001	TDC Mobil	Denmark	n.a.	First "Partner Networks" agreement. Vodafone offers co-branded services to Danish market
2001	China Mobile (Hong Kong)	Hong Kong	n.a.	Strategic alliance agreed
2001	Swisscom Mobile	Switzerland	n.a.	25% of equity acquired
2001	Airtel Movil SA	Spain	n.a.	Equity interest increased to 91.6%
2001	Japan Telecom and J-Phone	Japan	11 million	Acquired 69.7% of J-Phone, Japan's third-largest mobile operator and 66.7% of Japan Telecom, its parent
2002	Radiolinja	Finland and Estonia	n.a.	Partner Network Agreements signed
2002	Vizzavi	France/U.K.	n.a.	Vodafone buys out Vivendi's 50% share of the Vizzavi mobile internet portal for €142.7 million
2003	Mobilcom, Bité,	Austria, Lithuania	n.a.	Partner Network Agreements signed
2004	Cyta	Cyprus	n.a.	Partner Network Agreements signed
2004	AT&T Wireless	U.S.	n.a.	$38 billion offer fails; Cingular bids higher
2005	Connex	Romania	n.a.	Equity stake raised to 99%; also buys Czech mobile operator
2005	Oskar	Czech Republic	n.a.	Acquired
2006	Vodafone Sweden	Sweden	n.a.	Sold for €970 million (£660 million)
2006	Vodafone Japan	Japan	n.a.	97.7% stake sold to Softbank £6.9 billion
2006	Belgacom Mobile SA; Swisscom Mobile AG	Belgium & Switzerland	n.a	25% interests in the two companies sold for total of £3.1 billion
2007	Hutchison Essar	India	22.9 million	Acquired 52% of India's 4th biggest wireless operator for $10.9 bn
2007	Bharti Airtel	India	n.a.	Sold Group's 5.60% direct shareholding in Bharti Airtel for $1.6 bn

(*Continued*)

TABLE 19.4 (*Continued*)

Year	Company	Country	Subscribers	Notes
2007	Tele2	Italy and Spain	n.a.	Acquisition of 100% of Tele2 Italia SpA and Tele2 Telecommunications Services SLU for €775 million
2007	The Qatar Foundation	Qatar	n.a	A consortium comprising Vodafone and The Qatar Foundation was named as the successful applicant in the auction to become the second mobile operator in Qatar
2008	Arcor	Arcor	n.a.	Increased its stake in Arcor for €460 million and now owns 100% of Arcor
2008	Ghana Telecommunications	Ghana	n.a.	Acquired 70% of Ghana Telecommunications for £486 million
2008	BroadNet	Czech	n.a.	100% sale of BroadNet Czech a.s. shares to Vodafone Czech Republic
2008	Crazy John's	Australia	n.a.	Control of Crazy John's 83% stake
2009	Verizon Wireless/Alltel	U.S.	n.a.	Verizon Wireless acquires Alltel Corp. for $5.9 billion
2009	Hutchison Telecommunications (Australia)	Australia	n.a.	Joint venture formed between Hutchison Telecommunications (Australia) and Vodafone Australia
2009	Vodacom	South Africa	n.a.	Additional 15% of equity acquired for £1.6 billion
2009	Central Telecom	U.K.	n.a.	Acquired of U.K.-based systems integrator

n.a. = not available or not applicable.

Source: Vodafone annual reports.

International strategy

Under Chris Gent, Vodafone's international expansion had been opportunistic and aggressive but not lacking in strategic rationale. Group strategy director, Alan Harper, explained:

> We have always been mobile focused. In 1995, when I joined Vodafone it was mobile focused . . . It had a turnover of £8 billion, 80% in the U.K. Today we are still mobile focused with a turnover of £100 billion—only 10% in the U.K. . . .

Our vision has been to leverage scale and scope benefits, reduce response time and ensure effective delivery to customers. This we have achieved by collecting or acquiring national operating companies and giving them a mission of a challenger company . . . For example, Vodafone with SFR is a challenger to France Telecom in France, Vodafone U.K. is a challenger to British Telecom in the U.K., Vodafone Germany is a challenger to Deutsch Telecom in Germany. With this challenger mindset we nurture and instill an entrepreneurial spirit among Vodafone companies and in this respect we do not behave as a traditional telephone company . . . [T]he cultural alignment of people within Vodafone is a key issue in sustaining this challenger and entrepreneurial mindset. To focus on this cultural alignment we give autonomy to the local entity and reiterate that the local entity did not join a global company like IBM or HP. The local entity has to work within a matrix structure and keep alive the "challenger mindset" on fixed line telephony and other incumbents, challenge the status quo every day, and evolve by being local entrepreneurs.[3]

This notion of local autonomy meant that Vodafone did not deploy any standard template in integrating its international acquisitions. It preferred to migrate its subsidiaries to the Vodafone brand; in some cases this was almost immediate, in others (where the existing local brand was strong as in Italy and Germany) it took many years. In some cases Vodafone saw virtue in transferring its operating and marketing practices and its pricing structure—but only where there was adequate compatibility. Apart from promoting Vodafone as a global brand and encouraging challenge and entrepreneurship among its operating companies, Vodafone also encouraged a common competitive strategy across the group. In selecting acquisition targets and in developing its acquisitions, Vodafone sought to be first or second in market share in every country it operated—this was critical to spreading the fixed costs of infrastructure, technology, and marketing. In competing for market share Vodafone eschewed price competition in favor of differentiating itself through a premium offering through value-adding content, network quality and customer care.

Twenty-first Century Challenges

The new century saw the beginning of more difficult times for Vodafone. The company was hit heavily by two developments. First was governments' auctioning of licenses for third generation wireless communication. Between 2000 and 2001, Vodafone paid over $30 billion for the new licenses (including $9.5 billion for a single 3G license in the U.K.). It soon became apparent that, like many of its competitors, Vodafone had greatly overestimated the commercial potential of 3G wireless communication and had grossly overpaid for its licenses. The second factor was the bursting of the "TMT" (technology, media, telecommunications) stock-market boom. In the first quarter of 2001, Vodafone's share price hit an all-time peak. During the next 30 months it would decline by 72%.

The outcome was a massive hit to Vodafone's bottom line. During the four-year period 2001 to 2004, Vodafone's net losses totaled £45 billion—primarily the result of write-offs of goodwill on over-priced acquisitions and amortization of 3G license costs. The impact of these various "impairments" is evident from the difference between operating profit and adjusted operating profit in Table 19.1.

When Arun Sarin replaced Chris Gent as CEO in 2003, Vodafone's management changed in both substance and style. "All that Gent and Sarin have in common," noted one insider, "is a love of cricket." While Gent was a quintessential Englishman, Sarin was a citizen of the world; he was born in India but his career had primarily centered on the U.S. While Gent was a deal maker, Sarin was an operations man with a strong technological background.

The "One Vodafone" Project

During 2004 it became increasingly clear that the greatest challenge facing Vodafone was deriving additional value from its sprawling global empire. Towards the end of 2004, Arun Sarin launched an ambitious program to unify its disparate global network and derive value from its unrivalled global reach. The drivers of this quest for a new international strategy were threefold. First, Vodafone became pressured by investors—especially institutions—for improved bottom-line performance and shareholder returns. Second, the "bigger is better" mantra that accompanied the telecoms M&A binge was increasingly questioned by those who argued that international spread gave few benefits, most of the economies of size in telecoms related to market share within a single country. Finally, the potential offered by 3G offered opportunities for a global rollout of new services—mobile internet access in particular. *The Economist* describes some key features of the initiative:

> Sir Chris [Gent] collected the pieces: Mr. Sarin's mission was to fit them together to achieve economies of scale and so to justify Vodafone's bigger-is-better strategy. For the past 15 months, Mr. Sarin has been doing just that, though mostly behind the scenes. Only now is the curtain finally being raised, with the launch this month of "third-generation" (3G) mobile services in 12 European countries and a relaunch in Japan. The roll-out of 3G, Mr. Sarin agrees, will provide litmus tests of both his own leadership and Vodafone's ability to function as a unified entity.
>
> Redrawing organisation charts, rationalising back-room systems and cutting costs are hardly the sorts of activities that generate headlines, so Vodafone seems a less dynamic firm than it was under Sir Chris. But this dull-but-necessary work is what Mr. Sarin is good at, and what Vodafone needs to bring its sprawling divisions together. His "One Vodafone" project has sorted out the behind-the-scenes spaghetti at Vodafone's national affiliates, so that they are now all using the same technology. This cuts costs by making it possible to develop a new service once, and then introduce it in many markets simultaneously.
>
> Mr. Sarin has also restructured Vodafone's management. The bosses of its large regional operations now report directly to him. The head of marketing at each national operator now reports to the group head of marketing, rather than simply to his local boss, and so on. The aim is to bind the national operators together and give Mr. Sarin more direct control of his firm. Aligning structure with strategy in this way will, he hopes, enable the firm to "execute flawlessly."

This is not rocket science. Simplifying Vodafone's structure, he believes, is the foundation for making 3G a success, for it enables Vodafone to reap the benefits of its global scale. A single technology platform allows it to test handsets or services in one market and then deploy them everywhere. It ensures seamless international roaming, even for video calling. And it has allowed Vodafone to use its Japanese operation as a test-bed for 3G.

By far the greatest benefit of Vodafone's scale is its resulting clout with handset-makers. It has set strict standards for its 3G handsets, and even the biggest handset-makers have no choice but to comply with them if they want Vodafone's business. Using the same technology in both Japan and Europe means that Vodafone can offer Japanese handset-makers access to European markets and Western firms access to the Japanese market, while playing them off against each other.[4]

The One Vodafone strategy involved reorganizing the corporate structure to facilitate closer linkages between the corporate center and the operating companies and enhanced integration. The new structure introduced at the beginning of 2005 included:

- Six geographically defined businesses that would report directly to the CEO. These included: the U.K., Germany, Italy, Asia-Pacific, other EMEA subsidiaries,[5] and European and non-European affiliates (including the U.S., South Africa, China, France and several other countries).

- Strengthened global functions, each of which would report directly to the CEO. Marketing would include a new multinational corporate unit serving global corporate customers. Marketing would also take care of global handset procurement. Technology would be responsible for standardized network design and IT shared services. Business Development was a new function "responsible for driving Vodafone's product and services portfolio into affiliates and Partner Networks."

- The establishment of two management committees to oversee the execution of the strategy set by the main board. The Executive Committee would focus on strategy, financial structure and organizational development; the Integration and Operations Committee would be responsible for operational and budgetary planning, and product and service development. Both committees were chaired by Arun Sarin.

Alan Harper, head of strategy, explained:

. . . With acquisitions all over the world, one of our challenges is to integrate seamlessly not only technology (which, by the way, is more or less similar across the world) but also people . . . The challenge of this restructuring program is to balance the need for coordination and synergies with local initiatives . . . We are trying to integrate national operating units . . . and trying to leverage scale and scope while trying to retain the local autonomy and responsiveness of our challenger national units.[6]

The One Vodafone program involved business integration across a wide range of activities including billing (in 2005 Vodafone operated with eight different billing systems), network design, procurement, IT (including billing, back office, ERP/HR, and data center processes), service-center platforms, roaming, customer services and retail operations. According to Harper:

> What One Vodafone tries to achieve is to simplify the integration issues in terms of brand strength and integrating local culture and processes. We centralize all our marketing efforts, branding and product development. Technology is standardized. Network design is coordinated. Best practices are benchmarked by Advance Services. Knowledge is shared . . . We keep and encourage local initiatives such as customer services, and sales . . .[7]

Adjusting the International Strategy

The limits of the One Vodafone program were immediately apparent in three very important markets. Japan and the U.S. used cellular wireless technologies that differed from the GSM European standard used by Vodafone across most of its markets. Verizon Wireless used CDMA wireless technology. Its incompatibility with GSM meant that meant that Vodafone was unable to exploit any significant economies between its U.S. presence and the rest of its international operations. Vodafone's minority equity position in Verizon wireless and the absence of the Vodafone brand further isolated Vodafone's U.S. investment from the rest of Vodafone.

These technological distinctions were reinforced by other distinctive features of these markets. Japan (together with Korea) was regarded as the world's most advanced wireless market, adopting new wireless technologies at least two years earlier than Europe. Vodafone's introduction of its global range of handsets in Japan led to an exodus of Japanese subscribers: the phones were seen as technologically backward. The U.S., on the other hand, lagged both Europe and the Far East in the adoption of new wireless technologies—mainly because of its multiple incompatible wireless standards.

France, too, represented a problem in terms of integrating into Vodafone's global network. As with Verizon Wireless, Vodafone possessed a minority share of SFR (44%) and had not moved SFR to the Vodafone brand. Moreover, SFR supplied mobile, fixed line, and internet communication services, while Vodafone had avoided involvement in fixed line.

During the next 12 months, further changes in Vodafone's international strategy ensued. Strong competitive and regulatory pressures in the mature markets of North America, Western Europe, and Japan encouraged Vodafone to shift its focus to the growing markets of Eastern Europe, Africa, and Asia. Vodafone sold its majority holding in Vodafone Japan in March 2006. This was followed by divestments in Sweden, the Netherlands, Belgium, and Switzerland, and by acquisitions in Egypt, Hungary, Romania, South Africa, and India.

Vodafone also expanded its non-equity modes of internationalization. Initially, Vodafone's partnering arrangements with overseas mobile operators related only to roaming services. However, under Sarin, Vodafone's partner network moved to closer arrangements for supplying Vodafone services and content to partners' own customers. In 2006, Iceland became the first franchise partner to adopt the Vodafone brand.

Vodafone's International Strategy 2008–9

During his first 10 months as Vodafone CEO, Vittorio Colao made several changes to the international aspects of Vodafone's strategy initiated by Sarin. In particular:

- Colao slowed Vodafone's expansion into emerging markets. Under his leadership, the only significant emerging market acquisitions were of Ghana Telecom and an increase in Vodafone's ownership of Vodafone South Africa.

- Increasing Vodafone's presence in the corporate market through expanding Vodafone Global Enterprise, which manages relationships with Vodafone's 270 largest multinational corporate customers: "VGE simplifies the provision of fixed, mobile and broadband services for MNCs who need a single operational and commercial relationship with Vodafone worldwide. It provides a range of managed services such as central ordering, customer self-serve web portals, telecommunications expense management tools and device management coupled with a single contract and guaranteed service level agreements."[8]

- Colao sought to build Vodafone's influence in technology development in the industry—particularly in mobile internet applications. However, for the most part, Vodafone operated with a high degree of national autonomy. This is evident from Vodafone's organizational chart. Thus, each national operating subsidiary is headed by a CEO with profit-and-loss responsibility to headquarters.

Scale Economies in Telecom Services

In evaluating the benefits of international presence and the potential for cross-border linkages, a key issue for Vodafone was the sources and extent of global-level scale economies. There was little doubt that scale economies were very important at the national level: infrastructure, marketing, sales and billing all involved substantial fixed costs, which needed to be spread over a large base of users. However, at the global level these economies were less evident. Table 19.5 offers no clear evidence that profitability is associated with either size or international spread.

The most obvious cost benefit from global scale was in centralized purchasing. In addition to its own equipment and software needs, Vodafone was one of the world's biggest purchasers of handsets (in many countries consumers bought their handset bundled with a service contract). Vodafone's handset requirements gave it massive clout when striking deals with handset makers.

However, these scale advantages from purchasing depended upon all of Vodafone's subsidiaries using the same technology—in second-generation wireless (2G) this was largely true: Vodafone had adopted the European GSM standard. The major exception was the U.S. where its associate company, Verizon Wireless, used CDMA—an incompatible wireless technology.

A global brand also provided economies in advertising and brand development due to spillovers in advertising across national borders and the potential to use media and promotional events that attracted global audiences. Other economies were available from centralizing certain functions. Technology development, Web support, financial reporting and legal services were all centralized.

FIGURE 19.1 Vodafone: organization chart, March 2009

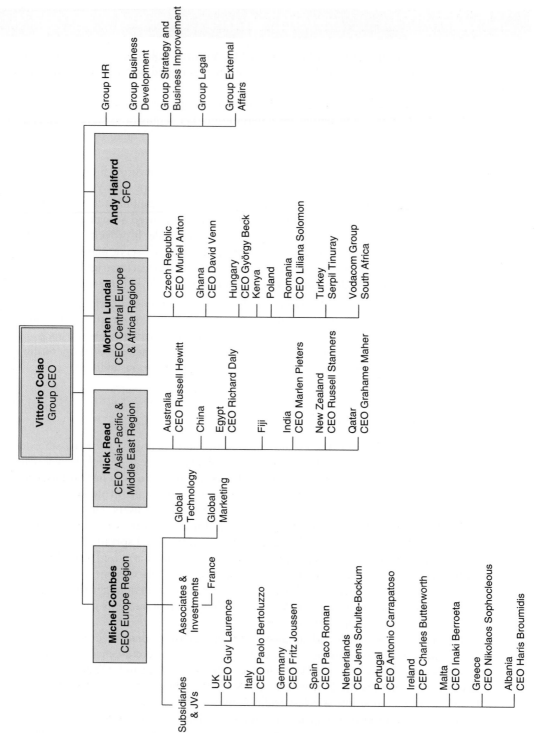

TABLE 19.5 World's largest telecommunication service companies, 2008

		Revenue ($ million)	Net profits ($ million)	Net margin (%)
1	AT&T	124 028	12 867	10.4
2	Nippon Telegraph and Telephone	103 684	5362	5.2
3	Verizon Communications	97 354	6428	4.4
4	Deutsche Telekom	90 260	2171	2.4
5	Telefónica	84 815	11 112	13.1
6	France Télécom	78 290	5956	7.6
7	Vodafone	69 138	5188	7.5
8	China Mobile Communications	65 015	11 442	17.5
9	Telecom Italia	45 118	3241	7.2
10	Vivendi	37 166	3810	10.2
11	BT	36 626	−140	(0.4)
12	Sprint Nextel	35 635	−2796	(7.9)
13	KDDI	34 814	2217	6.4
14	Comcast	34 256	2547	7.4
15	China Telecommunications	31 814	−51	(0.0)
16	América Móvil	31 012	5337	17.2
17	Softbank	26 608	430	1.6
18	Telstra	22 371	3304	14.8
19	China United Telecommunications	21 981	2840	12.9
20	Royal KPN	21 373	1950	9.1

Source: Fortune Global 500 (2009).

Economies were also available from standardizing administrative and operational practices. A key aspect of the "One Vodafone" project was that it sought opportunities for such standardization. Booz Allen describes its role in this process:

This program was not just an integration of two functions or two countries, or a merger of two companies, but really an integration program that spanned the 16 countries which had diverse people and diverse markets," says Klaus Hölbling, a principal in Booz Allen's Vienna office. "We couldn't assume we would integrate one operation the way we'd done another because the markets were very different. A customized approach was needed."

Wave 0 of the engagement focused on the business case for integration. Wave 1 established common planning and design standards, elevated management of the supply chain to a global level, and created the architecture for a common service platform. In Wave 2, the work encompassed new operating models, assessing how global and local business would be conducted, and development of a new organization structure and implementation plan . . .

Vodafone is still learning to find the right balance of local versus global—however, the transformation has already resulted in significant cost savings as well as innovative market strategies, more competitive and differentiated pricing, and leading product and service offerings. The new organization facilitates rapid movement of resources and talent, and sharing of best practices and expertise.[9]

It was also questionable whether exploiting the economies from a global brand or standardized global systems necessitated ownership of overseas telecom companies. Vodafone's partner network allowed Vodafone to earn licensing income from providing its brand and particular services to local operators without any need to invest in those countries.

Beyond these cost economies associated with global presence there were also user benefits resulting from international presence. This was certainly the case in serving corporate global accounts. In the case of individual users, international roaming could be offered through access agreements with local service providers. The key roaming benefits of having subsidiaries in different countries was the ability to offer "seamless" roaming services—identical services in each country. It also allowed the flexibility to offer promotional deals. For example, in summer 2009 Vodafone's Passport program offered: "No Roaming Charge in Over 35 Countries This Summer!"

Adapting to Local Market Needs

A key issue for Vodafone was not simply the existence and extent of these potential benefits from global scale but whether the pursuit of these benefits compromised Vodafone's ability to adapt to the local market requirements. Observing the failed international strategies of Swissair and DoCoMo, the Japanese mobile operator, the *Asian Wall Street Journal* drew three lessons for global strategy (see Exhibit 19.1).

EXHIBIT 19.1

Three Lessons for Global Strategy from Swissair and DoCoMo

[T]he first lesson is to start with the microeconomics: Understand what drives superior economic performance in your business and don't take your domestic success for granted. Both the airline and the telecoms businesses are highly regulated, technology driven and capital-intensive industries with high fixed and very low marginal costs (per airline seat or per mobile call minute) . . . In the mobile industry, the significant fixed-cost components of the business (networks, product development, and brand advertising and promotion) provide unit cost advantages to the national market leader compared with its followers . . .

Despite regulatory changes, the economics of the mobile industry remain primarily national in nature. That is, it is clearly better to be a market leader in one country than a follower in two countries. There are obvious trends suggesting that broader geographic scope adds value in mobile. Increased subscriber roaming and higher mobile penetration rates are shifting an increasing portion of cross-border traffic from fixed to mobile networks.

Both trends favor a mobile operator with domestic leadership positions in a number of major city markets within a continental regional market such as Europe or North America. Value has been created by such "regional" consolidators. Vodafone accomplished this in Europe, now owning the No. 1 or No. 2 mobile operator in most major national markets . . .

When both NTT DoCoMo and Swissair convinced themselves they needed to expand beyond domestic boundaries to survive, the race to fulfill their global aspirations seems to have resulted in a set of investments more focused on the number of flags on a boardroom map rather than on these basic economics driving superior profitability in their industries. The risks of these two aggressive expansion strategies were further compounded by not having control over most of their international investments.

That means the third lesson from the two companies' problems is to move to management control if you are serious about capturing acquisition synergies . . . Similarly, in short order DoCoMo accumulated direct or indirect stakes in nine mobile operators—most for cash, at the peak of the telecom bubble. But this acquisition spree resulted in equity stakes in only two market

leaders and these were in relatively minor geographic markets—KPN Mobile domestically in the Netherlands and Hutchison in Hong Kong. All the others were lesser players. DoCoMo acquired stakes in the No. 3 U.S. player AT&T Wireless, Taiwan's No. 4 player KG Telecom, U.K. No. 5 player Hutchison U.K., and distant followers KPN Orange in Belgium and E-Plus in Germany. Worse still, all these investments were minority stakes and so would appear to give DoCoMo limited ability to exert control over critical strategic and operational issues at these operators . . .

In contrast, Singapore Telecom appears to be pursuing a more focused strategy. Withdrawing from an early set of unfocused European investments, SingTel has focused more recently on mobile operators in South Asia. It now has stakes in the No. 1 or the strong No. 2 mobile operator in Singapore, Thailand, Indonesia, the Philippines and Australia.

Source: "When Global Strategies go Wrong," *The Asian Wall Street Journal* (April 4, 2002). Reproduced with permission.

Vodafone's experience in Japan underlined some of the risks inherent in a global approach to wireless telephony. Vodafone took control of J-Phone, Japan's third-largest operator, in 2001. Migrating J-Phone to the Vodafone brand, to Vodafone's European 3G technology (UMITS), and to Vodafone's global range of handsets proved disastrous. After losses in market share, Vodafone sold its Japanese subsidiary to Softbank in 2006. According to *The Economist*, the sale of Vodafone Japan signaled a definitive end to Vodafone's famous "big is beautiful" strategy, pointing the way towards a more focused regional strategy. For example, in Europe, Vodafone concentrated upon exploiting its scale advantage within an increasingly unified market.[10]

Compared to its nationally focused competitors, Vodafone was also looking disadvantaged by its mobile-only business focus. A key trend was towards the integration of fixed and mobile networks offering bundled services to customers. A number of operators offered "quadruple play" bundles comprising fixed and mobile telephony, broadband internet access and television services. Vodafone was slow in responding to the trend towards bundling: "Vodafone management has no strategy for convergence," observed one analyst in 2006.[11]

A key theme of Colao's November 2008 strategy review was a push into "total communications services":

> [T]he three target areas are mobile data, enterprise and broadband. Vodafone has already made significant progress on mobile data, with annual revenue of £3 billion, 26% higher on an organic basis than that of a year ago, but the opportunity remains significant as the proportion of the customer base that regularly uses data services is only around 10% in Europe. In the enterprise segment, Vodafone has a strong position in core mobile services, mainly amongst larger corporations. The aim is to build upon this position and expand into the broader communications market, serving small and medium sized businesses with converged fixed and mobile products and services and to continue to increase the Group's penetration of multinational accounts. In fixed broadband, the Group has a presence in all of its European markets and 4.6 million customers globally.[12]

Total communications involved Vodafone in leasing fixed line capacity from other telecom providers. In Britain, Vodafone is acting as a wireless partner to BT, Britain's fixed-line incumbent, which lacks a mobile network. Vodafone has also acquired some of its own fixed line capacity; in 2008 it acquired Tele2's fixed-line and broadband services in Italy and Spain.

Developments in Technology

Adding further complexity to the assessment of benefits and cost of internationalization were the technological changes affecting the industry. Vodafone, along with a number of other new wireless telephony startups such as Orange, Nextel and Wind, were created to exploit the new technology of cellular wireless communication. A quarter of a century later that technology was changing rapidly. Although several potential substitutes for cellular wireless communication had lacked commercial success (for example, paging systems, the Iridium satellite communication system), the pace of technological change appeared to be accelerating. The most visible technological changes were in hardware. Cellular phones were adding new functions and technological convergence was blurring functional distinctions between cellular phones, PDAs, handheld game players (such as Nintendo Gameboys) and portable music players. The remarkable success of Apple's iPhone pointed to the extent to which our conceptions of cell phones were changing.

The implications for wireless telephony providers were complex. At one level, the increasing number of wireless communication devices and the increased demand for mobile internet access greatly increased the total demand for wireless communication. However, an increasing range of alternatives was becoming available. The potential for WiFi to compete with cellular networks was being increased by the creation of city-wide WiFi networks and the advent of WiMax. More direct competition was likely through the opening of new segments of radio frequency for wireless communication. In March 2008, Federal Communications Commision auctioned licenses to the "C-block" spectrum, which conferred the right to operate the 700 MHz frequency band. A surprise bidder was Google. Together with its Android operating platform, Google was signaling a clear intention to become a central player in the development of mobile technology.[13]

While new technology offered opportunities for developing new content and services, the problem for Vodafone and the other cellular service providers was that the new technologies were controlled either by hardware companies (Nokia, Apple, Intel, Qualcomm, for example), or software companies (such as Google, Microsoft). The success of Apple's iPhone was especially alarming for Vodafone. Because of Apple's exclusive deal with O2 (owned by Telefónica), Vodafone was shut out of the widening array of mobile services provided for iPhone users.[14] The iPhone had also positioned Apple as a key gateway into the 3G mobile services through Apple's applications store, which offered support for third-party developers, creating services and content for the iPhone. In response, Vodafone launched its own software applications store—the Joint Innovation Lab—in May 2009. Verizon Wireless, China Mobile and Softbank partnered in the venture whose aim was to produce a single platform for developers to create mobile widgets and applications on multiple operating systems and access the partners' combined 1.1 billion customer base.[15] However, Apple was not the only hardware company seeking to build a strong strategic position from which it could influence the evolution of the wireless technology. Nokia was the world's largest handset supplier and it owned Symbian, the most widely used operating system for mobile phones.

The power battle between hardware suppliers and service provides had important implications for Vodafone's gobal strategy. If Apple, Nokia, Research in Motion, and Google were increasingly their control of wireless technology and content, there was a risk that wireless services would be increasingly commoditized. In this event, the potential for creating value from supplying wireless services across national boundaries would become progressively smaller.

Notes

1 "Captain Colao Takes the Helm and Changes Course in Stormy Seas," *Financial Times,* November 12, 2008.
2 "Vodafone," Lex column, *Financial Times,* May 19, 2009.
3 "Vodafone: Out of Many, One" (ESSEC Business School Case Study, 2005).
4 "Foundation and Empire," *The Economist,* November 25, 2004.
5 Europe, Middle East and Africa.
6 Quoted in "Vodafone: Out of Many, One" (ESSEC Business School Case Study, 2005): 9.
7 Quoted in "Vodafone: Out of Many, One" (ESSEC Business School Case Study, 2005): 9.
8 Vodafone Group Plc, Annual Report, 2009, p. 20.
9 See www.boozallen.com/media/file/06_2005AR_PEA .pdf, accessed April 16, 2008.
10 "Vodafone: Not-so-big is Beautiful," *Economist,* March 9, 2006.
11 "Vodafone: Calling for a Rethink," *Economist,* January 26, 2006.
12 Vodafone Group plc, Annual Report, 2009, p. 9.
13 "An Auction That Google Was Content to Lose," *New York Times,* April 4, 2008. See www.nytimes.com/2008/04/04/technology/04auction.html?_r=1&oref=slogin, accessed October 22, 2009.
14 "Vodafone in Consolidation Call," *Financial Times,* July 24, 2009.
15 See www.jil.org, accessed May 28, 2009.

Case 20 Richard Branson and the Virgin Group of Companies in 2007*

Despite celebrating his 57th birthday, Richard Branson showed no signs of flagging energy or loss of entrepreneurial vigor. During the last two weeks of January 2007, Virgin announced a slew of new initiatives. These included the creation of Virgin Bioverda—a joint venture to develop ethanol plants in the U.S.—a bid for a vacation company (First Choice) and a proposal to take over rail services between London and Edinburgh. At the same time, Branson was negotiating an alliance with Tata Group to establish Virgin Mobile in India and preparing to buy 50 acres of land in Macau to build a $3 billion casino and leisure complex. Meanwhile, Virgin

America—Branson's San Francisco-based low-cost airline—was struggling to get approval from the U.S. Department of Transportation. Some believed that Virgin Galactic—Branson's passenger spaceship service—might be first into the air.

Yet despite being lauded for his entrepreneurship, eccentricity and embodiment of "the friendly face of capitalism," his Virgin group of companies remained a mystery to most outsiders—and to many insiders as well. At the beginning of 2007 there were 215 Virgin companies registered at Britain's Companies House, of which 20 are identified as recently dissolved. However, most operations are conducted through the 36 companies listed on the Virgin web site (see the Appendix). While a number are Virgin companies identified as "holding companies"—they exist only to own and manage other Virgin companies—there is no overall parent company for the group.

The opacity of Virgin's structure and finances encouraged frequent speculation about the overall performance of the group. During the late 1990s, there was consistent evidence that the group as a whole was not performing well. *The Economist* observed that: "Virgin Travel is the only one of Virgin's businesses to make a large profit . . . The rest of Mr. Branson's firms lost money in total."[1] The *Financial Times* pointed to a net cash outflow and a negative economic value added for the group as a whole.[2] During recent years, overall financial performance was strengthened by profit growth at Virgin's wireless telecommunications businesses and the post-2002 recovery in the airline industry. Nevertheless, several Virgin companies continued to generate losses.

As ever, Branson was dismissive of outside criticism, claiming that analysts and financial journalists misunderstood his business empire. Each Virgin company, he argued, was financed on a stand-alone basis; hence attempts to consolidate the income and assets of the companies were irrelevant and misleading. Moreover, Branson had little regard for accounting profits, preferring cash flow and capital value as the critical performance indicators. Thus, most of the Virgin companies were growing businesses that were increasing in their real value and long-term cash-generating potential, even if accounting profits were negative:

> The approach to running a group of private companies is fundamentally different to that of running public companies. Short-term taxable profits with good dividends are a prerequisite of public life. Avoiding short-term taxable profits and seeking long-term capital growth is the best approach to growing private companies.[3]

Apart from questions about financial performance, outside observers also pondered the strategic direction of this motley collection of over 200 separate companies. The Virgin group covered a remarkable range of business, from airlines to bridal stores. In an era of corporate refocusing and the nurturing of core competences, what possible business rationale could explain the structure and composition of the Virgin group? It was not only Virgin's financial resources that risked being stretched. Was there a risk that the Virgin brand would become overextended and that its appeal and integrity would be damaged? With regard to Branson himself, should he attempt to involve himself personally in guiding the various Virgin companies? As the group expanded and Branson became more of a strategic and charismatic leader rather than a hands-on manager, did Virgin need to establish a more systematic approach to control, risk management, and strategy?

The Development of Virgin

Richard Branson's business career began while he was a student at Stowe, a private boarding school. His startup magazine, *Student*, was first published on January 26, 1968. The early success of the magazine encouraged Branson to leave school at 17 years old, before taking his final exams. Agreeing to the boy's request to leave, the headmaster offered the prophetic statement, "Richard, you will end up in prison or as a millionaire." Both predictions were to be fulfilled.[4]

This early publishing venture displayed features that would characterize many of Branson's subsequent entrepreneurial initiatives. The magazine was aimed at baby-boomers between 16 and 25 years old and was designed to appeal to the optimism, irreverence, antiauthoritarianism, and fashion consciousness of the new generation. It would also fill a "gaping hole in the market." *Student* was to be the "voice of youth" and would "put the world to rights." Its eclectic style reflected its founder's ability to commission articles by celebrities and to identify subjects not touched by many well-established magazines. Norman Mailer, Vanessa Redgrave and Jean-Paul Sartre contributed pieces, which appeared among articles on sex, rock music, interviews with terrorists and proposals for educational reform.

Virgin Records

Branson's next venture was mail order records. Beginning with a single advertisement in the last issue of *Student* magazine, Branson found that he was able to establish a thriving business with almost no up-front investment and no working capital, and could easily undercut the established retail chains. The name "Virgin" was suggested by one of his associates who saw the name as proclaiming their commercial innocence, while possessing some novelty and modest shock-value. Virgin Records brought together Branson and his childhood friend Nik Powell, who took a 40% share in the company and complemented Branson's erratic flamboyance with careful operational and financial management. In 1971 Branson opened his first retail store—on London's busy Oxford Street.

Expansion into record publishing was the idea of Simon Draper, one of Virgin's record buyers. Draper introduced Branson to Mike Oldfield, who was soon installed at Branson's Oxfordshire home with a fully equipped recording studio. *Tubular Bells*, launched in 1973, was an instant hit, eventually selling over 5 million copies worldwide. The result was the Virgin record label, which went on to sign up bands whose music or lifestyles did not appeal to the major record companies. Among the most successful signings were the Sex Pistols.

The recession of 1979–82 was a struggle for Virgin. Several business ventures failed and several of Branson's close associates left, including Nik Powell, who sold his share-holding back to Branson for £1 million plus Virgin's cinema and video interests. Despite these setbacks, the 1980s saw rapid growth for Virgin Records, with the signing of Phil Collins, Human League, Simple Minds and Boy George's Culture Club. By 1983, the Virgin group was earning pretax profits of £2 million on total revenues of just under £50 million.

Virgin Atlantic Airways

Virgin Atlantic began with a phone call from Randolph Fields, a Californian lawyer who proposed founding a transatlantic, cut-price airline. To the horror of Branson's executives at Virgin Records, Branson was enthralled with the idea. On June 24, 1984, Branson appeared in a First World War flying outfit to celebrate the inaugural flight of Virgin Atlantic in a second-hand 747 bought from Aerolinas Argentina. With the launch of Virgin Atlantic, Branson had embarked upon a perilous path strewn with the wreckage of earlier entrepreneurs of aviation, including Laker, Braniff and People Express. Unlike Branson's other businesses, not only was the airline business highly capital intensive—it also required a completely new set of business skills, in particular the need to negotiate with governments, regulatory bodies, banks, and aircraft manufacturers.

Private to Public and Back

By 1985, a transatlantic airfares price war and the investment needs of Virgin Atlantic had created a cash squeeze for Virgin. Branson became convinced of the need to expand the equity base of the group. Don Cruikshank, a Scottish accountant with an MBA from Manchester and Branson's group managing director, was assigned the task of organizing an initial public offering for Virgin's music, retail, and vision businesses, which were combined into the Virgin Group plc, a public corporation with 35% of its equity listed on the London and NASDAQ stock markets.

Branson was not happy as chairman of a public corporation. He felt that investment analysts misunderstood his business and that the market undervalued his company. A clear conflict existed between the financial community's expectations of the chairman of a public corporation and Branson's personal style. With the October 1987 stock market crash, Branson took the opportunity to raise £200 million to buy out external shareholders.

As a private company, Virgin continued to expand, using both internal cash flows—mainly from Virgin Atlantic Airways—and external financing. The retailing group moved aggressively into new markets around the world. The Virgin Megastore concept provided the basis for new stores in Japan, the U.S., Australia, the Netherlands and Spain. This growth was facilitated by the formation of a joint venture with Blockbuster Corporation, the U.S. video-store giant. New ventures launched during the early 1990s included Virgin Lightships, an airship advertiser; Vintage Airtours, an operator of restored DC-3 aircraft between Orlando and Key West; Virgin Games producing video games; West One Television, a TV production company and Virgin Euromagnetics, a personal computer company. Meanwhile, Virgin Atlantic Airways expanded its network to 20 cities including Tokyo and Hong Kong. It also won many awards for its customer service.

1990–2006: Continued Expansion, Selective Divestment

Expansion pressured cash flow and the Persian Gulf War of 1990–1 cut airline profits. Branson relied increasingly on joint ventures to finance new business development. The partnering arrangements were primarily in retailing and included one with Marui, a leading Japanese retailer, and another with W. H. Smith, a prominent U.K. retail chain.

Ultimately, the capital needs of Virgin Atlantic forced Branson to take drastic action. In March 1992, Branson sold his most profitable and successful business, Virgin Music, the world's biggest independent record label, to Thorn EMI for £560 million (close to $1 billion). Virgin Music's tangible assets had a balance sheet value of only £3 million. The sale marked a dramatic shift in focus for Virgin away from its core entertainment business towards airlines and travel. It provided the capital to support new business ventures.

In the meantime, Branson's long-standing rivalry with British Airways took a nasty turn. Evidence emerged that British Airways had pursued a "dirty tricks" campaign against Virgin. This included breaking into Virgin's computer system, diverting Virgin customers to BA flights, and spreading rumors about Virgin's financial state. The outcome was a U.K. court case that resulted in BA paying $1.5 million dollars in damages to Branson and Virgin.

The second half of the 1990s saw acceleration in Virgin's business development activities, with a host of new ventures in disparate markets. Virgin's new ventures were a response to three types of opportunity:

- *Privatization and deregulation.* The rolling back of the frontiers of state ownership and regulation in Britain (and elsewhere) created business opportunities that Richard Branson was only too eager to seize. Virgin's most important privatization initiative was its successful bids for two passenger rail franchises: the west coast and cross-country rail services. The resulting business—Virgin Rail—was a joint venture with transportation specialist, Stagecoach. Deregulation in the world's airline sector also created opportunities for Virgin. In 1996, Euro-Belgian Airlines was acquired and re-launched as Virgin Express, and in Australia, Virgin Blue began operations during 2000. Branson's bid to operate the British National Lottery was unsuccessful, but in 2001, Virgin Atlantic was part of the consortium that acquired a stake in the British air traffic control system.

- *Direct selling of goods and services to consumers.* Branson was continually on the lookout for business opportunities offering a "new deal" to consumers. Most of these ventures involved direct sales to consumers and passing on the cost savings from bypassing traditional distribution channels. Virgin Direct, launched in 1995 as a joint venture with Norwich Union, offered telephone-based financial services to consumers. In subsequent years, Virgin Direct expanded the range of financial products it offered and moved to the internet. Virgin Car and Virgin Bike challenged the existing dealership system of the automobile and motorcycle manufacturers by offering direct sales of cars and motorbikes at discounted prices. Virgin Wine was also launched.

- *TMT.* The "TMT" (Technology, Media, Telecom) boom of 1998–2000 created a tremendous buzz within Virgin. Virgin's origins lay in media, while the internet offered a new channel for Virgin to reach consumers. In 1997 Virgin Net, an internet service provider and portal, was launched as a joint venture between Virgin and cable operator NTL. The next year Virgin Mobile, a joint venture with Deutsche Telecom's One-to-One wireless telephone service began business in Britain. The success of Virgin Mobile in Britain—half a million subscribers were signed up within the first year and four million by 2004— encouraged Virgin to expand into the U.S., Australia, South Africa and South East Asia. Virgin's increasing online presence was seen as offering important e-commerce opportunities to the Virgin group as a whole. The Train Line Company (www.thetrainline.com) was set up as an online reservation service for train passengers. Virgin Direct offered music downloads. The Virgin.com portal became a shopfront for all of Virgin's consumer offerings.

Other new ventures appeared to be largely the result of Branson's whims and opportunism and defied any kind of categorization. These included a chain of health clubs (Virgin Active), space flight (Virgin Galactic), and biofuels (Virgin Fuels, Virgin Bioverda).

To fund so many new ventures, Branson sought to release equity from some of his established and growing businesses. Major divestments included:

- Virgin Atlantic: 49% was sold to Singapore Airlines for £600 million in 1999;
- Virgin Megastores, France was sold to Legardere Media in 2001 for £100 million;
- Virgin One: Virgin's home loan business was sold to Royal Bank of Scotland in 2001 for £100 million;
- Virgin Blue: 50% was sold to Patrick Corporation for £250 million in 2001; a further 25% of Virgin Blue was sold in that company's 2003 IPO, raising a similar amount;
- Virgin Mobile (U.K.) was acquired by cable operator NTL for £962 million in 2006.

Moreover, Virgin Express—Virgin's loss-making, Brussels-based airline—merged in 2005 with SN Brussels Airlines to form SN Airholdings, in which Virgin held a 30% stake. The appendix shows a timeline of Virgin's development.

The Virgin Group of Companies in 2007

Among the 200-plus companies forming the Virgin Group, the major businesses in terms of revenues and market presence are shown in Table 20.1. The principal commonalities between this diverse range of enterprises are, first, their use of the Virgin brand name and, second, the role of Richard Branson as their instigator and, in most cases, their major investor.

The Virgin Brand

The Virgin brand was the group's greatest single asset. There are few brands that encompass so wide a range of products as Virgin. Can a brand that extends from train travel and financial services to night clubs and music downloads have any meaningful identity? The Virgin web site explains the Virgin brand as follows:

All the markets in which Virgin operates tend to have features in common: they are typically markets where the customer has been ripped off or under-served, where there is confusion and/or where the competition is complacent. In these markets, Virgin is able to break into the market and shake it up. Our role is to be the consumer champion, and we do this by delivering to our brand values, which are:

- *Value for Money:* Simple, honest and transparent pricing—not necessarily the cheapest on the market.
- *Good Quality:* High standards, attention to detail, being honest and delivering on promises.

- *Brilliant Customer Service:* Friendly, human and relaxed; professional but not corporate.
- *Innovative:* Challenging convention with big and little product/service ideas; innovative, modern and stylish design.
- *Competitively Challenging:* Sticking two fingers up to the establishment and fighting the big boys—usually with a bit of humor.
- *Fun:* Every company in the world takes itself seriously so we think it's important that we provide the public and our customers with a bit of entertainment—as well as making Virgin a nice place for our people to work.[5]

These attributes were communicated to customers in a variety of ways. Virgin Atlantic pioneered a range of innovative customer services (principally for its business class passengers). These included inflight massages, hair stylists, aromatherapists and limousine and motorcycle home pickup services. In 1998 it offered speedboat rides along the Thames from Heathrow to the City of London, allowing executives and bankers to dodge London traffic jams. British Airways—huge, stodgy and bureaucratic—provided the ideal adversary against which Virgin Atlantic could position itself. When British Airways was experiencing problems erecting its giant Ferris wheel, the London Eye, Virgin positioned a blimp above the site bearing the message "BA Can't Get It Up!"

TABLE 20.1 Main businesses within the Virgin Group, 2006

Virgin Active	Chain of health and leisure clubs in the U.K. and South Africa
Virgin Atlantic	London-based airline serving 20 destinations in the U.S., Caribbean, South Africa and Asia
Virgin Atlantic Cargo	Air freight using Virgin Atlantic's network
Virgin Balloon Flights	Passenger balloon flights in the U.K., Holland and Belgium
Virgin Blue	Low-fare airline flying in Australia
Virgin Books	Publishes books on music, sport, TV, movies, and comedy
Virgin Brides	Chain of bridal retail stores
Virgin Comics	Collaboration with writer Deepak Chopra, filmmaker Shekhar Kapur and Sir Richard Branson
Virgin Cosmetics	Direct sales of specially formulated cosmetics
Virgin Credit Card	Credit card issued by Virgin Money
Virgin Digital	Online digital music collection
Virgin Drinks	Distributes Virgin-branded soft drinks
Virgin Experience Days	Offers innovative leisure experiences, from bungee jumping to Ferrari driving
Virgin Express	Brussels-based airline offering scheduled flights to U.K. and other European destinations
Virgin Galactic	Offers opportunities for space travel
Virgin Games	Online gaming
Virgin Holidays	U.K.-based tour operator specializing in long-haul holidays to America, the Far East, Australia, and South Africa, using Virgin Atlantic flights

TABLE 20.1 (*Continued*)

Virgin Jewellery	Offers a range of silver and fashion jewelry
Virgin Limited Edition	Offers vacation packages at exclusive hotels worldwide
Virgin Limobike	Motorcycle taxi service in London
Virgin Limousines	Limos serving northern California
Virgin Megastores	Eighty megastores in Europe, Japan, and North America sell music, movies, computer games and books
Virgin Mobile	Wireless telephone resellers offering easy-tariff service with no line rental or fixed-term contract
Virgin Money	Online financial services offering loans, mutual funds, and stock trading
Virgin.net	U.K.-based internet service provider
Virgin Play	Distributor, marketer, and promoter of computer and interactive games in Spain
Virgin Radio	U.K. digital radio broadcaster
Virgin Spa	Spa services in South Africa
Virgin Trains	Major U.K. operator of passenger train services and facilities and allows booking of Virgin Train tickets online
Virgin Unite	Charitable, volunteer organization supporting grassroots charities
Virgin Vacations	Vacation packages
Virgin Ware	Retail and online vendor of underwear
Virgin Wines	Direct seller of wines
V2 Music	Independent record label (artists include the Stereophonics, Tom Jones, Moby and Underworld)
Pacific Blue	Airline operating daily services between Australia and New Zealand

Source: www.virgin.com.

Some of Branson's ventures seemed to be inspired more by a sense of fun and eagerness to "stick it to the big boys" than by commercial logic. Virgin Cola was introduced in 1994 packaged in a "Pammy" bottle modeled on the body of *Baywatch* star Pamela Anderson. The goal, according to Branson, was to "drive Coke out of the States."[6] By 1997, Virgin Cola was losing £5 million on revenues of £30 million.

Virgin's ability to extend its brand so widely pointed to the broad appeal of Virgin's values and business principles. Much of this appeal was linked with Richard Branson's persona and style. The values and characteristics that the Virgin brand communicated are inseparable from Richard Branson as entrepreneur, joker, fair-playing Brit and giant killer. The Virgin brand was identified too with the innovation and unconventional strategies and marketing that characterized most Virgin startups. Branson went to great lengths to differentiate his new enterprises from established market leaders. Thus, the difference between Virgin Atlantic and BA, between Virgin Cola and Coke, and between Virgin Money and the leading banks was not primarily about products; it was more about the nature of the companies and how they related to their customers. As Virgin internationalized, a critical issue was whether Branson and the Virgin brand could achieve the same rapport with consumers in other countries as they did in Britain. Although Branson was well known in Europe and

North America, in many respects he was a quintessentially British character who was a product of time and place.

A continual issue for Virgin was the risk that the brand might become overextended. The head of brand identity at consultant Landor Associates commented: "He's still way too unfocused. He should get out of businesses that don't fit the Virgin/Branson personality, such as beverages, cosmetics, certainly financial services, or come up with another brand name for them."[7] Widespread public dissatisfaction with rail services in Britain suggested that Virgin's vision of new standards of service for rail travelers might be unattainable given the structural problems of Britain's congested rail infrastructure.

Despite his renown, Branson, too, might be waning in market appeal. Was there a risk that, having seen Branson as flight attendant, Branson in a wedding dress, Branson with successive prime ministers, and Branson attempting to fly around the world in a hot-air balloon, the public might tire of his exploits?

During the late 1990s, Virgin had moved to consolidate around a number of core businesses, notably travel, entertainment, and retailing. However, this trend was short lived: the telecom and internet revolution offered Branson a host of new entrepreneurial opportunities that were irresistible.

Branson as Entrepreneur

Almost all of the Virgin businesses were new startups. From the founding of *Student* magazine through to the formation of Virgin Galactic, Branson's primary strength as a businessman was in conceiving and implementing new business ideas—not that Branson was the source of all of Virgin's new business ideas. Branson acted as a magnet for would-be entrepreneurs and Virgin actively encouraged the submission of new business ideas to its corporate development offices in London, Sydney and New York. Virgin employees, too, were encouraged to develop proposals for new businesses. The idea for Virgin Bride had originated with a Virgin Atlantic employee dismayed by the products and services offered by existing U.K. bridal stores. Nelson Mandela once offered a business idea to Branson, suggesting that Branson acquire a South African health club chain that had gone bankrupt putting thousands of jobs at risk. Virgin Active South Africa is now the country's biggest chain of health clubs.

Yet Branson's leadership of the Virgin Group extended beyond his role as a source of entrepreneurial ideas. As the creator of Virgin and its unique corporate culture, and the primary promoter of its image and entrepreneurial spirit, Richard Branson was synonymous with Virgin. To many of his generation he embodied the spirit of "New Britain." In a country where business leaders were members of "the establishment" and identified with the existing social structure, Branson was seen as a revolutionary. Despite a privileged family background (his father was a lawyer and Richard attended a private boarding school), Branson had the ability to transcend the social classes that traditionally divided British society and segmented consumer markets. As such, he was part of a movement in British culture and society that has sought to escape the Old Britain of fading empire, class antagonism, Victorian values, and stiff-upper-lip hypocrisy. Richard Branson symbolized the transition from "Rule Britannia" to "Cool Britannia."

Informality and disrespect for convention were central to Branson's way of business. Branson's woolly sweaters, beard, windswept hair and toothy grin were practically a trademark of the Virgin companies. His dislike of office buildings and the usual symbols of corporate success was reflected in the absence of a corporate head office and his willingness to do business from his family homes, whether a houseboat in Maida Vale or Necker Island Caribbean retreat. This lack of separation between work, family, and leisure—indicated by the involvement of cousins, aunts, childhood friends and dinner-party acquaintances in business relationships—reflected a view of business as part of life which, like life, should involve excitement, creativity and fun.

An earlier case study on Virgin explains Branson's approach to new business startups:

> Much of the operating style was established not so much by design but by the exigencies of the time when Virgin was getting started. It has proved to be a successful model that Branson can replicate. His philosophy is to immerse himself in a new venture until he understands the ins and outs of the business, and then hand it over to a good managing director and financial controller, who are given a stake in it, and are then expected to make the company take off. He knows that expansion through the creation of additional discrete legal entities not only protects the Virgin Group, but also gives people a sense of involvement and loyalty, particularly if he trusts them with full authority and offers minority share holdings to the managers of subsidiaries. He is proud of the fact that Virgin has produced a considerable number of millionaires. He has said that he does not want his best people to leave the company to start a venture outside. He prefers to make millionaires within.[8]

His use of joint ventures was an extension of this model reinforced by his dealings with the Japanese. Branson was impressed by the Japanese approach to business, admiring their commitment to long-term development and focus on organic growth. His only major acquisition was the parts of British Rail that formed Virgin Rail. Prior to that, Branson had made only two significant acquisitions: Rushes Video for £6 million and the airline that became Virgin Express. He saw similarities between Virgin and the Japanese *keiretsu* system (multiple companies interlocking through managerial and equity linkages in a collaborative network). Virgin's network of small companies combined "small is beautiful" with "strength through unity." He explained this and other business maxims that he believed to be necessary for success in a speech to the Institute of Directors in 1993. "Staff first, then customers and shareholders" should be the chairman's priority if the goal is better performance. "Shape the business around the people," "Build don't buy," "Be best, not biggest," "Pioneer, don't follow the leader," "Capture every fleeting idea," and "Drive for change" were other guiding principles in the Branson philosophy.

Branson's values of innocence, innovation and irreverence for authority were apparent in his choice of new ventures. He drew heavily on the ideas of others within his organization and was prepared to invest in new startups even in markets that were dominated by long-established incumbents. His business ventures, just like his sporting exploits, reflected a "just live life" attitude and a "bigger the challenge, greater the fun" belief. In identifying opportunity he was particularly keen to identify markets where the conservatism and lack of imagination of incumbent firms meant that they were failing to create value for customers. Branson entered markets with a "new" and "anti-establishment attitude" that sought to offer customers a better alternative. An example of this was Virgin's entry into financial services. Into a business that was long regarded as conservative and stuffy, Branson hoped to bring "a breath of fresh air."

At the same time, the affection of the British public for Branson reflected the fact that Branson's values and his sense of fair play were consistent with many traditional values that defined the British character. His competitive battles against huge corporations like British Airways and Coca-Cola linked well with the heroes of yesteryear who battled against tyranny and evil: King Arthur, Robin Hood, and St. George. Resisting British Airways' "dirty tricks" campaign and his other battles with corporate giants resonated well with the British sense of decency. Even his willingness to appear in outlandish attire reflected a British propensity for ludicrous dressing-up, whether for fancy-dress parties, morris dancing, or the House of Lords.

Virgin's Management Structure

Of Virgin's 200-plus companies, the majority are operating companies that own assets, employ people, and offer goods and services. These operating companies are owned and controlled by some 20 holding companies; most of these own several operating companies within the same line of business. For example, Virgin Travel (Holdings) Limited owns Virgin Group's investments in Virgin Atlantic, Virgin Blue, Virgin America and SN Airholdings. Overall ownership of most of the Virgin Group lies in the hands of Virgin Group Investments Limited—a private company registered in the British Virgin Islands. Virgin Group Investments Limited is owned by Richard Branson and a series of trusts, the beneficiaries of which are Branson and his family members.

The most striking feature of the Virgin Group is its legal complexity. For example, Virgin's passenger train companies are Virgin West Coast Mainline and Virgin Cross Country. These are owned by Virgin Rail Group Holdings Ltd, 51% of which is owned by Ivanco (No. 1) Ltd, which is owned by Virgin Group Investments Ltd.

This financial and legal structure reflects Branson's unconventional ideas about business and his wariness of the financial community. The intricate structure involving offshore private companies cloaks the Virgin empire in a thick veil of secrecy. This is reinforced by the use of "bearer shares" by several of the Virgin holding companies through which minority shareholders (venture capitalists and other investors) cannot be identified. However, Branson also views the loose-knit structure of the group as consistent with his vision of people-oriented capitalism:

> We're structured as if we are 150 small companies. Each has to stand on its own two feet, as if they are their own companies. Employees have a stake in their success. They feel—and are—crucial to their company because they are one-in-fifty or one-in-a-hundred instead of one-in-tens-of-thousands. They indeed are all under the Virgin umbrella, but they are generally not subsidiaries. I'm over them to see if one company can't help another, but otherwise they are independent. Some people like the idea of growing fiefdoms—companies that brag about sales of over $5 billion a year—but there is no logical reason to think that there is anything good about huge companies. History in fact shows the opposite. Those huge corporations with tentacles and divisions and departments become unwieldy, slow growing, stagnant. Some chairmen want them like that so that one division's loss can make up for

another's profit, but we'd rather have a lot of exciting companies that are all making profits—as are all of ours.[9]

The Virgin Group has been likened both to a brand franchising operation and to Japanese *keiretsu*, where member companies have financial and management links and share a common sense of identity. The reality, according to *Management Today*,[10] is somewhere between the two. Will Whitehorn, Branson's long-time strategist and business developer, describes Virgin as "a branded venture capital organization."

The formal linkages between the companies include:

- *Ownership*. Most of Branson's equity interests are owned by Virgin Group Investments Ltd.

- *The brand*. Virgin's trademarks—including the Virgin name and logos—are owned by Virgin Enterprises Ltd. Neil Hobbs, intellectual property lawyer for Virgin Enterprises, explains: "Our role is both to optimize and enhance the value of the brand and to protect that by ensuring that that value is not diminished through infringement by third parties. VEL licenses companies both within and outside the Virgin Group to use the Virgin brand."[11] One third-party licensee is EMI Records, which owns Virgin Records and is licensed to use the Virgin name.

- *Management*. Virgin Management Ltd is the management arm of the Virgin Group. It manages the appointment of board members and senior executives to the different Virgin companies, assists in coordination between the companies, and is responsible for the development of new business enterprises. In 2005, Virgin Management Ltd had 87 employees at Virgin's London headquarters.

However, the key to the management of the Virgin Group is the informal relations between Branson and a small core of long-term associates who form the senior management team of the Virgin Group and occupy key executive positions within individual operating companies. Among Branson's inner circle are:

- Will Whitehorn, originally Branson's press spokesman, who has been Virgin's director of brand development and corporate affairs for the past decade and is currently CEO of Virgin Galactic. He is widely viewed as Branson's second-in-command and key strategic thinker.[12]

- Gordon McCallum, who joined Virgin in 1997 as group strategy director from McKinsey & Company. He has pioneered Virgin's entry into mobile telecommunications and since September 2005 has been CEO of Virgin Management Ltd.

- Patrick McCall, who was formerly an investment banker at UBS Warburg. At Virgin he is a director of Virgin Management and has been a board member of a number of Virgin companies, including Virgin Rail and Virgin Blue.

- Stephen Murphy, who joined Virgin from Quaker Oats. He was Virgin Group's finance director from 1994 to 2000, and since 2001 has been a board member of Virgin Management as executive director.

FIGURE 20.1 The Virgin Group of companies

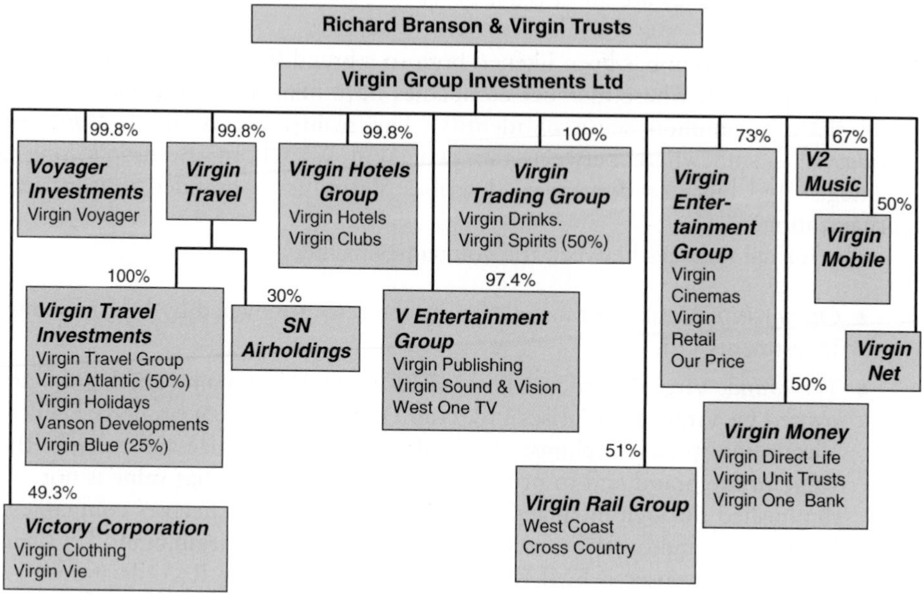

Source: *Financial Times,* August 13, 1998, p.25, updated from www.virgin.com.

Note: This figure is intended to provide a general view of the structure of the Virgin Group, but it includes only some of Virgin's 2001 companies.

- Rowan Gormley, who joined the Virgin Group as corporate development director after working as an accountant with Arthur Andersen & Co. He led Virgin's move into financial services in 1995 as chief executive of Virgin Direct. In January 2000, he became CEO of Virgin Wine.

- Frances Farrow, who joined Virgin Atlantic as commercial services director from the law firm Binder Hamlyn. She became CEO of Virgin USA, Inc.

Figure 20.1 shows the structure of the Virgin Group of companies, including some major operating companies and the holding companies that own them.

Virgin's Organizational Culture

The ability of the Virgin Group to operate effectively with so little formal structure or management systems owes much to the group's unique organizational culture. This is defined almost entirely by Branson's own values and management style. It reflects his eccentricity, sense of fun, disrespect for hierarchy and formal authority, commitment to employees and consumers and belief in hard work and individual responsibility. The group provides an environment in which talented, ambitious people are motivated to do their best and strive for a higher level of performance. While the working environment is informal, anticorporate and defined by the popular culture of its era, expectations are high. Branson expects a high level of commitment, the acceptance of personal responsibility and long hours of work when needed. Financial rewards for most employees are typically modest but nonpecuniary benefits include social activities, company-sponsored weekend getaways and impromptu parties.

The apparent chaos of the Virgin Group, with its casual style and absence of formal structure and control systems belies its sharp business acumen and forceful determination. It is easy for more traditional business enterprises to underestimate Virgin—a key error of British Airways. Virgin possesses considerable financial and managerial talent, and what it lacks in formal structure is made up for by commitment and close personal ties. The Virgin organizational structure involves very little hierarchy, offering short lines of communication and flexible response capability. Employees are given a great deal of responsibility and freedom in order to stimulate idea generation, initiative, commitment, and fun. The lack of formal controls is conducive to teamwork and entrepreneurial spirit.

Virgin's Financial Performance

Financial reporting by the Virgin companies was fragmented, hard to locate and difficult to interpret. No consolidated accounts existed for the group as a whole. Not only were there multiple operating companies but ownership of these companies lay with a number of holding companies, some of which consolidated subsidiary accounts while others did not. Tracking financial results over time was difficult because investments in Virgin operating companies were frequently transferred within the group. Individual Virgin companies (at least those registered in the U.K.) submitted audited financial statements to Companies House (a government agency). Table 20.2 shows results for some of the Virgin's operating and holding companies.

The financial structure of the Virgin Group has changed substantially over the years. In particular, Virgin's near collapse during the 1990–2 recession has resulted in a more conservative approach to financing. During the past 15 years, Branson has relied increasingly on equity partners to finance his new business ventures. Typically, joint venture partners have taken 49% or 50% of the equity of the new venture despite supplying the majority of the equity capital. The power of the Virgin brand and Branson's celebrity status and promotional capabilities has meant that Branson has acquired equity stakes in new ventures that were disproportionate to the size of his financial investment—which was typically small. For example, Branson put up only £2000 initially for minority stakes in Virgin Clothing and Virgin Vie; at Virgin Blue, Branson's initial investment was a mere A$12 million. Virgin's joint ventures include:

- Virgin Atlantic, which was 49% owned by Singapore Airlines.
- Virgin Rail, which was 49% owned by Stagecoach.
- Virgin Retail had different partners and investors. These included Blockbuster and Marui.
- Virgin Trading drinks ventures had been launched with investments from William Grant and Cotts.
- Victory Corporation, the fashion and toiletries company, was pioneered by entrepreneur and investor Rory McCarthy. In addition, outside investors owned 25% of the equity. McCarthy also held one-third of V2 Music.
- Virgin Express was a subsidiary of SN Airholdings in which Virgin held a 30% equity stake.
- Virgin Blue was a publicly traded company where Virgin held 25%.
- In addition, private investors (including major equity and venture capital funds) held equity stakes in some Virgin businesses.

TABLE 20.2 Financial results for selected Virgin companies

Company	Revenue (£ m)	Net profit (£ m)	Total assets (£ m)	Employees (incl. directors)	Financial year ending	Comments
Virgin Group Ltd	0.2	(151.4)	69.9	4	March 31, 2005	Investment holding company. Owns Voyager Group Ltd and Virgin USA, Inc. Exceptional loss of £151 m in 2005
Virgin Enterprises Ltd	13.3	3.3	129.3	4	March 31, 2006	Owns and licenses Virgin brand
Virgin Management Ltd	5.7	(13.3)	548.7	97	March 31, 2006	Management of other Virgin companies. Owns Virgin Bride Ltd, Virgin Mobile (Singapore), Vanson Group Ltd, and Virgin Life Care Investments Ltd
Virgin Travel Group Ltd	0	0.7	250.1	10	February 28, 2006	Holding company. Owns Virgin Atlantic Airlines Ltd and Virgin Holidays Ltd
Virgin Atlantic Ltd	1912.3	60.3	1196.7	8939	February 28, 2006	Airline
Virgin Leisure Ltd	0	36.9	216.2	n.a.	March 31, 2006	Investment holding company that owns Virgin Active Group Ltd
Virgin Mobile Holdings (U.K.) Ltd	563.1	44.9	106.3	1488	March 31, 2006	Telecommunications. Acquired by NTL on July 4, 2006
Virgin Mobile Group (U.K.) Ltd	80.0	65.8	374.8	3	March 31, 2006	Holding company. Owns Virgin Mobile Telecoms Ltd

Company				Date	Description
Virgin Money Ltd	51.1	12.8	20.0	4	December 31, 2005	Online financial services, primarily credit cards
Virgin Money Holdings (U.K.) Ltd	258.2	8.5	40.3	376	December 31, 2005	Online financial services, primarily personal investment products
Virgin Rail Group Holdings Ltd	717.1	(1.2)	372.6	4456	March 4, 2006	Owns West Coast Trains Ltd and CrossCountry Trains Ltd
Virgin Retail Group Ltd	0	(82.6)	39.2	4	March 31, 2004	Holding company. Owns Virgin Retail Ltd and Vspace Ltd (internet cafés).
Virgin Retail Ltd	376.3	(74.7)	203.7	3240	March 27, 2004	Holding company. Owns Virgin Atlantic Airways Ltd and Virgin Holidays Ltd
Virgin Trading Group Ltd	0	(7.0)	7.6	4	March 31, 2005	Investment holding company. Owns Virgin Drinks Group Ltd

n.a. = not available.

Source: Company annual reports submitted to Companies House.

Looking Ahead

During early 2007, Virgin Group appeared to be relatively free of the cash-flow and debt-service problems that had plagued it in the past. While a number of Virgin businesses were making losses and others (for example, Virgin Atlantic) were only marginally profitable, recent divestments had replenished the group's coffers. Longer term, however, there were fundamental strategic questions about the future shape and rationale for the Virgin Group. What kind of enterprise was Virgin? Was it a brand management and franchising company, an incubator of startup businesses, a vehicle for Richard Branson's personal ambitions, or a novel form of conglomerate? Was Virgin a unified, if diversified, business or a loose confederation of many independent businesses?

Whatever the identity and rationale of the Virgin Group, it was not apparent that the existing structure or organization fitted with any of these categories:

- If Virgin was a brand franchising organization, then the critical role for the Virgin Group was to develop and protect the brand and maximize the licensing revenues from its use by other companies. Clearly Branson would need to play a role in promoting the brand but it was not necessary that he should have any strategic, operating, or ownership role in the companies using the brand.

- If Virgin was to be an incubator of new startups then there needed to be a more systematic approach to evaluating new business opportunities and monitoring their progress and development.

- If Virgin was a conglomerate, then did this imply a stronger corporate role? What kind of strategic planning and financial controls were needed to ensure that value was not being dissipated? And could Virgin really perform across so wide a range of businesses?

Whichever path Virgin followed, it appeared that organizational changes would be needed in order to manage intercompany linkages. Although Branson liked to maintain that the different companies were independent and "stood on their own two feet," the reality was somewhat different. Some companies had been strong cash generators; others were heavy loss makers. Relationships between the companies were largely *ad hoc* and Branson was proud of the fact that no consolidated financial statements were prepared, even for internal management purposes. Moreover, changes to Britain's capital gains tax laws threatened to eliminate the advantages of multiple, offshore holding companies. Indeed, to obtain the tax benefits from Virgin's loss-making businesses, there were clear advantages in consolidation. Key questions also surrounded the management of the Virgin brand. To the extent that the brand was a common resource, how could it be best protected? The experiences of Virgin Rail suggested that adverse publicity from one company could negatively affect the overall status of the Virgin brand.

As always, the future of the Virgin Group could not be considered without taking account of Branson himself. What kind of role did he anticipate now that he had celebrated his 57th birthday? If Branson was to become less active as chief entrepreneur, public relations director and strategic architect for the Virgin companies, who or what would take his place?

Appendix

The history of Virgin

1968—First issue of *Student* magazine, January 26.

1970—Start of Virgin mail order operation.

1971—First Virgin record shop opens in Oxford Street, London.

1972—Virgin recording studio opens at The Manor near Oxford, England.

1977—Virgin record label launched with Mike Oldfield's *Tubular Bells*.
—Virgin Records signs the Sex Pistols.

1978—Virgin opens The Venue night club in London.

1980–2—Virgin Records expands overseas. Signs Phil Collins and Boy George/Culture Club.

1983—Virgin Vision (forerunner of Virgin Communications) formed to enter broadcasting and produce and distribute films and videos.
—Vanson Developments formed as real-estate development company.
—Virgin Games (computer games software publisher) launched.
—Virgin Group earns pre-tax profit of £2.0 million on sales of £50 million.

1984—Virgin Atlantic Airways and Virgin Cargo launched.
—First hotel investment (Deya, Mallorca).
—Virgin Vision launches The Music Channel, a 24-hour satellite-delivered music station and releases its first feature film, *1984,* with Richard Burton and John Hurt.

1985—Virgin wins Business Enterprise Award for company of the year.
—Virgin Vision extends film and video distribution internationally.
—Virgin Holidays formed.

1986—Virgin Group, comprising the Music, Retail & Property, and Communications divisions, floated on London Stock Exchange. Placement of 35% of equity raises $56 million.
—Airline, clubs, holidays, and aviation services remain part of the privately owned Voyager Group.

1987—Virgin Records forms subsidiaries in the U.S. and Japan.
—British Satellite Broadcasting (Virgin a minority partner) awarded satellite broadcasting license. (Virgin sells its shareholding in 1988.)
—Virgin acquires Mastertronics Group, distributor of Sega video games in Europe.
—Virgin Airship & Balloon Company launched to provide aerial marketing services.

1988—Recording studios opened in Barnes, London.
—New international record label, Virgin, launched.
—Virgin Broadcasting formed to further develop Virgin's radio and TV interests.
—Virgin Hotels formed.
—Virgin Megastores opened in Sydney, Paris, and Glasgow.
—Branson takes Virgin private with £248 million bid for outstanding shares.

1989—Virgin Music Group sells 25% stake to Fujisankei Communications for $150 million.
—Virgin Vision (video distribution) sold to MCEG of Los Angeles for $83 million.

1990—Virgin Retail Group and Marui form joint venture company to operate Megastores in Japan.
—Virgin Lightships formed to develop helium airships for advertising.

1991—W. H. Allen plc acquired. Merged with Virgin Books to form Virgin Publishing.
    —Sale of Virgin Mastertronic to Sega. Remaining part of the business
      becomes Virgin Games.
    —Virgin Retail Group forms 50:50 joint venture with W. H. Smith to
      develop U.K. retail business.
1992—Sale of Virgin Music Group to Thorn EMI plc.
    —Joint venture with Blockbuster to develop Megastores in Europe, Australia,
      and U.S.
    —Virgin Communications gains license for Britain's first national commercial
      rock station (Virgin 1215AM goes on the air in April 1993).
    —Virgin acquires Euro-Magnetic Products, distributor of personal computer
      consumables.
    —Vintage Airtours established to fly Orlando-Florida Keys in vintage DC-3s.
1993—Virgin Games floated as Virgin Interactive Entertainment plc with Hasbro
    and Blockbuster taking minority equity stakes.
    —Virgin Euromagnetics launches a range of personal computers.
1994—Virgin Cola Company formed as joint venture with Cott Corp.
    —Agreement with W. Grant to launch Virgin Vodka.
    —Virgin acquires W. H. Smith's 75% stake in Our Price retail music stores.
    —Virgin Retail Group forms joint ventures to develop Megastores in Hong
      Kong and South Korea.
    —Virgin City Jet service launched between Dublin and London City Airport.
1995—Virgin Direct Personal Financial Service is launched as a joint venture with
    Norwich Union (whose stake is later acquired by Australian Mutual Provident).
    —Acquisition of MGM Cinemas, U.K.'s biggest movie theater chain, to create
      Virgin Cinemas.
1996—Virgin Travel Group acquires Euro-Belgian Airlines to form Virgin Express.
    —V2 record label and music publishing company launched.
    —London & Continental Railways (in which Virgin a major shareholder) wins
      £3 bn contract to build the Channel Tunnel Rail Link and operate Eurostar
      rail services.
1997—Virgin Rail awarded franchise to operate the West Coast train services.
    —Virgin Net, an internet service provider, formed with NTL.
    —Branson acquires a 15% stake in the London Broncos rugby league team.
    —Victory Corporation, a joint venture with Rory McCarthy, launches the
      Virgin Clothing and Virgin Vie toiletry products.
    —Majority share in Virgin Radio sold to Chris Evans's Ginger Media Group.
    —Virgin Bride retail chain formed.
    —Virgin One telephone bank account and "one-stop integrated financial
      service" launched in collaboration with Royal Bank of Scotland.
1998—Virgin Entertainment acquires W. H. Smith's 75% stake in Virgin/Our Price.
    —Virgin Cola launches in the U.S.
1999—Virgin sells its U.K. cinema chain to UGC for £215 million.
    —Virgin launches mobile phone service in joint venture with Deutsche
      Telecom's One-to-One (November).
    —49% of Virgin Atlantic sold to Singapore Airlines for £600 million.
    —Restructuring and relaunch of loss-making Our Price record stores.
2000—Virgin Mobile launches U.S. wireless phone service in joint venture with Sprint.
    Virgin Mobile Australia (a joint venture with Cable & Wireless) launched.
    —Virgin Net, Virgin's portal and ISP venture, closes its content division.

—Virgin announces the closing of its clothing company (February).

—Virgin Cars, online sales of new cars, launched.

—Virgin and Bear Stearns form Lynx New Media, a $130 million venture capital fund.

—Inaugural flight of Virgin Blue, Virgin's low-cost Australian airline.

—Branson knighted by the Queen: becomes Sir Richard Branson.

—Virgin fails to win franchise to run Britain's government-owned National Lottery.

2001—50% of Virgin Blue sold to Patrick Corporation for A$138 million.

—Virgin expands into Singapore and SE Asia with joint ventures with local companies in radio stations, cosmetic retailing, and wireless phone services.

—Virgin.net merges its ISP and portal businesses.

—16 French Virgin Megastores sold to Lagardere Media for €150 million.

2002—Virgin Bikes (U.K.) begins direct sale of new motorcycles at discount prices.

—Virgin Mobile offers wireless telecom services in the U.S.

2003—Virgin Blue initial public offering; Virgin retains 25% of equity.

2004—50% stake of Virgin Money repurchased from AMP for £90 million.

—Virgin Digital launched. Offers online music store and digital music download capabilities.

—Virgin Cars and Virgin Bikes sold to MotorSolutions Ltd of the U.K. for an undisclosed amount.

2005—Virgin Mobile launched in Canada.

—Virgin Atlantic increases services to Shanghai and begins flights to Beijing.

—Virgin Atlantic introduces self-service check-in for all passengers.

2006—Launch of Virgin Atlantic credit card.

—NTL acquires Virgin Mobile.

—Virgin Mobile and Virgin Money launched in South Africa.

Source: www.virgin.com.

Notes

1 "Behind Branson," *The Economist,* February 21, 1998, pp. 63–6.
2 "The Future for Virgin," *Financial Times,* August 13, 1998, pp. 24–5.
3 Richard Branson, letter to *The Economist,* March 7, 1998, p. 6.
4 Branson is one of Britain's richest individuals, with a net worth exceeding $2 billion. Branson also spent a night in Dover police cells when arrested for tax offenses after he sold through his Virgin store a batch of Virgin records intended for export. The case was settled out of court.
5 "The Virgin Brand," www.virgin.com/aboutvirgin/howitallworks/, accessed October 23, 2009.
6 P. Robison, "Briton Hopes Beverage will Conquer Coke's Monopoly," *Bloomberg News,* December 14, 1997.
7 M. Wells, "Red Baron," *Fortune,* July 3, 2000.
8 R. Dick, *The House that Branson Built: Virgin's Entry into the New Millennium,* INSEAD Fontainebleau, France, 2000.
9 R. Dick, *The House that Branson Built: Virgin's Entry into the New Millennium,* INSEAD, Fontainebleau, France, 2000.
10 C. Blackhurst, "At the Court of King Richard," *Management Today,* May 1998, pp. 40–5.
11 "Consolidating and Protecting the Licensed Virgin Brand," www.cscorporatedomains.com/ downloads/ IPScan_issue1 0_virgin.pdf, accessed March 3, 2007.
12 "Will Whitehorn: Galactico of the Airways," *Independent,* November 27, 2006.

Case 21 Google Inc.: Running Amuck?

Google's announcement on July 7, 2009 that it would be adding a computer operating system to its Chrome internet browser set off shock waves through the IT community. The much-heralded battle between Google and Microsoft for dominance of cyberspace had taken a major step closer. This emerging "Battle of the Titans" was a gift for news editors. Stock analysts were less impressed; they were awaiting the announcement of Google's second quarter financial results on July 15. Their key concern was that Google's many ambitious new initiatives were adding cost and distracting management at a time when advertising revenues were being squeezed by the economic downturn. Chris O'Brien of the San Jose Mercury summed up the feelings of many in a blog entitled "Google's growing identity crisis":

> There are a handful of reasons people generally cite for Google's success. The power of its search engine algorithm. The elegance of a business model that matches text ads to searches. A restless, innovative culture continually striving to improve and evolve its products.
>
> Here's what always struck me about Google: its simplicity. At the start, Google did one thing phenomenally well. Its search engine was so superior that the company's name became synonymous with search itself. And its home page was, and remains, a visual model of simplicity: a sea of white space, the Google logo, a search box, a couple of links—and no ads.
>
> The homepage aside, though, Google increasingly feels like a company running in a thousand directions at once. Over the past year, it has released a steady stream of high-profile products that seem to have little or no relation to the core identity expressed on its corporate homepage: "Google's mission is to organize the world's information and make it universally accessible and useful." The problem is that in expanding into so many different areas—productivity applications, mobile operating system, a Web browser—that the identity of Google itself has become muddled. No doubt, this all follows some clear logic from inside the Googleplex. But from the outside, it's getting harder every day to articulate what Google is. Is it a Web company? A software company? Something else entirely?[1]

For Sergey Brin, one of Google's co-founders, the growing breadth of Google's empire was a source of pride:

> Every minute, 15 hours worth of video are uploaded to YouTube . . . Today we are able to search the full text of almost 10 million books. While digitizing all the world's books is an ambitious goal, digitizing the world is even more challenging. Beginning with our acquisition of Keyhole (the basis of Google Earth) in October 2004, it has been our goal to provide high-quality information for geographical needs . . . Last year, AdSense (our publisher-facing program) generated more than $5 billion dollars of revenue for our many publishing partners . . . In addition to Gmail and Google Docs, the Google Apps suite of products now includes Spreadsheets, Calendar, Sites, and more . . . Google Translate supports automatic machine translation between 1640 language pairs . . .[2]

The concern of many stock analysts was that most of Google's diversifying initiatives did nothing to boost revenue, let alone generate profit. The *Financial Times*' Lex column dubbed Google a "one-trick pony": "Google has what amounts to a license to print money. By inserting itself between the shops and shoppers of the world, the search provider takes a small commission every time it connects the two." Beyond its core search business, Google's activities only added cost:

> [J]ust look at YouTube, the video-sharing website Google bought for $1.8bn—paid mostly in stock—in 2006. The site supplies about 40 per cent of all videos watched online worldwide for free. That generosity comes at tremendous cost, as very few of its videos carry advertising. Credit Suisse estimates YouTube's running costs will be between $500m and $1bn this year, while revenues will only be in the region of $240m. Even with the addition of more professionally created content, the economics appear unsustainable.[3]

TABLE 21.1 Google Inc.: Key financial data

	2004	2005	2006	2007	2008
Income data:					
Revenues	3189	6139	10605	16594	21796
Costs and expenses:					
Cost of revenues	1469	2577	4225	6649	8622
Research and development	395	600	1229	2120	2793
Sales and marketing	296	468	850	1461	1946
General and administrative	188	387	752	1279	1803
Total costs and expenses	2549	4121	7055	11510	15164
Income from operations	640	2017	3550	5084	6632
Interest income and other, net	10	124	461	590	316
Income before income taxes	650	2142	4011	5674	5854
Net income	399	1465	3077	4204	4227
Balance sheet data:					
Cash and marketable securities	2132	8034	11243	14218	15845
Long-term liabilities	43	107	128,	610	1226
Total stockholders' equity	2929	9418	17039	22689	28238

Source: Google, 10-K Report, 2008.

With Google's revenue growth hit by the 2008 recession while its costs continued to rise rapidly, some investors believed that it was time to rein in Google's chaotic expansion and develop a more focused strategy founded upon a clear recognition that the basis of Google's business model was the advertising revenues that flowed through which its dominance of internet word searches. Table 21.1 shows financial data for Google.

Google's Founding

Google was created by Larry Page and Sergey Brin, PhD students at Stanford University. In January 1996, Page's search for a dissertation topic led him to examine the linkage structure of the World Wide Web. Page and Brin developed a page-ranking algorithm that used backlink data (references by a Web page to other Web pages) to measure the importance of any Web page. Although several rudimentary Web search engines were in existence, most selected Web pages on the basis of the frequency with which a particular search word appeared. They called their search engine "Google" and on September 15, 1997 registered the domain name google.com. They incorporated Google Inc., on September 7, 1998 in Menlo Park, California. Google's "PageRank" algorithm was granted a patent on September 4, 2001.

Google met an essential need of the rapidly growing number of people who were turning to the World Wide Web for information and commercial transactions. As the number·of web sites grew exponentially, locating relevant web content became a critical need. Page and Brin were not alone in recognizing the potential for a search engine. Among the early crawler-based Web search engines were WebCrawler, Lycos, Excite, Infoseek, Inktomi, Northern Light, and AltaVista. Several of these search engines became popular "portal sites"—web sites that offered users their first port of entry to the Web. Given that the primary purpose of a portal was to guide users to the information and commercial services offered by the web, other portal sites soon recognized the need to offer a search facility. Yahoo! licensed AltaVista's search engine, then in 1998 replaced AltaVista with Inktomi.

The Google search engine attracted a rapidly growing following because of its superior page ranking and its simple design—it did not compromise its search functionality by attempting to become a portal. In 2000, Google began selling advertisements—paid web links associated with search keywords. These "sponsored links" were brief, plain text ads with a click-on URL, which appeared alongside with Web search results for specific keywords. Advertisers bid for keywords; it was these "cost-per-click" bids weighted by an ad's click-through rate (CTR) that determined the order in which a sponsored links would appear. In offering a Web-based advertising system linking third-party advertisers to a search engine of informational web site, Google's system copied many of the features of the then market leader, Overture. After 2000, Google experienced explosive growth and was boosted in May 2002 by AOL's decision to adopt Google's search engine and its paid listings service.

Page and Brin's initial funding was a $100 000 contribution from Andy Bechtolsheim, co-founder of Sun Microsystems. In June 1999, larger funding was obtained from venture capital firms Kleiner Perkins Caufield & Byers and Sequoia Capital. On August 19, 2004 an initial public offering of about 7% of Google's shares raised $1.67 billion, giving Google a market capitalization of $23 billion.

Google's Expansion, 2004–9

The financial boost provided by Google's IPO fueled even more rapid development of its business. In its core Web search business, Google was continually seeking to improve users' search experiences while finding ways to better monetize its dominance of web search through advertising. However, the most striking feature of Google's development was its determination to grow beyond its core web search business. This expansionist urge reflected the company's *raison d'être*: it had never seen itself just as a supplier of an internet search engine, its declared mission was ". . . to organize the world's information and make it universally accessible and useful." Google's IPO prospectus had elaborated this intent:

> We serve our users by developing products that enable people to more quickly and easily find, create and organize information. We place a premium on products that matter to many people and have the potential to improve their lives, especially in areas in which our expertise enables us to excel.
>
> Search is one such area. People use search frequently and the results are often of great importance to them. For example, people search for information on medical conditions, purchase decisions, technical questions, long-lost friends and other topics about which they care a great deal. Delivering quality search results requires significant computing power, advanced software and complex processes—areas in which we have expertise and a high level of focus.[4]

Google's quest to meet the information needs of society caused it to continually seek opportunities for accessing new information and provide it through additional media channels. As Exhibit 21.1 shows, Google's quest to provide accessibility to the

EXHIBIT 21.2

Google Timeline

January 1996. Larry Page and Sergey Brin begin collaborating on a search engine called BackRub.

September 1998. Google Inc. establishes operations in a friend's garage in Menlo Park, California and hires its first employee.

June 1999. Google obtains $25 million in venture capital funding. Google moves to its new Googleplex headquarters in Mountain View, California.

September 1999. Google.com officially launched.

2000. Continued enhancements to Google including the Google Directory, the ability to search via wireless devices and the first 10 non-English language versions Google officially becomes the world's largest search engine. Google introduces AdWords, a self-service ad program that could be activated online. Introduction of the Google Toolbar allowing users to perform a Google search without visiting the Google homepage.

February 2001. Acquires the assets of Deja.com and begins organizing its huge Usenet archive into a searchable format.

August 2001. Dr Eric Schmidt, former CEO of Novell and CTO of Sun Microsystems, becomes CEO of Google.

September 2001. Google becomes profitable.

December 2001. Launch of Google Image Search and Google Catalog Search (allowed more than 1100 mail order catalogs to be searched). Year-end Google Zeitgeist summarizes search patterns, trends, and top search terms of 2001.

February 2002. Introduction of the Google Search Appliance allowing search to be extended beyond firewalls to company intranets, e-commerce sites, and university networks. Google Compute allows available processing on users' computers to help solve computation-intensive scientific problems.

May 2002. AOL selects Google to provide search and advertising to its 34 million members.

September 2002. Google News launched: access to 4500 leading news sources worldwide.

December 2002. Froogle, a product search service launched.

April 2003. Acquisition of Applied Semantics; launch of Google AdSense: generates revenue through placement of highly targeted ads adjacent to their content.

January 2004. Local Search allows geographically focused web search and personalized search on Google Labs, enabling users to specify their interests and customize their search results.

April 2004. Launch of Gmail, a web-based mail service. Gmail designed to deliver relevant ads adjacent to mail messages.

July 2004. Acquires Picasa, Inc., a digital photo management company that helps users to organize, manage and share their digital photos.

August 2004. Initial public offering of GOOG on NASDAQ through a Dutch auction process.

October 2004. Release of Google Desktop Search. Also Google SMS launched: instant, accurate answers to queries through text messaging, using a cell phone or handheld device. Acquisition of Keyhole Corp., a digital and satellite image mapping company.

November 2004. Google index of Web pages numbers 8 billion.

December 2004. Launch of Google Groups: allows users to create and manage their own email groups and discussion lists. Google Book Search begins scanning of books from many of the world's leading libraries.

January 2005. Launch of Google Mini, search tool for small and medium-sized businesses. Launch of Google Maps providing map views and satellite views.

June 2005. Google Labs offers Personalized Homepages. Launch of Google Earth.

August 2005. Launch of Google Talk: free internet telephony.

September 2005. Release of Google Blog Search.

October 2005. Launch of Google Reader combines blog, Web page and news sources onto a single screen.

November 2005, Launch of Google Base to upload content in a structured format that searchers can then find. Google Analytics replaces "Urchin" as an online advertising management tool.

January 2006. Google Video Store offers range of content using a new Google Video Player. Google domain in China announced.

February 2006. Google Chat: integrates email and instant messaging within a Web browser. Updated version of Google Desktop released. Google Page Creator facilitates simple design and creation of Web pages.

March 2006. Debut of Google Finance: financial and business information.

April 2006. Release of Google Calendar for easy accessing and sharing of personal calendars.

June 2006. AdWords launches click-to-play Video Ads. Launch too of Google Checkout to provide a faster, safer and more convenient online shopping. Google Maps available to businesses for embedding in their own web sites.

August 2006. Agreement with Fox to access their newly acquired MySpace. SketchUp acquired. Partners with EarthLink in a proposal for free WiFi for the city of San Francisco.

November 2006. Google Apps for Education expands offer of Google services to teachers and students. Google for Educators, a new outreach program offers elementary teachers

Google Certification through the Google Teacher Academy,

October 2006. Acquisition of YouTube. Release Web-based applications Docs and Spreadsheets. Acquisition of Jobspot, a collaborative wiki platform, which later becomes Google Sites.

December 2006. Release of Patent Search indexing more than 7 million U.S. patents.

January 2007. Partnership with China Mobile announced.

February 2007. Acquisition of Adscape, producer of in-game advertising producer.

April 2007. Acquisition of DoubleClick. Froogle changed to Google Product Search. Acquisition of Zenter, software to create and share online presentations. Acquisition of TiSP, a home broadband service.

May 2007. First steps towards universal search—integrated search of video, news, books, images and local results.

June 2007. Acquisition of Feedburner, provides tools for sitefeed management and analysis.

September 2007. AdSense for Mobile introduced. Presently, a new application for making slide presentations, added to Google Docs.

November 2007. Android, the first open platform for mobile devices, and a collaboration with other companies in the Open Handset Alliance, announced. Google.org announces REC for supporting low cost electricity from renewable sources.

January 2008. Google bids in the 700MHz spectrum auction.

February 2008. Launch of Google Sites (based upon the acquisition JotSpot), allows creation of collaborative web sites with embedded videos, documents, and calendars.

March 2008. Completion of acquisition of DoubleClick.

May 2008. Release of Google Health—allows secure online collection, storage and management of individuals' medical records and health information.

June 2008. Google Finance offers real-time stock quotes. Launch of Google Site Search—site owners can enable Google-powered searches on their own web sites.

September 2008. Announcement of Chrome, new open source web browser. T-Mobile announces the G1, the first phone built on the Android operating system.

February 2009. Google Latitude mobile devices allows sharing your location.

March 2009. Launch of Google Ventures, a venture capital fund to support innovation and new technology.

May 2009. Launch of Sky Map for Android: allows identification of stars and planets via Android phone.

world's information had taken it into new communication media (notably wireless telephony, but also radio, TV and video games) and sources of information beyond third-party web sites.[5] These new sources of information included images (Google Image Search), maps (Google Maps), academic articles (Google Scholar), books (Google Book Search), satellite imagery (Google Earth), news (Google News), patents (Google Patent Search), video (Google Video; YouTube), finance (Google Finance), and Web logs (Google Blog Search).

However, Google's entrepreneurial and technological dynamism also resulted in initiatives that extended beyond the accessing and organizing of information. Since the introduction of Gmail in 2004, Google offered a widening array of software and services for communicating, creating and manipulating 2D and 3D images, producing documents, creating Web pages, managing time and social networking. For example: Google Docs is a suite of software for creating, storing and sharing text documents, spreadsheets, and presentations; Blogger is software that allows individuals to create their own Web logs; Google Groups allows individuals to establish and support communication within a group formed around a particular interest or identity; Orkut is a social networking service; Picasa is downloadable software for organizing, editing and sharing photographs. The Appendix describes Google's products and services.

Most of these additional products and services offered no new revenue opportunities for Google. However, Google was also expanding its advertising-based revenue model. Google's primary source of advertising revenue is AdWords launched in 2000. Advertisers specify the words that should trigger their ads and the maximum amount they are willing to pay per click. When a user searches google.com, short text

TABLE 21.2 Google's revenues ($ millions)

	2006	2007	2008
Advertising Revenues			
Google web sites	6332.8	10624.7	14413.8
Google Network web sites	4159.8	5787.9	6714.7
Total advertising revenues	10492.6	16412.6	21128.5
Licensing and other revenues	112.3	181.4	667.1
Total revenues	10604.9	16594.0	21795.6

Source: Google Inc., 10-K Report 2008.

advertisements appear as "sponsored links" on the right side of the screen. AdWords also places advertisement on third party web sites through the Google Partner Network.

AdSense uses an advertisement placement technology developed by Applied Semantics which Google acquired in 2003. It allows Google to place ads on third party web sites. In 2008, 32% of Google's advertising revenue was derived from partners' web sites, and 68% from its own web sites.

The Appendix explains AdWords and AdSense in greater detail. Table 21.2 shows Google's revenues from advertising.

In 2007 and 2008, Google's diversification efforts took a dramatic new turn with Google's entry into mobile telephony and Web browsers.

Android and Mobile Telephony

In November 2007, Google, in collaboration with its partners in the Open Handset Alliance, announced its Android wireless communication software platform. *PC Advisor* commented:

> Google's announcement of the Android mobile development platform . . . is yet another example of the lengths the company will go to keep its advertising business growing at a jaw-dropping rate. It is also another awe-inspiring—or terrifying, depending on one's perspective—display of the engineering and business resources Google can unleash and of the power it has to influence, disrupt and rearrange markets . . .
>
> "What we have here is Google trying to move the whole mobile internet forward through this alliance," said industry analyst Greg Sterling of Sterling Market Intelligence.
>
> In a nutshell, Google announced a free, open-source application development platform called Android for mobile devices with the intention of eclipsing existing operating systems from Microsoft, Symbian, Palm and others . . .
>
> Android will have a complete set of components, including a Linux-based operating system, middleware stack, customizable user interface and applications.
>
> Google envisions that with Android, developers will flood the mobile market with new applications and online services that can be written once and deployed in many phones, something that, as Google sees it, the current mobile technical fragmentation prevents.
>
> The goal: to radically improve the creation, delivery and provision of mobile online services and applications, in the hope that as people find the experience more satisfying, their mobile web and internet usage will balloon, along with online ad revenue . . .
>
> Ultimately, what is propelling Google in this effort is its core advertising business, which the company recognizes it must extend to the mobile market. A small market today, mobile advertising is expected to attain a significant size in coming years. According to Opus Research, mobile advertising spending in North America and Western Europe will reach a combined $5.08bn by 2012, up from an estimated $106.8m at the end of this year. This represents a compound annual growth rate of 116%. Opus Research, which released the forecast last week, said that improving the mobile user experience will prompt more people to spend more time using the internet via their mobile phones. This in turn will fuel ad revenue growth.

In the end, independently of what ends up happening, Google's entry into the mobile market is a welcome development, Dulaney said. "We need powerful players from the 'wired' internet market to get into the mobile space to break up the tight control carriers have had on content," Dulaney said. "So far, carriers have controlled all the content and they've been bad at it. Innovation has been stifled."[6]

A few weeks later Google announced its intention of bidding in the Federal Communication Commission's upcoming auction of 700MHz wireless spectrum. The interesting feature of Google's bid was that it had no desire to win the auction. Its intention was to force the major telecom service providers into the auction so that a new section of the wireless spectrum would be developed for the wireless internet service. Google lobbying had already ensured that whoever developed this portion of spectrum would be required to allow users to download any software application they wanted on their mobile device and to use any mobile devices they liked on that wireless network. In January 2008, the FCC announced that AT&T and Verizon had won the auction bidding a total of $16 billion. Many observers believed that the real winner was Google: while AT&T and Verizon would bear the costs of developing the 700MHz waveband, Google would be able to offer its Android system and mobile internet services without any of the upfront costs.[7]

Chrome

Google's announcement of its Chrome Web browser on September 2, 2008, generated huge publicity, but little surprise. It was widely known that founders Brin and Page had wanted to launch a Web browser since Google's early days. For several years Google had been the main source of technical and financial support for Mozilla's Firefox browser. According to the Google's head of product development, Sundar Pichai: "Google's entire business is people using a browser to access us and the web." Google's explanation of its decision to launch its own browser emphasized the improved functionality for users: "Google Chrome is a browser that combines a minimal design with sophisticated technology to make the web faster, safer, and easier," claimed Google's web site. Microsoft's internet Explorer by contrast was limited by the legacy of its 15 year history, which meant that it was optimized for JavaScript or Web 2.0.

However, most observers believed that Google's strategic intent was not simply a superior user experience. An additional motive imputed to Google was its desire to protect the threat posed by the new version of Microsoft's internet Explorer (IE). Version 8 of IE launched in beta mode in August 2008 allowed an "InPrivate" protection mode that would delete cookies and make it more difficult to track users' browsing habits. The result would be to limit Google's ability to use such information for targeted advertising.

Others believed that Google's primary intention was not so much to protect itself against Microsoft as to launch a direct attack upon Microsoft's dominance of personal computing and to speed the transition of computing to a new online environment:

[Google Chrome] is an explicit attempt to accelerate the movement of computing off the desktop and into the cloud—where Google holds advantage.

And it's an aggressive move destined to put the company even more squarely in the crosshairs of its rival Microsoft.[8]

The announcement 10 months later that Google would add an operating system to its Chrome browser was seen as confirmation that the primary motivation of Chrome was to strike against the core of Microsoft's market strength.

Google's Management and Capabilities

Google's phenomenal growth and capacity for innovation rested upon a management system that was unique, even by the unorthodox standards of Silicon Valley. In his book, *The Future of Management*, Gary Hamel identified several key features of the management system built by founders Larry Page (President of Products) and Sergey Brin (President of Technology), and their "adult supervisor" Eric Schmidt (Chairman and CEO):

1. Hiring policy. Google only employs people who it believes to be exceptionally talented: "Google's leaders believe that one exceptional technologist is many times more valuable than one average engineer; hence they insist on hiring only the brightest of the bright—folks out on the right-hand end of the bell-shaped curve. They also believe that if you let one 'bozo' in, more will surely follow. Their logic is simple: A-level people want to work with A-level people—fellow savants who will spark their thinking and accelerate their learning. Trouble is, B-level people are threatened by A-class talent, so once they get in the door, they tend to hire colleagues who are as unremarkable as they are."

2. A "dramatically flat, radically decentralized" organization: "In many ways, Google is organized like the internet itself: it's highly democratic, tightly connected, and flat. Like so much of Google's culture, the source of the company's radical decentralization can be traced back to Brin and Page, both of whom attended Montessori schools and credit much of their intellectual independence to that experience. Says Mayer: 'They don't like authority and they don't like being told what to do.' Brin and Page understand that breakthroughs come from questioning assumptions and smashing paradigms."

3. Small, self-managing teams: "Roughly half of Google's 10 000 employees—all those involved in product development—work in small teams, with an average of three engineers per team. Even a large project such as Gmail, which might occupy 30 people, is broken into teams of three or four, each of which works on a specific service enhancement, such as building spam filters or improving the forwarding feature. Each team has an 'über-tech leader,' a responsibility that rotates among team members depending on shifting project requirements. Most engineers work on more than one team, and no one needs the HR department's permission to switch teams."

4. Rapid, low-cost experimentation. "Evolutionary adaptation isn't the product of a grand plan, but of relentless experimentation . . . Google's 'just-try-it' philosophy is applied to even the company's most daunting projects, like digitizing the world's libraries. Like every new initiative, Google Book Search began with a makeshift experiment aimed at answering a critical question; in this case: how long does it take to digitize a book? To find out, Page and Mayer rigged up a piece of plywood with a couple of clamps and proceeded to photograph each page of a 300-page book, using a metronome to keep pace. With Mayer flipping pages, and one half of Google's founding team taking digital snapshots, it took 40 minutes to turn the ink into pixels. An optical character recognition program soon turned the digital photos into digital text, and within five days the pair had ginned up a piece of software that could search the book. That kind of step-wise, learn-as-you-go approach has repeatedly helped Google to test critical assumptions and avoid making bet-the-farm mistakes."[9]

The result was a constant impetus towards creativity, innovation, and entrepreneurial initiative. Indeed, given the caliber and characteristics of Google's employees, it was difficult to see how Google could not be a hotbed for innovation:

> Our employees, who have named themselves Googlers, are everything. Google is organized around the ability to attract and leverage the talent of exceptional technologists and business people. We have been lucky to recruit many creative, principled and hard working stars. We hope to recruit many more in the future. We will reward and treat them well . . . Because of our employee talent, Google is doing exciting work in nearly every area of computer science . . . Talented people are attracted to Google because we empower them to change the world; Google has large computational resources and distribution that enables individuals to make a difference. Our main benefit is a workplace with important projects, where employees can contribute and grow . . . [10]

The culture of creativity and innovation was institutionalized through Google's "70-20-10" rule which stipulated that Google would devote 70% of its engineering resources to developing the core business, 20% to extend that core into related areas, with 10% allocated to fringe ideas.

Underlying Google's capacity for innovation and the effective implementation of new initiatives was a set of resources that few other technology-based companies could match. With an operating cash flow of $7.9 billion in 2008 and a cash pile of $15.8 billion, Google was a financial powerhouse matched only by Microsoft, IBM, HP, and Apple. This financial strength allowed Google to buy its way through acquisition into almost any market or area of technology. Most of the time Google did not need buy its way into new market: like Apple, its brand (valued by Interbrand in 2008 at $25 billion—the world's tenth most valuable) offered it instant credibility. Most important was a user base unmatched by any other IT company. With 776 million unique visitors to its web site every day, it reached an estimated 77% of the world's internet audience daily.

Future Challenges

For all Google's vitality and its manifest destiny to lead the next generation of information technology, there were those—both within Googleplex and outside—who perceived danger in Google's trajectory. Despite a slowing during 2008, Google was expanding rapidly. Between 2003 and 2007 its revenues had grown from $1.5 billion to $21.8 billion and employees from 1628 to 20 222.[11] Coordination was a growing problem; while the majority of Google's employees were concentrated at its Mountain View, California, headquarters, Google had additional research and development and sales and support offices in 18 other cities throughout the U.S., as well as facilities in Argentina, Austria, Australia, Belgium, Brazil, Canada, China, Czech Republic, Denmark, Egypt, England, Finland, France, Germany, Hungary, India, Ireland, Israel, Italy, Japan, Korea, Mexico, New Zealand, Norway, Poland, Russia, Singapore, Spain, Sweden, Switzerland, Taiwan, Turkey and United Arab Emirates.[12]

Growing size and complexity were recognized by Google as significant sources of risk:

> We have experienced rapid growth in our headcount and operations, which has placed, and will continue to place, significant demands on our management, operational and financial infrastructure. If we do not effectively manage our growth, the quality of our products and services could suffer, which could negatively affect our brand and operating results. Our expansion and growth in international markets heightens these risks as a result of the particular challenges of supporting a rapidly growing business in an environment of multiple languages, cultures, customs, legal systems, alternative dispute systems, regulatory systems and commercial infrastructures. To effectively manage this growth, we will need to continue to improve our operational, financial and management controls and our reporting systems and procedures.[13]

As Google increasingly displaced Microsoft as the world's pre-eminent IT company, it would be a target for criticism and regulatory pressures. Under the headline "Is Google Too Powerful?," the potential for Google to dominate the Web and media advertising was noted by *Business Week* early in 2007:

> . . . Google has come to represent all our hopes, dreams, and fears about the disruptive promise and dangers of the internet. As this clash plays out over the next couple of years, the outcome could determine the way we'll entertain ourselves, shop, socialize, and do business on the internet. The overriding question: Will the vast commercial landscape of the Net, like so many other tech markets in the past, condense to one dominant force for the foreseeable future? Will we just Google everything?[14]

By 2009, the dominant concern was less about market power in a traditional sense and more about the sheer mass of personal data that Google had access to. Google's cookies allow it to track every Google user's web browsing. Its online map service, "Street View," allows views inside individuals' home properties and the observation of visitors to those homes. Gmail allows Google an intimate view of personal communications of Gmail's 30 million account holders.

These growing concerns about privacy and market power would impose additional pressures on Google's top management team. Had the time come for Google's leading trio—Brin, Page, and Schmidt—to scale back Google's ambitions and draw boundaries around Google's corporate strategy?

Appendix: Description of Google's business and products (extracts from Google, 10-K Report for 2008)

Overview

Google is a global technology leader focused on improving the ways people connect with information. Our innovations in web search and advertising have made our web site a top internet property and our brand one of the most recognized in the world. We maintain a large index of web sites and other online content, which we make freely available via our search engine to anyone with an internet connection. Our automated search technology helps people obtain nearly instant access to relevant information from our vast online index.

We generate revenue primarily by delivering relevant, cost-effective online advertising. Businesses use our AdWords program to promote their products and services with targeted advertising. In addition, the thousands of third-party web sites that comprise the Google Network use our AdSense program to deliver relevant ads that generate revenue and enhance the user experience . . .

Our Mission

Our mission is to organize the world's information and make it universally accessible and useful. We believe that the most effective, and ultimately the most profitable, way to accomplish our mission is to put the needs of our users first. We have found that offering a high-quality user experience leads to increased traffic and strong word-of-mouth promotion. Our dedication to putting users first is reflected in three key commitments:

- We will do our best to provide the most relevant and useful search results possible, independent of financial incentives. Our search results will be objective and we do not accept payment for search result ranking or inclusion.

- We will do our best to provide the most relevant and useful advertising. Advertisements should not be an annoying interruption. If any element on a search result page is influenced by payment to us, we will make it clear to our users.

- We will never stop working to improve our user experience, our search technology and other important areas of information organization.

We believe that our user focus is the foundation of our success to date. We also believe that this focus is critical for the creation of long-term value. We do not intend to compromise our user focus for short-term economic gain.

How We Provide Value to Our Users

We serve our users by developing products that quickly and easily find, create, organize and share information. We place a premium on products that matter to many people and have the potential to improve their lives.

Some of the key benefits we offer include:

Comprehensiveness and Relevance Our search technologies sort through a vast and growing amount of information to deliver relevant and useful search results in response to user queries. This is an area of continual development for us. When we started the company in 1998, our Web index contained approximately 30 million documents. We now index billions of Web pages and strive to provide the most comprehensive search experience possible . . .

Objectivity We believe it is very important that the results users get from Google are produced with only their interests in mind. We do not accept payment for search result ranking or inclusion. We do accept fees for advertising, but the advertising is clearly marked and separated and does not influence how we generate our search results. This is similar to a newspaper, where the articles are independent of the advertising . . .

Global Access We strive to provide our services to everyone in the world and the Google interface is available in 120 languages . . .

Ease of Use We have always believed that the most useful and powerful search technology hides its complexity from users and gives them a simple, intuitive way to get the information they want. We have devoted significant efforts to create a streamlined and easy-to-use interface based on a clean search box set prominently on a page free of commercial clutter . . .

Pertinent, Useful Commercial Information The search for information often involves an interest in commercial information—researching a purchase, comparing products and services or actively shopping. We help people find commercial information through our search services and advertising products . . .

Multiple Access Platforms The mobile phone is the primary way that many people around the world access the internet. We have continued to invest in improving mobile search and have introduced applications that allow users to access search, email, maps, directions and satellite imagery through their mobile devices.

Improving the Web We want to make the Web experience as good as possible for users around the world. This includes providing platforms for developers to build, deploy and run increasingly rich applications. For users, we are investing in areas to improve their experience in using web-based applications, including making browsers more stable and powerful.

Products and Services for our Users

Our product development philosophy involves rapid and continuous innovation, with frequent releases of early-stage products that we then iterate and improve. We often make products available early in their development stages by posting them on Google Labs, at test locations online or directly on Google.com. If our users find a product useful, we promote it to "beta" status for additional testing. Once we are satisfied that a product is of high quality and utility, we remove the beta label and make it a core Google product. Our main products and services are described below:

Google.com—Search and Personalization We are focused on building products and services on our web sites that benefit our users and let them find relevant information quickly and easily. These products and services include:

Google Web Search In addition to providing easy access to billions of Web pages, we have integrated special features into Google Web Search to help people find exactly what they are looking for on the Web.

Google Image Search Google Image Search is our searchable index of images found across the web. To extend the usefulness of Google Image Search we offer advanced features, such as searching by image size, format and coloration and restricting searches to specific web sites or domains.

Google Book Search Google Book Search lets users search the full text of a library-sized collection of books to discover books of interest and to learn where to buy or borrow them . . .

Google Scholar Google Scholar provides a simple way to do a broad search for relevant scholarly literature including peer-reviewed papers, theses, books, abstracts and articles . . .

Google Finance Google Finance provides a simple user interface to navigate complex financial information in an intuitive manner . . .

Google News Google News gathers information from thousands of news sources worldwide and presents news stories in a searchable format within minutes of their publication on the Web . . .

Google Video Google Video lets users upload, find, view and share video content worldwide.

Google Blog Search Google Blog Search enables users to search the blogging universe more effectively and find out users' opinions on a wide variety of subjects. The Google Blog Search index includes every blog that publishes a site feed.

iGoogle and Personalized Search iGoogle connects users to the information that is most useful and important to them in an easy-to-use and customizable format . . .

Google Product Search Google Product Search helps users find and compare products from online stores across the web and directs users to where they can buy these products . . .

Google Custom Search Google Custom Search allows communities of users familiar with particular topics to build customized search engines . . .

Google Base Google Base lets content owners submit content that they want to share on Google web sites . . .

Google Webmaster Tools Google Webmaster Tools provides information to webmasters to help them enhance their understanding of how their web sites interact with the Google search engine . . .

Applications

Information created by a single user becomes much more valuable when shared and combined with information from other people or places. Therefore our strategy for products we develop in this space is simple: develop tools for our users to create, share and communicate any information generated by the user, thus making the information more useful and manageable. Examples of products we have developed with this strategy in mind include:

Google Docs
Google Docs allows our users to create, view and edit documents, spreadsheets, and presentations from anywhere using a browser . . .

Google Calendar
Google Calendar is a free online shareable calendar service that allows our users to keep track of the important events, appointments and special occasions in their lives and share this information with anyone they choose . . .

Gmail
Gmail is Google's free webmail service that comes with built-in Google search technology . . . We serve small text ads that are relevant to the messages in Gmail.

Google Groups
Google Groups is a free service that helps groups of people to connect to information and people that have interest in them. Users can discuss topics by posting messages to a group, where other people can then read and respond . . .

Google Reader
Google Reader is a free service that lets users subscribe to feeds and receive updates from multiple web sites in a single interface . . .

Orkut
Orkut enables users to search and connect to other users through networks of trusted friends. Users can create a profile, personal mailboxes, post photos and join or manage online communities.

Blogger
Blogger is a Web-based publishing tool that lets people publish to the Web instantly using weblogs, or "blogs."

Google Sites
Google Sites allows users to easily create, update and publish content online . . .

YouTube
YouTube is an online community that lets users worldwide upload, share, watch, rate, and comment on videos, from user generated, niche professional, to premium videos . . . YouTube offers a range of video and interactive formats for advertisers to reach their intended audience.

Client

Google Toolbar
Google Toolbar is a free application that adds a Google search box to web browsers (internet Explorer and Firefox) . . .

Google Chrome
Google Chrome is an open-source browser that combines a minimal design with technologies to make the web faster, safer, and easier to navigate.

Google Pack
Google Pack is a free collection of safe, useful software programs from Google and other companies that improve the user experience online and on the desktop . . .

Picasa
Picasa is a free service that allows users to view, manage and share their photos . . .

Google Desktop
Google Desktop lets people perform a full-text search on the contents of their own computer, including email, files, instant messenger chats and web browser history . . .

Google GEO—Maps, Earth and Local

Google Earth
Google Earth lets users see and explore the world and beyond from their desktop. Users can fly virtually to a specific location and learn about that area through detailed satellite and aerial images . . .

Google Maps
Google Maps helps people navigate map information . . .

Google Sketchup and Sketchup Pro
Google Sketchup is a free tool that enables users to model buildings in 3D . . . The Pro version of this tool is sold to professional designers and includes additional features.

Google Mobile and Android

Google Mobile
Google Mobile lets people search and view both the "mobile Web," consisting of pages created specifically for wireless devices, and the entire Google index. Users can

also access online information using Google SMS by typing a query to the Google shortcode and checking their email using Gmail Mobile. Google Mobile is available through many wireless and mobile phone services worldwide.

Google Maps for Mobile

Google Maps for Mobile is a free Java client application that lets users view maps and satellite imagery, find local businesses and get driving directions on mobile devices.

Blogger for Mobile

With Blogger for mobile devices, users can take pictures with their camera phones and then post their pictures and text comments to their blog using MMS or email.

Google Gmail, News and Personalized Home for Mobile

Several of our services, such as Gmail, News and Personalized Home are also available as mobile applications.

GOOG-411

GOOG-411 is a free, speech-enabled application allowing users to call 1-800-GOOG-411 to search for businesses by name or category.

Android

Android is a free, open-source mobile software platform which allows developers to create applications for mobile devices and for handset manufacturers to install . . .

Search by Voice

Search by Voice lets users do a Google Web search just by saying what they are looking for . . .

Google Checkout

Google Checkout is a service for our users, advertisers and participating merchants that is intended to make online shopping faster, more convenient and more secure . . .

Google Labs

Google Labs is our test bed for our engineers and adventurous Google users . . .

The Technology Behind Search and Our User Products and Services

Our Web search technology uses a combination of techniques to determine the importance of a Web page independent of a particular search query and to determine the relevance of that page to a particular search query.

Ranking Technology

. . . PageRank is a query-independent technique for determining the importance of web pages by looking at the link structure of the Web.

Text-Matching Techniques

Our technology employs text-matching techniques that compare search queries with the content of web pages to help determine relevance . . . By combining query independent measures such as PageRank with our text-matching techniques, we are able to deliver search results that are relevant to what people are trying to find.

Infrastructure

We provide our products and services using our homegrown software and hardware infrastructure, which provides substantial computing resources at low cost. We currently use a combination of off-the-shelf and custom software running on clusters of commodity computers . . .

How We Provide Value to Our Advertisers and Content Owners

Google AdWords

For advertisers seeking to market their products and services to consumers and business users over the internet, we offer Google AdWords, an auction-based advertising program that lets advertisers deliver relevant ads targeted to search queries or Web content across Google sites and through the web sites of our Google network, which is the network of online and offline third parties that use our advertising programs to deliver relevant ads with their search results and content . . . AdWords is accessible to advertisers in 41 different interface languages.

Advertisers in our AdWords program create text-based or display ads, bid on the keywords that will trigger the display of their ads and set daily spending budgets. AdWords features an automated online signup process that lets advertisers quickly implement ad campaigns on Google properties and the web sites of our Google Network members. Ads are ranked for display in AdWords based on a combination of the maximum cost-per-click pricing set by the advertiser and click-through rates and other factors used to determine the relevance of the ads. This favors the ads that are most relevant to users, improving the experience both for the person looking for information and for the advertiser who is generating relevant ads . . .

Google AdSense We are enthusiastic about helping content owners monetize their content, which facilitates the creation of better content to search . . . Our Google AdSense program enables web sites that are part of the Google Network to deliver AdWords ads that are relevant to the search results or content on their pages. It also allows offline media companies, such as television and radio stations, to deliver ads and audio ads to the content they provide. We share most of the revenue generated from ads shown by a Google Network member with that member. The key benefits we offer to Google Network members include:

Access to Advertisers Many small web-site companies and content producers do not have the time or resources to develop effective programs for generating revenue from online advertising. Even larger sites, with dedicated sales teams, may find it difficult to generate revenue from pages with specialized content. Google AdSense promotes effective revenue generation by providing Google

Network members access to Google's base of advertisers and their broad collection of ads . . .

Improved User Satisfaction Many web sites are cluttered with intrusive or untargeted advertising that may distract or confuse users and may undermine users' ability to find the information they want . . . Our AdSense program extends our commitment to improving the overall Web experience by enabling web sites to display AdWords ads in a fashion that we believe people find useful rather than disruptive.

Better Storage, Management, Access and Visibility We have developed new storage, management and access technologies to allow content owners and producers to distribute and, if they wish, monetize more types of online and offline content . . .

Syndicated Search We provide our search technology to partners of all sizes, allowing Google search service to be offered through these partners' properties. For commercial partners, we provide an extensive range of customization options.

Display Advertising

Display advertising is internet advertising that typically includes static or animated images as well as interactive audio or video media, such as the banner ads you see on the tops or sides of many popular web sites. Our goal is to make it easy for anyone to use display advertising. We want advertisers to realize a better return on their display advertising campaigns and publishers to maximize the value of the content on their web sites by providing tools, platforms and channels for ad management and delivery.

We completed our acquisition of DoubleClick in March 2008 and are in the process of integrating DoubleClick's online ad serving and management services into Google's advertising solutions. DoubleClick provides Google with a platform for delivering display advertising. DoubleClick also provides services related to the delivery of display advertising, including media planning, buying, implementation and measurement tools for advertisers and agencies and forecasting and reporting tools for publishers. Through these tools we also provide publishers with access to agencies and advertisers to help them sell their advertising inventory and ways to streamline the ad sales process.

We also offer advertising solutions on YouTube in a range of video, static or animated images, and interactive formats.

The Technology Behind Google's Advertising Programs

Our AdWords and AdSense programs serve millions of relevant, targeted ads each day based on search terms people enter or content that they view on the Web. The key elements of our advertising technology include:

Google AdWords Auction System

The Google AdWords auction system lets advertisers automatically deliver relevant, targeted advertising. Every search query we process involves the automated execution of an auction, resulting in our advertising system often processing hundreds of millions of auctions per day. To determine whether an ad is relevant to a particular query, this system weighs an advertiser's willingness to pay for prominence in the ad listings (the cost-per-click or cost-per-impression bid) and interest from users in the ad as measured by the click-through rate and other factors . . . The AdWords auction system also incorporates the AdWords Discounter, which automatically lowers the amount advertisers actually pay to the minimum needed to maintain their ad position . . .

AdSense Contextual Advertising Technology

Our AdSense technology employs techniques that consider factors such as keyword analysis, word frequency and the overall link structure of the web to analyze the content of individual web pages and to match ads to them almost instantaneously . . . Our display advertising programs provide advertisers and publishers services related to the delivery of branded display advertising. The key elements of our display advertising technology include:

DoubleClick Advertiser Platform

The DoubleClick Advertiser Platform provides tools for media planning, buying, selling, ad delivery, measurement, and optimization . . .

YouTube

YouTube offers video ads solutions to advertisers that provide advertisers with a way to promote their content to the YouTube community as well as to associate themselves with content being watched by their target audience . . .

Google Enterprise

Schools and businesses are increasingly moving towards Web-based applications and away from licensed software. Since Web-based applications require minimal up-front investment, businesses can pay as they use them and download updates.

Google Apps

Google Apps provides hosted communication and collaboration tools for organizations such as businesses, schools and groups. Google Apps includes communication features such as Gmail, Google Calendar, Google Video, Google Sites, and Google Talk and collaboration features such as Google Docs. It is available on an organization's own domain . . .

Google Mini

The Google Mini is targeted at small-and medium-sized businesses who want to let employees and customers search designated documents, intranets and web sites.

Google Search Appliance

The Google Search Appliance is similar to the Google Mini except that it can handle more documents and offers more advanced features. Some advanced features of the Google Search Appliance include integration with advanced corporate security protocols, integration with other enterprise applications, such as content management systems, portals and other systems and real-time search of business applications . . .

Notes

1 "Google's Growing Identity Crisis": Chris O'Brien's blog, July19, 2009, www.mercurynews.com/ci_ 12853656?IADID, accessed July 20, 2009.

2 Quoted in D. Rowan, "Inside Google: The Man with All the Answers," *Wired*, August 2009, p. 77.

3 "Lex: Google the One-trick Pony," *Financial Times*, April 17, 2009.

4 Google Inc. SEC form 424B3, filed November 23, 2004.

5 At the March 2008 Federal Communications Commission's auctioning of licenses to "C-block" spectrum, Google was one of the bidders. Google was delighted to lose out to winning bids to AT&T and Verizon that together amounted to over $18 billion because the FCC had decreed that the new spectrum owners would be required to open their networks to third-party providers. Hence, Google would be free to offer its wireless service without the need to invest in infrastructure. See: "An Auction that Google was Content to Lose," *New York Times*, April 4, 2008, www.nytimes.com/2008/04/04/technology/04auction.html?_r=1&oref=slogin, accessed October 23, 2009.

6 "Analysis: Google's Android Mobile Strategy Explained," *PCAdvisor*, November 6, 2007, www.pcadvisor.co.uk/news/index.cfm?newsid=11248, accessed July 21, 2009.

7 "Wireless Auction: Google Likely Out, and Happy," *Forbes*, February 6, 2008.

8 "Inside Chrome: The Secret Project to Crush IE and Remake the Web," *Wired Magazine*, October 16, 2008.

9 G. Hamel, *The Future of Management*, Harvard Business School Press, Boston MA, 2007.

10 Letter from the Founders, "An Owner's Manual" for Google's Shareholders, http://investor.google.com/ipo_letter.html, accessed 30 March, 2008.

11 These consisted of 7254 in R&D, 8002 in sales and marketing, 3109 in general and administrative and 1857 in operations.

12 Google Inc., 10-K Report to the SEC for 2007, p. 33.

13 Google Inc., 10-K Report to the SEC for 2008, p. 20.

14 "Is Google Too Powerful?" *Business Week*, April 9, 2007.

Case 22 Bank of America's Acquisition of Merrill Lynch

December 2008

On the afternoon of Monday December 22, 2008, Ken Lewis, Chairman and CEO of Bank of America Corporation, was preparing for a special meeting of Bank of America's board of directors, which would be held by telephone at 4 p.m.

The meeting was critical to the future of Bank of America and to the future careers of Lewis and his top management team. The meeting offered the board its final opportunity to pull the plug on its acquisition of Merrill Lynch & Company, which was to be consummated in ten days' time (January 1, 2009).

The acquisition, announced on September 15, 2008 (see Exhibit 22.1 for the press release), would create America's biggest financial services company in terms of total assets. It was the culmination of a quarter of a century of almost continuous acquisition by the Charlotte, North Carolina, banking corporation. Under Hugh McColl, its CEO from 1983 to 2001, North Carolina National Bank first became NationsBank, then, after its 1998 acquisition of San Francisco-based BancAmerica, it changed its name to Bank of America Corporation. Table 22.1 shows Bank of America's principal acquisitions.

Despite the size of the acquisition, it was not the result of careful strategic planning. The merger announcement came the same day that Lehman Brothers filed for Chapter 11 bankruptcy protection amidst growing fears that the global financial system was going into meltdown. Anticipating that Merrill Lynch might be the next major financial institution to fail, the acquisition was hastily brokered by Federal Reserve Board chairman Ben Bernanke and U.S. Treasury Secretary, Hank Paulson. Announcing the merger, Bank of America's Chairman and CEO, Ken Lewis, stated: "The fact that we

---

EXHIBIT 22.1

Press Release: Bank of America Buys Merrill Lynch Creating Unique Financial Services Firm

CHARLOTTE (September 15, 2008)—Bank of America Corporation today announced it has agreed to acquire Merrill Lynch & Co., Inc. in a $50 billion all-stock transaction that creates a company unrivalled in its breadth of financial services and global reach. "Acquiring one of the premier wealth management, capital markets, and advisory companies is a great opportunity for our shareholders," Bank of America Chairman and Chief Executive Officer Ken Lewis said. "Together, our companies are more valuable because of the synergies in our businesses." "Merrill Lynch is a great global franchise and I look forward to working with Ken Lewis and our senior management teams to create what will be the leading financial institution in the world with the combination of these two firms," said John Thain, chairman and CEO of Merrill Lynch.

Under the terms of the transaction, Bank of America would exchange 0.8595 shares of Bank of America common stock for each Merrill Lynch common share. The price is 1.8 times the stated tangible book value. Bank of America expects to

achieve $7 billion in pretax expense savings, fully realized by 2012. The acquisition is expected to be accretive to earnings by 2010. The transaction is expected to close in the first quarter of 2009. It has been approved by directors of both companies and is subject to shareholder votes at both companies and standard regulatory approvals. Under the agreement, three directors of Merrill Lynch will join the Bank of America Board of Directors.

The combined company would have leadership positions in retail brokerage and wealth management. By adding Merrill Lynch's more than 16 000 financial advisers, Bank of America would have the largest brokerage in the world with more than 20 000 advisers and $2.5 trillion in client assets. The combination brings global scale in investment management, including an approximately 50% ownership in BlackRock, which has $1.4 trillion in assets under management. Bank of America has $589 billion in assets under management. Adding Merrill Lynch both enhances current strengths at Bank of America and creates new ones, particularly outside of the United States. Merrill Lynch adds strengths in global debt underwriting, global equities and global merger and acquisition advice. After the acquisition, Bank of America would be the number one underwriter of global high yield debt, the third largest underwriter of global equity and the ninth largest adviser on global mergers and acquisitions based on *pro forma* first half of 2008 results.

Source: http://newsroom.bankofamerica.com/index.php?s= 43&item=8255, accessed August 13, 2009.

could put this transaction together in less than 48 hours is a great statement on the strength of both our teams, but also on the great strategic fit which, from the instant that we talked about it, became clear that this transaction would make a lot of sense."

Others were less convinced that the transaction made sense. The biggest concern was that Bank of America was overpaying. The *Financial Times*' Lex column commented:

Even if Merrill is being taken out at a third of its 52-week high, it is, in the circumstances, hardly a steal at 1.8 times tangible book value and 12 times 2009 earnings. Mr. Thain's willingness to accept market realities has enabled Merrill shareholders to escape a total wipe-out. As Jamie Dimon noted after acquiring Bear Stearns, there is a difference between buying a house and buying a house that's on fire. While flames are licking at Merrill's outhouses, Mr. Thain has persuaded BofA's Ken Lewis there is still plenty of time to douse them. But until Mr. Lewis can prove that Merrill has suffered only cosmetic damage, he will struggle to get investors excited about promised savings worth $7bn or 10% of the cost base. BofA's shares fell 15%, destroying $23bn of value.

TABLE 22.1 Bank of America's growth by acquisition

Year	Company acquired	Notes
1960	Security National Back of Greensboro merges American Commercial Bank of Charlotte	Merged bank names North Caroline National Bank (NCNB)
1982	First National Bank of Lake City (Florida)	First out-of-state acquisition by NCNB
1991	C&S/Sovren of Atlanta	NCNB changes its name to NationsBank
1993	MNC Financial of Maryland	
1998	BancAmerica Corporation of San Francisco	NationsBank renames as Bank of America
2004	Fleet Boston Financial Corporation	Expands into Northeast
2006	MBNA	Bank of America becomes largest U.S. credit-card issuer
2007	U.S. Trust	Bank of America establishes leading position in private banking for wealthy individuals
2007	ABN AMBRO North America	Principal subsidiary is La Salle Bank Corporation
2008	Countrywide Financial	Bank of America becomes largest mortgage lender in U.S.
2008	Merrill Lynch & Company, Inc.	September 15 bid to take effect January 1, 2009

If the deal proceeds to plan, BofA would secure the Merrill brand and the largest retail broker network in the U.S., with a 17 000-strong herd of financial advisers as well as a leading investment bank and wealth management franchise. There are, though, two big dangers. First, much of the risk Merrill has "offloaded" in its vendor-financed sale of toxic securities could come back to haunt its new owner. Second, a culture war between two workforces remunerated according to different pay systems seems unavoidable.[1]

During the final quarter of 2008, pessimism about the merger continued to grow—Bank of America's share price declined from $29.55 on September 16, 2008 to $13.53 on December 22. The critical concern was Merrill's balance sheet. On October 16, Merrill reported a third-quarter loss of $5.1 billion resulting mostly from a writedown in the value of its CDOs (collateralized debt securities and real-estate related assets).

By mid-December it was becoming clear that Merrill's fourth-quarter results would be even worse that the dreadful third-quarter figures. On December 14, 2008, Bank of America's Chief Financial Officer, Joe Price, advised Ken Lewis, Bank of America's CEO, that Merrill Lynch's financial condition was deteriorating. During the previous week Merrill Lynch's projected fourth-quarter losses had risen from $9 billion to $12 billion.

These revelations about the full horrors of Merrill's financial position removed any lingering doubts over whether Bank of America had overpaid for Merrill: current losses and future write downs probably meant that Merrill Lynch was worth absolutely nothing. The issue for Lewis and the board was whether to invoke the "MAC clause" in the merger agreement, which allowed the merger to be called off in the event of a "materially adverse event" occurring.

There followed a flurry of communications between Lewis, Federal Reserve Chairman Bernanke and Secretary Paulson and officials of the U.S. Treasury. After informing them of Bank of America's desire to exit the merger, Lewis became a target of sustained pressure from the Department of the Treasury in particular.

Secretary Paulson reminded Lewis of the risks to the entire U.S. financial system that would result from Bank of America's rescinding the merger agreement—risks that would inevitably have a major impact upon Bank of America itself. Paulson also indicated that, should Bank of America invoke the MAC clause, the U.S. government would seek the removal of Bank of America's board and top management team. However, if Bank of America went ahead with the merger, the Treasury and Federal Reserve System would provide whatever assistance was needed by Bank of America to restore its capital and to protect it against the adverse impact of "toxic" Merrill Lynch assets.[2]

As Lewis got ready to speak to his fellow board members, he realized that he was faced with the most difficult decision of his entire career. If Bank of America went ahead with the merger, Merrill's appalling financial situation would be a major drag on Bank of America's performance, would depress its share price and would undoubtedly anger shareholders. However, beyond the short term—probably the next two to three years—he believed that shareholders would reap considerable long-run benefit from the strategic advantages of the new global colossus. Rescinding the deal would free Bank of America from Merrill Lynch's acute financial problems—but the implications were troubling. It would postpone—possibly forever—Lewis's desire to create the world's pre-eminent universal bank. Even more serious, it might be the trigger for the financial calamity that President Bush had forewarned in his recognition that: "This sucker might go down!" The implications for Bank of America, especially if Paulson made good on his threat to remove Bank of America's board, were hardly appealing.

The potential conflict between Lewis's moral obligations to his shareholders and to his country was further complicated by his legal duties. As chairman and CEO, Lewis was required to inform shareholders of company matters relevant to their interests. Although shareholders had on December 5 approved the acquisition of Merrill Lynch, this was without the new projections of Merrill's fourth-quarter losses. When Lewis had raised issues of disclosure with Bernanke and Paulson he had been given the opinion that such disclosure would not be conducive to the stability of the U.S. financial system.[3]

The Strategic Issues Arising from the Merger

The strategic arguments in favor of the merger were outlined in a joint press conference by the two CEOs—Ken Lewis and John Thain—made on September 15, 2008. Lewis saw Merrill Lynch as adding critical strengths to Bank of America in relation to both individual financial services and corporate financial services. Figure 22.1 shows two slides from their presentation.

In terms of individual financial services, Merrill Lynch's U.S.-wide network of local offices and its army of financial advisers would represent a massive extension of Bank of America's existing brokerage and wealth-management services. In addition, Bank of America anticipated that the combination of the largest U.S. wealth-management organization with one of America's biggest retail banks with presence in 31 states would offer considerable opportunity for offering a wider range of financial services to the clients of each.

Merrill Lynch's much bigger presence outside of the U.S. would also offer Bank of America the opportunity to build a truly international wealth-management business.

In terms of Bank of America's corporate and investment banking, the merger would transform Bank of America from a provider of corporate banking services with comparatively small-scale investment banking activities into one of the world's leading investment banks. Not only was Merrill strongly positioned in all the world's major financial centers—it had also established a strong position in the emerging markets of Asia, Eastern Europe, Latin America, Africa and the Middle East—most notably in the BRIC countries. Appendices 22.1 and 22.2 provide information on the businesses and performance of the two companies.

Some of the contentious aspects of the merger extended beyond the specifics of the Merrill Lynch acquisition to the overall strategy of Bank of America. Bank of America was one of a small number of U.S. banks—the others were Citigroup and J.P. Morgan Chase—that had taken advantage of the repeal of the Glass-Stegall Act to combine commercial and investment banking. This so-called "universal banking model" was common in Europe where UBS, Deutsch Bank, Credit Suisse, BNP-Paribas, Barclays, Royal Bank of Scotland and Unicredit long combined conventional banking services with capital market activities, corporate advisory services, market making and proprietary trading.

The financial crisis of 2008–9 had confirmed the robustness of the universal banking model. Among the major U.S. investment banks, only Goldman Sachs and Morgan Stanley had survived. The universal banks were able to pick up the pieces: in addition to Bank of America's acquisition of Merrill Lynch, J.P. Morgan Chase had acquired Bear Stearns. The universal banks had demonstrated the advantages of risk spreading as a result of diversification, plus the stability advantages of financing through retail bank deposits rather than relying on wholesale money markets. In addition there were

FIGURE 22.1 Extract from Merger Presentation by Ken Lewis and John Thain

Creating the Premier Financial Services Company in the World

Ken Lewis
Bank of America
Chairman and CEO

John Thain
Merrill Lynch
Chairman and CEO

Strategic Rationale

- *Diversify business mix*
- *Significant enhancement to our investment banking capabilities*
  - *Creates leading positions in*
    - *Global Debt Underwriting*
    - *Global Equities*
    - *Global M&A Advisory*
- *Leadership position in retail brokerage and wealth management*
  - *20,000 financial advisors (16,690 Merrill Lynch advisors)*
  - *$2.5 trillion in client assets*
- *Brings global scale in investment management*
  - *50% ownership stake in BlackRock with $1.4 trillion in AUMs*
  - *Columbia funds have $425 billion in AUMs (total BAC AUMs $589 billion)*

(AUM = Assets Under Management)

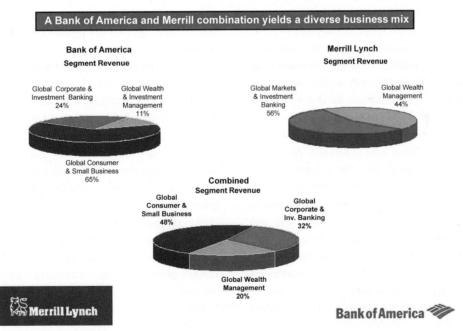

the strategic advantages that had traditionally been argued for the universal banks. First, the "one-stop-shopping" benefits in relation to both individual and corporate/institutional customers of offering a comprehensive range of products and services. Second, the vertical integration benefits of having a retail distribution network to support investment banking activities such as underwriting and securitization.

There were others who believed that the benefits of combining investment and commercial banking were small, while the costs were potentially great. These critics pointed to the fact that few financial institutions had been able to make "cross-selling" financial products work well, while the organizational and management difficulties of administering diversified, multinational financial service companies were huge. Citigroup was often quoted as an example of a financial service company whose size and complexity had made it unmanageable. Part of the problem was in designing management systems that exploit the synergies between commercial and investment banking while avoiding the inherent conflict of interests that multiple relationships with the same client posed (see Exhibit 22.2).

EXHIBIT 22.2
Universal Banks Need Careful Monitoring

The recent failure of Bear Stearns, Lehman Brothers and Merrill Lynch as independent banks has raised questions about the future of investment banking. The transformation of Goldman Sachs and Morgan Stanley into banking holdings is the last nail in the coffin for investment banks as we knew them for a century. At the same time, the growth of new giants such as JPMorgan Chase, Bank of America, Wells Fargo and Barclays looks like the triumph of the universal banking model over specialized banks.

As the U.S. Treasury and regulators attempt to stop the financial meltdown, they are also redefining the banking model in unintended ways that may sow the seeds of financial turbulence in the future. By encouraging or allowing banks such as JPMorgan, Bank of America and Barclays to rescue weaker banks, useful as it is in the short term, they are also nurturing bigger universal banks. Their sheer size will not only strengthen the unwritten TBTF principle ("too big to fail"). The emerging banking model, based on financial conglomerates with a high degree of diversification, also creates problems for banking stability.

Financial history tells us conglomerates are complex to manage. They usually run profitable business whose margins fund other under-performing units, which is one of the reasons why investors put a discount on their share price. But financial conglomerates also involve additional problems related to risk management, conflicts of interest and capital allocation, which create huge challenges for regulators and banking stability as a whole.

The first basic problem that universal banks face is risk management. On the one hand, these banks offer low-risk, traditional banking services—such as deposit-taking and commercial lending—with guaranteed deposits and an insurance mechanism set up by governments. Yet they also run trading units, lend money for mergers and acquisition, manage individuals' portfolios, invest their savings in exotic products and design complex structured loans. These banks look more stable because they are more diversified, but in this diversification lies the problem.

There are a few universal banks in the U.S., such as Bank of America and JPMorgan, which have weathered the storm so far reasonably well. It is also true that European banks such as Santander or BBVA have been successful with a universal model, although they are strong retail banks and not as diversified as their U.S. competitors. If one leaves these exceptions aside, managing the traditional banking business together with risky financial operations not only makes the basic banking function riskier, but also puts pressure on the whole bank. This is one of the reasons for the huge problems at the heart of the financial woes of Merrill Lynch, UBS, Fortis and Wachovia.

In universal banks, conflicts of interest are ubiquitous. This is an old story that often comes back. It happened during the internet bubble, when some banks played different roles for different parties: advising on M&A, lending to fund some acquisitions, leading initial public offerings or managing portfolios. Chinese walls were torn down and some bankers unethically exploited those conflicts of interest. Public uproar and some regulatory changes calmed the storm but did not eradicate the intrinsic problem.

Disclosure and shareholders' protection is another important issue. By definition, capital allocation in conglomerates is complex to make and complex to discern. Unless banks make a huge effort to explain it in a clear way, neither investors nor regulators really understand where their risk lies, as the recent crisis has shown.

The conflicts of interest inherent in universal banks are not enough to forbid their existence or to go back to the U.S. Glass–Steagall Act.

But regulators should monitor them more closely and ask them to separate legally and operationally the basic banking intermediary function from other financial services. Banks should fully disclose their capital allocation and risk in a clearer way, both for shareholders and investors.

Auditors can also help here. Just have a look at the annual reports of some of the failed banks over the past three years and one gets the feeling, most of the time, that they were almost immune to risk.

A dynamic economy needs well functioning banks. But the universal model needs a clear separation of regulated and unregulated activities and better transparency and disclosure. Unless we address this challenge, we may end up not only with larger banks but with a weaker financial system in the future.

Source: J. Canals, Universal banks need careful monitoring, *Financial Times,* October 19, 2008. Reproduced by permission of Prof. Jordi Canals, IESE Business School, University of Navara.

Appendix 1: Bank of America Corporation: The Business and Performance

General

Bank of America Corporation ("Bank of America" or the "Corporation") is a Delaware corporation, a bank holding company and a financial holding company under the Gramm-Leach-Bliley Act. Our principal executive offices are located in the Bank of America Corporate Center, Charlotte, North Carolina 28255.

Through our banking subsidiaries (the "Banks") and various nonbanking subsidiaries throughout the U.S. and in selected international markets, we provide a diversified range of banking and nonbanking financial services and products through three business segments: *Global Consumer and Small Business Banking, Global Corporate and Investment Banking* and *Global Wealth and Investment Management.* We currently operate in 32 states, the District of Columbia and more than 30 foreign countries. The Bank of America footprint covers more than 82% of the U.S. population and 44% of the country's wealthy households. In the U.S. we serve approximately 59 million consumer and small business relationships with more than 6100 retail banking offices, more than 18 500 ATMs and approximately 24 million active online users. We have banking centers in 13 of the 15 fastest growing states and hold the top market share in six of those states...

As of December 31, 2007, there were approximately 210 000 full-time equivalent employees within Bank of America and our subsidiaries. Of these employees, 116 000 were employed within *Global Consumer and Small Business Banking,* 21 000 were employed within *Global Corporate and Investment Banking* and 14 000 were employed within *Global Wealth and Investment Management . . .*

($ millions, except where indicated)	2007	2006	2005	2004	2003
Income statement					
Net interest income	34 433	34 591	30 737	27 960	20 505
Noninterest income	31 886	37 989	26 438	22 729	18 270
Total revenue, net of interest expense	66 319	72 580	57 175	50 689	38 775
Provision for credit losses	8 385	5 010	4 014	2 769	2 839
Noninterest expense, before merger and restructuring charges	36 600	34 792	28 269	26 394	20 155
Merger and restructuring charges	410	805	412	618	–
Income before income taxes	20 924	31 973	24 480	20 908	15 781
Income tax expense	5 942	10 840	8 015	6 961	5 019
Net income	14 982	21 133	16 465	13 947	10 762
Performance ratios					
Return on average assets (%)	0.94	1.44	1.30	1.34	1.44
Return on average common shareholders' equity (%)	11.08	16.27	16.51	16.47	21.50
Return on average tangible shareholders' equity (%)	22.25	32.80	30.19	28.93	27.84
Total ending equity to total ending assets (%)	8.56	9.27	7.86	9.03	6.76
Total average equity to total average assets (%)	8.53	8.90	7.86	8.12	6.69
Dividend payout (%)	72.26	45.66	46.61	46.31	39.76

($ millions, except where indicated)	2007	2006	2005	2004	2003
Market price per share of common stock					
Closing ($)	41.26	53.39	46.15	46.99	40.22
High closing ($)	54.05	54.90	47.08	47.44	41.77
Low closing ($)	41.10	43.09	41.57	38.96	32.82
Market capitalization	183 107	238 021	184 586	190 147	115 926
Average balance sheet					
Total loans and leases	776 154	652 417	537 218	472 617	356 220
Total assets	1 602 073	1 466 681	1 269 892	1 044 631	749 104
Total deposits	717 182	672 995	632 432	551 559	406 233
Long-term debt	169 855	130 124	97 709	92 303	67 077
Total shareholders' equity	136 662	130 463	99 861	84 815	50 091
Asset quality					
Allowance for credit losses	12 106	9413	8440	9028	6579
Nonperforming assets measured at historical cost	5948	1856	1603	2455	3021
Allowance for loan and lease losses as % of total loans and leases outstanding (%)	1.33	1.28	1.40	1.65	1.66
Allowance for loan and lease losses as % of total non performing loans and leases (%)	207	505	532	390	215
Net charge-offs	6480	4539	4562	3113	3106
Net charge-offs as % of average loans and leases outstanding	0.84	0.70	0.85	0.66	0.87
Nonperforming loans and leases as a percentage of total loans and leases (%) outstanding measured at historical cost	0.64	0.25	0.26	0.42	0.77
Nonperforming assets as % of total loans, leases and foreclosed properties (%)	0.68	0.26	0.28	0.47	0.81
Ratio of the allowance for loan and lease losses at December 31 to net charge-offs	1.79	1.99	1.76	2.77	1.98
Capital ratios (period end)					
Risk-based capital:					
Tier 1	6.87	8.64	8.25	8.20	8.02
Total	11.02	11.88	11.08	11.73	12.05
Tier 1 Leverage	5.04	6.36	5.91	5.89	5.86

Global Consumer and Small Business Banking

2007 ($ millions)	Total	Deposits	Card services	Consumer real estate	ALM other
Net interest income	28 809	9 423	16 562	2 281	543
Noninterest income:					
Card income	10 189	2 155	8 028	6	–
Service charges	6 008	6 003	–	5	–
Mortgage banking income	1 333	–	–	1 333	–
All other income	1 343	(4)	943	54	350
Total noninterest income	18 873	8 154	8 971	1 398	350
Total revenue, net of interest expense	47 682	17 577	25 533	3 679	893
Provision for credit losses	12 929	256	11 317	1 041	315
Noninterest expense	20 060	9 106	8 294	2 033	627
Income (loss) before income taxes	14 693	8 215	5 922	605	(49)
Income tax expense (benefit)	5 263	2 988	2 210	234	(169)
Net income	9 430	5 227	3 712	371	120
Net interest yield* (%)	8.15	2.97	7.87	2.04	n/m
Return on average equity	14.94	33.61	8.43	9.00	n/m
Efficiency ratio*	42.07	51.81	32.49	55.24	n/m
Period end—total assets	442 987	358 626	257 000	133 324	n/m

* The *efficiency ratio* measures the costs expended to generate a dollar of revenue; *net interest yield* evaluates how many basis points we are earning over the cost of funds.

The strategy for *GCSBB* is to attract, retain and deepen customer relationships. We achieve this strategy through our ability to offer a wide range of products and services through a franchise that stretches coast to coast through 32 states and the District of Columbia. We also provide credit-card products to customers in Canada, Ireland, Spain and the United Kingdom. In the U.S. we serve approximately 59 million consumer and small-business relationships utilizing our network of 6149 banking centers, 18 753 domestic branded ATMs, and telephone and internet channels. Within *GCSBB* there are three primary businesses:

- *Deposits* provides a comprehensive range of products to consumers and small businesses. Our products include traditional savings accounts, money market savings accounts, CDs and IRAs, and noninterest and interest-bearing checking accounts. Debit card results are also included in *Deposits*.
- *Card Services,* which excludes the results of debit cards (included in *Deposits*), provides a broad offering of products, including U.S. Consumer and Business Card, Unsecured Lending, and International Card. We offer a variety of cobranded and affinity credit-card products and have become the leading issuer of credit cards through endorsed marketing in the U.S. and Europe. During 2007, Merchant Services was transferred to *Treasury Services* within *GCIB*.
- *Consumer Real Estate* generates revenue by providing an extensive line of consumer real estate products and services to customers nationwide.

Consumer Real Estate products are available to our customers through a retail network of personal bankers located in 6149 banking centers, mortgage loan officers in nearly 200 locations and through a sales force offering our customers direct telephone and online access to our products. *Consumer Real Estate* products include fixed and adjustable rate loans for home purchase and refinancing needs, reverse mortgages, lines of credit and home equity loans. Mortgage products are either sold into the secondary mortgage market to investors while retaining the Bank of America customer relationships or are held on our balance sheet for ALM purposes. *Consumer Real Estate* is not impacted by the Corporation's mortgage production retention decisions as *Consumer Real Estate* is compensated for the decision on a management accounting basis with a corresponding offset recorded in *All Other*.

- The *Consumer Real Estate* business includes the origination, fulfillment, sale and servicing of first mortgage loan products, reverse mortgage products and home equity products. Servicing activities primarily include collecting cash for principal, interest and escrow payments from borrowers, disbursing customer draws for lines of credit and accounting for and remitting principal and interest payments to investors and escrow payments to third parties. Servicing income includes ancillary income derived in connection with these activities such as late fees.

Global Corporate and Investment Banking

2007 ($ millions)	Total	Business lending	Capital Market and advisory	Treasury Services
Net interest income	11 217	5 020	2 786	3 814
Noninterest income:				
Service charges	2 769	507	134	2 128
Investment and brokerage services	910	1	867	42
Investment banking income	2 537	–	2 537	–
Trading account profits (losses)	(5 164)	(180)	(5 050)	63
All other income	1 148	824	(971)	1 092
Total noninterest income	2 200	1 152	(2 483)	3 325
Total revenue, net of interest expense	13 417	6 172	303	7 139
Provision for credit losses	652	647	–	5
Noninterest expense	11 925	2 158	5 642	3 856
Income (loss) before income taxes	840	3 367	(5 339)	3 278
Income tax expense (benefit)	302	1 246	(1 977)	1 213
Net income (loss)	538	2 121	(3 362)	2 065
Net interest yield	1.66	2.00	n/m	2.79
Return on average equity	1.19	13.12	(25.41)	26.31
Efficiency ratio	88.88	34.98	n/m	54.02
Period end—total assets	776 107	305 548	413 115	180 369

Global Corporate and Investment Banking provides a wide range of financial services both to our issuer and investor clients, who range from business banking clients to large international corporate and institutional investor clients, using a strategy to deliver value-added financial products and advisory solutions. Global Corporate and Investment Banking's products and services are delivered from three primary businesses: *Business Lending, CMAS* and *Treasury Services* are provided to our clients through a global team of client relationship managers and product partners. In addition, *ALM/Other* includes the results of ALM activities and other *GCIB* activities (such as commercial insurance business, which was sold in the fourth quarter of 2007). Our clients are supported through offices in 22 countries, which are divided into four distinct geographic regions: U.S. and Canada; Asia; Europe, Middle East and Africa; and Latin America.

- *Business Lending* provides a wide range of lending-related products and services to our clients through client relationship teams along with various product partners. Products include commercial and corporate bank loans and commitment facilities, which cover our business banking clients, middle market commercial clients and our large multinational corporate clients. Real-estate lending products are issued primarily to public and private developers, homebuilders and commercial real-estate firms. Leasing and asset-based lending products offer our clients innovative financing solutions. Products also include indirect consumer loans, which allow us to offer financing through automotive, marine, motorcycle and recreational vehicle dealerships across the U.S. *Business Lending* also contains the results for the economic hedging of our risk to certain credit counterparties utilizing various risk mitigation tools.

- *Capital Markets and Advisory Services* provides financial products, advisory services and financing globally to our institutional investor clients in support of their investing and trading activities. We also work with our commercial and corporate issuer clients to provide debt and equity underwriting and distribution capabilities, merger-related advisory services and risk management solutions using interest rate, equity, credit, currency and commodity derivatives, foreign exchange, fixed income and mortgage-related products. The business may take positions in these products and participate in market-making activities dealing in government securities, equity and equity-linked securities, high-grade and high-yield corporate debt securities, commercial paper, mortgage-backed securities and ABS. Underwriting debt and equity, securities research and certain market-based activities are executed through *Banc of America Securities, LLC,* which is a primary dealer in the U.S.

- *Treasury Services* provides integrated working capital management and treasury solutions to clients worldwide through our network of proprietary offices and special clearing arrangements. Our clients include multinationals, middle-market companies, correspondent banks, commercial real estate firms and governments. Our products and services include treasury management, trade finance, foreign exchange, short-term credit facilities and short-term investing options. Net interest income is derived from interest-bearing and noninterest-bearing deposits, sweep investments, and other liability management products. Deposit products provide a relatively stable source of funding and liquidity. We earn net interest spread revenues from investing this liquidity in earning assets through client-facing lending activity and our ALM activities.

Global Wealth and Investment Management

2007 ($ millions)	Total	U.S. Trust	Columbia Management	Premier Banking and Investments
Net interest income	3 857	1 036	15	2 655
Noninterest income:				
Investment and brokerage services	4 210	1 226	1 857	950
All other income	(144)	57	(366)	146
Total noninterest income	4 066	1 283	1 491	1 096
Total revenue, net of interest expense	7 923	2 319	1 506	3 751
Provision for credit losses	14	14	–	27
Noninterest expense	4 635	1 592	1 196	1 700
Income before income taxes	3 274	741	310	2 024
Income tax expense	1 179	274	114	749
Net income	2 095	467	196	1 275
Net interest yield	3.06	2.69	n/m	2.70
Return on average equity	18.87	17.25	11.29	72.44
Efficiency ratio	58.50	68.67	79.39	45.31
Period end—total assets	157 157	51 044	2 617	113 329

Global Wealth and Investment Management provides a wide offering of customized banking, investment and brokerage services tailored to meet the changing wealth management goals of our individual and institutional customer base. Our clients have access to a range of services offered through three primary businesses: *U.S. Trust, Bank of America Private Wealth Management (U.S. Trust); Columbia Management (Columbia)* and *Premier Banking and Investments (PB&I)*.

U.S. Trust, Bank of America Private Wealth Management In July 2007, we completed the acquisition of U.S. Trust Corporation for $3.3 billion in cash combining it with *The Private Bank* and its ultra-wealthy extension, *Family Wealth Advisors*, to form *U.S. Trust*. The results of the combined business were reported for periods beginning on July 1, 2007. Prior to July 1, 2007, the results solely reflect that of the former *Private Bank*. *U.S. Trust* provides comprehensive wealth management solutions to wealthy and ultra-wealthy clients with investable assets of more than $3 million. In addition, *U.S. Trust* provides resources and customized solutions to meet clients' wealth structuring, investment management, trust and banking services as well as specialty asset management services (oil and gas, real estate, farm and ranch, timberland, private businesses and tax advisory). Clients also benefit from access to resources available through the Corporation including capital markets products, large and complex financing solutions and its extensive banking platform.

Columbia Management *Columbia* is an asset-management business serving the needs of institutional clients and individual customers. *Columbia* provides asset management products and services, including mutual funds and separate accounts. *Columbia* mutual fund offerings provide a broad array of investment strategies and products including equity, fixed income (taxable and nontaxable) and money market (taxable and nontaxable) funds. *Columbia* distributes its products and services directly to institutional clients and distributes to individuals through *U.S. Trust, PB&I* and nonproprietary channels including other brokerage firms.

Premier Banking and Investments Premier Banking and Investments includes *Banc of America Investments*, our full-service retail brokerage business and our *Premier Banking* channel. Premier Banking and Investments brings personalized banking and investment expertise through priority service with client-dedicated teams. It provides a high-touch client experience through a network of approximately 5600 client-facing associates to our affluent customers with a personal wealth profile that includes investable assets plus a mortgage that exceeds $500 000 or at least $100 000 of investable assets.

Appendix 2: Merrill Lynch & Co., Inc.: The Business and Performance (extracts from 10-K report for 2007)

The Business

Merrill Lynch was formed in 1914 and became a publicly traded company on June 23, 1971. In 1973, we created the holding company, ML & Co., a Delaware corporation that, through its subsidiaries, is one of the world's leading capital markets, advisory and wealth management companies with offices in 40 countries and territories. In our Global Wealth Management ("GWM") business, we had total client assets in GWM accounts of approximately $1.2 trillion at December 26, 2008. As an investment bank, we are a leading global trader and underwriter of securities and derivatives across a broad range of asset classes and we serve as a strategic advisor to corporations, governments, institutions and individuals worldwide. In addition, as of December 26, 2008, we owned approximately half of the economic interest of BlackRock, Inc. ("BlackRock"), one of the world's largest publicly traded investment management companies with approximately $1.3 trillion in assets under management at the end of 2008 . . .

Our activities are conducted through two business segments: Global Markets and Investment Banking ("GMI") and GWM. In addition, we provide a variety of research services on a global basis.

Global Markets and Investment Banking

The Global Markets division consists of the Fixed Income, Currencies and Commodities ("FICC") and Equity Markets sales and trading activities for investor clients and on a proprietary basis, while the Investment Banking division provides a wide range of origination and strategic advisory services for issuer clients. Global Markets makes a market in securities, derivatives, currencies, and other financial instruments to satisfy client demands. In addition, Global Markets engages in certain proprietary trading activities. Global Markets is a leader in the global distribution of fixed income, currency and energy commodity products and derivatives. Global Markets also has one of the largest equity-trading operations in the world and is a leader in the origination and distribution of equity and equity-related products.

Further, Global Markets provides clients with financing, securities clearing, settlement and custody services and also engages in principal investing in a variety of asset classes and private equity investing. The Investment Banking division raises capital for its clients through underwritings and private placements of equity, debt and related securities and loan syndications. Investment Banking also offers advisory services to clients on strategic issues, valuation, mergers, acquisitions and restructurings.

Global Wealth Management

Global Wealth Management, our full-service retail wealth management segment, provides brokerage, investment advisory and financial planning services, offering a broad range of both proprietary and third-party wealth management products and services globally to individuals, small- to mid-size businesses and employee benefit plans. Global Wealth Management comprises Global Private Client ("GPC") and Global Investment Management ("GIM").

Global Private Client provides a full range of wealth management products and services to assist clients in managing all aspects of their financial profile through the Total Merrill^{SM} platform. Total Merrill^{SM} is the platform for GPC's core strategy offering investment choices, brokerage, advice, planning and/or performance analysis to its clients. Global Private Client's offerings include commission and fee-based investment accounts, banking, cash management and credit services, including consumer and small business lending and Visa® cards; trust and generational planning; retirement services and insurance products.

Global Private Client services individuals and small- and middle-market corporations and institutions through approximately 16 090 financial advisors as of December 26, 2008.

Global Investment Management includes our interests in creating and managing wealth management products, including alternative investment products for clients. GIM also includes our share of net earnings from our ownership positions in other investment management companies, including BlackRock.

	GMI	GWM
Clients	Corporations, financial institutions, institutional investors, and governments	Individuals, small- to mid-size businesses, and employee benefit plans
Products and businesses	**Global Markets** *(comprising Fixed Income, Currencies and Commodities ("FICC") and Equity Markets)* Facilitates client transactions and makes markets in securities, derivatives, currencies, commodities and other financial instruments to satisfy client demands	**Global Private Client ("GPC")** Delivers products and services primarily through our Financial Advisors ("FAs") Commission fee-based investment accounts
	Provides clients with financing, securities clearing, settlement, and custody services Engages in principal and private equity investing, including managing investment funds, and certain proprietary trading activities	Banking, cash management, and credit services, including consumer and small business lending and Visa$^{(r)}$ cards Trust and generational planning Retirement services Insurance products

(continued)

GMI	GWM
Investment Banking Provides a wide range of securities origination services for issuer clients, including underwriting and placement of public and private equity, debt and related securities, as well as lending and other financing activities for clients globally Advises clients on strategic issues, valuation, mergers, acquisitions and restructurings	**Global Investment Management ("GIM")** Creates and manages hedge funds and other alternative investment products for GPC clients Includes net earnings from our ownership positions in other investment management companies, including our investment in BlackRock

Results by geographical area, 2008

($ millions)	2008	2007	2006
Net revenues			
Europe, Middle East and Africa	(2 390)	5 973	6 896
Pacific Rim	69	5 065	3 703
Latin America	1 237	1 401	1 009
Canada	161	430	386
Total non-U.S.	−923	12 869	11 994
United States	−11 670	−1 619	21 787
Total net revenues	(12 593)	11 250	33 781
Pretax earnings from continuing operations			
Europe, Middle East, and Africa	(6 735)	1 211	2 091
Pacific Rim	−2 559	2 403	1 204
Latin America	340	632	357
Canada	5	235	181
Total non-U.S.	−8 949	4 481	3 833
United States	−32 882	−17 312	5 977
Total pretax earnings from continuing operations	(41 831)	(12 831)	9 810

Results by business segment, 2008

($ millions)	GMI	GWM	MLIM	Corporate	Total
Noninterest revenues	(25 416)	10 464	–	(1675)	(166 27)
Net revenues	(26 460)	12 778	–	1 089	(12 593)
Noninterest expenses	15 084	10 432	–	3 722	29 238
Pretax (loss)/earnings from continuing operations	(41 544)	2 346	–	(2633)	(41 831)
Year-end total assets	568 868	97 849	–	826	667 543

(continued)

Results by business segment, 2008

($ millions)	GMI	GWM	MLIM	Corporate	Total
2007					
Non-interest revenues	(4950)	11719	–	(1068)	5701
Net revenues	(2668)	14021	–	(103)	11250
Non-interest expenses	13677	10391	–	13	24081
Pre-tax (loss)/earnings from continuing operations	(16345)	3630	–	(116)	(12831)
Year-end total assets	920388	99196	–	466	1020050

Appendix 3: "The Golden Age for Financial Services is Over" By Shawn Tully

The New Most Powerful Man in Finance, Bank of America CEO Ken Lewis, Talks about the Future of Wall Street and the Economy

To reach the new power center of Wall Street, hop into a cab to La Guardia, board a flight for Charlotte, stride into a beige granite tower, go past the allegorical murals of the common man at work, then take the elevator to the 58th floor. You're at the headquarters of Bank of America, and you're about to enter the glass-framed suite of CEO Ken Lewis.

A world away from Manhattan money and its ethos—which, by the way, he detests—Lewis presides over a company that represents the future of finance. BofA's deal to buy Merrill Lynch for $50 billion sets the template. Sure, rival institutions—notably J. P. Morgan Chase and Citigroup—combine investment and consumer banking. But the Bank of America/Merrill union creates a colossus of unprecedented size and scope.

It isn't clear whether the deal will enrich shareholders or how the market chaos will play out. But it's certain that Lewis is realizing the epic vision he has long dreamed of. "I approached [former Merrill CEO] Stan O'Neal a few years ago, but he showed no interest," says Lewis. Now the crisis brings the missing piece within his grasp: "We've fulfilled the strategic picture we sketched on blank sheets of paper."

The Merrill merger will make BofA just what Lewis wants it to be, the dominant player almost across the board in financial services. By capturing Merrill's "thundering herd" of 16700 financial advisors, BofA becomes the world's biggest brokerage, with $2.5 trillion in client assets. If both firms keep their current market shares, BofA will rise from the second tier in investment banking to first place in global debt and equity underwriting. After years of acquisitions that created the first true nationwide banking brand, BofA already ranks first in credit cards, retail banking (with 6000-plus branches) and mortgages via its recent acquisition of Countrywide. BofA is now a full-blown financial supermarket, a business model that is succeeding at J.P. Morgan under CEO Jamie Dimon but failing at Citigroup.

Lewis, who's 61, clearly thinks he has an advantage over those two because he's bigger—in more businesses, in more places. Seated in his sun-splashed office adorned with American Impressionist and Hudson River school paintings, he's describing the future of finance in terms perhaps best characterized as cautious exultation. He predicts an end to profligate pay and a witheringly tough market ahead that will leave a few giant champions and a field of casualties. That's not all bad news as far as Lewis is concerned. After all, he hates Wall Street's inflated pay; the market crisis brought him Merrill Lynch; and any decline in the rest of the investment banks out there is good for him. "We'll take a lot of their business," he says.

Lewis is under no illusion that the next few years will be easy. "The Golden Age for financial services is over," he tells Fortune. "It will never be the same, not in my career. Revenues will be far harder to get in the future." For Lewis the biggest problem is the plight of the consumer. He sees the credit pie shrinking as Americans, stretched by high mortgage payments and gas prices, their jobs frequently in jeopardy, recognize that they can't afford the debt they already have, let alone add more. "The consumer is deleveraging, just like many of the banks," says Lewis.

The banks, in his view, are just as weak as the consumer. As a result, they'll be hard-pressed even to satisfy the demand for mortgage, car and credit card loans. "We'll see big write-downs all the way through next year that won't abate until 2010," says Lewis. "Over that period a number of big banks won't have enough capital to make a lot of loans." Lewis sees a rare opportunity to grab market share by extending credit while his competitors languish on the sidelines.

Lewis says his edge isn't just a plentiful pool of capital. He also claims that he'll soon enjoy a big advantage over the best soon-to-be-ex-investment banks in the business, as well as the only ones that remain independent, Goldman Sachs (GS, Fortune 500) and Morgan Stanley (MS, Fortune 500). Both firms are turning into bank holding companies. That will allow them to fund their loans and investments with stable deposits rather than short-term debt that can evaporate in a financial crisis. But it will also force them to radically shrink their balance sheets.

But Lewis believes that transformation will make them far less formidable forces in capital markets. Why? It's complicated, but here goes: since Goldman and Morgan must shrink their balance sheets by reducing their towering leverage, they won't be able to offer the same financing options their corporate customers increasingly demand—that's because corporations that give Goldman and Morgan their underwriting business will expect the banks to extend revolving credit facilities and bridge loans as part of the package. Says Lewis: "As bank holding companies, Morgan Stanley and Goldman will be forced to shrink their balance sheets when expanding your balance sheet is a key to getting corporate business. That will make them less competitive." How does Lewis feel about facing the two storied firms in battling for credit card customers and branch deposits? "We have something of a headstart," he says with a sly smile. "I'm not losing any sleep."

Even as the world moves Lewis's way, he still faces some obstacles. One is the issue of BofA's capital. With the bank's acquisitions of Countrywide and Merrill, even BofA's war chest has become a bit crimped. Unless the bank bolsters its equity, its regulatory capital-to-assets ratio will fall to around 7.4% after the Merrill deal, below Lewis's target of 8% to 8.5%. Lewis is pondering a radical solution: cutting BofA's almost $3 billion quarterly dividend, which amounts to $11.8 billion annually. "For the first time, the dividend is on the table," says Lewis. "The Merrill deal is a factor, along with everything that's happening in the economy. The need to build capital is more apparent and intense."

Shrinking the dividend, however, will disappoint investors who flocked to BofA stock because of its reliable, ever-rising payout. It also represents a retreat for Lewis, who until recently told investors that a cut was unlikely. "A lot of investors will be upset, and the stock price may go down if he makes the cut," says Meredith Whitney of Oppenheimer & Co.

The other big issue for BofA is whether it overpaid for Merrill. Lewis calls the deal "the strategic opportunity of a lifetime." But was it really such a bargain? BofA is paying an extremely high price in a market where assets are going for a song, although the deal could prove profitable in the long run. Until Friday, September 12, Lewis was weighing the acquisition of Lehman Brothers, then on the verge of bankruptcy. Lehman had $85 billion in toxic real estate loans. "We figured that the $85 billion in troubled loans was at least $10 billion underwater," says Lewis. He calculated that the value of Lehman's good assets—its investment bank and asset-management arm—wasn't nearly enough to compensate for the potential $10 billion-plus loss on the mortgage assets. He wanted the government to take $65 billion to $70 billion of the most dangerous securities on its books. Over the phone on Friday evening, Lewis told Treasury Secretary Hank Paulson he couldn't buy Lehman without government assistance. When Paulson said he couldn't help, Lewis walked.

On Saturday morning, September 13, Merrill CEO John Thain phoned Lewis in Charlotte to propose a merger, and the two made the giant deal in 36 hours. The huge question is why Lewis paid $50 billion, or $29 a share, a 70% premium over Merrill's closing price on Friday. Over that weekend, with markets heading for a meltdown on Monday, Lehman's looming bankruptcy threatened to bring down Merrill as well. Indeed, Lehman failed on Monday morning; the following week Barclays got a sweet deal buying its North American investment bank and headquarters for $1.7 billion.

So why didn't Lewis wait until Monday, when Merrill might have faced bankruptcy or, even if it survived, been forced to settle for a fire-sale price? Lewis explains that if Merrill went bankrupt, BofA would have had a harder time buying the business it most coveted, Merrill's brokerage franchise. "In a bankruptcy we'd have to bid against other potential buyers, and that asset would have been worth a lot on its own," says Lewis. And if Merrill avoided bankruptcy, Lewis feared that Thain would make another deal. "Both Goldman Sachs and Morgan Stanley were in the mix," says Lewis. So Lewis eliminated his chance of losing Merrill by acting in a flash. He won't talk much about the negotiations with Thain. "He started at a higher price, and I started at a lower price," he says simply.

It may be true that Lewis would have lost Merrill had he waited. But he has no regrets about the price. "Merrill is worth significantly more than $50 billion," he says. He is promising shareholders that he'll cut costs by a staggering $7 billion before taxes. Unattainable? Not if you consider the extraordinary cost savings Lewis wrung from the Countrywide merger, and the Fleet acquisition in 2004. Lewis is especially anxious to attack Merrill's pay scales. "Merrill was paying typical Wall Street pay," he says. "Their staff people were making a lot more than our staff people. That won't last. We intend to pay market instead."

And if his new employees aren't happy about the pay—or any of Lewis's grand transformations, for that matter—they probably shouldn't waste their time griping to the CEO. Lewis isn't known for his tolerance of complaint. A few years ago one of his top lieutenants wrote the boss a long memo complaining that he'd been undermined by another executive. A few days later he found the memo on his desk. At the top, Lewis had scribbled three words: "Get over it."

Source: S. Tully, The Golden Age for financial services is over,' *Fortune*, September 29, 2008, http://money.cnn.com/2008/09/28/news/companies/tully_levis.fortune/index.htm. Reproduced with permisson.

Notes

1 "BofA/Merrill Lynch," *Financial Times,* September 16, 2008.
2 See: A.M. Cuomo, "Bank of America—Merrill Lynch Merger Investigation," State of New York Office of the Attorney General (April 29, 2009), http://online.wsj.com/public/resources/documents/BofAmergLetter-Cuomo4232009.pdf, accessed July 3, 2009.

3 The facts regarding conversations between Lewis and U.S. government officials are unclear on this point. See: A.M. Cuomo, "Bank of America—Merrill Lynch Merger Investigation," State of New York Office of the Attorney General (April 29, 2009), http://online.wsj.com/public/resources/documents/BofAmergLetter-Cuomo4232009.pdf, accessed July 3, 2009.

Case 23　Jeff Immelt and the Reinventing of General Electric, 2009

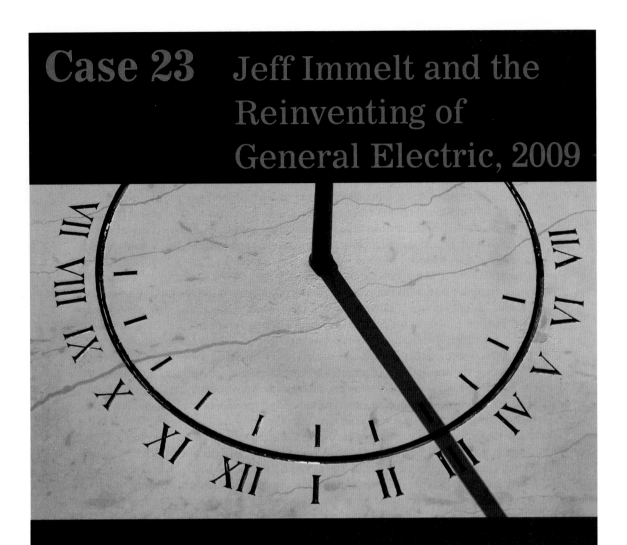

April 2009

On April 22, 2009, Jeff Immelt, chairman and CEO of the General Electric Company, was in Orlando, Florida, preparing for the annual shareholders' meeting—his eighth since becoming CEO. The meeting would lack the upbeat, celebratory atmosphere that had been the norm under his predecessor Jack Welch. General Electric's stock was trading a little below $12 that day—up from the low of $6 it reached six weeks earlier but well down on the $53 that GE's shares were trading at when Immelt's appointment had been announced late in 2000. Shareholders' anger was further fuelled by GE's decision to slash its dividend—the first dividend cut since 1938.

Since taking up the leadership of GE, Immelt had become familiar with adversity. If taking over from Jack Welch—"living legend" and "best manager of the past half-century"—was daunting enough, external events soon revealed just how tough his job would be.

Four days after Immelt took over the chairman's suite, two hijacked airliners ploughed into New York's World Trade Center, setting off a train of events that would profoundly affect GE's business environment. A month later, Enron's collapse precipitated a crisis of confidence over corporate governance, executive morality and financial reporting. The scandal at Tyco International—a company that had explicitly modeled itself on GE—and its decision to break up into three separate companies reinforced suspicion of the conglomerate business model. Controversy over financial statement manipulation and executive compensation soon engulfed GE. After being lauded by analysts for its smooth earnings growth it became apparent that GE systematically massaged its quarterly earnings through the use of reserves and end-of-quarter asset sales. More serious criticism was directed at GE's alleged disguising of the true risks of its businesses by consolidating the financial statements of its industrial businesses and its financial services business, GE Capital. In March 2002, Bill Gross, of the IPCO fund management group, argued that GE was primarily a financial services company but, with the support of GE's industrial businesses, GE Capital had been able to operate on a narrow capital base while maintaining a triple-A credit rating. Further problems for Immelt emerged when in September 2002 the details of Welch's startlingly generous retirement package from GE were leaked to the press.

By 2006, it seemed that Immelt was successfully exorcizing the ghost of Jack Welch and winning the war against external adversity. Between 2003 and 2006, Immelt's new growth strategy was achieving its targets for both revenue and profit. Better communication with the investment community and more detailed financial reporting were helping to restore investor confidence in GE. From 2003 to early 2007, GE's stock price experienced a sustained recovery. GE's rehabilitation was confirmed by its reclaiming the title of Fortune's "Most Admired Company" in 2005 and 2006.

Then came the financial crisis of 2008–9. The problems of sub-prime, mortgage-backed securities ballooned into a global credit crunch and forced the demise or government bailout of many of America's biggest financial institutions: Bear Stearns, Lehman Brothers, AIG, Fannie Mae and Citigroup. It profoundly affected GE. GE Capital, GE's financial services arm, was one of America's biggest financial services businesses. For two decades GE Capital had been GE's primary growth engine. It was now seen as "ticking time bomb" of bad debts and asset writedowns.

Two weeks before the end of the first quarter of 2008, Immelt confirmed that GE would meet its quarterly earnings expectations of $0.50 to $0.53 per share. The news, six weeks later, that GE had earned only $0.44 per share was a massive disappointment—GE had a long record of reliable earnings guidance and invariably meeting or exceeding its financial targets. Former CEO Jack Welch was outraged: "I'd get a gun out and shoot him if he doesn't make what he promised now. Here's the screw-up: you made a promise that you'd deliver this, and you missed three weeks later. Jeff has a credibility issue."

As the financial crisis deepened, Immelt was forced to take radical action to shore up GE's balance sheet. On September 25, he suspended GE's stock buyback program but reaffirmed that GE had no need for outside capital. Yet, one week later, Immelt made an agreement with Warren Buffett for a $3 billion equity injection with a guaranteed annual dividend of 10%. Investor confidence waned further: the fear for shareholders was that GE Capital, which had provided 42% of GE's profits in 2007, might bring down the whole of GE. As James Quinn observed in seekingalpha.com:

Most people know GE as an industrial conglomerate that makes light bulbs, appliances, and jet engines. The truth is that . . . GE is a bank disguised as an industrial conglomerate . . . Being a bank during the boom years of 2004 to 2007 did wonders for GE's bottom line. Being a bank now is a rocky path to destruction.[1]

Central to the "earnings magic of GE Capital" was GE's AAA credit rating, which allowed GE Capital to finance itself at a lower cost of capital and with a weaker balance sheet than other financial institutions. On March 12, Standard & Poor's (S&P) downgraded GE from AAA to AA+, further damaging the reputation of the company and its CEO.

The address by Immelt and CFO Keith Sherrin to the shareholders' meeting on April 22, 2009, focused on two key strategic issues. Sherrin addressed how GE was shoring up its financial strength in order to weather the current downturn. Immelt concentrated upon GE's longer term strategy. For the most part, he reiterated the principal elements of the strategy that he had been developing since he took over as CEO seven-and-a-half years earlier. In particular, Immelt emphasized GE's commitment to organic growth; exploiting technological innovation and globalization; creating new business opportunities through matching GE's existing capabilities to emerging opportunities in environmental conservation, infrastructure, and healthcare; and developing the leadership needed for GE to prosper in the coming era. At the same time, Immelt emphasized how the current financial and economic crisis represented a once-in-a-generation "reset." Key changes were likely to include a reduced role for financial services in the future, an increased role of government, lower levels of wealth, and a growing emphasis on reputation and trust.

Immelt identified five themes for how GE would "get through the cycle and then . . . build the franchise over the long term":

- "Build strong businesses." GE's four major businesses—energy infrastructure, technology infrastructure, GE Capital and NBC Universal—would be the foundation for GE's growth and cash generation into the future. GE had already divested its least attractive businesses (such as insurance and reinsurance, and plastics and silicones) and had entered several high-potential industries: renewable energy, oil and gas, water, healthcare information technology, avionics and cable. The principal change in the GE portfolio would be a shrinking of GE Capital through exiting some of the product lines and focusing increasingly on building links between GE Capital and GE's other businesses (as in leasing aircraft).

- "Invest in innovation, services, and globalization." During the current decade, GE had invested about $50 billion in research and development. Key innovations included GE's investment in Smart Grid, which would allow massive savings in energy. General Electric's new sodium battery offered vast improvements in power storage with potentially valuable applications to power generation and transportation (locomotives in particular). In media GE had developed Hulu, the world's largest video content site after YouTube. In brain imaging and clean power generation from coal GE was also a world leader. In all its industrial businesses, services in the form of customer and technical support and maintenance would be an important source of growth and a major contributor to the bottom line.

- "Position in essential themes." Essential themes are key areas of emerging opportunity for GE. The most important of these was "ecoimagination"— business innovation and development in environmentally responsible activities such as green energy. For the immediate future, GE had identified infrastructure as a tremendous opportunity. GE's quest for opportunities would also be focused on countries where the biggest increases in public expenditure on infrastructure, healthcare and energy were likely to be, these included the U.S., Canada, China, Brazil, U.K., France, Germany, and the Middle East.

- "Drive competitiveness." As always, ambitious performance targets were fundamental to GE's strategy. After a dominant focus on using top line growth as the primary driver of profitability, in 2009, Immelt shifted GE's priorities to cost cutting, setting a target of reducing costs by $5 billion annually.

- "Commitment to people." Immelt reiterated GE's commitment to developing people including investment in training, emphasis on retention, and nurturing of loyalty.[2]

Despite the greater financial stability and a recovery of GE's share price during March and April 2009, unease over GE's future prospects and the strategy being developed by its chairman and CEO continued. Most concerns related to the central role of GE Capital within the company. Despite Immelt's intention of shrinking GE Capital, it would continue to represent a major part of GE's assets for the foreseeable future. As such, it would be a continuing source of risk for GE. With the loss of GE's triple-A credit rating, the financial synergies between the industrial and financial parts of GE were less apparent.

A further concern was whether Immelt's strategy of organic growth based upon innovation and exploiting "essential themes" could deliver the long-term profit growth that investors had come to expect of GE. As Harvard's Clay Christensen observed:

> The major growth engine at GE has been GE Capital . . . But the fact that it's been a great growth engine in the past means it likely won't be in the future. That's my biggest worry for GE. I don't see a new engine of growth that's comparable to what they had in the past. One challenge is that the bigger a business gets, the less and less interest it has in small opportunities. And all the big growth markets of tomorrow are small today.[3]

GE has shown a capacity for internal growth. However, most of GE's growth has been the result of acquiring major new businesses then expanding them through internationalization and the application of GE's strong management systems.

Moreover, the major growth opportunities that GE was pursuing involved the development and sales of whole systems of products and services. In healthcare, GE was pursuing deals that involved supplying not just medical imaging equipment, but generators, technical support, training and finance. In infrastructure, GE is engaged in multi-faced deals that involve hardware systems, support services, finance and training. Developing these types of business opportunities required high levels of coordination across multiple organizational units—inevitably creating increased organizational complexity and making GE's systems for linking individual incentives to individual and organizational performance even more difficult to implement.

Ultimately, Immelt had to face the question of whether General Electric made sense any more. For close to 20 years conglomerates had been deeply unfashionable both with investors and management theorists. Most had either reorganized themselves as more focused businesses (for example, Textron, General Mills, TRW, BTR) or had broken up completely (ITT, Hanson, Vivendi-Universal, Tyco). While the break up of GE had been suggested many times in recent years, the idea had attracted little serious support: GE was the exception; its quality of management was such that it had avoided the problems that had beset other large, highly diversified corporations. That reasoning held less credence in April 2009. GE's broad diversification had done little to offer it stability throughout the economic cycle— the dividend cut was a clear indication of this. Even more serious, GE's managers had lost much of their hero status. Immelt's retractions of the assurances he had given on earnings, funding needs and the dividend and the inability to foresee the vulnerability of GE Capital's dependence upon the wholesale credit markets for financing its business had seriously undermined the credibility of Immelt and the belief that GE's management was wiser than the market.

For most of GE's 120-year history it had been a pioneer of modern management providing many of the principles and methods that form the basis upon which large companies are managed today. The critical question posed by Immelt's notions of a fundamental "reset" of the business environment following the 2008–10 recession was whether this new business environment would offer GE the opportunity for a new era in its corporate development or whether it would expose the frailties of a corporate giant whose business model rested on the management logic of a previous century.

Table 23.1 summarizes GE's financial performance during 2002–8.

TABLE 23.1 General Electric: selected financial data, 2002–8

($ millions)	2008	2007	2006	2005	2004	2003	2002
General Electric Consolidated							
Revenues	182 515	172 488	151 568	136 262	123 814	113 421	111 967
Net earnings	17 410	22 208	20 742	16 720	17 222	15 561	12 998
Cash from operating activities	48 601	43 322	31 455	37 691	36 493	29 229	28 766
Cash used for investing activities	(40 901)	(69 504)	(52 647)	(35 099)	(38 423)	(21 843)	(61 227)
Return on average shareowners' equity	15.9%	20.4%	19.8%	18.1%	18.8%	20.0%	25.2%
Stock price range ($)	38.52– 12.58	42.15– 33.90	38.49– 32.06	37.34– 32.67	37.75– 28.88	32.42– 21.30	41.84– 21.40
Year-end closing stock price ($)	16.20	37.07	37.21	35.05	36.50	30.98	24.35
Total assets	797 769	795 683	697 273	673 210	750 252	647 834	575 018

(continued)

TABLE 23.1 *(Continued)*

($ millions)	2008	2007	2006	2005	2004	2003	2002
Long-term borrowings	330 067	319 013	260 749	212 167	207 784	170 309	138 570
Total employees	323 000	327 000	319 000	316 000	307 000	305 000	315 000
U.S.	152 000	155 000	155 000	161 000	165 000	155 000	161 000
Other countries	171 000	172 000	164 000	155 000	142 000	150 000	154 000
GE data (industrial businesses)							
Short-term borrowings	2375	4106	2076	972	3252	2555	8786
Long-term borrowings	9827	11 656	9043	8986	7561	8388	970
Shareowners' equity	104 665	115 559	111 509	108 633	110 181	79 666	63 979
Total capital invested	123 545	137 824	128 172	123 899	128 230	91 684	74 763
Return on average total capital invested	14.8%	18.9%	18.5%	16.7%	16.9%	18.1%	24.0%
Borrowings as a percentage of total capital invested	9.9%	11.4%	8.7%	8.0%	9.0%	11.9%	13.0%
Working capital	3904	6433	7527	7853	7788	5282	3821
GECS data (financial services businesses)							
Revenues	71 287	71 936	61 351	54 889	50 320	43 513	38 456
Net earnings	7055	10 301	10 658	7577	8728	7974	2491
Shareowner's equity	53 279	57 676	54 097	50 812	54 379	45 790	37 202
Total borrowings	514 601	500 922	426 262	362 042	355 463	316 593	267 014
Ratio of debt to equity at GE Capital	8.76:1	8.10:1	7.52:1	7.09:1	6.45:1	6.62:1	6.48:1
Total assets	660 902	646 485	565 258	540 584	618 614	554 877	489 602

Source: General Electric, 10-K reports 2006 and 2008.

The General Electric Company

The GE that Jeffrey Immelt inherited in 2001 was the world's most valuable company and was widely regarded as the world's most successful. It is the only company to have remained a member of the Dow Jones industrial index since the index was created in 1896. The key to its success had been to combine massive size with constant adaptation. Over the decades GE had adapted both its business portfolio and its management systems to the demands and opportunities of a changing world.

It was founded in 1892 from the merger of Thomas Edison's Electric Light Company with the Thomas Houston Company. Its business was based upon exploiting Edison's patents relating to electricity generation and distribution, light bulbs, and electric motors. Throughout the twentieth century GE was not only one of the world's biggest industrial corporations, it was also "a model of management—a laboratory studied by business schools and raided by other companies seeking skilled executives."[4] Under the leadership of Charles Coffin, between 1892 and 1922, GE successfully married Edison's industrial R&D laboratory to a business system capable of turning scientific discovery into marketable products. After the Second World War, Chairman Ralph Cordiner, assisted by Peter Drucker, pioneered new approaches to the systematization of corporate management. Under Fred Borch (CEO 1963–72), GE established a system of strategic management based on strategic business units and portfolio analysis that became a model for most diversified corporations. Reg Jones, GE's chairman from 1973 to 1981, further developed GE's system of corporate management linking techniques of strategic planning to systems of financial management.

During his two decades at GE's helm, Jack Welch had led one of the most comprehensive strategic and organizational upheavals in GE's long history. General Electric's business portfolio had been reformulated through a massive exit from extractive and manufacturing businesses where GE lacked the potential for global leadership, together with a major shift into services—financial services in particular. By the time he retired, GE Capital was responsible for close to half of GE's revenues and the majority of its assets. At the heart of Welch's remaking of GE was the creation of a performance culture supported by comprehensive systems for setting and monitoring performance targets and providing powerful incentives for their achievement.

> Changing the culture—opening it up to the quantum change—means constantly asking not how fast am I going, how well am I doing versus how well I did a year or two before, but rather, how fast and how well am I doing versus the world outside. Are we moving faster, are we doing better against that external standard?
>
> Stretch means using dreams to set business targets—with no real idea of how to get there . . . We certainly didn't have a clue how we were going to get to 10 inventory turns [a year] when we set that target. But we're getting there, and as soon as we become sure we can do it—it's time for another stretch.[5]

Welch declared war on GE's elaborate bureaucracy and stripped out layers of hierarchy. His management style was based upon direct human contact—often confrontational—in which managers committed to ambitious performance targets, then pressured themselves and their own subordinates to deliver. Every aspect of GE's management systems was redesigned from the ground up, from strategic planning to human resource management. In addition to remaking the GE culture and infrastructure, every few years Welch would introduce a major new corporate initiative that would shift GE's strategic direction. These included: "Be #1 or #2 in your global industry"; "Work-out," a process for company meetings that allowed grassroots ideas about organizational change to be implemented; "Six Sigma," a program of company wide initiatives to improve quality and reliability; and "Destroy your business dot.com," an initiative to encourage exploitation of internet technologies.

The outcome was two decades of outstanding corporate performance. Between 1981 and 2001, revenues had grown from $30 billion to $126 billion, net income from under $2 billion to $14 billion, and stock market capitalization from $14 billion to $510 billion—an average annual return to stockholders of 24%.

Jeff Immelt

Jeffrey R. Immelt was appointed CEO of GE at the age of 44. He had previously been head of GE's Plastics business and, most recently, head of Medical Systems. He had an economics and applied math degree from Dartmouth and an MBA from Harvard. He claimed that his own experience of GE extended beyond his two decades with the firm—his father spent his entire career at GE. On being recruited from Harvard by GE in 1982, Immelt was identified as a "young high potential" whose progress was tracked by senior executives at GE. In 1987, Immelt was invited to attend the executive development course at Crotonville, GE's management development center. This course was considered the gateway to the executive ranks of GE. At GE Appliances, GE Plastics and GE Medical Systems, Immelt acquired a reputation for turning around troubled units, driving customer service and exploiting new technologies. He also demonstrated the ability to motivate others— an aptitude that he had revealed as an offensive tackler for Dartmouth's football team in the 1970s.[6]

In December 1994, the GE board began to consider possible candidates to replace Jack Welch. Immelt was one among a list of some 20 GE executives submitted by Welch for board consideration. After five years of careful monitoring and assessment the list had shrunk to three: Jim McNerney, Bob Nardelli and Immelt.

Immelt's emergence as front runner owed much to his outstanding success at GE Medical Systems, which he was appointed to lead in 1997. In addition to rigorous cost cutting and exceeding his budget forecasts, Immelt showed the ability to pick good managers, motivate them, pioneer new technologies, and expand the business. His strength was in energizing and motivating others: "He brought the life and energy that drives major growth," commented GE's head of HR.

Immelt had developed a personality and leadership style that contrasted sharply with those of Welch. Yet, they seemed to be similarly effective in driving business performance. *Business Week* observed: "Where Welch ruled through intimidation and thrived as something of a cult figure, Immelt opts for the friendlier, regular-guy approach. He prefers to tease where Welch would taunt. Immelt likes to cheer people on rather than chew them out. That style has given him a very different aura within

GE. He may not be a demigod, but it's his man-of-the-people nature that draws praise from the top ranks to the factory floor."[7] Immelt knew that his different style of leadership would have important implications for his role as CEO and the ways in which he would influence GE's strategy, structure, and systems. However, Immelt believed that the principal changes that he would initiate at GE would be a result of the changing environment and the shifting priorities that GE faced.

GE's Business Environment, 2001–9

The remarkable growth in profits and stock market valuation that Welch had achieved was against a backdrop of an economy effused by optimism, confidence and growth. The new century presented a whole new set of challenges. In his first letter to shareholders, Immelt observed: "The exuberance of the late 1990s and the inevitable downturn have created difficult times. Entire industries have collapsed, poor business models have been exposed, large companies have filed for bankruptcy and corporate credibility has been called into question."[8]

In a world of geopolitical and economic turbulence, Immelt believed that GE's diversified portfolio of businesses would provide GE the stability to weather business cycles: "The GE portfolio was put together for a purpose—to deliver earnings growth through every economic cycle. We're constantly managing these cycles in a business where the sum exceeds the parts."[9]

However, 2008–9 revealed the limits to this "stability through diversity" thesis. General Electric escaped the dire consequences of the credit crunch that engulfed many financial service firms, the problems of GE Capital posed a major threat to the whole corporation that required urgent remedial attention—including the equity injections from Warren Buffet.

A further key change in the business environment was the discrediting of the 1990s' obsession with shareholder value maximization. From the outset, Immelt was anxious to disassociate himself from cruder versions of shareholder value maximization. In all his communications to shareholders, Immelt was emphatic that the job of the CEO was not to manage the stock price but to manage the company for the long-term earnings growth that would drive the stock price: "We all want the stock to go up. But to do that we have to manage the company. In fact, the only way you can run GE is to believe that performance will ultimately drive the stock."[10] Apart from providing the underlying earnings growth, the only other influence that management could play was to offer transparency to investors through detailed financial reporting. If the annual report had to be "the size of the New York City phone book, that's life," commented Immelt. Nevertheless, despite the "new transparency" many of the fears that depressed GE's stock price during the first quarter of 2009 were exacerbated by uncertainty over GE Capital's financial obligations.

However, the most crucial issue for GE, Immelt believed, was to identify the likely sources of profit in the future. Under Welch, the potential for value creation through cost reduction and the elimination of underperforming assets had probably been fully realized. Immelt would need to look to new areas. Top-line growth would have to be the driver of bottom-line returns. Yet, opportunities for value creation were likely to be meager: "I looked at the world post-9/11 and realized that over the next 10 or 20 years, there was not going to be much tailwind." The primary driver of such growth, figured Immelt, was organic growth—given the level of M&A activity and the huge volume of funds flowing into private equity funds, acquisitions could easily destroy shareholder value. With a generally poor outlook for growth in the world economy, the central challenge was to identify where the most promising opportunities for profitable growth would lie.

In identifying opportunities for profitable organic growth, Immelt sought to identify key global trends that would offer business opportunities for GE. Between 2001 and 2009, there were several revisions in Immelt's view of what these trends would be. For example early in 2007, Immelt identified the key growth trends that GE could exploit as: infrastructure, emerging markets, environmental solutions, digital connections, global liquidity and demographics.[11] Two years later, the "big themes" were infrastructure, emerging market growth, clean energy, and sustainable healthcare.[12] Across the 2001–9 period as a whole, four key external trends were paramount:

- *Demography*. The aging of the world's population would create opportunities for goods and services required by older people—healthcare services in particular. Population growth in the developing world would also offer expanding demand for many other of GE's businesses—including entertainment.

- *Infrastructure*. GE predicted massive investments in infrastructure by 2015. GE's positioning in infrastructure products, services and financing offered it opportunities in energy, aviation, rail transportation, water, and oil and gas production.

- *Emerging markets*. China, India, Eastern Europe, Russia, Middle East, Africa, Latin America and South East Asia would offer rates of GDP growth around three times that of the world as a whole. These countries would be key centers of business opportunity for GE.

- *Environment*. The challenges of global warming, water scarcity and conservation would become increasingly pressing creating the need for technologies and innovatory responses to alleviate these problems.

GE's Growth Strategy

Growth—organic growth in particular—became the central theme of Immelt's strategy for GE. In 2002, he committed GE to an organic growth rate of 8% per annum (under Welch organic growth had averaged 5% a year) and to "double digit" earnings growth. This 8% revenue growth was based upon the idea that GE should be able to grow at between two and three times that of world GDP. Profits would grow faster than revenues, explained Immelt, because of reductions in general and administrative expense as a percentage of sales and higher margins resulting from new products and services. Between 2002 and 2007, GE comfortably met these targets: revenues grew at 13% each year, operating earnings at 14%. However, during 2008, revenue growth was only 6% and earnings declined by 19%.

Immelt's growth strategy comprised several elements.

Reshaping the Business Portfolio

To position GE for stronger growth, the company would need to exit slow-growth businesses, reallocate resources to businesses where growth prospects were strong, and enter new businesses. Despite Immelt's focus on organic growth, repositioning would require acquisition. Immelt stressed that GE's acquisitions would be selective and focused: "We don't acquire companies just because we can. We don't go for unrelated fields. We acquire companies that give us new growth platforms where GE capability can improve financial performance and build shareholder value."[13]

Immelt's first five years were a period of intense acquisition activity for GE. Between September 2001 and March 2009, GE's major acquisitions were in five major areas:

- *Broadcasting and entertainment.* The acquisitions of Telemundo and Bravo TV networks, Vivendi Universal's entertainment business, and Oxygen Media represented a massive expansion of GE's presence in movies and TV.
- *Healthcare.* Key acquisitions included: Amersham (U.K. diagnostics and medical equipment company), HPSC (financial services for medical and dental practices), and Abbott Diagnostics (the world's leading provider of *in vitro* diagnostics).
- *Energy.* Major growth areas were in alternative energy sources (e.g. acquisitions of Enron's wind energy business, BHA Group Holdings—emission reduction equipment, ChevronTexaco's coal gasification business, AstroPower—solar energy products; and Vetco Gray and Hydril Pressure Control (petroleum drilling equipment).
- *Technology infrastructure.* Key acquisitions were in security systems (InVision Technologies explosive detection systems; Edwards Systems Technology, fire detection; Interlogix, security systems); water treatment (Ionics and BetzDearborn); and aerospace (Smiths Aerospace, avionics and aircraft components).
- *Finance.* GE Capital continued to make acquisitions in the area of equipment leasing, commercial finance, credit cards and consumer finance.

Table 23.2 shows GE's main acquisitions and divestments during 2001–9. Table 23.3 shows basic financial data for GE's business segments, while Table 23.4 gives detailed information for GE Capital.

TABLE 23.2 General Electric's principal acquisitions and disposals, 2001–8

2001	NBC acquires Telemundo, a leading Spanish language television networks.
2003	GE Healthcare acquires Instrumentarium.
2003	GE Capital acquires Transamerica Finance from AEGON, who retained the rest of Transamerica Corporation.
2004	NBC acquires the entertainment assets of Vivendi Universal, excluding Universal Music. This forms NBC Universal, of which General Electric owns 80%.
2004	GE Healthcare acquires Amersham plc.
2004	GE Capital acquires Dillard's credit card unit for U.S.$1.25 billion.
2004	GE sells 60% stake in GE Capital International Services (GECIS) to private equity companies, Oak Hill Capital Partners and General Atlantic, for $500 million.

(continued)

TABLE 23.2 *(Continued)*

2004	GE's life and mortgage insurance businesses spun off as Genworth Financial.
2004	GE Security acquires InVision Technologies, a leading manufacturer of airport security equipment.
2005	GE Commercial Finance acquires the financial assets of Bombardier, a Canadian aircraft manufacturer for U.S.$1.4 billion.
2006	GE Healthcare acquires IDX Systems, a medical software firm, for U.S.$1.2 billion.
2006	GE Advanced Materials division is sold to Apollo Management for U.S.$3.8 billion.
2006	GE Water & Process Technologies acquires Zenon Environmental Systems for $758 million.
2006	Sale of GE Insurance Solutions and GE Life to Swiss Re.
2007	GE-Aviation acquires Smiths Aerospace for $4.6 billion.
2007	GE Oil and Gas acquires Vetco Gray for $1.4 billion.
2007	GE Plastics is sold to Saudi Arabia Basic Industries Corp. for $11.7 billion.
2007	GE NBC-Universal acquires Oxygen Media (cable TV channel).
2008	GE Co. acquires Vital Signs Inc. for $860 million.
2008	GE Energy Infrastructure acquires Hydril Pressure Control (oilfield equipment).
2008	GE Capital finance acquires Merrill Lynch Capital, CitiCapital and Bank BPH.

TABLE 23.3 General Electric: segment performance, 2004–8 ($ millions)

	2008	2007	2006	2005	2004
Revenues					
Energy Infrastructure	38 571	30 698	25 221	21 921	19 841
of which:					
Energy	29 309	22 456	19 406	–	–
Oil and Gas	7417	6849	4340	–	–
Technology Infrastructure	46 316	42 801	37 687	33 873	30 142
of which:					
Aviation	19 239	16 819	13 017	–	–
Enterprise Solutions	4710	4462	3951	–	–
Healthcare	17 392	16 997	16 560	–	–
Transportation	5016	4523	4159	–	–
NBC Universal	16 969	15 416	16 188	14 689	12 886
Capital Finance	67 008	66 301	56 378	49 071	43 750
Consumer and Industrial	11 737	12 663	13 202	13 040	12 408
Profit					
Energy Infrastructure	6080	4817	3518	3222	3100
of which:					
Energy	4880	3835	2918	–	–
Oil and Gas	1127	860	548	–	–
Technology Infrastructure	8152	7883	7308	6188	5412
of which:					
Aviation	3684	3222	2802	–	–
Enterprise Solutions	691	697	620	–	–
Healthcare	2851	3056	3142	–	–
Transportation	962	936	774	–	–

(continued)

TABLE 23.3 *(Continued)*

	2008	2007	2006	2005	2004
NBC Universal	3131	3107	2919	3092	2558
Capital Finance	8632	12243	10397	8414	6593
Consumer and Industrial	365	1034	970	732	601
Assets					
Energy Infrastructure	33836	31466	24456	–	–
Technology Infrastructure	58967	57670	49641	–	–
NBC Universal	33781	33089	31425	–	–
Capital Finance	572903	583965	491000	–	–
Consumer and Industrial	5065	5351	5740	–	–
Investment (Property, plant and equipment additions)					
Energy Infrastructure	1226	1054	867	–	–
Technology Infrastructure	1395	1954	1389	–	–
NBC Universal	131	306	352	–	–
Capital Finance	15313	17832	14489	–	–
Consumer & Industrial	284	363	373	–	–

Source: General Electric, 10-K Report, 2008.

TABLE 23.4 GE Capital Finance: financial data by business segment (in $ millions)

	2008	2007	2006
Revenues			
Commercial Lending and Leasing	26742	27267	25833
GE Money	25012	24769	19508
Real Estate	6646	7021	5020
Energy Financial Services	3707	2405	1664
GE Commercial Aviation Services	4901	4839	4353
Profit			
Commercial Lending and Leasing	1805	3801	3503
GE Money	3664	4269	3231
Real Estate	1144	2285	1841
Energy Financial Services	825	677	648
GE Commercial Aviation Services	1194	1211	1174
Total assets			
Commercial Lending and Leasing	232486	229608	
GE Money	183617	209178	
Real Estate	85266	79285	
Energy Financial Services	22079	18705	
GE Commercial Aviation Services	49455	47189	

Source: General Electric, 10-K Report, 2008.

A key theme in Immelt's reshaping of GE's business portfolio towards higher growth was the creation of new "growth platforms." Growth platforms could be extensions of existing businesses or they could be entirely new areas of business. For example, GE's expansion into Spanish language broadcasting (spearheaded by the acquisition of Telemundo) was an example of one of GE's businesses (NBC) expanding into a new, fast-growing market segment. Other growth platforms could be entirely new businesses that drew upon some of GE's existing strengths. For example, renewable energy and security services were entirely new areas of business for GE.

Identifying new growth platforms was established as a central strategic challenge for GE's businesses. The approach involved the analysis and segmentation of markets to identify high-growth segments that offered the potential for attractive returns, then to use a small acquisition as a basis for deploying GE's financial, technical and managerial resources to build a leading position. Immelt explained the role of his acquisitions as follows:

> We did a lot of heavy lifting in our portfolio because we didn't have enough juice. We saw where we needed to go and we found that we wouldn't get there with our existing businesses. So, we bought homeland security, biotech, water—businesses that would give us a stronger foundation for innovation.[14]

General Electric also exited from a number of low-growth, low-margin businesses including insurance and plastics, and consumer financial services in Japan. It was widely believed that appliances and lighting would also be candidates for divestment. Despite, Immelt's assurance that "We'll stay in those businesses. They both return their cost of capital,"[15] General Electric's Consumer and Industrial segment was conspicuously absent from Immelt's references to GE's efforts to "build strong businesses." The Appendix describes GE's main businesses at the end of 2008.

Technology

Immelt remarked on the fact that he represented a different generation from Jack Welch and that his generation had a much closer affinity for technology. He identified technology as a major driver of GE's future growth and emphasized the need to speed the diffusion of new technologies within GE and turn the corporate R&D center into an intellectual hothouse. His commitment to technology was signaled by expanding GE's R&D budgets. This began with a $100 million upgrade to GE's corporate R&D center in Niskayuna, New York and was followed by the construction of new Global Research Centers in Shanghai and Munich, Germany. By the end of 2008, GE Global Research had over 2500 researchers working in GE Global Research Centers in New York, Bangalore, Shanghai, and Munich.

Immelt's emphasis on technology reflected his belief that the primary driver of sales was great products: "You can be six sigma, you can do great delivery, you can be great in China, you can do everything else well—but if you don't have a good product, you're not going to sell much". [16] Increasing product quality and product innovation became a critical performance indicator for all of GE's businesses.

Under Welch, the emphasis of R&D had been short-term product development. Under Immelt, the time horizon lengthened and focused upon fewer, bigger projects: the number or projects was cut from over 1000 to just 100. Looking beyond the lifespan of individual projects, five broad areas of technology were given particular emphasis including nanotechnology, advanced propulsion and biotechnology.

Among new projects, Immelt was particularly interested in identifying and supporting projects that offered large-scale market potential. "Imagination Breakthroughs" were promising projects with the potential to create $100 million in sales over a three-year period. By mid-2006, some 100 Imagination Breakthroughs had been identified and individually approved by Immelt. Major Imagination Breakthroughs included

- *Evolution* hybrid locomotive: an energy-saving locomotive that would use energy lost in braking to be stored in batteries.
- *Smart Grid*: a marriage of IT with electrical infrastructure to support twenty-first century energy needs.
- *Sodium batteries*: a novel, patented battery technology for large-scale electricity storage.

Customer Focus and Integrated Solutions

A key feature of Immelt's career at GE was the extent of his customer orientation and the amount of time he spent with customers, building relationships with them and working on their problems. Looking ahead, Immelt saw GE using IT and redesigned processes to become increasingly customer focused. Soon after taking over as CEO, Immelt emphasized the primacy of customer focus: "We're dramatically changing our resource base from providing support to creating value. Every business has functions that add high value by driving growth. These are the functions that deal with the customer, create new products, sell, manufacture, manage the money and drive controllership. Call that the front room. Every business has backroom support functions that sometimes are so large and bureaucratic they create a drain on the system and keep us from meeting our customers' needs and keep us from growing. So we're going to take more of the back-room resources and put them in the front room—more sales people, more engineers, more product designers. We're changing the shape of this company and we're doing it during a recession."[17] The increased customer focus involved increased investment in GE's marketing function—including hiring talented marketing executives and developing processes for identifying new product and service offerings and unmet customer needs. Some of these are discussed below in relation to "Changing the GE Management Model."

An important outcome of GE's enhanced customer focus would be the ability better to meet customer needs through bundling products with support services and combining product and service offerings from different businesses. Every business was encouraged to create customer value through bundling products with a variety of customer service offerings, including technical services, financial services, training, and the like. Across businesses, enterprise selling was given greater prominence. For example, in the case of a new hospital development, there might be opportunities not just for medical equipment but also for lighting, turbines and other GE businesses as well. To exploit new opportunities that cut across GE's existing divisional structure, GE began to create cross-business, high-visibility marketing campaigns.

"Ecomagination" emerged from GE's 2004 strategic planning process as a way for GE to better capitalize on greater environmental awareness through combining initiatives in emissions reduction, energy efficiency, water supply, and scarcity management. The ecomagination proposal then went to the Commercial Council, which planned an initiative involving 17 products.[18]

Increasing GE's capacity to serve customers better with integrated solutions was a key consideration in Immelt's reorganization of GE's structure in which divisions were consolidated into a few broad-based business sectors—the aim being to facilitate closer integration of related businesses. (The changes in GE's organizational structure will be considered in greater detail in the next section.)

Immelt believed that some of the biggest payoffs from greater customer orientation would come from GE's increased success in international markets. This would involve more local product development and an increased emphasis on truly aligning products and services to meet local market needs rather than simply adapting product features. In terms of exploiting opportunities in major growth markets such as India and China, Immelt saw the need to go from a "defeaturing" mindset (providing a stripped-down American product) to a "customer-optimization" mindset.

Exploiting global opportunities also involved globalizing GE's own talent base. Under Immelt's leadership, GE sought to internationalize its workforce—including core corporate functions. By 2006, of 400 younger members of GE's audit staff, about 60 were Indian.

GE's Competitive Advantage

In GE's annual report for 2008, Immelt outlined the basis on which GE would build "solid competitive advantage over the long term":

OUR STRATEGY
Our strategy borrows our key strengths from the past and makes them relevant to a new era of global business:

Be Global. Our non-U.S. revenues have averaged 13% annual growth this decade. We expect our global growth to outpace the U.S. in 2009. This is a source of competitive advantage for GE. We are perfecting an approach called "connected and scalable localization" whereby we accelerate growth by expanding our local product lines, serving new customers, and creating strong partnerships with local champions. GE has 25 countries each with more than $1 billion in revenues, so empowering our local teams is critical to driving growth. Global diversity is important in this cycle because it diversifies revenues and risk. We expect Healthcare's diagnostic imaging business to suffer in the U.S. as our customers grapple with budget cuts. However, we have a $9 billion global healthcare business that we expect to experience strong demographic growth, offsetting weakness in the U.S.

Drive Innovation. We will invest $10 billion in technology and content in 2009, the same level as 2008. Since 2000, we have invested approximately $50 billion in product technology. We'll launch economical "value products" in

2009 such as the 2.6-megawatt wind turbine, which has high efficiency, more capacity, and lower cost. We'll continue to build our innovation pipeline. We launched a venture in digital pathology, which we think will be a $2 billion market over time. We launched hulu,™ a joint venture between NBC Universal and News Corp., which is an innovative digital content platform competing with YouTube.™ We have invested $150 million in battery technology that will power our hybrid locomotives. We will continue to fund innovation through the downturn.

Build Relationships. GE has many ventures and partnerships that help us grow and diversify risk on a global basis. Our multi-business structure makes us a particularly desirable partner for governments and other large investors. A great example is our spectacular success with the Beijing 2008 Olympic Games. This event produced $2 billion of revenues across multiple GE platforms, while building our relationships in China. In 2008, we announced a multifaceted partnership with Mubadala, the commercial investing arm of Abu Dhabi, which includes a commercial finance joint venture, projects in renewable energy, and a training center in Abu Dhabi. Mubadala will also become a "Top 10" GE investor.

Leverage Strengths. We have core processes centered on organic growth, operating excellence, and leadership development. The aim of these processes is to spread best practices across the Company. We compare our progress on common metrics in industrial organic revenue growth, margins, return on total capital, and productivity as measured by revenue per employee with a composite of world-class peers. We continue to perform. In addition, we continue to invest $1 billion annually in our people and leadership development. We value our team. We remain committed to developing broad and "battle-tested" global leaders.[19]

Changing the GE Management Model

The management system that Immelt inherited had been reformulated by his predecessor and mentor, Jack Welch, but as also a product of 120 years of continuous development. Immelt respected GE's management systems and process, and recognized that many of them were so deeply embedded within GE's culture that they were integral to GE's identity and the way it viewed the world. At the core of GE's management system was its management development—its so-called "talent machine"—and its system of performance management.

General Electric is unique among leading corporations for its reliance upon internally developed leadership: all of its CEOs were promoted from within the company. General Electric's meritocratic system of development and promotion was put in place by Charles Coffin, the CEO who succeeded Edison in 1892. Since then GE has been a "CEO factory" that has produced top management talent not only for GE, but for many other corporations. During the 1950s, GE worked on the two key pillars of its management development system: its corporate university at Crotonville, NY, and its "Session C" system of tracking, evaluating, and planning managers' careers and formulating succession plans for every management position at GE from department head upwards. Jack Welch greatly increased senior executives' emphasis on the management development and career planning process emphasis. The Session C reviews became all-day events at each of GE's businesses involving Welch and the business CEO reviewing the performance, values, and potential of each manager.

General Electric's management appraisal and management development processes formed one dimension of a management system devoted to driving high performance. The company's financial planning, strategic planning, and HR appraisal and development were all based upon sophisticated processes for measuring performance and identifying the determinants of superior performance. Under Jack Welch the GE's system of performance management became increasingly based upon quantitative targets that allowed focus and accountability. "Nothing happens in this company without an output metric," observed Immelt. All of Immelt's strategic initiatives—from the 8% organic growth target to productivity improvements, reductions in overhead costs and six sigma—were linked to precise quantitative targets. In 2005 GE standardized its customer satisfaction metrics, focusing on "net promoter scores" (the percentage of customers who would recommend GE to a friend, minus the percentage who wouldn't).

GE's commitment to management development and metrics-based performance management would continue to be the foundation for GE's management system under Immelt's leadership; at the same time, the redirecting of GE's strategy towards a greater emphasis technology, customer focus and increased integration across GE's different businesses also required significant changes to GE's structure and systems. As *Harvard Business Review* editor, Tom Stewart observed:

> Immelt put two of GE's traditional strengths—process orientation and the ability to develop, test, and deploy new management ideas in the service of a different goal. That meant designing a process that could reliably draw new revenue streams form existing businesses.[20]

Changing Organizational Structure

The most visible of the management changes introduced by Immelt concerned the overall structure of the organization. Between 2002 and 2008, Immelt reversed several of the major structural changes that Welch had introduced during the 1980s. As part of "delayering" and his effort to create a more responsive company, Welch had broken up GE's major industrial sectors into smaller divisions. In order to facilitate greater cross-business integration, the bundling of products and services into "systems", and the creation of new "growth platforms", Immelt progressively reorganized GE's divisions into a smaller number of broad-based sectors. Following an initial reorganization in 2002, a further reorganization was initiated in 2005: "In 2005, we restructured the Company into six businesses focused on the broad markets we serve: Infrastructure, Commercial Finance, Consumer Finance, Healthcare, NBC Universal, and Industrial. Each business has scale, market leadership, and superior customer offerings."[21] In 2008, these six businesses were reduced to five. Figures 23.1 and 23.2 show GE's organizational structure in 2001 and in March 2009.

FIGURE 23.1 General Electric's organization structure, 2001

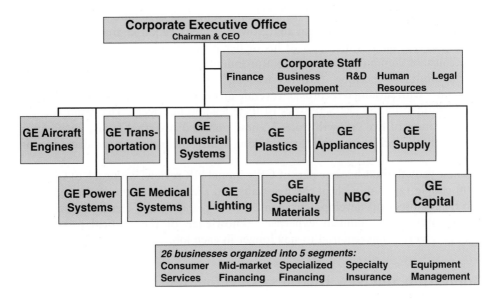

FIGURE 23.2 General Electric's organization structure: segments and businesses, January, 2009

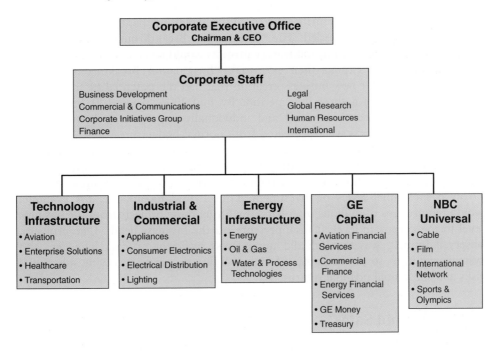

Leadership Development

As with Jack Welch, Immelt saw his most important task as helping to develop GE's managerial talent. To implement his growth strategy required that each of GE's employees internalized it as part of his or her personal mission. This required not only constant communication and reinforcement from the CEO but also the skills and aptitudes to become "growth leaders." A benchmarking exercise on 15 companies with sustained records of revenue growth (for example, Toyota and Dell) sought to identify the characteristics of their leading managers. The result was the categorization of five "growth traits." These included: external focus, imagination and creativity, decisiveness and clear thinking ability, inclusiveness and deep domain expertise.

These growth traits became part of GE's annual HR review, with each of GE's top 5000 people rated on each of the five traits and the results of the assessment built into their subsequent development plans. Career planning also changed: because of the importance of "domain expertise" (knowledge of the particular business), managers were being required to stay longer in each job.

Innovation and New Business Development

A key challenge was to reconcile GE's famous obsession with profitability and cost control with nurturing the innovation that would drive growth. Innovation, especially when it included big, long-term projects, involved substantial risk. The danger was that GE's obsession with performance metrics might discourage business unit heads from making big bets on promising new opportunities. Furthermore, given the fact that many of the biggest opportunities were likely to require cooperation across divisions further increased the likelihood that that they would fail to get the support they needed. The "Imagination Breakthroughs" initiative was designed to ensure that major, innovatory projects would receive the investment and attention needed to exploit their potential. "Imagination Breakthroughs" were promising projects for new business creation that had the potential to create $100 million in sales over a three-year period. By mid-2006, some 100 Imagination Breakthroughs had been identified and individually approved by Immelt. Once approved, these projects were protected from normal budget pressures. About half involved new products and the other half involved changing commercial structure. Immelt saw these Innovation Breakthroughs as a means of focusing attention on the goal of business creation and development. Given that some of these projects involved substantial levels of investment (GE's hybrid locomotive, for example, would require tens of millions of dollars), by lifting these projects from the business level to the corporate level, it took pressure off the business heads. One problem, observed Immelt, was that GE did not possess sufficient product managers and systems engineers to put in charge of high-visibility programs involving substantial risks and substantial possible returns.

Marketing and Sales

A key aspect of Immelt's creation of a customer-driven company was a revitalization of GE's marketing function. "Marketing was the place where washed-up salespeople went."[22] Upgrading GE's marketing was achieved through creating the new senior corporate position of Chief Marketing Officer, the recreation of GE's Advanced Marketing Seminar, developing an Experienced Commercial Leadership Program, and requiring that every business appoint a VP-level head of marketing. Most important was the creation of GE's Commercial Council, which brought together GE's leading sales and marketing leaders to develop new business ideas, to transfer best practices and instill a commercial culture within GE. A key initiative was "At the Customer, For the Customer," a program that deployed six sigma in marketing, sales, and customer relations activities, applied GE's six sigma methodologies to customers' own businesses, and used new metrics to track customer satisfaction and customer attitudes.

As with all aspects of GE's approach to management, marketing was subject to the same systematized, metrics-driven analysis as all other functions within the firm, often with some startling revelations:

> We're getting the sales force better trained and equipped with better tools and metrics. A good example is what we're doing to create discipline around pricing. Not long ago, a guy here named Dave McCalpin did an analysis of our pricing in appliances and found out that about $5 billion of it is discretionary. Given all the decisions that sales reps can make on their own, that's how much is in play. It was the most astounding number I'd ever heard—and that's just in appliances. Extrapolating across our businesses, there may be $50 billion that few people are tracking or accountable for. We would never allow something like that on the cost side. When it comes to the prices we pay, we study them, we map them, we work them. But with the prices we charge, we're too sloppy.[23]

The GE Growth Process

By early 2006, GE's various management initiatives with regard to changing GE's performance metrics, revising its management development process, fostering innovation and developing a stronger marketing function were integrated into what Immelt referred to the GE Growth Process. As Immelt explained:

> If you run a big multibusiness company like GE and you're trying to lead transformative change, that objective has to be linked to hitting levers across all of the businesses—and it must keep that up over time. So you've got to have a process. That's true from an internal standpoint, but it's also the only way you get paid in the marketplace. Investors have to see that it's repeatable.
>
> I knew if I could define a process and set the right metrics, this company could go 100 miles an hour in the right direction. It took time, though, to understand growth as a process. If I had worked out that wheel-shaped diagram in 2001, I would have started with it. But in reality, you get these things by wallowing in them awhile. We had a few steps worked out in 2003, but it took another two years to fill in the process.[24]

During 2006, Immelt's view of GE's growth engine as an integrated, six-part process was disseminated throughout the organization and became a key part of Immelt's communication to GE's external constituencies (see Figure 23.3).

FIGURE 23.3 General Electric's six-part growth process

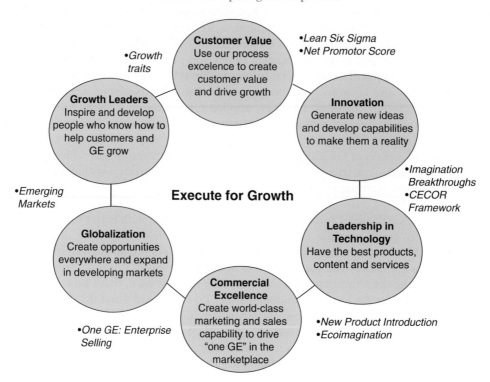

The Challenge of Integration and Complexity

Common to most of the organizational changes initiated by Immelt was the desire to create value through the many parts of GE working together more closely and more effectively. "Working at GE is the art of thinking and playing big; our managers have to work cross-function, cross-region, cross-company. And we have to be about big purposes," observed Immelt.[25]

However, greater integration across GE's different businesses created complex coordination problems. GE has gone beyond cross-selling and product bundling to embrace the concept of "enterprise selling":

> We've always done enterprise selling on an ad hoc basis, but we want to go beyond the convenient cross-selling opportunities and think more systematically about the kinds of customers that can benefit from our broad portfolio. If somebody's building a hospital, that might represent a total package of $1 billion, of which the GE market potential might be $100 million. We're probably already talking to the C-suite because we sell the medical equipment. What we need to do is set things up so that the medical rep can bring in the lighting rep, the turbine rep, and so on.[26]

This concept of enterprise selling has also been applied to whole countries:

> In Qatar, the emir wants to know everybody doing business in his country. In a dinner set up to talk about oil and gas bids, he might say, "Jeff, I'm going to

EXHIBIT 23.1

GE Medical Systems Customer Solutions Initiative

One of the earliest initiatives to exploit opportunities for bundling products and services was to combine the sale of medical imaging equipment with consulting services. In 2001, GE Medical Systems (soon to become GE Healthcare) created a new unit, Performance Solutions, to provide an integrated approach to hospital diagnostic imaging departments by combining equipment with technical support and patient-management systems. A lead customer was Stanford University Medical Center which transitioned to all-digital imaging for its hospital and outpatient unit.

After a promising start, by 2005, Performance Solutions was in trouble. The medical equipment

sales people had limited understanding of the consulting services being offered by the Performance Solutions unit and provided few sales leads for the new integrated offering. They were also reluctant to share their customers with sales personnel from Performance Solutions. Meanwhile, the sales personnel from Performance Solutions considered themselves as "solution providers" and felt constrained by having to limit their solutions exclusively to GE offerings.

Source: Based upon Ranjay Gulati "Silo Busting How to Execute on the Promise of Customer Focus," *Harvard Business Review* (May, 2007).

put $10 billion into a hospital," or he might mention that they're going to buy GE engines for Qatar Airways.[27]

Exploiting customer requirements across a range of products and services is highly appealing for a diversified company like GE, but it has complex organizational ramifications. Sales and marketing staff becoming less focused upon their particular business and more oriented towards the opportunities provided from across the company as a whole. In practice, this creates complex problems of organization, expertise, and incentives. Exhibit 23.1 describes the difficulties encountered in the apparently simple bundling of medical diagnostic equipment with consulting services.

As Immelt recognized, organizing to meet customer needs implied a different type of organizational structure from organizing for operational efficiency. Similar challenges existed in relation to GE's efforts to develop large-scale innovations that cut across its existing business-based structure. Reconciling these different coordination needs posed organizational challenges that even GE had not fully resolved:

I've found that few companies are actually structured to deliver products and services in a synchronized way that's attractive from a customer's perspective. Individual units are historically focused on perfecting their products and processes, and give little thought to how their offerings might be even more valuable to the end user when paired with those of another unit. It's not just that the status quo doesn't reward collaborative behavior—although the right incentives are also critical. It's that the connections literally aren't in place.

One way to forge those connections is to do away with traditional silos altogether and create new ones organized by customer segments or needs. Many companies, however, are understandably reluctant to let go of the economies of scale and depth of knowledge and expertise associated with non-customer-focused silos. A company organized around geographies can customize offerings to suit local preferences, for instance, while a technology-centric firm can be quick to market with technical innovations. In many cases, functional and geographic silos were created precisely to help companies coordinate such activities as designing innovative products or gaining geographic focus. A customer focus requires them to emphasize a different set of activities and coordinate them in a different way.

In their initial attempts to offer customer solutions, companies are likely to create structures and processes that transcend rather than obliterate silos. Such boundary-spanning efforts may be highly informal—even as simple as hoping for or encouraging serendipity and impromptu conversations that lead to unplanned cross-unit solutions. But the casual exchange of information and ideas is generally most effective among senior executives, who have a better understanding than their subordinates of corporate goals and easier access to other leaders in the organization.[28]

Extensive collaboration across divisional boundaries also mitigated against some aspects of GE's performance-management systems. Part of the paradox of GE was its reconciliation of cooperation and a one-enterprise culture with strong internal competition—not just competition for resources but also competition between people for recognition and reward. As Immelt pushed cross-business initiatives in innovation, new business development, and marketing and sales, it seemed likely that the intense internal pressures for meeting divisional performance targets would be compromised.

A key feature of the performance driven organization that Welch had created was a clear division between the role of the business division and that of the corporate headquarters. The business divisions with their individual CEOs were responsible for running their own businesses both operationally and strategically. The role of the corporate headquarters was both to support the businesses through various centralized services and to drive business performance by putting divisional top management under intense pressure to deliver.

As headquarters became increasingly involved in promoting and developing developmental initiatives such as GE's "Imagination Breakthroughs" and enterprise selling, increasingly the corporate headquarters became a partner with the business divisions rather than an overseer of divisional performance and interrogator of business strategies.

As a result, much of the simplicity and directness associated with Welch's management style was being supplanted by an emphasis on managing integration which inevitably involved more sophisticated approaches to strategy execution. Developing new products, businesses, and customer solutions required new and more complex cross-business and cross-functional coordination within GE. The new performance requirements were being built on top of GE's existing commitments to efficiency, quality and financial performance. Could this added complexity be borne by a company that was steadily growing larger and encompassing a widening portfolio of businesses and products? Management research pointed to the fact that most companies pursuing the combination of innovation and efficiency in fast-moving business environments were forced to become less diverse in order to maintain outstanding performance. Among the other top-20 companies on *Fortune's* "most admired" list in 2006, Procter & Gamble, Johnson & Johnson, Berkshire Hathaway, and 3M were widely diversified—the other 15 were much more specialized, with most being single-business companies (FedEx, Southwest Airlines, Dell, Toyota, Wal-Mart, UPS, Home Depot, Costco). As Immelt made clear to his top managers, GE was entering uncharted waters: "The business book that can help you hasn't been written yet." While Immelt was extolling the benefits of GE's diversity as a source of strength and opportunity, other companies were moving in the opposite direction, divesting businesses in order to achieve a narrower core-business focus. As Chris Zook, head of global strategy at Bain, commented: "The conglomerates are dead. With some rare exceptions, the conglomerates' business model belongs to the past and is unlikely to reappear."[29]

Appendix: General Electric's businesses (extract from 10-K Report, 2008)

Energy Infrastructure

Energy Infrastructure (21.1%, 17.8% and 16.6% of consolidated revenues in 2008, 2007 and 2006, respectively) is a leader in the field of development, implementation and improvement of products and technologies that harness resources such as wind, oil, gas and water . . .

Energy

Energy serves power-generation, industrial, government and other customers worldwide with products and services related to energy production, distribution and management. We offer wind turbines as part of our renewable energy portfolio, which also includes solar technology. We also sell aircraft engine derivatives for use as industrial power sources. Gas turbines and generators are used principally in power plants for generation of electricity and for industrial cogeneration and mechanical drive applications. We are a leading provider of Integrated Gasification Combined Cycle (IGCC) technology design and development. Integrated Gasification Combined Cycle systems convert coal and other hydrocarbons into synthetic gas that, after cleanup, is used as the primary fuel for gas turbines in combined-cycle systems . . . Nuclear reactors, fuel and support services for both new and installed boiling water reactors are offered through joint ventures with Hitachi and Toshiba . . .

Oil and Gas

Our technology helps oil and gas companies make more efficient and sustainable use of the world's energy resources.

Oil and Gas supplies mission critical equipment for the global oil and gas industry, used in applications spanning the entire value chain from drilling and completion through production, transportation and pipeline inspection and including downstream processing in refineries and petrochemical plants. The business designs and manufactures surface and subsea drilling and production systems, equipment for floating production platforms, compressors, turbines, turboexpanders, high-pressure reactors, industrial power generation and a broad portfolio of ancillary equipment. [O]ur service business has over 40 service centers and workshops in all of the world's main oil and gas extraction and production regions . . .

Water and Process Technologies

Water and Process Technologies offers water treatment solutions for industrial and municipal water systems, including the supply and related services of specialty chemicals, water purification systems, pumps, valves, filters and fluid handling equipment for improving the performance of water, wastewater and process systems, including mobile treatment systems and desalination processes . . .

Technology Infrastructure

Technology Infrastructure (25.4%, 24.8% and 24.9% of consolidated revenues in 2008, 2007 and 2006, respectively) is one of the world's leading providers of essential technologies to developed, developing and emerging countries. Around the world, we are helping build healthcare, transportation and technology infrastructure.

Aviation

Aviation produces, sells and services jet engines, turboprop and turbo shaft engines and related replacement parts for use in military and commercial aircraft. Our military engines are used in a wide variety of aircraft including fighters, bombers, tankers, helicopters and surveillance aircraft, as well as marine applications, and our commercial engines power aircraft in all categories of range: short/medium, intermediate and long-range, as well as executive and regional aircraft. We also produce and market engines through CFM International, a company jointly owned by GE and Snecma, a subsidiary of SAFRAN of France, and Engine Alliance, LLC, a company jointly owned by GE and the Pratt & Whitney division of United Technologies Corporation. New engines are also being designed and marketed in joint ventures with Rolls-Royce Group plc and Honda Aero, Inc., a division of Honda Motor Co., Ltd.

Enterprise Solutions

Enterprise Solutions delivers integrated solutions that improve customers' productivity and profitability. We offer integrated solutions using sensors and non-destructive testing, security and life safety technologies, power system protection and control and plant automation and embedded computing systems. From home to industry to national security, our technology covers the full spectrum of security solutions, including card access systems, high-tech video monitoring, intrusion and fire detection, real estate and property control, and explosives and narcotics detection. We design and manufacture equipment and systems that enable customers to monitor, protect, control and ensure the safety of their critical applications . . .

Healthcare

Healthcare has expertise in medical imaging and information technologies, medical diagnostics, patient monitoring systems, disease research, drug discovery and biopharmaceutical manufacturing technologies. We are dedicated to predicting and detecting disease earlier, monitoring its progress and informing physicians, helping them to tailor treatment for individual patients. Healthcare manufactures, sells and services a wide range of medical equipment that helps provide a fast, non-invasive way for doctors to see broken bones, diagnose trauma cases in the ER, view the heart and its function, and identify early stages of cancers or brain disorders. With X-ray, digital mammography, computed tomography (CT), magnetic resonance (MR) and molecular imaging technologies, Healthcare creates industry-leading products that allow clinicians to see inside the human body more clearly than ever. In addition, Healthcare manufactured technologies include patient monitoring, diagnostic cardiology, ultrasound, bone densitometry, anesthesiology and oxygen therapy, and neonatal and critical care devices . . .

Transportation

Transportation provides technology solutions for customers in a variety of industries including railroad, transit, mining, oil and gas, power generation and marine. We serve customers in more than 100 countries.

Transportation manufactures high-horsepower diesel-electric locomotives . . . We also offer leading drive technology solutions to the mining, transit, marine and stationary and drilling industries. Our motors operate in thousands of applications, from electrical drive systems for large haulage trucks used in the mining industry to transit cars and drilling rigs, and our engines are used for marine power . . .

Transportation also provides a portfolio of service offerings designed to improve fleet efficiency and reduce operating expenses . . .

NBC Universal

NBC Universal (9.3%, 8.9% and 10.7% of consolidated revenues in 2008, 2007 and 2006, respectively) is a diversified media and entertainment company focused on the development, production and marketing of entertainment, news and information to a global audience. NBC Universal, which is 80% owned by General Electric and 20% owned by Vivendi S.A., is engaged in the production and distribution of film and television programming; the operation of leading cable/satellite television networks around the world; the broadcast of network television through owned and affiliated television stations within the United States; and investment and programming activities in digital media and the internet. Our premier film company, Universal Pictures, is engaged in the production and worldwide distribution of theatrical, home entertainment and television programming. We own the world-renowned theme park Universal Studios Hollywood, operate and hold an ownership interest in the Universal Studios Florida theme parks and brand, design and develop international theme parks under exclusive licenses. Our cable/satellite television networks provide produced and acquired entertainment, news and information programming to households worldwide. Our cable/satellite television networks include the USA Network, Bravo, CNBC, the SciFi Channel, MSNBC, Oxygen, UniHD, Chiller, Sleuth, mun2, and branded channels across Europe, Asia and Latin America. The NBC television network is one of four major U.S. commercial broadcast television networks. Together, the NBC television network and Telemundo, our U.S. Spanish-language broadcast television network, serve 210 affiliated stations within the U.S. At December 31, 2008, we owned and operated 26 television stations each subject to U.S. Federal Communications Commission regulation. We have exclusive U.S. television rights to the 2010 and 2012 Olympic Games, National Football League Sunday Night Football and the Super Bowl in 2012 . . .

Capital Finance

Capital Finance (36.7%, 38.4% and 37.2% of consolidated revenues in 2008, 2007 and 2006, respectively) offers a broad range of financial products and services worldwide. Services include commercial loans, operating leases, fleet management, financial programs, home loans, credit cards, personal loans and other financial services . . .

Commercial Lending and Leasing (CLL)

Commercial Lending and Leasing offers a broad range of financial services worldwide. We have particular mid-market expertise and offer loans, leases and other financial services to customers, including manufacturers, distributors and end users for a variety of equipment and major capital assets. These assets include industrial-related facilities and equipment; vehicles; corporate aircraft; and equipment used in many industries, including the construction, manufacturing, transportation, telecommunications and healthcare industries . . .

GE Money

GE Money, through consolidated entities and associated companies, is a leading provider of financial services to consumers and retailers in over 50 countries around the world. We offer a full range of innovative financial products to suit customers' needs. These products include, on a global basis, private-label credit cards; personal loans; bank cards; auto loans and leases; mortgages; debt consolidation; home equity loans; deposit and other savings products; and small and medium enterprise lending . . .

Real Estate

Real Estate offers a comprehensive range of capital and investment solutions, including equity capital for acquisition or development, as well as fixed and floating rate mortgages for new acquisitions or recapitalizations of commercial real estate worldwide. Our business finances, with both equity and loan structures, the acquisition, refinancing and renovation of office buildings, apartment buildings, retail facilities, hotels, parking facilities and industrial properties. Our typical real estate loans are intermediate term, senior, fixed or floating-rate, and are secured by existing income-producing commercial properties. We invest in, and provide restructuring financing for, portfolios of mortgage loans, limited partnerships and tax-exempt bonds.

Energy Financial Services

Energy Financial Services offers structured equity, debt, leasing, partnership financing, project finance and broad-based commercial finance to the global energy and water industries and invests in operating assets in these industries. Energy Financial Services also owns a controlling interest in Regency Energy Partners LP, a midstream master limited partnership engaged in the gathering, processing, transporting and marketing of natural gas and gas liquids . . .

GE Commercial Aviation Services (GECAS)

GECAS is a global leader in commercial aircraft leasing and finance, delivering fleet and financing solutions for commercial aircraft. Our airport financing unit makes debt and equity investments primarily in mid-sized regional airports.

Consumer and Industrial

Consumer and Industrial (6.4%, 7.3% and 8.7% of consolidated revenues in 2008, 2007 and 2006, respectively) sells products that share several characteristics—competitive design, efficient manufacturing and effective distribution and service. Strong global competition rarely permits premium pricing, so cost control, including productivity, is key. We sell and service major home appliances including refrigerators, freezers, electric and gas ranges, cooktops, dishwashers, clothes washers and dryers, microwave ovens, room air conditioners, and residential water systems . . . Consumer and Industrial also provides integrated electrical equipment and systems used to distribute, protect and control energy and equipment. We manufacture and distribute electrical distribution and control products, lighting and power panels, switchgear and circuit breakers . . .

Notes

1 James Quinn "General Electric: Genuine Risk of Collapse?" *Seeking Alfa,* November 17, 2008) http://seekingalpha.com/article/106445-general-electric-genuine-risk-of-collapse, accessed October 24, 2009.
2 Transcript of Presentation to General Electric Annual Shareowners Meeting, April 22, 2009.
3 "The GE Mystique," *Fortune,* March 6, 2006, p. 100. "Less than the Sum of the Parts? Decline Sets in at the Conglomerate," *Financial Times,* February 5, 2007, p. 9.
4 "What Makes GE Great?" *Fortune,* March 6, 2006, pp. 90–6.
5 General Electric, Annual Report, 1993, p. 5.
6 "Running the House that Jack Built," *Business Week,* October 2, 2000.
7 "The Days of Welch and Roses," *Business Week,* April 29, 2002.
8 General Electric, Annual Report, 2002.
9 General Electric, Annual Report, 2002.
10 Address to shareholders, Annual Share Owners' Meeting, Philadelphia, April 26, 2006.
11 General Electric, Annual Report 2006, pp. 4–5.
12 General Electric, Annual Report 2008, pp. 4.
13 General Electric, Annual Report, 2002.
14 "Growth as a Process: An Interview with Jeff Immelt," *Harvard Business Review,* June, 2006.
15 General Electric, Annual Report, 2002.
16 "Growth as a Process: An Interview with Jeff Immelt," *Harvard Business Review,* June, 2006.
17 "Growth as a Process: An Interview with Jeff Immelt," *Harvard Business Review,* June, 2006.
18 "Growth as a Process: An Interview with Jeff Immelt," *Harvard Business Review,* June, 2006.
19 General Electric, Annual Report 2008, pp. 6–7.
20 "Growth as a Process: An Interview with Jeff Immelt," *Harvard Business Review,* June, 2006.
21 "Letter to Shareholders," General Electric, 2005 Annual Report.
22 "Growth as a Process: An Interview with Jeff Immelt," *Harvard Business Review,* June, 2006.
23 "Growth as a Process: An Interview with Jeff Immelt," *Harvard Business Review,* June, 2006.
24 "Growth as a Process: An Interview with Jeff Immelt," *Harvard Business Review,* June, 2006.
25 "Growth as a Process: An Interview with Jeff Immelt," *Harvard Business Review,* June, 2006.
26 "Growth as a Process: An Interview with Jeff Immelt," *Harvard Business Review,* June, 2006.
27 "Growth as a Process: An Interview with Jeff Immelt," *Harvard Business Review,* June, 2006.
28 "Growth as a Process: An Interview with Jeff Immelt," *Harvard Business Review,* June, 2006.
29 "Less than the Sum of the Parts? Decline Sets in at the Conglomerate," *Financial Times,* February 5, 2007, p. 9.

"If a man could flow with the stream, grow with the way of nature, he'd accomplish more and he'd be happier doing it than bucking the flow of the water."

W. L. Gore

Malcolm Gladwell (author of *The Tipping Point* and *Outliers*) described his visit to W. L. Gore & Associates:

> When I visited a Gore associate named Bob Hen, at one of the company's plants in Delaware, I tried, unsuccessfully, to get him to tell me what his position was. I suspected, from the fact that he had been recommended to me, that he was one

*This case was prepared by Robert M. Grant. ©2010 Robert M. Grant.

of the top executives. But his office wasn't any bigger than anyone else's. His card just called him an "associate." He didn't seem to have a secretary, one that I could see anyway. He wasn't dressed any differently from anyone else, and when I kept asking the question again and again, all he finally said, with a big grin, was, "I'm a meddler."[1]

The absence of job titles and the lack of the normal symbols of hierarchy are not the only things that are different about W.L. Gore & Associates, Inc. ("Gore"). Since its founding in 1958, Gore deliberately adopted a system of management that contrasted sharply with that of other established corporations. While the styles of management of all start-up companies reflect the personality and values of their founders, the remarkable thing about Gore is that, as a $2.5 billion company with 8500 employees ("associates") in facilities located in 24 countries of the world, Gore's organizational structure and management systems continued to defy the principles under which corporations of similar size and complexity are managed.

The Founding of W. L. Gore & Associates

Wilbert L. (Bill) Gore left DuPont in 1958 after 17 years as a research scientist. At DuPont, Gore had been working on new synthetic material called polytetrafluoroethylene (PTFE) which it had branded "Teflon." Gore was convinced that DuPont's commitment to a business model based on large industrial markets for basic chemical products had caused it to overlook a whole range of innovative applications for PTFE. In forming a business together with his wife, Vieve, Gore was also motivated by the desire to create the energy and passion that he had experienced when working in small research teams at DuPont on those occasions when they were given the freedom to pursue innovation.

Working out of their own home in Newark, Delaware, and with the help of son, Bob, the Gore's first product was Teflon-insulated cable (which was used for the Apollo space program among other applications).

The company's biggest breakthrough was the result of Bob Gore's discovery of the potential of Teflon to be stretched and laced with microscopic holes. The resulting fabric had several desirable properties; in particular, it shed water droplets but was also breathable. Gore-Tex received a U.S. patent in 1976. Not only did it have a wide range of applications for outdoor clothing, the fact that Gore-Tex was chemically inert and resistant to infection made it an excellent material for medical applications such as artificial arteries and intravenous bags. The potential to vary the size of the microscopic holes in Gore-Tex made it ideal for a wide range of filtration applications.

Origins of the Gore Management Philosophy

FundingUniverse.com describes the development of Bill Gore's management ideas as follows:

From their basement office, the Gores expanded into a separate production facility in their hometown of Newark, Delaware. Sales were brisk after initial product introductions. By 1965, just seven years after the business had started, Gore & Associates was employing about 200 people. It was about that time that Gore began to develop and implement the unique management system and philosophy for which his company would become recognized. Gore noticed that as his company had grown, efficiency and productivity had started to decline. He needed a new management structure, but he feared that the popular pyramid management structure that was in vogue at the time suppressed the creativity and innovation that he valued so greatly. Instead of adopting the pyramid structure, Gore decided to create his own system.

During World War II, while on a task force at DuPont, Gore had learned of another type of organizational structure called the lattice system, which was developed to enhance the ingenuity and overall performance of a group working toward a goal. It emphasized communication and cooperation rather than hierarchy of authority. Under the system that Gore developed, any person was allowed to make a decision as long as it was fair, encouraged others, and made a commitment to the company. Consultation was required only for decisions that could potentially cause serious damage to the enterprise. Furthermore, new associates joined the company on the same effective authority level as all the other workers, including Bill and Vieve. There were no titles or bosses, with only a few exceptions, and commands were replaced by personal commitments.

New employees started out working in an area best suited to their talents, under the guidance of a sponsor. As the employee progressed there came more responsibility, and workers were paid according to their individual contribution. "Team members know who is producing," Bill explained in a February 1986 issue of the Phoenix Business Journal. "They won't put up with poor performance. There is tremendous peer pressure. You promote yourself by gaining knowledge and working hard, everyday. There is no competition, except with yourself." The effect of the system was to encourage workers to be creative, take risks, and perform at their highest level.[2]

Bill Gore's ideas about management were influenced by Douglas McGregor's *The Human Side of Enterprise*, which was published as Gore's own company was in its start-up phase. McGregor identified two models of management: the conventional model of management, rooted in Taylor's scientific management; and Weber's principles of bureaucracy which he termed "Theory X." At its root was the assumption that work was unpleasant, that employees were motivated only by money, and that management's principal role was to prevent shirking. "Theory Y" was rooted in the work of the human relations school of management, which assumed that individuals were self-motivated, anxious to solve problems, and capable of working harmoniously on joint tasks.

A key element in Bill Gore's management thinking related to the limits of organizational size. He believed that the need for interpersonal trust would result in organizations declining in effectiveness once they reached about 200 members. Hence, in 1967, Bill and Vieve decided to build a second manufacturing facility in Flagstaff, Arizona. From then on, Gore built a new facility each time an existing unit reached 200 associates.

According to Malcolm Gladwell, Gore's insistence upon small organizational units is an application of a principle developed by anthropologist, Robin Dunbar.

According to Dunbar, social groups are limited by individuals' capacity to manage complex social relationships. Among primates, the size of the typical social group for a species is correlated with the size of the neocortex of that species' brain. For humans, Dunbar estimates that 148 is the maximum number of individuals that a person can comfortably have social relations with. Across a range of different societies, Dunbar found that 150 was the typical maximum size of tribes, religious groups and army units.[3]

Organization Structure and Management Principles

The Gore organization does include elements of hierarchy. For example, as a corporation, it is legally required to have a board of directors—this is chaired by Bob Gore. There is also a CEO, Chuck Carroll. The company is organized into four divisions (fabrics, medical, industrial and electronic products) each with a recognized "leader." Within these divisions there are specific business units, each based upon a group of products. There are also specialized, company-wide functions such as human resources and information technology.

What is lacking is a codified set of ranks and positions. Gore associates are expected to adapt their roles to match their skills and aptitudes. The basic organizational units are small, self-managing teams.

Relationships within teams and between teams are based upon the concept of a lattice rather than a conventional hierarchy. The idea of a lattice is that every organizational member is connected to every other organizational member within the particular facility. In the lattice communication is peer-to-peer, not superior to subordinate. For Bill Gore, this was a more natural way to organize. He observed that in most formal organizations, it was through informal connections that things actually got done: "Most of us delight in going around the formal procedures and doing things the straightforward and easy way."[4]

Leadership is important at Gore, but the basic principle is that of natural leadership: "If you call a meeting and people show up—you're a leader."[5] Teams can appoint team leaders, they can also replace their team leaders—as a result every team leader's accountability is to the team. "Someone who is accustomed to snapping their fingers and having people respond will be frustrated," says John McMillan, a Gore associate. "I snap my fingers and nobody will do anything. My job is to acquire followership, articulate a goal and get there . . . and hope the rest of the people think that makes sense."[6]

New associates are assigned to a "sponsor" whose job is to introduce the new hire to the company and guide him or her through the lattice. The new hire is likely to spend time with several teams during the first few months of employment. It is up to the new associate and a team to find a good match. An associate is free to find a new sponsor if desired. Typically, each associate works on two or three different project teams.

Annual reviews are peer based. Information is collected from at least 20 other associates. Each associate is then ranked against every other associate within the unit in terms of overall contribution. This ranking determines compensation.

The company's beliefs, management principles and work culture are articulated on its web site (see Exhibit 24.1).

EXHIBIT 24.1

W. L. Gore & Associates: Beliefs, Principles and Culture

What We Believe

Founder Bill Gore built the company on a set of beliefs and principles that guide us in the decisions we make, in the work we do, and in our behavior toward others. What we believe is the basis for our strong culture, which connects Gore associates worldwide in a common bond.

Fundamental Beliefs

- *Belief in the individual:* if you trust individuals and believe in them, they will be motivated to do what's right for the company.

- *Power of small teams:* our lattice organization harnesses the fast decision-making, diverse perspectives, and collaboration of small teams.

- *All in the same boat:* all Gore associates are part owners of the company through the associate stock plan. Not only does this allow us to share in the risks and rewards of the company; it gives us an added incentive to stay committed to its long-term success. As a result, we feel we are all in this effort together, and believe we should always consider what's best for the company as a whole when making decisions.

- *Long-term view:* our investment decisions are based on long-term payoff and our fundamental beliefs are not sacrificed for short-term gain.

Guiding Principles

- *Freedom:* the company was designed to be an organization in which associates can achieve their own goals best by directing their efforts toward the success of the corporation; action is prized; ideas are encouraged; and making mistakes is viewed as part of the creative process. We define freedom as being empowered to encourage each other to grow in knowledge, skill, scope of responsibility, and range of activities. We believe that associates will exceed expectations when given the freedom to do so.

- *Fairness:* everyone at Gore sincerely tries to be fair with each other, our suppliers, our customers and anyone else with whom we do business.

- *Commitment:* we are not assigned tasks; rather, we each make our own commitments and keep them.

- *Waterline:* everyone at Gore consults with other associates before taking actions that might be "below the waterline"—causing serious damage to the company.

Working in Our Unique Culture

Our founder Bill Gore once said, "The objective of the Enterprise is to make money and have fun doing so." And we still believe that, more than 50 years later.

Because we are all part owners of the company through the associate stock plan, Gore associates expect a lot from each other. Innovation and creativity; high ethics and integrity; making commitments and standing behind them. We work hard at living up to these expectations as we strive for business success. But we also trust and respect each other and believe it's important to celebrate success.

Gore is much less formal than most workplaces. Our relationships with other associates are open and informal and we strive to treat everyone respectfully and fairly. This type of environment naturally promotes social interaction and many associates have made lifelong friends with those they met working at Gore.

Do Something You're Passionate About

At Gore, we believe it's important to have passion for what you do. If you're passionate about your work, you are naturally going to be highly self-motivated and focused. If you feel pride and ownership, you will want to do whatever it takes to be successful and have an impact. So when you apply for an opportunity at Gore, be sure you're going to be passionate about the work you'll be doing.

The Lattice Structure and Individual Accountability

Gore's unique "lattice" management structure, which illustrates a nonhierarchical system based on interconnection among associates, is free from traditional bosses and managers. There is no assigned authority, and we become leaders based on our ability to gain the respect of our peers and to attract followers.

You will be responsible for managing your own workload and will be accountable to others on your team. More importantly, only you can make a commitment to do something (for example, a task, a project, or a new role)—but once you make a commitment, you will be expected to meet it. A "core commitment" is your primary area of concentration. You may take on additional commitments depending on your interests, the company's needs, and your availability.

Relationships and Direct Communication

Relationships are everything at Gore—relationships with each other, with customers, with vendors and suppliers and with our surrounding communities. We encourage people to build and maintain long-term relationships by communicating directly. Of course we all use e-mail, but we find that face-to-face meetings and phone calls work best when collaborating with others.

Sponsors

Everyone at Gore has a sponsor, who is committed to helping you succeed. Sponsors are responsible for supporting your growth, for providing good feedback on your strengths and areas that offer opportunities for development and for helping you connect with others in the organization.

Source: www.gore.com/en_xx/careers/whoweare/about-gore.html. Reproduced by permission of W.L. Gore & Associates.

Innovation

The success of Gore's unusual management system is its capacity for innovation. Between 1976 and July 2009, Gore received 918 patents. Even more remarkable has been its ability to extend its existing technological breakthroughs to a wide variety of new applications. Central to Gore's ability to innovate is its willingness to allow individuals the freedom to pursue their own projects: each associate is allowed a half day each week of "dabble time". The company's web site gives examples of the results of these initiatives (see Exhibit 24.2).

EXHIBIT 24.2

Examples of innovation at W.L. Gore & Associates

Change Music

How did the creators of GORE-TEX® products—worn by outdoor enthusiasts and people with active lifestyles all over the world—invent a new kind of guitar string?

Although manufacturers have coated their guitar strings for many years to make them last longer by protecting them from perspiration, oil, and dirt the coating severely compromised the quality of the sound.

Gore had no presence in the music industry until one associate envisioned a completely new type of guitar string that would prevent string contamination, last longer, and be more comfortable for musicians to play. Relying on the company's unique culture and mentoring system to support his efforts, he formed a cross-functional team—including Michael and John—to make it happen.

Each member of the Gore team had the knowledge and know-how needed to develop this exciting new product. With the entrepreneurial spirit characteristic of Gore, they took this innovative concept to the marketplace in less than two years.

But the team's commitment to integrity didn't stop in the lab. They asked 15 000 musicians to test the new strings for sound quality before the product was introduced. Since then, revolutionary ELIXIR® Strings have inspired a generation of musicians all over the world to pick up their guitars and play. And their ELIXIR® Strings experience and the challenges they overcame have changed their lives too.

Change Lives

How did the creators of GORE-TEX® products—worn by outdoor enthusiasts and people with

active lifestyles all over the world—invent material to patch human hearts?

For people with a serious heart problem known as an atrial septal defect, or "hole in the heart," open heart surgery was once the only treatment. The surgeon makes an incision in the chest to expose the heart; a heart-lung bypass machine pumps blood while the heart is stopped and the defect is patched. Many patients with this condition are infants and small children, for whom this surgery poses an even greater risk.

A dedicated team of Gore associates—including Hannah, Nitin, and Sarah—developed a minimally invasive device that physicians implant through a cardiac catheter to permanently close the hole without major surgery. Driven by Gore's core values of integrity, innovation, and quality, the team spent years perfecting the device before taking it to market. Patients treated this way experience much less pain, recover much more easily and quickly, and have less scarring.

Since then, the GORE HELEX septal occluder has changed the way doctors treat patients with this heart defect and has helped thousands of patients throughout the world—more than half of them infants and children—lead normal, healthy lives. And the team's experience with the septal occluder product changed their lives, too.

Change Industries

How did the creators of GORE-TEX® products—worn by outdoor enthusiasts and people with active lifestyles all over the world—invent material that protects firefighters from heat, flames, and hazardous chemicals?

Gore makes a line of protective fabrics based on its patented membrane technologies. These fabrics are used by Gore's customers—garment manufacturers—as one layer of protective clothing for military and law enforcement uniforms, medical protective wear, workwear, and turnout gear for fire and safety personnel.

Firefighters rely on protective gear—including boots, pants, jackets, gloves, and headgear—to keep them safe. While already incorporating waterproof and breathable GORE-TEX® fabric to improve the comfort and quality of their gear, the firefighting industry identified a need for barrier fabrics that also protected firefighters against bloodborne pathogens and common fire ground chemicals. Dave, Henri, and Ron were part of a cross-functional team that set out to engineer high-performance CROSSTECH® protective barrier fabric to meet this need.

By building relationships with firefighters, suppliers, and industry experts, the global Gore team came to understand the extreme conditions that firefighters are exposed to. Harnessing deep knowledge of Gore's membrane technologies and their passion for making a difference, they developed Gore protective barrier fabrics that change the way firefighters respond to emergencies. And their fire service experience and the challenges they overcame have changed their lives, too.

Source: www.gore.com/en_xx/careers/associatestories/12347 22965408.html. Reproduced by permission of W.L. Gore & Associates

Gary Hamel closes his discussion of W.L. Gore and Associates with the following challenge:

Bill Gore was a 40-something chemical engineer when he laid the foundations for his innovation democracy. I don't know about you, but a middle-aged polytetrafluoroethylene-loving chemist isn't my mental image of a wild-eyed management innovator. Yet think about how radical Gore's vision must have seemed back in 1958. Fifty years later, postmodern management hipsters throw around terms like complex adaptive systems and self-organizing teams. Well, they're only a half century behind the curve. So ask yourself, am I dreaming big enough yet? Would my management innovation agenda make Bill Gore proud ?[7]

Notes

1 M. Gladwell, *The Tipping Point,* Little, Brown & Co., London, 2000.

2 See www.fundinguniverse.com/company-histories/WL-Gore-amp;-Associates-Inc-Company-History.html, accessed October 25, 2009.

3 M. Gladwell, *The Tipping Point,* Little, Brown & Co., London, 2000, pp. 177–81.

4 Quoted by G. Hamel with B. Breen, *The Future of Management,* Harvard Business School Press, Boston MA, 2007, p. 87.

5 Quoted by G. Hamel with B. Breen, *The Future of Management,* Harvard Business School Press, Boston MA, 2007, p. 88.

6 W. L. Gore & Associates, Inc.: Quality's Different Drummer, IMPO, www.impomag.com/scripts/ShowPR.asp?RID=3923&CommonCount=0, accessed October 25, 2009.

7 Gary Hamel with Bill Breen, *The Future of Management,* Harvard Business School Press, Boston MA, 2007, p. 100.

Contemporary Strategy Analysis 7th Edition

Also Available:

Text Only
7th Edition

ISBN 9780470747100

Text and Cases
7th Edition

ISBN 9780470747094

www.contemporarystrategyanalysis.com